A TREATISE ON MIND

VOLUME 1

The 'Self' or 'Non-self'

in Buddhism

Other Titles in the Series

The I Concept

Volume 2: Considerations of Mind - A Buddhist Enquiry

Volume 3: The Buddha-Womb and the Way to Liberation

Cellular Consciousness

Volume 4: Maṇḍalas - Their Nature and Development

Volume 5: An Esoteric Exposition of the Bardo Thödol (Part A)

Volume 5: An Esoteric Exposition of the Bardo Thödol (Part B)

The Way to Shambhala

Volume 6: Meditation and the Initiation Process

Volume 7: The Constitution of Shambhala

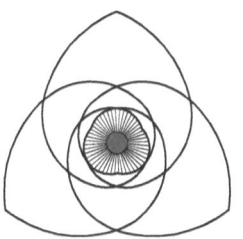

VOLUME ONE

The 'Self' or 'Non-self'

in Buddhism

BODO BALSYS

UNIVERSAL DHARMA
PUBLICATIONS
SYDNEY, AUSTRALIA

ISBN 978-0-9923568-0-4

2nd Edition 2025

Āḥ!

Homage to the Lord of Shambhala.
Inconceivable, inconceivable, beyond thought
Is the bejewelled crown of this most excelled Jina.
He whose Eye has taught many Buddhas.
And who will anoint the myriad,
that in the future lives will come.
As I bow to His Feet my Heart's afire.
Oh, this bliss, this love for my Lord
can barely be borne on my part.
It takes flight as the might of the Dove.
The flight of serene *nirvāṇic* embrace.
The flight of Light so bright.
The flight of Love so active tonight.
The flight of enlightenment for all to come to
their mind's Heart's attire.

Obeisance to the Gurus!
To the Buddhas of the three times.
To the Council of Bodhisattvas, *mahāsattvas*.
To them I pledge allegiance.

Oṁ Hūṁ! Hūṁ! Hūṁ!

Dedication

Thanks to my students, past, present and future, and in particular to those that have helped in the production of this Treatise.

Oṁ

Acknowledgments

Special thanks to Angie O'Sullivan, Kylie Smith,
and Ruth Fitzpatrick
for their efforts in making this
series possible.

Oṁ

Contents

Preface xi

1. The Rules of Interpretation of Sacred Scriptures 1
    - Introductory concepts 1
    - The relativity of things 9
    - The *saṃsāra-nirvāṇa* interrelationship 14
    - Direct awareness and interpretation 19
    - The nature of the serpent power 22
    - The *chakras* and esoteric lore 30
    - Levels of interpretation 38
2. The Two Truths 49
    - Some introductory questions 49
    - The two truths 56
3. Buddhist Schools and the Wheel of Direction in Space 110
    - The eight-spoked wheel 110
    - The Buddhist Schools 112
    - The four outpourings of Buddhist *dharma* 126
    - 'True existence' and the two truths 128
4. East and West, the Mahāmudrā of the Two Truths 137
    - The need for an Eastern and Western integration 137
    - The Mahāmudrā of the two truths 145
5. The Sevenfold Reasoning Part A: The Introduction 156
    - Relativity and Nāgārjuna's *catuṣkoṭikā* 156
    - Bodhicitta and the 'self' concept 160
    - The I-consciousness and *kliṣṭamanas* 163
    - The 'one and the many' 170
6. Essay on the One and the Many 180
    - Nothing ultimately arises 180
    - Enquiry into a single effect 183
    - The five Elements 185
    - The interrelatedness of the Elements 193
    - The role of consciousness 197
    - The production of a multiple effect 201
    - Causes and effects 212

7. The Refutation of Partless Particles 221
What is meant by partlessness? 221
Quandary concerning 'truly existent' atomic unities 226
The unitariness of things 231
8. The Sevenfold Reasoning Part B: Meditation on the 'I' 236
The 'I' and the aggregates 236
Mind, body and the 'I' 244
The base of mind and body 258
The base of the 'I' and its possession 260
The 'I' and composites of aggregates 264
The 'I' and the shape of the body 267
9. Dependent Origination 269
Definition of *pratītyasamutpāda* 269
The problem of the origination of phenomena 275
The middle way of consciousness 279
Karma and the containers of mind 285
The three synonyms of Dependent Arising 287
10. Chapter one of the *Mūlamadhyamakakārikā* 295
11. The Diamond Slivers 319
The Four-Cornered Proof 319
The expansion of the Four-Cornered Proof 323
Five stages to the evolution of the *buddhadharma* 330
The Diamond Slivers 331
12. Non-production from Other 342
Inherently existing otherness and production 342
Inherently existent production 349
Inherently existing otherness 351
13. The Four Extremes 355
14. The Four Alternatives and Refuting a Self of Persons 358
The Four Alternatives 358
The time line and the first argument 361
The second and third arguments 365
Refuting a Self of Persons 371
The 'self of persons' 379
The subtle 'self' of persons 387
Summary of the Prāsaṅgika and Svātantrika opinions 392

15. The Seven-Cornered Reason 398
The first reason 398
The second reason 401
The remaining reasons 405
Summary 410

16. The Pudgala Doctrine 413
The core doctrines 413
Correlation of the *pudgala* doctrine to the I-consciousness 417
The role of *jīva* 431
Fire and its fuel 435

Bibliography 442

Index 445

Figures

Figure 1. The Mahāyāna Schools, (the Dharma Wheel) 127
Figure 2. The Elements 197
Figure 3. The Middle Way of Consciousness 281
Figure 4. The Four-Cornered Proof 320
Figure 5. The Relationship of Śūnyatā to Saṃsāra 325

Tables

Table 1. The Elements 195

Preface

This treatise investigates Buddhist ideas concerning what mind is and how it relates to a concept of a 'self'. It is principally a study of the complex interrelationship between mind and phenomena, from the gross to the subtle—the physical, psychic, supersensory and supernal. This entails an explanation of how mind incorporates all phenomena in its *modus operandi,* and how eventually that mind is liberated from it, thereby becoming awakened. Thus the treatise explores the manner in which the corporeally orientated, concretised, intellectual mind eventually becomes transformed into the Clear Light of the abstracted Mind; a super-mind, a Buddha-Mind.

A Treatise on Mind is arranged in seven volumes, divided into three subsections. These are as follows:

The I Concept
Volume 1. *The 'Self' or 'Non-self' in Buddhism.*
Volume 2. *Considerations of Mind—A Buddhist Enquiry.*
Volume 3. *The Buddha-Womb and the Way to Liberation.*

Cellular Consciousness
Volume 4. *Maṇḍalas - Their Nature and Development.*
Volume 5. *An Esoteric Exposition of the Bardo Thödol.*
(This Volume is published in two parts)

The Way to Shambhala
Volume 6. *Meditation and the Initiation Process.*
Volume 7. *The Constitution of Shambhala.*

The I Concept represents a necessary extensive revision[1] of a large work formerly published in one volume. Together the three volumes investigate the question of what a 'self' is and is not. This involves an analysis of the nature of consciousness, and the consciousness-stream of a human unit developing as a continuum through time. It will illustrate exactly what directs such a stream and how its *karma* is arranged so that enlightenment is the eventual outcome.

The first Volume analyses Prāsaṅgika lines of reasoning, such as the 'Refutation of Partless Particles', and 'The Sevenfold Reasoning' in order to derive a clear deduction as to whether a 'self' exists, and if so what its limitations are, and if not, then what the alternative may be. The analysis resolves the historically vexing question of how—if there is no 'self'—can there be a continuity of mind that is coherently connected in an evolutionary manner through multiple rebirths.[2] In order to arrive at this explanation, many of the basic assumptions of Mahāyāna Buddhism, such as Dependent Origination and the Two Truths, are critically analysed.

The second Volume provides an in-depth analysis of what mind is, how it relates to the concept of the Void *(śūnyatā),* and the evolution of consciousness. The analysis utilises Yogācāra-Vijñānavādin philosophy in order to comprehend the major attributes of mind, the *saṃskāras* that condition it, and the laws by means of which it operates.

The enquiry into the nature of what an 'I' is requires comprehension of the properties of the dual nature of mind, which consists of an empirical and abstract, enlightened part. As a means of doing this, the *ālayavijñāna* (the store of consciousness-attributes) is explored, alongside the entire philosophy of the 'eight consciousnesses' of this School.

Volume three focuses on the I-Consciousness and the subtle body, by first utilising a minor Tantra, *The Great Gates of Diamond Liberation,* to investigate the nature of the Heart centre and its functions, then the

1 The book was inadequately edited hence contains many errors and grammatical mistakes that have been corrected in this treatise.

2 My earlier work *Karma and the Rebirth of Consciousness* (Munshiram Manoharlal, Delhi, 2006) lays the background for this basic question.

chakras below the diaphragm. This is necessary to lay the foundation for the topics that will be the subject of the later volumes of this treatise concerning the nature of meditation, the construction of *maṇḍalas,* and the yoga of the *Bardo Thödol.*

The focus then shifts to investigate where the idea of a self-sustaining I-concept or 'Soul-form' may be found in Buddhist philosophy, given the denial of substantial self-existence prioritised in the philosophy of Emptiness. Following this, the pertinent chapters of the *Ratnagotravibhāga Śastra* are examined in detail so that a proper conclusion to the investigation can be obtained via the *buddhadharma.* This concerns an analysis of how the *ālayavijñāna* is organised, such that the rebirth process is possible for each human consciousness-stream, taking into account the *karma* that will eventually make each human unit a Buddha. In relation to this the ontological nature of the *tathāgatagarbha* (the Buddha-Womb) must be carefully analysed, as well as the organising principle of consciousness represented by the *chakras.* I thus establish that there is a form that appears upon the domain of the abstract Mind. I call this the Sambhogakāya Flower. The final two chapters of this Volume principally define its characteristics.

The second subsection, *Cellular Consciousness,* is divided into two parts. Volume four deals with the question of what exactly constitutes a 'cell', metaphysically. The cell is viewed as a unit of consciousness that interrelates with other cells to form *maṇḍalas* of expression. Each such cell can be considered a form of 'self' that has a limited, though valid, body of expression. It is born, sustains a form of activity, and consequently dies when it outlives its usefulness. This mode of analysis is extended to include the myriad forms manifest in the world of phenomena known as *saṃsāra,* including the existence and functioning of *chakras.*

Volume five deals with the formative forces and evolutionary processes governing the prime cells (that is, *maṇḍalas* of expression), and the phenomenon that governs an entire world-sphere of evolutionary attainment. This is explored via an in-depth exposition of the *Bardo Thödol* and its 42 Peaceful and 58 Wrathful Deities. The text also incorporates a detailed exposition concerning the transformation of *saṃskāras* (consciousness-attributes developed through all past forms of activity) into enlightenment. The entire path of liberation enacted by a *yogin* via the principles of meditation, forms of concentration, and related techniques *(tapas, dhāraṇīs)* is explained. In doing so, the soteriological purpose of the various wrathful and theriomorphic deities is revealed. This Volume is published in two parts. Part A explores chapter 5 of the *Bardo Thödol* concerning the transformation of *saṃskāras* via meditating upon the Peaceful and Wrathful Deities. This necessitates sound knowledge of the force centres (*chakras*) and the way their powers (*siddhis*) awaken. Part B deals with the gain of such transformations and the consequence of conversion of the attributes of the empirical mind into the liberated abstract Mind.

The third subsection, *The Way to Shambhala*, is also in two parts. They present an eclectic revelation of esoteric information integrating the main Eastern and Western religions. Volume six is a treatise on meditation and the Initiation process.[3] The meditation practice is directed towards the needs of individuals living within the context of our modern societies.

Volume six also includes a discussion of the path of Initiation as the means of gaining liberation from *saṃsāra*. The teaching in Volume five concerning the conversion of *saṃskāras* is supplementary to this path. The path of Initiation *is* the way to Shambhala. As many will choose to consciously undergo the precepts needed to undertake Initiation in the future, this invokes the necessity of providing much more revelatory information concerning this kingdom than has been provided hitherto.

How Shambhala is organised is the subject of Volume seven, which details the constitution of the Hierarchy of enlightened being[4] (the Council of Bodhisattvas). It illustrates how the presiding Lords who govern planetary evolution manifest. This detailed philosophy rests on the foundation of the information provided in all of the previous volumes, and necessitates a proper comprehension of the nature of the five Dhyāni Buddhas. To do so the awakening of the meditation-Mind, which is the objective of *A Treatise on Mind*, is essential.

---

3 The word Initiation is capitalised throughout the series of books to add emphasis to the fact that it is the process that makes one divine, liberated. It is the expression of divinity manifesting upon the planetary and cosmic landscape.

4 The word 'being' here is not pluralised because though this Hierarchy is constituted of a multiplicity of beings, together they represent one 'Being', one integral awakened Entity.

How to engage with this text

In this investigation many new ways of viewing conventional Buddhist arguments and rhetoric shall be pursued to develop the pure logic of the reader's mind, and to awaken revelations from their abstract Mind. New insights into the far-reaching light of the *dharma* will be revealed, which will form a basis for the illustration of an esoteric view that supersedes the bounds of conventionally accepted views. Readers should therefore analyse all arguments for themselves to discern the validity of what is presented. Such enquiry allows one to ascertain for oneself, what is logical and truthful, thus overcoming the blind acceptance of a certain dogma or line of reasoning that is otherwise universally accepted as correct. Only that which is discovered within each inquiring mind should be accepted. The remainder should however not be automatically discarded, but rather kept aside for later analysis when more data is available—unless the logic is obviously flawed, in which case it should be abandoned. There is no claim to infallibility in the information and arguments presented in this treatise, however, they are designed to offer scope for further meditation and enquiry by the earnest reader. If errors are found through impeccable logic, then the dialectical process may proceed. We can then accept or reject the new thesis and move forward, such that the evolution of human thought progresses, until we all stand enlightened.

This treatise hopes to assist that dialectical evolution by analysing major aspects of the *buddhadharma* as it exists and is taught today, to try to examine where errors may lie, or where the present modes of interpretation fall short of the true intended meaning. The aim is also to elaborate aspects of the *dharma* that could only be hinted at or cursorily explained by the wise ones of the past, because the basis for proper elaboration had not then been established. This analysis of *buddhadharma* will try to rectify some of the past inadequacies in order to explore and extend the *dharma* into arenas rarely investigated.

There will always be obstinate and dogmatic ones that staunchly cling to established views. This produces a reactive malaise in current Buddhist ontological and metaphysical thought. However, amongst the many practitioners of the *dharma* there are also those who have clarified their minds sufficiently to verify truth in whatever form it is presented, and will follow it at all costs to enlightenment. The Council of Bodhisattvas heartily seek such worthy ones. The signposts or guides upon the way to enlightenment have changed through the centuries, and contemporary practitioners of the *dharma* have yet to learn to clearly interpret the new directions. The guide books are now being written and many must come forth to understand and practice correctly.

If full comprehension of such guide books is achieved those *dharma* practitioners yearning to become Bodhisattvas would rapidly become spiritually enlightened. Here is a rhyme and reason *for* Buddhism. The actual present dearth of enlightened beings informs us that little that is read is properly understood. The esoteric view presented in this treatise hopes to rectify this problem, so as to create better thinkers along the Bodhisattva way.

The numbers of Buddhists are growing in the world, thus Buddhism needs a true restorative flowering to rival that of the renaissance of debate and innovative thinkers of the early post-Nāgārjunian era. In order to achieve this it must synthesise the present wealth of scientific knowledge, alongside the best of the Western world's philosophical output.

Currently the *buddhadharma* is presented as an external body of knowledge held by the Buddha, Rinpoches, monks and lay teachers. This encourages practitioners to hero worship these figures and to heed many unenlightened utterances from such teachers, based on a belief system that encourages people to *uncritically* listen to them and adopt their views. When enlightened teachers *do appear* and find consolidated reasons for firing spiritual bullets for the cause of the enlightenment of humanity, then all truth can and will be known. The present lack of inwardly perceived knowledge from the fount of the *dharmakāya* on the part of many teachers blocks the production of an arsenal of weapons for solving the problems of suffering in the world. Few see little beyond the scope of vision in what they have been indoctrinated to believe, allowing for only rudimentary truths to be understood. While for the great majority this suffices, it is woefully inadequate for those genuinely seeking Bodhisattvahood and enlightenment. The cost to humanity in not being given an enlightened answer as to the nature of awakening, is profound.

We must go to the awakening of the Head lotus to find the most established reasoning powers. Without the 1,000 petals of the *sahasrāra padma* ablaze then there is little substance for proper understanding, little ability to hold the mind steady in the dynamic field of revelation that the *dharmakāya* represents. How can the unenlightened properly understand Buddhist scriptures, when there is little (revelation) coming from the Head centres of such beings? Much still needs to be taught concerning the way of awakening this lotus, and to help fill the lack is a major purpose of *A Treatise on Mind.*

Those who intend to reach enlightenment must go beyond the narrow sectarian allegiances promoted by many strands of contemporary Buddhism. Buddhism itself unfolded in a dialectical context with other heterodox Indian (and Chinese, etc.) traditions, and prospered on account of those engagements. When one sees the unfolding of enlightened wisdom in such a fashion, the particular information from specific schools of thought may be synthesised into a greater whole. Each school has various qualities and types of argument to resolve weaknesses in the opposing stream of thought. This highlights that there are particular aspects in each that may be right or wrong, or neither wholly right or wrong. Through this process we can find better answers, or if need be, create a new lineage or religion which is expressive of a synthesis of the various schools of thought.

The Buddha did not categorically reject the orthodox Indian religio-philosophical ideas of his time, nor did he simply accept them—he reformed them. He preserved the elements that he found to be true, and rejected those 'wrong views' which lead to moral and spiritual impairment. If the existing system needs reformation it becomes part of a Bodhisattva's meditation. The way a reforming Buddha incarnates is dependent on how he must fit into such a system. Thus he is essentially an outsider incarnating into it to demonstrate the new type of ideas he chooses to elaborate. If there is a lot of dogmatic resistance to the presented doctrine of truth, then a new religion is founded. If there is some acceptance then we see reformation. There is always room for improvement, to march forward closer to enlightenment's goal, be it for an individual or for a wisdom-religion as a whole. There is a need for reform throughout the religious world today.

By way of a hermeneutical strategy fit for this task, we ought look no further than the Buddha himself. The Buddha proposed that all students of the *dharma* should make their investigations through the *Four Points of Refuge*. These are:

1. The doctrine is one's point of refuge, not a person.
2. The meaning is one's point of refuge, not the letter.
3. The sacred texts whose meaning is defined are one's point of refuge, to those whose meaning needs definition.
4. Direct awareness is one's point of refuge, not discursive awareness.[5]

These four points can be summarised or rephrased as: the doctrine (*dharma*), true or esoteric meaning, right definition, and direct awareness are one's point of refuge, not adherence to sectarian bias, semantics, the dialectics of non-fully enlightened commentaries, or to illogical assertions. What may be long held to be truthful, but is not, upon proper analytical dissection, needs rectifying. Also, in other cases, a doctrine or teaching may indeed be correct, but the current interpretation leaves much to be desired, and hence should be reinterpreted from the position of a more embracive or esoteric view.

Hopefully this presentation finds welcoming minds that will carefully analyse it in line with their own understandings of the issues, and as a consequence build up a better understanding of the nature of what constitutes the path to enlightenment. Their way of walking as Bodhisattvas should be enriched as a consequence.

For a guide to understanding the pronunciation of Sanskrit words, please visit our website.
http://universaldharma.com/resources/pronounce-sanskrit/

Our online esoteric glossary also provides definitions for most of the terms used in this treatise.
http://universaldharma.com/resources/esoteric-glossary/

5 Griffith, P.J., *On Being Buddha, The Classical Doctrine of Buddhahood*, (Sri Satguru Publications, New Delhi, 1995), 52.

My eyes do weep as I stare into this troubled world,
For I dare not place my Heart in my brother's keep.
He would grapple that Heart with hands so rough
So as to destroy the fabric of its delicate stuff.
Oh to give, to give, my Heart does yearn,
But humanity must its embracive,
Humbling, pervasive scene yet to learn.
To destroy and tear with avarice they know,
But little care to sensitive rapture they show.
How to give its blood is my constant fare,
For that Love to bestow upon their Hearts I bemoan.
But they hide their Hearts behind mental-emotional walls.
No matter how one prods these walls won't fall,
So much belittling emotional self-concern prop their bastions.
Oh, how my eyes do weep as I stare.
I stare at their fearsome malls and halls.
That lock Love out from all their abodes
And do keep them trapped in realms of woe.

Oṁ Maṇi Padme Hūṁ

1

The Rules of Interpretation of Sacred Scriptures

Introductory concepts

In introducing this treatise the mode of interpreting sacred scriptures should be discussed at the outset. One should not necessarily follow traditional interpretations simply because that is the way it is presented by the instructor steeped in orthodoxy. Orthodoxy insists that one ought to accept the established interpretation because that is what someone higher up in the ladder of the hierarchy of one's school, or the founder, tells us is to be believed. The lineage of such interpretation may extend back many hundreds or even a thousand or more years, therefore it is venerated as authoritative and generally unquestioned as the source of the highest revelation and truth. The denoted antiquity of an unbroken line of lineage spells total acceptance. The student is compliant and becomes indoctrinated into an entire belief system without properly developing a proper rationale of discernment.

Generally the indoctrination serves well because the general beliefs purported are valid, and because of the spiritual calibre of the student. Such calibre is at a level where the knowledge-discernment capability of the student is completely saturated to the maximum level by the presented doctrines. There however exist superlative beings, excellent philosophers, Bodhisattvas, that from former lives have developed the capacity for high revelatory discernment. They often question the orthodoxy through having discovered problems with the established logic. Such logic will have been found to veil the real, to only indirectly lead to the development of enlightenment-attributes and in some cases to even mar its progress. This produces the eventuation of dissention and the appearance of different schools of developing valid cognition.

The veil of language often hangs like a cloud, obscuring true insight, marring the developing Clear Light of Mind[1]. The fare that is adequate for beginners upon the path will not suffice to feed the cognitive needs of the superlative thinker. Many more levels of interpretation will be found by such a one than by the novice. Therefore texts are often written with these two levels of thinking in mind; words are chosen by the wise with care to incorporate both needs. Their treatises *(śāstra), sūtras*[2] and Tantras, generally consist of multidimensional thought structures, where many levels of meaning can be derived. This *Treatise on Mind* hopes to reveal much concerning such multidimensionality, of the way the many veils of meaning can be uncovered and deciphered.

In Buddhism the question of correct interpretation has been traditionally answered by the 'four points of refuge'. These are:

> (1) The doctrine is one's point of refuge, not a person. (2) The meaning is one's point of refuge, not the letter. (3) The sacred texts whose meaning is defined are one's point of refuge, not those whose meaning needs definition. (4) Direct awareness is one's point of refuge, not discursive awareness.[3]

---

1 Mind is capitalised in this treatise when it refers to the abstracted enlightened Mind, compared to the concreted empirical unenlightened mind. Therefore the convention I shall use in this series is to capitalise the awakened Mind and keep the empirical mind in lower case.

2 *Sūtra:* 'thread', original discourses of the Buddha. These discourses are generally categorised in a triune way: first the discourses on the four Noble Truths are presented, next the *prajñāpāramita* teachings that emphasise emptiness are given, then finally the *Tathāgatagarbha sūtras* emphasising the Buddha-nature.

3 Shastri, *Abhidharmakośa,* 1202. Taken from P.J. Griffith, *On Being Buddha, The Classical Doctrine of Buddhahood,* (Sri Satguru Publications, Delhi, 1995), 52. See also La Vallée Poussin, *Madhyamakavṛttiḥ,* 43-44; Lévi, *Mahāyāna-Sūtrālaṃkāra,* 138-39. In his excellent essay on these Four Reliances Robert A.F. Thurman states that 'These four reliances are common in Universal Vehicle texts. The earliest instance of their mention and detailed analysis is in Asaṅga's *Bodhisattva Stages,* where they are given in Skt., BBh, (Dutt, *Bodhisattva-bhūmi,* 175-76). There are some variations from the final Tibetan tradition, in order and terminology, though the thrust is the same'. R.A.F. Thurman, *The Speech of Gold; Reason and Enlightenment in Tibetan Buddhism.* (Motilal Banarsidass, Delhi, 1989), 113-14, *fn.*

The *first* point means that when one analyses what is written concerning any teaching one must be able to ascertain its logical basis and evaluate its truth or worth for oneself. Seekers must consider the recesses of their own inner meditative reserves, and not rest upon faith in the fame of the author, or because some eminent person, guru, Rinpoche, or other, said that it is truthful. Such beings are rarely enlightened and thus are prone to errors in thinking. Also, even if the guru or authority was enlightened, the student needs to train his/her mind properly in logical and intuitive deduction, so as to overcome the impediments to lethargic thought. Only in this way can the limitations in consciousness be eliminated, the substance of the mind lacking in any area be strengthened, and the blocks to proper comprehension cleared. Thus true wisdom can be evoked. The *dharma* stands on its own merit and does not need authoritative validation to ascertain its viability. Students need to derive their own understandings from it. Eclectic discussion can help in the formulation of such validation. Discursive or straightforward reason can broaden the perspective of the student's thinking and lead to arenas not previously perceived. Ultimately, however, an enlightened one is needed to help properly awaken the inner tools and organs of perception[4] that allow multidimensional visioning.

The *second* point means that one must take care to not reify any form of information given in the *sūtras* and *śāstras* being studied. One must try to eke out the most esoteric interpretation possible, and not just rely upon the quick, exoteric, and thus often most literal interpretation (as meant by 'the letter' above). Much deep thought must therefore be given as to the meaning. The most conventional form of interpretation is generally the least important, and most limited, veiled, reserved mainly for those with 'dull minds', who are content with the most superficial deductions.

In order to obtain the higher esoteric meaning one should use the interpretive method (the seven keys or modes of interpretation) explained at the end of the last chapter of my book *Karma and Rebirth of Consciousness*. They are: literally, numerically (including geometrically), astrologically, allegorically, symbolically, physiologically, and esoterically.

---

4 *Chakras.*

The *third* point refers to the fact that original sources by an acknowledged enlightened one should be relied upon. If such an author later takes the time to elaborate a difficult section, then that explanation should be utilised as a base to evaluate the rest of the text. This does not absolve meditation upon the topic at hand, or relaxing one's mental guard in trying to eke out the definitive meanings of other passages of the text. It means rather that the definitive interpretations can be used as a tool to fathom the meanings of related subjects, not just in that text, but in all of the related texts belonging to that particular school of thought. Though the definitive interpretation may have stood the test of time, nevertheless there may be aspects of it never revealed, hence significant meditation should be given in order to ascertain the most valuable esoteric implication.

In *The Speech of Gold* Thurman quotes from the *Akshayamati Scripture:*

> Which scriptures are definitive in meaning? Which are interpretable? Those teaching superficial realities are interpretable in meaning. Those teaching ultimate realities are definitive in meaning. Those teaching various words and letters are interpretable. Those teaching the profound, the difficult to see, and the difficult to understand are definitive. Those introducing the path are interpretable. Those introducing the goal are definitive. Those scriptures that teach as if there were a lord in the lordless, using such expressions as "self," "living being," "life," "soul," "creature," "person," "human," "man," "agent," "experiencer," etc., are interpretable. And those scriptures that teach the doors of liberation, the emptiness of things, their signlessness, wishlessness, inactivity, non-production, non-occurrence, living-beinglessness, lifelessness, personlessness, and lordlessness, and so on, are definitive in meaning. You should rely on the latter, not the former.[5]

The statement 'You should rely on the latter, not the former' may be true, but one should endeavour to comprehend both. The form of interpretation one should take is entirely dependent upon the level of development of one's consciousness, of how awakened it is. If one is absorbed in the *śūnyatā* experience ('emptiness, voidness'), or is in the

---

5 Thurman, *The Speech of Gold; Reason and Enlightenment in Tibetan Buddhism*, 123, quoting: Tsongkhapa, *Essence of Eloquence*, III n. 2.

process of directly attaining such a state of awareness, then 'the latter' is preeminent and automatically incorporates the former. If one has not achieved *śūnyatā*, or who cannot in that life, thus has little ability to comprehend its meaning (which includes virtually the sum of humanity), then the former is the one that is of importance. The person has still much to gain and master from basic experiences in the material domain before absolutes can begin to be striven for. Such people are incapable of truly comprehending what absolute mastery necessitates. They may strive to achieve such, but still have many obscuring *saṃskāras*[6] blocking the way. The definitive interpretation therefore for them is a mystery, an objective to someday comprehend.

Next we have the middle level of interpreter, incorporating the bulk of Buddhist Scholars, who strive to rely upon the definitive interpretation, but must also comprehend the interpretive. This includes such things as understanding the nature of consciousness, *karma*, *saṃskāras*, higher metaphysics, the dynamics of psychological processes, the rationale of a 'non-soul'; all with keeping open an eye or view to comprehend, then identify with that which is definitive.

Finally there are the enlightened ones. They know the truth through direct perception. They need not interpret, but if they choose to do so their consideration is definitive and may reveal concepts previously not known or revealed in the texts.

Thurman further states:

> In fact, the absolute takes precedence over the relative, not intrinsically or ontologically, as it were, since the "two" realities are precisely presented as a conceptual dichotomy, but epistemologically, since the mind's orientation toward the absolute is more beneficial and liberating than its orientation toward the relative, which after all is the creation of misknowledge. Thus, the statement "there is no Buddha" contains

6 *Saṃskāra* (compounding of ideas): From the Sanskrit roots, *sam* and *kri*, meaning the action (*kri*) that will improve, refine or make an impression in consciousness. *Saṃskāras* are thus the impressions from actions done in former incarnations and which are carried through to this one and thus become the basis for one's present *karma*. It also refers to the effects of one's present actions that will bear fruit in later lives. *Saṃskāras* are thus those actions that tend to bind one to the wheel of rebirth; to repetitious pain or pleasing dispositions, mental constructs, the inception of imagery, and all emotions. They can also be the tendencies to enlightenment.

> the negation of the truth-status of a Buddha, and points to his ultimate status which is truthlessness, or realitylessness, or emptiness.[7]

I do not agree with the terms 'truthlessness', or 'realitylessness' here, as 'emptiness' can be conceived as truth or reality itself. It is not void of these. The inference is that because *śūnyatā* is 'empty' it does not intrinsically contain all truth and the real. It may be considered void of these things, but is the ground of the *dharmakāya*, the immaculate fount of pristine wisdom *(dharma),* which manifests as Truth (that which is definitive), and fecundates the Real wherever it manifests.[8] The statement 'there is no Buddha' therefore really means that ultimately, when one is in the process of gaining enlightenment, one can only rely upon one's own meditative experiences. One *cannot* look to any external source for such revelation, not even that of the Buddha. Therefore there is 'no Buddha' because through direct revelation that which is directly experienced *is* the enlightenment. Direct perception needs no external teacher. Conversely, such experience (the *fourth* point) *'is the Buddha'*.[9]

The statement that 'the mind's orientation toward the absolute is more beneficial and liberating' is correct, and from this perspective, the assertion 'You should rely on the latter' has its validation. However, that which is 'interpretable in meaning' is necessary if one wishes to function practically in the realms of consciousness and thus in

---

7 Thurman, 124.

8 How such terms as 'truthlessness', or 'realitylessness' are interpreted however is important. Semantics always plays its role in the definition of things, therefore though my interpretation may differ from Thurman's, his may be valid from his perspective. Similarly with other concepts treated in this book, various interpretations may be valid from particular viewpoints, and often the way I define words may not tally with the accepted view. My intention is to reveal the esoteric veiled by the philosophy presented, which will be evident as this series unfolds. For this reason some new definitions and concepts need to be presented that the Buddhist mindset is not accustomed to, but which hopefully the reader will find revealing.

9 Actually in practice, once the process of inner contemplative obeisance has begun then impressions from the *guru* (the representative Buddha in one's life) will eventuate in accordance with those established in past lives. The inner and outer have become one. We can also say that the perceiving consciousness of the enlightened one does not perceive a separative 'self', therefore though there may be the appearance of a Buddha, what appears is also intrinsic to all beings.

saṃsāra.[10] Without such a comprehension none of us could exist in a human body. There certainly could not be any striving for the 'definitive meaning'. The definitive interpretation leads one to experience that which exists 'outside' the empirical mind, and yet can also be inclusive of it. If most people relied exclusively on this form of interpretation without having properly developed their minds they risk being naïve optimists, or impractical idealists, immersed in conceptualisations they shallowly comprehend, hoping for attainments not possible in that life. An 'absolute' level of realisation is only obtainable by the greatest Bodhisattvas, and the vast majority of people have yet to be led to the Bodhisattva path. Many do not even conceive that such a path exists. They need education along these lines. Striving to comprehend such an ideal however is always useful, even if the attainment lies far in the future, if the mind is developed rather than mere belief. Here epistemological teachings set the path, ontology helps examine the nature of the definitive, which if phrased in terms of 'absolutes' such as *śūnyatā,* is intrinsic, because it lies at the core of our essential being.

The path to enlightenment therefore realistically necessitates that aspirants should first strive at excellence with the 'interpretable in meaning' and seek the latter form of interpretation when they have the capacity to do so. One should never stop striving and once mastery of conventional thinking has been obtained, then from that platform leap to obtaining the 'absolutely real' form of revelation. This introduces the epistemology of the so called 'Idealists', the Yogācāra-Cittamatra school. Thurman states that the Centrist Mādhyamika School looks at two Realities: 'superficial *(saṃvṛti)* conventional *(vyāvahārika)* reality *(satya)*', and 'profound *(saṃvṛta)* ultimate *(pāramārthika)* reality *(satya)*', whilst the Yogācārins have Three Natures in their place: 1. 'Imaginatively constructed *(parikalpita)* nature *(lakṣaṇa)*'. 2. 'Relative nature *(paratantra lakṣaṇa)*'. 3. 'Perfect *(pariniṣpanna)* nature *(lakṣaṇa)*'.[11]

---

10 *Saṃsāra:* cyclic existence, life-death cycle, the empirical realm. The ocean of causality, the perpetual turning of the wheel of births and deaths. Anything associated with the material worlds, to that which is ephemeral and ever-changing, and hence phenomenal, having no true substantiality of its own. It refers thus to the realms of illusion (corporeality) into which the personality incarnates and begins to identify with by means of the empirical mind.

11 Thurman, from the diagram, 118.

In his explanation Thurman refers to the 'Three Wheels of the Dharma'.[12] The first being the Hīnayāna mode of interpretation, the second being the general Mahāyāna mode, which however suffers from problems 'if taken too literally and interpreted nihilistically'[13] because of interpretations concerning the nature of *śūnyatā*. This necessitates a third Wheel, which endeavours to eliminate this problem, called 'the *Elucidation of the Intention* itself, known as the "subtly discriminative" type of Universal Vehicle teaching'.[14] What makes it 'subtly discriminative' is described by Thurman thus:

> At stake primarily is the interpretation of the frequent statements of the Buddha in the Universal Vehicle Scriptures[15] to the effect that all things are empty, often phrased as straight negations: that is, "there is no form, no feeling, no Buddha, no enlightenment, no non-enlightenment" and so forth. The Centrists[16] supply the qualifier "ultimately" in all texts other than the *Transcendent Wisdom Hundred Thousand*, where the qualifier is in the text. But for the Idealists,[17] Buddha considered this insufficient, and hence devised a scheme known as the "three natures" *(trilakṣaṇa)*. Things have three natures, an imaginatively constructed *(parikalpita)* nature, a relative *(paratantra)* nature, and a perfect, or absolute *(pariniṣpanna)* nature. When all things are said to be "empty of intrinsic reality," this only applies to them in their imaginatively constructed nature; they continue to exist as relative things, and their ineffable relativity devoid of conceptual construction is their absolute nature. Thus, the insertion of the relative category between the conceptual *(parikalpita)* and the absolute *(pariniṣpanna)* insulates the practitioner against nihilism.[18, 19]

---

12 See also D. S. Lopez, Jr., *A Study of Svātantrika*, (Snow Lion Publications, New York, 1987), 224-26, where the ways that the different schools interpret these are discussed.

13 Thurman, 117.

14 Ibid., 117. This turning of the Wheel also promulgated teachings on the *tathāgatagarbha*, the Buddha-germ or womb, which will be analysed later.

15 The Mahāyāna.

16 The Mādhyamika.

17 The Yogācāra.

18 Thurman, 117.

19 *A Handbook of Tibetan Culture* states that 'According to the *Cittamatra* school all things can be analysed according to these three natures or categories, namely: 1) the imaginary *(parikalpita)*, which includes the nominal (names and symbols) and the

Thurman then states:

> There are two main criticisms of this Idealist hermeneutic. First, mere literal acceptability is an inadequate criterion of definitiveness, since there are varieties of interpretability—some involve symbolism, some involve intention, some involve context, some merely involve restoring abbreviated expressions, and so forth. Hence the criterion is too rigid and simplistic to cope with the intricacies of the teachings. Second, for all its claims to fine analytical discrimination, three-nature theory and all, this hermeneutical strategy is still itself scripturally justified—it is, after all, the scheme set forth in the *Elucidation of Intention Scripture.* No abstract rational rule or criterion to distinguish between scriptural claims is disclosed, and hence the obvious circularity of invoking a scripture's own claim of definitiveness as proof of its own definitiveness. The great Centrists, especially Chandrakirti and Tsong Khapa, level these criticisms at the Idealist hermeneutic before setting forth their own strategies.[20]

The second criticism of the Yogācāra philosophy, relating to the disclosure of 'criterion to distinguish between scriptural claims' may or may not be true, however all Buddhist philosophy claims to be logical. Also the statement is irrelevant in view of what the Buddha has said in the *Kālāma Sūtra* about not believing anything because you have heard it, or because it is scripturally asserted (as is also the intent of the Four Reliances). Note that the lengthy quotes above have been provided to present a background of comprehension for the reader unfamiliar with these differing views, assisting thereby the understanding of the narrative that follows.

The relativity of things

When analysing the concept of 'relativity' and 'dependence', then such relativity refers to the quality of consciousness, i.e., how it identifies

---

delimited (mistaken view of self with respect to the individual and phenomena); 2) the dependent *(paratantra),* which includes impure dependence i.e., aggregates *(skandha),* elements *(dhatu),* sensory activity fields (*ayatana*), etc. and pure dependence, i.e., *buddha-*attributes; and 3) the absolute or thoroughly established phenomena *(pariniṣpanna),* which includes emptiness *(dharmadhatu)* and the irreversible states of cessation. Ed. G. Coleman, *A Handbook of Tibetan Culture,* (Rider, London, 1993), 397-398.

20 Thurman, 119.

with phenomena and to what degree. Initially consciousness is focussed towards the form, and *saṃskāras* are created through a combination of the aggregates, elements, and sensory activity. Because the person is primarily focussed via a self-concept, the 'I', he/she imaginatively mistakes phenomena to be real. This produces reifying of consciousness and fixation with *saṃsāra*. Differing degrees of attachment and knowledge-levels exist as to its nature, with consequent relative mastery of the related properties, creating different levels of interpretation of things, from that of primitive, animistic tribal societies, to the highly qualified scientific community, thence to Buddhist metaphysicians and yogic attainment. This in turn creates relative levels of ignorance.

At the later stages of evolution when actively treading the Bodhisattva path the Bodhisattva's focus is towards the development of Buddha-attributes. Accordingly, the *saṃskāras* concerning the fleeting phenomenal world are eliminated and converted into enlightenment attributes at a rate relative to the Bodhisattva stage that has been attained.

There are therefore two different types of orientation indicated:

a. Downward to the realms of the form, and intensification of attachment to its allurements, to which there are relative degrees of ignorant forms of activity. This refers to the 'imaginatively constructed *(parikalpita)* nature'. All exists as part of the experience zone in the mind, consequently is 'imagined'.

b. Upward to concepts of liberation from the form and the consequent lessening of the grip of *saṃsāra* and its illusions for such a person. The driving motivation *(vāsanā)* orients one towards right views and enlightening experiences. This produces the development of Buddha-attributes, which the Mādhyamika 'the *Tathagatagarbha* school take as absolute', whereas 'the Yogācāra take them as dependent', to quote Coleman *et al.* Such phenomena are integral to being enlightened, hence are 'absolute', but are capable of generating phenomena when interrelating with *saṃsāra,* thereby causing dependencies.

The way that people in these two broad categories interpret the 'real' is therefore different, as are the nature of the doctrines they would read and accept as being useful and true, e.g., scientific materialism versus the doctrine of the Void. The variety of religious presentations, philosophies, and 'isms' found in the world all present relative truths, however they are part of the one process that leads eventually to the bliss of liberation, once those truths have been assimilated and transcended upon the upward way.

There is a process that leads from reliance upon the 'imagined' phenomena around one to the reality experienced by a Buddha. This includes the epistemological conceptualisations described above in order to discern the truth. We then have the path of yoga-meditation, the perusal of the Tantras in order to experience direct perception of the real. The process persists (over many lives) until Buddhahood is obtained. One thing is dependent upon another, everything is relative, a flow of mutable interrelation until the immutable is realised. Relativity therefore should be interpreted as this flux of interconnectedness. Even Buddha-attributes are relative to each other. They are literally the application of potent forces and energies from domains far subtler than those of normal human livingness. They govern the laws conditioning *saṃsāra,* hence a Buddha has mastered the sum of its phenomena. From the domains of Mind via a clarified mind do these attributes (*siddhis,* psychic powers) manifest to command whatever is to be.

Whether these Buddha-attributes are 'pure dependents' *(paratantra)* because of their relativity to each other is a moot point, depending upon whether one thinks in terms of absolutes, as being the Buddha nature (intrinsic emptiness), or in terms of such a One's interrelation with phenomena that we can cognise (extraneous emptiness), or in terms of *the process* producing the appearance of that which is cognisable (the intrinsic mastering the extraneous).

That all things are relative is the contention posited throughout this series. Without such relativity we could not think and categorise things. Things are defined as 'things' only when viewed relative to each other. *Śūnyatā* is only conceived as such relative to an 'other', i.e., *saṃsāra.* Without *saṃsāra śūnyatā* could not be explained or defined. *Śūnyatā* may be the goal, breaking this flow, hence considered an absolute, but it is not the true goal of one seeking Buddhahood. It is effectively a mirror of the *dharmakāya* into *saṃsāra. Śūnyatā* may 'exist', but there are no reference points to its existence until valid cognition is achieved. Later the fact that it is the middle between extremes, bridging *saṃsāra* to the *dharmakāya* shall be explored. It facilitates the eventual integration of *saṃsāra* into/as the *dharmakāya*. The process necessitates the appearance of the human mind as a foundation for the demonstration of Mind. *Śūnyatā* can therefore be considered a vehicle of translation of such a mind into the *dharmakāyic* Mind. Considerable elaboration of what constitutes such a Mind is therefore imperative.

There is nothing rigid or simplistic in the concept of relativity, it allows all varieties of interpretation, and the definiteness of definitions as well as all subtleties of perception. It does not need scriptural justification, but scriptural authority can also be invoked as an interpretative tool if need be. (In reference to the Madhyamaka[21] criticism of the 'Idealist hermeneutic' given above.) Only the concept of relativity allows us to define anything. Epistemological deductions are certainly useful, but direct pristine (yogic) insight is best. The Clear Light of Mind is the fount of all wisdom.

Things are automatically categorised in the mind (the process of *parikalpita*) in accordance to their relativityness as part of the process of their definition, hence the 'varieties of interpretability'. This is but another way of stating the different ways things can be properly evaluated and defined, (i.e., how things stand relative to other things). This then determines how symbolism, intention, context, *etc.*, can be analysed. If a teaching or thing presented is symbolic, then the question that is automatically asked is 'In what way are we to derive meaning from it?'

The *bodhi*-tree, symbolising the Buddha's enlightenment, is one example. First it is conceptualised or imaginatively construed; then arises the concept of relativity, it's roots, trunk, branches, leaves, shade. They all pertain to aspects of enlightenment, from the foundations or roots (*saṃsāric* involvement), to the trunk, the main support or basis of the teachings or *dharma* from which branch out the main lines of reasoning, syllogisms, hermeneutics, pathways for knowledge. Each of these are relative to each other. Then come the myriad twigs and leaves, facets of knowledge forming the relatively differing sequences of the overall structure of *bodhi*.[22] They provide a comforting 'shade' of

---

21 *Madhyamaka*, derived from *madhymapratipad,* refers to the Middle Way School. Mādhyamika means 'pertaining to the middle way', an adherent of the Madhyamaka School.

22 *Bodhi*, enlightenment, full awakening, perfected knowledge, transcendental insight.

revelation over the meditating one, preparatory to the liberating Light that must come from within. Next we have the absolute or ultimate truth; that the entire structure of the tree is a unity, but its form and shape is relative to others around it (e.g., other Buddha-fields).

Furthermore, only in this ultimate view can certain other intangibles be seen, such as the way that sunlight falls upon the tree, and the shade it creates, i.e., the way it tones down the absolute source of all (the sunshine, representing the *dharmakāya),* making the experience bearable or comfortable for most. Is this not a reason why the Bodhisattva Gautama chose the shade of a tree to sit under, and wherewith his enlightenment was produced?

Many examples of this nature could be cited showing that rather than being 'too rigid and simplistic', the three nature concept (in the way outlined here) is an essential ingredient in all definitions of things. The utilisation of relativity allows fluidity and is automatically utilised in any definition. When the Mādhyamikas have to use the qualifier ultimately 'in all texts other than the *Transcendent Wisdom Hundred Thousand,* where the qualifier is in the text' then they are in fact utilising a *de facto* version of the three nature theory.[23] When put into context we have:

---

23 See A. Wayman, *Untying the Knots in Buddhism, Selected Essays,* (Motilal Banarsidass, Delhi, 1997) 79-80, where we also have the words from the *Bodhisattva-piṭaka-sūtra*:

> On the three truths *(satya)* of the bodhisattva *(saṃvṛti-paramārtha-,* and *lakṣaṇa),* conventional truth *(saṃvṛti-satya)* is as much as there is of mundane convention; and is expression with letters, speech, and discursive thought. When consciousness does not course, how much less the letters—that is absolute truth *(paramārtha-satya).* Truth of characteristics *(lakṣaṇa-satya)* is as follows: all characteristics are one characteristic, and one characteristic is no characteristic. On the bodhisattva's skill in truth: the bodhisattva does not weary of expressing conventional truth; he does not fall into direct realization of absolute truth, but matures sentient beings; he reflects on the truth of characteristics as no characteristic.

In short, it appears that there was circulating in Nāgārjuna's time this scriptural theory of a third truth—of characteristics as no characteristic, apparently underlying the other two truths, where 'characteristics' means 'characters of differentiation.'...this may explain Nāgārjuna's MMK, XXV, 19: "There is no differentiation *(viśeṣaṇa)* of Saṃsāra from Nirvāṇa; there is no differentiation of Nirvāṇa from Saṃsāra." That is to say, Nāgārjuna rejected the 'all characteristics' of the Sarvāstivādin that serves to differentiate Nirvāṇa from

a. The conventional interpretation, where there are things that appear to have an existence relative to other things.
b. The 'absolutely valuable reality', conceptualised as *śūnyatā*.
c. The term 'ultimately' uniting the two. This term means 'eventually, taking place in an unspecified later time', which necessitates a process of becoming, i.e., of manifesting one form of *relative* appearance in relation to another. These 'relative appearances' are the characteristics of *saṃsāra*, which become ultimately 'no characteristic' in terms of *śūnyatā*. The *process* of that which ultimately relates the two can also be considered that which is imagined because it is not yet manifesting. Thus this is but a version of the 'imaginatively constructed (*parikalpita*) nature' of the Yogācārins.

Therefore, when the two truths are explained later, so then the explication of the 'three natures' given above should be seen to be implicit in the presentation; namely that the term 'ultimately' is figurative for the progression of the relative appearances of things. It has implicit in it the 'relative (*paratantra*) nature' of the Yogācārins, as well as the 'imaginatively constructed (*parikalpita)* nature'. This eventually produces 'the ultimate', which is in itself relative to that which is 'not ultimate'. The truth of the matter is that ultimately the *dharmakāya* is all.

The *saṃsāra-nirvāṇa* interrelationship

From the perspective of the quote from Wayman,[24] where he states 'Nāgarjuna rejected the "all characteristics" of the Sarvāstivādin that serves to differentiate Nirvāṇa from Saṃsāra in the way the discriminating mind does', the view is from the perspective of Absolute

---

Saṃsāra in the way the discriminating mind does. With the 'eye of insight' there is one characteristic, or sameness; because with this 'eye' one sees *dharmas*, e.g., their dependent origination. But Nāgārjuna did not say that Nirvāṇa and Saṃsāra are the same. By insisting that Nirvāṇa and Saṃsāra have no characteristics of differentiation, he pointed to 'no characteristic', perhaps implicating the Mahāyāna Nirvāṇa, called 'Nirvāṇa of no-fixed abode' *(aprattiṣṭhita-nirvāṇa).* After the time of Nāgārjuna, the Mādyamika insisted there were just two truths, thus supporting my conclusion that the three-truth theory preceded Nāgārjuna.
See also page 87 of the text.

24 Ibid., 80.

Truth. From this perspective Nāgārjuna's statement, 'there is no differentiation of *nirvāṇa*[25] from *saṃsāra'* is interpreted as 'because everything in *saṃsāra* is void, so there is no differentiation between *nirvāṇa* and *saṃsāra'*. (Which is actually stating that in reality there is no *saṃsāra,* only the Void is true. Here the word *nirvāṇa* is given before *saṃsāra* as a technical device to indicate its priority.) When viewing things in terms of the discriminating mind, then we are conceptualising conventional truth, wherein *nirvāṇa* and *saṃsāra* are linked by means of the process inherent in the term 'ultimately'. It is this process that the first part of Nāgārjuna's statement refers: 'There is no differentiation *(visheṣaṇa)* of Saṃsāra from Nirvāṇa'. The first part of the statement therefore refers to the process that is productive of *nirvāṇa/śūnyatā* from out of *saṃsāra,* the second part refers to the mode whereby *saṃsāra* is perceived by one in *nirvāṇa.* (The technical device here is to place *saṃsāra* before *nirvāṇa.*)

Absolutely speaking there is 'no differentiation' in the process that relates the two modes of expression of *saṃsāra-śūnyatā* and *śūnyatā-saṃsāra,*[26] but conventionally there is; they are linked by a process: the term *relatively* by one brand of Buddhist hermeneutics, *ultimately* by another, and 'characteristics of differentiation' by the early Sarvāstivādins. The difference between these terms is that the words 'ultimately' and 'characteristics of differentiation' imply a time sequence *(saṃsāra* including or relating to *śūnyatā* as *saṃsāra-śūnyatā*), whereas the term 'relatively' *(śūnyatā* including or relating to *saṃsāra* as *śūnyatā-saṃsāra)* does not. It however categorises or distinguishes between the appearances of things within that time sequence. The

---

25 *Nirvāṇa*, 'extinguished'. State beyond sorrow, therefore ultimate sphere of emptiness *(śūnyatā).* All defilements are extinguished, producing perfect calm, thus the state of residing in *śūnyatā*. From the Sanskrit roots *nir, nis,* meaning out, forth, away from, and *va,* meaning to blow, as the wind, to move, to be agitated. The 'final' attainment of the evolutionary process with respect to the form. It thus concerns complete liberation from all forms of taintedness or identification with the realms of illusion. It concerns the liberation of consciousness into a state of 'Be-ness', into spaciousness, that which is neither being nor non-being.

26 I have used the terms *saṃsāra-śūnyatā* and *śūnyatā-saṃsāra* (which shall be used throughout this series) here because *nirvāṇa* has the connotation of the final liberation of a Buddha, whereas *śūnyatā* relates to the state of emptiness that exists in lieu of *saṃsāra*. The term *śūnyatā* is hence more technically correct for general considerations.

appearance of relativities therefore produces the 'ultimate' over a time sequence.[27] One term ('ultimately') thus describes a process of becoming, the other ('relatively') characterises the particulars of that process. Both terms are needed to properly describe the *saṃsāra-śūnyatā* interrelationship, therefore one cannot really use one without reference to the other when explaining this relationship. This leads us to the inevitable conclusion that the two truth approach (of the conceptual and the absolute) has implicit in it a third truth of relativity and the process of becoming, which binds all into a unity. Relativity allows the dualities to be adequately described and resolved.

The quotation from Tsongkhapa's *Essence of the Good Explanations* given by Lopez in *A Study of Svātantrika* states:

> Furthermore, when refuting [them],[28] one should affix the qualification "truly" [or "ultimately"] in relation to the thought of the opponent. Because, in general, [there are cases when the opponent's position] must be refuted in terms of both truths [ultimate and conventional], there are some cases in which it is not necessary to affix the qualification "truly." However, in most cases, the qualification "truly" must be affixed.[29]

The term 'truly' means 'honestly, without pretence', and indicates the way things exist in truth. *Truth* here referring to that aspect of the *dharma* pertaining to *śūnyatā*. We can also add a second stream of truth: that aspect of the *dharma* pertaining to the *dharmakāya,* which presents to the mind significant metaphysics beyond that of the Void, or 'Be-ness'. In Tsongkhapa's day the form of truth pertaining to *śūnyatā* mostly sufficed for exegesis and meditation, but not for the coming epoch of revelation of the nature of the *dharma*. It portends deeper revelatory insights into the way of enlightenment and its outcome in relation to the vastness of the multidimensional attributes of cosmos. Such progress is the expression of a natural process of the developing history of Buddhism.

---

27 One can also say that the ultimate *(śūnyatā)* inherently exists and the entire process of the removal of characteristics *(saṃskāras),* as explained in Volume 5A of this series, will simply reveal that which is the real all along. However, much more is implicated because wisdom is also generated.

28 Assertions from other schools.

29 Lopez, 370.

Tsongkhapa represented the end of an epoch. He came to precisely elucidate and aptly manifest a detailed critique of the sum of the Madhyamaka philosophy, and did this by placing into context all rival Buddhist schools. His efforts were therefore encyclopaedic, and in doing so he laid the foundation for further revelations to come. He produced the finalised books of all *dharma* that could be revealed preceding him. This allows succeeding new presentations of the *dharma*, once what he had to say was properly assimilated in the (Tibetan) Buddhist world. The present era is thereby introduced wherein further revelation can be provided of a deeper strata of *dharma.*

The use of relativity in analysis is needed to logically ascertain truth. It represents the part of the tree of *bodhi* where the main trunk splits off into its variegated branches. Therefore it needs no scriptural validation, but such can be presented as a means to greater revelation. Similarly with the word 'ultimately'—ultimately one gets to the leaves (attributes of the enlightened Mind, *bodhi)* by means of the variegated branches of the tree (avenues of thought, conventional reality). In the leaves the all-embracive truth of sunlight can be directly experienced. In this analogy the main trunk represents the conveyance of the principle of enlightenment, wisdom, which has its roots in the fertile ground of *saṃsāra*, where the soil represents the ignorance to be overcome. The air through which sunlight manifests represents *śūnyatā*, liberation, (the ultimate truth). The all-sustaining sun then is the *dharmakāya*. This is the *saṃsāra-śūnyatā* approach, and is the main way of interpreting the *bodhi*-tree.

The *śūnyatā-saṃsāra* relationship can be viewed in an analogy where the soil *(śūnyatā*—being vast, dark, 'unfathomable') contains the nutrients, enlightenment-attributes, sustaining the entire tree via the roots. In between the soil and the sky stands the full panoply of the tree, teeming with its myriad forms of hidden life and activity (revelatory experiences), which indicate the process of the relativeness of all that must ultimately manifest (the *dharmakāya).* The main trunk represents the support of the enlightened Mind (stemming from *śūnyatā).* The sunlight to which the branches and leaves of the tree aspire represents that aspect of *dharmakāya* that manifests as the cosmos. Seeds are caused to form which are then dispersed to distribute elements of the *dharmakāya* far and wide. Each new seed[30] has the capacity to germinate

30 The seeds symbolise the attributes of enlightenment that a Bodhisattva bequeaths

and sprout forth a new tree of revelatory capabilities and wisdom from out of the stable base that represents the soil/*śūnyatā*. In this analogy only the mind/Mind, *śūnyatā* and *dharmakāya* are players in the world. The mind is considered real, and though it contains aspects of *saṃsāra* its foundation is *śūnyatā,* and it is turned to the *dharmakāya,* of which it is an attribute. As it incorporates more of the attributes of *dharmakāya* so mind transmogrifies into Mind. The Mind integrates *saṃsāra, śūnyatā* and *dharmakāya.*

From the above perspective the earlier *saṃsāra-śūnyatā* approach has already been established, with the gains from *saṃsāric* activity in the process of being transformed and transmuted into *dharmakāya.* The abstract Mind contains *saṃsāra,* and the relativity is between the factors of transformation of the elements of mind/Mind (the leaves) into *dharmakāya,* supported by the stable ground of *śūnyatā* and its energies. This view therefore represents the practical meditative work in the Mind of a *yogin* or advanced Bodhisattva, when dealing with inner transformations.

An alternate view is that the soil represents the darkness of *saṃsāra,* which contains the nutrients of all that is to be. The roots of the tree represent the activity of the mind, whereby the essential nutrients (*karma*-forming tendencies) are extracted from the soil. The main trunk of the tree then is *śūnyatā,* with the branches and leaves representing the *dharmakāya.* This view is symbolically more correct because there is a consistent linear relationship from *saṃsāra* to mind to *śūnyatā* to *dharmakāya* and cosmos.

Though the detail of the *saṃsāra-śūnyatā* and *śūnyatā-saṃsāra* relationship has been explained here, it should be noted the way these terms are used throughout this series is that they signify the mechanism of the *tathāgatagarbha* (the Buddha-germ in us) in the way that it interrelates *saṃsāra* to *śūnyatā.* The tree then symbolises the *tathāgatagarbha's* interrelationship with the *personal-I* (the incarnate human unit). The detail is not exact, but the leaves represent the raincloud of knowable things emanated via the *tathāgatagarbha.* The branches and trunk represent the main body of the mind of the

---

to others. A seed can also refer to the Buddha germ *(tathāgatagarba),* but this statement hints at a vast ontology, somewhat explained in Volume 3.

personal-I, and the roots in the soil represent the extraction of basic understanding via the sense-consciousness in the soil of *saṃsāra*.

The various depictions of the nature of the *bodhi* tree as presented also illustrate how the various views of the schools of Buddhism can arise when rationalising the same set of factors.

Direct awareness and interpretation

The fourth point of refuge earlier given is: 'Direct awareness is one's point of refuge, not discursive awareness'. Historically, various teachings may have taken the form of intellectual conundrums, but this has served to maximally develop thought and the empirical mind. The texts were however not written for mere intellectual pursuits, to feed mentalistic pride, or conceptual forms of smugness, but rather as aids assisting the quest for enlightenment. If fruitful this quest awakens the Clear Light of non-discursive thought, wherein insight is instantaneous revelatory experience. Buddhist texts are effectively aids in meditation. They assist the mind to rightly focus the needed ideas to gain clear insight of the nature of reality. If correctly utilised the texts can therefore stimulate a direct awareness, an aim of all teachings given by the enlightened. In fact if a sacred text is truly sacred then it is the product of the expression of the meditation-Mind of the enlightened being that wrote it. It is conceived in meditation and presents the language of the nature of the awakened Mind. The text can therefore only be properly interpreted by those that at least have the mind reposed in a meditative state or engaged in *samādhi*.[31] If the mind is not meditative, then deeper meaning of the scriptures will be missed or distorted by the reader's ever too quick tendencies to emotively rationalise.

An enlightened One is like a Buddha (the prime example of a perfect teacher). Normally he will only partially explicate this or that fact about reality, because the emphasis is to lead the enquirer through a process of deductive and meditative logic wherewith truth (*satya*) can be deduced by that person. Words have their limitation, no matter how succinctly definitions are explained. There is always much more that

31 *Samādhi* can be defined as a concentration of the mind in a meditative equipoise upon the topic at hand.

could have been given, but could not be properly explicated through the extant language. Much can therefore only be hinted at, inferred, and also needs veiling for various reasons.

Over the millennia Buddhists have been overly concerned with modes of interpretation, producing many doctrinal disputes. Thus it may also be useful to the earnest student if the subject of interpretation is elaborated upon, allowing better comprehension of the meaning of the *sūtras*. P. J. Griffith states:

> Rules of interpretation will usually be framed by creating a hierarchy within the set of doctrine-expressing sentences, and requiring that those lower down the hierarchical order be interpreted in terms of those higher up. For example, such a rule might say *all doctrine-expressing sentences of this community are to be interpreted so that they are consonant with a particular subset of them.* The rule of interpretation used by some Buddhist communities, that Sūtras whose meaning is definitive *(nītārtha)* are to be used as guides for the interpretation of those whose meaning requires interpretation *(neyārtha)*, is of just this kind. Sūtras are, for Buddhists, collections of *buddhavacana*, Buddha's word, and as such are by definition collections of sentences expressive of doctrine for the community. But the assumption that all these sentences are of equal weight leads to problems, since there are many prima facie contradictions among them. Hence the specification of some subset of them as more authoritative: the prima facie meaning of these is to govern the interpretation given the rest.[32]

He further states:

> Buddhist scholastic literature, corpora are composed usually of a root- or core-text, sometimes in verse and sometimes in prose, surrounded by concentric layers of prose commentary, subcommentary, and subsubcommentary. The root-text is usually relatively short, and is essentially a mnemotechnical aid for the student, to be learned by heart as a first step in coming to grips with a particular corpus; the layers of commentary then proved exegesis and systematization, as well as extended discussion of controversial questions.[33]

32 Griffith, *On Being Buddha, The Classical Doctrine of Buddhahood*, 20.

33 Griffith, 28-29.

The *sūtras* were first written down centuries after the time of the Buddha. They were coded for recitation and came from the meditation-Mind of a disciple of the Buddha, such as Ānanda, who remembered the original discourses. The later Mahāyāna scriptures are the direct result of meditation in action, depicting the way that the author's Mind visualises, interprets and expounds pertinent information. Depending upon the relative enlightenment of the authors concerned (or if enlightened at all), so the *śāstras* etc.,[34] have differing value. Some concepts and terms may have become corrupted over the centuries of recitation, and there is always the case of translation or copying errors of scribes, as the sacred scriptures were copied from generation to generation. It is important therefore that the reader not take the text upon face value, but rather as guides for analytical deduction or reasoning for truth. Nothing written down can be considered absolute, and the different ways of interpretation of most scriptures are legion.

Accordingly Griffith states:

> It is claimed that whenever putative utterances of Buddha appear to some community not to be well said, not to conform to its own doctrinal system, its own tenets, they must be capable of an interpretation that makes them so conform.
>
> Such a rule of interpretation necessitated the development of complex theories about Buddha's intentions in speaking nonliterally, and a battery of technical terms was developed to label these intentions.[35]

Such 'complex theories' come about because the minds interpreting the *sūtras* and *śāstras* were not enlightened, or else the authors of the texts were not enlightened. That many hermeneutic schools exist also indicate that enlightenment can be of differing degrees, signifying various ignorance levels concerning the nature of fundamental reality. Differences can be considered to result from the many ways (views) the eye can observe the same object, affecting comprehension accordingly. Clearly, differing epistemologies can be rightly integrated in an awakened Mind and their content seen straightforwardly for what

34 *Sūtras* are the compiled rules, aphorisms and discourses of the Buddha, whereas *śāstras* are commentaries or treatises.

35 Ibid., 54.

they are. The forms of illogic can then be immediately discarded, and alternate views put in the proper category of legitimacy.

The nature of the serpent power

The source of inspiration of a sage's enlightened Mind is always presented in symbolic terms in a legend or myth concerning that person. This can be correctly interpreted by those comprehending the symbolism of the mysteries of being/non-being. The source always indicates the level of attainment of the originator of the scripture. Nāgārjuna, for instance, was said to have received his revelations from the realm of the *nāgas* (serpents). Serpents signify the way vital energy (*prāṇa*) in the body flows. Their realm represents the place of the store of such energies in the subtle body, which accomplished *yogins* can consciously access.

In considering the nature of the transformed *prāṇas* as a consequence of yogic practice serpents refer to the process of the development of *siddhis* (psychic powers) and consequent wisdom for those practicing the white *dharma*.

Saṃskāras and *prāṇas* are virtually synonymous. They convey all consciousness-attributes developed by any individual. The associated energies manifest in a serpentine fashion. Each different *saṃskāra* has a beginning (the tail), accumulates qualities as it travels through time (a body) and an eventual end (head). The symbolism of where Nāgārjuna obtained his revelations thus informs us that he was a very accomplished *yogin*. It implies that his highly refined *prāṇas* were of such a high order that the energy conveyed by the serpents manifested as *siddhis* of accomplishment.

The quality of the *prāṇas* in the *nāḍī* system[36] of the body is all important. They determine the extent to which the *chakras*[37] (psychic centres) are awakened, the degree of rotation of their whorls of petals,

---

36 *Nāḍi:* literally river. (Also from *nada*, a species of hollow reed.) *Nāḍīs* are finely reticulated channels for the conveyance of *prāṅa* in the etheric vehicle. These channels stem from the three principal ones in the central spinal column (*iḍā, piṇgalā* and *suṣumṇā nāḍīs*). They roughly follow the path of the nerves and blood stream. There are said to be 72,000 *nāḍīs*, though this number is symbolic. Each *nāḍī* allows the passage of the five different types of *prāṇas*, and their combinations.

37 The proper transliteration of this Sanskrit term is *cakra*, however I have retained the commonly used *chakra*, signifying how it is pronounced.

and the intensity of the colours. (The *chakras* are receptacles for the assimilation and transformations of the attributes of consciousness. They are Eyes with which to perceive multidimensional space.) This pertains to the ability of the meditator to receive impressions from higher sources, such as from *dharmakāya,* Bodhisattvas, or *ḍākinīs* ('sky-goers', feminine protectors of the law).

How serpents evolve to be conveyers of wisdom so that they can enlighten *yogins,* and through them inspire an entire corpus of Buddhist philosophy, is an intriguing subject for those wishing to develop the Eyes to see. The foundation of much of the Mahāyāna stream of revelation is based upon knowledge of many esoteric topics stemming from the awakening of *chakras.* Authors who did develop their Eyes arose to fill in some of the missing portions of the overall philosophy that for instance Nāgārjuna did not provide. Other scholars have relied upon purely empirical deductions, and so differing schools of interpretation developed. Various forms of concretions of mind reifying the esoteric logic were also produced. Tantric philosophy provides the answer for doctrines that come as a consequence of yogic practices, but the Tantras are not decipherable by the uninitiated, apart from the general meanings of the associated symbolism and underlying philosophy. Comprehending the esoteric background to sacred texts and of the internal processes constituting the making of an enlightened being should therefore be important for both practitioners and scholars if the reified knots of logic are to be untangled.

The symbolism of the serpent is inextricably interwoven with that of *the staff,* which is often one of the very few possessions retained by Hindu and Buddhist *yogins* and mendicants in their wanderings. They carry these not just to aid their physical bodies in their travels, but because the staff also symbolises their yogic prowess and austerities. It depicts the strait up central spinal column through which the subjective energies associated with their yogic practices must flow. The spinal column is the central support of the *yogin's* entire meditative being, without which his attainments *(siddhis)* would not be possible.[38] *Prāṇas* flow up the spinal column via the three major psychic channels that it houses.

---

38 For the esoteric significance of the cane staff that Milarepa possessed (who was perhaps Tibet's greatest accomplished *yogin),* see G.C.C. Chang. (Trans), *The Hundred Thousand Songs of Milarepa, Vol 1,* (Shambhala, London, 1977), Ch. 18.

At the base of the spinal column we find the energy of the Mother aspect, the primeval causative or formative energy that lies coiled in potential for liberating activity. This central reservoir of heat, or internal energy, that sustains the life of the dense material form, is called *kuṇḍalinī* ('serpent power').

Kuṇḍalinī is related to the fires deep within the heart of the earth and can be considered to have been, exist not, and yet is. It is an effect of the past (that has been), has no substantiality of its own ('exist not'), for in the last resort it is the Fiery subjective expression of the will, and is that which sustains the phenomenal, illusory universe (which is considered 'empty'). Yet it 'is' as long as this material world is sustained.

Its animating dynamo in a person is said to be the Base of Spine centre,[39] which in conjunction with the *chakra* at the sacral area psychically sustains life by means of fine channels *(nāḍīs).*

As well as the serpentine motion of this energy the symbol of the serpent is taken from a spiral path that two major *naḍīs* take around the central column. One of these paths (the *iḍā nāḍī*) conveys the psychically receptive feminine creative forces and energies in Nature (an attribute of *kuṇḍalinī)* sustaining the evolution of sentience. The energies that it bears also pertain to the *prāṇas* from the input of the sense-consciousnesses as correlated by the intellect and thus empirical rationalisations, which often blind one to enlightened perceptions. Thus it governs the expression of the mind *per se,* and being *manasic* (of the mind) the Elements associated with it are Earth and Fire.[40] It also conveys the general vitality (*prāṇa*) absorbed from the air and obtained from food (utilising that term in its broadest possible sense).

The *piṇgalā nāḍī* conveys the 'son energy', the consciousness-engendering factor, the result of experience-gathering activities when integrated into streams of loving cognitive perceptions and intuitive revelations. It channels the *prāṇas* of human emotions, desire, and the affections developed through family and group interrelations. These qualities are later developed into the energy of love upon the path of liberation. It is Watery or Airy in nature, and is fluidly embracive

39 *Mūlādhāra chakra.*

40 The alchemical Elements: Earth, Water, Fire, Air and Aether shall be capitalised throughout this series. Explanations shall be provided as to their attributes when needed.

of unities, as associated with thinking via the Heart. It then conveys the *prāṇas* of an expansive Mind-stream that is vibrantly sensitive to impressions from manifold directions in multidimensional space. (A definition of the enlightened-Mind.)

The symbol of the *iḍā nāḍī* is the moon, because like the moon, it conveys reflected light, which is associated with the form nature, the energies of the personality, and that of the psychic world. The symbol of the *piṇgalā nāḍī* is the sun, the greater luminary, because it expresses the illuminating light of wisdom *(prajñā)*. When the sun and moon are therefore spoken of in mystical, esoteric, alchemical, mythological, or religious texts, one can always assume that they refer to the energies associated with these *naḍīs*. The *iḍā* and *piṇgalā* streams of energy are said to relate to 'wisdom and method' where the feminine is the wisdom aspect and the masculine is the compassionate aspect (or 'method'), as stated in the introductory commentary on Tantric texts in Jamgön Kongtrul's *Treasury of Knowledge*.

> There are three main channels, the left, right and central channels, whose functions are of primary importance and whose positions within the body reflect the principles of method, wisdom and nonduality... The left channel, in Sanskrit *lalanā (rkyang ma)*, originates from the power of the white aspect of the glow of pristine awareness. It creates the illusion of an apprehender. Lalana is also called "wisdom" (*shes rab, prajñā*) because it causes the lunar wind (*zla ba'i rlung*) to flow from the left nostril....The right channel, in Sanskrit *rasanā (ro ma)*, originates from the power of the red aspect[41] of the glow of pristine awareness. It creates the illusion of an objective world, the apprehended. Rasana is also called "method" (*thabs, upāya*) because it causes the solar wind (*nyi ma'i rlung*) to flow from the right nostril.[42]

One should note that the details concerning the arousal and liberation of psychic energy have been *purposely made misleading* in all Tantric

41 It indicates the left channel as white, the male aspect, and the right channel as female and red. Note that though the terms *lalanā* and *rasanā* are commonly used in Tibetan Buddhist texts, I shall use the more commonly known terms *iḍā, piṇgalā and suṣumṇā* (the central channel) throughout this series when referring to these *nāḍīs*.

42 Jamgön Kongtrul Lodrö Tayé, *The Treasury of Knowledge*; *Systems of Buddhist Tantra*, (Snow Lion, New York, 2005), 37.

texts because of the inherent dangers. The concept of red and white flows of *prāṇa* is an example, as in reality there are five main *prāṇic* streams in each *nāḍī,* each possessing a different hue.[43]

Compassion (love) is the active expression of wisdom if it is to be truly efficacious, hence explained in terms of the skilful means of a Bodhisattva. Compassion generally relates to relieving sources of emotional pain or suffering, and wisdom relates to the right application of consciousness. Compassion arises spontaneously from the heart, whereas wisdom is derived from the mind when directed compassionately. From this Bodhisattvic perspective the assignment of compassion to the masculine gender is correct. Our concern here is literally an analysis of the dual Ray of Love-Wisdom. From another perspective the utilisation of correct analogy is assisted by the biological role of woman, which is to give birth to the child (the formed realm, *prakṛti)* and then to compassionately guide the child through its formative years (i.e., the demonstration of 'method'). The feminine nurtures the developing form, whilst the masculine principle should provide the right educative direction (i.e., 'wisdom') for the child's upbringing. This however, is the opposite to what is presented in orthodox Buddhism. When applying gender to any symbolic consideration one should always observe the different types of energy qualification. The more spacious and unfettering then 'masculine', the more receptive to and embracive of attributes of the form then 'feminine'. The nature of the 'view' however is the determinant factor, whether from above-down (e.g., with respect to the Bodhisattva attitude) or from below-up, as is the case with the feminine biological role.

Whatever the case may be for wisdom and compassion, the correct assignment for the *nāḍīs* is: the left (*iḍā)*—lunar, Earthy-Fiery, female, intelligence, activity; and the right (*piṇgalā)*—solar, Watery-Airy, male, consciousness, contemplation. Note that the Watery Element is sometimes assigned to the feminine because of its fluid changeability. The correct feminine assignment however is to the ubiquitous fusion of Water with Fire, producing the desire or emotional-mind *(kāma-manas).*

---

43 This allows the conveyance of the *prāṇas* of the five sense-consciousnesses and the development of the wisdoms of the five Dhyāni Buddhas through the *nāḍīs*. Many of the veils and blinds incorporated in Tantric texts shall be unravelled in this series, as will be evident by the time the mysteries of the *Bardo Thödol* are revealed in Volume 5.

The central channel, the *suṣumṇā nāḍī*, conveys the dynamically active 'Father energy' that impels the person onwards towards liberation. This is the energy that unites the highest aspect of being to the lowest, thus fully enlightening the person, providing the experience of *dharmatā* (actual reality, the Ultimate Truth of phenomenon).

Suṣumṇā is brought to activity when 'the Son', consciousness *(prajñā),* is in full compassionate expression whilst the person is meditating. The mind has become serene and yet manifests a powerful intensity, allowing receptivity to the vast reaches of all-encompassing space. The mind is then a fully prepared and endowed womb, into which the ripened Fiery seed of all potential *(kuṇḍalinī)* is ready to spread its energy to flower in space. This seed is liberated by a potent sound *(mantra)* conveying the most intense type of energy that reaches down into the deepest layers of substance, to the base of manifest being. There it awakens the feminine Fire sustaining the life of every atom, integrating it with the Fires of the evolved consciousness. The triune united Fire *(kuṇḍalinī, iḍā-piṅgalā* and *mantra)*[44] then rises up the central channel *(suṣumṇā),* fully vivifying the various psychic centres in geometric order as it does so. Once the Head centre becomes totally vitalised with the fused energies then the person is liberated from the throttlehold of the form. Enlightenment has ensued.

The picture presented here is a bare outline. It is not yet possible to give an accurate detailed picture of the nature of the 'raising of *kuṇḍalinī*' because of the immensity, subtlety, and esotericism of the subject. The entire story of manifest being, of evolution, and meditative unfoldment is hidden in it. Many have tried to satiate their curiosity by perusing the various meditation and occult texts on the subject. It should be noted however that such information is always veiled, purposely misleading, contradictory, or else cursorily treated, because of the potential dangers awaiting the unwise in their premature attempts to awaken this force. In its most material aspect (for it is many layered) *kuṇḍalinī* will burn and destroy the form or wreak havoc upon the psychic constitution of the person who has not the knowledge or the moral and psychic purity to rightly direct it, and who has utilised the force of the personal will to

44 *Piṅgalā* and *iḍā* have at this stage been united as Love-Wisdom, producing the lucidity that is their 'Son'.

'awaken' it. Its tendency will always be to reinforce or distort whatever subtle, uncontrolled desire, or base quality that exists. (For it manifests through the path of least resistance as it allegorically seeks to unite with the Father energies.) This is symbolised by the burning poison of the viper which produces psychic madness and spiritual death.

This introduces the secondary implication of the meaning of the serpent, as that of the *ability to poison;* which concerns engendering the little *prāṇic* serpents embodying qualities of desire, lust, spite, hatred, enmity, and vituperation. It thus also symbolises that which causes a person to be bound to the type of life associated with the sensual, illusion-forming material world. This domain is also implicit in the Watery (desire) world that Buddhist tradition states that *nāgas* (serpents) are said to rise from. Psychically, this means that their place of generation is associated with the Solar Plexus (naval) centre *(maṇipūra chakra),* which controls the expression of this Element. A serpent can thus refer to the ability to 'poison' (when the associated *prāṇas* are defiled or aberrant), or else to awaken wisdom.[45]

There are five types of *prāṇas*, as explained in my book on *karma* associated with the stages of yogic development, called *apāna, samāna, udāna, prāṇa, and vyāna.*[46] They convey the qualities of the five Elements. When the third Element conveying the Fiery (mental) principle becomes the major *prāṇa (udāna)* flowing in the *nāḍī* system then the serpents are Fiery. When the fourth of the Elements (Air)

---

45 Three serpents lie within you:
The adder of death,
that with poisonous venom feeds the sensual person.
The serpent of wisdom, transmuted poison is ambrosia,
joyous nectar of Light, Love, and of Life.
The Dragon of Fiery Life, the serpent has shed its skin,
is free and flies.
Oh humanity, where are the chords that bind you?
It is your task to find them, and release the power behind them
if in all-encompassing space you shall reside. (Though consciousness cannot delineate it, yet it is a zone of residence that is the natural state of Mind.)

46 Bodo Balsys, *Karma and the Rebirth of Consciousness.* (Delhi: Munshiram Manoharlal, 2006), 56-7. See also Tabulation One, page 60. *Apāna* conveys Earthy *prāṇas, samāna* Watery ones, *udāna* the Fiery *prāṇas, prāṇa* the Airy quality, and is a generalised term for all five types of *prāṇa.* Finally we have *vyāna* conveying the Aetheric *prāṇas.*

becomes the major *prāṇa* flowing in the *nāḍīs* then the associated *nāgas* conveyed are Airy in nature, and sprout wings. If also Fiery they are viewed as *Fiery flying serpents*. This signifies the ability to travel in consciousness in all directions in time, space, and beyond. Such serpents can also convey the experience of the spaciousness of *śūnyatā*.

When the fifth of the *prāṇas* become dominant in the *nāḍīs*, then the Fiery flying serpents transmute themselves into *Dragons of Wisdom*. This *prāṇa* conveys the Aetheric Element associated with the stage called *vyāna*, vivifying the combined Head and Ājñā centres, which evokes the Dharmadhātu Wisdom of Vairocana in combination with the All-accomplishing Wisdom of Amoghasiddhi. Such is the nature of enlightenment.

The above represents an esoteric consideration of the *prāṇic* constitution of the three main types of enlightened beings (Fiery serpentine, Fiery flying serpentine, and Dragons of Wisdom) that are responsible for the source material of Buddhist literature and most of the commentaries and subcommentaries. The three types of enlightenment shall later be elaborated via the terms *ālayavijñāna*, *śūnyatā* and *dharmakāya* enlightenments.

The remaining two types of *prāṇas* are *apāna* and *samāna*. The level of expression represented by *apāna* (Earthy *prāṇas*) concerns sluggish small serpents, worms, and even maggots, which convey common conventional empirical thoughts pertaining to the material world and its phenomena, producing *saṃsāric* entanglement and attachments.

The level represented by *samāna* (Watery *prāṇas*) concerns vipers and small serpents. They are the psychic emanations of the full gamut of emotional, imperilled thinking of the active desire-mind, producing various distortions of truth, glamours, and illusions. The small serpents are also associated with the development of *siddhis*, psychic powers such as clairvoyance. They are expressions of the psychic realms of deception and *māyā*.[47] Many beginners on the spiritual path derive their basic impressions from these realms.

---

47 *Māyā:* illusion, deceit. The aggregates of forces controlling one's *chakras* by excluding the controlling impressions from the realms of enlightenment. Therefore the perceptions derived from the three planes of human livingness to the exclusion of any higher perceptions. It incorporates the sum of the energies working through the *nāḍīs*, causing the individual to identify unduly with *saṃsāra* and its allurements. It thereby embodies the impressions that veil the real.

The relationship between the *viper* and *the Fiery flying serpent* can be seen in that the 'viper' is a person whose *kuṇḍalinī* energy has been expressed to the degree that the centres *(chakras)* associated with the emotional desire nature (the 'Waters') have been stimulated. (Often causing many psychic aberrations and problems.) The *Fiery flying serpent* symbolises one who is liberated from attachment to the bodily nature.

The *chakras* and esoteric lore

In relation to *kuṇḍalinī* one must also include a discussion of the *chakras*, for they are intricately linked. In its simplest connotation the word *chakra* means wheel, the wheel of motion. *Chakras* are vortices of energy delineating consciousness, and depending upon the particular *chakras* activated they connote the different desirous, emotional, mental and psycho-spiritual qualities experienced by a person. From another angle of vision, they can be perceived as Eyes, allowing the entry of light from one dimension of perception into another. They are thus doorways to and from the realms of being/non-being (depending upon the Element each *chakra* controls) through which the *yogin* can leave and enter at will. All depends upon the degree of attainment evidenced.

Chakras manifest as swirling saucer-like whorls of energy, stemming from points in the spine, and are divided by means of spokes of energy into regions that are likened to the petals of lotus blossoms. The seven major endocrine glands are their physiological externalisations.

In effect, the *chakras* are eddies of energy that gradually increase in luminosity from a dull glow to a brilliant incandescence as the person is able to increasingly utilise the energies that are the result of spiritual development. This happens very slowly, as in the course of normal evolutionary development, or else it can be greatly hastened by means of meditative practices, following the Eightfold Path and other spiritual disciplines. There are seven major *chakras,*[48] though they can be grouped in terms of the development of the wisdoms of the five Dhyāni Buddhas, the perfection of the five Elements, and of the attributes of the five *prāṇas,* as presented in Buddhist Tantric texts. We therefore have the Head lotus *(sahasrāra padma)* integrated with the Ājñā centre (the

48 Or eight when the powerful dual Splenic centre is also counted.

third Eye) that together are capable of processing all five Elements, plus the most refined expression of Aether. They are situated on top of the head and the brow. Next is the Heart centre *(anāhata chakra),* situated in the chest cavity. It specialises in processing the Airy Element. The Throat centre *(viśuddha chakra)* specialises in the development and assimilation of the Fiery Element. The Watery Element is processed by the Solar Plexus centre *(maṇipūra chakra),* situated in the naval area. The overlapped Sacral and Base of Spine centres *(svādiṣṭhāna* and *mūlādhāra chakras)* process the Earth Element.[49]

One of the main reasons for presenting such technical information is to explicate esoteric concepts veiled in the texts. A modernised mode of interpretation of Buddhist symbolism shall be introduced, presenting new terminology that will facilitate revelation of the truths coded into various texts by the enlightened. Indeed, many facts concerning the nature of the domains of enlightened beings shall also be revealed because there is a need for Buddhists to better comprehend whither they go as they aspire to become enlightened.

Not all enlightened beings are of equal realisation. The psychic constitution of some can be considered as *Fiery serpents,* others as *Fiery flying serpents,* and the very few that are the true *mahāsiddhas* (enlightened saints possessing great occult power, such as Padmasambhava and Milarepa) can be described as *Dragons of Wisdom.* Depending upon where they stand in this ladder of 'serpent power', so the quality of their writings and achievements differ. Thus one must interpret their works accordingly. Some works are Fiery (mentalistic) in nature, others Airy (pertaining to *śūnyatā),* and others truly esoteric (Aetheric, *dharmakāyic)* and thus contain coded information accessible to many levels of interpreters, to assist in the development of the inner

---

49 Comprehension of the nature of the *chakras* is paramount, if the esoteric significance of later Buddhist ontology, especially its yogic and Tantric basis is to be revealed. Therefore this subject is only introduced here, and their attributes shall be examined as needed throughout this series. Much information that is considered 'esoteric' in the texts, but is considerably veiled, will be elucidated as the veils are removed. Many of the views practitioners presently possess concerning Tantras will necessarily alter in the light of the revelations provided from unveiling the garbled to reveal the esoteric. Volume 5 specifically presents significant detail concerning the constitution and functions of the *chakras.*

Eyes and Ears, hence *siddhis* and great wisdom. Thus the degree of enlightenment of the author is important. It also sets the level of what is possible to reveal, i.e., the sources of the revelation, whether from Bodhisattvas, *mahābodhisattvas*, *ḍākinīs,* or from the Jinas.[50]

What the Bodhisattva has attained internally, i.e., the nature of the *prāṇas* developed, the quantity and quality of the empowering *nāgas*, or the Clear Light of his/her meditation-Mind, is what determines what can be received in vision. This is also conventionally understood, as shown in the statement by Griffith:

> The "[concentration called] 'stream of doctrine'" is a state of ecstatic trance wherein bodhisattvas obtain doctrinal instruction direct from Buddha or from some functional analogue thereof such as Maitreya. Both the source and the method are taken to guarantee the efficacy and accuracy of the instruction obtained, and that it is mentioned here points to the strong emphasis placed by this corpus upon the authoritativeness and accuracy of its own words. The words of the verses are thus *buddhavacana* because they are formed, made, and communicated by Maitreya, one who functions like Buddha, to Asaṅga, their human speaker, and because the latter's utterance of them reproduces Buddha's speech.[51]

In the case of Asaṅga, receiving impressions direct from Maitreya in the texts concerning the famous *Five Works of Maitreya,* such as the *Mahāyānasūtrālaṃkāra,* and *Abhisamayālaṃkara* (which are the foundation to the Yogācāra School of philosophy), the symbolism of the source should be noted, as was with Nāgārjuna.

The process of the evolution of the corpus of the Buddhist religion can be viewed in terms of the awakening process of a human unit. The sequence of the unfoldment of the *chakras* are similar. *Chakras* are organised to awaken according to a natural sequence, in conjunction with a person's mental-emotional activities. The Buddhist religion is naturally set at the high end of human development, related to striving to comprehend the nature of consciousness, and to master *saṃskāras* with view of liberation.

---

50 A Jina is a victorious one. An epithet of the Buddha. More specifically it refers to the Dhyāni Buddhas.

51 Griffith, *On Being Buddha, The Classical Doctrine of Buddhahood*, 36.

Maitreya, the next Buddha to appear, is the embodiment of the compassion of the Buddhas. Compassion is active love. As such it represents a fusion of both love and wisdom. The teaching provided however was the Yogācāra doctrine, hence the emphasis being the wisdom of the Mind. The esoteric objective of this doctrine for the *buddhadharma* was the complete awakening of the Fiery impetus of the Throat centre. Maitreya's guiding presence was needed in the formation of this doctrine to ensure that no residual aspect exists in it that may pertain to the natural separative tendency of the mind. (The activity of the 'left eye', esoterically speaking.) The compassionate tenor of the doctrines was thereby ensured. The Fires from the Throat centre, plus the Airy impetus from the Heart centre were needed to awaken the twelve major petals of the Head centre.

Centuries earlier the Heart centre *per se,* the source of the realisation of *śūnyatā,* was awakened in the form of the Mahāyāna ontology in its Mādhyamika form. From this basis Nāgārjuna received his major revelations, as his focus was the doctrine of *śūnyatā*. The Heart in the Head centre was also energised.[52]

Asaṅga's meditative concentration or purpose was towards awakening the complete Head lotus (the outermost tiers) for the *buddhadharma*. (Though the task fell more specifically to his brother Vasubandhu.) This was needed if later Tantric doctrines were to be disseminated and to thrive. The major twelve-petalled lotus of the Head centre, plus all of the subsidiary petals of this lotus (including the inner Throat tier), could then awaken for the entire corpus of Buddhism.

The Yogācāra doctrine of 'mind only' was thus a derivation of the awakening Head lotus (and by extension the Throat in the Head) for the religion, whilst the doctrine of *śūnyatā* of the Madhyamaka School was derived from the Heart centre (thence the Heart in the Head). Asaṅga being the 'human speaker' of Maitreya ('the latter's utterance of them reproduces Buddha's speech') means that Asaṅga functioned

---

52 The constitution of the Head centre will be detailed in Volumes 4 and 5 of this *Treatise on Mind*. The introductory information introduced here, plus by extension the hagiographies of all Buddhist sages and savants, can be correlated and adapted by Buddhist historians with what is provided in the later volumes to produce many interesting insights as to the esoteric history of the religion.

as a Throat centre, thus the doctrine of the Yogācāra is a Throat centre expression manifesting in such a way that the twelve main petals of the Head lotus could be compassionately awakened.

The Heart centre is located centrally between the Base of Spine and Head centres. It empowers the activity of the Bodhisattvas, engendering the powers of the eight *mahābodhisattvas* in accord to the movement of its *prāṇas* in the eight directions in space.[53] On the other hand, the five tiers of the Head centre are embodied by the qualities of the five Dhyāni Buddhas. The doctrine of *śūnyatā* concerns the 'middle between all extremes', which is what the Heart represents. Its true foundation is the energy or potency of love (compassion). The Yogācāra doctrine of the *ālayavijñāna* on the other hand, is that of the mind/Mind, needed to awaken the Head centre which is specifically constituted to process and embody the Fiery Element. The Yogācāra therefore exemplifies the wisdom aspect of the dual Love-Wisdom Ray.

Like the *yin-yang*[54] motion one doctrine counterbalances the other, making the expression of the *buddhadharma* more complete. The Yogācāra represents the feminine *(iḍā)* and the Madhyamaka the masculine *(piṅgalā)* view. The interrelation helps prevent both doctrines from becoming extremes. With respect to the other extant religious presentations they are effectively both expressions of the *madhyamapratipad,* the middle way or path between extremes of eternalism and nihilism, and thereby complimentary to each other. The way of the Mind overcomes the extreme of eternalism by its fluidity, thereby not identifying with any fixed 'permanent' object in space. The way of the Heart overcomes nihilism by the compassion developed when everything is integrated in the Void that is undefinable by mind. The energy of compassion can be considered a defining *effect* of the experience of *śūnyatā.* Consequently it is the driving energy impelling the Bodhisattva to act. The import of this dual expression is veiled in the important term *bodhicitta,*[55] where the *bodhi* part represents the

53 Throughout this series the nature of these eight directions shall be detailed, generally excluding the additional two directions (making 'the ten directions of space') that incorporate the past and future.

54 Yin-yang, the union of male and female (Tib. Yab-yum) principles in Nature.

55 *Bodhicitta:* the Heart's Mind, the Mind of enlightenment. The power or force

compassionate force, and the *citta* part the attributes of mind that are the foundation for the expression of wisdom. This integration is the basis to the Mahāyāna stream of Buddhism.

When we observe the two major preceding Theravādin schools, the Sautrāntika and the Sarvāstivādin-Vaibhāṣika, we find that they derived their essential doctrines from two major *chakras* below the diaphragm, the Solar Plexus centre *(maṇipūra chakra)* and the Sacral centre (*svādiṣṭhāna chakra*). The Buddha presented the foundational or Base of the Spine *chakra* teachings.

Kalupahana explains the differences between these two schools of thought:

> The Sarvāstivāda concluded their analysis of *dharmas* with the recognition of ultimate discrete atomic elements which they were unable to put together even with a theory of four basic relations. The result was that they were compelled to admit a singularly metaphysical conception of "self-nature" (*svabhāva*) to account for the experienced continuity of such discrete phenomena. This self-nature could not be looked upon as something impermanent and unchanging, for that would be to defeat the very purpose for which it was formulated in the first place. Therefore they insisted that this self-nature (*svabhāva, dravya*) of *dharmas* remain during all three periods of time[56]...One of the schools that reacted against this conception of "self-nature", ... was the Sautrāntaka school of Buddhism. As its name implies, this school was openly antagonistic to the "treatises" (*śāstra*) and insisted upon returning to the "discourses" (*sūtrānta*) as sources for the study of the Buddha-word[57]....Even though the Sautrāntikas were openly critical of the substantialist conception of *dharma* advocated by the Sarvastivādins, their reluctance to abandon the theory of moments (*kṣaṇa*) left them with the difficult task of explaining the experienced continuity in the individual person. The emergence of schools like "personalists" *(pudgala-vāda)* and "transmigrationists" *(samkrānti-vāda),* closely related to and sometimes identical with the

---

productive of awakened realisations, enlightenment that emanates from the Heart centre. The compassionate force of the liberating Mind. It is the mind of pure perfection, the authentic nature of Mind.

56 D. J. Kalupahana, Trans., *Mūlamadhyamakakārikā of Nāgārjuna. The Philosophy of the Middle Way*, (Motilal Banarsidass, Delhi, 1999), 22.

57 Ibid.

> Sautrāntikas, is indicative of the solutions that this school had to offer in order to overcome the difficulties arising from the acceptance of a theory of moments.
>
> The Sarvāstivāda and Sautrāntika schools thus presented a rather complicated set of theories, all contributing to philosophical confusion. The former perceived a "self-nature" *(svabhāva)* in the cause and emphasized the identity *(ekatva)* of cause and effect, while the latter, seeing no such "self-nature" but merely perceiving "other-nature" *(para-bhāva),* insisted upon the difference *(nānatva)* between cause and effect. The Sarvāstivāda conception of self-nature *(svabhāva)* was extended to all phenomena, including the human personality, while the Sautrāntikas, denying self-nature in phenomena, surreptitiously introduced a conception of self or person *(ātman, pudgala)* in a human personality.[58]

Here we can see that with their conception of self-nature in all phenomena the Sarvāstivādins derived their understanding via the attributes of the awakened Sacral centre, as this *chakra* is concerned with the vitalisation of the sum of the bodily form. The Sautrāntika derived their theory of 'self in persons' via impressions associated with the awakened Solar Plexus centre, which is the centre of the self-will, from whence the 'I' concept derives. We can therefore account for the evolution of Buddhism, from the centres below the diaphragm: the Base of the Spine, Sacral and Solar plexus centres (the Buddha's teachings, plus that of the early schools), to those above the diaphragm being embodied by the Mahāyāna schools. Finally, concerning the centres in the Head, general Tantrayāna gained revelation of the nature of the *dharmakāya,* which relates to the awakening of the Ājñā centre of Buddhism. The epoch of Maitreya will awaken the complete significance of the Head lotus, revealing many esoteric insights not possible before. All necessarily contribute to the complete bodily form of Buddhism as far as its psychic constitution is concerned, just as the *chakras* are necessary for the functioning of the human body.[59]

---

58 Ibid., 22-23.

59 This exposé is presented in terms of the *chakras* because such considerations are rarely thought of, but lies at the heart of all thinking of those that have progressed through yogic processes, as have all the Buddhist philosophers. It is, after all, a precedence set by the Buddha himself.

The psychic constitution (*nāḍī* system) is the true human unit, as the external corruptible form (the *māyāvirūpa)* is a body of illusion that automatically reflects whatever energies manifest through the *nāḍīs*.

The course of evolution outlined above hints at the significant millennial planning by the Council of Bodhisattvas whereby they chose a sequenced incarnating process that best suits the compassionate education of humanity according to the collective wisdom (*sarvajñāna*) of their united meditations.[60]

With the above in mind we can see that the only true way for one to properly interpret sacred scriptures and the writings of the major Buddhist metaphysicians is to develop the same form of meditative receptiveness that they did, either via the Heart centre, the Throat centre, or via the lower centres for the Theravādin schools. This does not mean that the Head centre was not awakened, but rather that the *prāṇas* that flowed through it to produce its awakening were principally from the lower centres, hence producing Earthy, Watery, Fiery or Airy forms of liberation.

The teachings concerning liberation by comprehending the nature of *dharmakāya* (hereafter called the Dharmakāya Way) necessitates the complete awakening of the Head and Ājñā centres, whereby Aetheric *prāṇas* become dominant. The Throat, Heart and Head lotuses are capable of producing higher transcendental wisdom. If the Fiery energy from the Throat centre dominates then the *ālayavijñāna* enlightenment is possible. If the Airy then the *śūnyatā* enlightenment *occurs* (for which the *prajñāpāramita* teachings lay the foundation) that produces direct spontaneous insight, without the conceptual process *(pratyakṣa)*. All is possible according to a *yogin's* capacity and Bodhisattva level. This does not mean that the higher forms of awakening are not possible for the present Theravādin schools, as always (even in the early formative period of Buddhism) an exceptional *yogin* can appear therein, but the disposition of the teachings favour the *ālayavijñāna* enlightenment, exoterically viewed as the *arhat* accomplishment.

---

60 It should be obvious for those that have contemplated the actions of Bodhisattvas that they work collectively with a united meditation-Mind as how best to alleviate the ignorance and suffering in the world, according to humanity's available *karma* and predisposition to generate *kleśas* (dissident emotions) and *saṃskāras*. Depending upon the course of action of humanity, so the Bodhisattvas can fine-tune their incarnations to assist. Nothing is haphazard, or left to chance, and esoteric law is obeyed in all their undertakings.

Levels of interpretation

This statement by Griffith can be used to further illustrate the nature of right interpretation:

> It is important, given the emphasis placed by many Buddhist theorists and more western interpreters, upon perception *(pratyakṣa)* and inferential reasoning *(anumāna)* as the only valid means of gaining knowledge *(pramāṇa)*, to stress, as a corrective, the importance given here to authoritative persons as the guarantors of textually transmitted doctrinal knowledge.[61]

'Authoritative persons' are those who have proved themselves enlightened via awakening higher perceptions through Mahāyāna meditation techniques. The results of such revelations are recorded in their writings. If sentences 'express meaning' and a *sūtra* or *śāstra* is composed of a number of meaningful sentences, then it expresses the context of all of the meaningful sentences tied together to produce an overview or stream of revelation that is the sum of the content of each sentence. In this way all revelation proceeds. In the meditation-Mind each sentence can be conceived as a visual import or image that can contain many strata or levels of understanding. The *sūtra* or *śāstra* is the completed meditation sequence.

Griffith further states:

> It is an ancient and standard Buddhist claim that the attainment of true wisdom somehow transcends language, and that the sphere of discursive awareness in which doctrine-expressing sentences necessarily have their being, although essential, is significant primarily because the claims made in that sphere are instrumentally effective in producing nondiscursive awareness *(jñāna)*.[62]

Jñāna[63] thus must be developed by anyone wishing to properly interpret, without which comprehension of higher revelation is not

61 Griffith, 41.

62 Griffith, 55.

63 It would be better to use the word *prajñā* here, because though *jñāna* can be interpreted as pristine cognition (of a Buddha Mind) it is a flexible term and is sometimes translated as 'worldly knowledge'. *Prajñā* on the other hand is generally translated as analytical wisdom, discriminative awareness, or transcendental knowledge.

possible. The wise must explain the doctrines of the texts in the most skilful way so that those without understanding can receive valid insights and develop such ability themselves.

There are seven modes of interpretation (keys) presented at the end of my book *Karma and the Rebirth of Consciousness* that should be utilised if the esotericism of a sacred text is to be understood. They denote the way the enlightened veil the wealth of their teachings through symbolism, numerology, the law of correspondences, astrological verities, allegory, physiological analogy, and esoteric considerations (such as knowledge of the subtle body and its functions). The nature of the language, symbolism, and way of transmission by the enlightened of information presented to the unenlightened is necessarily conveyed in such a manner. A vast amount of information can thereby be compressed in a short well written and coded text. Such understanding is necessary to rightly interpret sacred scriptures.

A principle aim of this series is to reveal the context of many of these keys, therefore analysis of some texts shall be in far greater depth than would normally be the case. The many levels of meaning in the writings of the enlightened can therefore be revealed as well as the shortcomings of many conventional assumptions.

The student should consider the levels of interpretation and the factor of relativity in everything considered sacred. Without comprehension of how a form of truth stands relative to something else, the danger of concretion of information and undue emphasis on things relatively insignificant manifests. The more subtle, but far more embracive interpretation will then be missed. The factor of relativity will of necessity be utilised throughout this treatise.

Griffith states further:

> This location of textual authority either in something akin to revelation (in the case of texts communicated by Maitreya to Asaṅga), or in the transmission of the insights of an authoritative human teacher through a line of reliable preservers and transmitters of those insights (through a *guruparaṃparā*) is not peculiarly Buddhist. It is, rather, pan-Indian, a feature of śāstric discourse generally. Its presence in the doctrinal digests is another indication of the extent to which Buddhist theorizing had, by the third or fourth century, entered the mainstream of Indian

> virtuoso intellectual life[64].....Some of the terminology used to describe the authoritativeness of these texts—their teaching is *abhrānta*, without error; their composers have *uttamaprajñā*, supreme discernment, or are like a second Buddha—sounds, indeed, as though one should assimilate the kind of authority given these texts to that given the text of the Bible by some Christian fundamentalists.[65]

The concept of *guruparaṃparā*, or of lineage traditions, is an important consideration in Buddhism and Hinduism, and rightfully so. It was essential in the past when books were comparatively scarce, and often the most sacred instructions or commentaries were not written down, but were 'ear whispered' from preceptor or guru to students, through a lineage or series of beings that have evolved to take the place (becoming the 'son') of the preceding guru. This was the way that the most sacred teachings were safeguarded in any particular school of thought. They remained sacred thereby, ensuring that the quality of teachings stayed at a very high level, so that the student would be assured of the best possible means to enlightenment if he/she found the right (enlightened) guru, to be initiated into an instruction lineage. The secrets of initiation into the mysteries of any particular lineage always took much time and earnest dedication, necessitating special skills to master. The student had to prove him or herself worthy. It was also necessary for some of the more dangerous Tantric and yogic practices to be safeguarded in this way.

However, apart from safeguarding against dangerous Tantric and yogic practices, the concept of *guruparaṃparā* is nowadays not as important as it used to be. This is because of the nature of modern mass-communications; the widespread availability of books containing an ever-increasing amount of formerly esoteric information in a translated comprehensible form. Also, the modern student has generally developed further and faster intellectually than his predecessors and thus can comprehend far quicker the nature of the information in manuals and texts. Shortcuts to learning have been developed, leading to many more people gaining individualistic forms of self-enlightenment or realisations. This does not obviate the need, ultimately, for an

---

64 Griffith, 40.

65 Ibid.

enlightened one to be found that can lead the *śrāvaka* ('hearer', or pious attendant of the doctrine) into the higher mysteries of the meditation-Mind. It does however mean that much of the preliminary learning can be wisely and relatively quickly learned from books (such as the present one), thus quickening the process of right interpretation and hence comprehension as to the way to enlightenment.

Dogmatism of all types must be carefully eliminated in one's search for truth and ultimate meaning. One should always strive to be as broadminded as possible and thus avoid adhering to doctrines that purport that they are 'without error' or that 'their composers have *uttamaprajñā*, supreme discernment, or are like a second Buddha', simply because it is so claimed by the majority of the community of which one happens to be a part. The teachings must undergo the most rigorous testings that the student can apply before acceptance. He/she must remain open-minded and be capable of accepting other teachings, if such come that may prove better, or that might shed further light upon the difficult passages that have not yet been properly comprehended. The student must always be wary of quick interpretations and commonplace understandings, as much imperceptible to the unenlightened lies hidden in the scriptures. I have already stated that enlightenment is relative, and that there are many levels of interpretation. This means that the level or signposts of interpretation continue to be raised, depending upon the level of enlightenment one possesses.

A statement by D.S. Lopez, Jr. is helpful here:

> Tibetan exegetes refined the process of determining whether a statement was of interpretable meaning through the delineation of four criteria:
>
> 1. The intended meaning *(dgongs pa)*
> 2. The foundation of the intention *(dgongs gzhi)*
> 3. The motive *(dgos pa)*
> 4. The contradiction if taken literally *(dngos la gnod byed)*
>
> Each of these requires discussion. The intended meaning *(dgongs pa, abhiprāya)* is what the Buddha says–that is, what he intends his audience to understand. This intended meaning is multiple and hence difficult to determine[66].....In any case, the intended meaning must

66 D.S. Lopez, Jr., 'On the Interpretation of the Mahayana Sutras', Ed., D. S. Lopez, Jr., *Buddhist Hermeneutics,* (Motilal Banarsidass, Delhi, 1993), 55.

> differ from the Buddha's own knowledge of reality in order for the statement to be interpretable *(neyārtha).* This knowledge of reality is the foundation of the intention *(dgongs gzhi),* the truth or fact that the Buddha has in mind when he says what is not ultimately true. The motivation (*dgos pa, prayajana)* is the Buddha's purpose, based on his knowledge of the capacities and needs of his disciples, in teaching what is not actually the case. The last criterion, the contradiction, if taken literally *(dngis la gnod byed, mukhyārthabādha),* refers to the contradiction by reasoning and by definitive scriptures if the statement were accepted without interpretation.[67]

Regarding the statement: 'In any case, the intended meaning must differ from the Buddha's own knowledge of reality in order for the statement to be interpretable', the question to be asked is why should the 'Buddha's own knowledge of reality' *not* be interpretable? We could answer that his enlightened perception simply is, i.e., 'is definitive' and therefore there is no interpretation needed, or indeed is not possible with the discriminative mind. Here we are again involved with the argument *re* what is 'definite in meaning' and what is 'interpretable', explained earlier. Therefore when we say 'not interpretable' we must add the qualifier 'by whom?' This then makes the statement more correct, especially when we look to those that may be functioning at any of the levels of enlightenment earlier explained. Once something has been comprehended then it has been interpreted. This also includes what is in a Buddha's Mind. He automatically interprets on many levels of perception at once, otherwise he could not explain anything properly.

The intended meaning may indeed be 'multiple' and hence 'difficult to determine', whilst the quality of the effort required to overcome ignorance by students is an important consideration for spiritual teachers. The evocation of considerable effort by students is preferred to spoon-feeding them with information. The intention is for them to learn to overcome *saṃsāra* through mastery of their *saṃskāric* impediments. However, what is interpretable or not interpretable depends upon the target audience. A Buddha has the ability to alter his language to make everything interpretable as well as to give the experience of *śūnyatā* to those qualified to receive it if he so wishes.

---

67 Ibid., 55-56.

They then can correctly interpret that experience. Such an interpretation is not necessarily different from a Buddha's own interpretation. Indeed, it is not really possible for a Buddha and a high grade Bodhisattva to be in disagreement about 'things', there is just a vaster capacity of content or context in a Buddha's Mind.

All things in a Buddha's Mind can be perceived by a fully enlightened being whose *sāmadhi* (meditative concentration) is *śūnyatā*, which according to the above definition is 'definite in meaning', but which will be viewed as relative to 'something else' in the Buddha's Mind, because though *śūnyatā* is the state of residence of that Mind it is not exclusive of the 'other'. We can state the above because we incorporate in our understanding the consideration that what is contained and revealable in a Buddha's Mind may be vaster and more subtle than in a ('lesser') enlightened being's Mind, but this does not abnegate comprehension. That vastness is yet to be fully attained by the Bodhisattva, but nevertheless its nature and general paradigm is experienced, and interpreted. Such interpretation, however, must not be thought of in terms of empirical deduction, but rather, as a spontaneous non-conceptual revelatory identification with the *tathatā* that is the Buddha Mind, as per the focus of meditation.

The next point is the 'foundation of the intention', 'the truth or fact that the Buddha has in mind when he says what is not ultimately true'. For example, the erroneous version of the doctrine of *karma* as was then expounded, as explained in my book *Karma and the Rebirth of Consciousness*. It is the perspective or angle of vision that determines the truth or otherwise of something. Many presented formulations are true in the current context but may not be true when viewed from a different perspective; when greater more embracive knowledge has been accrued. However, everything a Buddha says is true, or more precisely, interpretable as part of a greater truth, once the code that his teaching is veiled by has been properly comprehended.[68] This indicates the way the *dharma* manifests. Errors are perceived because only part of a more wholesome truth has been revealed and this 'part' is not seen

68 Even the erroneous doctrine of transmigration of consciousness into animal forms dealt with in my former book is correct from one perspective.

in its proper context by the interpreter.[69] This produces the problems of the 'foundation of intention'. To be able to see what 'the foundation of intention' actually is in a Buddha's Mind necessitates someone who is similarly (though not necessarily as comprehensively) enlightened. Having developed a similar Mind one can peer into the intention. Another method, where ascertaining the Buddha's intention is possible, is for the Buddha to convey such ideation to one who can receive telepathic impressions from him at the appropriate time. The presumption here is that the words attributed to a Buddha are correct, though this may not necessary be the case. Misrepresentation is always possible.

Lopez describes the third criteria as, 'The motivation is the Buddha's purpose, based on his knowledge of the capacities and needs of his disciples, in teaching what is not actually the case'. As above stated he does not teach what is actually not the case, but rather uses symbolism, allegory, etc., through which the true meaning can be derived and evaluated once such language is properly understood. Often the limitations of the interpreter's mind are at fault when he thinks that the teaching is false, because he has not taken a broad enough view, has not properly understood the meditative intent, or the coded mode the enlightened speak by.

Finally we are told 'the contradiction, if taken literally, refers to the contradiction by reasoning and by definitive scriptures if the statements were accepted without interpretation'. There will always be seeming contradictions if esoteric information is presented to those who have not evolved the capacity to understand. The wise one always takes possible misrepresentation of what he had said or written into account, and observes these effects over a long duration of time. Inevitably such 'contradictions of reason' must be rectified, and the wise one considers this part of the planned education. *Karma's* hand will deal mechanisms of comprehension in the normal course of events, whereby those that have formed wrong or contradictory opinions in past (lives) will learn to rectify them according to the enlightened view. It is just a matter of

69 One should also note that many things may have been purported to have been said by the Buddha by later authors that in fact were never his actual statements. Only enlightened beings can factually determine what was actually said through recourse to their meditation-Minds. Historical precedence and the logical metaphysics presented in the *sūtras* infer that they were actually the Buddha's words. We then impute that this is so.

time. Therefore 'ultimately' (to use the Mādhyamika form of logic) there is no contradiction, if the information proceeds from an enlightened being. If partially enlightened then error may exist producing logical contradictions. Such also need to be rectified over time.

The earnest student must always try to discover uttered or written contradictions by those that are not enlightened. Many are the claimants to enlightenment; rare are those who have attained. Such forms of illogic are major sources of *karma* for the teacher. The seeming 'contradictions' by an enlightened one are always based upon established truth, and present deeper insights awakening the ripened student's intuitive faculties. They lead to enlightenment, contrary to the forms of illogic presented by unworthy teachers. One way of discerning the difference is that the enlightened one *never* feeds glamour, pride, or forms of shallow thinking in the student, which offer quick rewards for relatively little effort. Nor do the enlightened proscribe exercises that cause pain and suffering, except in cases where cleansing *karma* is necessary, or through the many renunciations one must make of all attachments to ephemeral things. Nor is it possible to buy teachings from the wise. They give freely to all worthy supplicants. Worthiness comes from past life attainments and preparedness in this life for the teachings.

Esoteric statements made by the enlightened may appear contradictory because interpretation is determined by the spiritual standing of the viewer. Those that interpret concretely will never understand more than the most basic level of the statements made by the enlightened. The methods chosen to interpret spiritual information accords to the level of awakening attained in past lives of achievement:

1. One may be an exemplary Bodhisattva, well founded in enlightened reasoning from many lives of philosophic and meditative investigation. Being Initiated[70] into the mysteries associated with the doctrine, immediately an insight or revelatory response is invoked.
2. A beginner upon the Bodhisattva path will have meaningful, well thought-out responses derived from *sūtras* and related hermeneutics, but his/her deductions may miss the mark for the most esoteric presentations, which are generally contradictory to conventional

70 I will capitalise the words Initiate and Initiation in this series when it indicates the process of becoming enlightened, or one who is so.

thinking. Such a one generally has formed opinions as to the nature of enlightenment and its process, rather than the fluid, broadminded, revelatory approach of one farther travelled upon the road.

3. The intelligentsia, who see things in terms of the logic derived from this world and its phenomena. They possess much learning, but generally desire concrete proof for the subjective things that are immediately accessible to those of the first category.
4. Those driven by emotional-minds, who accept quick, often shallow-reasoned assumptions about this or that speculative philosophic argument, generally what best appeals to their emotions. Their thought life is glazed and self-opinionated. The problems concerning the 'foundation of the intention' arise when endeavouring to teach this vast and very broad category of humanity, because they do not listen properly. Their short-lived attention span and shallow thinking is catered for by simple, generally allegorical or metaphorical teachings. They are esoterically blind, and deep philosophic constructs fly past them.
5. Those engrossed in purely sensual and selfish activities. They care little for higher philosophical speculations, or the *dharma*. They are dull of hearing and what reasoning abilities they have developed is prostituted for selfish or sensual gain.

It should also be noted that the statement found in certain texts that the Buddha spoke nothing at all, or when Nāgārjuna said that he presented no doctrine at all, is only true from an absolutist sense. An example is the quote from the *Sūtra of the Adornment of Pristine Cognition's Appearance which Penetrates the Scope of All Buddhas*:

> Nothing at all is seen by the buddhas, nor heard, nor intended, nor known, nor is the object of omniscience. Nothing has been said or expressed by the buddhas. The buddhas neither speak nor make expression. The buddhas will not resort to speech and they will not resort to expression. The buddhas do not become manifestly, perfectly enlightened. The buddhas have not caused anything to become manifestly, perfectly enlightened. The buddhas have not renounced conflicting emotions. The buddhas have not actually disclosed purity. Nothing at all is seen by the buddhas, nor heard, nor tasted, nor smelt,

> nor known, nor cognised. If you ask why this is the case, Mañjuśrī, it is because all things are utterly pure from the beginning.[71]

The *'beginning of what'*, one may rightfully ask, because if 'Nothing at all is seen by the buddhas, nor heard, nor tasted, nor smelt, nor known, nor cognised' how can there possibly be a beginning? If there is a beginning, then there has to be a beginning of 'something', in which case the senses and cognition, etc, are activated. This means that then the Buddha can speak, will be heard, be made known, etc. The above quote is based upon consideration of absolute truth, whereas clearly one needs to incorporate conventional truth, if any soteriological consideration is to take effect for those whom a Buddha has incarnated.

Thurman states:

> Nāgārjuna, in the climactic chapter of his *Wisdom*, in which he analyzes the concept of "Nirvana" and finally equates Nirvana and samsara, anticipates the objections of those who will consider him to have made some authoritarian statement about Nirvana by listing a version of the "Fourteen Unpronounced Verdicts" of the Buddha and concluding with the following extraordinary verse: "The quiescence of all perceptions and fabrications, that is the Highest Bliss! No doctrine at all was ever taught by any Buddha to anyone."[72]

Such a statement can only be asserted because of considerations of the Buddha residing in the Void. It is *untrue* when looked at in the context of the phrase 'There is no differentiation *(viśeṣaṇa)* of Saṃsāra from Nirvāṇa, there is no differentiation of Nirvāṇa from Saṃsāra'.[73] Because in translating from *śūnyatā* to *saṃsāra* words are conveyed, meaning is relayed to consciousnesses, which then have the opportunity to act upon them in one way or another. If the Buddha literally spoke nothing at all then he would have chosen the *pratyekabuddha*[74] path after his *nirvāṇa* (which he seriously considered for a short while). But the

---

71 *Sarvabuddhaviṣayāyatārajñānālokāṃkārasūtra,* (Dudjom Rinpoche, Jikdrel Yeshe Dorje. *The Nyingma School of Tibetan Buddhism, Its Fundamentals and History, (*Wisdom Publications, Boston, 1991), 298.

72 Thurman, 128.

73 Wayman, 80.

74 A contemplative, self-absorbed in his/her own enlightenment.

unassailable fact is that he did choose to speak (rather than remain silent) and therefore we have what is known as the *buddhadharma* today. There are times, however, when a Buddha teaches in silence, in meditative equipoise, for those that have the ability to receive instructions in this way. Then he can be considered to not 'speak nor make expression' etc.

It is wrong to fall into extremist absolutist positions of the above type because they posit only a small part of the overall view. (Thus interpretation in reference to 'speaking nothing at all' should consist of no more than a footnote or two in philosophical texts.) The subject of how the Buddha communicated with those caught up in *saṃsāra*, as well as to the deities, *ḍākinīs*, Bodhisattvas and all the other categories of beings, needs a better dictum than zealously saying that he spoke nothing.

Therefore we say that he spoke a lot, in many different ways: verbally, telepathically (his thoughts could be perceived clairvoyantly), and through yogic direct perception as well, according to the nature of what was needed by the recipient. Certainly the foundation of what he spoke stemmed from the Void, but in reality it came from a vaster source, the *dharmakāya*, the nature of which the proponents of 'no speech' did not consider. The Void/*śūnyatā* is not the All, the *dharmakāya* is, and certainly therein there is speech, mantric Sound, but perceptible only to those whose basis is the Void. Such sounds no human ear can perceive, unless the *chakras* are ablaze with Light supernal. Literally the creation and destruction of whole galaxies of concepts can rest in a mantric sentence. Words and concepts are conveyed in silence, in the utmost stillness, where even the sound of a 'pin drop' from such a source, if emanated wrongly or aberrantly, could shatter a formed world.

Salutations to the great reforming ones!
The victory songs of all Jinas wings them on.
Oṁ

2

The Two Truths

Some introductory questions

For hermeneutic examination of the epistemology of Buddhist texts it only matters indirectly as to who the foes of any Buddhist philosopher were, be they the Sāṃkhyas, Mimāṃāsakas, or Buddhist logicians from other schools. What truly matters is that the logic contained within these texts can cogently answer all counter arguments. What is unassailable will stand the test of time, but what is uncertain must ultimately be modified accordingly to be unassailable, or be discarded. There can be no text or story that is considered so sacred as to avoid close scrutiny because it is purported to have been said or penned by a great one, even the Buddha. Indeed, because it has been a matter of long-held belief it should all the more be analysed for the possibility of inaccuracies before acceptance. Old concepts generally need to be assailed from a fresh viewpoint. The resultant deductions need not necessarily be 'new', for if the explanation is sound, all enlightened beings would have previously acknowledged the valid rhetoric or definitive view presented. The fact is however that certain concepts can only be brought to light at the opportune time, when the foundation for their acceptance has been wrought out in the society one resides in. An example is the scientific theorem that energy and matter are interrelated; that one can be exchanged with the other in accordance with the factor of the speed of light squared. The definitive concepts of how energy manifests and the laws governing its interrelation with matter was not part of the lingua franca of the early philosophers. Such understanding now needs to be incorporated into the ontology concerning the interpretation of any epistemic subject.

There were always many Bodhisattvas endeavouring to speak for Buddhas. The questions raised is to what degree were they enlightened when they wrote their treatises, and from what Bodhisattva level is the source of their information derived? The sound ontology of the writings and its soteriology can provide many hints as to their sources, especially if definitive in nature. Even so, correct interpretation of that which is profound is imperative. If the test of proper analytical scrutiny fails, they must then be relegated to the shelves of a textual museum for students of history to catalogue.

There is a tendency of many interpreters of the two truths, the conventional truth *(saṃvṛti satya)* and the ultimate truth *(paramārtha satya),* to enter into a reductionist rhetoric where the ultimate truth becomes the *de facto* only 'truth', as the conventional truth is considered 'illusional' and therefore can be dismissed as inconsequential, based on the idea that we are deluded by it and hence must overcome our delusions. Certain epistemic considerations in relation to the two truths need answering, as the concept of 'absolutes' needs querying. I shall list them here but shall only briefly deal with some of the issues in this chapter because subjects, for instance, such as what *śūnyatā* may or may not be and its relation to the *dharmakāya* necessitates considerable foundational rhetoric before something definitive can be ascertained. Many other topics need to be discussed before a sound ontology is derived. A variegated explanation of many of these and other topics concerning the *buddhadharma* will consequently be offered throughout this series. The objective is to discern the truth concerning much of the hermeneutic presented as *dharma* via the 'filter' of an esoteric approach that can be ascertained as a 'new view'. Much will consequently be revealed that was formerly veiled. Hopefully this new view will be accepted as valid cognition by my readers.

1. A complete accounting of the way *saṃskāras* of an individuating, reincarnating 'being' are continuously sustained, as well as their method of transmutation needs, to be provided. Are their transmuted essences annihilated with respect to *śūnyatā* (if we take that to be absolute truth), or is there some aspect that remains? If so, in what form and in what capacity does this remainder manifest? Logically

there must be a remainder, otherwise we would have annihilation. The various exponents of the *buddhadharma* are careful to avoid this trap of nihilism.

2. A consideration of the way the course of the various ignorance states spiral through cycles of negation, thence revelation, to inevitably bring about the 'view of selflessness', which is the basis of Madhyamaka polemics. Soteriological considerations become paramount, how wisdom and compassion upon the path to liberation are developed must be comprehended, otherwise querying the relation between the two truths becomes meaningless.

   Each 'ignorance state' is relative and thus represents a sphere of darkened substance to be inevitably transmogrified, made transmundane in light. This concerns the nature of the darkness-light interplay. For instance, what is light with respect to *śūnyatā*? How is light generated and sustained through the process of the rebirth of consciousness, and what is its 'status' in *śūnyatā*? We can ask if ignorance (darkness) is totally annihilated in *śūnyatā*, and if so, then has all of the darkness been transformed into light? What then does the developed luminosity and radiance of an enlightened Mind mean in relation to its establishment via *śūnyatā?* From this perspective we perceive that *śūnyatā* is but a sphere of intensified light. Is it therefore like a blazing sun, if so of what hue? What is the true status of ignorance in the nature of things? Is it possible for the *śūnyatā* experience (absolute truth) to have annihilated ignorance, if the Buddha attributes of the *dharmakāya* have not yet been attained?[1] If so, does this mean that the *śūnyatā* experience is not void of ignorance? In other words the ontology of the different levels of enlightenment need comprehending.

3. The concept of relativity must be considered, as it is utilised in all forms of analysis. In relation to *what* does one make observations? How does conventional truth relate to ultimate truth? What are the gradations of mergence from one to the other? Is this from the point of view of the sentience developed by a plant, frog, dog, the consciousness of a human, the perceptions of a Bodhisattva at one

---

1 The reference here is to the attainment of high level Bodhisattvas that have experience of *śūnyatā,* but are not yet Buddhas.

or other of the Bodhisattva stages of unfoldment, the enlightened stance of a *ḍākinī*, the *dhyāna* of a Buddha? If one says that they 'make no observations at all', then are the observations of others to be discarded? Is it possible to manifest a reductionist polemic until a void is obtained to actually arrive at the true nature of *śūnyatā*, which in the last analysis must be experienced in order to know. The observations stemming from yogic and meditative practices are necessary for this. *Śūnyatā* may inherently exist, but the veils of substance obscuring it must be progressively transformed into their Void attributes if it is to be revealed. Semantical processes, no matter how cogent will not produce this.

4. Phenomena cannot simply be negated because it is transient, or because it is inherently empty. The existence of phenomena, or purpose for its existence, must be properly accounted for. If it is tacitly asserted to not exist, then how can we have a consciousnesses to register the fact of phenomena? For what purpose does consciousness exist, and *karma* for that matter, if they are said to be likewise illusional, but inevitably help produce the experience of the Void? The technicalities of how *śūnyatā* sustains phenomena, or conversely, if phenomena sustains *śūnyatā*, needs to be properly explained in any consideration of the two truths. Many questions arise in this context. For example, how did the wheel of Dependent Origination come to originally exist? Why is *saṃsāra* not instantly annihilated by the existence of *śūnyatā*? What is *śūnyatā* really, how does it relate to *svabhāva* (for which there are a number of interpretations[2]), and to consciousness-transformations within energy fields?

5. The philosophy must account for the way that evolution works, and therefore the way that consciousness evolves, or of the evolution of the human species as a whole. One must also envision the nature of further expression and development of Mind in *śūnyatā*, as there is no such thing as stasis in cosmos, nothing is annihilated, only transformed from one 'entity' to another. *Dharmakāya* is inclusive of the evolution of Mind, and encompasses the multidimensionality of space within the vastness of cosmos. What actually 'evolves' therefore

2 The main definition being the self-existent, self-becoming plastic essence of substance, that causes the existence of things.

needs comprehension, because the nature of the *Tathāgata* has only been viewed in terms of, or in relation to, the human condition. What exactly is 'It' that lies beyond or is an extension of the 'ultimate truth' when the human condition no longer is a factor of consideration?

6. Great philosophical flexibility also needs to be developed to incorporate the effects of a future esoteric science, one which asserts conclusive proof on what was once highly debatable ponderables developed in the West, such as the nature of the atom. The deductions of modern physics, biology, chemistry, and astronomy now need to be interpolated into any philosophy, if that philosophy is to reflect irrefutable cogent logic expressing unassailable truth along ontological or heuristic lines. Scientific revelations have not altered the nature of absolute truth, however they have offered the bonus of a significantly sophisticated expression for the approaches that reveal truth. Relative truth has much yet to reveal on the march to consider the 'ultimate'. The nature of the *saṃsāra-śūnyatā* fusion that an enlightened one awakens to becomes comprehensively experienced as a consequence.
7. What needs to be explained therefore, are the further implications of the effects of *karma*. If *karma* exists, then that which acts to create it must also exist, and that something must be defined as a 'self', the *personal 'I',* or conscious awareness of an identity separate from another 'self'. This 'self' is perpetually changing, and continuously modified by *karma*, via the accompanying agents, *skandhas* and *saṃskāras*. Due to its transience it is fundamentally illusional, but has a temporal reality as part of a process of becoming during a sequence of time. It is an individualised store of conscious volitions that have *śūnyatā* as its base, which is conceived of as absolute truth. The process of rectifying *karma* (normally seen as an attribute of conventional truth) however is that which reveals *karma* as something more than what appears conventionally, inevitably making the two truths the same.
8. We therefore need to comprehend the nature of the personal-I, and its expression as an 'I-consciousness', that outlives the duration of the personal-I, surviving after its death to take further rebirth. This consciousness of an 'I' refers to the expression of a consciousness-stream that is separated from other similar streams, allowing

the appearance of individuality over successive rebirths of that consciousness. The 'personal-I' or 'I-concept' then refers to the individualised mind developing consciousness-attributes during any particular incarnation of a consciousness-stream.

Intricately interwoven with the concept of an 'I' is the topic of the *skandhas* and *saṃskāras*. The *skandhas* are bundles or groups of attributes that together constitute the human personality and are responsible for the evolution of consciousness. Exoterically, there are five *skandhas*: 1. form, or body, the sense organs, sense objects and interrelationships (*rūpa*), 2. perception or sensation, feelings and emotions (*vedanā*), 3. aggregates of action, or the motives to thus act (*saṃskāras*), 4. the faculty of discrimination (*samjñā*), 5. revelatory knowledge (*vijñāna*). Effectively, all of these forms of activity are attributes of the *saṃskāras* that are carried through from life to life collectivised in their various groupings. Of the *skandhas, rūpa* represents the sense-consciousnesses, whilst *vedanā* and *samjñā* are together the *kāma-manasic* (desire or emotional-mind) aspects of consciousnesses. The *saṃskāras* are expressed in the form of the five different types of *prāṇas* conveyed throughout the *naḍī* system. They are one's karmic accumulations that must be worked with in that life, and are eventually transmuted into the seeds of enlightenment *(vijñāna).*

In the esoteric account provided in this series I relegate the term *skandha* more purely to consideration of form *(rūpa)*[3] and of the mental substance *(manas)* that incorporates the body of expression of the material world. Indeed most people view things with a materially focussed consciousness. However, *yogins* (practitioners) manifest a multidimensional view, where experiences via the outer sense-perceptors are not as important as those derived via the subjective perceptions of the inner organs *(chakras)* by means of which they are experienced. The focus of this series is upon this inner world of experiences of *yogins,* which represents the *esoteric* view. Consequently the other attributes of the *skandhas* have been treated ontologically as categories in their own right. Hence *saṃskāras* have been differentiated from the *skandhas,* because all interrelations with phenomena by means of the

3 This is the way they are treated in the Uttaratantra, where the *skandhas* are relegated to the Earth Element. See Tsultrim Gyantso Rinpoche, Rosemary Fuchs, *Buddha Nature, The Mahayana Uttaratantra Shastra with Commentary* (Snow Lion, New York, 2000), 27.

faculty of discrimination is carried by them. (They also convey the transcendent attributes of Mind.) They therefore convey the constituency of consciousness. The term *kāma-manas* is used instead of *vedanā* and *samjñā*. *Kāma-manas,* the mental-emotions, represents the main content of the *saṃskāras* normally conveyed as a consequence of sense contact with phenomena and interrelations with humans.

The esoteric view is proffered in the light of the teaching of the dimensions of perception. Proper analysis of the concept of multidimensionality, which will be treated later in the series, necessitates the redefinition of the way some terminology is generally viewed.

As *karma* dictates the way it all manifests, including the progress to reveal *śūnyatā,* does it necessarily follow that *śūnyatā* is karmaless, or does a new form of *karma* manifest? For instance a 'thus gone' Buddha has left the *karma* of the earth sphere behind him as he enters *parinirvāṇa,* but what about any *karma* he may posses concerning the immensity of cosmos?

The existence of an independent consciousness of a 'self' is customarily negated in general Buddhism and thus by the Prāsaṅgika-Madhyamaka school,[4] or else cursorily dismissed as something irrelevant, because it is an outcome of ignorance. Reasons exist for such postulations, however this viewpoint needs to be modified. This is essential, for without the appearance of an I–concept there could be no striving for liberation, consequently no appearance of a Bodhisattva or eventually a Buddha. The I-concept thus does matter, and though an integral philosophy exists to explain 'it' in Buddhist terminology to counterbalance the teachings on *śūnyatā,* further exposition however needs to be provided to account for certain shortcomings in what has been presented. The two concepts are diametrically opposed extremes, yet are integrally interwoven in the *maṇḍala*[5] of being/non-being, and within the context of the two truths. From this perspective the I-concept may be an integral aspect of the realms of ignorance, but from another standpoint its ramifications are borne out as reality, as its transmuted

4 The Prāsaṅgika-Madhyamaka ontology of Tsongkapa, Buddhapālita and Candrakīrti (following from Nāgārjuna's work) shall be the focus of this Volume, as it may be considered as the 'most refined' or 'extremist' version of the Madhyamaka teachings.

5 *Maṇḍala*: 'that which circumscribes', a specific form or blueprint of what is to be, used as a visualising tool.

source lies in the *dharmakāya*. The significance of this important concept will be explored throughout this treatise.

The two truths

I shall now use a number of quotes from eminent authors to help establish the views of various Buddhist schools concerning these truths. My purpose here is not to write a dissertation as to the differing views concerning the two truths, but rather to present an overview of some of their main tenets, and comment upon the arguments presented. I hope thereby to bring into perspective certain ideas that need elucidating which are not necessarily covered by the available literature. The subject is not straightforward, as there are various views concerning the two truths in the Mahāyāna stream. In many ways this subject lies at the heart of Buddhist philosophy.

One of the purposes of presenting these quotations is to emphasise the importance of 'conventional reality' as the basis to establishing 'absolutely valuable reality' (ultimate truth) because It produces the path to enlightenment. A cogent comprehension in relation to the way of the manifestation of phenomena, and indeed what it consists of, and its relation to *śūnyatā* can thereby be gained. Comprehensive consideration of this method of approach will unveil revelations concerning the relation of *saṃsāra* to *śūnyatā*. This necessitates an investigative reappraisal of the 'self' concept, as much can yet be revealed to supplement epistemological polemics. Here conventional reality refers to the way that 'things' are perceived by means of the awakening or the awakened Mind with respect to manifesting phenomena. 'Things' have a tangible and perceptible reality in that they can be touched, or otherwise contacted by means of the five senses, and thereby incorporated into consciousness, even though the contactable is transient.

It should be noted that the doctrine of the two truths is effectively a later Mahāyāna discourse, as Kalupahana points out. He is of the opinion that the 'Buddha's epistemological standpoint' did not allow for speculations on the nature of an 'absolute reality'.

> The theory of dependent arising *(praṭiccasamuppāda)* explaining the phenomena that are dependently arisen *(paṭiccasamuppanna)* thus accommodates the four truths as well as the two truths. All truths being pragmatic, there is here no place for an "absolute or ultimate

reality." The Buddha's epistemological standpoint does not allow for such speculations.

This, however, was not the case with the metaphysicians. It is significant to note that when the Buddhist metaphysicians were faced with the problem of reconciling the four truths with their conception of substance *(svabhāva),* they were compelled to fall back on the conception of two truths *(Akb* p. 33). However, their interpretation of the two truths is totally different from the Buddha's and, in fact, seems to be contrary to it.[6]

With respect to the *two truths* a quote from an article by Kapstein, where he speaks of the two truths in terms of 'conventional reality' and 'absolutely valuable reality'[7], is useful:

In addition to the categories of substance and attribute, individuating and generic characteristic, concretum and abstractum, which Mi-pham explicitly assigns to conventional reality, his tradition maintains that, for example, what we would term necessary truths are to be classed here as well. The conventional aspect of the principle of reality further plays a foundational role with respect to the concept of causality, as will be indicated below...

The principles of efficacy, dependence, and reality, as introduced thus far, are all principles belonging to the conventional logic of investigation. The absolute logic of investigation is presented as a second aspect of the principle of reality[8]...The "great arguments" *(gtan tshigs chen mo)* of the Madhyamaka are now called upon to demonstrate that there is no causal agent which acts to generate the result, that results do not come to be depending upon such causal agents, and that individual essences are merely convenient fictions. The three gates to liberation *(rnam thar sgo gsum)* are thus thrown open: causes stripped of efficacy are unmarked *(mtshan ma med pa);* results that are not dependent entities can no longer be objects of expectation *(smon pa med pa);* and reality itself cannot be hypostatized through such fancies as individual essence *(ngo bo nyid med pa).*[9]

---

6 David J. Kalupahana, *Mūlamadhyamakakārikā of Nāgārjuna,* 332.

7 M. Kapstein, 'Mi-pham's Theory of Interpretation', *Buddhist Hermeneutics,* (ed., Donald S. Lopez, Jr.) 156.

8 Ibid.

9 Ibid., 156-157.

Concerning these 'great arguments' of the Mādhyamika, the footnote given states that:

> The argument applied to causes, called "Diamond Fragments" (*rgyu la dpyod pa rdo rje gzegs ma*), proceeds from the assumption that if an individual thing comes into being as the result of some cause, then that cause must either be the thing itself or something other. The supposition that it is the thing itself leads to an infinite regress, whereas the assumption that the cause is other cannot be sustained owing to the absence of any intrinsic relationship between the supposed cause and its result. Having denied these two alternatives nothing is gained by supposing that their conjunction might explain causation; and their joint negation leads to the absurdity of things coming into being causelessly. The argument is intended to demonstrate that the concept of cause is radically defective, i.e. empty[10]...The argument employed here intends to reduce to absurdity the notions of the one and the many (*ngo bo la dpyod pa gcig du bral*), with the result that the concept of individual essence is overthrown[11]...in the case of spiritual substance it depends on the denial of the unity of consciousness.[12]

This and associated logic supporting a conclusion as to the nature of the absolute truth are treated in later chapters of this book ('The Sevenfold Reasoning', 'The Essay of the Many and the One', etc.). These 'great arguments' are ontological dissertations into the question of the nature of a 'self', or of that which can query the fact of the two truths. Such must be established before any detailed empirical discussion can follow concerning the nature of truth.

There is an inherent falsehood in 'the denial of the unity of consciousness', unless if by 'consciousness' one is referring to the intellect, which is born and dies with each new human personality.

Consciousness (the mind/Mind *per se*) has unity because it survives at the death of a human personality and it flows into the next successive personality, concerning which the related *saṃskāras* and *karma* manifest in order to continue the process that leads a person to liberation. Also, once we understand the nature of consciousness, and

10 Ibid., 170.

11 Ibid.

12 Ibid.

the way it manifests on its own realm of expression, then indeed there is a 'unity of consciousness', which allows consciousness to be stored in the *ālayavijñāna*. Because consciousness persists after the demise of the physical body it can only do so in a unified form, otherwise there could be no coherent after-death experiences. Nor could an enlightened being trace anyone's previous birth, because there would be nothing coherent to gain such impressions from, there would only be a chaotic mess from which nothing could be gleaned. *Karma* can only manifest via coherent 'unities', as was explained in my book *Karma and the Rebirth of Consciousness*. This theme shall be further elaborated in this series, as well as the mode of consciousness transference from one life to the next.

Donald S. Lopez Jr., states:

> A conventional truth *(saṃvṛtisatya, kun rdzob bden pa)* is a truth for a concealer. The concealer is an ignorant consciousness that misapprehends the nature of phenomena[13]....conventional truths are not truths in the sense that ultimate truths are. Ultimate truths, emptinesses, are truths because they exist in the way in which they appear to a wisdom consciousness. Conventional truths are truths only for a concealer *(samantādvaraṇa, sgrib byed)*. They are displayed by the conception of true existence as ultimately existent to ignorant conceptual consciousnesses. These consciousnesses conceive phenomena to exist truly, to exist in the way in which they are displayed by the conception of true existence. In this way, phenomena which appear to exist truly are truths only for ignorance, they do not in fact exist in the way they appear.
>
> Phenomena other than emptinesses do, however, validly exist as is indicated by the two other etymologies of *saṃvṛti*.....[14]
>
> In general, there are three meanings of the *saṃvṛti* of *saṃvṛti-satya*.[15] The first is the ignorant consciousness for which truths for a concealer are true. The second meaning of *saṃvṛti* refers to objects that are mutually interdependent *(parasparasaṃbhavana, phan tshun rten pa)*. In this sense, one may say that emptiness exists conventionally

---

13 Donald S. Lopez Jr., *A Study of Svātantrika*, 205.

14 Ibid., 206.

15 *Saṃvṛti:* from the prefix *sam* plus the verbal root *vṛt*, to cover, to involve, thus relative, empirical, deceptive, a false conception, worldly knowledge, being the basis to illusion. *Satya*, means 'truth'.

> because emptiness is a dependent arising[16].....The third meaning of *saṃvṛti* is "conventions of the world" *(lokavyavahāra, 'jig rtan pa'i tha snyad).* It is this meaning of the term that is used to translate *saṃvṛtisatya* as "conventional truth," although truth for a concealer is a more evocative translation.[17]

Concerning these three levels of *saṃvṛtisatya* we can say that the first level concerns various ignorance states, indicating increasing levels of sophistication of knowledge about things. Each level of ignorance is relative to the next, producing a graded series of expansions and increasing clarification of consciousness. Knowledge about things and human interrelationships is consequently gained, right through to discovering the *dharma* and following its path. Next we have the dependent arising of phenomena, whereby everyone and everything is dependently interrelated, as will be explained in the chapter on Dependent Origination. All is illusional, hence 'empty'. Dependent Origination is not concerned with ignorant states per se, but rather with a process of interdependence, of moving lines of energy interrelationships, of the mode of the transformations of *saṃskāras* from one state of expression to the next. 'Conventional truth' can be thought of in terms of the conventional understanding of people in our societies, of science, philosophers, and the arts, concerning the tangibility of phenomena taken thus to be real though transient. Another aspect of conventional truth can be considered, namely, that which is imaginatively construed *(parikalpita),* which many people revel in.

Lopez further states:

> Not only are objects of knowledge the basis of division of the two truths, all objects of knowledge are exhaustively included in the two truths; everything is either a conventional truth or an ultimate truth, as is stated in the *Meeting of the Father and Son Sutra (Pitāputra-samāgamasūtra):*
>
> > It is thus: the Tathāgata comprehends the two [truths], conventional and ultimate. Furthermore, objects of knowledge are thoroughly exhausted in these conventional and ultimate truths.

16 Donald S. Lopez Jr., *A Study of Svātantrika,* 206

17 Ibid., 207.

There is no third truth because, like one and many, the two truths are a dichotomy and mutually exclusive. Two things are a dichotomy if it can be said that something does not exist if it is not one or the other of them. A dichotomy includes all phenomena such that there is no third category, there is nothing which is both, and there is nothing which is neither. Kamalaśīla says in his *Illumination of the Middle Way:*

> Regarding phenomena which have the character of mutual abandonment, if [something] is refuted as one and is not established as the other, it does not exist. Therefore, even the conception of a class which is neither is infeasible. ...Those which have the character of mutual abandonment pervade all aspects. Those which pervade all aspects eliminate another category, for instance, physical and non-physical.

The reason why the two truths are considered a dichotomy is that ultimate truths are truths whereas conventional truths are falsities, truths only for ignorance, as will be explored. If something is identified as a deceptive object, it is impossible that it is also a non-deceptive truth. If something is non-deceptive, it cannot also be a falsity. Therefore, deceptive object and non-deceptive object are mutually exclusive and a dichotomy; every phenomenon is either one or the other.[18]

There are really only two ways to the obtaining of truth (i.e., enlightened perception):

1. Through a deep heuristic introspection of the phenomena the body is sustained by and of its consciousness. One can gain an experience of *śūnyatā* and thus come to know (it) through the development of serene mental equipoise via eliminating attachment to *saṃsāra.* This necessitates control of the many types of input from sense perception in combination with the development of *bodhicitta.*[19] It represents the way inwards to the awakening of the powers of the Heart *chakra* (and by extension the Heart in the Head centre). This depiction concerns the general methodology chosen by Buddhists,

18 Ibid., 193-194.

19 *Bodhicitta:* the Heart's Mind, the Mind of enlightenment. The power or force productive of awakened realisations, enlightenment, that emanates from the Heart centre. It is the Mind of pure perfection, the authentic nature of Mind.

being the way of approach to the attainment of truth to ascertain absolute reality.

2. Looking outwards through a careful and minute study of the phenomenal universe. One ascertains truth by adamantly striving to logically and systematically comprehend the laws governing phenomena. This method starts through scientific deduction and research into the nature of the atom, the universe, and of how matter interrelates with energy. Investigative philosophers incorporate such discoveries to analyse the nature of what is, and is not. There is also the type of philosophical investigation as found in Western mathematical texts, the writings of the various empirical and metaphysical philosophers and the practices of many religious traditions. Atheistic considerations may begin the process but inevitably must be set aside so that the direct perception of the divinity governing the expression of all forms can be experienced. A necessary higher level of this methodology lies in the study of Astrology, esoterically understood, as well as the nature of the alchemicalisation of substance. This is not yet accepted by empiricists, but nevertheless holds the clue to many of the mysteries of what is known as Life, in, through, and beyond evolutionary forms. Such study necessitates a complete comprehension of the nature of the subtle body, with its *chakra* and *naḍī* system. What is generally presented in Astrological texts is the conventional reality described above. However, there is a higher *esoteric* form of Astrology that interprets attributes of the *dharmakāya*, which shall be introduced in this series. Esoteric comprehension of the true informational content of the world's myths also reveals much, as well as Buddhist and Hindu eschatological metaphysics.

For the complete picture of what 'truth' is to emerge, both keys thereto must be fully turned, as they provide complementary information. The integration of both forms of investigation awakens the enlightenment path by means of the Dharmakāya Way. The interrelatedness of these two modes of obtaining truth are symbolised by the images depicting the highest states of bliss obtained by Buddhas in sexual union with their divine Consort. The Buddha, or the penetrative mechanism, represents the inwards contemplative method, where the seed capable of producing the child of compassion goes inwards into the womb of being/non-being. The female Consort represents the outwards explorative method, of the conventional reality that provides added substance that envelops the inward method, and gives birth to the fruit of their combined union. It envelops *śūnyatā,* whereby *śūnyatā* acts as a seed for further growth. The phenomenal world, the Consort, plays the active role in the love making, whilst the Dhyāni Buddha is the stable base playing the passive role. Together they produce all that is and is not. The Consort represents the dynamic active interrelationship between the forces of *karma* inherent in the external universe and the stable divinity within. It allows for the projection of the qualities of the divine into manifestation.

The Dhyāni Buddha (the *absolute reality)* is the inherent quiescent Power that sustains the drive to evolutionary fulfilment and projects the seed *(śūnyatā)* as the foundation of every creative act. This 'seed' sprouts in the fertile ground of *saṃsāra,* clothed in the paraphernalia of conventional truth. As it grows out from the soil of the material domain and sloughs off (by transformation into wisdom attributes) the ephemera of empirical considerations, then the luminosity of the sun of the ultimate experience remains. There can be no expressed bliss, or the sounds, colours and the laws of Nature without this union between the Buddha and his Consort. The way to Buddhahood can thus be via the Consort, the complete affiliation with the laws of Nature that are a result of the union, or it can be directly through obtaining the absolute quiescence of the Dhyāni Buddha.

Treading the Bodhisattva path concerns travelling within the consciousness-space representing the womb of the Consort, with Buddhahood being obtained when one has progressed outside of that earthly womb of space-time and its evolutionary process. This means that to travel the Bodhisattva way one needs to master both methods of revelation, necessitating finding a means to unite them into unity, a fusion, a *mahāmudrā* of dynamic expansive love and wisdom.

The union or integration of both lovers, or modes of enquiry, provides the *complete* picture of the bliss of the Buddha nature *(dharmatā).* The philosophy concerning the methodology of such integration is presented in this *Treatise on Mind*. What needs explaining therefore is the product of the union between Buddha and Consort, the child to be, which represents the third method of revelatory attainment, the nature of which is neither one or the other, but partakes of both within the womb of the Mother. When properly analysed, this exploratory path is the harbinger of much revelation of an entire developed universe of possibilities, yet to be explored ontologically and eschatologically. The term 'eschatologically' here does just not refer to the human afterlife, but also to the transcendental purpose of the planets, stars, galaxies and universes, of their modes of evolutionary attainment.

It is the nature of *a third truth*, of relativity, because born in a Tathātagata-Womb, it is the result of the fusion of Buddha and Consort, and therefore is *neither* one or the other. Full elucidation of this truth is an important heuristic tool, or key, needed to be used by Buddhists to unravel greater mysteries of being, of awakening into increasing degrees of absolute relative Truth. (Indeed there are levels of 'absolutes' to be considered in this multidimensional universe.)

Seven categories of views concerning the two truths will herein be discussed.

1. The view of conventional thinkers.
2. The three natures of the Yogācāra.
3. The view of the extremist Prāsaṅgika Mādhyamikas.
4. The Svātantrika Mādhyamika view.
5. The Tsongkhapian Prāsaṅgika view.
6. The Yogācāra Mādhyamika view of the Nyingmapa.
7. The integrationist view of the Dharmakāya Way.

These differing schools of thought have valid rhetoric from one or other perspective, but incongruent aspects are successfully distilled out as we move from the first to the seventh view.

1. The view of conventional thinkers

This view is the simplest to consider. Conventional thinkers take the phenomena seen around and perceived by the five senses as real, conventionally existing. It may be deceptive, illusional, everchanging, nevertheless the truth of its existence is self-evident to them because of experiences derived from the five senses as ascertained by the mind that integrates the experiences. Theirs is a normative view based upon empirical observation of the world around. The multidimensional experiences derived from yoga-meditation is normally not part of their mind-set, but certain forms of religious or psychic experiences may be countenanced. For such beings (if not atheistic) a God concept manifests as their ultimate truth, and many follow the hermeneutic of religious orthodoxy. For atheists the gain of scientific enquiry and methodology becomes their ultimate truth.

2. The three natures of the Yogācāra.

First a quote from Pettit:

> In both Sautrāntika and Cittamātra, as in Madhyamaka, conventional reality—specifically concepts and reasoning—is the means *(upāya)* for realizing the ultimate. But in the final analysis, the conventional and ultimate realities of the proponents of true existence do not have an identical ontological status in emptiness as they do in Madhyamaka. More important is the meaning of "emptiness" that obtains in these systems. For Cittamātrins and proponents of extrinsic emptiness, emptiness and ultimate reality are established as the absence of what does not exist *(parikalpita)* in that which does exist *(paratantra).* In other words, pure relativity *(paratantra)* truly exists, and is the ultimate, with respect to the absence of the false appearances of projection. It is not devoid of its own nature, but of something extrinsic to it. A similar relation of relative and ultimate truths is obtained in the context of Sautrāntika.[20]

A way of viewing this problem of ultimates is that though the big toe and the brain consciousness appear to be separate from each other, they are nevertheless not mutually exclusive: there are pathways—bones, blood veins, sinew, flesh, nerves, and electro-chemical impulses, linking the two, to make them part of one functioning unity. We see that all aspects of the body function to produce one result: consciousness. From this perspective the brain consciousness represents 'the ultimate' for the organisational procedures and sentience of the cells and organelles of

---

20 John W. Pettit, *Mipham's Beacon of Certainty. Illuminating the View of Dzogchen, the Great Perfection*, (Wisdom Publications, Boston, 1999), 144, 145.

the rest of the body. The entire interconnected transiency of the form produce the pathways to the development of intelligent perceptions.

This is the way it is throughout Nature. There will always be relative 'ultimates' to be found, e.g., one genus or species ahead of a former one; the evolution of the animal kingdom from out of the plant kingdom, and of a thinking human from out of the animal kingdom. There are innumerable transitional subspecies, representing lesser 'ultimates', even if the pathways are not at first obvious and directly perceptible. So it is also in the field of being/non-being. Pathways therefore exist between consciousness and *śūnyatā*, and between *śūnyatā* and consciousness, otherwise enlightenment and liberation would not be possible. Any cogent rhetoric concerning the nature of gaining enlightenment must account for such in order to be viable.

This introduces the concept of the 'three nature' theory of the *Yogācārins* (imaginatively constructed *(parakalpita)* nature *(lakṣaṇa)*, relative *(paratantra)* nature and perfect *(paraniṣpanna)* nature). The 'relative nature' is that of the continuum, or rail track, which links the conventional (the 'store depot' of transient bits of information, 'goods') to the Void (the final terminal, where those bits of information are offloaded, i.e., perfectly assessed). In this analogy the 'goods' do not remain unchanged as they move from the store to the final depot, but are continuously modified, processed, and refined as they do so. My analysis, therefore, does not take on the Yogācārin position verbatim, but rather the general outline. The way that the doctrine is modified is presented throughout the discourse.

Here analysis of the result of Nāgārjuna's meditation, presented in the *Mūlamadhyamikakārikā* is useful.

> *Saṃsāra* (i.e., the empirical life-death cycle) is nothing essentially different from *nirvāṇa*. *Nirvāṇa* is nothing essentially different from *saṃsāra*...The limits (i.e., the realm) of *nirvāṇa* are the limits of *saṃsāra*. Between the two, also, there is not the slightest difference whatsoever.[21]

If this is true, then logically one can gain realisation of *nirvāṇa* through *saṃsāra*, i.e., through a thorough (meditative) examination of

21 Kenneth K. Inada, *Nāgārjuna. A Translation of his Mūlamadhyamikakārikā with an Introductory Essay*, (Sri Satguru Publications, Delhi, 1993) verse 19-20, p. 158.

its properties, and then to methodologically follow revelation of how to process the related phenomena to its 'ultimate' conclusion. This means therefore, that there is a way to *nirvāṇa*[22] via the expression of conventional truth. *Saṃsāra* thus becomes a prime heuristic tool wherein the solipsistic attitude concerning phenomena pertaining to an 'I' can be used as a means to ascertain whatever the Real may be. By thoroughly analysing the 'I' one can induce revelations of the existence of a not-'I' (non-being). *Śūnyatā* is just as real as *saṃsāra* and *saṃsāra* as real as *śūnyatā*, if they can be equated with each other. Both can be considered ultimate truths relative to each other. *Saṃsāra* is effectively sustained via *śūnyatā* and thus ultimately emanates from the *śūnyatā-saṃsāra* relation. 'Ultimately' *śūnyatā* is experienced through *saṃsāric* interconnectiveness. When *saṃsāra* emanates from *śūnyatā* then *śūnyatā* is obscured—'obliterated' for a continuum (of time), when *śūnyatā* is experienced then *saṃsāra* is obscured, 'obliterated' for a continuum (of being/non-being).

The fact is that though a person may become liberated and experience *śūnyatā*, *saṃsāra* still persists for the rest, and whilst *saṃsāra* exists, so too does *śūnyatā* as a potential for human experience. This simply means that what really distinguishes the two is that they exist upon a different time continuum. It is like the quandary of the seed and the sprout. They are not different, yet are. This is because the sprout *will* emanate from the seed, given time and the right environmental conditionings. (The seed therefore is intrinsic to the sprout, which in time will produce more seeds, given the right conditions.) The passage of time is the 'railroad track' that allows the maturation or germination of the sprout from the seed, whilst right environmental conditions (moisture, warmth, nutrients) constitutes the 'goods train' travelling thereon from depot to depot, from the raw seed to its maturation into a plant.

So it is also with the *saṃsāra-śūnyatā* interrelationship. Given time the 'seed' (here the human consciousness, relative truth) will mature into a human plant that can and does experience *śūnyatā* (absolute truth). The 'goods train' (the relative nature) thus represents all of the environmental conditionings that first create and mature human consciousness, allowing it to become wise and stabilised in *bodhicitta*,

22 Note that *nirvāṇa* can be considered to be a state of residing in *śūnyatā*.

which then provides the consciousness transformations necessary to experience *śūnyatā*. This train links every intermediary and factor of expression from depot to depot, and therefore exists relative to each. This relativityness can be considered in terms of dependent originations, where all such originations are viewed as aspects of the sphere of consciousness. They therefore manifest a continuum of increasingly subtler states of diminishing ignorance, hence vaster levels of experiential knowledge. Eventually such knowledge pertains to the real because consciousness becomes exceedingly refined and perceptive. Eventually its consciousness-bits are stilled, made serene, and the continuum then no longer moves—hence the experience of the ultimate truth. In other words, the train has either stopped or else runs so smoothly that no characteristics whatsoever are experienced as a consequence of its motion.

Over time various formative forces emanate from (or via) *śūnyatā* to 'create' the conditionings governing the movement of *saṃsāra* to its inevitable conclusion. Such forces are intrinsic to the warp and weft of Nature. Human consciousness can here be seeded, wherein it can grow and mature to finally eliminate the formative conditionings allowing *śūnyatā* to be experienced as part of a process that produces Buddhahood. Human consciousness is that which interrelates 'one' *(saṃsāra)* to 'the other' *(śūnyatā)*. Its activity *relative* to both extremes inevitably produces the transformations and refinements of phenomena so that the outcome is experience of the Void. Relativity here *(paratantra)* simply relates to the degree that consciousness is awakened or awakening to the need to act to bring about the needed transformations.

The Yogācāra viewpoint concerning the nature of phenomena is excellently presented by Lopez:

> Persuaded by the argument from illusion, that the same thing sometimes appears differently to different people, the Yogācārins sever the relationship between the external object and its aspect that the Sautrāntikas maintain, asserting instead that external objects are utterly non-existent and that the object is not a cause of the consciousness perceiving it. The Yogācārins hold that subject and object arise simultaneously, both arising from the same latency *(vāsanā, bags chags)* or seed *(bīja, sa bon)* that resides in the mental consciousness or mind-basis-of-all *(ālayavijñāna, kun gzhi rnam shes)*. A seed is activated, causing the appearance of the object and the consciousness

> perceiving it. Subject and object are the same substantial entity, arising from the same cause; there are no objects that are not of the nature of consciousness. Thus the Yogācārins maintain that there are sensa without objects external in entity to the perceiving consciousness and that these sensa are of the nature of mind...The Yogācārins assert that objects composed of material particles do not exist.[23]

It is true that all phenomena exists in the mind. However everything that we experience by means of sense contact can only be done so because of the fact that objects of the senses can be contacted and experienced. The sense-perceptors need to exist in order to experience phenomena, and electro-chemical impulses are sent through the nervous system to the brain to register the effects of the objects contacted. The mind (the intellect) then processes the experiences. Nothing however can be known by a cogniser outside of the processes of the mind, this however does not mean that external objects are non existent. Without them the mind could not exist or evolve. Neither could the *ālayavijñāna* exist to store the proceeds of consciousness-volitions. Similarly the seeds *(bījas)* therein had to have come from some prior existent state of awareness gained from experience with phenomena. They cannot simply be self-generated entities perpetually existing in this universal store of *manas* that contain the sensa of everything that can possibly be experienced in *saṃsāra*. Each *bīja* would then effectively be a permanent entity, an existent 'self'. Such a concept may exist for the Hindu view of an *ātman*, but is anathema to the Buddhist ontology. The *bījas*[24] themselves consequently must have evolved, and how is this possible without the appearance of extrinsic phenomena that consciousness experiences and which modifies consciousness. Each new experience either causes a new *bīja* to appear, or else the modification of an existing one.

Phenomena, stars and galaxies, have existed before the appearance of human intelligence. However, without the appearance of a mind the duration of galaxies stretching over many tens of billions of years would be meaningless. Even if many such universes appeared and disappeared,

---

23 Lopez Jr., *A Study of Svātantrika*, 157-158.

24 *Bīja* (Tib. yig 'bru): Seed (syllable), seminal point. The essential part of a mantra. The seed germ, the starting point for the display of power or creativity, for a *maṇḍala*, or as a focus for meditation.

with no intelligence, whatever appeared or not is irrelevant. There would be absolutely nothing to register the fact, as no consciousness exists to even query such an event. We can see from this that the Yogācāra position has merit in that without the mind (or sentience for that matter) to register the fact the manifestation of any phenomena effectively does not happen. Only in our minds does the appearance of phenomena, or of a universe to experience things in, have any meaning. However, in order for that mind to so act it must have evolved the ability to do so from the phenomenological appearance of an evolutionary process from primal substance. Later in this series I shall pursue the concept of a hylozoistic universe, in relation to the evolution of Buddhas in cosmos (the making of an Ādi Buddha) and thereby the appearance of Logoi, meaning that all phenomena is Mind-conceived, proceeding from the meditation-Mind of such a One. Hence this entire debate needs to move beyond consideration of just the human condition, and to take into account a grander *dharmakāyic* view which constitutes the Dharmakāya Way.

From the above we can see that the Yogācāra view is both correct and incorrect, depending upon one's angle of vision. In relation to the Svātantrika critique of the Yogācāra view Lopez states:

> The Sautrāntika-Svātantrikas, in the person of Bhāvaviveka, reacted strongly against the Yogācārin view, holding that external objects do exist as they appear to direct perception, although they do not truly exist. The Yogācāra-Svātantrikas assimilated the Yogācārin idealism, asserting that subject and object do not exist as separate entities conventionally, but rejected the Yogācārin contention that consciousness truly exists.[25]

Concerning the Yogācāra view one can say that consciousness, like all phenomenal appearances, is transient as far as empirical observations and their processing by the mind goes, as well as imputed ideas and images. Thoughts are continuously born and consequently die. Inevitably they are clarified and transmuted into enlightened perceptions, the development of a higher abstracted Mind, finally being extinguished in the *śūnyatā* experience. This does not mean that the gain of the sum of one's conscious experience is annihilated, rather the substance of thoughts has been transformed and stilled, but the essence, the impressions of what once

25 Lopez Jr., Ibid., 158.

manifests continue, in *bīja* (seed) form. If this was not the case a Buddha could recall nothing after his *nirvāṇa.* Hence the corporeal mind is eventually transformed (transcended) into the Mind that is *dharmakāya.* From this perspective the Yogācāra view is both correct and incorrect. It is correct with respect to the concept of mind/Mind, but not with respect to an enlightened view as to the nature of the phenomenal world.[26] The Sautrāntika-Svātantrika view as it is presented here is correct.

A further quote can here be added in relation to the three nature doctrine of the Yogācāra *(Cittamatra)*:

> According to the *Tathagatagarbha* school,[27] the imaginary nature and impure dependent nature are exactly the same, but the pure dependent nature is intrinsic emptiness or *rangtong* (the lack of inherent existence in imaginary phenomena) rather than *buddha*-attributes, and the absolute nature is the *buddha*-attributes themselves which are extraneously empty *(shentong)* of the dependent nature. Scholars sometimes refer to the former *(Cittamatra)* view as the 'pivotal model' of the three natures because the transformation of the imaginary into the absolute is effected by a pivotal movement from the impure dependence of *aggregates* etc. to the pure dependence of *buddha*-attributes, while the latter *(Tathagatagarbha)* view is called the 'pyramidal model' because, in succession, the pure dependent nature is experienced as the intrinsic emptiness of the imaginary and the absolute nature as the extraneous emptiness of the dependent, i.e., intrinsic emptiness and its scope. In other words, the *Cittamatrin* views *buddha*-attributes as dependent while the adherent of the *Tathagatagarbha* school views them as absolute'.[28]

Logically one would presume the Buddha attributes to be expressions of the absolute truth. Even when his teachings concern the interpretable, directed to common intellects, he has deduced what to impart from his residence in *pariniṣpanna.* His phenomenal appearance (*nirmāṇakāya*) however is a *māyāvirūpa* (illusional body of form) and must die like all other attributes of *saṃsāra.*

---

26 Even here they can be correct from the viewpoint of what exists in a Logoic Mind. This subject can only be understood when the nature of a Logos is comprehended. (Explained somewhat in the later volumes of this treatise.)

27 The Madhyamaka.

28 Ed. G. Coleman, *Handbook of Tibetan Culture,* 397-398.

3. The Prāsaṅgika Mādhyamika extremism

Though the entire Prāsaṅgika view evolved from Tsongkhapa's astute mind, nevertheless there appears two differing ways that the philosophy is perceived. In this section the extremist perception of Prāsaṅgika Mādhyamikas[29] views shall be analysed, which can be contrasted to the depiction of a more moderate consideration presented later.

Pettit states:

> According to the Gelug scholar 'Jam dbyangs bzhad pa, in Madhyamaka "the two truths are objects, not vague concepts...[t]hey are phenomena *(dharma, chos),* objects *(viṣaya, yul),* existents *(sat, yod pa),* and objects of knowledge *(jñeya, shes bya).* They are logically distinct—complementary, but mutually exclusive. Though the two truths are known by different kinds of consciousness—conventional and ultimate—they are not simply different perspectives on the same thing. Instead they are understood as "different isolates of one entity" *(ngo bo gcig la ldog pa tha dad),* referring to the ultimate emptiness of the conventional distinction of "conventional" and "ultimate."
>
> Gelug Prāsaṅgika here seems close to Svātantrika, which according to Mipham emphasises the valid cognitions that cognize the truths and the logical distinction of the two truths. If ultimate truth is validly cognized by means of rational analysis that investigates the ultimate status of a thing, the object known through such analysis is obviously distinct from that known by conventional analysis. However, if the definitive ultimate *(don dam mtshan nyid pa)* is an emptiness of absolute negation exclusive of appearance, then the coalescence of the two realities—for example, form and emptiness or appearance and emptiness—cannot be established because the two realities are, on the basis of this definition of the ultimate, mutually exclusive. Thus, according to Mipham, the definition of the negandum as utterly nonexistent, and its basis as conventionally existent, is not adequate to the nature of coalescence, which is realized as the absence of conceptual elaborations *(niṣprapañca, spros bral)* of existence, nonexistence, and so forth.
>
> Mipham, Go ram pa, et al., were not the only ones to notice the problematic nature of Tsongkapa's Prāsaṅgika system on this account. Napper notes that there is a "danger that, because Dzong-ka-ba chose

29 Utilised by the Gelugpa.

> to emphasize a verbal distinction between existence and inherent existence which cannot be realized in ordinary experience, people will miss the Mādyamika message altogether. They will not understand that Mādyamika is attacking and refuting our very sense of existence and, misled by the verbal emphasis on inherent existence, will see Mādyamika as refuting something merely intellectual".[30]

This quote establishes certain premises from various viewpoints, firstly we have the relativistic nature of all things *(paratantra).* The conventional is needed to define the absolute, and 'paradoxically' the conventional is contained in the absolute, they are not mutually exclusive in terms of the attributes of the liberated Mind. (Though they are mutually exclusive mathematically and logically.) Just because an enlightened one resides in *parinispanna* (absolute perfection) does not mean that the conventional is not cognisable from that place of residence. Therefore although the statement, the 'definitive ultimate (don dam mtshan nyid pa) is an emptiness of absolute negation exclusive of appearance' may appear true logically, it is not applicable in reality. If we understand them as 'different isolates of one entity' then intrinsically they are that entity, meaning that 'the definition of the negandum as utterly nonexistent' would also apply to ultimate truth. In fact they are that entity in the liberated Mind, whereas the ordinary mind perceives two truths. The dichotomy exists because the enlightened view of residing above or beyond *saṃsāra* has not been attained. Finally, the criticism of the Gelug (Prāsaṅgika) view on the two truths provided by Napper *et al* should be noted.

Lopez gives the Prāsaṅgika viewpoint on the nature of phenomena in *A Study of Svātantrika:*

> The Prāsaṅgikas assert that phenomena do not inherently exist even conventionally, and, therefore, when they negate inherent existence or existence from the object's own side, they find it unnecessary, indeed redundant, to add the qualification "ultimately" or "truly"

30 John W. Pettit, *Mipham's Beacon of Certainty. Illuminating the View of Dzogchen, the Great Perfection,* 145. His quote is from: Elizabeth Napper, *Dependent Arising and Emptiness.* (Wisdom, Boston, 1989), 147. Mipham (1846-1912), a great Nyingma scholar, is noted as an important member of the nineteenth century Eclectic Movement (*ris med*) in Tibet.

> because, according to them, if something exists by way of its own character or inherently exists, it necessarily also truly exists and ultimately exists. Whereas the Svātantrikas assert that phenomena exist by way of their own character, exist from their own side, and inherently exist while negating true existence, ultimate existence, and real existence, the Prāsaṅgikas assert that existence by way of the object's own character, existence from the object's side, inherent existence, ultimate existence, true existence, and real existence are synonymous and refute them all.[31]

The Prāsaṅgika argument presented here is unsound, from the point of view that they have their eye so fixated upon the 'absolute' they forget that it is *only* the Void they are describing in their form of denial, not the *śūnyatā-saṃsāra* relation,[32] nor indeed the vast certitude of *dharmakāya*. Furthermore, they forget *what* they are utilising to thus deny 'things'. It is something like a viewer so engrossed in the imagery of a movie that he or she is watching that they forget that they are sitting upon chairs, and have eyes which are viewing the images appearing in their consciousness. The Prāsaṅgika view *here* implies that they look only to *when* the ultimate has been experienced absolutely (presuming that there is even such a thing as an 'ultimate'), and take that as the beginning and ending of their logic, forgetting entirely that they are not 'there yet', and if they were they would have no form of mind to conceptualise with or to reason to all others who likewise are not 'there'. They have put the proverbial cart before the horse, expecting the cart to pull the horse. They must look to the *reality* of their actual incarnation in a phenomenal form (which the Prāsaṅgika view presented later does accomodate), and to properly explain *what* it is that has incarnated into such a form, *why* that form exists, *what* they are asserting their belief structures with, *why* they have a capacity to do so, and from that point of view come to a true middle way of revelation, one which will get them to the 'other shore', utilising the very substance they deny the existence of. Indeed, even then an existent exists, otherwise there is annihilation.

31 Lopez, *A Study of Svātantrika*, 150.

32 That is, the *śūnyatā-saṃsāra* nexus, the bridging mechanism that allows *dharmakāya* to incorporate *saṃsāra* in its scope.

It is a specious argument at best to acknowledge that one is utilising an equipment of response, the personality vehicle, yet ardently deny that it exists. At the ending of evolutionary time this might be so, but then an 'equipment of response' no longer has validity. What is designated as 'the ultimate' may exist, but then there is nothing it can communicate with. The objective of the functionality of *saṃsāra* is real, otherwise no enlightenment would be achievable. The functionality of the horse of mind must thus be truly acknowledged. It must then be rightly utilised to pull the cart of discernment and reasoning along the right track of overcoming different degrees (increasingly subtler levels) of phenomena (i.e., ignorance) to *śūnyatā* and beyond.

How can one accept the existence of conventional reality for conventional minds, but then manifest a denial of this acceptance by stating that 'existence by way of the object's own character, existence from the object's side, inherent existence, ultimate existence, true existence, and real existence are synonymous' and 'refute them all'? In doing so, they deny the actual means or processes that allow them to evolve, and to eventually experience the Void. If the means produces the real, then the means is also real. If the process of the continuum that leads from one to the other produce 'the ultimate', then the ultimate must also be the guiding principle all along. In other words, the experience of the ultimate is inclusive of the process of getting there.

All things exist relatively, allowing the Void to eventually be experienced. The Prāsaṅgika denial of phenomena ignores one half of the debate to fixate upon an extreme, an ultimate, to produce the type of conclusion desired.

Again the question to be asked is 'what is it in this time or life continuum that produces the changes from *śūnyatā* to *saṃsāra* and from *saṃsāra* to *śūnyatā*, and how does it do this?' It implies that the statement earlier quoted by Lopez (who was explaining the Mādhyamika attitude), 'conventional truths are falsities, truths only for ignorance', is basically untrue. They are 'truths only for ignorance' if one learns nothing from them, however, they prove (or disprove, if nothing is learned) the existence of the pathways to the Void, to enlightenment. This the Buddha aptly demonstrated in his life, by first accepting and thence rejecting one after another of these conventional truths, until he was lead to sit under the *bodhi* tree. If there was no process of acceptance and rejection then there would be no *bodhi* experience, consequently no Buddha. The process of analysing conventional truths is therefore the source of his great wisdom, meaning that which leads to the evocation of wisdom is not a falsity. The process leads to the elimination of ignorance.

Lopez's following statement: 'If something is identified as a deceptive object, it is impossible that it is also a non-deceptive truth' can from this perspective also be viewed to possess an inherent falsity, because that which is deceptive, even the mistakes one makes in one's life, can ultimately lead to the highest realisations if one learns from them. Each *level of truth is relative,* and can be perceived as an 'ultimate' in its own category, if never experienced before, and once experienced produces a profound revelation that produces an incremental journeying to *śūnyatā*. Thus it was for the Buddha when he first perceived the nature of disease, sickness, old age, and death. Each of these experiences was but a veil that once comprehended eliminates an ignorance level towards revealing the *śūnyatā* experience. By utilising cogent reasoning the consequences inevitably led him to his liberating conclusion. They were 'deceptive' only because of relativity, i.e., in relation to absolutes, but were non-deceptive for him in the moment of his aspirational journeying to the highest realisation. Wherever there is a liberating revelation, at whatever level of expression it manifests (i.e., at whatever 'ignorance level' one is positioned), there indeed is the process manifesting whereby *śūnyatā* incrementally manifests its potency.

Thus *śūnyatā* is not simply 'the ending', *it is in fact manifesting continuously during the process of becoming.* If this was not the case there could not be any liberated being, there would simply be 'a dichotomy' (between two extremes, two truths) 'that is mutually exclusive' of any process that could produce enlightenment.

That which unites the two truths can be called 'conventional reality' according to the line of reasoning that it is conditional or relative. However, this interrelating characteristic is neither one or the other, but partakes of both, being the bridge that allows the attainment of the ultimate and the transmutation of the conventional. The term 'transmutation' is used here because there is really no such thing as annihilation, there is only change from one form or state of existence to another. Yet from another perspective all forms of change represent an annihilation of that which was changed. Therefore there is no annihilation (as all is retained in mind/Mind), there is annihilation (because of the changes that are the outcome of the transience of *saṃsāra),* there is both annihilation and non-annihilation (which refers to the consciousness-stream which persists throughout all of the changes) and also there is neither both annihilation and non-annihilation (referring to the *śūnyatā* state).

In reference to *śūnyatā* it can be said that emptiness is more than just manifesting an empty mind, though that is one definition commonly presented. It also necessitates the transformation, transmutation and sublimation of *saṃskāras* until they are empty of the characteristics of *saṃsāra.* What remains is identified as the 'ultimate truth', though in reality this Void is but a mirror reflecting the 'ultimate' that is *dharmakāya.* This process is also accompanied with an intensification of the energy states involved. It consequently produces a luminosity and radiance of the Mind that must contain the intensity of the energies liberated. It therefore takes the most gifted *yogins* considerable time, measured in years or decades, to produce a Mind that can bear the energies involved when *saṃsāra* is transformed into *śūnyatā.* No epistemic, hermeneutic or other logical deduction, can produce such a result. Theories remain theories until consistent meditative practice produce experiential results. The 'empty mind' produced by simply eliminating thoughts consequently is not the Void. A mentally incapacitated person can also do this. This theme will be developed throughout this series, and detailed in the fifth Volume on the Tantric precepts of the *Bardo Thödol.*

Another form of emptiness indicated above is the process that comes from the transmogrification of one form of phenomena into the next. As phenomena changes it reveals the emptiness of its inherent nature, such as when fire burns the pages of a book. More fundamentally, we have the change of the intrinsic nature of substance in a nuclear reactor or a sun, from one element into the next, or into pure energy. There are also similar processes that can occur within *chakras* to produce psychic heat and the alchemical effects of the *siddhis.* Here we must view the relation of energy to substance, and also the way that the mind/

Mind controls the process of transmutative change. *Śūnyatā* is but a state of energy devoid of empirical mind, but nevertheless manifests forces that produce the transformation of phenomena. Inevitably the phenomenal will be abstracted back into its primordial state, producing the onset of *pralaya* (dissolution) at the ending of a great evolutionary cycle *(mahāmanvantara).*

We can therefore view *śūnyatā* in terms of the human condition and of the alchemical processes engendered by a human mind (examined by the various Buddhist logicians), as well as in terms of the slow relentless evolutionary march that transmogrifies the forms in Nature. This is assisted by the effects of a greater supramundane Mind that embodies and oversees the way that things must come to be. This subject (which shall be revealed throughout this series) is vaster than what the astute polemics of the Buddhist philosophers asserted over the past two millennia, nevertheless their astutely perceptive conclusions are the fundamental basis for further enquiry into the nature of Mind.

From the above it can be deduced that the statement of Candrakīrti from his *Clear Words* where he quotes and comments on the *Treatise on the Middle Way* is both true and untrue.

> Whatever exists inherently is permanent
> Since it does not become non-existent.
> If one says that what arose before is now non-existent,
> Then it follows that this is [an extreme] of annihilation.

> Since inherent existence is not overcome, that which is said to exist inherently never becomes non-existent. In that case it follows that through asserting it to be just inherently existent, one has a view of permanence. Because one asserts that things inherently exist at an earlier time and then asserts that now, later, they are destroyed and thus do not exist, it follows that one has a view of annihilation.[33]

If a phenomenon is truly existent, it must be unchanging in nature; thus, for it to cease, it must become utterly non-existent. Since the Vaibhāṣikas, Sautrāntikas, and Yogācārins assert that these impermanent phenomena, which they hold to be truly existent, disintegrate every moment, they thereby come to hold the extreme

---

33 Tsongkhapa's *Great Exposition of Special Insight, A Study of Svātantrika,* 44.

> of annihilation. The Yogācārins explicitly fall to the extreme of annihilation by asserting that sense objects do not exist even conventionally as entities separate from a perceiving consciousness.[34]

The term *inherent* means 'belonging to the essential character of something'. When some thing exists inherently then this means that it has a specific (inherent) characteristic which is experienced for the duration of its existence. If that thing inevitably changes this does not necessarily mean that the inherent characteristic does not change, but rather may take added characteristics to reflect changes that have produced permanent effects. Therefore the phrase 'Whatever exists inherently is permanent. Since it does not become non-existent' does not hold true from the perspective of what lies inherent in individual categories of things. When that category ceases to exist, i.e., the dinosaurs that roamed the earth millions of years ago, then what is inherent to them also ceases. However one can make the argument that the dinosaurs did not simply cease, but evolved into birds, in which case that which was inherent in the species also changed to incorporate what is the essential characteristics of the avian kingdom. Also, wood of a certain species of tree remains wood no matter what one carves into it, but if left a long time in the sun it may harden significantly, crack and change its colouration, no longer have a scent, etc. It may still be wood from that type of tree, but many of the inherent qualities that characterised it have altered. If it is burnt that wood is destroyed (has been annihilated) and becomes ash, with an entirely different set of inherent characteristics. No phenomena is free from change, yet each species of phenomena manifests characteristics that are unique, inherent to it.

We can also say with respect to the human condition that when internal changes occur (e.g., ups and downs in emotions) the overriding *inherent* consciousness may be basically stable, because such emotions inevitably die down to the base level of that consciousness. This base level is normally resistant to major change, but will do so if sufficiently challenged. When the emotions subside the inherent experiencing consciousness gains from their activity in some way, and accordingly

34 Ibid. (Kensure Yeshe Thupten, oral commentary.)

that which is inherent changes to accommodate the gain. Thus we evolve from childhood to mature age. In contradistinction Candrakīrti provides a rigid view, where he will not allow any change at all to the inherent attribute because the only inherent attribute considered real is *śūnyatā*.

What is it then that is 'inherent' in a human unit that makes such a one 'human'. One could say that this is the ability to think, to react to external observation and then to form opinions. One could go deeper than this and look to the foundational base of their existence, the *tathāgatagarbha,*[35] and the processes that will unveil it. Many superficial changes of form may only result in incremental changes of inherency. For instance, there are basic inherent characteristics to any species of animal or plant life, but many modifications of the nature of the form can take place due to environmental changes. Many millions of years may pass however, before there is a radical change to the inherent characteristic of that species, to change it to another species. (Through the altering of the genetic code.) This is similar to the way that consciousness works.

There are thus degrees of permanence to consider, for inherency can be defined as a form of permanence, but not in terms of absolutes. When Candrakīrti states:

> Whatever exists inherently is permanent
> Since it does not become non-existent.
> If one says that what arose before is now non-existent,
> Then it follows that this is [an extreme] of annihilation.

He is only considering absolutes, rather than necessary relative states of permanence. When someone views something as 'now non-existent' because it has ceased from the view (of his consciousness) it does not mean that it has ceased permanently, because the *saṃskāras* of the experience of that thing can be recalled, and indeed will be recalled as *karma*, and also in the form of memory. Hence there is no true annihilation.

Whenever there is change, however, there is also the perception of the annihilation of part or all of the characteristics of that thing.

---

35 *Tathāgatagarbha:* Womb or germ of the Buddha nature. The subject of the *tathāgatagarbha* will be fully explored in Volume 3 of this series. It has a form of permanence as it outlasts the birth and death of the incarnate personality.

This is an inevitable consequence of the process of change, because consciousness must move on to more fertile fields of revelation, and thus cannot be fixated upon an unchanging or immovable form. To argue that any aspect of phenomena must be 'unchanging in nature' is therefore incorrect, but nevertheless each 'thing' can and must have a real duration of its existence (and thus an inherent life) in the temporal world, which allows consciousness to experience that thing. Without such experiences enlightenment could not come to be. There certainly wouldn't be any Mādhyamika philosophers to argue about anything. Therefore 'things' can be considered to inherently exist, and also to not have inherent existence, i.e., any substantial lasting, permanent nature. (The view here is that because they lack *inherent* existence they are non-permanent.)

Inherent existence can also be considered from the point of view that though non-permanent, the duration of each experiential moment of each particular thing is a harbinger of *śūnyatā*, because it can act as a signpost for the way thereto. The 'existence' part refers to that which remains and is not annihilated by *śūnyatā* when consciousness is no longer a consideration.

What also must be considered is that each particular thing has within its constitution the seeds to its own destruction and disintegration, because it is composed of unstable elements. This means that annihilation of each and every thing *must* occur. However, as above stated, whatever has been experienced *becomes permanent* in that it can be recalled at any time from memory. It is even retained in the state called *dharmatā*,[36] as part of a Buddha Mind. How can something become 'utterly non-existent' if that thing has been experienced and retained in memory? Indeed, we have noted that the experiences become aspects of recurring *saṃskāras* conditioning the individual from life to life. This then makes its existence 'permanent', i.e., annihilation has *not* happened, even if the originating object of experience has long gone. The *saṃskāras* may become gradually purified and refined, but they hold a record of everything that has transpired in the past which any enlightened being can recall at will.

We therefore see that there is a case for annihilation (the destruction of some phenomena), for non-annihilation (the factor of memory), for

---

36 *Dharmatā* (Tib. chos nyid): actual reality, ultimate truth of phenomenon. Also, the natural force of things. Inherent nature, essence of existence.

a state where neither annihilation or non-annihilation exists (as in *śūnyatā*), and also for the simultaneous appearance of annihilation and non-annihilation—the viewing of whatever 'is' or 'is not' exactly as it 'is' or 'is not', such as via a Buddha Mind (where the *saṃsāra-śūnyatā* nexus is expressed *in toto*).

From one perspective *śūnyatā* can be considered the place of annihilation of *saṃsāra*, from another it is simply its container or 'upholder'. From this viewpoint *śūnyatā* is that which permanently exists to stabilise *saṃsāra,* making possible the continuous changes therein to persist for the extent of any necessary duration that allows the purpose of whatever is to be made manifest. Every phenomenal existence has a purpose.

What things may be, what they truly represent, why they persist for a duration (or a continuum of moments, long or short), and how they do so is not addressed by Candrakīrti's rhetoric above. The Prāsaṅgika also need to explain what *vāsanā*, the inherent driving force behind existence is, why it functions thus, and how it makes *skandhas* and *saṃskāras* move to instigate the phenomena we come to experience. They need to explain how and why this force drives all things through perpetual change on towards the final 'extinction' that *śūnyatā* represents.

The train of consciousness will not stop just because the extremist Prāsaṅgika rhetoric informs us that everything is Void, and thus empty of characteristics. It will still proceed to its destined depot and on the way will visit many stations representing signs of further accomplishment, refinement, and transmutation of formerly erroneous views. Upon arrival at its destination (*śūnyatā*) it will not be annihilated, but rather, has become transformed, transmogrified into something altogether useful for the expression of the *dharmakāya* Reasoning. This is because *śūnyatā* is not really the end of the line, but rather represents the middle between two extremes:

a. the extreme represented by *saṃsāra*.
b. the extreme represented by the *dharmakāya*.

It represents the mirror which reflects the expression of the *dharmakāya* (from whence comes the Mirror-like Wisdom of Akṣobhya) into *saṃsāra* so that the All-accomplishing Wisdom of Amoghasiddhi can be experienced. If the *dharmakāya* is reflected into/as *saṃsāra* then the 'extremes' are unified by a bridge, a nexus, that expresses the common denominator between both.

According to modern physicists energy cannot be destroyed, but simply changes from one form to the next. Consciousness likewise, cannot really be destroyed; rather, it changes from one form to the next, finally transmogrifying into the wisdoms of the Dhyāni Buddhas. For this reason a Buddha (who resides in *nirvāṇic* bliss) can recollect past experiences and communicate with human beings still possessing consciousness. *Śūnyatā* is effectively the 'containment' of that which has been transmogrified, but not destroyed.

The Prāsaṅgika-Mādhyamika rhetoric presented above consequently is problematic and needs re-evaluation because of lack of inclusivity, where fundamental processes concerning the way one experiences 'things' are omitted. It may be accurate if one views 'things' apart from consciousness and the way it works; if so, it has little bearing upon the human condition and of the road to enlightenment. However, the way this problem of relating the doctrine to the human condition has been solved is presented in the section on the Tsongkhapaian Prāsaṅgika view.

4. The Svātantrika view

What is seeded by the Buddha in the Womb of his Consort is but a form of consciousness-containment that expands to fill the limits of the capacity of that 'Womb' before its liberation from such a confined space. Indeed, the mode of consciousness-expansion and its transcension into *dharmakāya* (absolute truth) is the ultimate gain of this enquiry into the nature of the two truths.

From this perspective we have conventional truth, which is integrated with the process of consciousness-expansion. Then there is the path of exacting its thorough refinement, producing a consequent utter quiescence of the remainder, viewed as 'emptiness', 'absolute valuable reality'. Emptiness is the bridge between conventional truth and its inevitable transmogrified expansion into 'cosmos', which is herein termed *dharmakāya* (the ultimate truth whence the Dharmakāya Way leads).

Emptiness (*śūnyatā*) is effectively not a 'truth' per se, rather an undefinable experience. What therefore is often equated in these quotes as 'ultimate truth' is really the middle between extremes, the foundation via which the 'ultimate' may be experienced. What lies on either side of this 'bridge' therefore represents the two truths. I have also indicated a third truth (contrary to Lopez's quotes from Kamalaśīla) which is the process of becoming (therefore of 'relativity'), which is neither one or the other, producing various enlightenment states as the Bodhisattva *bhūmis* (stages) are trod. Even cosmos presents many graded levels of further expansive Bliss known only to Buddhas. From this perspective we can analyse five 'truths'.

1. The conventional truth of the 'concealer'.
2. The relative truths gained by those upon the enlightenment path, who experience both the real and the unreal.
3. The truth of *śūnyatā*.
4. The ultimate truth of *dharmakāya* for the enlightened ones still earth-bonded.
5. Further revelatory zones of expansive Bliss for 'thus gone ones'. (Buddhas that have relinquished *karma* to a earth-sphere.)

What is depicted here is but an extension of Jang-gya's summary from the quote below, where he explains 'that there are ultimates that are objects and ultimates that are subjects and that each of these can be further divided into actual and concordant ultimates'. The gaining of relative truths being the mechanism whereby these 'concordant ultimates' are experienced.

Lopez states, quoting from Bhāvaviveka, the founder of the Svātantrika view[37]:

> As Bhāvaviveka makes so clear, conceptual reasoning consciousnesses are indispensable tools of the Bodhisattva who is seeking to dispel all forms of ignorance. By designating conceptual reasoning consciousness with the term "ultimate," Bhāvaviveka certifies their place in the path.
>
> Like Bhāvaviveka's hypothetical opponent, Murti sees the ultimate, which he calls "the Absolute," as utterly transcendent and totally beyond comprehension by thought and analysis. Bhāvaviveka on

37 As other basic postulates of this view have already been commented upon I shall focus upon the ramifications of this statement as it provides considerable room for debate.

the other hand, recognizing the rigidity of such a view, is able to expand the category of the ultimate to include not only emptiness but consciousnesses by which it can be known.

Jang-gya provides a useful summary of the various meanings of the term ultimate in the Svātantrika. He explains that there are ultimates that are objects and ultimates that are subjects and that each of these can be further divided into actual and concordant ultimates.

Emptiness—the lack of true existence—is an actual ultimate in that it is free from the elaborations of true existence as well as the elaborations of dualistic appearance when it is directly realized by a Superior's exalted wisdom of meditative equipoise. When emptiness is realized by a conceptual reasoning consciousness, it is free from the elaborations of true existence but appears dualistically, that is, emptiness and the conceptual consciousness realizing it remain separate. The conceptual consciousness is not directly realizing emptiness; it understands it through the medium of a generic image or meaning-generality *(arthasāmānya, don spyi),* which is the appearing object of that consciousness. Emptiness is its referent object. When emptiness serves as the referent object of a conceptual consciousness, it is called a concordant ultimate because, for that consciousness, it is not free from the elaborations of dualistic appearance. Thus, the two types of objective emptiness, actual and concordant, are differentiated from the point of view of the type of consciousness realizing them, non-conceptual and conceptual wisdom consciousnesses respectively[38]... Therefore, whatever is ultimately existent must necessarily exist for a reasoning consciousness analyzing the ultimate. Is it also true that whatever exists for a reasoning consciousness analyzing the ultimate is necessarily ultimately existent? No, because emptiness exists for a reasoning consciousness but does not ultimately exist. If the reasoning consciousness turns its light of analysis on the lack of ultimate existence that it has found when searching for ultimate existence and investigates that lack of ultimate existence in an effort to discover whether it ultimately exists, it will find that the lack of ultimate existence itself does not ultimately exist; emptiness is empty of true existence. Thus, although emptiness—the lack of ultimate existence—exists in the face of a reasoning consciousness, it does not ultimately exist.[39]

---

38 Lopez Jr., *A Study of Svātantrika*, 140-141.

39 Ibid., 142.

One could use the paradoxical statement that ultimately such a thing as an 'ultimate' does not exist, if by the designation 'ultimate' we mean the infinite or the absolute. This is because as soon as one gets to the border of the ultimate and then enters into the 'ultimate' then one must enter into a zone or level of realisation that completely transcends anything that we have come to know or formerly experienced, otherwise it could not be called 'the ultimate'. By this is meant the transcension of what was known before as the 'finite', or limited perspective. It cannot be reasoned with any certainty that the ultimate is inclusive of the finite, or whether it is a self-enclosed sphere of something incomprehensible, or if it is open ended, spacious, manifesting to the far bounds of the infinitude.

Therefore, it is questionable if there really is such a thing as ultimate truth, it is in reality but a conventional designation placed by those who, for lack of a better term, need to describe a concept of finality. However, the relativityness of all things is not included or discussed above, for we could easily say that what is known as 'ultimate' is only so relative to the human consciousness that would try to comprehend it. What is implied in the term 'ultimate' in relation to whatever 'exists for a reasoning consciousness analyzing the ultimate' is the process of becoming. 'What is the ultimate?' is the question asked, and then: 'how can the empirical mind come to comprehend the ultimate when the ultimate is beyond any conception of thought or cognition attainable by the empirical mind?' This implies that the ultimate is beyond comprehension. By this deduction then there could be an infinite succession of (concordant) ultimates. For an 'ultimate' to be experienced there must be a process of priming the mind so that it can make the quantum leap into a state of experience beyond what a mind could normally comprehend.
When the 'ultimate' is conceived of as *śūnyatā* then a process of the negation of attributes of mind is generally pursued. But what if the 'ultimate' is the *dharmakāya,* does this alter the 'process of becoming'? I would say certainly. Both the negation of attributes of mind, plus the development of others into wisdom attributes are needed.

One could also eliminate the concept of 'ultimate', taking the concept to be inherently impossible to obtain. Even *śūnyatā,* though designated 'ultimate', cannot truly be so, because the *dharmakāya* is beyond it. The word ultimate implies finality, ending, no more. Finality implies or confers limitation, the circumscription of some set, category of thing, or sequence of activity. There may be an ultimate that thus circumscribes, but is it in reality an absolute? It may circumscribe one set of phenomenological activity, but may be open ended with respect to whatever is the 'remainder'. If there is an ultimate that is limited it could not in reality be absolute, but if it is open ended, then there is room for expansion, for growth of some sort. If the 'ultimate' is conceived of as spaciousness that is inclusive of everything, then that 'everything' is flawed, because it contains aspects that are perpetually changing and adapting (within spheres of circumscription, which is but a way of describing the starry universe). Thus there is room for a concept of expansion for growth. If this form of spaciousness is said to be 'empty' of all forms of phenomena, of everything that is 'caused', then it may be the 'ultimate', but it is not inclusive of everything, as *saṃsāra* is beyond its scope of being, neither does it incorporate the way that the *dharmakāya* incorporates *saṃsāra.*

Whichever way one wishes to look at it, the ultimate is relative to that which is not-ultimate. The ultimate is decisively final, producing an impossibility to proceed further. Such a concept may inevitably be true for the cycles of human incarnations, and for aspects of consciousness, but *not for existence*—it persists, and for this persistence there is *no ultimate*, only a continuum moving towards distant goals. When something other than consciousness manifests as its means of Identity then the condition termed *śūnyatā* is experienced. Since it is said that it 'does not ultimately exist', meaning that it is not a 'thing', an existent, it must therefore be reckoned as something 'other'. What this something 'other' is, is difficult to explain, other than indirectly through such terms as *tathatā*, *mokṣa,* Thusness. Other endeavours are veiled in terms of the Buddha nature *(tathāgatagarbha)* and the concept of the *dharmakāya.*

The key here is the word *continuum.* What exactly is a continuum? Is it mind/Mind-borne, or is it carried by some other vector, by both, or neither? This is the major question needing answering. How does a continuum of the principle of Life work in relation to time, and to the directions in space? Or is there such a thing as time-space in relation to it, or merely cycles of appearance and non-appearance of phenomena? Existence (Life) continues in *śūnyatā.* Nothing is annihilated, thus the continuum *(vāsanā)* that propelled the existent (One) does not cease in that state. What is known as 'consciousness' may have ceased, but not the awakened Mind, and *vāsanā* continues to drive Mind onwards and upwards through multidimensional Space (of which *śūnyatā* can be conceived of as representing one such dimension).

From this perspective the statement earlier given that there 'is no third truth' is a falsity, because this 'third truth' is indeed hidden or veiled by the meaning of the word 'ultimate' and the relativity of the continuum of existence. This is because that which links the conventional to the ultimate is a process of becoming 'the last in a series' to produce that 'beyond', past which it is impossible for consciousness to proceed, but not for that into which it has transmogrified. We thus have the concept of the ultimate nature of things when taking consciousness to be a 'thing'. It is the nature of *the process* that produces an ultimate (which is a truth in itself) that is subtly omitted or avoided by many Mādhyamika philosophers in their concept of two truths. They have turned a blind eye to that which links one to the other. These truths are thus *not* 'mutually exclusive and a dichotomy', any more than a railway depot is mutually exclusive to the destination station to which a train travels. They are linked by the railway track, and everyday commerce, carriages (bits of information) can travel both ways. There are always tracks, trails, or signs, made upon the way concerning the process of how one gets 'there', to the final port, or 'other shore' of being. This is certainly the case with the two truths; one is *inclusive* of the other.

There are in fact two approaches to understand absolute truth, in that:

a. It is aloof and excludes relative truth totally.
b. It is truly inclusive of the all.

If we analyse point (a) then its sheer aloofness harbours the possibility of annihilation. Analysis of point (b) shows us that one cannot exclude the factor of an 'existent' that first cognises relative truth and then absolute truth, for that truth to be inclusive of 'the all'. Such an 'existent' however need not be an 'I', which Buddhist polemics focuses upon, but rather a principle that 'exists' and which survives the changing scenarios of *saṃsāra* and continues on through various stages of progressive enlightenment to Buddhahood. When 'the all' is conceived to include the sum of cosmos, then it is not possible to exclude conception of an 'ultimate existent'. Questions to be asked with respect to what an 'ultimate existent' may be are: 'what is "it" that moves into space as a "thus gone one"?', 'for how vast a duration of untold *manvantaras* of expression have "thus gone" Ones appeared?', and 'to what extent have their further development of cosmic Mind manifested?' These questions need to be sequenced by further questioning: 'what are the laws governing the expression of such a Mind', and 'how does this relate to the appearance of the phenomenon of a universe?' Such questions must be asked and then answered, and in answering them we discover what might be called the 'esoteric' in Buddhism. Consequently, Buddhists must move beyond merely questioning the existence of the Hindu concept of *ātman* in their search for the truth of what an 'ultimate existence' may be.

Concerning *śūnyatā* we see from the generalised Mādhyamika consideration that it is considered exclusive. Yet if it is exclusive then it could hardly be equated with enlightenment, the expression of great wisdom. Where then does this leave *śūnyatā?* The theme in this series is that it is the middle between extremes. To truly be the base of the Buddha-Mind it must contain the pathways to be inclusive of the all. Thus absolute truth could not be so if it did not contain the sum of what can be considered 'the finite' in it, whilst the finite or conventional truth is but the seed or paradigm that is the eventuation of the absolute. They are but the terminals of the same track (continuum) of consciousness unfolding, until that consciousness is superseded via the *śūnyatā* experience. This experience does not necessarily mean the ending (i.e., exclusion) of the conventional truth, but rather can be inclusive of it, when *śūnyatā* is extended to the *dharmakāya.*

The argument by Bhāvaviveka informs us that the 'tracks' or mechanism concerning the process of how one gets 'there' is consciousness as it tries to conceptualise *śūnyatā,* and then manifests the activity that allows it to directly experience the taste of the 'ultimate'. This conceptual consciousness therefore recognises 'dualistic appearances', the *saṃsāra-śūnyatā* relation, because it is the bridge between the two. It is that which recognises the signs along the way, allowing one *(saṃsāra)* to be mastered and transcended and the other *(śūnyatā)* to be realised in terms of direct non-conceptualising awareness.

The paradox is that for *śūnyatā* to be experienced by the conceptualising consciousness, consciousness must cleanse from itself all forms of conceptualisations, all images and ideas. It must therefore no longer function, and thus for it 'ultimate existence' does not exist. What is actually experienced in *śūnyatā* is beyond conceptualisation; beyond the changeability of forms, and the appearance of things associated with phenomena. *Śūnyatā* therefore 'exists',[40] but it may not necessarily be the ultimate, except with reference to the phenomena that *saṃsāra* represents. It is but a stage in the river of continuum where consciousness has been transmuted and *saṃsāric* conditionings have come to rest, absorbed into the essence of whatever it was that caused it to originally appear. This place of absorption is *śūnyatā*.

With respect to Bhāvaviveka's statement that 'emptiness—the lack of ultimate existence—exists in the face of a reasoning consciousness, it does not ultimately exist', it could be said that this is only in terms of a 'reasoning consciousness', which cannot exist if it is to experience *śūnyatā* (emptiness). Thus if the interpretive consciousness does not exist how can that which it endeavours to interpret exist? However, whether there is a consciousness there to experience it or not, emptiness does exist (even though no 'existent' denoted as an 'I' may be found within it, and leaving aside the polemics of what an 'existent' may or may not be), as it can be experienced by direct non-discursive perception. Whatever can be experienced 'exists', even though it may not be an 'existent' in terms of being a describable appearance or form. Without it a totally materialistic universe would exist with no capacity for transcendental evolutionary change. The nature of the continuous changes we observe requires a state of emptiness to exist as a type of flux allowing transition from one state or stage to the next.[41] Otherwise

---

40 We could in fact apply the Nāgārjunian *catuṣkoṭikā* to *śūnyatā* and state that *śūnyatā* exists, does not exist, both exists and does not exist, and neither exists and does not exist, depending upon one's point of view.

41 Scientists will also inevitably have to think of transmutative change in these terms. They need to comprehend that *yogins* have been involved in manifesting phenomenological alchemical changes for millennia. Scientists have discovered nothing essentially new along this line, other than the materialistic study of phenomena, plus technological methodology to achieve the goal of transmutation of substance. They have provided valuable information concerning the nature of the phenomenal universe in its most concreted form, but have much yet to discover in order to solve their remaining quandaries and paradoxes in physics.

there would be an impossible rigid stasis in the scheme of things.

A reasoning consciousness can deduce and accept facts such as the above because they are within the bounds of reason. Such reasoning is however transient (thus 'empty' of the permanency that it is said would make something 'real') and does not partake of the 'ultimate', which is non-transient, and not empty, but is empty of the faculty of reasoning. A reasoning consciousness can however be empty of thoughts, but such 'emptiness' is not *śūnyatā*.

If *śūnyatā* did not 'ground' or support the existence of *saṃsāra* then *saṃsāra* could not exist. (Thus the entire universe becomes an impossibility.[42]) *Saṃsāra's* transience would have no stable matrix to sustain its activity or to provide a conclusive solution for its steady march to evolutionary perfection.[43] *Śūnyatā* contains the energy fields via which all that is known as *saṃsāra* comes to be. It represents the fabric of space that ties the transience into a unity. It cannot be experienced by consciousness in any coherent manner, because a reasoning consciousness immediately clothes the energy qualifications with images, thoughts, which veil the real. To experience the real therefore the thought processes (modifications of the mind) must be stilled and the energy fields directly experienced for what they reveal.

If *śūnyatā* is the place into which *saṃsāra* is absorbed, then it also contains that which is the cause of its origination, its eventual cyclic re-emanation (for the process of rebirth happens for all beings, not just for the human consciousness). This means that *śūnyatā* allows that which Exists beyond it, to manifest through it so as to cause the originating impetus for each successive rebirth of phenomena. *Śūnyatā*, being passively Void, does not act so of its own accord, but rather manifests as a mirror to reflect the expression of primal Mind to effect the appearance of phenomena. This theme, lying outside of general Buddhist ontology, has vast ramifications and consequently will be elaborated in the later volumes of this series.

---

42 One could make an argument that the 'nothingness' that 'existed' before the universe was created as a consequence of the 'Big Bang' (according to scientific opinion) is but *śūnyatā* applied upon a vast universal scale.

43 This is an interpretation of chapter 24:18 of Nāgārjuna's *Mūlamadhyamakakārikā:* 'We state that whatever is dependent arising, that is emptiness. That is dependent upon convention. That itself is the Middle Path'. (Kalupahana, 339.)

Buddhists must yet properly explain how and why *saṃsāra* initially came into existence. Can anything be really explained by a reasoning that postulates that if, originally there was nothing but the Void, then there is truly nothing but the Void, and there will also 'ultimately' be nothing but the Void? When however we look to the fact that the Void is also conceived as being empty of emptiness then it must be composed of a 'residual' that is not definable by consciousness. This 'residual' by implication thus also contains seeds *(bījas)* for future (cyclic) emanation of *saṃsāra*. Nothing is annihilated, otherwise a Buddha or Bodhisattva could remember nothing whatsoever when attaining *nirvāṇa*.

Buddhists must also account for the force, viewed in terms of energy-processes, that sustains the phenomena of *saṃsāra*, not just for the human *mahāvirūpa*,[44] but for the entire phenomenal universe of cause-effect.

Regarding the phrase the 'conceptual consciousness is not directly realizing emptiness: it understands it through the medium of generic image or meaning generally *(arthasāmānya, don spyi)*, which is the appearing object of that consciousness. Emptiness is its referent object', we should understand that like nature can only perceive like nature. The only reason why consciousness can perceive material things is because consciousness is likewise material, albeit of a much finer nature. *Śūnyatā* is by definition not material, is void of such, so what is there that consciousness can perceive or cognise? How can consciousness perceive *śūnyatā* if the very nature of *śūnyatā* is to annihilate consciousness, like the matter and anti-matter interrelation of modern physics? They exist as two completely different universes, consciousness and *śūnyatā*, with no possible mechanism of interrelation in the extremist version of Madhyamaka philosophy. From this perspective we see that consciousness understands *śūnyatā* in terms of 'the medium of generic image or meaning generally *(arthasāmānya, don spyi)*, which is the appearing object of that consciousness'. In other words such a 'generic image' can only exist in consciousness if it has something there to model its image upon. It is said that no such 'thing' exists, as there is only the Void, so how is it possible for consciousness to know anything of the Void? A mechanism however there must be, otherwise there could

44 *Mahāvirūpa:* the illusional body of appearance.

be no means to enlightenment, to liberation, for we would not even be able to conceive that liberation from *saṃsāra* was a path to follow; or a conception that something like *śūnyatā* could exist.

The only way for such a mechanism to exist is for consciousness to convey *śūnyatā* in some way, to contain an aspect of 'it', and then to utilise a 'mirror-like wisdom' to perceive it. How consciousness can perceive *śūnyatā* (which is said to be 'empty of true existence') shall be revealed in this treatise. Because it does we can consequently come to know of and experience aspects of the Buddha-Mind.

Such a mechanism needs to be accounted for in Madhyamaka philosophy, and indeed is existent, but in a veiled form, as we shall later see. 'True existence' in this context would relate to any form of lasting or permanent phenomena that consciousness would delegate to be real. The reasoning consciousness however, when thoroughly examining the properties of what it deems to be 'real', such as the *ātman* of Hinduism,[45] will form the conclusions obtained by Buddhist logic, that such will be found to lack 'ultimate existence'. Upon deep analysis, it will further deduce that 'the lack of ultimate existence itself does not ultimately exist: emptiness is empty of true existence'. 'True existence' being either an ephemeral or an unchanging form cannot be truly existent, however there is an 'ultimate existent', the Life that persists through to Buddhahood and beyond.

5. The Tsongkhapaian Prāsaṅgika view.

In this view Tsongkhapa argues that though conventional truth is illusional and deceptive it nevertheless is a genuine truth and is equally valid with the ultimate truth. He bases his logic on such texts as chapter 24 of Nāgārjuna's *Mūlamadhyamakakārika,* the ramifications of the philosophy of Dependent Origination originally espoused by the Buddha, and Candrakīrti's *Madhyamakāvatāra.* To explain this view I shall primarily use an article by Sonam Thakchoe, who states:

> Following the arguments of Nāgārjuna and Candrakīrti very closely, for Tsong khapa, emptiness and dependently arisen, therefore ultimate

45 *Ātman:* the innermost essence, a Self or 'soul' of the individual, seen to be eternal, unchanging, as well as the universal 'Self'.

and conventional, truths are mutually coextensive. The doctrine of emptiness is incoherent unless it is applied to dependently arisen phenomena, hence conventional truth, and so too is the concept of dependent arising incoherent unless it is applied to empty phenomena, hence ultimate truth. In the *Eulogy of Dependent Arising (rTen 'brel stod pa)*, Tsong khapa advances several arguments to reinforce the unity between the two truths[46]...For Tsong khapa this follows on the grounds that both emptiness and dependently arisen are ontologically coextensive, and hence are non-contradictory (18). It therefore follows that: 'in spite of the fact that whatever is dependently arisen is albeit primordially empty of essence, it *exists* and is proclaimed as illusion-like' (27)[47]...The efficacy of empty phenomena—namely, emptiness as the bearer of cause and effect—is particularly significant to this view, as presented in Nāgārjuna and Candrakīrti's arguments[48]...Tsong khapa also argues, moreover, that the realisation of phenomena as dependently arisen is the necessary condition for the realisation of both the truths. For one cannot realise phenomena as dependently arisen unless one sees phenomena as empty—therefore, the simultaneous realisations of the two truths is essential. In the *Lam gtso rnam gsum*, the argument reads: 'So long as the understanding pertaining to conventionally regularity of appearances—dependently arisen—and the understanding pertaining to the empty [phenomena]— free from all claims—are seen as mutually exclusive', on Tsong khapa's view, 'the purport of the Buddha is not yet understood' (11). Therefore the philosophical inquiry, argues Tsong khapa, is incomplete until the simultaneous realisations of the two truths is achieved. The philosophical inquiry, on the other hand, is complete whenever the realisations of conventional truth and ultimate truth operate simultaneously—without taking alternate turns—and attains freedom from all mistaken views, as its consequence, by merely seeing dependently arisen phenomena/empty phenomena.[49]

---

46 Sonam Thakchoe, 'Status of Conventional Truth In Tsong Khapa's Mādhyamika Philosophy', *(Contemporary Buddhism, Vol. 8, No. 1, May 2007)*, 33.

47 Ibid., 34.

48 Ibid.

49 Ibid., 34-5. Concerning the unity of the two truths Thakchoe further states: 'Tsong khapa corroborates the claim in the following way: that the buddha's form-body (rūpakāya) is accomplished as a result of the exhaustive accumulation of moral virtue (bsod nams kyi tshogs); therefore, its accomplishment depends upon engaging the world with the wisdom of dependent arising whereas the

There is a completely different tenor of expression in the above extract to the Prāsaṅgika attitude earlier presented, where they assert that phenomena does not exist even conventionally and 'negate inherent existence or existence from the object's own side', therefore find it redundant, to qualify the process of moving from the conventional to the ultimate with the words ultimately or truly. In contrast to that presentation, focused almost entirely upon the ultimate truth, is the view to be now analysed where we find that Tsongkhapa eulogises the process of striving to obtain a simultaneous experience of both truths. (The associated teaching of Dependent Origination, the basis of the Prāsaṅgika deductive reasoning, will be examined in a later chapter.)

First we have the statement that when one realises both truths simultaneously 'without taking alternate turns' then one 'attains freedom from all mistaken views, as its consequence, by merely seeing dependently arisen phenomena/empty phenomena'. What this means is that an enlightened Mind integrates both the conventional and the ultimate in one all-encompassing Mind-stream. Both are seen conjointly and dependently integrated in one integral *maṇḍala* of cause and effect. The enlightened one automatically discerns phenomena to be empty because of its transience, and also real because of its epistemic and soteriological effects on consciousness.

Also the statement that the 'efficacy of empty phenomena—namely, emptiness as the bearer of cause and effect' has significance in terms of the emanation of *karma,* because the implication is that *karma* (of the external universe) emanates from emptiness, is sustained by it, and is that into which *karma* is eventually resolved. With *karma* the entire field of expression of *saṃsāra* manifests. Much yet needs to be revealed concerning this subject of *karma.* After all, it is that law that drives the entire evolutionary process on to its ultimate conclusion, to Buddhahood for every human unit. Consequently it is a prime directive force that *inherently exists*, affecting both *saṃsāra* and the path to liberation, wherein the experience of *śūnyatā* is a factor. Freedom

buddha's truth-body (dharmakāya) is accomplished as a result of the exhaustive accumulation of penetrative wisdom (yeshe kyi tshogs), hence its accomplishment depends upon engaging the world with the wisdom of emptiness...which requires the transcendence of worldly conventions by means of achieving a direct vision of emptiness in the meditative equipoise.' (Ibid, 36.)

from personal *karma* may be accomplished in *śūnyatā,* but if both *śūnyatā* and *saṃsāra* are experienced simultaneously, karmic expression persists, which is the nature of the enlightened Mind of any Bodhisattva compassionately concerned with liberating sentient beings. Also, it is wrong to think that a Buddha is absolutely free of *karma*. Such a one has simply relinquished karmic ties to the phenomena of this earth sphere, but not with cosmos. The ontology of why this is so and what it implies has yet to be cogently revealed. The 'simultaneous realisations of the two truths' has greater ramifications than is normally realised, because the ontology of the nature of the content of an enlightened Mind hasn't been properly contextualised. Much still needs revealing as the esoteric in Buddhism is unveiled, which constitutes unfolding the Dharmakāya Way.

Lopez states:

> The Prāsaṅgikas are realists in that they assert that external objects exist as separate entities from the perceiving consciousness. They are skeptics in that they deny the veracity of sense-perception in terms of the appearance of inherent existence. From another point of view, they are not realists in that they do not accept that all of the characteristics of the object that appears to a sense consciousness are true; a sense consciousness correctly perceives the general object and its primary characteristics but misperceives the object as inherently existent. In this way they go beyond the position of the critical realists, who hold that in veridical perception those characters that appear to the senses are the actual characters or properties of the external object. The Prāsaṅgikas also are not sceptical in a certain sense in that they do not deny that indubitable information can be gained about the nature of things. For them, external objects exist, but they do not exist in the way that they appear. Objects appear to exist inherently, and this false appearance is perceived by the non-conceptual sense-consciousness. There are two factors that appear to the sense-consciousness, the appearance of inherent existence and the mere appearance of the imputedly existent object. For common beings these two appearances are mixed. There are thus true and false aspects present in the sensa which ordinarily cannot be distinguished. The Prāsaṅgikas turn to the other valid source of knowledge, inference, to discern and destroy with reasoning the conception of inherent existence by thought and the perception of inherent existence by the sense consciousness. Reasoning

> reveals that the object does not exist in and of itself but is empty of inherent existence. By becoming accustomed to this emptiness again and again from the viewpoint of many different reasonings, the false factor in sense perception can be identified and, through developing direct perception of emptiness and accompanying that practice with altruistic deeds, that false appearance can finally be eliminated at Buddhahood[50]...The Prāsaṅgikas concur that phenomena do indeed appear to exist in and of themselves but argue that this is a false appearance, undefinable under analysis.[51]

This view is correct, as far as it is presented here. Indeed, reason *(pramāṇa[52])* is necessary to obtain valid cognition. Such cognition can then assert the illusionality of all phenomena that extraneously appear real to the sense-perceptors. Similarly with attributes of mind that produce images, reveries, daydreams, fantasies, hallucinations, and constantly changing ideas. All are empty of inherent existence, but have the capacity to assist the attainment of enlightenment. The objective of the nature of the ever-changing phenomena is thus important, as it produces the inculcation of a path to Buddhahood.

Thakchoe's statement concerning one of the arguments Tsongkhapa uses to purge erroneous extreme views is that *'appearance avoids the extreme of existence* on the ground that a thing's ontological framework is due to its interdependent existence—characteristics of causally produced phenomena—thus counteracting an inherently existent essence'[53] needs commentary. Namely that an 'inherently existent essence' *(svabhāva)* does not necessarily prevent the appearance of 'causally produced phenomena'. It can be conceived of as a stratum of plastic elementary substance (or energy field) that embodies forms by adapting and changing to accommodate each new appearance of phenomena. There is no reason why a matrix of elementary particles (such as the atoms discovered by science, and the quarks they are constituted of) cannot accommodate those changes as per the rearrangement of atoms for every

50 Lopez Jr., *A Study of Svātantrika* 158-159.

51 Ibid., 159.

52 *Pramāṇa:* (from *pra-mā* to measure out correctly), valid cognition, first hand knowledge, both empirical and inferential.

53 Thakchoe, 34.

physical change. The plastic essence may represent a Void Element (or Elements) that accommodates the characteristics of the appearance of phenomena and 'congeal' or 'condense' an aspect of itself to do so, which can then revert back to its primal state, as per the implications of the formula $E=mc^2$ (energy equals mass times the speed of light squared). Here energy can be considered such an 'essence', from which phenomena (mass) can appear, and recede again. Also, the substance conveying thoughts, and of which an idea is constructed from, allows a mental continuum to exist after the death of an individual. The subject concerning *svabhāva* is not straightforward and shall be relegated to a later chapter. (The Essay on the Many and the One.) *Svabhāva* can be the recipient of the gain of the expression of such phenomena, when integrated with the law of *karma*. Much also shall be made clear when the doctrine of the *tathāgatagarbha* (the 'Buddha-womb') is explored in Volume 3. We shall see exactly what 'it' is that *drives* a consciousness-stream progressively onwards (with the aid of *karma)* to gain Buddhahood. The methodology is therein explained whereby *samalā tathatā,* Suchness (the condition of the *tathāgatagarbha*) that is defiled with *saṃsāric* attributes, is converted into *nirmalā tathatā,* where no such defilements exist. All such considerations come into view when the two truths are simultaneously integrated into unity.

Tsongkhapa's soteriological consideration must also be taken into account:

> ... the undermining of the soteriological significance of conventional truth would also undermine the possible fruit thereof since the conditions by which enlightenment is made possible would be undermined. This is because enlightenment is possible only through the medium of conventional truth, after all enlightenment is a correct realisation of conventional truth *qua* conventional phenomena and moreover enlightenment itself is a conventional phenomenon. Any preferential treatment of the two truths—namely, looking down upon the conventional truth as less significant than its ultimate counterpart—would render such a position unsustainable.[54]

The entire Bodhisattva path comes into play here, for what indeed could be salvaged or liberated from *saṃsāra* if phenomena does not even

54 Thakchoe, 35.

exist conventionally? Such phenomena includes the mind one would reason with to follow the path to enlightenment. There is a purpose to the evolutionary path, for the cycles of pain and pleasure, of the slow accumulation of knowledge via conventional experiences, whether valid or imaginary, that humans experience. Wisdom and compassionate ideals must be gained as one awakens to the revelations that the liberated Mind provides. Such is not possible if the experiences gathered from the phenomena was not real, if validly cognised and not just imagined chimeras. It may also be inherently empty, but such emptiness is the end result of cycles of durations of existence of various categories of phenomena, and each such duration, such as the life of a chair before it is consumed by fire, produces a real cognisable effect upon any sense-perceptor experiencing it. We see also that the 'emptiness' implicated here may differ from the Prāsaṅgika view, as the concept of a medium of expression *(svabhāva)* is not excluded, but is empty of the types of phenomena consciousness perceives as real and tangible.

If Dependent Origination is a fact and annihilation does not occur, then the proponents of the two truths must be able to explain *exactly* what is 'it' that 'exists' in *śūnyatā,* and if not dependent therein, then how does 'it' move through various Bodhisattva stages *(bhūmis)* to Buddhahood. That which is not annihilated must be an 'existent' and if *not* an 'existent', what then? The descriptive term 'Void' used throughout this text depicts a condition experienced by some entity that:

a. Retains memory.
b. Can demonstrate supramundane *siddhis.*
c. Possesses inestimable wisdom.
d. Possesses the capacity to 'move on' to *parinirvāṇa.*
e. Can generate a Buddha-field[55] in cosmos, once having 'moved on'.

One can then ask a question: 'Is such a Buddha-field a singularity or is it dependent upon the existence of other such Buddha-fields?' Consequently, 'What is the purpose of such Buddha-fields and what is their relation to the appearance of the phenomena of space, the comings and goings of stars, galaxies and universes?' The answer to

55 *Buddha-field:* described in various *sūtras,* each Buddha-field is said to contain innumerable Bodhisattvas.

all of these questions lies in a comprehension of the term *dharmakāya,* the body or field of expression *(kāya)* of the *dharma,* the moral law and quintessential truth concerning all things knowable and supramundane. This entire field of expression necessarily inhabits cosmos, otherwise it could not be universal, 'absolute', a Buddha-Mind. Such must be revealed at the nexus, or point of interrelation between *śūnyatā* and *saṃsāra* when experienced simultaneously. Consequently pathways of understanding can be conveyed to empirical minds, even if such understanding is not complete, and cannot be properly understood until the nexus is sought and resided in. Such explanation is then the objective of this series, its foundational basis being mainly developed in the three volumes denoted *'The I Concept'.* It cares not for labels, such as being Buddhistic, theistic or agnostic; it cares simply to extract the truth of what 'is-is not' (fusing the two concepts into a unity) equated with the expression of a Buddha-Mind. In fact, when established the philosophy will present an ontology that is the middle between the extremes of the general Mahāyāna Buddhist and Hindu rhetoric,[56] a true *madhyamaka* that combines the best of all views, and which herein is called the Dharmakāya Way.

Tsongkhapa's argument is based on the fact that:

> ... ultimate truth is portrayed as 'ultimate' not because of its ontological absoluteness, or its having primacy over the conventional truth, but simply because of its *steady* character—coherence between the ultimate mode of its appearance and its mode of being—in contrast with the *conflicting* character of conventional truth—incoherence between the conventional mode of appearance and its mode of being. Ultimate truth is non-deceptive for the same reason, hence, Candrakīrti writes, in his *Yuktiṣaṣṭikāvṛtti* '[Interlocutor]: Why is nirvāna said to be the ultimate truth? [Reply]: Nirvāna is said to be ultimate truth purely based on worldly conventions *('jig rten gyi tha snyad kho nas),* because its nature *(bdag nyid)* does not deceive the world[57]...Therefore, the thrust of the arguments behind speaking one of the two truths as 'ultimate', 'non-deceptive' or 'true', and the other as 'conventional', 'false' or 'deceptive', so far as Tsong khapa is concerned, is not suggestive of any ontological hierarchical relation between the two truths; rather, it

56 Specifically the Advaita Vedanta.

57 Thakchoe, 37-8.

> points to the contrasting epistemic features that exist between the two truths in terms of the consistency between their mode of appearance and their mode of existence, or in terms of the mode of presenting themselves to their respective cognising consciousnesses.[58]

These two truths may indeed present 'contrasting epistemic features', however the conventional is eventually absorbed into the 'absolute', and henceforth becomes irrelevant, except as a foundation of the developed wisdom. Wisdom is the gain, being the mode of communion of one that resides in the domain of the awakened state to those immersed in conventional attitudes. Silence is the true form of expression of the liberated one, because rarely is it possible to provide esoteric information to conventional thinkers, the 'concealers'. They bury the truth within the vacillating convolutions of their turbulent emotional or desire-minds. Only those upon the path of gaining relative truths have the capacity to truly hear such instructions as a guide to whence they are travelling. Eventually the disparity between the liberated one and the prospective hearers is so great that a 'thus gone one' arises to make strides in cosmos, far away from earth evolution. Always however, that domain can be instantly accessed, because all exists within the domain of Mind. Communion then is only with the liberated Minds or those directly becoming such.

Next to consider is a pragmatic injunction provided by Tsongkhapa to his students.

> However, the most critical point to understand in this discussion is as follows: the distinctions made between real/unreal, truth/false, deceptive/non-deceptive are *conventional practices*, and therefore need to be understood strictly within the context of ordinary *conventional discourse.* This also means that these conventional distinctions are not contrived by the Mādhyamikas themselves.
>
> Although the Prāsangika Mādhyamika, on Tsong khapa's account, does not accept the assumptions underlying the conventional distinctions, it values the linguistic convention, adopts similar conventions within its system, and insists that the Prāsangika Mādhyamika must conform to worldly conventions.[59]

58 Ibid., 38.

59 Ibid., 41.

Here we have a version of the adage 'when in Rome do as the Romans do'. Such action however is a necessity for the wise. They live a dual life of adhering to the results of the experiences and awarenesses derived from their own meditation-Minds (in non-deceptive truth) and yet obey worldly conventions (deceptive truths) when interrelating to those not awakened. Such interrelation is minimalised because rarely will those ensconced in deceptive conventional truths listen to the harbingers of necessary change. A serene quietness is thus evidenced by the liberated one. Though always seeking to uplift, inspire and help awaken those whom they come in contact with, when opportunity so arises, they will however not squander energy and time when such effort is known to be fruitless. Wise soteriological considerations consequently reign supreme, as compassion is the modus operandi of their lives. Wisdom is evidenced as to right timing and the most efficacious words spoken. That spoken emanates from the liberated domain but must be phrased conventionally. 'For Tsong khapa, the causal effectiveness of a thing is precisely what determines its being true. As long as a reflection of a face is causally effective, thus empirically functional, even if not necessarily consistent with its appearance, then it is true, in the ordinary sense, in its own right.'[60]

The eminent pragmatism of Tsongkhapa's view means that the liberated do not try to impose their views upon 'concealers'. All reconciled in *saṃsāra* gain the consequences of whatever truth they seek, either through ignorance, or to aspire for the elucidation of truth for enlightenment's sake. Enlightenment is not possible if phenomena does not exist because there is nothing to gain enlightenment with. Indeed the entire objective to enlightenment would be meaningless because there would be no soteriological basis to its expression. If both truths are integrated simultaneously in one *mahāmudrā* of realisation, then we have discovered the *śūnyatā-saṃsāra* nexus, the realisation of which constitutes the Dharmakāya Way.

I shall conclude this section on the Prāsaṅgika rhetoric with a quote from Garfield's excellent essay where he stresses the importance of conventional truth, wherein even ultimate truth can be considered a conventional truth.

---

60 Thakchoe, 41.

> Tsong khapa argues, following Candrakīrti very closely, that the ultimate truth—emptiness—is an external negation, a mere elimination of any intrinsic existence in things, and of any conceptualization (*Ocean* 52–23). But this in the end amounts to the same thing, since to be merely existent is to lack any intrinsic identity. The ultimate truth is, hence, even for Tsong khapa, that the conventional truth is all that there is[61]...The important point here, and the principal topic of this essay, is that for both Candrakīrti and Tsong khapa, it is the fact of epistemic authority that guarantees truth in convention and the reality of the conventional. When we ask why is conventional truth a *truth,* the answer will turn on the fact that there is a difference to be drawn *within* the conventional between truth and falsehood, as well as a truth *about* the conventional. There is something that counts as getting it right about conventional reality[62]...Nāgārjuna's deepest insight was that despite the vast difference between the two truths in one sense, they are in an equally important sense identical. We can now make better sense of that identity, and of why the fact of their identity is the same fact as that of their difference. The ultimate truth is, as we know, emptiness. Emptiness is the emptiness not of *existence* but of *inherent existence.* To be empty of inherent existence is to exist only conventionally, only as the object of conventional truth. The ultimate truth about any phenomenon, according to the analysis I have been defending, is hence that it is merely a conventional truth. Ontologically, therefore, the two truths are absolutely identical. This is the content of the idea that the two truths have a single basis, which is empty phenomena. Their emptiness is their conventional reality; their conventional reality is their emptiness.[63]

Conventional truth is what we come to know by the deductive processes in our minds, whilst the development of Mind merely clarifies[64] the conception of such truth and interweaves with it a vast

---

61 Jay L Garfield, 'Taking Conventional Truth Seriously: Authority Regarding Deceptive Reality', (*Philosophy East and West,* University of Hawaii Press), 342.

62 Ibid., 343.

63 Ibid., 351.

64 I use this term both in the sense of making something more comprehensible, plus the effect of a refinement process wherein the most intrinsic aspect of a concept or of mind is distilled out, hence converting attributes of mind into Mind.

multidimensional overlay of awareness of cosmos under the rubric of absolute truth. The epistemic pursuit of conventional truth, specifically throughout the first three volumes of this series, to produce a revelatory ontology concerning the nature of the ultimate truth is a major reason why these volumes are attributed as part one of this series, termed *'The I Concept'*. The reason being that in pursuit of the conventional view, in order to ascertain the 'ultimate' one must thoroughly analyse the 'I' that appears at the centre of the enquiry. It is an important actor upon the road to ultimate liberation. The concept of the 'I' is not as easily dismissed as many suppose. It persists as long as there is a conventional mode of expression.

6. The Yogācāra-Svātantrika-Mādhyamika view of the Nyingmapa.

For the explanation of this system I shall utilise the writings of Dudjom Rinpoche. His focus is the results of meditative absorption, rather than mere analytical deduction. He calls the Nyingmapa view the 'Great Madhyamaka'. His thinking is essentially a syncretic approach where he finds no real difference between the different Madhyamaka views during meditative absorption:

> When balanced in the expanse of reality without conditions to be clarified or established, both modes of Madhyamaka make no distinction regarding the cessation of all elaborate signs of subject-object dichotomy therein. However, during the aftermath of meditative absorption, they are distinguished between the former [Outer Madhyamaka] which classifies the two truths, allocating emptiness to the ultimate and appearances to the relative, and the latter [Great Madhyamaka] which determines the two truths to be [respectively] the harmony and disharmony of the abiding and apparitional natures.[65]

Concerning the Prāsaṅgika system, which Dudjom Rinpoche states is proven and that it:

> Also holds the ultimate reality without synonyms, the expanse of reality in which appearances and emptiness are coalesced, is the ground attained in the single, conclusive vehicle. Therefore it is spoken of in the mantra texts as E-VAM, the continuum of the basis, the

65 Dudjom Rinpoche, *The Nyingma School of Tibetan Buddhism,* 206.

> embodiment of indestructible reality, the great seal, the emptiness endowed with all supreme aspects, the mind in its natural state, the naturally present pristine cognition and so forth. If known as such, no one can contradict that this reality is the conclusive definitive meaning.
>
> The mode [of ultimate reality] is identical in meaning to those modes mentioned in the outer tantras of the way of mantras, namely, one's own real nature *(bdag-gi de-kho-na-nyid),* the blessing which is the ultimate truth without symbols *(don-dam mtshan-ma med-pa'i byin-rlabs)* and the deity of the expanse of indestructible reality *(rdo-rje dbyings-kyi lha).* It is also identical to those modes of the inner tantras, namely, the indivisible truth free from the range of the intellect according to Mahāyoga, the indivisible pristine cognition and expanse of reality according to Anuyoga, and the original ground in which primordial purity and spontaneous presence are coalesced according to the conclusive Great Perfection *(rdzogs-pa chen-po).*[66]

Having established the means whereby the ultimate truth can be realised Dudjom Rinpoche then further analyses the attributes of the Svātantrika and Prāsaṅgika views. He states:

> Therefore, when one meditates [according to these two kinds of Madhyamaka], they are found to make the same essential point. When the pristine cognition or ultimate reality experienced during sublime meditative equipoise according to the greater vehicle, which the all-knowing great Longcenpa expressed within our own [Nyingma] tradition, is objectified, it is impossible for conceptual elaborations such as the postures of clinging to explicit negation and implicitly affirmative negation to exist therein, regardless of the concepts of being and non-being upheld by philosophical systems.
>
> There is no philosophical system to be upheld during the great sameness, which is a coalescence free from conceptual activity. However, when the aftermath of that meditative equipoise is conventionally objectified, the structure of the ground, path and result and so forth is differentiated in accordance with quotations from the authentic literary transmissions.[67]

Here he is saying that in meditative equipoise all Mādhyamika views are integrated into 'the great sameness, which is a coalescence free from

---

66 Ibid., 207.

67 Ibid., 208.

conceptual activity', because the absolutely valuable unifying reality is experienced in the Mind. It is only when the meditator comes out from *dhyāna* and experiences life in the material world again that the various permutations of conventional reality manifest. The meditation-Mind sees all [things] in a timeless absorption in the truth that is the universal *dharma (dharmakāya)* in 'indivisible pristine cognition' that is error-free. Or as Dudjum Rinpoche says 'This is why the expanse of reality, the conclusive ultimate truth without synonyms in which appearances and emptiness are coalesced, should be well established as sameness throughout the extent of existence and quiescence'.[68] Later he provides four qualifications possessed by this meditative reality (referring to Maitreya's *Supreme Continuum of the Greater Vehicle):*

> In its own essence, this reality or pristine cognition possesses four enlightened attributes of hidden meaning beyond the range of childish intellects of inhibited perception. Namely, it is pure because it is originally uncovered by minute blemishes, permanent because it is naturally without change, blissful because it is never oppressed by suffering, and true self because it pervades all saṃsāra and nirvāṇa and pacifies elaborate concepts of self and selflessness.[69]

I shall add three other points to this list, namely, that it is *compassionate* because it sees the suffering pursued by the ignorant that manifest conflicting opinions, emotions, and separative attitudes. It demonstrates as *universal Life* because it incorporates all perspectives and lives in one timeless embrace. The term 'Life' here incorporates the sum of the Entities (Minds) that inhabit the *arūpa* (formless) universe. Finally it manifests a *cosmic Identity,* incorporating the multidimensional view of a vast expansive vision far exceeding the happenings upon our little planet. Conventional truth is then not a consideration, rather the many Minds of the 'thus gone ones' manifesting as One universal Mind. Unseen and unknown by ordinary minds, the vast order of being/non-being of cosmic space and the phenomenological universe is maintained and directed by this Mind. Its nature and content is gradually revealed to Bodhisattvas as the highest *bhūmis* are trod.

68 Ibid., 209.

69 Ibid., 212.

A Buddha is liberated into such a Mind-Space wherein he plays a role, one of milliards of such Minds in an awesome Hierarchy of transcended Ones. Consequently the universe becomes populated by stars and galaxies, each being embodied and empowered by such Minds.

This last point is hinted at by Dudjom Rinpoche's statement:

> Furthermore, all the outer and inner phenomena subsumed by the components, psychophysical bases and activity fields are apparitions which arise from reality, and yet, by the power of its natural purity, with reference to the conclusive abiding mode, they do not stray from the natural sameness of the Original Buddha [Samantabhadra[70]] and are of the nature of the buddha-body and pristine cognition. They are seen as such by the conclusive buddha-eye which is free from all obscurations.[71]

Also:

> The intentions of the sūtras and the tantras agree that the pure array of the buddhas' fields and bodies and so forth appears through the purity of one's own mind.[72]

This 'buddha-eye' is the all-seeing Eye (Ājñā centre) centred in the forehead, and when thoroughly awakened allows multidimensional visioning.[73] If the entire Head centre (*sahasrāra padma*) is taken to represent such an Eye and focussed veridically northwards then the entire cosmos and the Buddha-fields[74] therein is open for viewing and communion with in the Mind's Eye. This lotus is built upon the paradigm of the Real and reflects the truth of *dharmakāya* once its 1,000 petals have been awakened.

To clarify the fact that the Nyingma view of the two truths presented here is focussed upon the esoteric or Tantric aspects of the *dharma* we have the statement;

---

70 The primordial, Ādi Buddha.

71 Dudjom Rinpoche, *The Nyingma School of Tibetan Buddhism*, 212.

72 Ibid., 214.

73 The process whereby this Eye is awakened is explained in Volume 5.

74 Later in this series I shall speak of these Buddha-fields in terms of being the domains of Logoi.

> It is said particularly in the tantrapaṭika of the unsurpassed way of mantras that [the buddha-bodies and fields] originate through the purity of the internal structure of the energy channels, currents and seminal points and of mind-as-such. Therefore, while all things are not truly existent apart from being mere labels designated by the ideas of one's own mind, the infallibility with which these objects designated by thought appear in circumstances dependent on different intellects, is called proof by the logic of convention. Not one of us at the present time, who has gathered the appropriate deeds and awakened to the appropriate propensities, can contradict in the case of fire, for example, the statement that fire is hot, since it is validly proven that the nature of fire does appear to be hot; and the same would appear to be true for virtue, evil and the like. Ultimately, however, no such one-sided determination can be made. This is known because fire does not appear to be hot to the creature Agniśuci and so forth, and because empowered beings can display various emanations and transformations of substance.[75]

We see from above that once yogic powers *(siddhis)* manifest then what is know as conventional truths, and the conventions concerning the appearance of things disappears. A new set of perceptions take their place, derived from the esoteric inner world of the *nāḍī* system and the psychic centres *(chakras)*. Once the *chakras* awaken then the integration of the two truths into one can easily be seen. Such is the accomplishment of a *siddha* (one who has mastered *siddhis*).

7. The integrationist view of the Dharmakāya Way

The Dharmakāya Way incorporates aspects of all the other views either in part or in full, as already indicated, and is an extension of the Nyingma view presented by Dudjom Rinpoche. The development of the meditation-Mind is necessary in order to fuse the conventional and ultimate truths into Oneness. Tantric methodology is used to achieve this aim. The Dharmakāya Way however modernises the epistemic and ontological scope of the concepts, introducing a greater more cogent rationalisation of the implications of all aspects of the *buddhadharma*. It consequently elaborates the meaning of the term *dharmakāya* by

75 Dudjom Rinpoche, *The Nyingma School of Tibetan Buddhism*, 214.

presenting an esoteric vision depicting some of the constituency of an enlightened Mind.

More is consequently revealed concerning the experience of the *dharmakāya,* of the scope of life in cosmos for 'thus gone' ones, of the types of concepts they consider, and of the parameters governing multidimensional visioning than was hitherto possible. The exegetical and lexical constraints of the past mind-set that enlightened ones had to conform to prevented the complete turning of the keys of the esoteric *dharma* that is now possible. The limits of the Buddhist lexicographical and hermeneutic terminology can also be transcended through inclusion of concepts from the world's esoteric traditions that come from enlightened Minds. Consequently the Dharmakāya Way represents the continuation of the evolution of the *buddhadharma* for future generations, especially for the Bodhisattvas that have incarnated into or are conditioned by Western civilisation with its materialistic and technological bias, and consequently no longer live in an overtly Buddhistic environment. The *dharma* must adapt to meet the needs of their enquiring minds.

The conventional and esoteric ('ultimate') views shall consequently become increasingly merged within the exoteric domain of enquirers as they take on new more embracive ideas than currently available. A greater number of Bodhisattvas will consequently appear to order the apparitions of human civilisation towards more wholesome activities. Inevitably the planet will be transformed through a new era of cooperative identity, allowing *siddhas* to openly flourish, and 'thus gone' Ones to exit earth space in groupings rather than singularly, as at present. The earth will then be a sanctified domain because the *dharma* will rein supreme in all minds. Inevitably, even its substance shall become liberated as *pralaya* (dissolution) ensues, where material phenomena becomes transmogrified into its Void attributes.

3

Buddhist Schools and the Wheel of Direction in Space

The eight-spoked wheel

The purpose of this chapter is to present technical information concerning the major Buddhist schools, so that later reference to any of their founders and related teachings will be better understood. A basic comprehension of their doctrines is important, allowing one to understand the context of the evolution of the exegetical and epistemic views of the religion, as well as some of the main issues that confronted the exponents of the *buddhadharma* over the epochs. I will present an interpretation of these diverse and somewhat abstruse views via the esotericism of the directions of the eight spoked wheel of the *dharma*.

This wheel is also that of the eight spoked wheel (or cross) of direction in space (*aṣṭadiśas*). It is an important epistemic tool for the analysis of the context of any scripture, consequently its analytical methodology will be regularly used throughout this series.

Buddhist texts normally abound in the usage of this technique to empower the ontology and eschatological doctrines they contain with greater meaning. This cross concerns the four cardinal directions, north, south, east, west, and their intermediate points, and is the basis of most *maṇḍalas* that detail formed space. Sometimes ten directions are mentioned in commentaries, which incorporate these eight directions, plus a forwards and backwards motion through time, providing therefore a concept of evolution of the *maṇḍala*. While this is a valid conception, consideration of such motion would complicate significantly the exegesis concerned, hence shall be omitted in my explanations of the presented facts. Maṇḍalas incorporate the nature of the movement of *prāṇas,* the organisation of *chakras,* arcane, even pedestrian or technical subjects, such as the appearances of the Buddhist schools.

Indeed, the subject of *maṇḍalas* that incorporate such devices as this cross is so important that the fourth Volume of this treatise is devoted to their explication. Buddhist academics and practitioners should thoroughly familiarise themselves with the way the texts are structured as *maṇḍalas.* To properly interpret them one must deduce the way the four and eight armed crosses, the twelve-spoked wheel (of the Heart centre unfolding) and other numerological considerations, such as the doctrines of the five Dhyāni Buddhas, and five sense-consciousnesses are veiled throughout the texts. The enlightened beings that provided us the texts and Tantras thought *maṇḍalically* and numerologically, which is self-evident for all that seriously analyse their works. More effort should thus be taken by readers to unveil the hidden *maṇḍalas* within texts, and for this purpose a thorough understanding of the *aṣṭadiśas* is a major key.

In general the directions northeast, southeast, southwest and northwest manifest in the form of a mutable cross, of continuous cyclic activity. The *northeast* represents the direction of 'unity', wherein the unified philosophy, or grouping of forces exists. The direction *southeast* represents the projection of that unified force as an 'expression' into the field of *saṃsāra.* Here it is seeded into and accordingly modified by an individual's developing mind, which undergoes a genesis of a belief system wherein the philosophy associated with the northeast is heuristically developed. The direction *southwest* concerns the resultant gain as 'understanding', and different derivations of that realisation, causing further experimentation and consequent aggrandisement of knowledgeable bits, hence the evolution of the intellect. The direction *northwest* represents an emanatory demonstration of the mastery of what has been gained through evolutionary development in the southern portion of the eight-armed cross. This is denoted as 'goodwill' in the field of human consciousness, or as the will-to-good upon a higher level of expression. It represents the movement upwards, of aspiration to higher fields of endeavour, from that strictly relegated to the world of human relationships (west).

The cardinal directions (north, east, south and west) represent the fixed cross aspect, indicating a steady flow of energies to these four main orientations that inevitably represent the nature of the direct expression of the field of consciousness, and inevitably the development of compassionate considerations. The *north* is upwards to liberation, divinity, the mount of achievement. The *east* represents the way inwards to the Heart of life, the Void experience. The *south* represents the direction downwards to the little ones ensnared in *saṃsāra,* the world of form. The direction *west* represents travelling to the field of service that represents humanity, and all related social interactions.[1]

The Buddhist Schools

The following section concerning the Buddhist schools is presented in order to put all of these schools of thought into context utilising the *aṣṭadiśas* to do so. The reader can then better appraise their distinctions and the associated complexity of thought. The philosophical views differ, nevertheless their rich tapestry is a worthy study, allowing one to better appreciate the arguments later presented when the school of thought of an author of a text is known.

Lopez states:

The hierarchy established by the Ge-luk-bas[2] is as follows:

1 My rendition of the meaning of the directions of the eight-armed cross is adapted from the information given on pages 189-194 of Alice A. Bailey's *Discipleship in the New Age II* (Lucis Press, 1968). The books by Alice Bailey were written telepathically by an enlightened Tibetan Rinpoche under the pseudonym of D.K. (Who was at that time a senior official at the Tashi Lungpo monastery at Shigatse.) The teachings in her books show the context of the working of an enlightened Mind, which though Tibetan, uses a non-sectarian methodology to impart timely, necessary esoteric information to the world according to a Plan formulated by the Council of Bodhisattvas. Detractors of these teachings show a prejudiced opinion or lack of spiritual insight as to the way great Bodhisattvas use skilful means, and the appropriate use of *siddhis* (psychic powers) to teach a far vaster audience than would otherwise be possible. The theistic or Christian terminology utilised via Alice Bailey's mind needs to be properly accommodated by intuitive broadminded deductive reasoning and adequate cross referencing, such as converting references of Christ to Maitreya, and 'God' to the concept of a Logos, the meaning of which will be explained later in this series. All true esotericism has Buddhist philosophy at its heart, as my series of books will demonstrate.

2 The Ge-luk-bas (Gelugpa) are the philosophical school in Tibetan Buddhism that express the Prāsaṅgika-Mādhyamika line of reasoning.

Prāsaṅgika-Mādhyamika
Sautrāntika-Svātantrika-Mādhyamika
Yogācāra-Svātantrika-Mādhyamika
Cittamātra (Yogācāra) Following Reasoning
Cittamātra (Yogācāra) Following Scripture
Sautrāntika Following Reasoning
Sautrāntika Following Scripture
Vaibhāṣika

From the lowest to the highest there is an increase in the subtlety of the two extremes identified by the individual schools. The Vaibhāṣikas abandon the extreme of permanence by asserting that all conditioned phenomena are impermanent and abandon the extreme of annihilation by asserting that the past and the future are substantial entities *(dravya, rdzas)*, that is, that the past of an object exists after its present existence and the future of an object exists before its present existence. The Sautrāntikas abandon the extreme of permanence by asserting that uncaused phenomena are not substantially existent and abandon the extreme of annihilation by asserting that objects are naturally established as places for imputing designations and as bases of conception by thought. The Yogācārins abandon the extreme of permanence by asserting that objects are not naturally established as the bases of conception by thought and as places for imputing designations. For example, a table is not established by way of its own character as a basis for the affixing of the name "table." They assert that dependent phenomena and consummate phenomena are truly established, thereby abandoning the extreme of annihilation. As we have seen, the Svātantrikas abandon the extreme of permanence by asserting that no phenomenon is established from the side of its own objective mode of subsistence without being posited by the power of appearing to a non-defective awareness. They abandon the extreme of annihilation by asserting that all phenomena are established from their own side, that they exist by way of their own character. The Prāsaṅgikas abandon the extreme of permanence by asserting that phenomena are not established from their own side and under their own power, and abandon the extreme of annihilation by asserting that phenomena are imputedly existent, being mere designations by terms and thoughts[3]...The Sautrāntika-Svātantrikas, in the person of

3 D. S. Lopez Jr., *A Study of Svātantrika,* 153-154.

> Bhāvaviveka, reacted strongly against the Yogācārin view, holding that external objects do exist as they appear to direct perception, although they do not truly exist. The Yogācāra-Svātantrikas assimilated the Yogācārin idealism, asserting that subject and object do not exist as separate entities conventionally, but rejected the Yogācārin contention that consciousness truly exists.[4]

Lopez presents many other differences, however the above suffices to present the case to rearrange the listing, eliminating the Prāsaṅgika philosophy from the head of a hierarchy, but rightfully puts it into place as part of a *maṇḍala* in relation to the others. This is necessary, as each of these schools have flaws in their logic, as will be further seen when I examine the *Sevenfold Reasoning, Diamond Slivers,* and the *Four Extremes,* which are criteria of the epistemic constructs of the Prāsaṅgika. The synthesising Dharmakāya Way that is presented in this *Treatise on Mind* must also be correctly positioned in relation to these Buddhist schools.

More examples concerning the eight-armed cross of direction in space will be presented throughout this series and elaborated in the book *Maṇḍalas, Their Nature and Development.* Below is the pertinent information concerning these eight directions. Only basic information concerning the major schools of Buddhism needs to be given, as readers can research the subject elsewhere if desired. It can be said that virtually all major teachers have their own variant of a particular school of the *dharma.* It should also be noted that this listing is based upon what is presented by Tibetan exegesists, the division between the Svātantrikas and the Prāsaṅgika for instance, never existed in classical Buddhism.

In utilising the *aṣṭadiśas* the direction *south* represents the way downwards into the realm of 'things', the objects of perception that the sense-perceptors utilise (the realms of the little lives embodying the forms contactable) and from which the mind can gain empirical deductions. Here we find the first of the schools to have arisen, the Vaibhāṣikas, who 'abandon the extreme of annihilation by asserting that the past and the future are substantial entities *(dravya, rdzas),* that is, that the past of an object exists after its present existence and the future

4 Ibid.,158.

of an object exists before its present existence'. This is the most basic, or foundation philosophy, from which the other schools derive more sophisticated doctrines. This school is generally termed the 'Analysts', the Sautrāntikas are termed 'Traditionalists', the Yogācārins 'Idealists', and the Mādhyamika, 'Centrists'.

The Vaibhāṣikas and the Sautrāntikas are further explained in the book *Buddhist Ethics*:

> Analysts derive their name and also their tenets from the *Great Detailed Exposition (Mahāvibhāṣā),* a compendium of the class of phenomenology *(abhidharma, mngon pa).* They could also be called "Atomists", since one of their major beliefs is in the existence of partless and indivisible atoms, as well as partless and indivisible moments of consciousness. For the Analysts, these phenomena, being partless and indivisible (therefore subject to neither material destruction nor division through analysis), are held to be ultimate truths, as opposed to anything that is an aggregation of particles or moments, which they consider to be conventional truths. Both truths, conventional and ultimate, are real for the Analysts, who therefore, in terms of Buddhist philosophy, stand as "Realists" *(bhāvavādin, dngos por smra ba).* Theirs is a philosophy expounded mainly by adherents of the Individual Way and no doubt characterized the tenets of the original schools of Buddhism in India.
>
> Traditionalists are so called because their assertions are based mainly on the scriptures that record the word of the Buddha. Though Traditionalists are Realists, the Traditionalist followers of reason differentiate themselves from Analysts by negating the substantial status of conceptually imputed phenomena and by propounding a finer concept of conventional and ultimate truth. For them, a phenomenon able to produce an effect *(arthakriya, don byed nus pa)* is ultimate truth, and one not able to do so is a conventional truth. Traditionalists were followers of the Individual Way[5], but their tenets may have been the spark that originated the finer thought of the Universal Way.[6]

5 The 'followers of the Individual Way' are the Hīnayāna, and those of 'the Universal Way' are the Mahāyāna.

6 Jamgön Kongtrul Lodrö Tayé, *Buddhist Ethics,* Trans. and Ed., International Translation Committee founded by V.V. Kalu Rinpoché. (Snow Lion Publications, New York, 2003), 359-360.

The atomist view, wherein existents are espoused and experienced as 'moments of consciousness' naturally relates to the southern direction of the *aṣṭadiśas.*

The direction *southeast* represents the process of assimilating or integrating general philosophical teachings in accord with impressions gained from the phenomena associated with *saṃsāra*. This concerns the way the Sautrāntikas following Scripture derive wisdom from naturally established objects, in accord with their interpretation of doctrinal passages (*sūtras*), which represents that which emanates from the northeast direction.

Snellgrove states that:

> An interesting school so far as later developments are concerned is one known as Sautrāntika, meaning "Ending with the Sūtra" in the sense that they do not accept the Abhidharma as canonical. Although none of their scriptures survives they are known from the views that are attributed to them by their opponents. Thus while the Sarvāstivādins[7] believed that the elements of existence maintained a real existence in the past and the future as well as the present, the Sautrāntikas asserted that the elements only existed in any real sense as they manifested themselves momentarily in a continual transient present time. They also rejected the theory of nirvāṇa as being an element in its own right, for like space, they argued, it was physically nonexistent. Teachings such as this, which reduced physical existence to a bare minimum while leaving nirvāṇa free of any realistic designation, would appear to be halfway between what was later regarded as typical Hīnayāna and Mahāyāna opinions.[8]

As the Sautrāntikas *following reasoning* 'abandon the extreme of annihilation by asserting that objects are naturally established as places for imputing designations and as bases of conception of thought', so this school relates to the direction *southwest.* In this direction such imputation refers to the way in which experiences are made an essential part of the unit of consciousness, producing an identification with

7 The most important Vaibhāṣika school, of which some information has survived over the millennia.

8 D. Snellgrove, *Indo-Tibetan Buddhism,* (Shambhala, Boston, 2002), pp. 80-81.

them, so that new *bījas* are created for the future activities of that consciousness to recall and reason with when needed. This school follows the type of reasoning found in Dignāga's (and Dharmakīrti's) works, such as *pramāṅasamuccaya* (The Compendium on Prime Cognition). Snellgrove's comments relating to the Sautrāntikas that 'appear to be halfway between what was later regarded as typical Hīnayāna and Mahāyāna opinions' can also be relegated to this direction.

The direction *east* represents the way inwards to the heart of life via contemplative introspection. This necessitates a properly established mode of ascertaining what is, via the art of meditation, and which leads to the establishment of the understanding that consciousness is the foundation to the process of realisation, of life.

This direction is occupied by the Yogācārins who 'assert that dependent phenomena and consummate phenomena are truly established, thereby abandoning the extreme of annihilation'. Here we have the Yogācārins *following scripture* (the *sūtras,* plus that established by Asaṅga), because the teachings followed (concerning the nature of consciousness and its relation to form and to *śūnyatā*) are rudimentary (at least in a manner that compliments the doctrines of the other schools) for a proper understanding of all Mahāyāna doctrines. The Yogācāra are so named because their assertion is that only by the practice of appropriate yoga can the impure *saṃskāras* be properly cleansed or transmuted so as to produce enlightenment. Without an understanding of the nature of the mind the art of meditation is not possible, and it is this art that produces revelation as to the way of the Heart. Such understanding incorporates the nature of mind as basis of all (the *ālayavijñāna*) and also of the Clear Light of Mind that abides in its natural state. This is only obtainable through a proper cultivation of *bodhicitta* and the Bodhisattva ideal, which is the way of the Heart.

For the Centrist (Mādhyamika) view this way to the Heart also sees the mind as an illusion, producing the realisation that all is Void *(śūnyatā).*

The book *Buddhist Ethics* states concerning the Yogācārins:

> Idealists, whose system was pioneered by Asanga, are so called because they assert that all phenomena are the nature of the mind that perceives them. For this reason, they are also called "Proponents of

the Aspect of Consciousness" *(vijñānavādin, rnam rig smra ba).* The lack of substantial duality between observer and observed is for them the subtle selflessness of phenomena, the ultimate truth. This view provided the support for the experientialist approach to meditation; for this reason, they are also called "Experientalists" *(yogācārin, rnal 'byor spyod pa).* This approach, however, led them to overemphasize perception or mind and to attribute to the mind a true or ultimate status. A branch of the Idealists, which follows the scriptures, also subscribes to the belief in a fundamental consciousness *(ālayavijñāna, kun gzhi rnam shes)* as the storehouse of cumulative imprints of actions and as the person itself. Idealists are followers of the Universal Way, and their tenets, along with those of the Centrists, are said to have formed the conceptual frame of reference for the tantric systems.[9]

The direction *west* represents the way outwards into the world of human interrelationships in general. This involves gaining the knowledge obtained from human social interactions via the mental environment. The observation is that all that is observed exists in the mind, therefore only that which exists in the mind is real. This concerns the Yogācārins *(Idealists) following reasoning*, as they follow the art of meditation in relation to what they empirically observe by means of mind as the primary means of gaining revelation. Meditation is the means whereby this mental environment constituting the sum total of human thought life incorporated as the *ālayavijñāna,* plus that expressed as the higher Mind, can become fully experienced. All empirical philosophical schools can be considered expressions of this direction, some by extension also ascribe to the directions east or north, and others to the southern directions, especially that of materialistic science, with its atomic theory as the basis to all things.

The direction *northeast* represents *unity,* in that it concerns the mode of expression of the doctrines concerning *śūnyatā* and of its relationship with *saṃsāra. Saṃsāra* consequently becomes an existent that is experienced by means of the sense perceptors so that wisdom can be gained, even though what pertains to *saṃsāra* is an illusion. The Centrist (middle way) doctrines of the Mādhyamika come into view because they incorporate the path that is purported to be the

9 Jamgön Kongtrul Lodrö Tayé, *Buddhist Ethics,* 360.

middle between extremes, taking all of the other views into account. In this direction therefore all the fundamental Mādhyamika Schools are represented, specifically however, the position held by the Sautrāntika-Svātantrikas, in the person of Bhāvaviveka, who dismissed the Yogācārin view, by accepting the existence of external objects. Also the extreme of annihilation is abandoned 'by asserting that all phenomena are established from their own side, that they exist by way of their own character'. In the concept of 'own character' the Sautrāntika-Svātantrikas hold views similar to common humanity who accept external phenomena to be real. This facilitates the education of human units through similarity of views, allowing presentation of a sound empirical basis for their comprehension of the true nature of the material world as a basis for the establishment of the ultimate truth of the Void. This allows the expression of a more sophisticated doctrine of the true nature of life to the southeast direction held by the Sautrāntika *following scripture.*

The Mādhyamika are described thus in *Buddhist Ethics:*

> Centrists, whose system was pioneered by Nāgārjuna, are so called because they follow the "centre" (*madhya, dbu*) or "middle way" which does not fall into the two extremes of negating conventional reality and asserting the true existence of phenomena. They advocate the complementarity of the two truths, the conventional as the dependent arising of phenomena and the ultimate as the emptiness of true status of everything that exists. Centrists are subdivided into "Dogmaticists" (*svāntantrika, rang rgyud pa*) and "Consequentialists" (*prāsaṅgika, thal 'gyur pa*), the former advocated by Bhāvaviveka and the latter by Candrakīrti, Shantideva, etc. Their main difference lies in their analyses of whether or not a phenomenon has an "essence." The former asserts that it does, but does not say what it is exactly. The latter asserts that when a phenomenon is analyzed, nothing is found that can be said to constitute the phenomena itself. Consequentialists assert that everything is just a name, a mere imputation of the mind, and nothing ever has any true existence, even conventionally. The tenets of Centrists represent the prominent part of the Universal Way philosophy, as well as the view based on which tantric practice is performed.[10]

10 Ibid., 360.

The direction *northwest* concerns the process of *outward expansion* of the entire sphere of identification into that which is beyond the present sphere of action-reaction. It involves the forward-progression of the individual towards the 'beyond', the liberation ahead, to project whatever is/is-not, the gain of the experiential process, to the other shore of whatever was conventionally understood. This position is held by the Prasaṅgika, who 'abandon the extreme of annihilation by asserting that phenomena are imputedly existent, being mere designations by terms and thoughts', and by properly asserting the doctrine of *śūnyatā*. Consequently the exclusion of the factor of *saṃsāra* other than as a field to derive experience of the ultimate truth, represents the emanation of the will-to-good of this school, where the liberation gained by access to *śūnyatā* is 'the good'.

The direction *north* represents the way upwards towards that which represents the Divine—to the *ālayavijñāna*, *śūnyatā*, and thence the *dharmakāya*, depending upon the level of attainment of the person. This position is logically held by the Yogācāra-Svātantrika-Madhyamaka,[11] who have 'assimilated the Yogācāra idealism, asserting that subject and object do not exist as separate entities conventionally, but rejected the Yogācārin contention that consciousness truly exists'. In endeavouring to assimilate elements from both major Mahāyāna schools they pave the way for a fusion of all extremes.

This refutation of mind concerns the nature of the empirical mind, which because of its attachment to *saṃsāra* is ephemeral. It does not include the awakened (abstract) Mind. Here we should look specifically to the 'Great Madhyamaka',[12] as it is known by the Nyingmapa who

---

11 Normally simplified to Yogācāra-Madhyamaka.

12 This title is somewhat contentious, as is indicated by Shakya Chokdan, Trans. Komarovskilarolslav in the *Three Texts on Madhyamaka*. (Library of Tibetan Works and Archives, Dharamsala, 2000), 62, *fn*. 33. (*Note* here that the term Niḥsvabhāvavādin refers to a proponent of entitylessness, i.e., emptiness of oneself, as propagated by Nāgārjuna. The Yogācāra school proposes emptiness 'of other'.)

There are two ways of identifying the Great and Middle Madhyamikas: When Yogācārins identify themselves as Great Madhyamikas, Niḥsvabhāvavādins become [for them] Middle Madhyamikas. When Niḥsvabhāvavādins identify themselves as Great Madhyamikas, Yogācārins become Middle Madhyamikas. Nevertheless,

practice it. Dudjom Rinpoche states:

> Concerning the subtle, inner Great Madhyamaka of definitive meaning, it is stated in the *Jewel Lamp of the Madhyamaka* by the master Bhavya *(skal-ldan):*
>
> > The Madhyamaka of the Prāsaṅgika and the Svātantrika is the coarse, Outer Madhyamaka. It should indeed be expressed by those who profess well-informed intelligence during debates with [extremist] Outsiders, during the composition of great treatises, and while establishing texts which concern supreme reasoning. However, when the subtle, inner Madhyamaka is experientially cultivated, one should meditate on the nature of Yogācāra-Madhyamaka.[13]

In the accompanying footnote it is stated that:

> The Great Madhyamaka *(dbu-ma chen-po)* is also known as Yogācāra-Madhyamaka. As such it is not to be confused with the Yogācāra-Svātantrika school. It integrates the view that all things of saṃsāra are intrinsically empty *(rang-stong)* of their own inherent substantiality with the view that all enlightened attributes are empty of those extraneous phenomena (*gzhan-stong*).[14]

The text furthermore states:

> It would indeed be a grave error to equate the tenets of mundane Mind Only[15] with the Great Sage's buddha-body of reality and the mass of its inseperable enlightened attributes, exceeding all the sands of the River Ganges, which are inclusively known as the uncorrupted expanse, the inconceivable expanse, ultimate virtue, unchanging and firm reality, truth in the ultimate abiding nature of reality, the primordially liberated buddha-body, freedom from all conceptual elaborations of the four extremes, and renunciation of the two concepts

according to Shakya Chokden both Yogācāra and Niḥsvabhāvavādin traditions have to be identified as Great Madhyamikas, since their claims to be Great Madhyamikas are equally powerful.

13 Dudjom Rinpoche, *The Nyingma School of Tibetan Buddhism*, 169.

14 Ibid., Notes 14, *fn.* 169.

15 The Yogācāra school.

of selfhood. These are spontaneously present, utterly transcending the phenomena of consciousness.[16]

This list of superlatives describes attributes of the *dharmakāya,* or fully liberated Mind, which is the objective espoused by the Yogācāra-Madhyamaka to achieve, as provided in the rDzogs chen practice. A further, more detailed explication of the nature of the *dharmakāya,* and the method of its attainment, is also an objective of this *Treatise on Mind.* Continuing with Dudjom Rinpoche's text:

> In general, those whose intelligence is authoritative, without falling into prejudice, do not differentiate between the two modes of emptiness [*rang-stong and gzhan-stong*] when abiding in the Madhyamaka [view], which is the summit of the four philosophical systems dependent on different traditions of promulgation which have been precisely enumerated. This is clearly understood through the respective treatises of the two great masters, Nāgārjuna and Asaṅga[17]...It is difficult to destroy attachment to superficial characteristics (*mtshan-'dzin).* However, in order for the discriminative awareness born of study and thought to refute it, the Prāsaṅgika and the Svātantrika reasoning which cuts through conceptual elaboration is sharp. But when the experiences of meditation are established, it is this tradition of the Great Madhyamaka, as taught in the third promulgation,[18] which is supremely profound and vast. This naturally present pristine cognition, the ultimate truth of the naturally pure expanse, is the original abiding nature of all things, and it is the pristine cognition to be experienced by individual intuitive awareness.[19]
>
> Thus, absolute reality is the pristine cognition of the non-dual nature of just what is. It is indicated by the words buddha-body of reality or essential buddha-body which genuinely transcends the phenomena of consciousness. Yet, also comprised within this doctrine, which is misrepresented as the philosophical system known as the Mind Only, are: the definitive order of the three continua as taught in the way of secret mantra; the definitive order of the ground,

---

16 Dudjom Rinpoche, *The Nyingma School of Tibetan Buddhism*, 184.

17 Ibid.

18 The Tantrapiṭaka, which incorporates the teachings of Secret Mantra of the Great Madhyamaka.

19 Dudjom Rinpoche, *The Nyingma School of Tibetan Buddhism*, 185.

> path and result of purification and so forth which are adhered to by followers of the greater vehicle in both its causal and resultant aspects, and which include [the terminology] of deities, mantras, embodiments of indestructible reality, supreme bliss, emptiness endowed with all supreme aspects, the imperishable seminal point which is the fundamental support of body, speech and mind; and also the uncommon definitive order of the ground, path and result.
>
> One should know that the intention of the final promulgation, even though not within the path upheld by the proponents of intrinsic emptiness *(rang-stong-pa),* is without contradiction by examining, one by one, the commentaries of the great lords of the tenth level[20] and the teachings belonging to the tantrapiṭaka of the way of the secret mantra.[21]

The development of the schools can also be viewed in terms of the awakening of the *chakras:*

- The Vaibhāṣika, and the other schools that evolved directly from the time of the Buddha, embody the Base of the Spine/Sacral centre combination.
- The Sautrāntika the Solar Plexus centre.
- The Yogācāra the Throat centre.
- The Svātantrika and the Prāsaṅgika Mādhymika the Heart centre, and its control of the centres below the diaphragm.
- The Great Madhyamaka and the Dharmakāya Way the combined Head centre.

It can also be said that the three schools of the northern direction embody the qualities of the Ājñā centre. The left lobe of the centre is embodied by the Prāsaṅgika. Here the *iḍā naḍī* aspect of Buddhism is fully unfolded by means of discursive dialectics. Ideally, they produce a version of *śūnyatā* without residue in the way that they cut all bridges to *saṃsāra* by the means of the reduction of all syllogisms, or assertions of other schools concerning phenomena to absurdities, or unwanted deductions, rather than positing their own views. In order to do so they,

20 The highest Bodhisattva level. The next step is Buddhahood.

21 Dudjom Rinpoche, *The Nyingma School of Tibetan Buddhism*, 185-186. Secret Mantra is another name for the Vajrayāna or Tantrayāna.

paradoxically, must develop the mind (conveyed by the *iḍā naḍī)* to its sharpest, most refined peak, though they deny the very existence of that which is their major tool for analysis, to achieve their reductionist consequences. Their conclusion that 'nothing is found that can be said to constitute the phenomena' makes *śūnyatā* the consequence.

The right lobe of the Ājñā centre, conveying the *piṇgalā prāṇas* of Buddhism is embodied by the Svātantrika Madhyamaka. They produce a version of *śūnyatā* with residue, meaning that they neither fully reside in *saṃsāra* or *śūnyatā*, but fuse them both into a *mahāmudrā*[22] of revelatory being. This 'residue', which is the 'essence' that the Svātantrika Madhyamaka states phenomena posses, can be seen to be the Void Elements explained later (in 'The Essay on the Many and the One'), as well as memory *bījas* (seeds) of everything that happened, which can be recalled by an enlightened one at will. Also, similar to the Yogācāra-Madhyamaka, this school takes meditation as the core method of obtaining truth.

The Yogācāra-Madhyamaka take the quality of the integrating central position of the Ājñā centre because they abandon neither *saṃsāra* or *śūnyatā.*[23] They work with meditative techniques to transform all five Elements and sense perceptions in the form of the true Vajrayāna.[24] Having not abandoned the essential aspects of the doctrine of Mind only, it can utilise the five aspects of mind to gain empowerment of the qualities of the five Tathāgata families (of the five Dhyāni Buddhas), and thereby the all-embracive Dharmadhātu Wisdom in the form of the pristine awareness of Samantabhadra and Consort.

Despite the objective of their teachings, the brilliance of most of the scriptures, and the methodology of meditation techniques, all of the traditional schools flounder through the obscurations of symbolic, veiled, exoteric doctrines, and literal interpretations wherein exaggerations are rife. We therefore have beliefs, such as that of the transmigration of

---

22 *Mahāmudrā:* The great Seal or Symbol of revelatory attainment, signifying the natural state of the Buddhas. It is called *mūdra* or 'gesture' because revelation of the three bodies of a Buddha is sealed in supreme unchanging bliss.

23 Representing therefore the *prāṇas* of the left and right lobes of the Ājñā centre which become integrated by means of the *śūnyatā-saṃsāra* nexus.

24 The path of the indestructible power of the *vajra*/dorje in Tantric Buddhism.

the human consciousness into animals; which my book *Karma and the Rebirth of Consciousness* has aptly demonstrated as fallacious.[25] The extremist version of the Prāsaṅgika rhetoric of ultimates would even make the activity of Bodhisattvas meaningless, because all *saṃsāric* activities are deemed 'non-existent', Void.

The Dharmakāya Way[26] lifts the veils on such conceptualised gloss, properly interpreting the meaning of the presented scriptures, and teaches the unadulterated truth, as well as simplifying meditation techniques. In this way the practitioner is lead to the objective, *samyuksambodhi* (the highest enlightenment, for those that have the capacity in any life) the quickest possible way without distortion or mishap. It presents the externalisation of the esoteric 'ear whispered truths' that were only hinted at formerly, or deeply veiled in the texts and Tantras.[27] It integrates the essentiality of all traditions of Buddhism, as well as all truly esoteric doctrines of the various religions, past and present. It is the revelation of the *dharmakāya* to those that are to be Initiated into its ways, thus represents the empowerment of all 1,000 petals of the Head centre.[28]

The complete flower or eight-spoked wheel of all the Buddhist schools is shown in Figure 1. The eight directions represent pathways within the Head lotus for obtaining revelations governed by the epistemologies of these schools. When encircled by the fundamental concepts that are common to all, which unify all schools into oneness, then the esoteric *dharma* wheel that is the key symbol of Buddhism is depicted.

For the deepest insights into the enlightenment path aspirants should first astutely analyse the truth of the nature of life in *saṃsāra* to comprehend it in relativistic terms, and then cogently research the

---

25 The subtler esoteric interpretation of rebirth into animal form in terms of the physical body being an animal form, and the theriomorphic forces contained therein that must be mastered by those upon the liberation path, is presented in the later volumes to this series.

26 Which will be continuously explained as this treatise unfolds.

27 The Sanskrit term for this veiling is *sandhyābhāṣa*, the intentional veiling or incorporated code in Tantric texts, secret, esoteric, intentional, hence 'twilight language'. However, controversy exists amongst scholars whether this word or *sandhābhāṣa* is the correct term for the esoteric code in the Tantras.

28 In this respect the three Madhyamaka schools embody the processes of unfolding the three major tiers of the Head lotus, which are explained in Volume 5 of this treatise.

ontology and tenets of the various Buddhist schools. The polar opposites of the various schools should be noted, as the philosophies presented by the schools at the end of each arm of the cross are those that are either the most diametrically opposed, or else they work together in a congruent way.

When the Dharmakāya Way (or the *dharmakāya)* is placed in the central position, then we see that it is the integrating source of all *dharma*. It represents the true middle way for all; the Way inwards, onwards, and outwards in all directions to greater revelatory standing of the *buddhadharma*. It expresses the omniscient *dharma* that is the Buddha-body externalised and inclusive of them all. Being the heart, it can at once be viewed as the centre of the *maṇḍala*, and also its boundary (and beyond into cosmos), as it represents both the inner and outer means of attainment for all of the schools. It is also not restricted to the terminology peculiar to Buddhism, but manifests a universalist approach that is the efflorescence of the esoteric truths that have existed throughout time immemorial and contained in the prodigious memories of the enlightened.

The four outpourings of Buddhist dharma

Figure 1 posits the three times in terms of the appearance of the schools, making the ten directions of Buddhist literature, with the central Dharmakāya Way being expressive of the continuum from the past to the future. Śākyamuni Buddha represents the past attainment, in that though he is steeped in the *dharmakāya* Reasoning, the source of all that was, is, and which is to be, he released the initial exoteric doctrines of the *sūtras* that sustained the early schools, from which developed the teachings of the Vaibhāṣika and the Sautrāntika. (The esoteric doctrines that he gave were only presented to a relatively select few.) This represents the First Outpouring (or Turning of the Wheel) of the *dharma*. The doctrines of later Mahāyāna dispensation of the Madhyamaka and Yogācāra were esoteric at his time. The Mahāyāna schools represented the Second Outpouring, and was externalised through the meditative revelations of great Bodhisattvas. The two outpourings represent the main corpus of Buddhism up to the present epoch, affecting principally those of the East. The Third Outpouring generated the most esoteric aspects of the *dharma* in the form of the highly veiled Tantras, being the basis of the Vajrayāna, the indestructible diamond vehicle.

The Fourth Outpouring will rectify philosophic and hermeneutic errors of the past, and will fuse the epistemic and metaphysical approaches of both the Eastern and the Western religious and philosophical streams. It is therefore a true *mahāmudrā* (the 'Great Symbol') for the world at large. Its promulgation is logically the main task of Gautama's successor, Maitreya, whose dispensation, or expression, can also be viewed in terms of a collective awakening of many Bodhisattvas scattered throughout the world, rather than in one geographical area. The true glory of the Dharmakāya Way will then be revealed, because high calibre Bodhisattvas that are suitable vehicles for this new transmission will have appeared everywhere to disseminate the doctrines.

Figure 1. The Mahāyāna Schools, (the Dharma Wheel)

Figure 1 can be viewed as a basic triplicity, with the schools of the southern direction representing the first turning of the Wheel. The schools involved with the second turning of the Wheel are represented by the northern direction. The Yogācāra schools are positioned centrally, acting as a type of medium between the Madhyamaka doctrines of the northern schools and the more empirically focussed schools of the south. The basic doctrine of the *ālayavijñāna*, of mind/

Mind as the basis of all, can find acceptance by all schools, once rightly modified, as the mind and its conjectures allow all philosophies and syllogisms to be grounded in such a way that various doctrines can be understood. The *ālayavijñāna* is effectively the bed of the *dharmakāya* for humanity. Through it the *dharmakāya* can be experienced, i.e., understood by means of a non-conceptual Mind expressing Clear Light. *Śūnyatā* is the bridge between the two. Without the *ālayavijñāna* there can be no quest for enlightenment for anyone. Within it the meditative process unfolds. All need to meditatively experience the higher realms of thought by yogic methods (which then become a liberating experiential zone), so that mind can be transformed into Mind, the basis for the *saṃsāra-śūnyatā* integration.

The second turning of the Wheel depicted in the Northern direction incorporates the Tantric teachings of all three Madhyamaka schools, with the focus being the Yogācāra-Svātantrika-Madhyamaka.

Each of the schools of thought have contributed to the *buddhadharma.* All have veridical thought constructs and sound semantics, yet flaws have appeared in their doctrines, lessening in scope as we move from south to north. Nevertheless, all have produced excellent children of the *dharma* that have accomplished much on the road to liberation. It is in the demonstration of superlative wisdom wherein Buddhism has truly set itself apart from other religious dispensations. The evolutionary process proceeds as earlier philosophers reincarnate, and riding upon the horse of earlier semantics, fix their errors, and accordingly manifest a new view that represents the march of the times. The schools have developed this way, as Bodhisattvas continuously incarnate to rectify past mistakes and consequently help to push the wheel to turn upon higher cycles of endeavour. Our hearts shall always leap out for these victorious ones of great striving and accomplishment.

'True existence' and the two truths

We see from the above that the case putting the Prāsaṅgika philosophy as the highest position is flawed. Also the statement that all forms of phenomena are empty of true existence needs a qualifier as to the exact meaning of the term 'existence'. Indeed, the subject of what 'existence' is or is not is worthy of a complete treatise. Indelibly bound to this subject is the question of *what exactly is* a Buddha, and how does such a one 'exist' after all *saṃsāric* attributes have been eliminated. The question of existence is answered by focussing upon the Void, where experience of it proves the existence of an experiencer, an 'existent'. In existing thus we have an example of what can be considered a 'true existence' that is not annihilated. In many ways the doctrine of the Void has historically been the 'middle way' for Buddhists. It is the 'middle' because *śūnyatā* stands between *saṃsāra* and *dharmakāya*.

Since the appearance of Tantric philosophy the focus has moved from *śūnyatā* to the *dharmakāya*, the higher ground from which the entire epitome of Buddhist wisdom stems. Here then the teaching of the Dharmakāya Way rests, and in time will reveal a new 'middle way' wherein *śūnyatā* is the base and the verities of cosmos (cosmic Mind) represents the higher attribute for which to aspire, making what is now considered as the *dharmakāya* the 'middle way'. Such progression of the possibilities of the human psyche is not inconceivable, in fact it is well within the grasp of the highest Bodhisattvas.

Again quoting from Lopez:

> It is the position of the Mādhyamikas—both the Svātatrikas and Prāsaṅgikas—that the two truths are neither exactly the same nor completely different.
>
> Four reasonings that refute the position that the two truths are different entities are set forth in the *Sutra Unravelling the Thought (Saṃdhinirmocana)*. If conventional truths and ultimate truths were different entities, then the reasoning consciousness realizing the final mode of being of an object could not eliminate an ignorant consciousness conceiving that object to be truly existent because the final nature of the object—an ultimate truth—and the object itself—a conventional truth—would be different entities such that the emptiness of the object could not be the final mode of being of the object itself. In other words, understanding the final nature of the object—its emptiness—would have nothing to do with understanding the object itself, whereby it would be possible to understand the object's final nature while conceiving the object to be truly existent. It would thus be impossible to overcome the conception of true existence and highest enlightenment would be impossible.[29]

29 Lopez, *A Study of Svātantrika*, 212-213.

Three further rationalities are presented demonstrating the sameness of the two truths. Similar arguments are then put forth explaining why the two truths cannot be exactly the same:

> Thus, the sutra presents four absurd consequences that would be entailed if the two truths were different and four absurd consequences if the two truths were not different. Gyel-tsap notes that all eight of these are consequences that imply the opposite. Thus, the first four imply that the two truths are not different and the last imply that they are different. Is this one of the so-called "paradoxes" that allegedly abound in Buddhist literature, leaving us exactly where we started? The sutra has explained why the two truths must be the same and why they cannot be exactly the same. According to the Ge-luk, the relationship of the two truths is one of being the same entity but different reverses (*ngo bo gcig dang ldog pa tha dad*). For the two phenomena to be the same entity means that they do not appear to be different to direct perception (*pratyakṣa, mngon sum*); they are indivisible. If this is the case, an apparent problem arises when it is asserted that the two truths are the same entity. According to Mādhyamika, when emptiness—an ultimate truth—is directly perceived by a non-Buddha, the phenomenon which is the basis of that emptiness—a conventional truth—does not appear. When a conventional truth is directly perceived by a non-Buddha, emptiness does not appear. The two truths are only perceived simultaneously by a Buddha. In this case, how can the two be the same entity if they appear separately to direct perception? The answer given is that to be the same entity means that the two phenomena in question do not appear *to be different* to direct perception. This does not imply that they must appear simultaneously to all direct perceivers. Form does not appear to a sentient being directly realizing the emptiness of a form. Emptiness does not appear to a sentient being directly perceiving a form. This does not mean, however, that the two appear to be different. When both a conventional truth and its emptiness appear to a direct perceiver, that is, when they appear to a Buddha, they do not appear to be different. Form and emptiness are the same entity, but this does not imply that they both must appear to all consciousnesses directly perceiving one or the other.[30]

30 Ibid., 215-216, where Lopez quotes in depth from the *Saṃdhinirmocana*.

From my earlier comments we can see why 'the two truths are neither exactly the same nor completely different', because they are in the process of an unfolding continuum of one perpetually manifesting by way of the other by means of their 'relative nature'. If there was no such relative nature then the two truths would be completely different, and we would get the absurdities explained above. Relativity is what unravels 'the so-called "paradoxes" that allegedly abound in Buddhist literature'. When one is seen in context of the other then 'the ultimate' will be seen to include the conventional and its emptiness will be observed in stark clarity.

Also, from the perspective of relativity, we see that the statement 'The two truths are *only* perceived simultaneously by a Buddha' is also partly an untruth. Upon the path to liberation a 'direct perceiver' may indeed either reside in the domain of conventional truth, or else gain the 'taste' of *śūnyatā*. However, once a being has stabilised his/her awareness in *dharmakāya* then from that vantage point *saṃsāra* is accessible at will without losing the stance in *śūnyatā*. The path of liberation is a process, a continuum, that is not a sluggishly flowing stream, but more like a torrent, with many vortices of realisation wherein high revelations of the ultimate truth are possible before merging back into the general current (conventional truth). As well as receiving enlightened perceptions, before falling back into mundane states of consciousness, different degrees of enlightenment can be gained. There may be a final end result, the attainment of a Buddha, but the path of getting there and the many revelations upon the way are important and cannot be dismissed. The great ones, such as Nāgārjuna, Milarepa, or Tsongkhapa, can therefore arise to describe the process to us, and present the benefits of their enlightened experiences before and after their enlightenment.

The difference between such great ones and the Buddha, is that the Buddha has 'thus gone'[31] to the other shore of cosmic livingness, whereby his 'time-continuum' or 'true existence' is no longer relegated to our earth sphere of activity, whereas theirs is. Because Buddhists have not developed the language or concepts whereby they can adequately explain the activities of such a 'thus gone' one in cosmos they often, through the haze of devotional accolade, exaggerate the characteristics of

31 The translation of the term Tathāgata.

a Buddha. We thus have concepts such as the only ones who can perceive the two truths simultaneously are Buddhas. Except the qualification I have just given, little distinguishes a Buddha and those that have attained a similar degree of enlightenment as he, but who have relegated to stay on a while longer with earth realm activities for compassionate grounds because their Bodhisattvic activity is still needed. Not all that have attained a similar degree of enlightenment as he did manifest as world teachers. Many other roles exist for them in the halls of Shambhala. Confusion has arisen because some Buddhist authors have hypothesised that there aught to be a real distinction. There is little however to be made[32] because when an enlightened awareness transcends space-time considerations it can be anywhere and know everything (e.g., of the contents of a Buddha's Mind-Space). Certainly direct perception of such relatively simple identifications as the nature of the simultaneity of the 'two truths as one' is automatically obtained.

Ultimately—phenomena may be empty, but the meaning of the word 'existence', or more succinctly stated, 'Life', needs to be better analysed by Buddhists, and must be studied as such. It is more than just the appearance and disappearance of forms, it is more than the Void. It is that which is the causative agent for the changing phenomena, which uses periodical vehicles, and 'objects', which are not truly existent. It is that which utilises the Void as a zone of comprehensive rest from phenomena, an interlude before further outward expansion. *'True existence',* seen in terms of the principle of Life, but not substance, is in reality all there is and nothing is void of it. It is inclusive of the being/non-being dichotomy. Without true existence nothing could be, and for this reason *saṃsāra* and the consciousness that perceives it exists (which is accepted by the Prāsaṅgika as conventional reality). Therefore I agree with the statement 'It would thus be impossible to overcome the conception of true existence and highest enlightenment would be impossible', if it refers to objects or things. However if it also refers to the principle of Life, then the statement is untrue. Indeed, this thesis purports that the highest enlightenment is *only possible* because of 'true existence', the *Life* governing the evolutionary process, that directs forms and things to ultimate Buddhahood.

32 The distinctions that exist are perceived of in terms of Ray lines, the chosen cosmic Path, and Initiation status; subjects dealt with in the later volumes of this series.

Life connects all periodical changes from one appearance to another appearance of any form of phenomena, and tracks the associated changes of bundles of aggregates and related *saṃskāras* to conclusion in a progressive manner. No change of any form is wasted or uselessly occurs (except through the ignorant manipulations of human beings), because it is all directed by a higher embodying principle that is not a form *per se,* but is actively aware and wilfully directive according to the principles of an enlightened Mind in operation. Indeed, understanding exactly what this principle called 'Life' (explained later in terms of the *tathāgatagarbha*, the Buddha-womb within us all[33]) is, and the process producing its outward expression, constitutes what I here call the Dharmakāya Way. Once this Life is understood then many of the above-mentioned paradoxes disappear.

How the Mādhyamika define 'true existence' may be different from the way I have,[34] but the fact remains that there is true existence, otherwise there would and could not be the inherent urge of consciousness to progress towards enlightenment. From darkness (ignorance) to the demonstration of great light (awareness) is the way set for all human units to travel, if Buddhahood is to eventually be gained by all. Without such a principle there could be no evolutionary process in Nature, or any way for that defined as *saṃsāra* to appear[35] or be sustained in such a manner that Buddhist philosophers could arise and argue or deny the fact of 'true existence'. It is the principle of Life that calls all into being, and that same principal works to its ending also. In this light the Buddha can be defined as one that has so firmly identified with the principle of Life that he embodies all of its characteristics without reservation. A Buddha is thus in complete command of the phenomena found in the known universe, as he embodies the laws governing all forms of transmutations from one state of existence to another. For this reason the two truths become one for him, because from the still reservoir of the Void come the Sounds (mantras) that control the manifestation of *saṃsāra*. These Sounds are the resonating energy that are an effect of adamantine Law,

---

33 Later extended in terms of the concept of a Monad.

34 Presumably their focus is upon the Hindu concept of the *ātman*.

35 The other reason said to be the cause of its appearance is the blind chance of materialist thinkers, but in such a case there could be no directive *karma,* or progressive evolutionary development to Buddhahood. Chaos would reign supreme.

and which are not transient, or perceptible to phenomenal change, but which causes modifications, ripples, in the fabric of space-time whereby phenomena, such as known and analysed in the conventional mode, can be made to appear or disappear.[36]

Accordingly, the mode of persistence of *saṃsāra*, i.e., the root cause of the cycle of Dependent Origination, as well as the question 'where does ignorance stem from?', needs to be adequately explained by the Mādhyamika. Answers must be provided in their current ontology not just for the human kingdom, but for all other kingdoms in Nature, where such a thing as 'ignorance' does not effectively exist. Ignorance, after all, is a human label for lack of knowledge *by humans*, who have developed consciousnesses/intellects possessing varying degrees of ignorance levels. (Therefore the Buddha was only concerned with educating humans when he gave out the teachings of Dependent Origination.) How can one possibly define 'ignorance levels' for entities that do not have consciousness or intelligence? Where is the proverbial yardstick that can measure such? Ignorance consequently is not an applicable term to the kingdoms below the human. A crystalline rock, a tree or insect, for instance, is ignorant of nothing, it simply does not have the capacity to know or to not know, and from this perspective it could be existing in a form of serene enlightenment. This is because from where it is at, on its own level, it may have reached the end point of the evolutionary march of its particular kingdom.

The fact that ignorance is the foundation to the cycle of Dependent Origination is meaningless, except for humans. If ignorance is the start of the wheel of Dependent Origination then logically this implies that ignorance drives all that we come to know to be, even the quest for liberation on to conclusion. Here, right from the start the entire philosophy of Dependent Origination falls apart, unless a different tact is used, which centres around the question 'what is it that drives the quest to overcome ignorance from the beginning of things, so that ignorance can be overcome and the quest for liberation brought to a conclusion, where even an enquiring mind ceases?'[37] The answer provided above is 'the principle of Life', yet exactly what this principle

36 Sound here equates with what Dudjom Rinpoche calls 'Secret Mantra'.

37 The later chapter on Dependent Origination shall further delve into this philosophy, and is introduced here by way of introduction.

is still needs definition. Many more words and concepts must yet flow before a reasoning mind is enlightened.

For general *saṃsāra* something other than ignorance must produce progressive evolution, and what this 'something other' is, is not answered by mere acceptance or by asserting the dogma of the Void. Also, how are ignorance and *vāsanā* (the driving energy causing the evocation of *saṃskāras)* tied in such a way that liberation from the wheel is possible for the lesser kingdoms in Nature? (Here the questions of exactly what is sentience, how does it come about, and what does it evolve into, arises.) A major query for all Buddhists consequently should be 'What in fact is ignorance, how did it come to be in the first place to start the wheel of dependence turning?' Also, if 'something' is truly ignorant then it is void—void of everything that it is ignorant of*?* Is therefore ignorance but another term for the Void? Or does ignorance (a state of not being aware) represent the beginning of something of which enlightenment is the ending? (A vast philosophy of causation of phenomena is veiled in all of these questions.) By this is meant that clearly there is the process of evolution, and this is the evolution of 'something', not merely consciousness, and that 'something' is not the Void. This leads us to the inevitable conclusion that there is an inherent 'true existence' underlying phenomena, that until a better term is found we can call 'Life'. We could even use that much denigrated and maligned word in Buddhist metaphysics, *'soul'*. It is a term that needs to be resurrected and dressed with cogent unassailable reason to produce its proper colouring and apparel of light. This is unavoidable.

This thing called Life *is true existence*,[38] and certainly is not destroyed upon experience of the Void. In fact there could be no such experience without it, and because of it the Void itself can be considered void of being void, meaning that there is really no true Void, because it is permeated with Life.

38 The Hindu concept of an *ātman* is not the factor here, as the errors in the ontology related to it have been adequately demonstrated by Buddhists. In denying this principle however, through the formulation of an alternative philosophy, certain flaws, or rather 'gaps' in the Buddhist rhetoric manifested, which will be revealed and rectified in this treatise. Fundamental to this rectification process are the concepts revolving around the principle of Life. Terminology shall be found, and some already introduced, whereby this new view can be elaborated and made consistent with the *buddhadharma*.

Also it is said by the Prāsaṅgikas that *karma* is a conventional truth. This may be true from one perspective. Their reasoning is that because transient things are 'annihilated' when absorbed into *śūnyatā*, so then the type of *karma* that caused the transience to flower in the first place is also annihilated. Yet logically we can deduce that without *karma* there can be no *śūnyatā* (the quest for it or for the actual experience). In reality *karma* is not annihilated, or ended, it simply changes from one form to another, in one case it accommodates the process of perpetual change, and in another the quiescence of the Void, and then the mode of travel of a Buddha in cosmos. For a Buddha therefore the *karma* that ties one to the earth sphere has changed to the type of *karma* that facilitates his experience in *parinirvāṇa* and the way he interrelates with similar 'thus gone' ones. *Karma* can therefore also be considered an ultimate truth in the same way that *śūnyatā* is. There is much concerning it that is ill-conceived and omitted in Buddhist hermeneutics and logic. By presenting only part of the truth Buddhists have not properly answered the fundamentals as to what makes up life as we know it, and this produces a complacent attitude of knowingness, which in reality is but knowledge of half-truths.

4

East and West, the Mahāmudrā of the Two Truths

The need for an Eastern and Western integration

To obtain enlightenment in this age of the internet both Eastern and Western thought processes must be comprehended. This is because a mass of information is available at one's fingertips and our libraries are crammed with a multitude of books containing the gain of thousands of years of religious and philosophic texts. The ability to quickly access the information needed concerning esoteric and religious subjects has therefore enabled a far faster learning procedure for people, and this is reflected in the requirements to be developed by those aspiring for enlightenment in modern times. Such a path necessitates uniting the meditative thinking style of the Eastern Mahāyāna Buddhists (whose focus is the philosophy concerning the Bodhisattva path) with the ordered Western process of storing concrete bits of information in such a way that logical and computer-like quick, accurate deduction of information is obtained. No longer should we allow meditative analytical processes that lack adequate attention to the detail of numbers, dates, and the accuracy of empirical facts, that Buddhism has presented. No longer can we have a full mind without heart-based understanding, that is the main Western approach. In one case a detailed rational mind in all religious and philosophical pursuits needs to be developed, and in the other case the principle of love must be utilised via scientific investigation. All must be harmonised via a meditative approach.

When developed this will allow the two halves to coalesce, making a pyramid, a vessel of light focussed upon the northern direction, wherewith aspirants to enlightenment can ascend and descend at will. We thus have the ascension of consciousness for enlightenment and the descent of revelation for the compassionate education and liberation of the all. The East-West interrelation produces the base of the pyramid. Thus will manifest a mystical experience of revelatory awareness as presented by the Easterners, but be fully expressed scientifically, as understood by the empirical consciousness of the Western mind. It must then be applied in detail to comprehend the great Plan or revelations from 'beyond the other shore' of the empirical mind. This Plan (emanating from the upholders of the principle of Life) is anchored into the consciousness of humanity in such a way that the 'beyond' is not so far away.

Indeed, the Buddhist enlightened consciousness is needed, and we need the Western mind. Together they form the two truths externalised in our civilisation, neither of which are currently manifesting properly. There are too many veils to enlightened reason or revelation still to be removed and revealed to humanity. When this finally happens on a large scale then the current cycle of human evolution will have reached its climax.

Too often Buddhists are found to be excessively engrossed in invocatory rituals focussed upon personality desires, whilst at the same time manifesting altruistic pronouncements. Such forms of activity produce benefits and should not be totally discarded, but need to be modified if the advanced stages of the path are to manifest. Practitioners should have a broad holistic view that is truly reflective upon the way others can be helped by what they do. Self focus must disappear altogether. Gaining right knowledge should not be ignored through zealous dogmatic focus upon ritualistic detail. Such focus can produce the manifestation of forms of ignorance, akin to a child ensconced in a game or a toy he likes which is based upon a vaster world of reality. Much depends upon the enlightenment level of the preceptor as well as the inner qualifications of the practitioner if beneficent fruit is to be produced.

The problem generally with Buddhist thought is that it is not properly universal. It lacks a continuing stream of thought-moments sequenced into a broad picture of detailed knowledge of everything pertainable to *saṃsāra*, which is needed if one is to wisely activate *bodhicitta*. This Eastern approach manifests a vertical meditative impression, but what also needs to be encompassed is the Western approach which is a horizontal or broad field of empirical knowledge. Easterners thus generally need to possess more facts about things in order to properly serve humanity and develop the enlightened Mind in this present epoch.

That experienced by either the present Western or Eastern approach is a major part of the circle or sphere of expansive inclusive enlightenment. The particular forms of experiences by these parties are however generally too curtailed into a narrow schema of activity, where little understanding manifests of the repercussions flowing from the types of experiential forms of activity undertaken. Mental-emotional walls of non-acceptance by either party are created by their aura of knowingness, where emotional zeal feeds the wrongly faceted mind. We therefore have walls of limitations blocking moments of possible revelatory standing.

The evils of the Western approach are well known, producing the separative, competitive and avaricious forms of societies and governments we now have. The cupidity evolved is antithetical to the best interests of the whole. We also have the marvels of Western technology leading to the war machines of the nations. The errors of the Eastern approach are harder to ascertain because they are subtler, but they lack proper perceptiveness of practical holistic approaches to meeting the world's needs. Energy contacts (e.g., types of ideas) manifest via a wall of belief systems, which gets focussed back onto, or into the personal self and its little world of activity, thus feeding pride and a sense of accomplishment. Accordingly, the appearance of a falsely contented 'mindfulness' and/or state of love for the 'other' manifests with no true knowledge bank for the understanding of how to properly give. Such a one cannot thus truly serve as a Bodhisattva should.

A sense of timelessness by those engrossed in the Eastern form of consciousness creates an illusional cul-de-sac which leads to a misuse or ignorance of the importance of time. Western forms of activity on the other hand become too focussed upon time considerations, whereby consciousness becomes over focussed upon its tiny part in the scheme of things, thereby creating illusion. The mental-emotional walls in both cases are formed due to a type of wilful resistance to broadening one's thought horizons.

Those prone to 'empty mind' have to be initiated into knowing the empirical nature of things, right timing sequences, and all other accomplishments that the West can offer, if the enlightened bliss-state of a complete revelatory knowing is to be attained. The intellect should not be irrationally dispensed with; it is included in the all, so it has to be exposed, made valid, enlightened, and fully activated when rising above the waters of emotion. True intelligent awareness means being consciously aware of the now, by being receptive to the intuitive awareness of the Heart (which is often confused with the mind in Buddhism).

The consciousness of the Heart allows one to truly conceive of the whole or 'the all'. This whole manifests something like a cell containing the orifices of expansion and thus enlightenment. It envelops the forces of dissecting, piercing, segregating, discriminating, building and of naming all that holds consciousness together. It is made firm, cognizable, by the path it creates through space. It is revealed in its entirety by light, with aspects of its deeper secrets instantly illumined by a lightning flash of revelation.

One should learn to think as or with lightning; it cuts asunder truth from grey matter, that substance which is void of the vibrancy that is the basis of all vital life. Substance that is vibrant is brightened ethereal matter, that like light, pushes aside darkness. Darkness has many shades of semi-dark. There is no darkness in a light beam—it cuts its trail and illumines the mind—hence enlightenment. People need to be perceptibly aware of the abstracted nature of illumined space, which manifests via etheric substance of different qualities in the one integral cellular system. Perception traverses through layers of substance that either offer resistance to or facilitate illumined perception, according to the hue or density of the grey. When the grey has been dissipated then illumination proceeds like lightning. Thus we can define the nature of the path to liberation in terms of the nature of the substance encountered, which must be refined through right livingness and meditative unfoldment, if the Clear Light is to be perceived.

There needs to be a meeting of minds between the theistically inclined religionist of the West and the (Eastern) Buddhists or Hindus, where the secret doctrines of both forms of attainment are exchanged. The Christian[1] is concerned with an upward aspiration to a central omnipotent Demiurge, thence through faith in the providence provided, and via the vicarious atonement of Christ-Jesus who died for the sins of many (therefore pursuing the ideal Bodhisattva life), salvation from the woes of this life are possible. His Buddhist brother looks inward, through a denial of the concept of 'self', to develop wisdom and *bodhicitta*, for the liberation of all sentient beings from *saṃsāra*. Both have much to teach the other, though first the exoteric of both religions must give way to the esoteric (as is expounded in this treatise), then a philosophical congruence, effectively a mergence, of the two seemingly diametrically opposed dispensations is possible. Indeed, this is a necessity.[2] They should be viewed as two parts of a unified system, the *iḍā and piṅgalā naḍīs* revolving around the *suṣumṇā* channel of absolute unassailable truth.

Ignorance is the state of mind of the uninitiated. They see not how enlightenment shapes consciousness into blue, green, yellow and red. All These colours are then admixed to make brilliant white. Green makes the blue of love active in the mind. Blue illuminates the love of the all. Yellow unifies or harmonises the wilful discriminative abilities of red, producing inner vision. The brilliant white flashes lightning-like through vistas untold, fusing these cardinal colours; very meaningful to behold. (All produce the mastery of the All-accomplishing Wisdom.)

Such thinking is virtually meaningless to Westerners, but holds esoteric truth to Buddhists who are accustomed to meditative thought, here considered in terms of the colourings of the five Dhyāni Buddhas. But there are also inconsistencies in Buddhist thought needing amending. Illogic should not be purveyed as fact. It produces a lack of faith in the remainder of the doctrine that is perspicaciously correct, producing *karma* for the perpetuators. Clearly the illumined Mind must be brought

---

1 One could incorporate here the ideas and practices of the religions of 'the Book'; Christianity, Judaism, Islam, but such considerations would overly complicate matters. Hence I shall stay with a Buddhist/Hindu verses Christian paradigm, where the other two religions are broadly implied in the Christian approach (religious fundamentalism, belief in one God, etc).

2 My various writings will demonstrate the nature of this mergence.

to the West in its natural state and explained appropriately, not veiled with paradoxes, fantastical digests of mythical happenings or glossed by wistful speculative rhetoric concerning the supernatural or psychic domains. These domains do exist, and also the *siddhis* (psychic powers) of accomplished *yogins,* but more appropriate, logical explanations should now be promoted. Errors in logic such as the concept of transmigration of consciousness into animal bodies also need rectification.

So how do we weave the Western style of esoteric (and scientific) reasoning into Eastern thought to see where the errors might lie? If there indeed are errors, then correct pristine logic will weed them out, if not then the presented doctrine, which has stood the test of time will last forevermore, and little more need be said. The Western mind continuously looks mentalistically for contradictions, whereas the Eastern approach is to accept as truth mythologised accounts, if intuitively the information 'feels right', or accepted as right according to the traditions of a particular school of thought.

No matter the school of thought one belongs to, it is best to ascertain what truth is by seeking the wisest in that society, who are specialists in the target field of investigation. Universities are set up for this purpose in the West. In the Eastern monasteries, the teachings given to earnest practitioners of the *dharma* concern the gaining of enlightenment. The aspirant is often exhorted to seek the best teachers irrespective of the lineage. This is certainly correct. Results are ascertained if truth is sought at all costs by the earnest seeker.

Whenever the mind is active then we have the question of interpretation and of different pathways of analytical deduction, which can produce controversy between the schools of thought. The same topic analysed from different views (e.g., the Eastern and Western approaches, theistic and non-theistic religions) often generate contradictory statements to those not initiated into the subtleties and terminology of the views. The point of integration between various truthful philosophies, albeit with differing rhetoric or terminology, is rarely attained, except by the most astute thinkers. These thinkers are the enlightened in our societies.

Even the Buddha was accused of giving contradictory statements, as the extract below from *Buddhist Hermeneutics* asserts.

At the beginning of the seventh chapter of the *Saṃdhinirmocanasūtra,* the bodhisattva Paramārthasamudgata is puzzled by the apparent contradiction in the Buddha's teaching. He points out that on numerous occasions the Buddha has taught that the aggregates *(skandha),* the truths *(satya),* and the constituents *(dhātu)* exist by their own character *(svalakṣaṇa),* yet on other occasions he has said that all phenomena lack entityness *(svabhāva),* that all phenomena are unproduced, unceased, originally quiescent, and naturally passed beyond sorrow. The Buddha responds:

> Listen, Paramārthasamudgata, and I will explain to you what I intended when I said that all phenomena are without entityness, all phenomena are unproduced, unceased, originally quiescent, and naturally passed beyond sorrow. Paramārthasamudgata, I was thinking of these three aspects of the nonentityness *(niḥsvabhāva)* of phenomena when I taught that all phenomena are without entityness: the nonentityness of character, the nonentityness of production, and the ultimate nonentityness.

The Buddha's answer, briefly stated, is that his teaching that all phenomena lack entityness should be taken as a qualified apophasis. He had in mind three different types of nonentityness which qualify the three natures (*trilakṣaṇa*), the imaginary *(parikalpita),* the dependent *(paratantra),* and the consummate *(parinṣpanna).* The meaning and implications of the doctrine of the three natures are topics of considerable controversy among the Yogācāra, Svātantrika, and Prāsaṅgika philosophers. According to the sūtra, imaginary natures are the entities and qualities that thought imputes to conditioned phenomena. These imputations are merely mental designations and thus do not exist by their own character. Dependent natures are the conditioned phenomena which are the objects of thought's operation and which serve as the bases of imputation of thought and terminology. These impermanent phenomena arise in dependence on causes and cannot produce themselves, and thus are said to lack entityness of production. The consummate nature is the fact that the imaginary nature is not established in conditioned phenomena. It is the selflessness of phenomena *(dharmanairātmya),* according to the sūtra.[3]

---

3 Lopez Jr., *Buddhist Hermeneutics,* 57.

When analysing the apparent contradictory statements above; 'the Buddha has taught that the aggregates *(skandha),* the truths *(satya),* and the constituents *(dhātu)* exist by their own character *(svalakṣaṇa),* yet on other occasions he has said that all phenomena lack entityness *(svabhāva),* that all phenomena are unproduced, unceased, originally quiescent, and naturally passed beyond sorrow', we see but a version of the two truths. The Buddha therefore did not have a lapse of reason, he plainly knew what he was saying, and was referring to an esoteric truth that was not properly understood at that time, but which later became the normative line of Madhyamaka rhetoric. There is the interrelated nature of phenomena with mind, and their antithesis, needed for the obtainment of enlightenment. At first conventional truth is presented, when he states that the aggregates, the truths, and the constituents 'exist by their own character', i.e., have a phenomenal reality. We next have the ultimate truth presented to us in that 'all phenomena lack entityness'. This could be understood because of the foundations laid in the Hindu society by *yogins* who had become *arhats.*

This quote is important as it clearly indicates that the Buddha had in his mind a form of logic concerning the interdependent nature of the two truths. They appear contradictory, but in reality are together responsible for the enlightenment of all sentient beings.

One type, the ultimate truth, concerns the realisation of *śūnyatā.* However, when the nature of the conventional reality is simultaneously explored to conclusion via the evocation of *bodhicitta* then an awakening into the *dharmakāya* is produced. If just the process of unfolding the conventional reality is fully realised then the revelation of what the *ālayavijñāna* confers is experienced. The three abovementioned terms are not interchangeable, they have distinct meanings in relation to each other, but all are interrelated, part of the same integral process of revelation. The esoteric implications of the Buddha's statements therefore relate to obtaining the three enlightenment levels. They also have a direct relation to the Yogācāra doctrine of the 'three natures'. The 'imaginary nature', of what conspires in the domain of mind, evokes the *ālayavijñāna.* The 'consummate nature' expresses *śūnyatā.* The 'dependent natures' producing the conventional truth lead eventually to the *dharmakāya* revelation, where the imaginary, the dependent and the consummate are all integrated into a blissful union of revelatory expression. Here we see that the 'imaginary' does not necessarily refer just to illusional images, but to all phenomena that appears in the mind by way of awakening Mind. Such phenomena can therefore pertain to the real as well as to the unreal. By 'real' here is meant that which is experienced in the inner universe of the liberated ones.

The Mahāmudrā of the two truths

It should be noted that the basic doctrine elaborated in this treatise is actually a detailed version of the Mahāmudrā uniting the two truths. The endeavour is to extend the lines of reasoning concerning the fusion of these two truths to their logical conclusion, and to explain, as much as possible, the ramifications of such an investigation. Concerning the basics of this union Geshe Kelsang Gyatso states:

> The mahamudra that is the union of the two truths is also known as the union needing practice. The union not needing practice is attained at the first moment of the path of no more learning, which is simultaneous with the attainment of perfect buddhahood[4]...According to the mahamudra of secret mantra it is the pure illusory body that is the deceptive truth and the meaning clear light that is the ultimate truth. In general, according to sutra, any phenomena other than emptiness itself is a deceptive, or conventional, truth. Because meditation upon the illusory body emphasizes such deceptive truths the illusory body itself is known by this name. In a similar fashion, because meditation upon the meaning clear light emphasizes emptiness, it itself is called ultimate truth. However, the meaning clear light is not actually an ultimate truth; because it is a mind it must necessarily be a deceptive truth. It is the *object* of this mind that is the ultimate truth[5]....The pure illusory body develops from the very subtle wind upon which the mind of initial meaning clear light is mounted and is attained automatically and without effort the instant this mind ceases. Thus, the pure illusory body is attained at the first instant of the mind of black near-attainment of the reverse order[6]....Afterwards, by depending

4 Geshe Kelsang Gyatso, *Clear Light of Bliss, Mahamudra in Vajrayana Buddhism,* (Wisdom Publications, London, 1982), 209.

5 Ibid., 210.

6 Ibid., 210-211.

> upon one of the internal or external methods mentioned earlier, the yogi will experience all the serial order signs from the mirage up to and including the all empty clear light. These signs are experienced in conjunction with meditation upon emptiness and when the all empty sign is perceived this is again the meaning clear light. When this is attained the yogi simultaneously reaches the mahamudra that is the union of the two truths. That yogi has assembled the pure illusory body and the meaning clear light at the same time. Even though the union needing practice has now been attained, the yogi will again arise from the meaning clear light. Thus in order to attain buddhahood there are further practices to be performed.[7]

In speaking of 'wind' (*prāṇa*) Kelsang was trying to elaborate the way that the two truths manifest in the form of *prāṇas* flowing, producing effects in a *yogin's* mind. The entire yogic process (denoted 'secret mantra') then works to refine gross attributes of consciousness ('deceptive truths', the *saṃskāras* conveyed by the *prāṇas)* until the 'pure illusory body' develops. Presumably the implication here is that of a *nirmāṇakāya,*[8] a manifestation body totally controlled by the yogin's Mind. Eventually the attributes of consciousness become so refined that the 'empty clear light' is obtained. The term 'Clear Light' utilised here and throughout this treatise is a descriptive phrase indicating the radiance achieved that is the Mind of an enlightened One, that though 'empty', nevertheless is replete with wisdom and compassionate insight. The term 'emptiness' really means empty of transient phenomena, of any form of clinging or attachment to *saṃsāra.* It does not mean an absolute vacuum, or the annihilation of whatever one can conceive of as existence. Hence what remains is Mind, an abstracted prescient, non-attached perceiver of whatever is/is-not. The entire subject of yogic transformation of *saṃskāras* is provided in Volume 5, where the *Bardo Thödol* is treated as a meditation text, and introduced earlier under the heading of the 'Yogācāra Mādhyamika view of the Nyingmapa'.

The concept of 'cessation' does not explain this Clear Light or

---

7 Ibid., 211.

8 *Nirmāṇakāya:* 'transformation body', the emanation (form) body of a Buddha. One of the three bodies or vestures of a Buddha *(trikāya).* It is the outer or phenomenal appearance, the tangible something that can be contacted on the realms of illusion, the incarnation body. The other two vestures are *dharmakāya,* and *sambhogakāya.*

what it actually reveals. If there is light then it must shine in relation to 'something', i.e., it must illumine 'something' in order for revelation to be obtained. Emptiness/*śūnyatā* is a medium for the expression or conveyance of that light. It represents but one half of the equation of the fusion of the two truths, the other is phenomena of some sort (i.e., as an aspect of the clarified Mind), albeit highly refined. How the two stand together, fused as one, is what this light reveals. Hopefully, the philosophical foundation for the explanation of what exactly *is* revealed thereby can now be laid. A pathway for such understanding can be presented within the framework of what presently exists in the Madhyamaka and Yogācāra philosophy, forcing a fusion of both streams of realisation, as the two truths are really exemplifications of the different ways these two philosophical systems view the nature of consciousness. Consequently, the nature of *what* is identified with when the *yogin* simultaneously assembles 'the pure illusory body' and the Clear Light is a major topic of this treatise. In relation to this the mechanism that makes the rebirth of consciousness possible, and indeed a necessity, shall also be provided.

A clear understanding of all the issues involved concerning the seminal Madhyamaka doctrine of the two truths allows us to delve further into other related subjects. We can then correctly assert a position, or to find counter arguments, if any exist, to the given position of the concepts of the negation of a 'self'. It also enriches the background philosophy from which one may proceed to probe deeper into the nature of being/non-being. Consequently I shall quote from the book *Jñānagarbha on the Two Truths*. (An eighth century Svāntantrika Mādhyamika philosopher.) What is provided from these extracts from Jñānagarbha is *a cogent methodology* whereby the *sūtras, śastras* and Tantras of Buddhism can be analysed. I shall utilise this methodology throughout this treatise so that the veiled meanings of the texts can be found. The extract therefore provides a valuable key for any hermeneutic investigation.

> Bhāvaviveka set the pattern for the Svāntantrika tradition when he argued that a Mādhyamika accepts *(siddha)* the existence of things in a relative sense, but denies them ultimately. With this distinction in hand, he was able to unravel the contradictions in some of Nāgārjuna's most paradoxical verses. Verse 18.8 of the *Madhyamakakārikās* is a good example. Here Nāgārjuna says:

> Everything is real or unreal, real and unreal, and neither real nor unreal – this is the teaching of the Buddhas.

This is a truly bewildering utterance—at least until the commentator begins his work. Bhāvaviveka explains the verse as follows:

> All *dharmas* are like *nirvāṇa*; but we accept as real, in a mundane sense, certain things that are conducive to the acquisition of prerequisites *(saṃbhāra)* for the understanding of ultimate truth and are real according to ordinary conventional usage. We also accept that some are unreal. Therefore, *conventionally*
>
> Everything is real or unreal.

As the Lord said. "Whatever ordinary people accept as real, I speak of as real. Whatever ordinary people do not accept, I speak of as unreal."

On the other hand, [the Lord] also said that everything is real, in the sense that the sense media *(āyatana),* such as the eye, and objects, such as form, do not contradict *conventional truth.* He also said that everything is unreal, since *ultimately* nothing is established in its own right *(svabhāvena),* like magic. Hence nothing is what it seems. With regard to both truths, then,

[Everything] is real and unreal.

At the moment of insight *(abhisamaya),* a yogi is completely free from concepts of the reality of *dharmas;* therefore,

> [Everything] is neither real nor unreal –
> this is the teaching of the Buddhas.

Bhāvaviveka dissolves the paradoxes by treating the verse as a mixture of the relative and the ultimate perspectives—perspectives that yield first one result and then another.[9]

Bhāvaviveka treats the interpretation of the verses in true esoteric fashion. Here we can add that the phrase:

1. *'Everything is real or unreal'* refers to conventional truth, which is ultimately productive of the *ālayavijñāna.* This happens via the knowledge and wisdom obtained through *bodhicitta* directed

---

9 M.D. Eckel, *Jñānagarbha on the Two Truths*, (Motilal Banarsidass, Delhi, 1992), 35-36.

to the phenomena of *saṃsāra*, and which allows one to master it completely. The resultant mental gain is collectively stored as the *ālayavijñāna*. The 'unreal' here refers to images and phantasms of the mind. The mind knows such images to be untrue, through comparison with what is obtained from stable impressions obtained via sense perceptions and through intellectual deduction, thus proving to itself that the objects of the phantasm do not exist. The conventional mind can also perceive the unreality of *saṃsāra*, once the logic pertaining to phenomena has been cognised. This mind can accept the truth of suffering and understand the need to escape suffering (which it experiences) by treading the Eightfold Path, and the way of the Bodhisattva. The conventional mind then begins to transform into unconventionality as higher truths are experienced and one enters the esoteric world of enlightened being. The collective knowledge of all minds, the *ālayavijñāna*, can then be experienced for what it is. *Śūnyatā* and the *dharmakāya* are accessible via the *ālayavijñāna* if the elements of mind are transformed into the Clear Light by the yogic process.

2. *'[Everything] is real and unreal'* refers to the true middle way of the *dharma* that ultimately produces complete comprehension of the nature of the *saṃsāric* universe and also to *śūnyatā*. It accepts both conditions of being/non-being, of *śūnyatā* (here 'the real', non-being) and phenomena ('the unreal', being) and works with both to the exclusion of neither, thus inevitably comes to know all that is/is-not. This then is the way to the *dharmakāya*.
3. *'[Everything] is neither real nor unreal'*, refers to the ultimate truth that is an expression of the experience of *śūnyatā*. It is a negatively worded aphorism (adopted by the Prāsaṅgika Mādhyamika) that neither accepts or rejects anything (hence their concept of 'middle way'). In their experience they can thereby come to know that which is real, the emptiness that is *śūnyatā*. But can a system of denials truthfully produce Buddhahood? A system of positive affirmations should logically produce a far more embracive level of revelation. Indeed this is so. The *dharmakāya* can eventually be experienced via a process of non-denial of every form of sensory data and then transmuting that which upon careful analysis is proven to be flawed and hence must be superseded. Nothing is at first rejected, but rather all is

accepted for analysis of what might provide a basis for transformation or transmutation. This transmuted base is then used as a platform for further realisation and revelation. Thus is established the stairway to complete enlightenment, the complete liberation of the Tathāgatas. The basis to such a path is well established in the Mahāmudrā and Vajrayāna teachings, but must also be fully integrated with the Western Way if the complete *maṇḍala* of accomplishment is to be achieved.

The Prāsaṅgika methodology therefore may produce liberation, but complete enlightenment, in the sense of what the *dharmakāya* pertains to, must be found by a different route. A system of denials cannot produce full comprehension of the nature of the all. The Dharmakāya Way concerns a fusion of all the other views indicated by the eight-armed cross of direction earlier explained, so that the result is not one or the other, it is both, and neither. Thus it is the *true middle way.*

We can add that one may follow the Mādhyamika path and progress relatively quickly to *śūnyatā*, but as a Bodhisattva one will not 'rest' there entirely, one will *still have to* build pathways backwards to the *ālayavijñāna* and forwards to the *dharmakāya* if progress into the mysteries of the Dhyāni Buddhas and Buddhahood is a goal. To be a Jina, a victorious one, means complete mastery of everything in the known and unknown universe. It cannot be obtained through a subtle avoidance of all extremes, or a denial of phenomena, thereby manifesting a form of non compliance with it. Thus, as Kelsang Gyatso stated, 'in order to attain Buddhahood there are further practices to be performed'.

If we interpreted the above in terms of Set Theory, then we get:

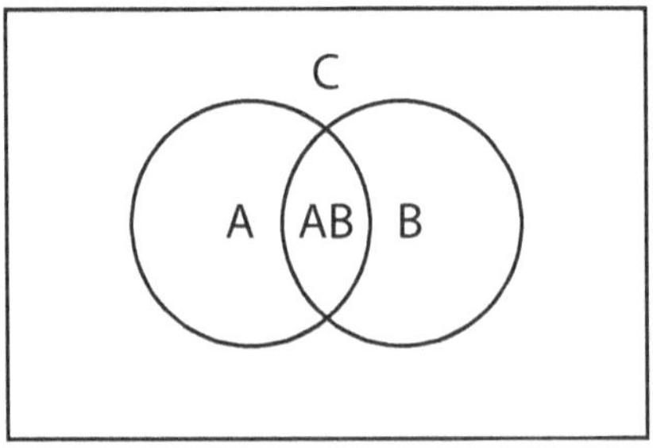

- A is inclusive of everything concerning the set of what is considered real, where the 'real' is translated as *śūnyatā*.

- B can be considered as the set of everything that is unreal, where the unreal is interpreted as *saṃsāra* .
- AB can be considered the set of that which combines portions of the real and unreal, which here can be translated as either the *śūnyatā-saṃsāra* integration, or the *tathāgatagarbha* residing in the *ālayavijñāna* environment, which will be explained later.
- C can be considered as the set of that which is neither the real or unreal, as well as both. It can thus be interpreted as the *dharmakāya.* Though C is enclosed (bounded) within a square for diagrammatical purposes, it can be considered as boundless, the All, that is inclusive of all the sets.

Eckel continues:

> If the argument [concerning the two truths—my note] stopped with the negation of distinctions it would be much less challenging than it is and, given Madhyamaka presuppositions, much less cogent. It would be equivalent to saying that there are two truths, but that from the perspective of one of them the other is groundless. To favour one perspective so completely over the other may seem necessary, but it offends the sense of balance that makes the Mādhyamikas search for the "middle" between extremes.
>
> Once Jñānagarbha has shown how the relative and ultimate perspectives produce different conclusions, the next step in the argument is to apply the ultimate perspective to the ultimate itself:
>
> > 16. From the standpoint of reason, the meaning of the words "ultimately [things] do not arise" also does not arise. Other [such statements] should be interpreted the same way.
> >
> > 17. [The Buddha] considers the relative and the ultimate to be identical in nature, because there is no difference between them. This is because reason also corresponds to appearances.
>
> To say that reason *(nyāya)* corresponds to appearances *(yathādaśana)* in Jñānagarbha's terminology is to say that the ultimate *(paramārtha)* is relative *(saṃvṛti).* This is a striking conclusion, but one that is consistent with everything that has gone before. Up to this point, he has tied affirmative statements that distinguish the two truths to statements showing that the distinctions do not ultimately apply. The ultimate is a rational cognition, as he explains in verse 4, but not a *real* cognition, as he explains in his refutation of self-cognition in verse

> 6. The relative is something that arises dependently, but ultimately nothing arises dependently. Now even the distinction between ultimate and relative falls away. From one perspective he states that the two are different, from another he says that even the ultimate is no more than a reflection of the relative.
>
> This argument is reminiscent of the contradictory, yet complementary relationship between the two truths in their moral aspect. From one perspective the two truths are distinct and have to be kept apart for the system to function, but from another perspective the two reinforce and complement each other. Someone who understands the system can hold the two perspectives together and not be confused by their apparent contradictions. To give up the attachments that stand in the way of action, it is important to understand that all distinctions are empty. But it is just as important to keep from being dazzled by the absence of distinctions and failing to put the awareness into practice. When Jñānagarbha turns the ultimate on the ultimate and finds it no different from the relative, he is giving the classic Madhyamaka argument for the return to the relative. The emptiness of emptiness itself compels a person to reappropriate and affirm, in a transformed way, the distinctions of the relative world.[10]

In the quotation above the point to be made is that the Mādhyamika's 'sense of balance that makes the Mādhyamikas search for the "middle" between extremes' gave us the wonderful system of philosophy revolving around the concept of *śūnyatā*. At the time it was formulated and developed this was the middle way between the then extant philosophic presentations. My contention is that it may form the middle ground between the Yogācāra-Vijñānavāda at one end of a see-saw and Tantric philosophy at the other end, yet from another perspective it forms one end of a see-saw and the Yogācāra-Vijñānavāda at the other. The fulcrum that integrates the two is the *dharmakāya* philosophy here disseminated (which can also be called the Mahāmudrā of the union between the Buddha and his Consort[11]), and which has previously been presented to Buddhism in a much more veiled form via their Tantras.

What is to be emphasised, and has already been somewhat elaborated, is Jñānagarbha's revelation that 'the ultimate *(paramārtha)* is relative *(saṃvṛta)*'. We can concur with this point wholeheartedly and

10 M.D. Eckel, *Jñānagarbha on the Two Truths*, 40-41.

11 The meaning of which shall be fully explored in the fifth Volume of this treatise.

can say that everything must be looked upon in relation to its relativity to everything else, even *śūnyatā* has its attributeless characteristics relative to that which is perceived to have attributes. It is specifically the philosophy of *relativity* that is to be expounded, for the concept opens the doorway to many revelations about the true nature of things.

Finally, the statement *'ultimately nothing arises dependently'* is not quite true (except from the perspective of that which *resides in* the ultimate and *never* leaves). It would rather be best to posit that ultimately everything arises from the meditation-Mind, is sustained by the activities of the mind/Mind, and is extinguished in the meditation-Mind. Everything is dependent upon what 'other' exists in that Mind for the formulation of whatever 'is' to come into being in the first place. What is known as Buddhist Philosophy is the outcome of such a process. Of course, one could contend, as Nāgārjuna tries in his *Vigrahavyāvartanī* (verse 29), that he has not presenting any philosophy (view) and therefore should be absolved from errors, but the fact is, if there is such a thing as truth, even the 'truth' of *śūnyatā*, then it 'remains', i.e., 'exists', and the meditation-Mind exists to cognise and utilise it for whatever purpose it has. Whether the mode of its utilisation constitutes a philosophy or not is open to debate. However, the meditation-Mind, or a Buddha-Mind, is self-sustaining, and self-evolving, irrespective of whether any mind attached to a mouth denies its existence. By 'self-evolving', it is meant that it has come from somewhere, and is going from there–to 'the other shore' of whatever was.

This phrase (of having gone 'to the other shore'), which is the central pillar or concept of the *Heart Sūtra (Vajrachhedeka)* is generally meant to refer to the attainment of utter liberation, of never having to return to incarnation. It can however, work both ways, i.e., a liberated Buddha can 'return' to *saṃsāra* to seed a receptive mind with enlightenment-impressions at the opportune moment, which may instigate a form of action that ultimately affects phenomena. It is an error to think that a Buddha cannot and does not work in this way, even after being 'utterly liberated', i.e., after having gained *parinirvāṇa*. There are many reasons for the continued manifestation of compassionate acts by 'thus gone' Buddhas, because *the karma* of the *dharma* transmission[12] remains between a Buddha and his disciples who are now high grade Bodhisattvas.

The statement in question may thus be true, relative to what is perceived as *śūnyatā*, but it has an invalidity in relation to the qualities of

12 *Guruparamparā*, or lineage tradition.

the *ālayavijñāna*, for therein are contained the *bījas* for things to arise, dependent upon other things or conditions, that allow consciousness to move. It is not true relative to the *dharmakāya*, for the *dharmakāya* supports both *śūnyatā* and the *ālayavijñāna*, and it empowers the *tathāgatagarbha* for all future Buddhas. Also the existence of the *ālayavijñāna* is dependent upon the *dharmakāya*. Herein arise the processes associated with the five Dhyāni Buddhas that appear relative and dependent upon each other. *Saṃsāra* is conditioned by the permutations of the five Wisdoms derived from these Jinas.

Humans who have not developed a meditation-Mind produce volitions and resultant *karma* through:

a. mental activities
b. desire-mind projections
c. pure automatic emotional or sense responses to external stimuli.

Even so, all such activities exist within the embrace of the meditation-Minds of the Lords of Karma, who adjust all volitions so that they eventually rebound on the perpetuator, producing a state of equalising harmony, leading ultimately to *śūnyatā*.

But how *śūnyatā* and the meditation-Mind relate to each other still needs clarification. Is *śūnyatā* but the extension of such a Mind, or does such a Mind arise from *śūnyatā*, or is neither the answer, or both? The volumes of this treatise will delve into such questions, however the explication necessitates the proper grounding of significant background information before the questions can be satisfactorily answered.

Having said this, it is also important to reemphasise that the two truths actually represent a Madhyamaka reasoning, whereas Vasubandhu implicates *three natures* in his treatise *Commentary on the separation of the Middle from Extremes.* Anacker states:

> Nāgārjuna posits only two kinds of truth, conventional and ultimate. It is here where Vasubandhu may argue. For a dual truth-scheme perhaps does not make the existence of confusion and suffering "real" enough. Vasubandhu's expedient of dividing reality into three, rather than two, fulfils this purpose.[13]

13 S. Anacker, *Seven Works of Vasubandhu*, (Motilal Banarsidass. Delhi, 2005), 194. Asaṅga and his brother Vasubandhu were the major instigators of the Yogācāra-Vijñānavāda system of philosophy.

Anacker states, quoting verse 1.2. from the above Commentary:

> "Therefore, everything is taught as neither empty nor non-empty, because of *its* existence, *its* non-existence, and *its* existence, and *this* is the Middle Path."

It is not empty, either because of emptiness or the construction of that which was not. Neither is it non-empty, because of the duality, object apprehended and subject apprehendor, and thus it has been taught, that "Everything compounded is called 'the construction of that which was not'; everything uncompounded is called 'Emptiness'", because of the existence of the construction of that which was not, because of the non-existence of duality, and the existence of emptiness in the construction of that which was not, and the existence of the construction of that which was not in emptiness. And *this* is the Middle Path: that everything is neither totally empty nor totally non-empty. And this is in accordance with passages in the *Prajñā-pāramitā-sūtras,* etc., which say: "All this is neither empty nor non-empty." Cf., *Kaushika-prajñā-pāramitā-sūtra.*[14]

The concept of 'the separation of the Middle from Extremes' is another way of depicting the major postulate elaborated in the section of this series termed *The I Concept,* where the nature of this 'middle ground' will be elaborated on, especially in relation to the philosophy of the *tathāgatagarbha.* We shall therefore gain a proper view as to why 'All this is neither empty nor non-empty'. First, a continuation of the analysis of the Mādhyamika reasoning needs to be undertaken, as found in 'The Seven-Fold Reasoning', 'Dependent Arising', the 'Diamond Slivers', the 'Non-Production from Others', the 'Four Extremes', etc. They provide the syllogistic and epistemic narrative whereby many aspects of the *dharma* can be correctly reasoned. A new analytical view dissecting ancient philosophy and its semantics can be accordingly provided, which should indeed prove valuable.

14 Ibid., 212.

5

The Sevenfold Reasoning Part A: The Introduction

Relativity and Nāgārjuna's *catuṣkoṭikā*

Having analysed the two truths the ground for the analysis of further facets of the Madhyamaka philosophy has been established. Now we shall specifically focus upon an exegetical enquiry into the ontology of what may or may not constitute a 'self'. In an attempt to fulfil this aim I shall quote extensively from the book *Meditation on Emptiness* by Jeffrey Hopkins,[1] as this is probably the most extensive coverage of the Prāsaṅgika-Madhyamaka philosophy by a Western author. Hopkins uses a detailed systematic approach to explain the logic of this school. This allows counter arguments to be produced where necessary.

During the translation of Sanskrit and Tibetan texts into English, meanings can change (thus of ideas that have developed over the course of millennia), however Hopkins has undoubtedly maintained as high a degree of accuracy as is possible regarding the intended meaning. Accordingly, this exposé hopefully will do justice to the integrity of the *buddhadharma* and can assist in comprehension of the difficult aspects of revealed texts for many generations of enquirers.

We shall start with the chapter of Hopkins' book entitled *Meditative Investigation.*[2] The sources for which he quotes, are Jam yang she pa's *Great Exposition Tenets,* Nga wang bel den's *Annotations,* and

1 J. Hopkins, *Meditation on Emptiness,* (Wisdom Publications, London,1983).

2 Ibid., 47.

translations from the works of Nāgārjuna, Buddhapālita and Candrakīrti. Therein he presents the sevenfold reasoning as set forth by Candrakīrti.

The first of these is given as *'Identifying the object negated in the theory of selflessness'*.[3] This concerns the thinking of 'I' and endeavouring to analyse its qualities.

The second is termed *'Ascertaining that selflessness follows from the reason'*. There it is stated:

> If the I is found to be neither inherently the same entity as the mind and body nor a different entity from them, then the I does not inherently exist.
>
> Through the seven-fold reasoning, one attempts to infer that the I does not inherently exist as it appears to do. Such an inference cannot be generated if one has not ascertained that non-inherent existence pervades, or occurs with, every instance of not being inherently the same as or different from the aggregates.[4]

Here we are given the basic duality, 'the same', 'or different', and this is a reasonable assumption to make because the already established logical fact is that both mind and body are transient. If this is so, the 'I' or I-concept is also transient and does not inherently exist. Also, if it is different from this transience, then it is real, eternal, and Buddhists have already logically rightfully presented the argument countermanding this, again denying the existence of an 'I'. The second possibility of a 'different entity' being *śūnyatā* also disproves the existence of an 'I', as *śūnyatā* is void of all such. So far, as the argument stands the Mādhyamika have already scored victory, and the rest of the dialogue is really redundant, except to present conclusive detail of evidence why there is no 'I'.

However, there are normally at least three answers or pathways to any analysis or definition of things, often four, five, and even seven or twelve. The major three constitute a basic duality, this or not this, with a third postulate somewhere in between, that is allied to either or both of the opposites. It stands in the middle and relates one to the other. Such a possibility is not hinted at in the above questioning, but in the middle between extremes important answers can normally be found.

---

3 Ibid.

4 Ibid., 47-48.

Such a possibility was in the mind of Vasubandhu, as shown in the earlier quotation from the book *The Seven Works of Vasubandhu*, and also that of Jñānagarbha, quoted earlier, where he states (including part of Eckel's commentary):

> 17. [The Buddha] considers the relative and the ultimate to be identical in nature, because there is no difference between them. This is because reason also corresponds to appearances.

> To say that reason *(nyāya)* corresponds to appearances *(yathādaśana)* in Jñānagarbha's terminology is to say that the ultimate *(paramārtha)* is relative *(saṃvṛti)*.[5]

Jñānagarbha, a Svātantrika Madhyamaka philosopher, would presumably ascribe to the sevenfold reasoning, but nevertheless his statement posits relativity in relation to two extremes. This automatically means that that which is relative to the seeming two extremes must act via a process involving a third factor that like glue unites one to the other. What Jñānagarbha is essentially saying is that if one thing is relative to another thing then 'there is no difference between them'. This is because the link that binds one to the other partakes of both, integrating them into a unity, a complete system.

Another factor to be taken into account is that accorded by Nāgārjuna's reasoning of any of the four pillars of his *catuṣkoṭikā*,[6] that something is 'this' or 'not this', 'neither this and not this', or 'both this and not this' (which is similar to Jñānagarbha's statement above). The duality 'this' or 'not this' refers to the mind's ability to determine that something is valid or not. The phrase 'both this and not this' is integral to the understanding of *saṃsāra*. It has the quality of pertaining to illusionality ('not this'), where we have *saṃskāras* that separate one karmic factor from another, each of which can be perceived in the mind's eye as being 'real', but in fact only manifest a temporal reality for an ephemeral period of time. It is also 'this', real, because of the inherent emptiness of *saṃsāra*. The phrase 'neither this and not this'

5 M.D. Eckel, *Jñānagarbha on the Two Truths*, 40-41.

6 Nāgārjuna's fourfold system of dialectics; negation of the positive, the negative, of both, and of neither. Four categories of existence; being, non-being, both being and non-being, neither being and non-being. (Also denoted *catuṣkoṭi*.)

is integral to *śūnyatā*, where *saṃsāra* has been properly cleansed of all defiling attributes, producing the 'real' that is not ephemeral, because there is no time factor to be included in its analysis.

From this line of reasoning we see that the phrases 'both this and not this' and 'neither this and not this' are integrally related, where we have the concept of the two truths, with *śūnyatā* and *saṃsāra* somehow integrated with each other. The first line of enquiry, relating to both the mind and aggregates, concerns enquiry into the conventional truth, the second line of enquiry, of being different from mind and aggregates relates to ascertaining the ultimate truth. Also we had earlier analysed a quotation from Nāgārjuna ascertaining the identity of this pair, that 'Between the two, also, there is not the slightest difference whatsoever'. The nature of the *nirvāṇa-saṃsāra* integration is what concerns us here; the determination of what constitutes their nexus, the zone of interrelation that eliminates the difference.

As we saw earlier the standard answer is that they are the same because they are both empty. This however does not really answer the question of how one accesses *śūnyatā* whilst residing in *saṃsāra*. This necessitates a bridging mechanism (nexus) otherwise *saṃsāra* would be *instantly annihilated* by the expression of the Void. (The phenomena represented by *saṃsāra* would instantly implode into the dearth of phenomena representative of the Void.) The question of how *saṃsāra* is sustained if it is intrinsically empty is quite important and as far as I know is not explained in Buddhism, *but needs to be*. It cannot be glibly dismissed. This subject therefore is also a major theme of this treatise, necessitating much foundation to be laid before it can be appropriately tackled. Such an answer is concomitant with the *dharmakāya* type of reasoning that offers a fusion of extremes, rather than relying upon an undefinable attribute (*śūnyatā*), which is one of the extremes. The question as to the nature of this *dharmakāya* type of reasoning, and how it manifests must then be answered.

Where all this leads is the conclusion that the phrase 'If the I is found to be neither inherently the same entity as the mind and body nor a different entity from them, then the I does not inherently exist' may not necessarily be a true statement, as it may logically partake of them both, as well as be different. It *depends upon how one defines* the 'I' concept.

Bodhicitta and the 'self' concept

The third of the seven-fold reasoning presented by Hopkins is:

> *Establishing the presence of the reasons of the subject.*
> *The seven-fold reasoning in brief is:*
>
> 'I' do not inherently exist because of (i) not being the aggregates, (ii) not being an entity other than the aggregates, (iii) not being the base of the aggregates, (iv) not inherently being based on the aggregates, (v) not inherently possessing the aggregates, (vi) not being just the composite of the aggregates, and (vii) not being the shape of the aggregates.[7]

Hopkins then presents the *first* of five statements under the heading '*Establishing that the I is not the mind and body*'.

> The I is not the mental and physical aggregates because then the assertion of an I would be senseless. 'I' would be just another name for the aggregates.[8]

In answer, we can say, precisely, the 'I' *is not just* the aggregates, but can be 'another name for the aggregates', if by 'aggregates' you mean the *skandhas* and specifically the *saṃskāras* constituting the person, which also incorporates mind. This constitutes the equipment that deluded individuals take to constitute themselves.

However, the reality is that this is not all that constitutes a human personality; it is more complex than that, as intellect alone (the translation of 'mind' here) is just a classifying and correlating tool, as well as a storehouse of information. It can be wed to the emotions, which then produces all of the desire-mind attributes. So far (when we add physicality—that which the intellect is identified with), all we have described is that which relates to the world of the materially profane (which constitutes the *skandhas* and *saṃskāras*), and the atheistic universe. But what about *bodhicitta*, how is it generated from the intellect, which expresses the opposite qualities to *bodhicitta*? (The intellect segregates and dissects aspects of *saṃsāra* in order to classify because of attachment to it, whereas *bodhicitta* unifies diverse elements of *saṃsāra* in order to liberate one from it.) The various types of desire-mind mean only intense self-focus; again disallowing the expression

7 J. Hopkins, *Meditation on Emptiness*, 48.

8 Ibid.

of *bodhicitta*. If intelligence is wedded to sensual pleasure (any of the aspects of the five senses and their combination), then (hedonistic) self-focus is obtained, the opposite of *bodhicitta*.

How *bodhicitta* is generated from the 'I' as well as where it actually comes from (when viewed in terms of a force to be invoked) needs to be understood. As it inevitably is a force driving the 'I' towards liberation via the Bodhisattva ideal much needs to be said as to its inherent nature and the way that it is expressed by an 'I'. *Bodhicitta* must enter into the debate concerning what is and is not real, valid, definitive, in relation to how it comes to incorporate a Buddha-Mind, yet exists prior to the establishment of such a Mind. It is a subject that cannot be avoided in one's quest for truth (enlightenment).

For the mind to be transformed by means of *bodhicitta* another factor is required in our consideration—a 'consciousness container'. It can be inferred that the mind must be encapsulated to become a *seed* or Buddha-womb (the *tathāgatagarbha),* which manifests as an integral part of the process of liberation (via the Dharmakāya Way). Without the containment of the substance of mind so that it survives death and continues on in a consciousness-stream that is continuously encapsulated with the appearance of a new personal-I in such a way that there is a progressive evolution of mind into Mind, no such thing as a Buddha could evolve. Such a one has the ability to recall past lives at will because of the fact of the existence of a 'consciousness-container'. Everything is ordered and progresses according to certain spiritual laws, such as that of *karma,* otherwise chaos would be the result, and the undue dissipation of all of one's past life's achievements.

This is but another way of saying that some concept of a 'self' must come to the fore that is effectively non-illusional because it is the expression of *bodhicittta* and the directive integration of the consciousness-stream of any reincarnating ego towards Buddhahood. It is the sustaining power of the force of the 'contained *bodhicitta*' that is the impetus of the Bodhisattva *bhūmis*.[9] This is a necessary extension

9 *Bhūmi:* progressive levels of realisation. From the verbal root *bhū* to become, grow into. The ten *bhūmis* or stages of perfection of the Bodhisattva. They are described under the rubrics: 1. great joy, 2. stainless purity, 3. illumination, 4. intense wisdom, 5. invincible strength, 6. direct presence, 7. the far-reaching stage, 8. steadfastness, 9. meritorious wisdom, 10. the *dharma* cloud. Bodhisattvas progressively develop the *bhūmis* over a series of lives.

of the logic of the texts presenting the teachings of the *tathāgatagarbha*, the Buddha-womb within us, as we shall later see.

Buddhists however have maintained for millennia that within Buddhist philosophy any concept of a 'self' presents contradictions, and certainly a Buddha or his 'womb', is freed from 'self' or a 'self concept'. This may be true, but it does not alter the fact that something akin to 'self' must exist to properly transform the impressions gained from mere sense-contact into the higher wisdoms, and thence produce the drive to liberation. If there was no such soteriological force acting then enlightenment would not be possible of its own accord. Instead of 'self' we could resurrect the term 'soul' and define it appropriately. Here this 'soul' can be defined *as an aspect of the thought-projection of the enlightened Mind of a primordial Buddha,*[10] which manifests as a paradigm of liberation for each human unit, for the sum of the evolutionary process of that life-stream. This Buddha-Mind collectivises such 'unitary streams' into overall patterns, *maṇḍalas* of activity, as part of the overall evolutionary pattern for the entire human race.

The concern here is the form that such a 'thought-projection' may take, i.e., the shape, as well as the mechanism in the realms of consciousness, that will allow or help cause the transformation and transmutation of *saṃskāras* to take place. It must also *act as a store* of all that has been gained, and thence to manifest through the utilisation of karmic purpose in such a way that enables it to present increasingly higher cycles of accomplishment until liberation is gained. Also, its emanatory quality and sustaining power must be what is known as *bodhicitta*.

This is the outline of what shall be presented in this treatise. The detail will follow, and though difficult to explain, it is possible, and necessarily so, as part of the furtherance of the progress of the *buddhadharma* well into the new millennia of striving to push the human race to greater heights of revelation; states of increasingly transcendental supernal Being, until all is merged into the *dharmakāya*.

So let us progress forth with this view of the *dharma* for those minds that will bear with it, and accordingly gain enlightenment.

---

10 The function of an Ādi (primordial) Buddha is here brought to light.

The I-consciousness and *kliṣṭamanas*

Referring to the previous quote from Hopkins, one can say that when perceiving or exploring *more than* just the aggregates, then such a construct can be called the *I-consciousness,* rather than just the personal-I of self-identity. The I-consciousness can then be viewed as the collective consciousness of all past activity, including that of past lives, that coherently utilises the aggregates and directs them to further gain evolutionary experience.[11] These aggregates flow in different streams within a continuum (*santāna*) from one life to another, and any portion of them are collectivised during any life by the mind (consciousness) that interrelates them into a 'personality', known conventionally as a '*self*', for the duration of the appearance of the *saṃskāras* concerned. (Which evolve through the educational process of birth, adolescence, maturity, old age and death, as depicted by the twelve links of Dependent Origination.) These aggregates are then modified by that 'self' (or personality) for the duration of the consciousness that *has free will* and *perceives action to be committed.* New *saṃskāras* (and associated *karma*) are then produced that modify the future accordingly. Consciousness focussed upon the slowly changing appearance, or form, wrongly identifies with it, calling it an 'I'.

In reality the 'I' is the quantum of *saṃskāras* and *skandhas* manifesting through it at any time, collectivised by the consciousness reacting to the impact of external stimuli from the environment of which it is a part. Such a 'self' thus has no lasting permanence, but a relative one, relative to other individualised units of self-consciousness that appear in the same space-time continuum that it is occupying. They are all evolving and interrelating together, producing a similar karmic flow, karmic patterning, or weaving, that coherently interrelates them all into one organism, or flux of coming and going (into and out of incarnation).

It should be noted that the I-consciousness is an aspect of the *ālayavijñāna* and interrelates freely with it, and also with the personal-I,

---

11 Note that the subject of this definition and enquiry does not involve a quest to reinstate what was meant by the Hindu technical term *'ātman'.* Another type of identity is the subject of consideration, derived from proper analysis of Buddhist ontological thought. Later the term I-consciousness will be replaced with more appropriate terminology.

when the personal-I is manifesting (as an aspect of the I-consciousness) in the three worlds of human interrelationships.

To better understand what is meant by the term I-consciousness I should weave in here a little of the Yogācāra philosophy concerning the 'eight consciousnesses'. This is necessary, as we endeavour to understand the nature of mind (*manas*) and the way it self-identifies. Lama Anagarika Govinda states:

> It is said in the *Laṅkāvatāra Sūtra:* 'It is because of the activities of the discriminating-mind that error rises, an objective world evolves and the notion of an ego-soul becomes established.'
>
> This discriminating consciousness is *mano-vijñāna,* the intellect, which conceives *manas* as the ego, because it is the apparently constant centre of reference, in which the previous moment of consciousness is reflected. This follows from the *Laṅkāvatāra Sūtra,* where it is said that *manas*, like *ālaya-vijñāna* or universal consciousness, cannot be the source of error.
>
> In other words, though *manas* contributes to the arising of the ego-concept, since it has the function of self-consciousness (by keeping up the connexion between past and present moments of consciousness and thus creating a sense of stability), it cannot be called the cause of the actual source of error, but merely a contributing factor or condition – just as a mirror which, by reflecting objects, may lead to the error that the reflections are the actual objects. But this error does not lie in the mirror, but in the mind of the observer. In a similar way the error is not committed by *manas* but by the intellect, which therefore is also called *kliṣṭa-mano-vijñāna,* 'afflicted' (namely, by error) 'intellectual consciousness'.
>
> The double-nature of *manas* which, as we have seen, participates in the empirical-intellectual as well as in the universal (intuitive) consciousness, is the reason why *manas* and *mano-vijñāna* are often mixed up and treated as synonyms and that even in the non-buddhistic Sanskrit literature a higher and lower aspect of *manas* is discerned, depending on whether *manas* is turned towards the empirical world or not.
>
> Therefore it is said in the *Mahāyāna-Śraddhotpāda-Śāstra:* 'The mind (*manas*) has two doors from which issue its activities. One leads to a realization of the mind's Pure Essence, the other leads to the differentiations of appearing and disappearing, of life and death. What, however, is meant by the Pure Essence of Mind? It

> is the ultimate purity and unity, the all-embracing wholeness, the quintessence of Truth. Essence of Mind belong neither to death nor rebirth, it is uncreated and eternal. The concepts of the conscious mind are being individualized and discriminated by false imaginations. If the mind could be kept free from discriminative thinking there would be no more arbitrary thoughts to give rise to appearances of form, existences and conditions.' [12]

When *manas* is turned to the empirical world and identifies with the form via the sense perceptions, through which it functions, then I call this *the personal-I.* When *manas* is turned towards the realisation of 'mind's Pure Essence', or rather, when the nature of that essence is directed towards the personal-I (producing intuitive flashes of insight), then here we find the activity of the *I-consciousness.* The I-consciousness can also be described in relation to the seventh of the eight consciousnesses, termed *kliṣṭa-mano-vijñāna* (or *kliṣṭamanas*). Tsongkhapa describes *kliṣṭamanas* thus:

> The *kliṣṭa-manas* is defined as that obscured *(nivṛta)* [mind], not the subject of moralizing, which views the maturation part of *ālaya-vijñāna* as self and has only nine [mental factors like contact, attachment, etc.].[13]

The text further states:

> By *nivṛta* is meant repeatedly polluted by afflictive emotions *(kleśa)* because this *[kliṣṭa-]manas* has been repeatedly polluted by the four root afflictive emotions *(kleśa)*[14].....How could its surrounding [mental factors] be only nine? Are there not also the following six: a) distraction *(vikṣepa)* implicit in [the opinion] "I am here," b) carelessness *(pramāda)* implicit in attachment and stupidity, c) fixation implicit in attachment; and d) absence of faith *(aśraddhā)*, e) laziness *(kausīdya)*, and f) dullness *(styāna)* implicit in the stupidity part? Are there not, therefore fifteen [mental factors] surrounding [*kliṣṭa-manas*]?

---

12 Lama Anagarika Govinda, *Foundations of Tibetan Mysticism, The Esoteric Teachings of Tibetan Buddhism*, (E.P Dutton & Co., Inc. New York, 1960), 78-79.

13 G. Sparham, (Trans.) *Ocean of Eloquence, Tsong-ka-pa's Commentary on the Yogācara Doctrine of Mind,* (Sri Satguru, Delhi, 1995), 107.

14 Ibid.

> [Response:] Although those [six mental factors] are said to be there, still the number [of mental factors associated with *kliṣṭa-manas*] is exactly nine. This is because the bases for imputing these six are the material realities (Tib. *rdzas)* of the four afflictive emotions [opinion about I, stupidity about I, pride in I, and self love]. [The six] do not exist apart from these four. That there is no mental factor beyond the material realities of these nine can be understood in detail from the *Vivṛta-guhyārtha-pinda-vyākhyā.* Fearing prolixity and because it is not really a difficult idea, I will not pursue it here.
>
> Fifth, investigation of the levels.
>
> Question: Is the *kliṣṭa-manas* [on the same level as] the level on which the person, in whose [mind-]stream it exists, was born or not? If the former [i.e., if the *kliṣṭa-manas* is always the same level as its *ālaya-vijñāna*], when an ordinary desire-[realm] person [35a] becomes freed from attachment to objects of the desire-[realm] he would, [absurdly], still not have removed [desire-realm] *kliṣṭa-manas* [because the desire-realm *ālaya-vijñāna* remains and, in this first case, the *kliṣṭa-manas* and its *ālaya-vijñāna* are said to be the same level]. Hence desire[-realm] afflictive emotion [such as the four afflictive emotions associated with the *kliṣṭa-manas*] would, [absurdly], still be manifestly operating in the [mind-]stream [even when they have been removed]. If the latter, [i.e., if *the kliṣṭa-manas* is not always the same level as its *ālaya-vijñāna*], given that the *kliṣṭa-manas* and its surrounding [mental factors] cling to the person's *ālaya-vijñāna* as I, since there would be impartiality, desire[-realm] afflictive emotions would not increase.[15]....The *kliṣṭa-manas* is associated with the ingrained view of I, however, and until the power of its antidote – uncontaminated wisdom – is produced it cannot be removed.[16]

Kliṣṭamanas is the name given to the many types of afflictive emotions (*kleśas*), stored as *bījas* (seeds) in the *ālayavijñāna.* They are projected in the form of related *saṃskāras* when the personal-I is focussed upon an object of desire. When these emotional *saṃskāras* surface they immediately fuse with the mental consciousness (*manovijñāna*), to produce such things as desire-mind, self-will (i.e.,

15 Ibid., 110-111.

16 Ibid., 111.

the four types of 'afflictive emotions'), or forms of ego-clinging. The emotions always manifest in relation to a concept of 'self', executing the will to appropriate things desired. They thus produce attachments for all things deemed pleasurable, glamorous, or needy by the personality, and react to that which they dislike.

There are said to be nine mental factors to *kliṣṭamanas*. Five of these are expressions of the five sense-consciousnesses, and are really five Watery attributes of the five Elements, of which the five senses come to be expressions. The emotions and the factor of desire are governed by the Watery Element (emotions, desire), and thus *kliṣṭamanas* is really 'afflictive' whenever the mind is conditioned by this Element in any way. There are Fiery emotions (mental emotions), as well as teary ones, of desire-mind, and those prompted by visual stimulus, as well as derived from the sense of touch. These need not be analysed here, as the reader can do this with the information presented in this series. The remaining four factors are those related to the production of a concept of 'self' or 'I', and will be dealt with later.

Manovijñāna designates things into their various categories, and thus can be also called the intellect or rational mind, minus the factor of desire or the emotions. It is discriminatory, separative, imaginative, creative, and a collector of facts based on impressions from the five senses. The added desires and emotions associated with *kliṣṭamanas* entangle the concepts and images of the *manovijñāna* with an identification of things experienced, and draw all experiences into a relation with concepts of 'I' or ego. The resultant attachment to things causes ignorance concerning the real nature of what is desired and appropriated for the little self. The two qualities, *manovijñāna* and *kliṣṭamanas*, together with the five sense-consciousnesses, and the five aggregates make the personal-I.

Another aspect of *kliṣṭamanas* to be considered is that it is the store of the emotional volitions. It is therefore an integral part of the process of the transmutation of these volitions; from attachment to things, glamour, and images of things desired into *love,* which is clear, calm, non-emotional. Love is pure reason, which draws all into a unity, fusion, oneness, in such a way that the true nature of all interrelatedness with 'things' are known for what they are.[17] When experienced in terms of lightning flashes of revelation this quality is called the 'intuition',[18] and is an expression of *śūnyatā*, because its effect is the liberation from phenomena.

It is also said in the *Ocean of Eloquence* that:

> The *kliṣṭa-manas* and its associated [mental factors] only leave neutral perfumes since they always remain, in essence, what is not a subject of moralizing.[19]

Earlier on the same page Sparham states that the group of six consciousnesses consists of all three types of mind 'such as a virtuous [mind]'.[20] The concept of *kliṣṭamanas* here therefore does not refer to a 'mind' per se, but something that is an adjunct to mind. What therefore presumably is implied is the desire principle that is attached to mind. This principle that *kliṣṭamanas* evokes may not appear neutral as it is highly polarised according to the object of desire. However it manifests in either a good or bad way, i.e., hindering or non-hindering the path to enlightenment, consequently is neutral. The seeded attributes can manifest either way, otherwise no gain in consciousness could be accrued. Desire is a force of attraction to the object desired, there is no rationality there. It is the intellect that rationalises, judges, and therefore 'moralises', according to its own set of conditioned images and beliefs, and it may utilise the desire principle in its judgements of things, but the desire-principle cannot moralise of its own accord. Hence when it is said that one 'desires enlightenment', that is an intellectual decision, because of observing the consequences of the effects of wanton desire upon the psyche. The emotions are similar, however when wedded to the mind, to produce the predominant human characteristic, the desire or emotional mind *(kāma-manas),* then moralising often happens, because of the analytical factor of mind that is conjoined to the desire

---

17 Sparham states (Ibid., 113): It is said that 'when *kliṣṭa-manas* fundamentally transforms it is to be called the transcendental wisdom of the sameness [of all]'. The accompanying footnote (Ibid., 120) states that: Sa skya Paṇḍita in his *Thub pa'i dgongs pa rab tu gsal ba* (47.3.4) says the statement comes from Candragomin's *Sangs rgyas kyi sa.*

18 Intuition: a term denoting the expression of *bodhicitta.*

19 Ibid., 65.

20 Ibid.

or emotions. It is this form of *kliṣṭamanas,* the mind *(manas)* that is defiled *(kliṣṭa)* with desire/emotions, that shall be my rendering of this term throughout this series. However I shall generally use the term *kāma-manas* as it more accurately describes the attributes of defilement.

Kliṣṭamanas, plus the *ālayavijñāna* (the portion of the *ālayavijñāna* containing *kliṣṭamanas*), is an important factor for the I-consciousness, because when downward focussed it seeds the 'I' or self concept for the purpose of gaining experience from *saṃsāric* interrelation via the principle of desire. An instrument is thereby produced in the phenomenal realms that can evolve the need to liberate all sentient beings. *Kliṣṭamanas* thereby becomes the mechanism for the development of *bodhicitta.* At the latter stages of human evolution *kliṣṭamanas* is transmuted into the 'mind of enlightenment' *(bodhicitta),* and in the process of its transmutation it has the capacity to not just cleanse and convert the emotional defilements, and 'unentangled ignorance',[21] but also to untangle the ignorance evolved by the formation of appropriate *saṃskāras.* It achieves this through fostering aspiration to high ideals from out of the desire principle, and then love for all beings, thereby destroying the 'self'-concept. The 'transcendental wisdom of the sameness' of the all is evoked instead. Whatever has the capability to seed something (e.g., the emotions) also has the capability to 'unseed' it, to abstract the originating causes back from whence they came.

It is therefore the desire or emotional attribute associated with *kliṣṭamanas* that expresses the defilement of mind, and the essence of the path to enlightenment concerns the conversion of these aspects *(saṃskāras)* into the attributes of the Heart centre that embodies the principle of Love, and it is wherein *śūnyatā* can be experienced. The

21 Ibid., 143. There it is stated: 'This ignorance always blocks direct witness to the meaning of selflessness, and is present whenever any virtuous, nonvirtuous or neutral state of mind arises. Now, since this [unentangled ignorance] is a mental factor *(caitta)* it must be associated with a single principle mind. But since it is a *kleśa* ('afflictive emotion') and lasts without a break in its continuum until the Ārya path, it could not be possessed by either the *ālaya-vijñāna* or by the set of six [consciousnesses]'.
I take this form of ignorance to be that inherent in Nature, and which also conditions the substance of the (concrete) mind, which entangles forms of ignorance through normal human activity. It must eventually be transformed, so as to act as a proper conduit for enlightenment upon the *ārya* (noble) path of right meditative activity.

desire at first produces attachment to the objects of perception, from which knowledge *(manas)* is obtained concerning the interrelatedness and characteristics of these objects. Without the foundation of desires such as sensuality, carnal love, attraction to the 'other', then what is known as *bodhicitta* could not evolve, because these attributes are the primary elements that lead to the development of selfless love. From such a foundation evolves the compassionate wisdom of a Bodhisattva.

Attachment to things, and desire for the 'other' become an expression of the manifesting personal 'I' via *kliṣṭamanas. Manovijñāna alone* will not produce such attachments, grasping, or clinging to anything; it's nature manifests in a separative manner because of its categorising function. First we have desires for all attractive, pleasurable things, in relation to the needs and wants of an 'I'. Later, because of the pain associated with being attached to transience (as per the four Noble Truths), such desire gets transmuted, when wedded with logic, into the desire for liberation from pain. This then produces the revelation that the only way this can be is to renounce all attachments, even to the 'I', and so we have the basis to the Eightfold Path.

The 'one and the many'

The *second* of five statements given by Hopkins is:

> The I is not the aggregates because just as the aggregates are many, so the selves would be many, or just as the I is one, so the aggregates would be one.[22]

Though the 'I' is much more that the aggregates, as established above, nevertheless the 'selves' can indeed be many, when you look at the fact that there are *many* personality incarnations of any individual life stream. Also, though these aggregates may be many they are also collectivised under the five main categories denoting the *skandhas*, and any *one* grouping normally dominates a particular stage of the evolution of the personal 'self'. Also, there are cycles within cycles of activity, wherein *saṃskāras* appear and then become obscured, thus there are

22 Hopkins, *Meditation on Emptiness,* 48. See *A Study of Svāntantrika,* 356*ff.*, for more information concerning the refutation of the one and the many.

many aggregates appearing and receding into objectivity at any period of experiential activity. Not one of them is the 'self' *per se*, but any collection of them appearing as the five *skandhas,* manifesting for the purpose of karmic clearing from any particular cycle of incarnation from the past, and for further experiential growth can be considered a 'self', conventionally considered, for the duration of their appearance (where a mind processes their manifestation). Thus, just because there are many aggregates, it does not necessary follow that the 'selves would be many', rather, we would see 'one-self' collectivising the aggregates as a unity by means of consciousness, and conscious volitions. Consciousness utilises past aggregates in order to receive present-future results seen in terms of consciousness shifts or growths. (There must however be a higher guiding principle that directs their overall progression towards the development of a Buddha-Mind. The separative 'I', functioning as a mind, will not do so of its own accord.)

The aggregates are possessed for the duration of their experiential effect, and then recede into the background of the *maṇḍala* governed by the consciousness principle. Thus the aggregates change with consciousness. Because both the aggregates and consciousness change, so the 'I' changes accordingly, as everything is in a constant state of mutual flux. An 'I' consequently exists for as long as a consciousness can hold an appropriate quota of such a flux in consciousness, and to direct it by means of its will to achieve a purpose. All forms of activity of the aggregates, as well as the integrity of the directive consciousness exists for differing durations. The sum of the flux of aggregates contained in one overall sphere of consciousness-containment (*maṇḍala*) constitutes the duration of the existence of an 'I' or 'self'. There is however, another aspect, an I-consciousness, that as already postulated, is responsible for the overall comings and goings of these 'selves'. Its parameters for existence will be established later in this treatise.

Thus, 'just as the I is one, so the aggregates would be one' is true, if all of the aggregates are collectivised as the focus of attention of the manifesting personal-I for the duration of a gained or received impression, e.g., in the sensation of touch, or the experience of any image by means of sight. In fact, this is the way the personal-I almost always functions. Consciousness moves, as the object of perception moves from one form of experiential arena to the next. Similarly, each human individuality, a 'one' contains many aggregates, all of which are incorporated by, and move according to the directive impulses of the overriding consciousness.[23] When groups of the aggregates act contrary to that control then sickness may happen, and if severe enough then the death of the 'I' may occur, and consequently also for the aggregates, which are scattered into the elements. Later a new 'self' appears to incorporate the most important of these aggregates *(saṃskāras)* into a new field of endeavour upon a slightly higher cycle. Such is the way with the law of *karma*.

Obviously the Mādhyamika view the concept of aggregates in relation to an 'I' from a different perspective than I have. They probably had the ontology of the Sarvāstivādin, other early Buddhist schools, or the Hindu concept of the *ātman* in mind. Also their arguments are generally focussed upon one aspect of the two extremes (*saṃsāra-śūnyatā*), that of the Void (*śūnyatā*), and that all changes of phenomena have the Void as their base. Existence of *śūnyatā* does not explain the fact that the other extreme (*saṃsāra*) is constituted entirely of the 'one and the many', of which there are more examples than the proverbial uncountable 'grains of sand to the Ganges'. For example, the human body [a 'one'] is seen as a unity, yet has many diverse parts [the many]. Trees, for instance, are a unity [a 'one'] and yet contain many branches, leaves and cells to their constitution [the many], as does every other form in the phenomenal universe. Also, if one wishes to analyse homogenous units, consisting of many exactly the same parts constituting the form or appearance of the thing [a 'one'], then one need only look to pure elements as discovered and described by modern science.

From *A Study of Svātantrika*:

> The subjects, those things propounded by ourselves and others, are not established as a truly existent plurality because of the lack of a true existent unity. [If there is no truly existent unity, a truly existent plurality cannot be established] because a plurality has the character of a composite of ones. To explain this, Śāntatarakṣita's *Ornament for the Middle Way* says:

23 Or via parasympathetic directives.

> When anything is analysed
> It is without unity.
> That which does not have unity
> Also is without plurality.

And the commentary following that says:

> For a plurality has the character of a composite of unities. If a unity does not exist, [plurality] also does not exist, just as if trees and so forth do not exist, forests and so forth do not exist.[24]

It is interesting that the above quote starts with the phrase 'when anything', in order to try to deny the existence of 'anything'. In other words, the entire sentence structure begins with the presumption that 'things' exist. If they don't then the Mādhyamika could not even speak to convey 'anything', any rhetoric whatsoever. Thoughts are also 'things', which they *must utilise* to try to convey to us, absurdly, that such things do not exist. They do exist, they are real in the sense that they aid one's subsequent progress to enlightenment, though they have a form of transience.

Śāntatarakṣita then (absurdly) provides an analogy, of an accepted realisation of the 'one and the many' in order to disprove such a possibility 'just as if trees and so forth do not exist, forests and so forth do not exist'. Trees and forests are objects of perception and exist as such. They demonstrate the existence of a non-homogeneous 'one and the many'. The concept of 'unity' really is rhetorical, depending entirely on how one wishes to define this term. Multiplicity and diversity in unity, a completed *maṇḍala* of expression, is all that needs to be considered as far as the path to enlightenment goes. This is what allows the expression of the richness of experience that instigates the development of the wisdom of the Buddhas. Each such unity is composed of a plurality of lesser unities, and each unity is a plurality, and so forth, until we get to the atomic and subatomic world. Plurality therefore 'has the character of a composite of unities'. In the subatomic world the distinction between unity and plurality becomes merged with talk of energy fields, quarks, and the various paradoxes of quantum physics.

24 Lopez Jr., *A Study of Svātanrika,* 370-371.

The Madhyamaka doctrine also presents the concept that the Void is 'void of being void' to overcome the problem of annihilation. However, then we still have the problem as to where *saṃsāra* comes from, which when answered allows one to account for the *saṃsāra-śūnyatā* integration. We see therefore that the relation of *saṃsāra* to *śūnyatā* cannot easily be dismissed by denying the existence of a 'one' or 'many'. But what form does an existence take to experience the *śūnyatā-saṃsāra* integration? Such a form must exist. That which produces enlightenment, the wisdom of the Buddhas, must have some type of coherent integrity for it to inevitably be accommodated as a Buddha-Mind. The truth lies neither in *saṃsāra* nor in *śūnyatā*, but somewhere that represents the fusion of the two.

With respect to the phrase: 'For a plurality has the character of a composite of unities. If a unity does not exist, [plurality] also does not exist' it has already been explained that it is difficult to establish the non-existence of a unity, unless we categorically state that the Void is void of any concept of a unity. We cannot however logically decide whether the Void is itself a unity or not. Because, if all of the unities inherent in Nature, of which there are milliards, are ultimately absorbed into the Void, then logic can presume that the Void represents one primordial Unity from whence all proceeds and ultimately recedes. From another perspective we can view that Void to represent the annihilation of all the unities associated with the phenomenal universe; it is both unitary and not unitary, so as to accommodate *saṃsāra* and accomplish this annihilation process. Others may categorically state that it is not unitary, therefore it can have nothing to do with the atomic, singular, and egoistic states associated with phenomena. In other words, the Void and the phenomenal world exist in two different universes, and there can never be any contact or association between the two. (Such an argument would therefore deny the *saṃsāra-śūnyatā* integration.)

Another could say that the Void is neither unitary nor non-unitary, that it is simply indescribable, to produce a fourth view, and so our philosophic conundrum proceeds. Also, from another perspective, we could list the properties of the Tathāgatas, which manifest as (seeming) unities within that Void (as one characteristic is differentiated from another). Also, is each Tathāgata a unity, part of a plethora of unities within the context of one universal Buddha-Mind (another unity)?

If they are not unities, then why do we call one, Dīpeṅkara, another Gautama, another Ratnasambhava, and so forth?

Nothing comes out of nothing, so if the Void does not 'exist' as such, then what does, to account for all that we are, and which we experience around us? If it does exist, then we have the problem of the ways of viewing it given above to sort out. In essence there lies the rut within which many Buddhist thinkers are found, and which envelops their present form of reasoning. Thus without an understanding of the mode of relating between the 'one and many' throughout the domains of being/non-being then nothing at all can be achieved. We would have a nihilistic non-universe, a non-event, with not even the Void existing. However, if we accept that both *śūnyatā* and *saṃsāra* exist (albeit not according to the conventional way people view existence), then why or how they interrelate via the 'one and the many' is the quandary needing answering.

It can also be added that the Prāsaṅgika doctrine of reducing all to the Void (by means of the process known as *reductio ad absurdum*) does not account for the existence and the reason for the appearance of all these examples of the 'one and the many'. The recourse to ultimates denies the reality of the present, or the way that the eternal Now manifests.

One cannot manifest a syllogism containing two distinct parts to an argument, and then act as if only one of the two parts (i.e., the Void) is relevant. Both sides of the picture or equation must be accounted for. Also, how does the doctrine explain the *saṃsāra-śūnyatā* fusion? If the two are fused then the one and the many in *saṃsāra* must be properly considered, otherwise one can fall into the extreme of annihilation, the denial of the existence of *saṃsāra*, even conventionally.[25]

The presented logic must be able to:

a. Explain the abundant existence of the 'one and the many' in *saṃsāra*.
b. Explain how this 'one and many' came to be, and what its purpose is.
c. Explain the *saṃsāra-śūnyatā* fusion in such a way that the duration of the *saṃsāra* (of the 'one and the many') is sustained in conjunction

25 Note that there may be many subtle mitigating Prāsaṅgika arguments to be considered not yet presented here.

with the fact that *śūnyatā* is empty of being empty, and which must interrelate with *saṃsāra* in some way.

d. Address the conundrum that the 'one and the many' may also exist in *śūnyatā*, for is not the doctrine of the 4, 16 or 18 *śūnyatās*,[26] depending upon source material, but a version of the 'one and the many'? We can conceive of one ultimate all-encompassing *śūnyatā*, and nothing more need be said, and/or there are divisions, categories, of *śūnyatā* stemming from or are aspects of the one, in which case there are 'one and the many', even in *śūnyatā*. It is after all *'not empty'* of anything other than transient phenomena. There is a remainder, otherwise one would have annihilation, and how this 'remainder' is organised is in question here.

e. Look also to ultimates, where the 'one and many' are *apparently* done away with. In the light of the reasoning of the Dharmakāya Way they may in fact not have necessarily been done away with. Do we not manifest a paradigm shift in our discernment here to view the true nature of what IS without allusion to *saṃsāric* conditions? However once that paradigm shift has manifested then a new View arises, a new landscape where a transcendental version of 'one and the many' do exist with *ḍākinīs,* Bodhisattvas, Jinas, etc. One must thus view with an enlightened Mind purely within the context of what exists in the enlightened domains without reference to *saṃsāra*. What really exists in such a View is not referenced in Mādhyamika epistemology and logic.

With respect to *śūnyatā* we can also refer to the twenty-fifth of the 40 Nidana verses of the *Guhyasamājātantra,* as translated by Wayman:

---

26 There are said to be sixteen types of emptiness, which are really negations based on the categories of phenomena. These are said to be: (1) Emptiness of the internal, (2) Emptiness of the external, (3) Emptiness of both internal and external, (4) Emptiness of emptiness, (5) Emptiness of the vast, (6) Emptiness of the ultimate, (7) Emptiness of the produced, (8) Emptiness of the unproduced, (9) Emptiness of the extremes, (10) Emptiness of the without beginning and without end, (11) Emptiness of that which is not to be abandoned, (12) Emptiness of self-identity, (13) Emptiness of all things, (14) Emptiness of self-defining characteristics, (15) Emptiness of the non-referential, (16) Emptiness of the absence of substantiality. Adapted from: G. Coleman, ed., *The Handbook of Tibetan Buddhism* (Rupa & Co., New Delhi, 1995). Other sources quote eighteen emptinesses, as listed for instance in Jeffrey Hopkins, *Meditation on Emptiness*, 204-5.

> Thought *(citta),* thought derivative *(caitasika),* and nescience *(avidyā)* are also called respectively Insight *(prajñā),* Means *(upāya),* Culmination *(upalabhdika)* : as well as Void *(śūnya),* Further Void *(atiśūnya),* and Great Void *(mahāśūnya).*[27]

Wayman later presents a commentary on this verse, quoting the 'Pradipoddhyotana, Mchan ḥgrel edition' that explains that:

> The 'diamond sun' *(vajrārka)* is characterized by the attainment of the 'means' gnosis *(upāya* kind of *jñāna),* hence Spread-of-Light. When this sets, there is the form of 'insight' *(prajñā),* hence Light. Then before the Clear Light can emerge, that Light must pass into Culmination-of-Light, which is the initial appearance of dawn, or nescience *(avidyā).* Then, on the basis of the three gnoses, namely voidness, further voidness, and great voidness (Light, Spread-of-Light, and Culmination-of-Light), riding on the winds,[28] the *yogin* soars to the Clear Light and perfects the *mahāmudrā* ('great seal').[29]

Here the Light (Void) refers to that Void that ultimately characterises substance of mind *(citta).* The Spread-of-Light Void relates to the emptiness of the further characteristics of mind *(manas)* in the form of *kliṣṭamanas.* The culmination-of-Light (Great Void) to the emptiness that ultimately characterises the sum of one's perception *(vijñāna),* and is expressed as the *ālayavijñāna.* Finally there is a universal Void, denoted as the Clear Light.[30] This description of the main characteristics of mind being converted into Voids by means of 'riding on the wind' (*prāṇas*), meaning the eventual conversion of *saṃskāras* by yogic means into the Clear Light, is quite important. The reason being that the statement referring to the winds by means of which 'the *yogin* soars' implicates the entire philosophy that shall later be described associated with gaining the wisdoms of the Dhyāni Buddhas via the alchemicalisation of consciousness into the five Void Elements. If

27 Alex Wayman, Yoga of the *Guhyasamājatantra, the Arcane Lore of Forty Verses,* (Motilal Banarsidass, Delhi, 2005), 15.

28 *Prāṇas,* of which there are five main ones, from which then we can derive five Voids associated with the Dhyāni Buddhas, as was shown on page 33 of my book: *Karma and the Rebirth of Consciousness.*

29 Wayman, 323.

30 Refer to the tabulation given by Wayman on Ibid., 194.

we incorporate the Dhyāni Buddhas as aspects of the Womb of the Consort of the Ādi Buddha (explained in Volume 5 of this series) then effectively we can derive seven different Voids pertaining to *śūnyatā,* that are veiled by the Clear Light.

In presenting four (or seven) versions of Void here, or the abovementioned 16-18 we see that Madhyamaka philosophers have enunciated a type of philosophic *faux pas,* when we are told that 'one and the many' do not exist, when clearly there is one overriding Void presented, the 'Universal Void' and a number of subsidiary ones. Neither can they deny the abundant appearances of 'one and the many' found throughout *saṃsāra*, when assuring us that *saṃsāra* exists (conventionally) simultaneously with *śūnyatā*. If *śūnyatā* can be categorised in a way that we can conceive of a number of forms of Void, how then can it be used as a basis to deny the existence of one and the many in *saṃsāra*? If you talk exclusively about the doctrine of the Void then you can deny anything or everything because of the way you choose to define the Void, but if you want to include *saṃsāra* in your discussion, then putting aside semantics, you cannot deny the existence of the one and the many. *Saṃsāric* phenomenon must be truly accounted for, and not merely shrugged away as being non-existent.

Also, ultimately, everything can be said to be brought back to the one—the Void. However, by utilising Madhyamaka philosophy, this is not possible, because in reality from the one comes the possibility of the many arising, as the many is but a compound of the one, and this they disallow. So if the Void also cannot be a 'one', what then is it if not one or many? Here we are omitting the problem of the many varieties mentioned above, because if it posses, or if there are, these varieties, then is it a one, or one of many? Which version of the presented doctrine are we then to believe: that it is an 'ultimate one' into which all phenomena proceeds after being stripped of all characteristics; not one or many, but something 'other' that partakes of neither; or that it is one and many? We see in fact that when it comes to *śūnyatā* paradoxically all of these are possibilities. (If we omit these various possibilities because they are 'really negations based on the categories of phenomena' we still need to account for the Void Elements, and the way that the wisdoms of the Dhyāni Buddhas manifest, which are explained later.) *Śūnyatā* is in fact an inexplicable experience of a oneness devoid of the vicissitudes of mind, but not of the all-expansiveness of the Mind that is cosmos. Indeed in cosmos there is One and Many (Bodhisattvas and Buddha-fields, to use conventional terminology) all integrated into one vast omnipresent and infinite (as far as that term has meaning) Mind-Space. One must reside in *śūnyatā* to experience the varieties of existence that abound in the *arūpa* universe (formless space). Within *dharmakāya* both the Oneness of *śūnyatā* and the 'many' discerned in *saṃsāra* are experienced simultaneously.

Our conceptualisations of 'one and many' may differ, so let us analyse some of the source material (briefly, because of the large amount there is) and see if these essential questions are answered, sidetracked, or ignored; in which case the syllogisms and logic presented will be found lacking.

For this purpose I shall quote extensively from the book *Jñānagarbha on the Two Truths, an Eighth Century Handbook of Madhyamaka Philosophy.*[31] The numbering system given by Eckel in his translation of the various verses will be utilised.

The remaining three verses of 'The Sevenfold Reasoning' (the probandium) shall be explained in Chapter eight.

31 M.D. Eckel, *Jñānagarbha on the Two Truths.*

6

Essay on the One and the Many
from Jñānagarbha's Commentary on the Two Truths

Nothing ultimately arises

Jñānagarbha's thesis here is that 'nothing ultimately arises'.[1] Verse 14 of the translated text states:

> Many do not produce one, many do not produce many, one does not produce many, and one does not produce one.[2]

This verse presents the main subject headings for the presented logic. First we have the assertion that 'Many do not produce one'.

> Many do not produce one, for if a single effect arises from a multiple [cause], such as the eye and so forth, the multiplicity of the cause does not produce multiplicity [of the effect], since the cause is multiple but the effect is not. [Moreover] absence of multiplicity [in the cause] is not the cause of the absence of multiplicity [in the effect], because the effect lacks multiplicity, even when the cause does not lack multiplicity. Thus the multiplicity or lack of multiplicity [in the effect] would not have a cause. Since nothing is excluded from [the categories of multiplicity and non-multiplicity], nothing would have a cause. If this were the case, [everything] would either exist permanently or not exist at all.[3]

---

1 Lopez provides an excellent essay on the meaning of the concept of the ultimate in his chapter on 'Ultimate Existence' in *A Study of Svātantrika,* 134ff.

2 M.D. Eckel, *Jñānagarbha on the Two Truths*, 80.

3 Ibid., 80-81.

The subcommentary given is:

> Why do many not produce one? He says: 'For if a single effect arises from a multiple [cause], such as the eye and so forth...' 'And so forth' includes form *(rūpa),* light *(āloka),* mental activity (*manaskāra*), and so forth. 'A single effect' refers to a visual cognition *(cakṣur-vijñāna).* If you accept that [a single effect] arises [from a multiple cause], then the multiplicity of the cause would not produce multiplicity [in the effect]. Why? Because the cause would be multiple, but the effect would not be multiple. In that case, absence of multiplicity in the cause would not be the cause of absence of multiplicity in the effect, because the effect would lack multiplicity, even in the absence of a lack of multiplicity in the cause. If the multiplicity or lack of multiplicity in the effect were related by invariable concomitance *(A)* to multiplicity or lack of multiplicity in the cause, [the effect] would have a cause. But this is not the case. Therefore, the multiplicity or lack of multiplicity in the effect does not have a cause. If you say that multiple and non-multiple effects have no cause, he says, 'Since nothing is excluded'—that is, nothing is excluded from [the categories of] multiplicity and non-multiplicity—'nothing has a cause'. And if nothing has a cause, everything must either exist permanently or not exist at all. The word 'everything' is to be supplied. Why [must everything either exist permanently or not exist at all]? Because it does not depend on anything else as a cause. If it did [not?] depend [on other causes], things could appear at random *(kadācit).*[4]

Why does it matter if the effect is not multiple? This is consistent with the way things happen in Nature, and in the field of human relationships and technological constructs. We could choose any one of a myriad of subjects to illustrate the point. There is, for instance, the conventional existence of a sword. It's creation can be considered a single effect, yet there are a multiplicity of causes that have gone into making it. First the originating iron ore had to be found somewhere and smelted to produce iron, then the iron had to be processed to make steel. Each of these processes themselves are the products of a number of causes, the construction of a furnace, the addition of fuel, the blowing of air, etc. The steel did not appear out of thin air. Then there is the craftsman that

4 Ibid., 130.

has to temper the steel and fashion the blade by hammering it again and again, a cause compounding upon cause, until finally we have a single effect, the finished sword. The same goes for the construction of anything in the material domain, cart, car, house, radio, etc. We could also look to Nature, where many causes produce a single effect, such as a tree—the factor of the originating germination of the seed, the factor of continual nourishment, the cyclic appearance of rain, necessary sunshine, and all of the cellular processes happening. Without any one of such causes the phenomena, tree (a single effect), would not happen. So how do the Mādhyamika account for the appearance of such things as swords, houses, trees, and cars if they will not allow causes?

Obviously the sword could have many other effects, depending upon the way it is put to use (i.e., its functionality), it could be used to cut things asunder, to kill (because of the fact that it conventionally exists, and because of the fact that it is a unity, a 'one' and thus can be utilised by another such 'one', a human personality), or may simply rust away over a long period of time, because of the inevitability of change in *saṃsāra*. This means that the 'single effect' inevitably is transmogrifying, changing into multiplicity. Inevitably, therefore, *multiplicity produces multiplicity, through the temporary appearance of the 'single effect'*. Again everything depends upon one's view, from where in the standpoint of time or the evolutionary process one is looking at something, which is what also concerns the word 'ultimately'.

Our view concerns the entire doctrine of *karma*, of causes and effects; which the Mādhyamika philosophers actually deny the existence of in this doctrine of 'many do not produce one'. The doctrine presented is actually saying that we live in a *karmaless* universe. This is because there are many *karmic* factors that produce the phenomenal appearance of any unity. If *karmalessness* is the case, then how do the Mādhyamikas explain the process of rebirth, the appearance of *saṃskāras*, the quest for enlightenment, enlightenment itself, or the appearance of anything at all? The Mādhyamika thinking here is that as a consequence of the fullness of time 'the many' ultimately get abstracted into a 'one', a unity, the Void, however because this Void is considered a no-thing so there is nothing to label as a 'one' or 'many'. No-thing therefore has come and no-thing therefore has gone ('has been caused'). The entire doctrine is based upon this simplistic view.

Again, the old standby words of 'ultimately' or 'truly' must be relied upon, presenting us once again with a doctrine of extremes or absolutes, where only lip-service is paid to the existence of conventional reality, because only the extreme of the Void is seen as worthy of consideration, as if that alone is what constitutes life. In effectively observing only one side of the *saṃsāra-śūnyatā* interrelation their logic is inherently deceptive, because it does not account for the sequence of time wherein the entire truth of what actually is/is not evolves. The true nature of the beginning of the sequence is not understood at all. In other words, where does the 'one' or the 'many' observed everywhere *come from*, and how does consciousness arise in the first place, that classifies and segregates the 'one' from the 'many'? Also, how can 'the ultimate' be achieved without that consciousness striving via its interrelationships with 'the one and the many' to perceive the need for aspiring to experience that which is Void?

It was stated in the previous chapter that even this doctrine of absolutes is not free from the concept of 'the one and the many', because of the existence of various forms of *śūnyatā* all integrated into a single one. So, if something already inherently is 'one and many' how can it be used to refute such?

Enquiry into a single effect

Now we can analyse the phrase a 'single effect', as referring 'to a visual cognition *(cakṣur-vijñāna).* ('If you accept that [a single effect] arises [from a multiple cause], then the multiplicity of the cause would not produce multiplicity [in the effect]'.) Here we see that any visual cognition, such as the images seen in the mind's eye when looking at a landscape, is the result of seeing many factors, many images at once (or rather in rapid sequence of many individual images forming a panoramic view), any number of trees, rocks, plants, mountains, sky, etc., each of which can be considered causes of the images. If they were not there they would not be included in what is seen, comprehended, and interpreted as such. Thus the phrase 'the multiplicity of the cause would not produce multiplicity [in the effect]' is untrue, because though the image may be (momentarily) 'single' the mind immediately interprets it in a number of different ways, i.e., it produces a multiplicity of effects. The mind may comment upon the different hues of green of the various trees, one large tree may stand out and be appropriately noticed, one peak of one mountain in the view may have snow upon it and the mind notes that, and another may not have, with the mind immediately trying to ascertain why this difference is so, and so forth. Many effects therefore arising out of the single image, though dependent upon a mind to register and interpret those effects.

We can clearly see here, that indeed, 'nothing is excluded', and for this reason, contrary to Jñānagarbha's line of reasoning, everything actually has a cause, and because it has a cause it also manifests phenomena of some type, and consequent change. Therefore his thesis 'everything must either exist permanently or not exist at all' is also erroneous, except in the ultimate sense, after things that have existed transiently have fully and finally served the purpose for their appearance within the continuum of time and space. Also things cannot and do not 'appear at random' because all causes and effects are governed by incontrovertible law, such as that of *karma*, and those of physics. All causes are ultimately interrelated, and if so then they derive either from *śūnyatā* or from some primal matrix of elementary substance (*mūlaprakṛti,* or *svabhāva*) that is integrated with and evolves into *śūnyatā*.[5] The mechanism of such transmogrifying evolution incorporates the alchemical furnaces that are the *chakras,* and the transmutative agency of human consciousness.

We also see that *śūnyatā* is the constantly recurring theme in Madhyamaka philosophy with regards to the word 'ultimately. Ultimately.....there may be the experience of *śūnyatā*, i.e., a state of 'no causes', but the process of manifesting or becoming 'ultimately' is one of a concomitant potpourri of causes and conditionings. The real question is *not* whether or not there are causes, but *'what or where is the nexus between the causeless state that śūnyatā represents and the myriads of causes and effects seen in Nature?'* This is what must be properly accounted for and explained in any philosophy that presents a complete view. This the Madhyamaka philosophy has not done.

---

5 Hinted at here is the philosophy concerning the ultimate cause for the appearance of the phenomena that characterises 'things'. The ontology of such a cause and its ramifications is vast and necessitates an incorporation of Hindu concepts, such as that of *mūlaprakṛti*. This subject will only be partly dealt with in this series, but will be properly explicated in later books.

The five Elements

There is an objection in the commentary given on the grounds of the cause of the effect being a 'combination', so how can the effect have no cause? The answer given is:

> This is wrong, because there is nothing that can be called "combination" apart from the elements [such as the eye and so forth] that make up the combination. Furthermore, these [elements] are multiple (*bhinna*), since they are mutually exclusive. How can they produce a single, non-multiple effect?
>
> Furthermore, why would elements [such as earth and so forth] that are included in another combination not produce the [same] effect [i.e., visual cognition]?[6]

The subject of the 'elements' is complicated in Buddhism. The Abhidharma states that there are eighteen 'experiential elements',[7] of which the five senses, plus the intellect are seen as the basis, and from which we get the six types of consciousness and their six modes of expression (which are the basis of production). In other lists we get 4 or 8 'elements'. Yogic philosophy, with its doctrine of the *naḍīs* will allow five, which are concomitant upon the development of the wisdoms of the Dhyāni Buddhas. This is the system I use. These five are termed Earth, Water, Fire, Air, Aether (Space).

The sixth 'element' given above: intellect (mentality), is really an aspect of the Fire Element.[8] In my book on *karma* I present a critique of Kalu Rinpoche's explanation of the 'elements' in his book *'The Dharma'*,[9] to which the reader is directed for further information.[10] The

---

6 Ibid., 131.

7 Thurman, *The Speech of Gold,* 134.

8 I capitalise the word Element for these five Elements in order to distinguish these alchemical principles and fundamental attributes of the human psyche, as well as for all of Nature, from the commonly designated scientific concept of elements, as well as the elements (or *dharmas)* of the Abhidharma system, and its derivates, which is the basic conception in Buddhism.

9 Kalu Rinpoche, *The Dharma That Illumines All Beings Impartially Like the Light of the Sun and the Moon,* (State University of New York Press, Albany, 1986).

10 See Bodo Balsys, *Karma and the Rebirth of Consciousness*, 44ff.

92 naturally occurring elements described by materialistic science are aspects of this Earth Element, as explained in my book. Each of the five Elements have five subdivisions to them.

In a footnote commentary to Nāgārjuna's *Precious Garland,* Hopkins states:

> The four elements conventionally exist in mutual dependence; the one cannot exist without the others. However, one of them is not the others because then it would have the character of the others whereby the character of the elements would become confused. They also do not inherently depend on each other, because then they would be inherently existent others, capable of standing alone whereas they are not. They also cannot subsist without the others. This is the fourfold analysis (dependence being considered two ways) which establishes that the elements do not inherently exist, that is, are not established as their own reality.[11]

Contrary to Hopkin's commentary, though 'pure', each Element manifests gradations of their essence that allow the interrelation and transference of attributes between them in the manner shown below. They are therefore interdependent and yet allow each to convey the characteristics of the others, without 'confusion'. Consequently they can 'stand alone' in a similar sense that the body of air 'stands alone' from the earth, and the earth from the bodies of water and air, yet all are interdependent, and to some extent conveyed by the other. Hence the earth carries the moisture so vital for life, and bodies of water (rivers, lakes, etc), the air carries moisture and fine particulate matter (dust), and water carries the air necessary for fish to breathe, and also earthy particles. Similar to what is observed in Nature there is the transformed subjective version concerning the Elements, which constitute the dimensions of perception via which we experience the all, and by utilising the related substance we can move 'things', direct thoughts, manifest psychic powers (the mundane and supramundane *siddhis)* and experience the Void.

Wayman states:

> The first fundamental is analogical thinking : "As without, so within" *(yathā bāhaṃ tathā 'dhyātmam iti).* The Sanskrit is from Abhayākaragupta's *Niṣpannayoāvalī.*[12]

11 Hopkins, *Meditation on Emptiness,* 896.

12 Wayman, *Yoga of the Guhyasamājatantra,* 62.

Such analogical thought is an excellent means for the derivation of wisdom, and not only for that which is without to within and its reverse, but also for that which is 'above' to 'below' and vice versa. Here then we have the movement of the four-armed fixed cross of steady sanctified purpose earlier explained.

The five Elements need proper consideration, and the detail of this subject will be explicated throughout this treatise. This is another area of incongruous thinking in Buddhism, like the subject of *karma*, which similarly was adapted from earlier Brahmanical philosophy.

The Elements are pure essences of what is/is not at whatever level of expression one is cognisant. The terms Earth, Water, Fire, Air, Aether denote the properties of their pure qualities. All formed things are composed from them: thoughts/consciousness, emotions/feelings, gross physical forms, all forms of empirical phenomena, plus that coexistent with the Buddha-spheres in the *dharmakāya*, and in *śūnyatā*.

Without such primal substance (*svabhāva*, meaning 'inherent existence'), nothing could exist or be conceived of. They become the basis for the demonstration of the wisdoms of the five Dhyāni Buddhas. All things therefore can be considered expressions of the law of Dependent Origination, except the Elements. They are the substratum (in their five layers) that support the origination of the All, from which all forms, feelings, thoughts, and that 'beyond' are constructed. If this was not so, then nothing could exist whatsoever. This includes the Void, which is principally constituted of the substance of one of the five Elements, manifesting the (transmuted) quality of Air.[13] Similar to *śūnyatā*, (physical) air is apparently 'empty' of characteristics, but is life-sustaining and allows the expression of light and wind (energy) to be expressed through or by means of it. One could also consider an aspect of *śūnyatā* that is 'defiled' because of its interrelation with *saṃsāra* (thereby integrating *saṃsāra* with *śūnyatā),* as is air with regards to smoke and steam. The defilements symbolise the expression of the effects of the various Elements carried as *prāṇas* (the Airy substance) through the *nāḍīs*.

It is an erroneous presumption to have a concept of 'no annihilation' (the state of experience in *śūnyatā)* and yet have no idea what actually supports that which is 'not annihilated', or that which constitutes what

13 See the doctrine of the five Void Elements below.

is 'not annihilated'. It is absurd to say that there is no inherent substance or existence, and yet state that annihilation of the 'life flux' (or whatever it is that is conceived of as taking rebirth) does not happen upon the attainment of *śūnyatā*. What then is 'it' that attains *śūnyatā* and how can 'it' be sustained? If one points to such terms as the *tathāgatagarbha*, Thusness, and the like, then the questions still remain: 'what is it and how can it be sustained if there is no inherent substance or existence?'

Note that there are two meanings to the word *svabhāva*, as Elizabeth Napper points out:

> As Dzong-ka-ba sees it, Nāgārjuna indicates in chapter fifteen, [of the *Treatise on the Middle Way*] the Analysis of *Svabhāva (rang bzhin),* two distinct meanings of the term *svabhāva:* one is *inherent existence*, the object of negation, which does not exist in the least; the other is emptiness, the *final nature* of each and every phenomenon. Final nature is what Dzong-ka-ba, following Chandrakīrti, sees as intended by the last two lines of the second stanza of chapter fifteen:
>
> > It is not reasonable that an [inherent, or final] nature *(svabhāva)*
> > Arise from causes and conditions.
> > If it did arise from causes and conditions
> > That [inherent, or final] nature would be something made.
> >
> > How could it be suitable
> > For an [inherent, or final] nature to be "made"?
> > An [inherent, or final] nature is non-fabricated
> > And does not depend on another. (XV.1-2)
>
> Numerous modern interpreters, not distinguishing in this way two separate meanings for *svabhāva*, see such passages as paradoxical, whereas for Dzong-ka-pa, again, paradox and even misunderstanding are avoided by a careful delineation of terminology.[14]

In this thesis, the second of the two meanings for *svabhāva*, as a form of emptiness, 'the final nature for each and every phenomenon' is further analysed.

If *śūnyatā* was not composed of such a substance then it simply could not exist, and the attainment of its conditioning would utterly be the end of everything, of existence. There could then be no Buddha-nature.

---

14 E. Napper, *Dependent-Arising and Emptiness,* 127-128.

Śūnyatā exists because the Elements are ultimately real.

Another way of viewing the Elements is that they represent five Voids, constituting the pristine elementary substance or energy; five different energy qualifications, from whence the five wisdoms of the Dhyāni Buddhas are evolved. These wisdoms are the modes of the distributing energy modifications of the five Elements. There needs to be five principal *chakras,* where, of the major seven, the Head and Ājñā centres are integrated, as well as the Base of Spine and Sacral centres. These five are needed, as depicted in the Buddhist Tantric literature, to convey the extended properties of the five Elements. Their modifications are seen in terms of the five *prāṇas* conveyed in the *naḍīs.* From their substance all formed and formless states of being/non-being, and the related entities associated with each respective level, can come to be, undergo various changes, and then continue (being fully clarified and refined) after liberation. They then manifest in terms of the Jina wisdoms. They are the five Tathāgata *bhūmis* that liberated beings utilise in *dharmakāya.*

The Elements therefore cannot be said to be illusions. We thus have:

1. The intrinsic Earthy *prima matrix* (*svabhāva*) that is Void of the vicissitudes and shapes of the forms of all phenomenal things which undergo dependent origination.
2. The intrinsic Watery *prima matrix* that is Void of the afflictive emotions, the substance constituting the denizens of the hell realms, of *pretas, asūras* and the sum of the feeling and emotional projections and thought forms constructed by humanity, as well as the emotive and sensitive sensory apparatus of the lesser kingdoms in Nature.
3. The intrinsic Fiery *prima matrix* that is Void of the vicissitudes of mind, whence we find the abode of the gods. It is present whenever things are to be consumed in cognition, in the blaze of reasoning, and later in the intense Fiery furnace of enlightened revelation. It is the base that supports the existence of the *ālayavijñāna.*
4. The intrinsic Airy *prima matrix* that is void of the qualities of inertia, the attributes of the three *guṇas,*[15] and *manasic* activity. It

15 *Guṇa* (Tib. Yon tan): 'fundamental quality'. All manifest objects are structurally

allows *śūnyatā* to be void of being void.

5. The intrinsic Aetheric *prima matrix* that is both Void and yet the cause of 'phenomena'. It consists of the *akāśa* or space-like substratum that supports the *maṇḍala* of the unity of the other forms of *svabhāva*, and from which comes the motivating potency of the three times. It is the foundational matrix for the omnipresent pervasiveness of the *dharmakāya*.

These five distinct types of primal Void substance (Void Elements) from whence all forms, modifications, and qualities of activity evolve, are the five types of Voidness that convey the wisdoms of the Dhyāni Buddhas.

1. The Dharmadhātu Wisdom of Vairocana—Ādi *śūnyatā* is conveyed by the Aetheric Void, where the space-like substratum becomes the base for the revelation of the gnosis of the omnipresent *dharma*.
2. The Mirror-like Wisdom of Akṣobhya—Clear Light, or Mahāyāna *śūnyatā* is conveyed by the Airy Void, which stands as the middle between all extremes.
3. The Discriminating Inner Wisdom of Amitābha—Culmination-of-Light, or Arhat *śūnyatā*. This refers to the Fiery Void, where the energy of mind has been clarified from all impediments, allowing the expression of Mind to manifest. The qualities of the *guṇas* and *manas* are hypostasised attributes, reflections of the true nature of Mind.
4. The Equalising Wisdom of Ratnasambhava—Spread-of-Light *śūnyatā*. This refers to the Watery Void, where the afflictive emotions have been transformed into the principle of Love, which unifies all life into a fusion of being/non-being.
5. The All-Accomplishing Wisdom of Amoghasiddhi—Light *śūnyatā*. This refers to the Earthy Void, where the vicissitudes and shapes of the forms of all phenomenal things have been transmogrified

---

composed of the three *guṇas: sattva, rajas* and *tamas*. *Sattva* (truth) embodies what is pure and subtle, *rajas* (kingly) embodies activity, and *tamas* (darkness, inertia) embodies heaviness and immobility. *Sattva*, signifying rhythm or balance, represents the quality that must be realised; *tamas* is the obstacle that opposes this realisation; and *rajas* is the force that overcomes *tamas*. In terms of consciousness, *sattva* manifests as peace and serenity, the base for the realisation of the truth of whatever is. *Rajas* is the activity of the mind that establishes knowledge, and *tamas* represents laziness, lack of interest, and stupidity arising from ignorance.

into their *essence*. The 'remainder' is Light and mantric sound, from whence the teachings of Secret Mantra of the Nyingma come.

From the fifth to the first Element we have a natural gradation of increasing subtlety, providing a different level or dimension of perception for transcendental experience. The lowest three levels can be considered the experience of 'tainted *nirvāṇa*', associated with factors governing the *śūnyatā-saṃsāra* integration. In the highest two levels, we have the experience of true *nirvāṇa* and the bliss of transcended *nirvāṇa (pariniṣpanna)* respectively. *Dharmatā* is herein experienced. The generalised Mahāyāna doctrines concerning *śūnyatā* relate to the second Void. The most rarefied Void expresses the attributes of the *dharmakāya*, and what I also exemplify in terms of the qualified term cosmos. Here are expressed the unified gnosis of the five Dhyāni Buddhas.

It is important to note that the rendering of the Elements pertaining to the Jinas utilised throughout this series differs from the traditional account, as derived from the *Bardo Thödol*.[16] In that account to Amoghasiddhi is attributed the Element Air, Ratnasambhava the Element Earth, Amitābha the Element Fire, Akṣobhya the Element Water and Vairocana Aether. The relationships I use relates the attributes of the Dhyāni Buddhas to the planes of perception *(lokas)* that they embody via their Consorts. These are the five Alchemical Elements, of which the *saṃskāras* and *prāṇas* are composed. This arrangement allows proper esoteric correspondences to be made upon all levels of perception, and to the way that these energies manifest via the *chakras*. The reasons for this assignment will be self evident to all who read the volumes of this treatise, wherein the veils and blinds in Buddhist doctrines are logically unveiled, providing revelatory information in their place. The nature of the planes of perception will be partially treated in Volume 4, and with more detail in Volume 6.

Once the doctrine of the Elements is rightly attributed to the Jinas and the families of deities deriving from them, then the entire *maṇḍala* of the manifestation of mind/Mind and the way it affects phenomena falls into place. This allows the attributes of the *chakras* to be comprehended. This subject shall be detailed in Volume 5. In

16 See Anagarika Govinda, *Foundations of Tibetan Mysticism*, 115-125 for an excellent account of this teaching.

this way the esotericism hidden within the exoteric Buddhist lore can be unveiled, providing a much richer accounting of Tantric philosophy than was ever possible to previously reveal. Once the attributes of the Dhyāni Buddhas are corrected then great vistas of revelation are possible, as they and their Consorts are central to the comprehension of the nature of the sum of the appearance of phenomena, and of the means of its transformation into *dharmakāya*. (Note that as there are actually seven major *chakras,* so there are effectively seven Elements. Two therefore are esoteric, being experienced by Buddhas.)

Each *chakra* is depicted as a lotus flower in the process of unfoldment and contains a central jewel, i.e., in the heart of the lotus (the Maṇi part of the mantra Oṁ Maṇi Padme Hūṁ). The jewel is the matrix of the purified essence of the Element of which the *chakra* expresses the potencies and forces. The floral shape, size, number of petals, intensity of hue and internal movement of energies to each *chakra* represents the Padme part of the mantra. This is governed by conscious or enlightened delineation (the Oṁ part of the mantra). All these aspects are the medium of expression conveying the possible types of energies (i.e., *prāṇas* or component aspects of the Elements) from the jewel to be expressed in the form (the Hūṁ part of the mantra). This form is the containment of the *naḍīs* of which the *chakras* are a component part, and by the organs in the body that the *naḍīs* vitalise.

We thus have multiplicity or diversity making up the unity that is a conscious or sentient response to whatever it is that the *naḍīs* come to express into the outer or tangible medium of response (the physical body). This phenomenal form is what consciousness identifies with and takes to be real until it has been trained to view things otherwise. The reality however is that the *chakra* and *naḍī* system stem from the *maṇḍala* of the five Voids that they are the expressions of, allowing the *śūnyatā-saṃsāra* interrelation to manifest the way that it does from flower to flower.

This is the way that each truly accomplished *yogin* views life. By finding his centre of consciousness, travelling through any one of the open doors to multidimensional space (the central 'jewels' at the heart of the *chakras*) the *yogin* (or *yoginī*) can come to experience the type of Void that the mastery of the attained pristine purity of body, speech, and mind, entitles him/her to experience. Buddhahood ensues when all five Voids are mastered and expressed simultaneously. Enlightenment can be experienced through any door. This is the secret that the mantra Oṁ

Maṇi Padme Hūṁ conveys, when coupled to the information associated with the symbolism of the 1,000 armed Avalokiteśvara (esoterically understood), whose mantra it is said to be.

The *chakras* can be conceived of as transformers of *prāṇas,* moderating energies from incoming sources in accord with the need; i.e., the capacity of the rest of the organism to bear the relevant potencies. They are also reservoirs of the type of *prāṇa* of the Element which they are uniquely constructed to bear. The *naḍīs* are conduits of potencies from petal to petal of the different *chakras.*

The difference between the *maṇḍalas* for the central jewels plus *naḍīs,* and the flowers, is that the jewels stem from a grid work pattern based upon the properties of the pentagram (of the five wisdoms), whereas the flowers are based upon a *maṇḍala* of the hexagram, which when doubled (allowing the expression of positive and negative) gives us the qualities of the Heart *chakra.* That which interrelates them is the *maṇḍala* based upon the square. (The foundation of the seat of power in a person, embodied by the qualities of the four petals of the Base of the Spine Centre.) This 'square' then becomes the basis of the foundation of a twelve-petalled Heart *chakra,* when interwoven with the properties of the triangle, four interwoven triangles making three squares. Such is the geometry of the sphere of Life, into which all is contained.

By analysing the doctrine of the Elements and the five Dhyāni Buddhas in this esoteric fashion we can raise our vision higher than considerations pertaining to the Element Earth, and therefore move beyond the focus of many contemporary accounts.

The interrelatedness of the Elements

Jñānagarbha's commentary continues in an objection-reply fashion:

> [Objection:]...But the cause of the effect is a combination *(sāmagrī).* The multiplicity or lack of multiplicity in the effect is related to the multiplicity or lack of multiplicity of that [combination] and is related by invariable concomitance *(anvaya-vyatireka).* So how can [the effect] have no cause?
>
> [Reply:] This is wrong, because there is nothing that can be called 'combination' apart from the elements [such as the eye and so forth] that make up the combination. Furthermore, these [elements] are

> multiple *(bhinna),* since they are mutually exclusive. How can they produce a single, non-multiple effect?
>
> Furthermore, why would elements [such as earth and so forth] that are included in another combination not produce the [same] effect [i.e., visual cognition]?
>
> [Objection:] [earth and so forth] do not produce [visual cognition] because they are different [from the eye and so forth].
>
> [Reply:] Our answer is the same. [Haribhadra's version of the argument repeats the earlier question: 'How can the eye and so forth, which are mutually distinct, produce (a single effect)?']
>
> [Objection:]...Those [elements] which, as causes of experience, possess an additional factor *(svabhāvātiśaya)* that causes [visual cognition], are the causes of [visual cognition]. The others [such as earth and so forth] are not.
>
> [Reply:] This is also mistaken. To claim that [these elements] possess a single additional factor that causes [visual cognition], when the eye and so forth are mutually distinct, is to contradict perception and so forth. Furthermore, the [additional factor] that causes [visual cognition] would have to be multiple if the eye and so forth are multiple. So the argument that the eye and so forth are diverse shows that this position is not very satisfactory.[17]

As our definitions of the term 'elements' differ, so obviously, will our concepts. Our vocabulary essentially manifests from two completely different perspectives, producing little concordance, as for instance, 'the eye and so forth', as given in Jñānagarbha's text, are not Elements in my accounting. They are simply organs of perception. Through the higher correspondences of the organs *(chakras),* the Elements can come to be known. So the argument as to the 'additional factor' becomes meaningless here, except for the factor of the mechanism of the eye that allows cognition of what is seen, and its stereo-visioning function, that allows perception and gauging of depth, i.e., the three-dimensionality of objects. If such are the 'additional factors' discussed, then fine, they can be factored in, but they are not the Elements.

---

17 Eckel, 130-131.

However, we can look to the statement 'these elements are multiple and mutually exclusive. How can they produce a single non-multiple effect?' I have posited five main Elements (to which there are 5 x 5 subdivisions), presenting the concept of multiplicity, but they are, and yet are not, mutually exclusive, in a similar manner that the five Dhyāni Buddhas are exclusive and yet integrated with respect to each other. Why is this? The answer lies in the fact that though distinct, each carries or bears aspects of the others, and are also the bearers of a process, a continuum from one to the next, where none can in reality, 'ultimately' be viewed as distinct from another. This can be borne in mind from the following table of their subdivisions with respect to increasing density.

Aether	Air	Fire	Water	Earth
Aether-Aether				
Aether-Air	Air-Aether			
	Air-Air			
Aether-Fire		Fire-Aether		
	Air-Fire	Fire-Air		
		Fire-Fire		
Aether-Water			Water-Aether	
	Air-Water		Water-Air	
		Fire-Water	Water- Fire	
			Water-Water	
Aether-Earth				Earth-Aether
	Air-Earth			Earth-Air
		Fire-Earth		Earth-Fire
			Water-Earth	Earth-Water
				Earth-Earth

Table 1. The Elements

In the above table we see that the bolded aspects represent the pure Elements from each of the categories. They can be considered interrelated, yet mutually exclusive, i.e., Aether-Aether is exclusive of Air-Air and of Fire-Fire, etc., yet to each column there are natural intersecting points where the qualities of the Elements comingle, producing thereby variegations of the pure Elements, allowing the assimilation of each other's qualities. Thus we have Air-Fire—Fire-Air. There are also the minor intersecting points, for instance, Aether-Earth with the Earthy aspects of all the other Elements. There is also a natural descent and translocation of *prāṇas* from one column to the next, e.g., Aether-Earth to Air-Earth, thence Fire-Earth, etc. The process of ascension of any *prāṇa* must be viewed similarly to that which occurs within a fractional distillation column, whereby grosser *prāṇas* bearing energy quotients unable to reach the subtler potency of a higher level of expression are syphoned off. The quality of consciousness is transmuted from grosser states to the more refined, thus higher perceptions are evoked and the nature of the developed *siddhis* defined within the *samādhi* of the accomplished *yogin*. Hence there is no sharply defined boundary between one gradient and the next, simply a gradual refinement from a denser gradient with the characteristics of being Earthy, to the next, with characteristics of being Watery, etc.

The fact that one Element bears aspects of all the others allows for the immense multi-diversity of forms and phenomena seen on all levels of expression. It is what facilitates 'multiple-effects' rather than non-multiple ones, contrary to Jñānagarbha's theory. It also allows evolution up the 'ladder' of being/non-being.

Table 1 presents an incomplete picture. A different perspective is presented in Figure 2. Each circle in Figure 2 represents another swastika, with the pure Element, e.g., Fire-Fire being the locus for the centre of the swastika. The swastika is but the animating power behind the actuality of a dorje/*vajra*. Here we see the way these Elements interrelate by way of moving vortices of energies (manifesting as *naḍīs* when viewed as a spiral motion over time). They produce the propagation of *saṃsāra*, or else provide the means whereby liberation can be gained. The Elements either bind or liberate, according to whether the swastikas are spinning from left to right (the liberating means) or from right to left (which produces increased immersion into *saṃsāra*, and hence bondage to it).

Depicted here is a cross section of a *naḍī*, indicating the way that *prāṇa* flows therein. It should be noted that the *prāṇas* are moving winds that manifest in the form of the *saṃskāras* that are generated during the life processes. The Elements are the substance constituting the *prāṇas*, and form the basis (*upādhi*) which supports phenomenal existence. Swastikas represent the dynamics of how things are moved or propelled through space. It is more accurate to consider each arm of a swastika as a spiral moving through space and time rather than a point in space.

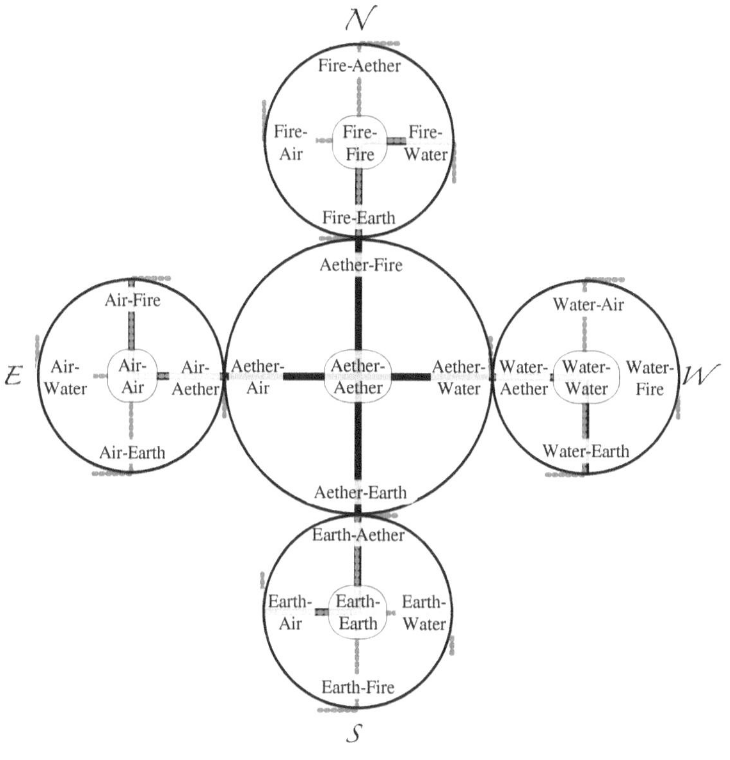

Figure 2. The Elements

The role of consciousness

Returning to Jñānagarbha's commentary, which states: 'why would elements [such as earth and so forth] that are included in another combination not produce the [same] effect [i.e., visual cognition]?' The esoteric answer is quite simple, all Elements go to produce 'the same effect', but specifically the *prāṇas* of the one whose quality relates directly to that of the effect will predominate. Visual cognition relates directly to the energies of the mind, therefore the Element Fire is the major purveyor of the ability to see, however, one can 'see' not only via the mind, but also through mental-emotions, etc. The Elements interrelate in the way shown in the swastika above and according to the way that the *prāṇas* and *saṃskāras* flow. Accordingly, the capacities of any of the senses is either stimulated or impaired. In the case of a debilitating sickness, the *prāṇas* conveyed to the area of sickness are of a greyish nature and have a devitalising effect. If the *prāṇas* being conveyed to the eyes, for example, are intensely of this nature one's sight could fail if the aberrant *prāṇas* are not rectified.

One can also state that there is really no such thing as a 'single non-multiple effect', as all things are a composite of many factors, even *śūnyatā* (when for instance the five Void Elements are incorporated into its constitution), so why would one to try to produce a 'single non-multiple effect', unless that effect be Buddhahood? But Buddhahood itself is the composite of many factors. It may be a moot point whether Buddhahood is a single effect or a multiple one, depending upon how one interprets the enlightenment concerned, as well as the wisdoms of the five Dhyāni Buddhas, however not all Buddhas are the same, they have different auras and manifest differing Buddha-spheres. We can thus argue, or simply say that 'many' (i.e., the compositional factor of the five Elements) produce One, the *swastika*/dorje of the five Dhyāni Buddhas that is enlightenment.

This doctrine of Elements is an elaboration of the Madhyamaka logic:

> Just as here, from those empty reflections and so forth,
> There are produced consciousnesses having their aspects [i.e., an eye consciousness seeing the reflection],
> Similarly, even though all things are empty, [383b]
> From those empty [things, effects] are thoroughly produced.[18]

Furthermore, these 'empty things' are constituted of the five distinct types of emptinesses (like the five fingers to the one hand) that are the basis of the phenomenal appearances of all things, viewed conventionally. Concerning the question that 'if things do not inherently exist what then manifests to perform functions?' The answer from the Prāsaṅgika Mādhymika viewpoint, via Chandrakīrti's *Commentary*

---

18 Chandrakīrti's *Supplement to (Nāgārjuna's) Treatise on the Middle Way* (VI, 37-38ab). Quoted from Elizabeth Napper, 196.

on Āryadeva's 'Four Hundred' is:

> In that case, regarding any object, [it is said]:
>
> > With respect to production, it does not come [here from somewhere]
> >
> > And, similarly, with respect to cessation, it does not go [from here to somewhere]. (XV.10ab)
>
> [Hence], it definitely does not inherently exist.
>
> Should someone ask, "If these do not inherently exist, then what is there?", the answer is as follows: Those [objects] that are dependent-arisings, entities produced from the thoroughly afflicted and the very pure acting as causes, exist.[19]

The answer with respect to the appearance of phenomena via Dependent Origination is only possible because of the existence of the Void Elements and their mode of manifestation, as outlined above. Concerning the non-appearance from somewhere of the production of phenomena, or in its cessation that it goes somewhere, it lies on the presumption that as all is Void ('ultimately') so how could there be a coming or going from anything. That may be so from the point of view of ultimates, but with respect to the appearance of the experiential phenomena there are causes and conditions, appearances and cessation, of moving events from an origination and ceasing at a destination. The duration of the manifesting phenomena is important, thus the relative entityness of things, as well as the manifest functions of those things. The manifestation of the wisdom in a Buddha's Mind depends upon this interdependent relative entityness as well as residence in *śūnyatā*. What consequently needs to be explained is a mechanism whereby 'things' that intrinsically lack entityness can also manifest functions, i.e., produce 'multiplicity'. This mechanism is the mind, which calls forth *saṃskāras* of past actions and integrates them with the experience of manifesting phenomena, generating any number (or multiplicity) of new *saṃskāras*. The question of the appearance of these *saṃskāras* and how they are converted into the Void Elements then constitutes the nature of walking the path to enlightenment.

Also (quoting from Elizabeth Napper's translation of *Dzong-ka-ba's*

19 Elizabeth Napper, 214.

Great Exposition):

> Therefore, through realizing that all phenomena are, from the beginning, without even a particle that is established by way of its own entity, you do not fall to an extreme of existence. And, when you induce an ascertaining consciousness which ascertains that even so [i.e., even though they lack inherent existence], things such as sprouts and so forth, without coming to be non-things empty of the capacity to perform functions, have the power to perform their own functions, you abandon the extreme of non-existence.[20]

It is relatively easy to perceive how things, being transient, inherently lack their 'own entity', because of the nature of their transience. The statement then introduces an 'ascertaining consciousness', but does not explain where such a consciousness has come from, i.e., how it has evolved in order to ascertain things that 'have the capacity to perform functions'. The assumption is that it has come from a human unit, a personal-I, who can thus query or look. Some conundrums arise here. Firstly we have the problem of falling into the 'extreme of existence' (i.e., the concept of an *ātman*, or permanent soul, a philosophic, 'all' or unity, a 'one', to which the main thesis of 'One and Many' really refers), which according to this philosophy is to be avoided. Then we have the problem of falling into the extreme of 'non-existence' or nihilism. This produces an atheistic universe, where many things exist, but are not causally related, other than through physical laws, likewise to be philosophically avoided. Avoidance of these two extremes is understandable, and a major part of the Mādhyamika logic concerns the methodology whereby one can do this. However, what is introduced in an endeavour to try to avoid the extremes is actually the factor of *consciousness*. (The *raison d'état* of the Yogācārin school of thought.)

This means that consciousness (which in its own way is transient, productive of the conventional truth) is the pathway to the real. It is the mechanism of realising the ultimate truth. It is the middle path, the Madhyamaka way. Yes! Then what is it in consciousness that is the saving grace of this philosophy, that allows its adherents to fall to neither extreme? The answer lies in the fact that via its forms of activity the

20 Ibid., 200.

ālayavijñāna, *śūnyatā*, and the *dharmakāya* can come to be experienced. They can only be experienced if there is a continuum of consciousness contained in a form, a coherent 'bundle' of attributes. Such a form allows consciousness to evolve in a steady and measured way that outlasts the birth and death of the personal-I's, by integrating the *karma* of the interrelated unfoldment of each personal-I. (It takes more than just one life to develop highly qualified and sophisticated consciousness-states.) The continuum therefore represents a type of 'soul', otherwise there could be no progress to any of the three abovementioned goals. It can also be gathered that this 'soul-form' does not fall into the category of 'extreme-existence', neither does it partake of 'non-existence'. So far so good. But this is not the preferred Mādhyamika view. However the logic is impeccable, and is definitely a pathway of revelation stemming from Tsongkhapa's[21] statement given above. Such a 'soul-form' we will see can also be considered to be grounded in the lack of 'entityness' denoted by a 'Void of the vicissitudes of mind', and also comes to manifest functions, i.e., produces 'multiplicity', the virtually never ending sequence of personal 'I's'.

The production of a multiple effect

In continuing Jñānagarbha's text we see that the opponent now presents a view that 'a multiple (*aneka*) cause produces a multiple [effect]'.[22] Jñānagarbha's reply to this is:

> This is wrong. If the cognitive nature and so forth [which are the cause] are mutually distinct, the cognition *(vijñāna)* [which is the effect] must also be multiple, because it is not different from them.[23] If it were different, they would not be its cause, because it would have to be associated with another efficient cause *(hetu-kāraṇa)*.[24] [If the effect is not multiple,] the particular aspects of the cause cannot be

21 Or alternatively rendered Dzong-ka-ba, Tsong Khapa, Tsong-ka-pa.

22 Eckel, 81.

23 The footnote provided, Ibid., 131: 'Different from the cognitive nature and so forth, which are the particular aspects of the cause'.

24 The footnote provided, (Ibid): 'By "efficient cause" Jñānagarbha seems to mean some additional, intervening factor to mediate the cause, which is multiple, and the effect, which is not'.

mutually distinct, because the cognition *(vijñāna)* [which is the effect] cannot be multiple. There can be no possible benefit from imagining the cause to be multiple. This is why [the opponent's] position is wrong.

[Objection:] By nature the effect is not multiple, but it is a phenomenon *(dharma)* that we imagine *(kalpita)* to be multiple because of its association with the cause. So the multiplicity of the effect, which is caused [by the cause], is imagined.

[Reply:] All right. If the efficient cause *(hetu-kāraṇa)* is conceptually constructed (*kalpanoparacita*), then in a real sense *(tattvā-rthena),* it is only imagined *(kalpita).* In that case, the effect has no cause, because it is associated with an efficient cause that is imagined.

Furthermore, if you say that the particular aspects [of the effect] actually (*vastutaḥ)* are multiple, but the effect is not, then the subject *(dharmin)* is different from the properties *(dharma),* since [the properties] are multiple, and [the subject] is not. This leads to the problem mentioned before [namely that the effect must be associated with some other efficient cause].

If the particular aspects are only imagined, it is wrong to say that multiple aspects arise from multiple causes. If the multiplicity [of the aspects] is conceptually constructed, it does not depend on an efficient cause.[25]

It should be noted that causes produce effects irregardless of whether there is any 'cognitive nature' to perceive of their happening. The universe was in existence long before there were human beings that developed cognitive faculties to perceive anything. It had to be, otherwise no humans could have evolved to perceive anything, or to develop the faculties with which to imagine things. To deny the existence of causes is to deny the existence of humans with their thinking and imaginative capacity. Humans are prime causative agents in this world system, because they can think, and thereby manifest premeditated actions in a wilful manner designed to manipulate things in the environment around them. That the things that they manipulate may be ultimately illusional is undeniable. However, until the time sequence eventuates when the 'ultimate' becomes the reality, such things are manipulated

25 Eckel, 81-82.

and changes happen that alter our perceptions, and we consequently grow conceptually in the knowledge of the way things are. *Karma* works in this way, and without the process of change (part of the second of the Four Noble Truths) there would be no evolution to Buddhahood. Wherever there is change there is something that has been caused, produced from something else.

So we can say that *ultimately* 'many do not produce many', but the reality of the phenomenal world is that conventionally many *do* produce many, as long as there is a universe composed of many things continuously interacting to produce the sum total of all that is. Ultimately there will be no universe, but that is *not the reality* now, and we must work with *present reality structures,* not try to live as if we were sometime in the unimaginable distant future, otherwise we will never evolve to get 'there'.

Now, if we say that *ultimately* 'many do not produce many', what is really meant by this statement? Myriads of changes have gone on throughout the process of the evolutionary experience wherein consciousness grows, strives to master, then finally conquers the condition known as *saṃsāra*, and enters into a causeless zone. So, ultimately a causeless zone is eventuated, where 'many do not produce many'. However, the process of getting there involves numerous steps along the way of *causes and effects,* each gradually being cleansed of defilements, with the *saṃskāras* becoming more sublime, then transcended, until only one effect is left, the 'ultimate'. So, is this 'ultimate' truly causeless if myriads of causes and effects have passed by to produce it?

The process is something like a distillation column (with five major fractional levels, i.e., five Void levels) where the most volatile and refined fractionate reaches the highest fractionating unit at the top of the column. Those possessing higher boiling points and consisting of heavier components are treated and fractionated off lower in the column. (Note that the spinal column in the human body symbolises such a unit, and from it stem the various *chakras*, each of which can be considered a fractionating unit.) It is from this position that all aspects of the Elements can be mastered, making one a *siddha* with respect to them; allowing one to perform what in the West are termed miracles.

One can therefore experience different levels of *śūnyatā*. This means that a Bodhisattva focuses upon attaining one particular level at a time (via any particular incarnation that has manifested for that purpose), but always the others are simultaneously worked upon to differing degrees.

These Voids are attained once one has distilled away the *saṃskāras* of change with respect to each of the Elements, until only the pure essence is left, the *svabhāva*, plus the wisdom of the corresponding Dhyāni Buddha. What is left then is a 'causeless' condition, at whichever level of the five Voids you discern. However the effluvium that has been discarded, in this respect, is not Void, but will be transmuted in order to abide in this condition. It gets recycled, to be utilised by those units of consciousness and sentience that can still gain from contact and experience with it.

This is another way of saying that this 'causeless condition' inadvertently acts as a cause or seed point (*bīja*) for the manifestation of the phenomena associated with the Element that it is expressive of. This is what sustains the *śūnyatā-saṃsāra* interrelation. The mechanism, when taking all of the five Voids into account, actually is a *viśvavajra*, but the detail of the philosophy of how such a *vajra* (Tib: dorje) and the moving swastika of the Voids are interrelated cannot be presently given.

We can also see that it is erroneous for Mādhyamika philosophers to focus mainly upon a small part of the overall philosophy, which I have described as the 'causeless condition' above. Scholars, such a Chandrakīrti and Jñānagarbha however are products of their era and civilisation, hence the factors conditioning their philosophic speculation was limited to what was possible at their period of time in history. (There was for instance a lack of scientific understanding of the nature of phenomena and its laws.) Thus they presented a syllogistic framework which was a more veracious derivation of the logic of their opponents. It was simply an extension of a similar mind set, through which their opponents were found to be inadequate to find proper responses in debates. Essentially, therefore, they were both talking along the same lines, with some very similar premises, e.g., of the concept of transmigration, and of 'the elements' that are the phenomenon *(dharma)* spoken of above; preventing true veridical logic from both camps. Present day Buddhists therefore need to evolve and extricate their thinking somewhat from that of the past epochs.

Of course the enlightened *knew,* but they were handicapped in what they could say by their enlightened perception of what could be given at any time with respect to the nature of the prevailing mindsets of the unenlightened. For this reason 'ear-whispered truths' that were *not* written down were reserved for those who had the capacity to Know, i.e., had the good *karma* to gain enlightenment in that life. This is a reason why the Buddha refused to discuss certain subjects, such as whether a Tathāgata was 'extinguished' or 'remained' after his *parinirvāṇa.* The enlightened could see for themselves and hence did not have to be told, whilst the unenlightened did not have the capacity to understand, and would only distort what was proffered, creating *karma.* Therefore the Buddha could not speak, but *sūtras* were written by others to inform the unenlightened.

This treatise proposes to unveil the esotericism in Buddhism by presenting much that formerly had to be veiled and heard only through esoteric transmission from a guru.

Now back to Jñānagarbha's syllogism, which was quoted above:

> This is wrong. If the cognitive nature and so forth [which are the cause] are mutually distinct, the cognition *(vijñāna)* [which is the effect] must also be multiple, because it is not different from them.

Why is it presumed that the cognition is 'not different' from the multiple causes? Cognition must be different from any multiple causes of phenomena. Indeed it is (vacuously) ignorant of most of the causes and rightfully so, otherwise it would be so enmeshed in a multifarious panoply of causes and effects stretching through incalculable aeons that it would become totally dysfunctional and not be able to perform its most basic activities. If one were to utilise Yogācārin philosophy then the above statement of Jñānagarbha is deemed true, because everything experienced and known is by means of consciousness, which must thereby be identified with what is experienced, for all happens because of and exists within the precincts of consciousness. However, in what has been presented above we are presented with rhetoric as to why cognition being different from any multiple causes of phenomena is untenable. The consciousness that cognises may be the effect, but it is both multiple (because many little cognitions go into the analysis or observation of manifesting phenomena) and singular, because it posits an overview and consequently can predict the probable future of the sequence of events manifesting a phenomena. An example is the deduction that the signposts on a highway will lead one to the city they point to. Being both unitary and multiple eliminates the main purport of Jñānagarbha's syllogism.

Consciousness cannot be so easily particularised as Jñānagarbha seems to assert; it is much more fluid, spacious, and graceful than that. Indeed, as we have already seen, consciousness is Tsongkhapa's salvation in his battle to find the middle way between extreme existence and non-existence. Obviously cognition is but a part of the functioning of consciousness whereby information is selected and integrated into consciousness, and Jñānagarbha is specifically speaking of it, but cognition is an integral part of consciousness and therefore cannot be separated from it in one's considerations.

If it is said that the 'cognitive nature and so forth' *are the cause*, then we can query how can this possibly be? The cognitive nature is that which registers and analyses an effect of a cause *after* the effect has been produced. It is like walking into a darkened room and then someone turns on a light switch. The cognitive nature suddenly apprehends light and surmises that this is because the light switch has been turned on (a cause), allowing the flow of electricity to the bulb (another cause), which then produces light because of the factor of electrical resistance (another cause) and the way that the light bulb was constructed to capitalise upon this factor (another cause). If it was not for any or all of these factors, no light switch, no electrical current, no appropriate wiring, no functioning light bulb connected to it all, then the cognitive nature would still be in darkness and perceive nothing.

It certainly is not the cause of all these things, or the cause of the phenomena of light. It has the ability, however, to register the fact that when a switch is turned on (all of the causative factors being *in situ* and rightly functioning, including the mechanism of the eye and eye-brain consciousness coordination), and light appears so with it comes the unlimited opportunities for activity that such light affords. (Thus the cognitive nature can be considered to be causative with respect to the realm of ideas, but generally needs visual input and other stimuli to formulate such ideations.)

Now, all of these factors are mutually distinct, because the omission of any one of them (e.g., if there was no electricity) would prevent the appearance of light, and consequently all of the further forms of activity that are possible because of it. This does not mean in any way that the cognition must be multiple, simply that it must be functioning, as part of a chain of cause-events, a sequence or continuum of such happenings through time that eventually or *ultimately* produces the effect of the registering of light (and everything that it reveals) in consciousness.

The word 'ultimately' is emphasised here because it is such an important term in Madhyamaka philosophy and I wish to point out one of its significant properties, namely that it can refer to something that will appear at the end of things, of finality. Therefore the ending of a particular time sequence, e.g., if we are counting milliseconds (with the passage of time slowed down so that the duration of each millisecond can have a noticeable effect upon consciousness), then 'ultimately' one minute will have passed and one hour appears as a very long period of time indeed. The term ultimately therefore refers to that which must achieve completion at the end of a time sequence, but the pace of the registration of time depends upon the nature of the consciousness (or sentience) that is experiencing it. The cognisance of consciousness therefore has reference to the type of 'time warp' it is in.

Is it attuned to and working with fast time, i.e., with picoseconds, nanoseconds or the comparatively slow milliseconds, wherewith the world of subatomic particles can be experienced? Herein one hour of normal human time may be an eternity; a subatomic particle may have lived out its entire life-span and died almost an 'eternity ago'. Or are we looking at slow time wherein events may be measured in terms of years, or hundreds of thousands or even millions of years (e.g., as in genetic adaptation). So how is this word 'ultimately' actually to be defined; in terms of atomic time, human time, evolutionary time, cosmological time, absolute time? It is obvious that the Buddhist philosophers really only thought in terms of human time (in relation to the human condition and the nature of its consciousness). It is all that really concerned them, but is this truly an enlightened stance, or must one alter one's thinking to properly account for all of the ways that time is reckoned?

Now, the consciousness (that registers the effect) may be considered to be not different from the rest of the factors in the chain of cause-effects to produce the light, however it is another factor needed in the equation: darkness + switch + electrical wiring + electricity + bulb + eye + nervous system + functioning brain produces the conscious registering of light. Or rather; all of the factors leading to the bulb produce light because the eye, nervous system and functioning brain have registered the appearance of such.

Yet the cognitive nature is also different because the light appears whether or not that consciousness is around to register it. If a blind person turned the switch the light will appear and be registered by another consciousness, even though it won't be registered by the eye-consciousness of the blind person. The sun, for instance, has been generating light long before humans were around to analyse its properties. The proof of it exists in the fact that the earth is existing, alive, and able to support the life of a human being and his consciousness-stream because of it. Consciousness may be able to acknowledge the fact, but the earth needs not this 'consciousness' in order to support life, though it needs the sun.

We see also that the cognitive nature need not be multiple, even though the causes are multiple. In fact, if the cognitive nature were multiple many problems could occur:

a. The factor of schizophrenia, where one aspect of the consciousness is saying one thing, and another aspect of the consciousness something else, the two aspects then clashing with each other.

b. One aspect of the consciousness may choose not to view something whilst the other consciousnesses wishes to. The two consciousnesses will thus fight over possession or control of the eyes, with one trying to keep the eyes closed and the other open. If such happened throughout the body with respect to other organs the body simply could not function.

c. One consciousness could be clearly superior in deductive abilities and the other an ignoramus, preventing the functioning of any proper reasoning, with the appearance of occasional lucidity. Such a 'split personality' would become increasingly pronounced according to the number of consciousnesses there were.

d. One consciousness could be programmed to see only one type of thing (being blind to everything else), and another to something else, again there would be a warring.
e. One consciousness could be asleep at the time of turning on the light and another awake, and when the sleeping one awoke there could be a clash of opinions.

The functioning of consciousness under any or all of the above conditionings would be severely impaired. (This being directly proportional to the number of cognitive natures there actually was.) Clearly in the normal person (schizophrenics and the blind aside) there is only one cognitive factor,[26] not many, analysing the many causes of the appearance of light, because that cognition is different from the light, but part of the same chain of interdependence. Light appears in consciousness because that chain of interdependence exists.

The cause consequently needs not to be imagined by the singular consciousness; it simply is thus, otherwise the singular phenomena of light could not appear. It is a singular phenomena that produces multiple effects, e.g., the lighting up of all of the objects of the room, which consciousness can find one by one, or sweep the room with panoramic vision to get an overview of what is there. Then, even going to find hidden objects, such as the words on a page that can be read when a book is opened, and which is part of a non-imagined sequence of events, which cannot happen in the dark. It necessitates the appearance of light, the flicking of a switch, and so forth.

It is here that the opponent is also in error, because he conceded that 'By nature the effect is not multiple, but it is a phenomenon *(dharma)*

---

26 There may however be aspects of the normal consciousness that at times appear to clash with other aspects in a relatively minor way, as for instance, when the alarm goes off, the lazy part of one's consciousness protesting and campaigning for more sleep, whilst the fastidious and responsible part demands to get up. When such happens then consciousness is normally partially impaired for the duration of the confusion, until its assertive dominant reason takes control of the situation.

that we imagine *(kalpita)* to be multiple because of its association with the cause. So the multiplicity of the effect, which is caused [by the cause], is imagined'. The fact is that it is not imagined, but deduced by impeccable logic to be there, because of known facts with respect to the material world of phenomena. From another perspective, everything in the phenomenal world can be considered a type of *imagining,* making us live in a type of dream world until we wake up to the reality of the enlightened state that is void of all such imaginings. But this is not the gist of the logic, which speaks of 'cognitive consciousness', 'eye consciousness', 'elements', and the like, i.e., of the world of conventional reality.

This is but an example of the opponent manifesting a similar mind set, not allowing him to properly think through to find proper reasoning in debates. Once the opponent falls into the trap of speaking of phenomena in terms of imaginings, then Jñānagarbha can pounce and say that if things are imagined, then there can be no cause, because such a cause would have no substantiality in fact. We however, do not go that way in our reasoning, but rather speak in terms of experiential fact, whereby consciousness grows along the road to attaining Buddhahood in the end, as per example the turning on of the light in a darkened room, or in one's mind for that matter. If there was no factor of turning on light then ignorance would never be conquered, and where would Jñānagarbha's logic stand then—in the dark, or the dark ages?

So we have a cause, the turning on of a light switch, and an eventual, ultimate, consequence—the attainment of Buddhahood. This brings us to the statement that the 'particular aspects [of the effect] actually *(vastutaḥ)* are multiple'. Yes this is indeed so, because there is a long list of causes and effects before Buddhahood is attained as a consequence of turning on that light switch. This does not necessarily make the subject different from the properties, because a Buddha (to be) includes all of the manifold vicissitudes of the process of the turning on of that light switch in consciousness. Yet the person is different, because he/she is more than just the process of turning on that switch. It is just one of the factors that has made one evolve. And it is true that 'the effect must be associated with some other efficient cause', because there are a myriad of such causes to take into consideration when the term 'ultimately' is utilised in our consideration. It is the continuum or process that is of importance, not just a single instance, or cause, such as turning on the light switch. (Though some commentators have likened the attainment of enlightenment simply just to that, i.e., the turning on of a light switch, where once one stood in darkness as to his perceptions of the true nature of things, one now stands completely in unadulterated light.)

Consequently, this entire concept of 'many do not produce many', etc., has gone astray because of:

1. An incomplete understanding, or confusion, of the nature of the Elements, *karma*, the evolutionary process, and of the way they function.
2. An improper use of the word 'ultimately' by ignoring the processes happening as part of a sequence of events. There is a sequence of conscious development and transformations between *saṃsāric* causes and conditionings and the ultimate attainment of *śūnyatā*, yet the presented philosophy makes out as if there is none, and that this attainment has happened. Ultimately yes....but not for a long while or duration of experiential development (of causes and effects, as governed by *karma*) can the ultimate be experienced. We can say that ultimately such a duration must cause the attainment of *śūnyatā*. The causes, conditionings, and effects, cannot simply be imagined, otherwise no experiences productive of anything real (like *śūnyatā)* could eventuate, but ultimately experience in *saṃsāra* will appear like a dream and *śūnyatā* the real.
3. An incorrect understanding of the way *saṃsāra* and *śūnyatā* interrelate. The presented logic that 'Many do not produce One. Many do not produce Many. One does not produce Many. One does not produce One', simply does not include the fact that *saṃsāra* and *śūnyatā* incorporate each other, i.e., the factor of *saṃsāra* as a viable entity is excluded in the reasoning. *Śūnyatā* alone is grasped and the fact that it is attributeless (to the reasoning mind) allowed the Mādhyamika philosophers to manifest an attributeless syllogism. It is in this unitary focus that the main error lies.

This triune foundation of error can consequently be found throughout the Madhyamaka philosophy, but can now be rectified.

Causes and effects

Jñānagarbha then gives seven additional verses to support his theses, which I shall briefly comment upon:

> (1) If you think that the effect is not multiple, but its particular aspects are multiple [and there is no difference between them], it must be an act of God![27]

I shall not examine the interesting subtleties of the meaning of the term 'God' (*Īśvara*) here, as this would take us too far away from the main theme. His exclamation however simply implies it would then be a miracle. However, if we take a god to be a human unit, capable of manifesting conscious volitions of self-will that can manipulate substance in such a way that consciousness is affected, then Jñānagarbha's expression is correct. (After all, the human unit is a god to the cells, the sentient units of his body.) I have already pointed out that nothing stands in isolation, thus we can say that an effect, the manifestation of light from a light bulb, once someone has flicked the switch on, can be considered a singular effect that has multiple ramifications (e.g., the lighting up of all the objects then seen in a room), depends upon how one defines or views the happening. This is because the sudden appearance of light actually has more causes than just the flicking on the light switch, for this will only happen if certain conditions, such as the existence of electricity, are manifest. One also effectively acts as a god when one flicks on the light switch, because it would appear so to one who has never come into contact with electricity and modern technology.

> (2) If [a cognition] is not different from its cognitive nature, it cannot arise from form *(rūpa)*. If it is not different from the *ākāra* [of the object], it cannot arise from form *(rūpa)*.[28]

How can a cognition be different from its cognitive nature? It is composed of the same elements, the substance of the mind that perceives, plus the rest of the apparatus that allows connection of the

27 Eckel, 82.

28 Ibid.

mind with the brain structure of a human. The only difference is that the cognitive nature is the substratum from whence the cognition derives its ability to perceive something, i.e., a *rūpa*, or a composite number of forms, to make a complete picture. The cognition can deduce this to be phenomenally real, and thus analyse because of the mental apparatus (etc) that utilises it. The cognition *does not* arise from the form; rather, the form is but a stimulus that allows the cognitive nature to gain something experientially from it. The form and the cognition that perceives are consequently two different things, passing fleetingly in the light. The form gives rise to stimuli that *can grow* into *saṃskāras* if the god that is the human unit wishes to interrelate with it in a definite manner so as to produce a pattern in consciousness that necessitates recollection at a later time. Cognition depends upon the conscious volitions, the will of the human unit (the thinker) and is not a property of the form (unless it be the human god's own body consciousness). The form however possess properties determining what can be experienced by the human unit that the human sense-perceptors and brain consciousness can gather sensory input from, in accordance with its inherent properties.

Many might see the mountains in the distance (forms) but very few will want to experience them to the extent of climbing to the pinnacles. For the great majority the interaction stops with the visual cortex and brain consciousness. The few that choose to climb will suffer the bruises, pains, joys, sights, and smells of the close-up view of the form. Without the factor of such conscious exertion by use of the will, nothing can arise from interaction with the form. The [external] form does nothing of itself but provide an opportunity for a human consciousness to experience its phenomena in one way or another.

It should also be noted that consciousness is constituted of aspects of the Fiery Element and the form is constituted of the Earthy Element. (The Watery Element refers to human emotions.) The Earthy Element concerns the sum of the physicality observed everywhere, including water and physical fire. It is therefore different from 'the *ākāra* [of the object]'. There is however a mechanism of interrelation, as indicated by the tabulation of the Elements. Each step of this ladder of the Elements can be considered a refined, distilled, or transmuted correspondence of the step below it.

> (3) If a single [effect] both arises and does not arise, and if [a single cause] both causes and does not cause [the effect] to arise, explain why there is no contradiction.[29]

From the point of view of conventional truth there is an obvious contradiction here because nothing phenomenal can both arise and not arise simultaneously. Some action either does or does not happen, like a sprout emerging from a seed, that given the right conditions can do so. If those conditions are not there then the seed will remain a seed, with only a potential to sprout. The moving time line of possibilities explains the process of arising of a sprout from seed, and finally of the emergence of a seed from the grown sprout. There is only one or the other, both do not exist at the same time. (The imagination can however visualise the process as a single continuum of timelessness.) With respect to ultimate truth however, a single effect can both arise and not arise if we look to the *saṃsāra* and *śūnyatā* interrelation. It arises in *saṃsāra* and plays its role in the interdependent continuum of causes and effects therein, but does not arise in *śūnyatā*, which acts as a stable support for the entire play. From this perspective there is no contradiction. Wherever you have an effect there you have a preceding cause and the same *saṃsāra* and *śūnyatā* interrelation applies.

> (4) If you think that all [of the effect] arises from all [of the cause], then it is clear, from the standpoint of reason, that a multiple [cause] and a single [effect] cannot be causally related.[30]

I have already shown that multiple causes can be causally related to a single effect, from a certain viewpoint, such as all of the factors (a multiple cause) that go into the construction of a house, or any other object used by people. Of course one can say that such things do not ultimately exist, and therefore there is no cause. However, this statement is basically an untruth, because such things *do exist* as long as this condition 'ultimately' has not been attained in the space-time continuum one lives in. Perhaps to counter the words 'ultimately' or 'truly' as

29 Ibid.

30 Ibid.

used in this Madhyamaka philosophy we should liberally splatter our commentary with the words 'basically', or 'realistically through time'.

> (5) If you think that [an effect] arises from specific conditions (*pratyaya*), then the individual [conditions] separately cannot be the cause of its arising, and the effect cannot have a cause.[31]

The specific conditions do not bring about a cause separately. The cause happens when the sum total of all the conditionings are working *in situ,* in the right time sequence, and then interacts with human consciousness that observes and experiences the factors that are the cause of whatever it is that is experienced. This will happen providing that the human god interacts with the conditionings in a manner whereby he can cognitively experience. Only within the processes of human imagination and thought can 'things' be taken out of context. This cannot occur elsewhere.

An effect therefore necessitates:

a. A correctly sequenced potpourri of causes.

b. The correct time sequence for its occurrence.

c. A principal trigger or action precipitating or effecting its outcome. (Like turning on the abovementioned light switch.) The trigger may be the result of previous causes, but without its action the specific outcome will not happen. The addition of water for instance, is necessary to trigger the germination of a seed. A trigger is therefore a certain necessary action or ingredient that will cause something that has the potential for action to manifest action. A light switch will not turn itself on of its own accord, it needs an external agent to do so.

   Karma also works according to how various triggers activate to awaken aspects of it into action. Without the appearance of such triggers these aspects are simply forces that are held in potential.

d. A continuation, leading to new causes and effects which will eventually outlive the 'original' effect. As everything in *saṃsāra* is transient so the house built (of concepts, temporal constructs) must one day crumble or be destroyed.

e. A cognitive process to experience it, if it is to have relevance for a human unit.

---

31 Ibid.

f. Eventually the attainment of a causeless-condition by a human unit working to cleanse *saṃskāras*.

g. Consequently the generation of unmitigated wisdom and mastery of all forms of phenomena, which is the accumulation of all experiences via the development of wisdom. This concerns the formation of a conclusive stance to benefit from it all, and to benefit the all as a result.

> (6) If you think that a [single] effect arises from [several] conditions, it follows, as before, that [the cause], which is multiple, and [the effect], which is not multiple, are not causally related.[32]

This point has been answered earlier, where I pointed out that 'a single effect' is just a matter of the way one defines things, that inevitably there is no such thing as a single effect, but effects there certainly are.

> (7) If [you think that] the two are not different, how reasonable is it to distinguish [aspects of the cause from aspects of the effect]? You fall back into the same problems, like an elephant after a bath.[33]

As cause and effect are different, which is obvious when one observes the darkness before the switch is flicked with the light thereafter, so there is no problem with this concept and observation.

Generally speaking we can say that rather than conceptually wallowing in dust, like an elephant after a bath, it is best to keep on cleaning the mind from ungainly concepts, and ignorant opinions, so that it can appear diamond-like from out of the many causes of the various types of murk that has prevented the clear unadulterated light from manifesting. Let us demonstrate how to turn on the switch to the awakening of enlightenment-consciousness.

Next we are presented with the third main contention of his logic, that 'One does not produce Many'.

> Furthermore, if an additional factor *(atiśaya),* such as the eye, produces an effect, does it also produce a second [effect]? If it does, this would be another case in which single and multiple [cause and effect] would have no causal relationship, since the effect would be multiple, but not the cause. If a second [factor produces the second effect], there

32 Ibid.

33 Eckel, 83.

would no longer be a single cause, since [the cause] would no longer be identical to the additional factor.[34]

It has already been illustrated that the eye (as an 'additional factor') is but part of a process of cause-effect that is necessary for the appearance of the phenomenon of light in a darkened room. Before the flicking of the switch the eye exists with the potential to see, and plays its part when the light appears. Once the light appears then the consciousness utilising the mechanism of the eye and eye-brain coordination decides what it wishes to look at. The eye then manifests in a different mode (other than just the immediate registration of light). This is part of the continuum of cause-effect interrelationships that makes up the development of consciousness. Whatever the eye looks at there is a new causal relationship established, with a new effect in the brain consciousness. The fact is that the time sequence, the continuum, has moved on, wherewith new causes and effects can be established.

Jñānagarbha's logic, however, which states: 'If it does, this would be another case in which single and multiple [cause and effect] would have no causal relationship, since the effect would be multiple, but not the cause', would freeze all happenings into one moment of time. (We thus have the appearance of an image, as in a photograph. The image is singular, depicting a captured moment in time, but the effect may be multiple, depending upon how various minds react to the image.) This means that this observation would be correct *if time did not evolve or move,* but it does. This is one of the most fundamental aspects of *saṃsāric* life, and with each new passing moment comes a fresh opportunity for consciousness to evolve, to move with it, because of new causes and effects of the ever-changing phenomena coming into play. Thus for each moment in time, there is but one cause-effect interrelationship happening for any one consciousness to experience. As these moments are sequenced throughout the passage of time, so too is the moving imagery of the consciousness experiencing it. Thus, over time, many effects come from a single cause, and that cause itself has a multiple number of causes preceding it, if one were to look backwards in time at the flow of events happening.

34 Ibid.

His statement therefore, 'If a second [factor produces the second effect], there would no longer be a single cause' is correct, because the sequence of time has caused all to move on, but this 'second factor' is an effect (probably one of many) of the earlier cause (i.e., of one producing many). The cause need not be identical to the 'additional factor', because time has seen to it that it will not be so. Also, the 'additional factor' (here the mechanism of the eye) is but a mechanism for the experience of an effect, not the effect itself, as the effect is what is registered in consciousness, and what is registered therein (the images it contains) continuously moves with new causes appearing due to the factor of time.

Finally, we have his treatment of the part of the logic concerning the phrase, 'One does not produce one'.

> It is not right even to say that one cause produces one effect, because if the eye and so forth only produce the next moment *(kṣaṇa)* in their own continuum *(santāna),* everyone would be blind and deaf. If they produce the cognition to which [they are related], their own continuum would be cut off. Neither [of these two options] is either possible or acceptable.[35]

Here Jñānagarbha deals with the time issue. However, he has the concept of time skewered, because it is not 'the eye and so forth' that 'produce the next moment *(kṣaṇa)* in their own continuum *(santāna)*', because that 'next moment' will flow on irregardless of what the eye etc., does. But he is correct with respect to the qualifying statement 'in their own continuum', which refers directly to the way the eye etc., act in a sequence of causes. However the fact is that most people are not blind and deaf, because the eye and ear do not function in isolation from anything else, but are part of an entire integrated and complicated physiological system, wherein the composite parts work in co-ordination with each other. (At the speed of light, in this case for sight, and the speed of sound for the ear.[36]) So the impact of light to the eye, or sound to the ear, is immediately relayed to the brain, and the brain consciousness then decides what to do with the input of sensory data before sending the messages to the eye and ear as how to react. The next stage of the

35 Ibid.

36 Note that the speed of sound is much slower than that of light.

eye's and ear's 'own continuum' then proceeds, and further messages are conveyed to the brain, which then instantaneously 'sees' and 'hears' deductively before giving new messages, and so forth. So we have the brain consciousnesses' 'own continuum', the eye's 'own continuum' and the ear's 'own continuum' all working together in a synchronised fashion to produce the images and sounds we all can experience. All factors, all 'own continuums' in the physical universe, are interrelated and work harmoniously in perfect accord (barring the factor of human free will). Thus we have a world system manifesting through which we can evolve and gain enlightenment.

Therefore, contrary to Jñānagarbha's logic, most of us are not blind and deaf precisely because 'one cause produces one effect' in any sequence of happenings in the 'own continuum' of the eye and the ear, as coordinated with a properly functioning brain consciousness. This is because no such continuum in an integrated closed system, such as is that of the human body, works entirely separately from any other; all factors in such a system are linked in some way and function congruently, cooperatively, and constructively with the purpose as directed by the central processing unit. In the case of a human being this is the brain mechanism and the consciousness animating it. Myriads of seemingly separate factors may be part of the expression of the next moment of its 'own continuum', producing the cause for further action by any factor, such as eye, toe, mouth, ear, under its control. There is also that part of the brain (the medulla oblongata and the parasympathetic nervous system) dealing with the autonomous functions of the body, such as the heartbeat and breathing.

Consequently, the statement 'If they produce the cognition to which [they are related], their own continuum would be cut off' is also not correct because 'their own continuum' is dependent *upon* them producing the cognition to which they are related. This is because a causative happening, such as the registering of light once a light switch is turned on in a room, is immediately conveyed to the brain consciousness, and this consciousness then reacts to the effect of the causative impulse and sends a message, a new causative impulse (in the next moment of the eye's own continuum) regarding how to respond. Therefore the eye's own continuum is produced because of the fact that it has produced a cognition (in the brain consciousness). If it can produce no such cognition then the presumption is that the eye itself is impaired and cannot register the appearing light, or the nerves from the eye to the brain is impaired, or the site for the registering of such impressions in the brain is impaired, or that consciousness has left the body in some way (being asleep, in a catatonic state, or death has occurred).

As noted 'one cause produces one effect' if we freeze time at the moment of the cause producing the effect, like taking a photograph of a scene. There is one cause, the light that has entered the camera from the object, and one effect, the resultant photograph. Viewed in isolation this is true, and is much like how we receive images in our minds from the external universe, but when viewed in relationship to the time continuum not so.

We see therefore, that Jñānagarbha's thesis that 'Many do not produce one, many do not produce many, one does not produce many, and one does not produce one' has definitely not been proven, except maybe in the case of being ensconced in *śūnyatā,* rather a contrary assumption has often been proven the case.

There are also concluding verses, which I shall not deal with here, as the above suffices to demonstrate the fallacies of the thesis.

7

The Refutation of Partless Particles

What is meant by partlessness?

An associated problem or derivation of the phrase 'one does not produce many', etc., concerns the refutation of partless particles. This is because the desire here is to refute the concept of there being a 'one', and if a one cannot be found, then the logic is that likewise there cannot be 'many', because many are composed of a number of ones. The logic is well explained in *A Study of Svātantrika:*

> Śāntarakṣita argues that to be truly unitary means to be partless, and he logically proves that nothing is partless. It is easy to understand that phenomena with perceivable parts are not partless; this is evident to direct perception. But those phenomena imputed to be unitary and partless that are inaccessible to direct perception are more difficult to refute. For this reason Śāntarakṣita's refutation of permanent unities and partless particles warrants special consideration.[1]

One could argue that 'to be truly unitary means to be partless', as Śāntarakṣita does, but this is an academic pursuit that misses the point as to what life, existence, the quest for enlightenment, and the attainment of Buddhahood, is all about. In other words, there is no point or purpose to partlessness. A Buddha is not partless, from the perspective that he possess an aura, an enlightened Mind, a Buddha-sphere around him, as well as manifesting in the form of the *trikāya*. His consciousness

---

1 D. S. Lopez Jr., *A Study of Svātantrika,* 182.

also manifests in the mode of the five Dhyāni Buddhas. From another perspective, these are all aspects of one ineffable Buddha-Mind, and therefore cannot be considered to constitute 'parts'. His awareness may also be 'non-dual' with respect to the *saṃsāra*, but it certainly has attributes on its own sphere or realm of being. *Śūnyatā* can be considered partless from the fact of being Void, but we do know from the above that various forms of *śūnyatā* do exist. Is the Void therefore 'truly unitary', as Śāntarakṣita posits that something that is partless must be? If it is truly unitary is it then a 'thing', a permanent entity of some sort? Is it possible to give a definite answer to such a question?

We can however leave such lofty speculations aside and directly answer the question 'what then is partlessness'? One could logically argue that a partless entity, or form of existence/non-existence that exhibits no characteristics, or attributes considered in terms of subdivisions, is not possible, unless one is directly experiencing the Void. (Hypothetically partless entities may however exist in Nature in the realm of the super-small or the unimaginably super-large, as will be explained below.)

So why bother with a theory of partlessness, except for academic curiosity, as to what such a state could mean? What this does is produce concepts, something like the mathematical conception of zero-dimensional space—a point in space, with no attributes, length, breadth or depth. It is simply an attributeless point that has no relation to anything else. However, when lines are drawn at right angles to this zero-dimensional point (i.e., the process of connecting it to something else), then inevitably we get the formation of two dimensional space, such as a flat sheet of paper, where one can draw lines of direction (e.g., of the eight points of the compass), but there cannot be any conception of depth, of distance, i.e., of three dimensionality. Three dimensionality is obtained when we draw a line at right angles to the representation of two dimension space, which when extended gives us the conception or appearance of solid objects possessing volume, and from whence we can measure distances, perceive the depth of things, with our sterioscopic vision. A greater magnitude or dimension of perception of 'things' or 'particles' can thereby be connected to it.

I do not wish to delve into the philosophy of dimensions of perception here, as that will be relegated to a later book, because of its importance in relation to the understanding of what constitutes consciousness. I wish to note here however the relative irrelevance of querying about partless particles from the point of view of the quest for enlightenment. Consciousness simply accepts the subdivisions and categories (its parts) of phenomena, utilising such acceptance as the basis for the derivation of wisdom.

Astrophysicists however have a similar concept to a partless particle in their hypothesis of the beginning of the universe, where they speak of a 'singularity' from which the entire universe explosively emanated.

Concerning this concept of singularity Gribbin states:

> Singularity: A point of infinite density and curvature of space-time where the laws of physics no longer apply. Every black hole contains a singularity:[2]...Hawking realized that by turning the equations around it might be possible to prove that the *expanding* Universe must have been born out of a singularity. He spent several years refining the mathematics, in collaboration with Penrose, and in 1970 they published a joint paper which proved that the Universe we observe must indeed have been born in a big bang singularity if general relativity is correct.[3]

Śāntarakṣita was obviously not thinking of such a singularity when he was considering 'partlessness', but this is exactly what the philosophy of partlessness implies, or can be deduced is productive of, from the point of view of modern physics, and logic, if the appearance of the physical universe is somehow to be explained by it. Is this singularity but another name for *śūnyatā*, if one conceives *śūnyatā* to be 'partless'?

Another way of considering partlessness is to try to imagine an absolute vacuum, where nothing whatsoever exists. (Such a vacuum does not actually exist in Nature.) An unimaginable force would have to exist to prevent the universe of forms, atoms, and elementary particles from being sucked into it, as the pressure to do so would be enormous. What about energy, which is omnipresent—it has parts too, wave frequencies, would it exist in such a vacuum? Science postulates that energy can exist in a vacuum, but if all mass is extinguished do we observe a black hole, from which nothing can escape, not even light? What exists

---

2 John Gribbin, *In Search of the Edge of Time. Black Holes, White Holes, Wormholes* (Penguin Books, London, 1992), 252.

3 Ibid.

inside such a black hole we can only speculate. Such physical plane observations by the scientific community may yet have something of value to say concerning rhetoric as to the nature of *śūnyatā*. Can we unequivocably say that black holes are not symptomatic of the nature of *śūnyatā*, if the concept is brought to speculating as to what exists beyond consciousness?

We can see the difficulty of conceiving an existence of a partless universe or state of existence, if it is to co-exist someway with our physical universe. How can the interrelation actually be explained?

Also, what is really being postulated in a theory of partlessness is the search for an absolute beginning, or else the most minute components of 'things'. Physicists have been hunting for such a speck of matter for decades in their investigation of the nature of the sub-atomic universe. They have come up with a number of representatives, such as one of the six flavours of quarks, and even the photon, which is indivisible, and acts as both a particle of matter and part of a wave front. To quote from K.N. Mukhin's book:

> Besides nucleons and electrons, three other particles related directly to the atom and the nucleus were known at that time [1932]. These were the photons (γ-quanta) emitted by an atom (nucleus) during energy transitions, and neutrinos and positrons which are emitted by the nucleus during β decay. Of course, none of these particles can be considered as a constituent of the atom or the nucleus since they are formed just at the instant of their emission by the atom or the nucleus. However, these particles were also called elementary particles since none of them can be imagined to "comprise" of other "more elementary" particles.[4]
>
> The modern concept of really elementary particles has been developed in recent years. It is assumed that six quarks (five discovered) and six leptons (five discovered) constitute really elementary particles: Four types of interaction take place between these particles: strong (really strong) electromagnetic, weak and gravitational. The respective quanta of these interactions are eight gluons, a photon, three heavy bosons and a graviton. Nucleons, mesons and other strongly interacting particles (hadrons) consist

4 K.N. Mukhin, *Experimental Nuclear Physics, Volume II, Elementary Particle Physics*, (Mir Publishers, Moscow, 1987), 138.

> of quarks and gluons. Nuclear forces between nucleons and strong interaction between hadrons in general are considered as secondary manifestation of the really strong interaction between quarks. Weak and electromagnetic interactions have been unified into a single theory in which four vector bosons appear in a natural way: the massless photon responsible for electromagnetic interaction...[5]

All things are said to be composed of such quarks, or photons in the case of light. There are other subatomic particles they also consider, scientifically disproving Śāntarakṣita's theory. Be that as it may, let us analyse his theorem a little more closely.

To be 'unitary' does not mean to be 'partless' but rather to manifest as a closed system of some sort, i.e., a unitary object is a coherent organism (as is a human being) that is constituted of many parts, each of which is dependent upon the other for the proper functioning of the entire organism. There is true unity in such diversity. This may be a conventional viewpoint, but it also works equally well on the realms of enlightenment, such as the unitariness of the five Dhyāni Buddhas, or the *maṇḍala* of the eight Mahābodhisattvas, the Kalāchakra *maṇḍala*, or any other such esoteric representation. If we add the qualifier 'truly', to make something 'truly unitary', it does not necessary mean that it is 'partless', but rather to have no connection with any other entity or system. It is a 'oneness' completely separate from any other entity, abiding by its own laws. But our universe does not work this way, neither does the world of human interrelationships. None are truly unitary, all are 'particles', entities within a larger system, and that system similarly manifests as an entity within a larger one, and so forth.

In reality it is meaningless to think in terms of the 'truly unitary existence' of Śāntarakṣita. It is not a consideration of enlightened beings. In fact the opposite is the case for them, for as the consciousness of Bodhisattvas expand and broaden they increasingly look to larger and vaster wholes, away from the world of the human unit living in the environment of his relatively microscopic world in the universe. They perceive vaster concepts of 'complete systems', such as the integrated unity of the myriad lives ('unitary existences') constituting the solar

5 Ibid., 140.

system, and of their way of evolution. They know of the manifold ways they have gained or will gain enlightenment, not necessarily related to earth concepts at all.

Existence therefore is constituted of 'unitary' species, but they are not *truly* unitary, in the sense of being composed of 'partless particles', except maybe when we look to the sub-atomic realm. Śāntarakṣita's 'refutation of permanent unities and partless particles' on *prima facie* evidence may have merit from his perspective. Nevertheless, unitary existences have been shown to abound in Nature, and if we were to extend this observation to the domain of what may constitute a 'soul' then we would conclude that such a hypothesised entity would likewise be unitary, but would upon close analysis be seen to possess discernable 'parts' or attributes.

Quandary concerning 'truly existent' atomic unities

Donald S. Lopez Jr. states:

> The refutation of partless particles is important because if minute particles are proven to have parts, all physical phenomena will necessarily be proven to have parts, since they are composed of minute particles. The Vaibhāṣikas assert that physical forms *(rūpa, gzugs)* are aggregations of minute partless particles. In order to prove that the existence of partless particles is impossible, Śāntarakṣita takes as his subject a minute particle which is surrounded on all sides by other minute particles. If the minute particle positioned in the middle of ten other particles in the four directions, the four intermediate directions, and above and below did not have parts, it would be impossible for the other particles to be located around it because the central particle would occupy no space. It could not have an eastern surface or a western surface because it would have no parts; all of its sides would be the same. It would absurdly follow that all ten surrounding particles would contact the central particle in the same place, that is, all ten particles and, by extension, all particles in the universe would occupy the same place, in which case physical objects such as the earth would not exist; they would have no dimension. If it is admitted that the central particle has sides that face the surrounding particles, then it must be accepted that minute particles have parts.

If minute particles are not truly existent unities, the objects composed of them are not truly existent unities. Also, if the objects of the five sense consciousness are not truly established, the sense consciousnesses themselves are not truly established because they depend on the sense objects for their production; as Bhāvaviveka argued, anything that depends on something else cannot be truly or ultimately established. Therefore, based on the refutation of partless particles, it can be inferred that sense consciousnesses and their objects do not truly exist. However, Śāntarakṣita goes on in the *Ornament for the Middle Way* to refute the truly existent unitary consciousnesses propounded by the Mimāmsākas, Sāṃkhyas, Vaiśeṣikas, Jainas, Cārvākas, and Vedāntins among the non-Buddhists, and the Vaibhāṣikas, Sauntrāntikas, and Yogācārins among the Buddhists.

The pivotal point in establishing that truly existent unities do not exist is that everything has parts, and Śāntarakṣita goes to some length to prove this. He shows that anything that can be asserted by a Buddhist or non-Buddhist can be logically demonstrated to be composed of physical parts, such as minute particles, or temporal parts, such as moments of consciousness. By refuting truly existent unity, that anything is truly one, Śāntarakṣita is not saying whole and part do not exist conventionally or that the terms "one" and "many" cannot be used. He is proving that there is nothing which is truly one that ultimately exists.

The proof that there is nothing which is truly many is accomplished more quickly. Śāntarakṣita says:

> When anything is analysed
> It is without oneness.
> That which does not have oneness
> Also is without manyness.[6]

First we should note that the Vaibhāṣika argument 'that physical forms (*rūpa*, gzugs) are aggregations of minute partless particles' is really a version of the theory of atoms, such as that presented to the world by the ancient Greek philosopher Democritus (460-370 BC). The theory that atoms were minute elementary partless particles persisted in the West right up to the advent of the modern era and the

6 Lopez Jr., *A Study of Svātantrika*, 183-185.

experiments of such men as Rutherford and Niels Bohr, who in the early twentieth century successfully showed that the atom consisted of at least two particles, an electron and a nucleus, whilst the nucleus was later shown to be composed of two main particles, protons and neutrons. Experimentation continued through the decades until physicists could conclusively demonstrate the existence of the 'really elementary particles' in the constituency of atomic structures, explained above.

Whatever may be the internal constituency of the atom, the fact is that all of Nature, every form in the manifest universe, is constituted of them, arranged in the manner of the 10 directions of space, and as far as the way that their forms interact with each other they can be considered as possessing *spherical shapes*, and are 'partless', for all intents and purposes, except for the nature of the electron exchanges between them that cause them to adhere together and to form compounds with each other, the electrons being negatively charged and the nucleus of the atom being positively charged.

Śāntarakṣita's argument does not take into account the real nature of a sphere.[7] If all of these particles were spherical then the central particle certainly would occupy space and there would be literally an infinite number of points that the other spheres could contact it with, as a sphere has no sides. This would be especially so if the balls are spinning. Ideally they would all be spinning at different rates and directions, though controlled overall by the motion of the central ball. (Physically however, the central spin would cause the others to spin in relation to it.) By having no sides, speculation relating to 'all of its sides would be the same' becomes meaningless.

The idea that it cannot be seen because it is enclosed by ten other particles does not mean that it is not there, as one can prove for oneself if one places a central ball in the midst of others surrounding it in the ten directions. Also, if the central ball was omitted there would still be a space created for it by the arrangement of the other balls. That the balls are constituted of 'parts', e.g., of atomic units is relatively immaterial,

7 He states: 'a minute particle which is surrounded on all sides by other minute particles. If the minute particle positioned in the middle of ten other particles in the four directions, the four intermediate directions, and above and below did not have parts, it would be impossible for the other particles to be located around it because the central particle would occupy no space'.

for if we could arrange 'really elementary particles' in this fashion (and we can deduce that such arrangements actually do exist in Nature, for instance with a large grouping of atoms, or photons acting as particles) then we will find that for each grouping of ten there will be an eleventh in the centre of them. We could even converge our vision to an ultimate unitary starting point, an *aṇu,* a seed, egg, germ, or 'singularity' if we wish and note that such primal *maṇḍalic* structures exist throughout Nature, to produce the beginning of anything. Why therefore not for the start of a human mind's ability to recognise itself as distinct from everything else, i.e., of all that is/is not, and also of the nature of its birthing/explosion/liberation into *śūnyatā*?

Therefore, the postulate that 'all ten particles' and, by extension, all particles in the universe, would occupy the same place, in which case physical objects such as the earth would not exist, having 'no dimension',[8] is certainly incorrect from this perspective.

Now, when observing the qualities of a photon, we find that it paradoxically acts both as an elementary particle and a wave front. This actually means that the particle/wave front could simultaneously be everywhere at once, for who can predict how vast the wave truly is in the cosmos. It can simultaneously manifest upon the earth and be extended to the far reaches of the universe. The photon therefore effectively appears anywhere or technically can appear simultaneously everywhere when it manifests as a particle. (In fact, all photons are effectively one, as there is no way to distinguish one from the other.) The quarks of physicists could likewise be an expression of a similar type of phenomena, though their appearance would be conditioned by the atomic structures by which they are bound.[9]

This attribute of photons therefore makes Śāntarakṣita's comment 'It would absurdly follow that all ten surrounding particles would contact the central particle in the same place, that is, all ten particles and, by extension, all particles in the universe would occupy the same place' correct, where such 'absurdity' is but a principle of physics, i.e., of the nature of a particle that behaves both as a wave front and a particle. It

8 Though of course it could be viewed as a zero-dimensional point if viewed from far enough away in space.

9 Note that the properties of minute particles will be further analysed in a later discussion of fourth dimensional space in Volume 4 of this series.

also denies Śāntarakṣita's subsequent statement: 'in which case physical objects such as the earth would not exist; they would have no dimension'. The truth being that despite such phenomena, physical objects, such as the earth, still continue existing because of all the subsequent laws, and the laws of probability, which 'bind' 'really elementary particles' into specific locations in time and space. It does not matter which particular photon appears at a certain location at a particular time, as any constituting the wave front will do. They are all identical, and as a consequence the phenomenal appearance of things is sustained.

Things that flash momentarily and randomly into and out of objectivity on a minute subatomic scale do not change the appearance of the macrocosmic object, because that object is composed of trillions of such subatomic particles. The reality is that when one elementary particle is in another time-space continuum sufficient numbers are appearing at the same time in the physical dimension to maintain the illusionality of the macrocosmic form. The laws maintaining the appearance of that form are in place at all times. Therefore his argument that such forms do not exist is not supported by factual evidence. That the universe is constituted of such particles as the basic building blocks of all that is, is now considered a basic truism.[10] That they are part of closed systems of different sizes and complexities, constituting the things of the phenomenal world around us, is also true, and this is the basis for conventional wisdom.[11]

An assertion that minute particles can indeed be 'truly existent unities', is dependent upon a proviso that we agree upon the meaning of the word 'truly'. If 'truly' is considered to refer to that which is 'unchanging, and therefore not in perpetual motion', then we can

10 These particles were not part of the conceptions of the earlier Buddhist philosophers and their opponents. One could speculate that if modern knowledge was indeed part of their ken, then how much would their philosophical investigations have had to change to accommodate the increased knowledge we now have of the physical universe?

11 Despite being 'closed', meaning being part of a unitary existence, they nevertheless are interrelated with all other things, and are altered according to the nature of the impact of energies, forces, and substances external to them, as well as manifesting their own internal changes.

conclude that no such particle exists in *saṃsāra*.[12] However, if we define the word in terms that the 'existent unities' truly or factually exist in Nature, then the supposition would be correct. Now, taking this second definition, we can see that 'the objects of the five sense consciousnesses' are in fact 'truly' established in consciousness, where they leave a lasting imprint as memory. This is because these objects exist on a macrocosmic scale, and therefore are not affected by the minute changes manifesting in the atomic universe. (Unless those effects manifest in such a way that a vast number of such changes happen within a time scale reckoned in microseconds, as in a nuclear explosion.) From this point of view 'sense consciousnesses and their objects' do exist, but ultimately are superseded by higher faculties of perception, born from that experienced via *chakras*. These objects are however not truly established because they are impermanent, transitory and hence ultimately illusional.

From the above point of view, 'existent unitary consciousnesses' can be considered to exist, but whether truly or not is debatable, but 'ultimately' (using that device again to refer to the far distant future, which is thus essentially an imagining) become transcended or transmogrified into *śūnyatā*. A form of 'truly existent unitary consciousness' is actually developed by a practitioner of black magic (such as a sorcerer, who has evolved the natural separative attributes of the mind to its ultimate materialistic conclusion), whereas his enlightened counterpart trained in white *dharma* has developed an inclusive, not exclusive, consciousness.

The unitariness of things

Now, we can analyse the final statement of the quotation: 'By refuting truly existent unity, that anything is truly one, Śāntaraksita is not saying whole and part do not exist conventionally or that the terms 'one' and 'many' cannot be used. He is proving that there is nothing which is one that ultimately exists'. In this regard, due to the peculiarities of the meaning of that word 'ultimately', we can agree with him. We can also

12 This however is a presumption, as we need to leave the question to whether protons, electrons or quarks, etc., 'change' to physicists.

come to the conclusion that that which is 'one' must ultimately exist. This is because all of Nature, and the entire evolutionary process, tends towards unification, towards oneness. Smaller elementary particles combine to form larger ones (e.g., atoms), atoms combine or unify to produce compounds and solid objects. The solid objects combine to produce what we can experience on a macrocosmic scale. All of the time we are moving from unities to greater unities. In a sense this is the foundation of what is perceived by consciousness. That is, it views a seeming diversity or plurality, made up of many, and indeed, countless unities, countless 'ones'. Thus our perception grows and expands in thinking or viewing, from a microcosmic scale of atoms and molecules to the macrocosmic scale of solar systems, galaxies and the universe itself, as the ultimate 'one'. An enlightened being's perception increasingly grows to incorporate both the minutiae and the vast complexity of this universal ordering, all in terms of unities, of 'ones' and of the way they interact as part of groupings, such as the way a chemist may look at the interaction of molecules in a beaker. The enlightened being's perception, however, is not limited to the universe of things, but views the interrelationships between the all, via a multidimensional perspective.

We will find that consciousness expands because of its increasingly sophisticated ability to integrate a progressively greater number of, as well as vaster, unities. Each unity is made up of myriads of component parts, each being unities in themselves. Thus within the field of consciousness many of our answers lie. *Śūnyatā* has also been considered to be a diversity, that manifests as a unity. It should be noted however that *śūnyatā* as a unitary 'something' can be considered an erroneous view. From the point of view of its spaciousness, unitariness is and is not definable within *śūnyatā,* yet *śūnyatā* can be conceived to be the unitary all that is. Whichever way one wishes to view it, therefore, all that we see is 'truly existent' unitary states of awarenesses. Here the term 'truly existent' is interpreted in terms of self-contained existences totally absorbed in their own field of expression. They interrelate with similar self-contained ones and such interrelatedness of planets, stars or galaxies for instance, may incorporate the entire scope of the universe in which it resides. They are 'truly existent' conventionally. When we look to that beyond consciousness, *śūnyatā*, being 'truly existent' and 'unitary' it is from the perspective of the 'unitary consciousness' having been transcended, because *śūnyatā* exists on a different plane of being/non-being. It can be considered a different transcendent parallel universe to that of consciousness, but we have merely swapped one form of unitariness with another. We can also integrate the different types of Void into a unitary state of Voidness. Śāntarakṣita's contention in the *Ornament for the Middle Way,* refuting 'the truly existent unitary consciousnesses' is therefore incorrect, except maybe in the way he chooses to interpret the word 'truly', however, the argument then is brought down to a consideration of points of view.

That 'everything has parts' does not prevent something from being a unity, or alter the fact that each of these parts are also integral unities. Whether these unities are composed of homogeneous or heterogeneous parts does not really matter, what matters is that together they function as a coherent whole, a total organism, or are seen by consciousness to do so, like a rock, a plant, animal, or a human unit.

Also, if one goes to the extreme to try to deny the existence of consciousness, one is doing this with one's own consciousnesses, and therefore is proving nothing, other than the fact that one is conscious and has the faculty of reasoning as well. We can also speculate whether *śūnyatā* does, does not, neither does and does not, or both does and does not function as such a 'coherent whole'. Is it a coherent unity that an enlightened being can experience accordingly? Is there logic to its existence, if so, is then its existence bound by the laws of logic? Or is it an illogical assumption? Or is such an experience of the enlightened considered irrational? In other words, are enlightened beings irrational? They certainly would be if their experiences were not composed of interrelated closed systems, i.e., many unitary thought-structures integrated into a patterning of awareness of all possibilities of past and future attainment.

If everything was open, i.e., there being no unities in anything, then their thoughts and meditations would have no beginning or ending, they could not be structured in a coherent way, therefore they could not communicate their awarenesses or realisations to any being (a unity); they could not come to conclusions about anything, as conclusions would be impossible to attain. Also, all thought and meditation-streams would merge into each other. (There being no containers; unitary 'things' holding anything into any semblance of form that allows a being to count or to compare.) There would be a vision obtained through a non-discriminatory awareness of an incoherent jumbled mess, like a myriad of different smokes and perfumes mingled together. This would disallow the discernment of anything, thus preventing consciousness (or whatever faculties one has to reason with) to carry out its discriminating function. Nevertheless an openess is also needed, to integrate the unities into Oneness.

We see that the capacities of a Buddha or Bodhisattva to reason perfectly logically, and effortlessly, lies in the fact that unities exist within one great unifying whole. The process concerns observing the ordering of the patterning of things, *maṇḍalas* within any unity, within a vaster structure, like that of a galaxy, and then viewing the increasing diversity of its component parts. With respect to a galaxy we see that it is composed of constellations of stars, and that each constellation has a certain number of stars. When observing an individual star, we can expand our vision to view its constituency of planets and around them moons, and so forth. Ordered structures, and the secret of how to quickly unravel the ordered patterning of each unity, is the key to understanding the nature of the miraculous instantaneousness of an enlightened being, of his/her seeming ineffability of reasoning. The pathways linking one unitary system with another can be travelled at the speed of thought or greater (when analysed from the *dharmakāya).*

Clearly Śāntarakṣita has not taken into account how an enlightened being actually does evaluate and integrate diverse streams of information in his denial of 'unities', and for this reason his theory can also be considered flawed. (Even though he 'is not saying whole and part do not exist conventionally or that the terms "one" and "many" cannot be used'.) He has not understood the way that the laws of being/non-being are interrelated and of the way that they function, so that a rational universe can exist, and which also allows one to rationalise *śūnyatā* as being a true unitary existence, as the experience therein integrates the All into Oneness, instantaneously. The philosophy of the way the (cellular) unities constitute the sum of being/non-being is well developed and explained in Volume 4. An agreement with Śāntarakṣita can however be reached in relation to emptiness being free of concepts, of the one and many, in the statement:

When anything is analysed
It is without oneness.
That which does not have oneness
Also is without manyness.

One must however make the proviso that this is only true when one is completely focussed upon the *śūnyatā* aspect of the two truths, ignoring entirely conventional truth and how it is the basis for gaining enlightenment. This state of residing in the Void is only part of the true nature of enlightenment. In conclusion it should be said:

When anything is analysed
The spaciousness of Oneness
will be found to be at the Heart of all that is.
Without a Heart that unifies all into true unity
How can love (compassion) manifest at all?
Without compassion there can be no Bodhisattva activity.
Without Bodhisattva activity a Buddha could not evolve.
Without a Buddha life would be meaningless.
Oneness incorporates manyness.
Manyness is productive of oneness.
Thus it is with the *śūnyatā-saṃsāra* relationship.
Thus it is with the *saṃsāra-śūnyatā* experience.

Oṁ Maṇi Padme Hūṁ

Homage to the Buddha, the *dharma*, and the *saṅgha*.

The Buddha unifies the multiplicity of diverse human unities into a communality, a oneness, by means of the universal *dharma*. The community (*saṅgha*) acts with one accord, where once there was a panoply of views and ignorant chaotic action, now there is order, governed by the liberating principles of *dharma*. Such is the way with the law of evolutionary attainment. Such is the way with enlightened Being.

Oṁ

8

The Sevenfold Reasoning Part B: Meditation on the 'I'

The 'I' and the aggregates

We can now continue the consideration of *The Sevenfold Reasoning* from the book *Meditation on Emptiness*. In endeavouring to establish that the *'I is not the mind and body'* five statements were presented, two of which were explained in Part A of *The Sevenfold Reasoning*. The remaining ones shall now be dealt with.

The third of five statements given is:

> The I is not the aggregates because the I would be produced and would disintegrate just as the aggregates are produced and disintegrate. The I is not inherently produced and does not inherently disintegrate because if it did, memory of former births would be impossible. For, the two I's of the different lifetimes would be unrelatedly different because they would be inherently other.[1]

Obviously, the 'I' cannot be considered 'the aggregates'. Because impermanence rules all in *saṃsāra*, so there will be a dispersal of the aggregates constituting the personality 'self' (personal-I), when its purpose for any particular major cycle of activity has ended. This is part of the process involving death and the eventual rebirth of the consciousness that coheres all *saṃskāras* into unity. Each aggregate that arises to play its appointed karmic role manifests a continuum for the future to unfold as

1 J. Hopkins, *Meditation on Emptiness*, 48-49.

a karmic moment. This happens in accord with the way it is changed or moulded by the conscious volitions of the personal-I that utilises and acts upon the aggregate concerned. The aggregates, as well as the personal-I, die to their former state of being and are changed into a new form to be experienced or reborn at the next karmic opportunity. The I-consciousness on the other hand, incarnates via a succession of personal-I's and persists for the duration of many of such births and deaths, until it is liberated and incorporated into the *dharmakāya*, as everything eventually must, once stripped of *saṃsāric* qualities.

Concerning the statement: 'The I is not inherently produced and does not inherently disintegrate because if it did, memory of former births would be impossible', we know that many have remembered their different 'I's' of past lives. Most have experienced the *saṃskāras* of being a woman in one life and in another the *saṃskāras* of being a man. This is because consciousness persists from life to life, from transformation to transformation of *saṃskāras* and *skandhas* (the aggregates conditioning a particular form). Because memory of every change, even the most minute, is stored in consciousness, so it can be recollected by one who has sufficiently cleansed the grosser *saṃskāras* that muddy the vision from any particular life. This clarifies the links to the past, allowing one to see the volitions, and thus remember what had transpired in a particular life upon the reappearance of the particular *saṃskāras* concerned. From this we can deduce that it is the I-consciousness that possesses the qualities alluded to as the 'I' here.

The keyword in the quotation is the word 'inherently'. By this is meant that it cannot be produced or disintegrated in reality. One can basically agree to this, if that which is not inherently produced or disintegrated refers to an I-consciousness manifesting for the duration of evolutionary time needed for the incarnating personal-I's to attain liberation. Thus it refers to a form of consolidated existence in the realms of consciousness that is sustained for the duration to Buddhahood. Inherently however, there *is* a beginning and an ending to *everything,* even for the *śūnyatā* experience, e.g., there are different *śūnyatās* or *śūnyatā* levels to experience, and finally the *dharmakāya*. There are thus different levels of attainment concerning Buddhahood, seen for instance in Gautama's case from the beginning, his *nirvāṇa* under the *bodhi* tree, to his *parinirvāṇa,* and then *beyond, mahāparinirvāṇa* (the nature of which is understood only by the highest Bodhisattvas).

What is implied in the quotation above is that if the 'I' was essentially produced then it would be finite and there would come a time when it would have to disintegrate. This is because its phenomena is illusional, like a mirage. The presumption is that upon disintegration there would be annihilation, producing total loss of such things as memory. How a 'mirage' can retain memory of anything, is the contention that is thus actually given. However, when we reckon with the reality of what consciousness actually is, and how it is produced, we see that it does not suffer such disintegration upon the death of the personal-I. Thus if the 'I' were an aspect of consciousness, or consciousness an aspect of an 'I', then the quoted logic does not ring true, because consciousness persists (after the death of the personal-I) and thus is the faculty that allows one to retain memory of past lives. It is inherently produced and eventually is transmogrified into the Clear Light (of instantaneous Revelation).

The real question here thus does not concern the appearance and disappearance of the aggregates, but rather the consciousness that collectivises the interrelated 'I's' of each successive personality on the chain or sequence of rebirths. How does it do this?

It does thus not follow that 'the two I's of the different lifetimes would be *unrelatedly* different because they would be inherently other'. Yes they might be 'other', as a male life in one country and a female life in another, the forms are indeed different, but the *saṃskāras* and *skandhas* of past conscious volitions still flow through and condition the evolving personality, his/her emotional and thought life, and they affect consciousness. The forms or appearance may be 'other', but the reality, that which manifests within such a body of 'flesh, blood and bones', the internal psychic constitution, remains the same or is similar, altered only by the awareness of new environmental conditionings, and the appearance of the form. We have all had many lives of being male or female, therefore many *saṃskāras* of each have been produced that can be drawn from to produce the qualifications of any particular incarnation of 'self'. Thus we can conclude that they are *not inherently* other. Consciousness carries through and unites the successive 'I's' into a collective continuum, allowing the past *saṃskāras* and *skandhas* of awareness to be recycled upon progressively higher, and finally, more sublime turns of the wheel of life. The purpose of each incarnation is to produce increasingly refined *saṃskāric* attributes. This allows Bodhisattvas and Buddhas to evolve from out of the mired turmoil of *saṃsāra*. As they do so, then each Bodhisattva and Buddha becomes expressively different, 'other', and yet there is a complete congruence of enlightened Minds.

Once incarnate the new personal-I utilises whatever is needed from the impressions stored by the I-consciousness (thus evoked from the activities engendered in past lives) for it to gain the awareness needed for that life.

The *fourth* of five statements given is:

> The I is not inherently produced and does not inherently disintegrate because then deeds done (*karma*) would be wasted as there would be no transmission of the potencies accumulated from actions since the I's of the different lifetimes would be unrelated others.[2]

Again, the role that consciousness plays in integrating one life, one cycle of 'I' to the next is disregarded here. It integrates 'deeds done' in a similar manner as it integrates one thought with the next thought. Each thought can be considered as an 'I', for it functions in a similar way, in that it appears separate from a previous thought-structure, just as each new human birth appears separate from the previous one, yet there is a continuum of flow from one to another. The 'I' is therefore 'inherently' produced, because it is based upon the stratum of attributes previously developed. However, it does not 'inherently disintegrate', as the essence of what was incorporated is passed on to the next one, or else it lays the foundation for the ones that follow sequentially, or even at some unrelated time in the thought life.

By 'inherently' here, is meant that though mirage-like, the thoughts consequently persist as an essential or relatively permanent part of a thought stream or continuum. Thus, as each thought dies and is reborn into a new one, there is continuity. Though one appears to have died to give place to the new one, this 'dying' is not death in the true sense

2 Ibid., 49.

of annihilation because its qualities live on in the new thought, though transformed, modified in some way, and sometimes even transmuted. It has conditioned the future patterning of the thought to be. Thus the past thought acts as a base for the new one, its qualities and images being retained or modified for the new idea. At any time a past idea or thought can be recalled from the store of consciousness called memory. There is a continuity of thought-substance. (This is what gives validity to the term 'inherent' here.) This gives that thought immortality, eternal life, because it is not even eradicated in the Mind of a liberated one, who is able to recall any of the thoughts from past lives, and indeed of any other human consciousness, if he/she so chooses.

So, how does Chandrakīrti's supposition explain such ability, in the light of the doctrine of impermanency? The fact is, that though a thought is 'inherently produced' the 'deeds done *(karma)'* are not 'wasted', because, contrary to Chandrakīrti's supposition, there will indeed be 'transmission of the potencies accumulated from actions'. This is testified by a Buddha's ability to remember past thoughts, thereby making them as immortal as he is.

So it is also with each successive rebirth. Whatever is needed for the new incarnation is recalled from the collective consciousness that acts as a store (*ālayavijñāna*) of all the past volitions of the conscious entity that is the reincarnating 'self'. For this reason there is no *karma* wasted, indeed, the opposite happens. The reincarnating consciousness chooses the necessary streams of consciousness-volitions called *karma* it needs to work upon, or to cleanse, for each successive appearance of the 'I' that is its manifest expression. Buddhist philosophy presently cannot precisely explain how a 'store consciousness'[3] is able to do this. A major, necessary theme of this treatise is therefore to try to rectify this flaw.

Without continuity of consciousness, each successive 'I' certainly would be unrelated, but there is continuity, and although past lives are not normally remembered, they can be if the ability is properly developed, such as through yogic prowess. The fact that enlightened beings can do so is a guarantee that all other conscious unities, each human 'self', can do so, and is a proof of the continuity of consciousness. Once again we

---

3 Effectively a soul-form.

find Chandrakīrti's reasoning incomplete because he has omitted the part or function that consciousness plays in the scheme of things.

Because thoughts can be recalled from within a person's consciousness, they are *inherent*; and because they can be recalled forever, as long as a Buddha-Mind can evolve and exist, so these thoughts can be said to inherently exist. However, we know that they can also be changed or modified, and therefore they can be considered transitory. Be this so, however, the fact is that change happens as part of a continuum, through the sequence of time. In reality, therefore, the originating thought is not what is changed, but rather its continuation in time.

In fact the originating thought persists unchanged and unmodified, because it is part of a thought-stream, where the sequence of thoughts can be traced backwards in that stream to the originating *bīja* of a thought. Literally therefore the thoughts never die or disintegrate, as long as there is a mind/Mind that can recollect. The mind-structure concerned can be of an ordinary reincarnating human being (which can be recalled in any future life), or of the omniscience of any enlightened one.

We can see quite clearly that Chandrakīrti's supposition is not substantiated in the realm of consciousness, and we must still analyse why it doesn't. Even the *śūnyatā* experience does not spell the end of such a thought structure, otherwise a Buddha, or any enlightened one, would not be able to remember anything after their enlightenment.

The *fifth* of the five presented statements is:

> The I is not inherently produced and does not inherently disintegrate because the I would meet with the results of actions not done by itself. If, on the other hand, the potencies accumulated from actions were transmitted, an I which was totally different from the I that committed the deeds would undergo the results of those deeds.[4]

As per usual the problem with interpreting this statement is with the word 'inherently', meaning existing as a permanent or essential attribute. What exists as a essential attribute is the factor of change with respect to the concept of an 'I'. It is effectively continuously produced and rather than disintegrating, it changes as each successive *saṃskāra* is experienced and either altered or transmuted. The 'I' has

4 Hopkins, 49.

changed accordingly and thus no longer stands the same. The form (or phenomenal appearance) may not have disintegrated (until death has happened), but aspects of consciousness have changed, they are no longer *in situ*.

The overseeing encompassing consciousness, utilising this continuously changing personal-I persists, and moreover has grown in consciousness-stature through the process. The same goes for each successive birth and death of the incarnate personality. A new mind is recreated for each birth, just as a new thought is recreated at the death of each old one. The primal coalescing causative thought that caused that personal-I to come to being (i.e., to incarnate) however persists, just as the originating thought described above (which can be recalled at any time by an enlightened one). The various personal-I's incarnate into and out from manifest space, but the cause for their appearances does not integrally change, otherwise the rebirthing process would not occur. One may ask 'What can this originating cause be?' For the answer we must look to the *tathāgatagarbha*, which will be explained in detail in Volume 3, for which the foundational concepts are established hereafter.

We see also that there must be a continuity of the consciousness-stream, via aspects of the store of the *saṃskāras* of the past that must be carried through into a particular life, in the form of the necessary *karma* that flows onwards to seed the actions of the future. Indeed, the *karma* that needs to be expressed conditions the overall process of birthing and dying, but there are streams of action-reaction of *conscious* volitions at play here. We have sequences of events happening in consciousness, as well as separate incidences happening in the world of the sense perceptions. This produces the appearance of individual happenings. Individual volitions do happen, but they are not uncorrelated, they are conditioned by past volitions in that life, by past *saṃskāras*, thus a new 'I' is continuously produced, otherwise there would be no evolutionary progression towards the Bodhisattva path. New cycles from an entirely different life stream can come in at any time, producing a new life circumstance.

For example, the sequence of time when Milarepa was involved in sorcery involves one distinct type of karmic stream. The transformation process when he actively sought out his guru Marpa, who set him on the road to enlightenment, involves another. When he finally achieved his enlightenment, then another karmic stream ensued, that enabled him to take disciples for training, producing their consequent enlightenment. So there are really three different 'I's' implicated here in his life. (The third one is not an 'I' in the technical sense, but an enlightened being does possess a means for self-expression, for identity, which makes him an 'I' during the process of that 'identity'.)

a. That of sorcery, of gross involvement in *saṃsāra*, of karmic accumulation.

b. That of actively treading the Bodhisattva path, of karmic cleansing.

c. The transcended 'I/non-I'.

Nevertheless there is a sequence, a continuity uniting the 'I's', allowing the actions of one to be cleansed by the other. Such is always the case, but for most of the lives the 'I's' are separated by the process of physical death. In Milarepa's case such a 'death' was incurred by the educational process given to him by Marpa, and his consequent meditative development. Consciousness persists, and when progressed through to enlightenment, upon the attainment of *śūnyatā*, it has been thoroughly cleansed of defilements. (Such is the 'ascertaining consciousness' of Tsongkhapa that saves his philosophy from falling into the quagmire of the two extremes.) This is but a way of saying that the *karma* is transmuted, but not eliminated. It then manifests in a form not related to the patterns of *saṃsāric* involvement. The *karma* produced leads one away from the formed realms and the need to incarnate therein. That is all. *Karma* is all. In this context *śūnyatā* can be considered as the foundational expression of the *karma* of the All, which is incomprehensible to the experience-reservoir of the empirical mind (the establisher of the I-concept). The *karma* pertaining to *śūnyatā* therefore is void of the experience of *ahamkāra*.[5] It is liberated from the constraints of any form and manifests via a far more spacious and embracive *maṇḍalic* patterning, that pertaining to *dharmakāya*.

The attainment of (or rather the revealing of) *śūnyatā* therefore concerns riding through the *saṃskāras* of the successive manifesting personal-I's in such a way that they are transmuted through conscious volitions that are a progressive continuum of cleansing gross defilements into the sublime. The process continues until the *saṃskāras* and

5 I-am-ness, the tendency towards definiteness, origin of all manifestation.

associated *skandhas* become transformed into the wisdoms of the five Dhyāni Buddhas. Then the onus of the *karma* is not for manifestation, but to reveal the non-manifested that is the gain of the cause-effect world of human experiences. Without the I-concept therefore, the transformation process of the *saṃskāras* and *skandhas* is impossible, thus Buddhahood could not be obtained from out of the mud of human *saṃsāric* activity.

This is also symbolised by the spotless lotus blossom, effectively the 'I' growing out of the mud of the swamp (our murky emotional-minds) to greet the light of the spiritual sun—the enlightenment-principle. It is an 'I' because it is 'separate' from other such flowers that share its pond habitat. Thus such an I-consciousness is what the Tathāgatha actually *sits upon* (as shown in the imagery of thankas) as a symbol of his ultimate attainment and prowess. It is the base *chakra* of his spiritual Life. Without it he would have never come to be what he is.

It is interesting also to note with respect to the phrase 'because the I would meet with the results of actions not done by itself', that *karma* allows this, because all around the personal-I are such 'results of actions not done by itself'. This is the general environment in which the 'I' lives, and for which it has free will, allowing it to choose whether to interrelate with it or not. As well as this there are many hidden karmic clauses in that environment that predispose the way that 'I' ought to act, *because* the *karma* is there interrelating every iota of Nature's kingdoms.

Mind, body and the 'I'

Next we are presented with the heading: *'Establishing that the I is not different from mind and body'*, to which there are four subsidiary statements.

> 1. The I is not an entity other than mind and body because if it were, the I would not have the character of the aggregates, such as production, disintegration, abiding, form, experiencing, and realizing objects.[6]

The statement is saying that the 'I' is transient, because the mind and body are transient and therefore the 'I' has no basis in fact. If it were something else altogether, then it could not possess the aggregates

6 Hopkins, 49. I have added numbers to this section.

in any way, and thus it could not exist as such. (They are transient, and if it is non-transient, it can not hang on to that which is fleeting.) This is true, however what is not stated here is the purpose for the existence of the phenomena of the 'I', or of the 'character of the aggregates'. It has already been posited that there is an 'I' that incorporates more than the 'mind[7] and body', and this 'something more' is what has been termed consciousness, which also incorporates the faculty of *bodhicitta*. From this perspective this 'I' can be considered other than a mind (the intellect) and the body. Yet it has 'the character of the aggregates', plus that faculty of higher revelatory reasoning and the driving will that can lead the person, the 'I', out of the confines of *saṃsāra* altogether, wherein such things as 'production, disintegration, abiding, form, experiencing, and realizing objects' both exist, and also do not exist. (Otherwise it would not be beyond *saṃsāra*.) They exist temporarily, because the process relating to the formation of *saṃsāra* and its disintegration (or rather, the relinquishing of ties thereto), is projected from realms beyond thought, but are moulded by thought when the conditioning impulses appear in the guise of form.

Having 'the character of the aggregates' does not necessarily mean that it is annihilated when the aggregates are destroyed (as in the process of bodily death). If we view this 'character' to be the interrelated *saṃskāras* then it is not in fact destroyed, but stored, to be resurrected, and transmuted upon a higher cycle of emanatory being.

> 2. The I is not a separate entity from the mental and physical aggregates because if it were, there would be no basis for the designation I. The I would be a non-product, and non-products are changeless whereas the I obviously changes.[8]

Here we must include the emotional aggregates in terms of that which changes, and also broaden our concept of mind to include all that consciousness represents. Consciousness, in the form of the I-consciousness, is not separate, because it is inclusive in its expression of the all which it comes into contact with, yet is separate, because it is not limited to the

7 Taking the mind here to refer to the sixth sense, the intellect, which is the identifying or self-conscious factor of the personal-I.

8 Hopkins, 49.

duration of the transience of the 'mental and physical aggregates' (here interpreting the term 'mental' as that which pertains to the intellect).

The I-consciousness is also sustained by *śūnyatā*, otherwise there could not be any striving for enlightenment. The existence of *śūnyatā* allows the threading all the successive personal-I's together, consolidating their unitary purpose. In this process *śūnyatā* is at the beginning of things and *śūnyatā* is at the ending, and thus at the heart of everything, something like a string that joins the pearls of each successive birth and death together. The entire process of evolution exists inbetween, as part of the *śūnyatā-saṃsāra* nexus, allowing Bodhisattvas to appear as aspects of the process leading all to *śūnyatā* by eliminating the obscuration of perception of what truly is.

If there were no factor of *śūnyatā* acting thus there could be no evolutionary progression of the 'I', no chance for the appearance of a Bodhisattva over evolutionary time. If *śūnyatā* was not the 'beginning and the ending', then there could be no middle process of the ever-changing 'I's', there could be no *saṃsāra* that changes, because ultimately, change can only be so in reference to something that is stable, that does not change relative to it. Only that which is stable can measure or gauge the process of rate of change, or mode of change of anything. Everything can be said to be changing together, in some way or other. For some things, the rate of change may be exceedingly fast, reckoned in milliseconds, and for others so exceedingly slow that the rate of change can hardly be detected at all. For the awareness manifesting the exceedingly rapid rate of change, the exceedingly slow rate can appear to be changeless, eternal.

Śūnyatā can be considered a *changeless state* from the point of view of human consciousness. Changes (in the fabric of the *maṇḍalic* nature of enlightened being) however *must* appear therein,[9] because the evolutionary gain by all Bodhisattvas on the journey to Buddhahood, and its attainment, is to be accounted for. No two Bodhisattvas are the same, each enlightened Bodhisattva adds a unique aspect of his/her evolutionary gain to the overall *maṇḍala* of liberated being. Myriads of sentient beings have evolved to become Bodhisattvas throughout the

9 Viewed from the vast perspective of cosmic evolution.

aeons of time, the process being established long before the earth was formed, and each have contributed their quota to the overall richness of *dharmakāya*. A Buddha can observe such change, because his type of awareness has increased to such an unimaginable speed that it appears instantaneous to us, and is inclusive of such a vast time-space continuum that makes ordinary human thinking, by comparison sub-atomic, microscopic.

Such important concepts may be hypostasised in Buddhism in terms of the attributes of a Buddha-Mind. However, all too frequently such a Mind is depicted to be in a kind of stasis. Having gotten 'there', the other shore of being/non-being, a Buddha need progress no further, so the doctrines imply. However, nothing can be further from the truth. There is always more, far more, to awaken to (or develop) in the multidimensional cosmos that such a one is born into. There are far distant goals to aspire to, after leaving the speck of matter in cosmos called earth behind. Buddhists must therefore broaden the scope of their ontology to include the vast panorama of cosmos into their perspective, allowing greater comprehension as to where a Buddha actually fits in the scheme of things. Buddhists have never comprehended the vastness of this universe of things and of non-things. The true depth and scale of its multidimensionality, of the way transmuted states of consciousness and how their cosmic identifications relate with respect to each other, and to the world of normal human perception, still remains veiled in their epistemology. The exoteric religion needs to accommodate such concepts, thereby changing in accordance with evolutionary Law. Nothing ephemeral, including the corpus of the religion, can stay rigid. Change is inherent in all such forms, or else there will be a slow decay of the life principle and eventual death of the form.

What also needs to be elaborated, to develop the thesis of the doctrine of an I-consciousness further, is the earlier introduction of a concept of a 'soul'.[10] This 'soul' was defined *as an aspect of the thought-projection of the enlightened Mind of a* primordial *Buddha,* which manifests as a paradigm of liberation for each human unit, for the sum of the evolutionary process of that life-stream. This Buddha-Mind collectivises

10 Presented in Chapter five of this book.

such 'unitary streams' into overall patterns, *maṇḍalas* of activity, as part of the overall evolutionary pattern for the entire human race.

Note that the soul-form implied here is separate from, yet is attached to the 'I', and incorporates it, otherwise the 'I' could not come to be in the first place. This soul-form does not directly partake of *saṃsāra*, but abstracts the distilled essence (or 'perfumes') from it, according to the activities manifested by the transient 'I', in a manner yet to be explained. It is therefore separate, and yet non-separate for the duration of the existence of the personal-I. There is also the 'non-product' (*śūnyatā*), which paradoxically, sustains the functioning of the 'I', for without it the 'I' would have no purpose for its progressive evolution. The intellect would cling tenaciously to an ego, but the expression of *bodhicitta* could not be grounded as an evolutionary fact, except maybe to a fictional, totally permanent unchanging soul, a concept which has been philosophically debunked. Only *śūnyatā* purports that ultimate release from phenomena that *bodhicitta* instigates, but the process necessitates the 'I' to manifest as the crucible of transmutation of base substances into the elixir of liberating bliss.

Without a stable, regulating force or anchor for the ship of life, then all that we would have is the chaotic clashing of destructive forces; 'I's' clashing with each other and destroying the ordered sequence of events that we all see around us. This is what appears to happen amongst humanity, because our civilisation is governed by the destructive potency of many egotistic people, 'I's', vying for personal power and wealth. Nevertheless there is an observed evolutionary push to the march of human history within the genteel ordering of Nature's domain. But *śūnyatā* alone will not guarantee such an evolutionary process, something else is needed to help propel the process along in a given direction. *Karma* is generally alluded to as productive of this, but *karma* as a mechanism necessitates the process of *individuation,* as explained earlier and in my book on *karma*. Individuation then demands a concept of a soul (that which causes the formation of an I-concept from out of the streams of consciousness, utilising available *karma* to do so), and a mechanism that allows *bodhicitta* to evolve and work in Nature.

Also, a soul-form is needed as an intermediary between the realm of a Buddha and that of the human unit. The units that measure time, the 'seconds', in a Buddha's realm (the *dharmakāya*) tick over at an exceedingly slow rate. It is effectively an 'infinite' duration or zone of experience, compared to that of the realm of human perception. The Buddha's realm can be compared somewhat to an hour hand of a clock, the soul realm (consciousness) to the minute hand, and that of the human personality to the second hand with respect to the rate of experience of time, however here the concept of time should be considered as the durations of cycles.

The intermediary is needed to plan for, direct, and to accommodate the gain of experience of any human life-flux for the number of incarnations it must manifest in human form, from the originating inception of such a form, to its eventual discarding as no longer necessary upon the attainment of Buddhahood. In these thoughts lies the reality that the doctrine of the three bodies of a Buddha (*trikāya*) actually symbolises, or rather veils. The normal Buddhist parlance becomes here an exoteric doctrine.

- The *dharmakāya,* or body of truth, representing the state of awareness of a Buddha on his own natural level of expression.
- The *sambhogakāya,* the bliss body of a Buddha. This is a Buddha's (or of the great Bodhisattvas) perfected or idealised state of manifestation upon the abstracted realms of the Mind. It can thus be perceived by consciousness as representational of an ideal form manifesting within the domain of Mind. Esoterically, the term is really but a pseudonym for 'soul' form, when relegated to the subjective realms of human development, as a term for such a form could not be conveyed any other way through the logic presented by classical Buddhist eschatological, epistemological, heuristic, or ontological doctrines. Buddhists would have immediately rejected and ostracised such a direct teaching as heresy, having already logically refuted the Hindu concepts of *ātman.*
- The *nirmaṇakāya*, the body of appearance of a Buddha (or literally of any fully enlightened being) in the realm of normal human interrelations.

We thus have, as an essential part of the process related to the establishment of conscious phenomenal life:

1. *Śūnyatā*, being the stable base, wherewith all things are sustained.
2. A soul-concept, the *tathāgatagarbha* (or I-consciousness), producing the process of individuation. (Yet to be fully explained.)
3. The appearance of the phenomenal, the personal-I (ego), manifesting in the three worlds and undergoing conscious experiences via the sense-consciousnesses.
4. *Karma*, working with available *skandhas* and *saṃskāras* upon and through the aspect of consciousness that has been individualised.
5. The life process, the gaining of conscious awareness, old age and death, followed by subsequent incremental repetitions of the process upon higher cycles of attainment, as per the teaching of Dependent Origination.

It should also be reiterated that if there was just *śūnyatā* and the personal-I existing side by side, then what is known as the 'I' *would be instantly annihilated*, as *śūnyatā* will not allow such a 'thing' to be. We can hypothesise that *śūnyatā* is too positive and (destructively) dynamic with respect to the transitoriness of the 'I', and is totally 'antithetical' (if such a term can at all be used for that, which in itself is really passive and acts not) to the ephemeral attributes of the 'I'. If we have the Void and we have the ephemeral universe, with its myriads of separate existences, separate egos or forms of 'self', so *why then is all that ephemera not instantly annihilated,* if *śūnyatā* alone represents the reality of what is? This is effectively what this second postulate of Chandrakīrti's infers, as *śūnyatā* is obviously a 'non-product', and thus will not allow any 'basis for the designation I'. If we define the 'I' as something that is separative, a unit of sentience, or of 'mind and body' that is transitory, then such a thing could not exist if it is incongruous with *śūnyatā*. How then can such 'things' exist simultaneously with the Void? Blithely stating that these 'things' exist simultaneously with the Void because they are intrinsically empty, cannot answer the question, because the substantiality of the appearing phenomena is ignored.

Annihilation of the phenomena clearly does not happen, except for a few liberated ones, that have through yogic *tapas* gradually refined mind into a state that can accommodate the Void. This therefore is a major area where Buddhist logic as it presently stands needs rectifying, because it gives no true mechanism to explain why phenomena and *śūnyatā* appear simultaneously. One may point to *karma*, but we have already seen in my book *Karma and the Rebirth of Consciousness* that Buddhists have not really understood this law, for what is given in the texts is but an exoteric account. If something is not understood, then how can it be used to explain the veridicality of something else?

Also the refinement process of consciousness and of *saṃskāras* that allows one to approach the Void produces greater intensities of energy for the *yogin* to experience. This is a product of the transforming and transmutation process, and what remains upon the experience of *śūnyatā* is an intense energy field. This is not made clear in most descriptions of *śūnyatā*. If the existence of such an energy field did not exist then many imbeciles, possessing vacuous minds could theoretically experience the Void, and therefore be already 'there', enlightened. If however a high energy state must first be attained, such an outcome would not be possible.

What is needed to prevent instant annihilation from happening is a third party, a mediator between the separative 'I' of a human personality, and the annihilator of 'self', of separativeness, which *śūnyatā* represents. We must thus redefine a soul-concept,[11] as above outlined, much to the chagrin of orthodox Buddhist thinkers. This mediator in the realm of consciousness, in the *ālayavijñāna*, must be of sufficient clarity in its energy state to contain or 'hold' *śūnyatā* in its embrace, and yet at abeyance. At the same time it must be able to absorb or abstract that which is the gain from the *saṃsāric* play by the sequence of personality-I's reincarnating in the *māyā* (illusion). From the perspective of the intensity of the energy of *śūnyatā* the 'soul-form' acts not just as a consciousness store, but also as a medium between the potent energy field of *śūnyatā* and the sluggish attributes of phenomena.

This mediator is the fount of the principle of *bodhicitta* for the personal-I, and is not annihilated by *śūnyatā* because it has *śūnyatā*

11 Note, as shall be later elaborated, the Buddha never denied the validity of such a concept, he merely remained silent on the issue. As well as an individual soul-form for each human unit, one would also have to posit a world-soul *(anima mundi)*, to prevent the sum of the world of phenomena disappearing into the Void.

at its heart (which allows it to string the 'pearls' of each personality incarnation into a unified progression to liberation), and because it is fabricated from the *dharmakāya* upon the highest possible level of consciousness (thus manifesting as part of the *ālayavijñāna*). Such a mediator must exist to facilitate the transmutation of forms of ignorance in *saṃsāra* into fields of light, so that consciousness can eventually be liberated into the 'emptiness of concepts' that *śūnyatā* represents.

The theory of the existence of *śūnyatā* and of *saṃsāra* demands the presence of a mediator between the two. We can anthropomorphise the concept of triplicity as Father - Son - Mother; or Bliss - Consciousness (Soul) - Form; Emptiness - Revelation - Experience; Power - Love–Wisdom - Active Intelligence. We also have the concept of the three *guṇas*, and of the *trimūrti* of Śiva - Viśnu - Brahmā in Hinduism; then the triple gem in Buddhism of Buddha - *dharma - saṅgha,* and the three bodies of a Buddha.

The above list is not in any way exhaustive. Such fundamental trinities can be found in their myriads in Nature and is a necessity in the process of life, of being–liberation–non-being. Note that this last triad can be read in two ways, the first takes 'being' as representing manifest *saṃsāric* life, and thus 'non-being' is viewed as *śūnyatā*. The second interpretation, takes 'non-being' as the illusion of all that is in *saṃsāra*, and 'being' as that which is representative of the *dharmakāya*. What is termed 'liberation' here is the effect of the process that leads from one to the other. It is a shorthand notation for a process, and that process can always be represented by triplicity. We have for instance, the three times: past, present, and future, that gets one from 'here' to 'there' (the 'other shore' of being/non-being).

Some Buddhists may be perplexed by the esoteric undertones of their philosophy, when stripped of exoteric misconceptions, because it *seemingly* flaunts millennia of ontological speculations by their greatest philosophers, but the logic is sound and revelatory. Many may try to deny it, and if there be sound reasoning, good, but others will try to ignore and ostracise the challenge to conventionality and consequently continue following outmoded doctrines that should be relegated to a spiritual museum for old books with flawed syllogisms and theories. Such repositories can serve the historian of ideas and of how they evolved, but it does not really serve seekers of truth, of those who are truly seeking to gain enlightenment. They need better fare to digest, more wholesome food that will get them there quicker.

So let the earnest Buddhist reader seeking truth (despite the costs to fixed belief systems) read on, to see just how this philosophy of intermediaries, of the I-consciousness, develops. The purpose is not to destroy Buddhist thought, but to enrich it, by adding further understanding as to what the universe, consciousness, and the nature of enlightenment consists of. Lets bring Buddhism into the twenty-first century and make it truly the *rāja,* the king of religions, as far as the soundness of its philosophical ontology and epistemology are concerned. Let it take on board the necessary reformation that it needs and consequently grow inwards and outwards towards the *dharmakāya* experience.

The third point of the presented logic associated with the phrase 'that the I is not different from mind and body' is:

> 3. The I is not a separate entity from the aggregates because if it were, there would be no object to be apprehended as I. The I would be a non-product like nirvana or a non-existent like a flower in the sky.[12]

By *nirvāṇa* here I presume is meant *śūnyatā*, which is said to be a 'non-product', because it is not a product of anything at all.

The above is true only to the extent that the sum total of the aggregates, the *saṃskāras* and *skandhas*, constitute the evolving personality. However they must be tied together by means of a mind, which possesses the ability to manifest conscious volitions. Without this ability the aggregates that manifest would not be able to do anything at all. Without consciousness they would effectively be 'non-existent like a flower in the sky'. What is the true cause of this conscious volition? Desire for gross sensual pleasure, intellectual striving for discursions in the realms of thought, former aggregates pushing through to the surface awareness of things, or some impulsion from an overriding consciousness? Buddhists will point to the cycle of Dependent Originations, saying that one thing depends upon another, and thus all is foundationless. But this does not really answer the question. The question needing answering is *what* caused Dependent Origination to happen in the first place and why?

12 Hopkins, 49.

A subsidiary question is what sustains it all in such a way that incarnations happen as perfectly integrated as they do on a mass world-wide, or even cosmic scale? Is the law of *karma* sufficient to explain it? If so, how does *karma* account for such perfect multidimensional interdependence throughout evolutionary time?

If there were simply aggregates acting out a sequence of events, then a person's progress would be like a train on a track, going only in the direction that the railway line will allow, for in reality that is all that these aggregates from past actions will cause to happen. It would make extremists out of humanity, all with lop-sided mental or emotional development. People with broad-minded, well-balanced development could not exist. The intellect would be pushed along in a given direction, deeper into separative, self-centred, and concreted thought patterns. It could go no other way, because of the nature of the substance that constitutes it. We thus would only have fanatics, as the railroad can lead only along the line of development instigated by the aggregate. Any type of aggregate surfacing would only tend to develop its type of quality, not any other. The person would be fixated there, unless there was a way out, i.e., *a higher type of Mind* than the intellect, producing new consciousness volitions.

This is a somewhat obscure point, as we are analysing the product of lines of development that are inclusive of this higher type of Mind. This higher Mind may not be expressed in all humans, but the potential and the faculties are already in place for its development.

One way of observing the problem is if one imagined what life would be like without any emotions whatsoever. For most this is a difficult assignment, as their consciousness is intricately interwoven with them. *Yogins*, however, are achieving just that. People manifest the emotions without being aware of them. The same goes with Buddhist philosophers regarding this higher consciousness; they use it, but have not properly thought out where it has come from. The higher consciousness is certainly not strictly composed of the aggregates and mind alone because this mind and the aggregates are drawn to transmogrify themselves by a higher force, by that which stands beyond (them) and which works upon them, like yeast that in a sugary solution produces alcohol. Pure consciousness exhilarates, producing awareness sublime, and leads to vast, expansive vistas beyond the realms of form, beyond the personal-I.

Such 'exhilaration' is carried along a different line, separate from the gross aggregates, but is inclusive of them, and has its expression in the *intuition*. Intuition functions as an inner prompting to act according to *conscience*, to go a new direction in life, despite what the logical mind asserts or the way the emotions are pulling. There is a subtle inner voice telling the individual what to do, or how to act in a given circumstance, or where to be at a particular time, even who to be with, given any number of options. Such inner promptings can, and generally do, change the entire life of the person. These promptings are thus not (just) the result of the aggregates, but are something 'other', influencing for the betterment of the individual concerned. The prompting therefore is to cleanse material *karma*. It generates the Bodhisattva path, the nature of which thus concerns developing the ability to assuredly listen to this inner voice. It is the Heart's Mind speaking to a receptive, calmed mind.

The existence of the intuition implicates a higher faculty than the mind. It is a 'non-product', in the sense of not being (inherently) derived from the aggregates, and is separate from them, and yet incorporates them in its mode of action.

Another way of viewing the phrase 'there would be no object to be apprehended as I' is that it can refer to unconsciousness, to one who is not aware of the 'self, the mind and aggregates' that he/she has incarnated into. The state of being unconscious thus makes 'not an I', and can be considered to make the personal-I 'non-existent like a flower in the sky'. It could also mean that the unconscious one is focussed elsewhere, upon an 'other', not 'here', but 'there'. However, unconsciousness is obviously not what our author is referring to in his postulates.

Continuing with the quotes from *Meditation on Emptiness:*

> 4. The I is not a separate entity from the aggregates, because if it were, the I would be apprehendable apart from the aggregates just as the character of form is apprehendable separate from the character of consciousness. But it is not.[13]

Again, this is only true if *citta* (the substance of mind) is tied

13 Hopkins, 49.

to the aggregates in such a way that conscious volitions *cannot* be made. Therefore though the aggregates may be an integral aspect of the personal-I, the 'I' necessitates something to distinguish itself, to incorporate aspects of itself from the flowing streams of aggregates. Aggregates possessing the needed qualities must be incorporated into the structure of the personal-I, causing others to be rejected, and most must be modified in diverse ways in accord with the will or purpose of the 'I'. It is not feasible for the aggregates to control such a process of their own as they are passively manipulated in a similar way that a person can manipulate clay to make pots. If they are flowing just of their own accord, then there is *no change,* or means thereto. They could then be considered a 'non-product like *nirvāṇa*', but this is not the case. They are quantified by self-identifying units of consciousness that manifest conscious volitions modifying *saṃskāras* in the way desired.

Once conscious volitions are manifested in such a way that they act differently to the way the aggregates are flowing, or modify them in some way, then there is an 'I' that is apprehendable, apart, and yet still integral to the constituency of the aggregates. This is what happens all the time with normal human personalities, when they use their *wills* to go against the karmic agenda set for them. New *karma* is created, and every time this happens so a new set of aggregates are formed, which are not the former aggregates, though adapted from them. They are apprehendable, thus apart from the former aggregates. Whatever utilises the *will* in such a way therefore, can be considered an 'I', conventionally, what I term the personal-I. However it is consciousness that is the over-riding decision maker with respect to the karmic flow, of the manifestation of the aggregates that must come to be in the future life-stream of the 'I'.

The main postulate of the quote is thus essentially untrue, as *santāna*[14] alone does not constitute the 'I'. Where would be the beginning

14 *Santāna:* psychical continuum, series, likened to the incessant flow of a stream. Literally the stream of consciousness and karmic actions, that has moulded or made our present and future lives. It is the stream of action-reaction, cause-effect volitions that have made us what we are. If one however follows the *santāna* of one's Heart centre then one will tirelessly and desirelessly cleanse the path of karmic impulsions, so that the stream of ever-expanding consciousness that is the effect of an awakening Heart can manifest without hindrances. This way concerns the development of enlightenment from life to life.

or the ending of such a flow, and indeed what would cause it to move without the *will* that manifests from a focal point of consciousness, which is the personal-I?

Wherever you have conscious volition, meaning the existence of a will to modify actions, or things of the three worlds, there you have the appearance of an 'I'. There can be no other way of doing this. Only through the manifestation of an identity, something which identifies itself as distinct from that which it consciously modifies, is such possible. There is the actor (the 'I'), and that which is acted upon (the aggregates). The actor will be aware of essential phenomena, incorporating the props (the aggregates) in his consciousness, and of the stage play of the character played, so the illusionality of phenomena is thus maintained. Though constituted of the aggregates, the unity of being stands apart from them. It possesses something more, and can counter the pressure of the *santāna* of the aggregates upon consciousness. Ultimately we have the appearance of an enlightened being, who has complete control of the *santāna*, because his/her consciousness has been freed from 'self'. In such a one however the self-will manifests via the flow of the *santāna* of the Heart in order to sustain the duration of any action. To modify something one must act as a 'self', an 'I', to do so.

Essentially, therefore, the will can only come via the self-assertion of an 'I', even if this 'I' is transitory, it must exist to assert conscious volitions or manipulate things. *Śūnyatā* will not thus assert, neither will a flow of aggregates, for aggregates are simply a moving stream and will not move anything but itself and what it carries along with it. Thus what is necessary for something new to happen is something 'else' to produce it, and this something is an 'I', as would be a rower in a boat rowing against the flow of the stream. If it is transitory, then the question would be for how long does it last, for one moment, the duration of a thought, a human life time, a million years, an aeon, a duration of a universe? All of these time spans are transitory, *but have a relative permanence,* and this is the crucial point or truth for the appearance of each creative 'I'. Transience may rule, but each transient factor has a relative permanency.

This concept of relative permanency is extremely important, because without it there could be no evolutionary progression, no road to Buddhahood. This is because there would be no ability to account for karmic interrelations, and no reckoning of time, therefore no ability for anything to progress in any ordered sequence. Having established this fact, it should consequently be noted that each unit of relative permanence that has the creative (conscious) ability to move things can in fact be considered an 'I'.

It should be further pointed out that such conscious wills can also exist upon the subjective realms, e.g., be manifest by disincarnate humans, and also in the realms of consciousness wherein the I-consciousness exists—for a duration, a cycle of aeons. We must use such terms for the reckoning of 'time' in this arena, because what we know of as time does not exist anywhere but in physicality, as it is defined in terms of cycles of physical events.

Finally, the phrase 'the character of form is apprehendable separate from the character of consciousness' is here considered a truism. It is a valid assumption, but not from the Yogācāra viewpoint that 'mind is all there is', thus the character of the form is non distinguishable from that of the consciousness that experiences it. Whatever the view, the important thing is that once the mind has processed something gathered by means of the sense-perceptions then all that the 'I' has experienced and known relating to it has been collated and stored in memory, and the experience can be recalled when needed.

The base of mind and body

The next heading given by Hopkins is '*Establishing that the I is not the base of mind and body*'. There is only one accompanying statement:

> The I is not inherently the base of the mental and physical aggregates like a bowl for yoghurt or like snow that exists throughout and surrounds a forest of trees because if it were, the I and the aggregates would be different entities. This has already been refuted in the second reasoning.[15]

From one perspective the 'I' *is* the 'base', because without it the mind and body, *karma,* and mental-emotional *saṃskāras,* could not come to be in the first place. Yoghurt is yoghurt without the bowl, but

---

15 Ibid., 49-50.

the bowl *quantifies* it in terms of edible portions, snow may melt, but the trees feel its presence during the winter and are fed by it during the thaw. So also the 'I' quantifies the mental and physical aggregates (and also the emotional ones) into 'edible portions'. Without such activity the *saṃskāras* would simply flow without being modified by anything at all. Each successive appearance of the 'I' allows the modifications of the *saṃskāras* in such a way that Bodhisattvahood can be attained in the end. By 'edible' is meant assimilable experiences out of the sum total of the panoply of possibilities that represents the environment, the banquet table in general. If everything was experienced at once then there would be an information overload causing insanity, as the personal-I could not cope. That such insanity does not occur in the majority of people is another proof for the existence of an 'I', because if the aggregates simply flowed without being modified or contained by anything that collectivises them into discrete packets of 'chewable' bits, then the sum total of the aggregates of myriads of past lives would be experienced all at once, producing a total inability for a coherent consciousness to function.

Also, like the effect of the melting snow upon the trees, the activity of the 'I' affects the appearance (e.g., the future *karma*) of the aggregates. From this perspective it is also the 'base'. Of course the 'I', like the snow, ultimately disappears, yet its effect upon consciousness, which has presumably gained through experience memories that it can remember at will, and new *saṃskāras* that can be brought to the surface at need, lives on. In a similar manner, a tree grows in stature from the water that it absorbs into its system as a consequence of the melting snow. The disappearing 'I' is not a true base in itself, but that which causes the continuous succession of 'I's' is, for without this succession no mental or physical aggregates could appear or be sustained, and acted upon. Each successive unit of consciousness is linked together by the overall consciousness, the I-consciousness. This consciousness thus continuously expands and intensifies itself. Inevitably it works at its own rarefication and transmogrification, until in the end, upon the attainment of Buddhahood, that which it embodied is merged into *dharmakāya*.

Observing the totality of the picture, the base here is thus the I-consciousness that collectivises these personal-I's, having sent each one out upon its incarnate errand.

From another perspective the base can be considered to be *śūnyatā*, because *śūnyatā* does not change in relation to the evolution of the successive 'I's', and by means of it they can be strung together into a unity. A base is something stable that acts to support something else.

The base of the 'I' and its possession

The fourth heading given by Hopkins is '*Establishing that mind and body are not the base of I'*. There is only one accompanying statement:

> The I is not inherently based on the aggregates like a person living in a tent or like a lion living in a forest because if it were, the I and the aggregates would be different entities. This has already been refuted in the second reasoning.[16]

The personal-I and the aggregates flow together, the 'I' quantifying the aggregates, thus one can be considered the base or foundation of the other. There could be no 'I' without the aggregates, and certainly the aggregates would be meaningless without the 'I'. They are thus not different, in that they do not exist of different elements, but the personal-I is based on the aggregates, metered out according to the vicissitudes of the law of *karma*, and it also provides access to aspects other than the aggregates for its experiential growth. Both change, the aggregates (constituting *saṃskāras*) are transmuted into the *qualities* of the wisdoms of the Dhyāni Buddhas, whilst the 'I' reincarnates into progressively wise unities and expands to become inclusive of the 'I' of the All that is not a separative 'self'—which is another definition of Buddhahood.

As the 'I' is inherently based upon the aggregates, therefore at this level of visioning they are not different *per se;* however, from a broader perspective, the 'I' is more than just the aggregates because it has modified them, utilises what has been modified, and also can gain from consciousness-awakening forms of perception that are not based on the aggregates.

Next we have the heading '*Establishing that the I does not inherently possess mind and body'*. There is only one accompanying statement:

16 Hopkins, 50.

> The I does not inherently possess the aggregates in the way that a person possesses a cow because if it did, the I and the aggregates would be different entities. The I does not inherently possess the aggregates in the way that a person possesses his body or tree its core because the I and the aggregates would inherently be the same entity. These positions have already been refuted in the second and first reasonings.[17]

This statement is correct from the perspective that if the 'I' is perpetually changing, hence illusional, and the aggregates also are continuously changing, how then can either of these 'possess' anything other than the illusional, that which is their own co-mutability? The I-consciousness, however 'possesses' both in its embrace, because through the faculty of memory and the creative imagination, it can instantaneously recall and re-experience any *saṃskāra* that has occurred through any volitional experience of the 'I'. It can also seed the personal-I with images and desire impulses in order to lead that 'I' to progress along a specially ordained path, like a cow being led along a path by its master. Thus some individuals are fated to achieve preordained activities. For example, when Gautama was born it was prophesised by a soothsayer that he would either become a universal monarch or a fully enlightened sage. The actuality however, was that despite all of the efforts of his father to make of him a universal monarch, the preordained destiny was for the Bodhisattva to become a Buddha. Nothing in fact could prevent him from fulfilling his pre-ordained purpose.

As far as I am aware, a detailed mechanism of predestiny is not presented in the Prāsaṅgika or general Mahāyāna logic. However, all rhetoric purporting to deny the existence of a 'self' must be able to explain such destiny satisfactorily, otherwise the rhetoric will be found to be flawed. If the law of *karma* is evoked to explain this phenomena then how it can do so must be precisely detailed. A naïve assertion that this law exists and acts in this way suffices not. All of the factors showing how and why *karma* works must be shown.

To briefly define the 'I' we can say that it is an expression of consciousness integrating the activities of the mind, emotions, and subtle and physical bodies, for the duration of any completed cycle of activity,

---

17 Ibid.

which can incorporate many related sub-cycles. What is termed 'mind' here is the concrete (empirical) mind, the intellect that self-identifies. Consciousness possesses the concrete mind (for the duration of the existence of an individualised 'I') but also incorporates an abstract or enlightened Mind that is not conditioned by the 'self' concept. The I-consciousness thus 'possesses' the mind and body for the duration of the sensory experience that produces a modification in consciousness, or for cycles of experiences, but then loses possession when the purpose for experiences no longer exist. A new 'I' is then caused to incarnate when a new cycle of experiences is needed. An example of this is when one goes to sleep, both the personal-I and the I-consciousness (which can be considered a greater or overshadowing 'I') no longer needs the bodily mechanism, does not overtly 'possess it' (apart from sustaining a life-thread) for the duration of its experiential progress in what is known as the dream or deep sleep state. It has momentarily disincarnated from the physical shell, and reincarnates into it upon the waking experience. A similar process happens in the process of actually dying to one body and the consciousness reincarnating into a new one. But in this case the personal-I no longer exists. Inevitably the overshadowing I-consciousness helps to build a new personal-I in a new child to be born.

Deep sleep is actually a good example of the fact that the aggregates of themselves are meaningless without the I-consciousness 'possessing them' in some way to produce its purpose. When the personal-I is not functioning then we have the sleep state ensuing, but consciousness is still functioning, and the proof thereof is dream states, from very lucid dreaming, to precognitions of what the future is to be. We also have mindless ramblings. In precognitive dreams we see that consciousness imposes certain images (those that can be interpreted to have meaning) upon the mind-space of the personal-I at a time when this personal-I is not in possession of the bodily form. Consciousness retains its link, otherwise the breath will stop, the heart will no longer beat, and the body will die. From this perspective it is consciousness that 'possesses' the body, the related *skandhas* and *saṃskāras*, for the duration of the purpose of the existence of the form, because during sleep, the personal-I for all intents and purposes, does not exist as a functioning entity. It possesses nothing of its own, and is not in charge of the karmic factors that propel it along through time and space, but the overshadowing I-consciousness does direct the *saṃskāras* and the related *karma*.

Actually, nothing can be possessed that is transient in nature, the aggregates are merely *borrowed* for a cycle of activity, and must be returned, once the gain from the handling of the unit of transience has been made. Though the aggregates (or objects desired) are often profoundly affected by, or nonexpectantly taken from the personal-I, through war, fire, theft, etc., all such (drastic) experiences are designed for people to grow in consciousness, to relinquish desire for any aspect of *saṃsāric* mire.

We can quite clearly see that the statement that the 'I does not inherently possess the aggregates' is only partly truthful. Though all forms of transience are borrowed for durations of experiential existence, it can however be stated that the I-consciousness 'possesses the aggregates' in a similar way that 'a person possesses a cow', because here we see that the person possesses the cow for the duration of the life of that cow (or of that person) as long a purpose exists for the person to possess the cow, otherwise he will dispose of it in some way. Both the possession of the cow and possession of the aggregates are consequently transitory in nature. However the duration of possession of the aggregates by the I-consciousness may last for many cycles of lives and eventually be transmuted into Buddha-qualities. How else could the attributes possessed by a Buddha have come about?

We see therefore that indeed, the I-consciousness and the aggregates of an incarnate personal-I are effectively 'different entities', in accordance with Chandrakīrti's supposition. But this does not stop the I-consciousness from absorbing the results of the experiences of such 'possession', and retaining them as memory, *in perpetuity,* despite the eventual disappearance or loss of that which was once 'possessed'. Also, the fact that a farmer once possessed a cow is not lost when the cow dies, because the cow had helped sustain the farmer's livelihood during its existence, and the effects persist. Indeed, sufficient resources may have been accumulated during the cow's life (as a result of conscious planning by the farmer) to be able to replace it, or it may have had progeny, thus continuing its purpose for the farmer. So it is with respect to the 'possession' of the aggregates by the I-consciousness, upon the death of a personal-I a new one can be successfully established as per the rebirth process, perpetuating the purpose for this 'farmer' of life experiences.

The next supposition that the 'I does not inherently possess the aggregates in the way that a person possesses his body or tree its core because the I and the aggregates would inherently be the same entity' depends upon the mode whereby one interprets the word 'inherently'. Also it has already been established that a person does not 'inherently possess' his body. It is a moot point if a tree possesses anything at all, because the concept of possession comes only with consciousness being active, and it could be argued that a tree is unconscious, but not unaware (e.g., of insect pests, for which it has mechanisms of defence), with respect to its form. The definition of 'person' in the above quotation also leaves much to be desired, as it clearly does not take consciousness into account, but only the aggregates as bound by the intellect, which we have already ascertained does not possess the body. Otherwise it would be in complete control during the process of sleeping, or be in complete control of autonomic nervous system functions, such as the beating of the heart, and also of the process of sickness and death.

Even if the I-consciousness can be considered to 'possess' the aggregates, then it does not follow that they would inherently be the same entity, any more than a person possessing a cauldron full of acid can be considered the same as it. It merely manifests a useful functionality for him. Inherently, the I-consciousness can derive something (e.g., experiences) from what has been possessed and incorporate this into its own structure, and from this perspective Chandrakīrti's supposition that they 'inherently be the same entity' can be correct. However, this 'same entity' has been transmogrified into a type of (Mind) substance that is integral to the realm of existence of the I-consciousness. Inherently, within the abstract realm of the Mind therefore, what has been absorbed can be considered 'of the same essence'. This persists, even though the phenomena of the form (of what was once possessed) has long since gone.

The 'I' and composites of aggregates

The sixth heading presented by Hopkins is '*Establishing that the I is not the composite of mind and body*'. There are three statements substantiating the point given.

> 1. The I is not just the composite of the aggregates because the aggregates are the basis of the designation I and an object designated is not its basis of designation.[18]

This point is true as it goes, for we have already ascertained that the 'I' is more than just the aggregates, or its *composite of mind and body*, for consciousness must be added and its duration over many lifetimes, as well as its purpose defined or delineated.

> 2. The I is not the composite of the aggregates because the composite of the aggregates does not inherently exist; if the composite of the aggregates were inherently one with the aggregates, the composites would be many like the aggregates, or the aggregates would be one like the composite.[19]

The first portion of this statement concerning the illusionality or 'non-existence' of the composites has been explained above. Presumably, Chandrakīrti has the concept of the *ātman* in mind, conceived as a singular permanent soul, indicating that this would necessitate many *ātmans*, re the second portion that 'the composites would be many like the aggregates, or the aggregates would be one like the composite'. Maybe so, but we do not support this concept of *ātman*, and therefore the argument is relatively irrelevant.

The statement, however, omits to inform us that the composites being many like the aggregates is what *actually* abounds in Nature. The body for instance, is seen as a unity, yet it is a composite of many milliards of cells, and the complex groupings of organs, blood vessels, nerve plexuses, etc., that together make it a functioning unity. All are necessary for the proper functioning of the body, so that it can achieve its purpose of being a mechanism of response with the outer environment for the inner integral consciousness. This consciousness utilises the sensory experiences gained for its own purpose, its own advancement within the world of personal-I's, and later upon the spiral ladder of evolutionary being. Everywhere there is unity and diversity bound together into forms that together evolve intelligence or else sentient states. Why should such unity also not exist for the 'I' as a composite of all aspects

18 Hopkins, 50. I have added the numbers to this section.

19 Ibid.

of mind, *saṃskāras* and *skandhas,* that the law of *karma* interrelates for a purpose during the appearance of any given cycle of activity?

The phrase 'does not inherently exist' is important, and informs us that in the light of *śūnyatā* such things as the aggregates and the 'I' do not exist; but we can just as well say that some aspect of them does, when using Nāgārjuna's classic statement already quoted equating the identity of *saṃsāra* with *nirvāṇa*.

When dealing with the phenomena of *saṃsāra* on its own terms, utilising the terminology of conventional truth, then we cannot willy-nilly turn to abstracts to deny the existence of anything as an argument. Nihilism is not the logic we seek to entertain. We must be consistent in our reasoning. If we say that nothing 'inherently exists' we can thus end all further speculation and debate about anything at all (because of its purposelessness). However, if we agree that this phenomena has a temporary reality and purpose for its existence, our need is to then manifest proper philosophical logic as to why. We can also query 'what aspect of it does exist, and how?' Also, 'what exactly, therefore, is a Buddha liberated from?' He has not entered a nihilistic universe, but rather one that is Life, and a plenitude at that.

This is the proper or logical course of action, because it allows us to find answers to all facets of life on that long journey to Buddhahood. Possessing these answers is what will make us Buddhas in the end, not their avoidance. Fixation upon *śūnyatā* alone can produce results, but not that pertaining to the ultimate path that the Vajrayāna conveys. The avoidance of knowing about all things sustains forms of ignorance, which is antithetical to enlightenment. Utilising such non-avoidance we can proceed to analyse the concept of the 'I' and the logic relating to its necessity in the scheme of things, allowing us to find an approach that will produce liberation.

To be fair to Candrakīrti, it should be noted that he had the Brahmanical philosophy and the Hīnayāna schools in mind in his dissertation, and if he were alive today he would of necessity had also to look to philosophical development since his time, and thus his rhetoric would differ.

The third statement states:

3. Also, if the composite of the aggregates were a different entity from

> the aggregates, it would be apprehendable apart from the aggregates and would not have the character of the aggregates. But this is not so.[20]

I have however postulated that the composite of the aggregates *is* and *is not* a different entity from the aggregates. It is inclusive of the aggregates, with added consciousness, and bound together by karmic law. It therefore has the characteristics of the aggregates, but is moulded at any time by the perception of things that consciousness has. This 'perception of things' is conditioned by many factors, such as the external environment of which it plays a part. For example, the aggregates may be manifesting through a male or female vehicle, a Buddhist, Muslim, or Western society with the consciousness experiencing things and accordingly adapting to what it is learning. It may also be 'apart from the aggregates' because perception can draw upon higher principles than is possible of the aggregates, such as *bodhicitta*, and the intuitive perception of a preordained destiny. The character of the aggregates produce such things as emotional reactions, fear, etc., in response to presented stimuli, but consciousness determines the overall view of how these reactions fit into the general pattern of its existence in the society of personal-I's of which it is a part.

As the distinction between the personal-I and the I-consciousness has already been explained, so the mode of their interrelation, as well as the way that the I-consciousness is 'apprehendable apart from the aggregates', shall also be explicated in this treatise.

The 'I' and the shape of the body

The seventh and final heading in this investigation given by Hopkins is *'Establishing that the I is not the shape of the body'*. In relation to this he quotes:

> The I is not the shape of the body because shape is physical and if the I were merely physical, it would not be conscious. Also, the shape of the body does not inherently exist because it is a composite of the shapes of the limbs of the body.[21]

20 Ibid.

21 Ibid.

The first statement is self-evident and needs no further comment. However the statement that 'the shape of the body does not inherently exist because it is a composite of the shapes of the limbs of the body', is pedantry provided for the completeness of the arguments. The shape of the body by definition is the composite of the overall shape of its component parts. There are differences, but the overall shape of all bodies are similar for all humans; two hands, two feet, torso and head, unless there are individual deformities. That many identify with these things as if they were the 'I' is indeed true, but all are aware that this overall shape changes as a person matures from childhood to old age. Their consciousness is aware of these changes and generally take them into account in the way they act in the environment, and most know that they are more than just a body, they also have emotions and intelligence, of varying degrees and capacities, which together makes up their personal-I, their personal identification that separates them in their consciousness from all other seeming 'I's'. Their perceptions of things may not necessarily be correct, or enlightened, but this perception of 'I' is what allows them to evolve from one incarnation to the next, to eventually strive for *bodhicitta* and enlightenment. This is the purpose of all such self-identification.

The above line of reasoning can be carried through to either refute, modify, or to agree with the rest of the Prāsaṅgika system of reasoning for the establishment of selflessness. We can therefore conclude that their form of semantics is not error-free and needs to be modified, or redefined to be truly philosophically sound.

This then concludes the section concerning 'the sevenfold reasoning', one of the main forms of 'reasoning for establishing selflessness', as stated by Hopkins:

> In the Prāsaṅgika system, the sevenfold reasoning, dependent-arising, and the diamond slivers are the three main forms of reasoning for establishing selflessness. Three other forms are the refutation of the four extreme types of production, the refutation of the four alternative types of production, and the reasoning establishing the lack of being one or many.[22]

22 Ibid., 61.

9

Dependent Origination

Definition of *pratītyasamutpāda*

The foundation for the concept of the Buddha's formula of Dependent Origination *(pratītyasamutpāda),* which states that all phenomenal things arise dependent upon everything else, is ignorance. The concept of ignorance needs elaboration, as it is considered the 'root of all *karma*-formations' and effectively is the central characteristic of the twelvefold formula of Dependent Origination, which runs as follows:

1. Through ignorance are conditioned the *saṃskāras*, i.e., the rebirth-producing volitions *(cetanā),* or 'Karma-formations'.
2. Through the Karma-formations (in a past life) is conditioned Consciousness (in the present life).
3. Through Consciousness are conditioned the Mental and Physical Phenomena (*nāma-rūpa*—the mind that names and the form that receives sensations), i.e., that which makes up what is known as individual existence.
4. Through the Mental and Physical Phenomena are conditioned the six Bases—the five physical sense-organs through which impressions can come, and consciousness as the sixth which correlates those impressions.
5. Through the six Bases is conditioned the (sensorial mental) Impression.
6. Through the Mental Impression is conditioned Feeling.
7. Through Feeling is conditioned Craving.
8. Through Craving is conditioned Clinging.
9. Through Clinging is conditioned the process of Becoming,

consisting in the active and passive life process, thus the rebirth process.

10. Through rebirth, the *karma*-producing process is conditioned.
11. A consequent rebirth.
12. Thus we get old age, grief, sorrow, lamentation, despair, death and the repetition of the cycle.[1]

Ignorance is relative to everything else, thus it conditions the entire sequence of this formula, however at each successive turn of the wheel the qualities associated with the sequence become progressively cleansed of grosser qualities (*saṃskāras),* through knowledgeable experiences gained. Eventually that knowledge is transmuted into wisdom signifying the ending of one level of ignorant activity. The continuous turning of the wheel for instance produces increasingly sublime and transmuted forms of desire for things. (Signifying the process of cleansing the related *saṃskāras.)* Thus craving for sensual pleasures and transient material objects become transmuted into desire for liberation from *saṃsāra* in a later life. This then becomes ardent striving to cleanse defilements, overcome hindrances, and finally an inherent spontaneous drive to liberation. Once liberation is achieved, then the awesome potency of the momentum of *bodhicitta* pushes a Bodhisattva forward into transcendent, sublime states of compassionate desire, void of any aspect of desire known by humans still attached to *saṃsāra*. (Such compassionate 'desire' is related to the levels of suffering experienced by all lives manifest upon the earth sphere and elsewhere.)

No matter how enlightened one is, there is always a degree of ignorance, as indicated by the ten stages of the Bodhisattva path (*bhūmis*). By extension the logic also applies to the condition known as Buddhahood, though we shall not hypothesise further as to whatever form of transcendent 'ignorance state' a Buddha may possess. One can, however, categorically state here that ignorance has been totally transcended by a Buddha with respect to the state of being human. There are, however, experiential zones in all constellations and galaxies in cosmos yet to explore. The multidimensional universe is far vaster than

---

1 This list is adapted from Nyanatiloka, Nyanaponika (ed.) *Buddhist Dictionary, Manual of Buddhist Terms and Doctrines,* (The Corporate Body of Buddhist Educational Foundation, Taiwan, third edition, 1970), 128-129. The Pali term for *pratītyasamutpāda* is *paṭiccasamuppāda.*

anything imagined by our empirical scientists, and Buddhist philosophers alike. The *bhūmis* can be redefined as the ten levels of lessening ignorance concerning the nature of *śūnyatā* and then the *dharmakāya*. Everything is relative to something else, therefore if we look at Dependent Origination, ignorance *(avidyā)* is the start of this list, so we see that there is always a new beginning, a new series of Dependent Origination every time a new contrary wisdom *(vidyā)* has been attained.

Nāgārjuna's Madhyamaka philosophy puts this doctrine of Dependent Origination at the very core of its ontology, so that it can not be accused of nihilism. Because it accepts Dependent Origination, so it accepts conventional viewpoints about the 'reality' of the phenomenal world, but gives us the proviso that ultimately such phenomena is empty of 'things'. Donald S. Lopez, Jr., explains the Mādhyamika view further:

> Mādhyamikas are so-called because they abide in the middle free from all extremes. They are able to do this because of their understanding of the relationship between emptiness *(śūnyatā, stong pa nyid)* and dependent arising *(pratītyasamutpāda, rten 'byung)*. An emptiness is a phenomena's lack of true existence. Each phenomenon is empty of true existence and that mere absence of true existence is the final nature of that phenomenon. Dependent arising is, loosely speaking, the positive implication of the absence of true existence. All phenomena are dependent arisings in the sense that they either arise in dependence on causes and conditions, are designated in dependence on their basis of imputation, or are imputed in dependence on a designating term or thought. This third type of dependent arising is most subtle and is asserted only by the Prāsaṅgikas.
>
> Only the Mādhyamikas assert that all phenomena are empty of true existence and that all phenomena are dependent arisings[2]...The other schools of Buddhist tenets assert the true existence of at least some phenomena and limit the category of dependent arisings to impermanent things, taking the term "arising" *(samutpāda, 'byung ba)* in "dependent arising" to mean arising in dependence on causes and conditions. Since whatever is a caused phenomena is necessarily impermanent *(anitya, mi rtag pa)* according to the Sautrāntikas, Yogācārins, Mādhyamikas, dependent arisings must be impermanent. The Mādhyamikas, however, take the term *samutpāda* also to mean "established" and assert that all phenomena, caused and uncaused,

2 Lopez, Jr., *A Study of Svātantrika*, 39.

impermanent and permanent, are dependently established[3]...

The emptiness of a phenomenon such as a sprout and the sprout's dependent arising are synonymous because if the sprout were truly established it would not be a dependent arising and if it were not a dependent arising, it would be truly established. Technically, however, emptiness and dependent arising are not synonymous because, in that case, whatever was a dependent arising would have to be an emptiness. Although whatever is an emptiness is necessarily a dependent arising, the converse is not true because an emptiness is necessarily a permanent *(nitya, rtag pa),* non-affirming negative *(prasajyapratiṣedha, med 'gag)* phenomenon, whereas dependent arisings include all phenomena, permanent and impermanent. Nonetheless, it is accurate to say that whatever is empty of true existence is a dependent arising and whatever is a dependent arising is empty of true existence.

Dependent arising is called the king of reasonings because it allows the Mādhyamikas to refute both extremes simultaneously. The Yogācārins, for example, need two separate reasons to abandon the two extremes as they define them. They claim that they abandon the extreme of annihilation because they assert that impermanent phenomena truly exist as the same entity as the consciousness perceiving them. They abandon the extreme of permanence by asserting that impermanent phenomena do not have a nature separate from that of consciousness. The Mādhyamikas refute both extremes merely by asserting that all phenomena in the universe are dependent arisings. Specifically, the fact that they are "dependent" refutes the extreme of permanence. Whatever is dependent cannot be truly existent. The fact that they are "arisings" or "established" refutes the extreme of annihilation because whatever is arisen or established cannot be utterly non-existent.[4]

For those wishing to properly comprehend the subtleties of the viewpoints of the various Buddhist schools concerning this difficult subject, more technical detail is provided by Hopkins:

Prāpyasamutpāda, apekṣhyasamutpāda, and *pratītyasamutpāda* are synonyms; however, they are sometimes explained with individual meanings. *Prāpyasamutpāda*, "arising through meeting", is taken as referring to the dependent-arising which is the production of things by their causes. This is the meaning that the Vaibhāṣhikas, Sautrāntikas,

3 Ibid., 39-40.

4 Ibid., 40-41.

and Chittamātrins give to 'dependent-arising'; for them, however, dependent-arising is a sign of things' true existence, not a sign of their non-true existence. 'Meeting' can even be taken literally in the sense of indicating that a cause's approaching cessation and its effect's approaching production are simultaneous.

Apekṣhyasamutpāda, 'existing in reliance' or 'relative existence' is taken as referring to the dependent-arising which is the attainment by products and non-products of their own entities in reliance to their parts. This meaning of dependent-arising is a distinguishing feature of the Mādhyamika system and is said to be the Svātantrika-Mādhyamikas' favoured means of proving no true existence, but is also shared with such Prāsaṅgika masters as Āryadeva. Things undeniably appear to the mind to be separate from their parts as when it is in thought, 'This house has ten rooms'. The house appears to be one thing and the ten rooms appear to be another.

Pratītyasamutpāda, 'dependent-existence', is taken as referring to the dependent-arising which is the designation of all phenomena in dependence on the thought that designates them. Without thought to designate the existence of phenomena, the arising of phenomena does not occur. However, phenomena undeniably appear to common beings as if they exist in and of themselves, appearing from the object's side toward the subject rather than appearing to be imputed by the subject toward the object. 'Existing in dependence on a designating consciousness' is the special meaning of dependent-arising in the Prāsaṅgika system. The other two meanings are also wholeheartedly accepted by the Prāsaṅgikas, but their own special interpretation is to take *pratītyasamutpāda* as referring to the designation of phenomena as dependent not just on their parts or bases of designation but also on the thought that designates them[5]....

Dependent-arising is the king of reasonings because it can, without residue, overcome both extremes. The reasoning is:

> All phenomena do not inherently exist because being dependent-arisings.
>
> Or, in its most powerful form:
>
> All phenomena do not inherently exist because of being dependently imputed.

Here 'all phenomena' means 'each and every phenomenon'. Through ascertaining the reason – that all phenomena are dependent arisings

5 Hopkins, *Meditation on Emptiness,* 166-167.

– the extreme of annihilation is avoided, and realization of the dependent-arising of causes and effects is gained. Through ascertaining the thesis—that all phenomena do not inherently exist—the extreme of permanence is avoided, and realization of the emptiness of all phenomena is gained.

Furthermore, through ascertaining the reason—that all phenomena are dependent-arisings—the extreme of permanence is also avoided because it is realized that phenomena are just interdependently existent, not inherently existent. Through ascertaining the thesis—that all phenomena do not inherently exist—the extreme of annihilation is also avoided because it is realized that only inherent existence is negated, not existence in general. As a yogi progresses in understanding dependent-arising, realization of how the reason and the thesis each avoid the two extremes become subtler and subtler.

All other reasonings that prove no inherent existence derive from this king of reasons, dependent-arising[6]....

It is even said that emptiness and dependent-arising are synonyms, but this is not in the sense that 'pot' and its definition 'that which is bulbous and able to hold water' are synonyms. Also, the synonymity of emptiness and dependent-arising does not mean that a consciousness which ascertains that effects arise dependent on causes and conditions also ascertains the meaning of their being empty of inherently existent production. Furthermore, the meaning of the term 'dependent-arising' is not asserted to be the meaning of emptiness. An explicit ascertainment of a dependent-arising does not even carry with it an implicit ascertainment of emptiness. Rather, emptiness is synonymous with dependent-arising for Mādhyamikas who through valid cognition have refuted inherent existence.

Not just anyone who realizes dependent-arising can realize its synonymity with emptiness since many even see dependent-arising as a reason for asserting inherent existence. However, when a Mādhyamika ascertains that external and internal things are dependent-arisings, he realizes, based on the force of this very understanding, that being empty of inherent existence is the meaning of being a dependent-arising. For, he has realized that what inherently exists does not rely on anything, and he has realized that inherent existence and dependent-arising are contradictory.[7]

6 Ibid., 168-169.

7 Ibid., 170-171.

The problem of the origination of phenomena

For the Mādhyamikas that refute inherent existence and assert that 'emptiness is synonymous with dependent-arising' the question again arises 'how *exactly* does *saṃsāra* arise in the first place? If all aspects of it 'do not inherently exist', everything being void, 'ultimately', then how does phenomena dependently arise from that Void?' *Saṃsāra* may ultimately be 'empty', but it manifests a tangible appearance, which if projected backwards through time to the beginning of whatever was, before originating actions were accomplished, taking also originating mental formations into account, we will then see that emptiness/ *śūnyatā* is all that remains. If *śūnyatā* is empty of 'self', and *saṃsāra* is built on the concept of individualities, particulars, unities, 'selves' (such as atoms, minerals, compounds, cells, and organisms), then how can that which is totally contradictory in nature arise (spontaneously) and be dependent upon that which is *true, selfless,* thus materially unsubstantial? How can empirical phenomena arise from a phenomenon that 'is necessarily a permanent *(nitya, rtag pa),* non-affirming negative *(prasajyapratiṣedha, med 'gag)'* or exist dependently in relation to that which is essentially antithetical to its very existence?

Also, if 'only inherent existence is negated, not existence in general', then what exactly is 'existence' to the Mādhyamikas, if it has no basis in fact, there being no inherent life? What is it then that does the actual evolving and attains Buddhahood in the end? If the answer is the *tathāgatagarbha*, then again, how does phenomena originally arise for this *tathāgatagarbha* to be defiled with it, and what is the purpose of this tainting illusional phenomena that has no 'inherent existence' in relation to this Buddha-germ? Is the *tathāgatagarbha* then an 'inherent existence or life' that does this evolving? It evolves in the sense that its obscuring defilements are removed, whilst everything else, changing and dancing around it, also evolves with respect to it. By 'evolution' here is meant the progressive development of substance to become the Void Elements. Is this the answer we seek, or is there more to the equation of the appearance of phenomena, than simply to be utterly stripped of characteristics? What is the development of the wisdom of a Buddha in relation to this, as this wisdom is evolved via the manifestation of the ever-changing attributes. We could say that the evolution of the attributes and the attainment of wisdom are a synonymous process. The attributes themselves are evolving sentient states and eventually consciousness, as part of their *raison d'être.* Cannot such activity be a reason for the appearance of a Buddha womb *(tathāgatagarbha),* so that phenomena can be organised and directed to an eventual goal, namely Buddhahood?

There is more to the appearance of phenomena than meets the eye. A vast evolutionary attainment is here hinted at, one that provides a rationale for the existence of the phenomenal universe and all of the kingdoms of Nature incorporated within it. The doctrine of *śūnyatā* holds only a part of the answer. Is therefore the assertion 'that what inherently exists does not rely on anything...that inherent existence and dependent-arising are contradictory' a truism? Could there not be a third party, such as the *tathāgatagarbha* to act as a mediator between them? Coming to a correct solution to this query is then an objective of serious meditation.

If the phenomena (e.g., the *saṃskāras of consciousness,* plus the objects of perception) evolves then it can be considered to have an 'inherent life', contrary to the Prāsaṅgika-Mādhyamika position. It stands to reason that the substance animating human forms, and the constituency of mind, has to come from somewhere. Also, the quality of its constituency must evolve in accordance with the progresses achieved by a succession of human personal-I's in order to have the karmic predisposition to be utilisable by the I-consciousness (*tathāgatagarbha).* All human units possessed of a mind (constituted of attributes) evolve wisdom via the rebirth process over time. This is an undeniable fact. *Karma* must bind the substance of the form and the indwelling consciousness inextricably together for a reason. If the phenomena does not evolve, and there is nothing in fact removing the defilements from the *tathāgatagarbha* (limiting our perspective to human units), then what in fact is that phenomena's aetiological basis? In relation to *what* is its progress sustained? Also, if the *tathāgatagarbha* does *not evolve*, then what is the meaning of it all, if the entire basis to our existence is perfect from 'the start'? Does this mean that we are already Buddhas and there is no more need to strive (that is, to continue existing) for any purpose?

The philosophy that *saṃsāra* and *śūnyatā* are aspects of each other (i.e., dependent arisings) may endeavour to solve these problems[8]—but we are left with a credibility gap of how they interrelate. The Yogācārins tried to fill this gap with their doctrine of the *ālayavijñāna*; giving us a more conclusive argument, and by acknowledging what is given in the passage quoted from Lopez above 'the true existence of at least some phenomena and limit the category of dependent arisings to impermanent things, taking the term "arising" *(samutpāda, 'byung ba)* in "dependent arising" to mean arising in dependence on causes and conditions'. This however still does not properly explain how this *śūnyatā-saṃsāra* identity actually is possible, and therefore how anything actually came to 'be'. Humans have dependently evolved from 'something' somehow so that they can actually exist to experience (the arising of) 'things' by means of sense contact and gain comprehension by means of the intellect.

The way that *śūnyatā* becomes dependent upon *saṃsāra*, and *saṃsāra* upon *śūnyatā* and why this is so determines the life process. Therefore it is imperative that the above questions are satisfactorily answered. It may indeed be possible to say that *saṃsāra* is 'empty', i.e., 'being empty of inherent existence is the meaning of being a dependent-arising', but this does not explain how phenomena can be sustained by emptiness, or indeed, what the nexus or ground upon which *saṃsāra* sits is. Any point of interrelation between the two here would be empty of whatever could cause such a contact. The concept of phenomena being sustained by emptiness is effectively absurd, unless we can posit emptiness as real, as well as presenting a method that allows 'something' that is 'empty of itself' to co-exist with that emptiness, without that which is 'itself' from being annihilated. So we get the statements with respect to *śūnyatā,* of it being 'empty of emptiness', meaning that *śūnyatā* is not empty in itself, but empty of 'things'. Again we are left with the conundrum that if these 'things' pertain to *saṃsāra*, what is it precisely that allows *śūnyatā* and *saṃsāra* to co-exist? The quandary arises because that which is 'empty of itself' is only ultimately so, but *not* whilst it has relative permanence. The question therefore

8 As given in the *Mūlamadhyamakakārika of Nāgārjuna,* Ch. 25:19-20 and above with respect to the phrase 'Emptiness is synonymous with dependent-arising for Mādhyamikas who through valid cognition have refuted inherent existence'.

arises in the face of the existence of experiencable phenomena on one hand, juxtaposed with the demonstration of *śūnyatā* on the other. That demonstration in any case *demands* a human unit to appear that is capable of undergoing the yogic processes that can transmute substance into their Void Elements. Again an evolutionary process is needed, intricately tied to the meaning of the word 'ultimately'.

A hint to the answering of this question lies in the qualifying statement by Lopez that 'emptiness and dependent arising are not synonymous because, in that case, whatever was a dependent arising would have to be an emptiness. Although whatever is an emptiness is necessarily a dependent arising, the converse is not true because an emptiness is necessarily a permanent *(nitya, rtag pa),* non-affirming negative *(prasajyapratiedha, med 'gag)* phenomenon, whereas dependent arisings include all phenomena, permanent and impermanent'. It implies a close approximation between *śūnyatā* and phenomena, that there is a process that must unfold before the impermanence (phenomena) becomes a permanent 'non-affirming negative' phenomenon. It is this process unfolding that ultimately produces a Buddha's wisdom that needs thorough investigation, for therein lies the heart of the matter interrelating *śūnyatā* to *saṃsāra.*

Hefty tomes can be written on this subject (the causation of 'things' and its ramifications) to elucidate why the Void and phenomena can and do coexist. Until this is properly explained, this twelve-fold chain of cause and effect (*pratītyasamutpāda*) is really foundationless. The term 'foundationless' here does not refer to *śūnyatā*, but to the fact that there is no foundation to the start of it all. Buddhists say that it is ignorance, but ignorance coming from what—*śūnyatā*? *Śūnyatā* and ignorance would then be identical from this equation, which is clearly false. Viewing it all from this angle we can see that the doctrine of *pratītyasamutpāda* has its problems, so much so that Nāgārjuna had to ponder hard on this subject.[9] What then is *saṃsāra* if it is 'empty'? Is it that which one assumes to be existent, but really is not?

9 Though he knew what he was postulating was correct, indeed praising *pratītyasamutpāda* as the most wonderful of the Buddha's doctrines, and his entire doctrinal discourse is based thus in truth, he could not put into words (in correct Buddhist terminology) the missing quanta of information that would make his philosophy complete in *every* respect, except in highly veiled terms.

The middle way of consciousness

The statement: 'All phenomena are dependent arisings in the sense that they either arise in dependence on causes and conditions, are designated in dependence on their basis of imputation, or are imputed on a designating term or thought' can now be analysed. What this Prāsaṅgika philosophy actually informs us of, is that apart from causes and conditions it is thought, consciousness, which is the basis to Dependent Origination and which sustains *saṃsāra*; because as we think of something, so it comes to 'exist', and thereby is dependent—upon the imputation of our thoughts. In analysing this line of reasoning we have:

śūnyatā—thought/consciousness—*saṃsāra*.

Thought/consciousness is therefore that which mediates between *śūnyatā* and *saṃsāra* and allows the existence of both. It is that, therefore, which makes the interrelation possible, and grounds Dependent Origination in the realm of meaning, in such a way that we can experience and gain from it in some way. It is also that which, according to Tsongkhapa as quoted earlier, allows the Prāsaṅgika to avoid 'the two extremes' in their reasoning.

The philosophy can now be completed by filling in the middle ground between *śūnyatā* and *saṃsāra*, to show how the one can interrelate with the other, allowing the entire chain of cause and effect to manifest. The nature of the relationship can be illustrated by the Figure below, where we can see that *śūnyatā* and *saṃsāra* are interrelated by the I-consciousness, which partakes of both. It has the ability to make conscious volitions in *saṃsāra* and therefore is able to move substance or things therein. It also has the ability to cleanse itself of defiling thoughts and to quieten the remainder[10] for it to then manifest in its natural state,[11] allowing the experience of *śūnyatā* and to utilise its emanatory quality (*bodhicitta*) to assist the liberation of the all.[12]

10 By a process known as *śamatha* (*zhi gnas*), meaning 'serene abiding', the elimination of external distractions in meditation.

11 Denoted as a Clear Light, or *luminosity*.

12 This process is generally depicted as *vipassanā, (lhag mthong),* special insight, penetrative or analytic insight.

Note that I generally use the term *bodhicitta* in the manner utilised by the rDzogs chen philosophy, as Reynolds explains:

> The Base of all existence is our own Primordial State, which is our inherent Buddha-nature. In the Dzogchen texts there exist many different designations for this Primordial State, but especially in the Dzogchen Semde Series, it is called Bodhicitta, as pointed out above. Here Bodhicitta does not mean what it does in the Sutra system, that is to say, "the thought of enlightenment" or the resolute intention to attain Buddhahood for the sake of liberating all sentient beings.[13]... In the Dzogchen context, the Sanskrit word *bodhicitta* is translated into Tibetan as *byang-chub kyi sems.* This Tibetan word is interpreted as follows: *byang* means "pure" from the very beginning, that is, *kadag,* or "primordially pure," and *chub* means "perfected," that is, *lhun-grub* or "spontaneously self-perfected." Finally, *sems* means not "mind," the conditioned thought process, but *sems-nyid*, "the nature of mind." This primordial purity and this spontaneous perfection exist in inseparable unity *(ka-dag lhun-grub dbyer-med)* as the two aspects of a single Primordial State that is Buddhahood.[14]

The nature of the enigmatical *bodhicitta* being the 'Base of all existence is our own Primordial State, which is our inherent Buddha-nature' can be better understood when the *tathāgatagarbha* is explained in detail. *Bodhicitta* can be considered to be both evolved by the awakening personal-I who cleanses the *saṃskāras* of the afflictions of mind (in which case it can be defined as 'the thought of enlightenment'), as well as being evoked from the inherent *tathāgatagarbha,* being a fundamental aspect thereof. (Then the meaning associated with the phrase '*byang-chub kyi sems'* is applicable.) That part of it that is evolved concerns the development of wisdom. That part that is inherent is the principle of love. Hence we obtain the dual Ray of Love-Wisdom.

Once any consciousness generates activity in *saṃsāra* then it must be grounded, contained in a form to do so, otherwise consciousness will be amorphous, acting upon nothing in particular and everything all at once. It must therefore manifest as an *individuality* (thus 'en-

---

13 J. M. Reynolds, *The Golden Letters,* (Snow Lion, Ithaca, 1996), 85.

14 Ibid.

souling' something) in order to exert a particular *will* to effect or move form. (This is indicated by the space occupied where the two spheres of this Figure interact.) This is specific for each individual human unit, and must be so, otherwise the incarnation process in a logical, continuous evolutionary purpose is not really possible. Scattered chaotic incarnations would exist instead.

But many would say that '*karma* sees to it' (rebirth), but then cannot explain exactly how *karma* does this. They do not understand that *karma* similarly needs enlightened agencies, Lords of *karma*, *mahābodhisattvas* and *ḍākinīs*, to rightly direct this law and its general patterns on a vast scale. There are also lesser *karmic units of consciousness*[15] to carry out the law to exactitude. If *karma* were not *wisely* directed it could not so inviolably and correctly act as a universal law.

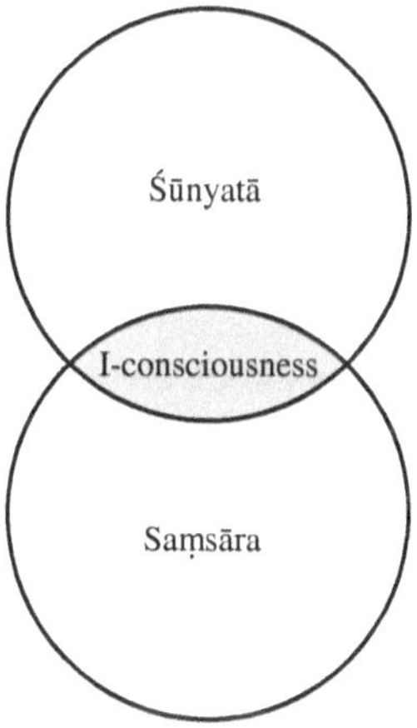

Figure 3. The Middle Way of Consciousness

Consciousness can also be abstracted into *śūnyatā* through the appropriate yogic processing. This is well known, but much is yet to be revealed concerning the detail of how it works in relation to the above Figure, and the dependent-arisings. Consciousness rather than *śūnyatā*

15 In a later book this function will be shown to be the responsibility of what is described therein as *devas*.

is what organises the appearance of phenomena. When consciousness and *śūnyatā* work together then phenomena is distilled, transformed, and abstracted from *saṃsāra*. But consciousness also is something that is often depicted as illusional. Consciousness, however, is not illusional *per se,* because its activities are what inevitably brings about Buddhahood, and this is the purpose of the entire *saṃsāra-śūnyatā* interplay. It therefore has a veridical nature that sustains the entire drive of a Bodhisattva, whose purpose is to eliminate illusion via the process of driving all towards the attainment of Buddhahood. Even then it remains and must be utilised if interrelation with *saṃsāra* is to happen. Indeed, its transmuted nature is incorporated into the nature of the Wisdom of the Tathāgata. Such a nature is all-knowing. J.M. Reynolds presents similar views with respect to the rDzog chen tradition:

> If one observes the mind and searches for where a thought *(rnam rtog)* arises, where it remains, and where it goes, no matter how much one researches and investigates this, one will find nothing. It is this very "unfindability" *(mi rnyed)* of the arising, the abiding, and the passing away of thoughts which is the greatest of all finds. Thoughts do not arise from anywhere *(byung sa med),* they do not remain anywhere *(gnas sa med)*, and they do not go anywhere *('gro sa med).* They do not arise from inside the body, nor do they arise from outside the body. They are truly without any root or source (*gzhi med rtsa bral*). Like the clouds in the sky, they arise only to dissolve again. Thoughts arise out of the state of emptiness and return again into this state of emptiness, which represents pure potentiality. We only have to observe our mind to discover this for ourselves. And this shunyata, this state of emptiness, is in fact the very essence of the mind (*sems kyi ngo-bo stong-pa nyid*). [16]

The 'essence of the mind' may have emptiness as its foundation, but such an emptiness manifests as a mirror that facilitates the reflection of the wisdom of the Dhyāni Buddhas into manifestation, and thereby the transmuted correspondences from the gain of the sense perceptions into *dharmakāya*.

The aspect of consciousness that is illusional is its volatile substance and the part that *is not* an illusion is what appertains and develops

16 Reynolds, 75.

wisdom. The translation of ignorance to wisdom, and of intelligence to enlightenment is the nature of the functioning I-consciousness.

The Prāsaṅgika deem consciousness an illusion, the question however arises, 'how can something that is an illusion be faithfully true as a directing principle projecting the illusionality of *saṃsāra* to be abstracted into *śūnyatā*?' If we correlate the I-consciousness (the directing principle here) with the *tathāgatagarbha* then it is but a way of stating that all sentient beings possess a Buddha-germ and hence will inevitably become Buddhas. If we eliminate *skandhas* and *saṃskāras* or *śūnyatā* as a driving force for the transmutation of *saṃsāra,* then this leaves consciousness, the Buddha-germ, or that which drives *karma* as the directing agents. Most logically however the directing agent must integrate the function of all three. Obviously the mind of an individual in any one life does not have this capacity, unless that mind is enlightened. It is known that the wisdom of an enlightened being can rightly direct *karma*. This may be so for an enlightened Mind, but what for the unenlightened, the great majority of humanity? Clearly something else, that is veiled and yet is enlightened, must direct their *karma*. This then leaves the Buddha-germ, the *tathāgatagarbha* working via a mind. The precise mechanism of expression of how it does this is what needs to be revealed to prove this assertion, and will be shown in Volume 3.

The fact is that neither consciousness, *karma*, or the *tathāgatagarbha* are truly illusional, from the perspective that they all appropriate *saṃsāra* and drive its elements to be stripped of their characteristics so that the remainder is the Void. Without such activity the Void Elements would not be experienced. In this trinity consciousness is the veil of the Buddha-germ, the apparel allowing it to function in *saṃsāra,* because it appropriates *saṃsāra* as its *modus operandi*. The Buddha-germ is the true directing agent that is focussed via consciousness to produce liberation from *saṃsāra*. The appearance of the manifesting phenomena is the *karma* utilised by the wisdom aspect of an enlightened consciousness (or Buddha-germ) to direct the process of the transformation of *saṃsāra* to liberation. Consciousness can thereby also be seen to be an agent or medium of expression for *karma*. *Karma* consequently is not illusional, it never acts in an inconsequential manner, rather it unfailingly manifests according to the precepts of *bodhicitta*, acting upon that which is illusional. Why so?

The answer lies in the fact that it is an aspect or expression of a higher principle, the *dharmakāya*, which can be deduced to be the expression of a transmuted state of consciousness, called the Buddha-Mind. *Karma* therefore is the law, an expression of the *dharma,* projected via the realm of consciousness to sustain Dependent Origination by fusing *śūnyatā* with *saṃsāra*. In this way *karma* arises in the sphere of consciousness to blend the extremes together, and indeed, start the entire cycle of cause-effect that is dependently arising. Without *karma* Dependent Origination could not be.

The philosophy concerning the origination of *karma* is not as simple as generally imagined, which is that it originates with the actions of an ignorant one. It may be so for human units that first appeared possibly aeons ago. However, the *karma* that caused the appearance of a world-sphere, one of a vast number of similar world-spheres in our galaxy, each of which have karmic interrelations (as they are all part of the same body of manifestation), is not so easily explained. It concerns the nature of the genesis of the phenomena into which an ignorant human unit is born, and who can manifest karmic actions for that consciousness-stream. The laws of causation producing the appearance of phenomena, hence starting the cycles of Dependent Origination, has its origins in the Mind of the wise, compassionate Will of a Tathagāta, a primordial, Ādi Buddha, manifesting His purpose via *saṃsāra* that has been established by his Consort (by utilising the primordial substance in her Womb) via the serene mirror-like qualities of *śūnyatā*.[17] The mode of the manifestation of the *tathāgatagarbha* (Buddha-germ) existing upon the highest abstracted domain of Mind also needs to be incorporated in this story of *karma*. The *maṇḍala* of the *tathāgatagarbha* has been seeded with purpose and with conscious volition by the meditative action of the Ādi Buddha and Consort. The rebirthing process then ensues whereby an ignorant personal-I can manifest volitions in *saṃsāra* and then reap the consequent karmic rewards. Outlined here is a very brief synopsis of what incorporates an aeonic evolutionary process.

17 This subject can only be introduced here. See Volumes 4 and 5A for further detail.

The cycle of *pratītyasamutpāda* has its own rebirths, similar to the sequence of births and deaths of the personal-I's of an individuating I-consciousness. Each cycle is based upon the proceedings of the former actions of all that is caught up within that cycle. The overview of the collectivisation of myriad cycles of *pratītyasamutpāda* for all humans and sentient beings alike is what the meditating Buddha directs from the realm of the *dharmakāya*.

Karma and the containers of mind

One should carefully analyse the subject of *karma* with respect to Dependent Origination, because without *karma* there could not be any form of dependency. *Karma* is also set to propel all to Buddhahood. It is consequently (as before stated) the law of compassion, *bodhicitta* in action.[18] Yet karmic action is said to be sown in ignorance. Ignorance consequently sets the wheel of Dependent Origination in motion. The conditions inside that wheel are however arranged by *karma,* which consequently determines the process of liberation from that wheel.

If ignorant states are correlated to the *karma* that directs them and the objective of *karma* is to drive all to liberation through the process of Dependent Origination, then a case may be made that it is not ignorance, but great wisdom that establishes Dependent Origination. Here one must ask 'what is the cause of this karmic law, and what is the mechanism whereby it is directed, that allows it to so govern the process of liberation?'

Ignorance is effectively the state of a lack of varying degrees of refined consciousness. There are consequently relative states of ignorance. The purpose of consciousness is to make itself more inclusive of states of awareness, of forms of intensified light, where there was formerly darkness. We have the expression of ignorance and 'ultimately', *śūnyatā*. In between exists the entire twelve-fold chain of cause-effect called *pratītyasamutpāda* allowing one to consciously gain wisdom.

---

18 How this force of *karma*, which can be considered the compassionate expression of a Buddha-Mind, 'creates' the conditions of the phenomenal world or appearance of *saṃsāra* from out of the seeds/*bījas* that are the residues of past turnings of the cycle known as *pratītyasamutpāda,* will be detailed in the later volumes. See specifically Volume 5A, chapter 3 in the section entitled 'The Six Realms'.

These are all well known concepts, but again we have an essential triplicity; ignorance-consciousness-*śūnyatā*.

Pratītyasamutpāda represents a container of the life processes leading to liberation whereby consciousness can develop and overcome various ignorant states. The reader similarly possesses an individualised thought structure, based around a mind, the 'container' of thought, or that which en-souls. If not possessed then one could not think logically in any way at all. (In a similar manner the bones of the cranium are a container for the grey matter of the cellular structure involved with the physicality of thought.) One's mind would be a chaotic mess of thoughts floating in and out, with no ability to resolutely act upon anything, except for a brief moment, until the next floating thought appears. (Unless acted upon by a strong external consciousness, a strong will, which will dominate such a person.) This is but a definition of insanity, and schizophrenics come close to this state of fragmentary mentation, but they are aware of their thoughts, of the self-concept, and have agonizing episodes whenever a new 'them' takes over, or tries to.

If the law of *karma* is not appropriately structured in contained segments it similarly would act in a chaotic way. All things are bound by cycles of containment, and then a period of release from containment so that a new cycle can begin upon a higher level. This is but one way of viewing the rebirthing principle. It is interesting to read the philosophy of 'no container for mind' (as given in *The Diamond Slivers*) written and thought out by those utilising such 'containers' to do so, but not noticing the fact. It is like children that are so engrossed in a game of make-believe that the game eventually becomes a reality for them, forgetting that it was their imagination that produced the imagery they are revelling in.

It is wrong to think that an originating Buddha is actively focussed upon the detail or minutiae of the actions of each and every human unit manifesting actions (of cause and effect), upon their own little cycles of dependent-arising. This is not his concern, anymore than observing the activities of any particular cell or cells constituting one's bodily form is the concern of any person. A Buddha's meditation is upon the great whole, the great collections and reservoirs of energy and consciousness; of karmic interrelatedness composed of vast groupings of human unities and of the myriad forms of sentience in Nature. These groupings are seen as *chakras* by the enlightened that possess the faculties of vision to do so. (There is a similarity of the process to a human unit, who certainly responds when a large group of cells start malfunctioning, producing diseases, cancers, ailments.) *Chakras* are but containers of different attributes of consciousness.

Logically, therefore, mediators are needed that are actively concerned with the relative small scale activities of respective human unities and of their incarnation process. The *karma* of each such unity, and of its developed mind must be contained and correlated in such a way that it integrates seamlessly with the all-encompassing environment of which it is a part. Again this advocates the I-consciousness; the idea of an overshadowing consciousness-form responsible for the directing of the respective karmic stream and seeding the *bījas* of activity for each new cycle of *pratītyasamutpāda* for any individual. (Bodhisattvas work thus for collectivised human groupings.) The logic that demands this is there, the Law is there imposing such evolutionary attainment, and the human players are in place *en masse* overcoming the cycles of ignorance because of this. Thereby chaos and insanity is avoided. The I-consciousnesses or *tathāgatagarbhas*[19] of humanity are the lesser karmic units of consciousness mentioned above.

The three synonyms of Dependent Arising

The earlier stated synonyms of Dependent Arising are:

1. *Prāpyasamutpāda,* 'arising through meeting' (referring to 'the production of things through their causes'), utilises the conventional reality mode of investigation. This mode focusses upon the phenomena of the external universe, upon the way *karma* is generated and conditions us via the related *skandhas* and *saṃskāras.*
2. *Apekṣhyasamutpāda,* 'existing in reliance', refers to the 'attainment by products and non products of their own entities in reliance of their parts'. It therefore attempts to utilise the ultimate truth as a mode of investigation. The exponents of this logical stream use their minds to

19 As units of *karma* they can be considered soul-forms, as they govern individual karmic life streams of any evolving entity on the road to Buddhahood, if one were to use a conventional term for such a subjective form they are 'containers of consciousness'.

further categorise the external show into increasingly smaller parts, hoping to lead us thereby to a cognition of *śūnyatā* as the reality of it all. Modern scientists have also utilised this reductionist approach (using conventional reality alone) to a far greater extent than was possible for the Mādhyamika. Scientists have discovered atoms, sub-atomic particles, quark theory, Quantum Electrodynamics, photons, and have speculated with string theory. Matter and energy have been determined to be interchangeable, thus can be expressed in terms of energy alone, similar to the way that *śūnyatā* can be depicted. The astrophysicist's concept of the 'Big Bang',[20] where it is said that the universe started from an attributeless singularity wherein the laws of physics break down, can be but another way of describing *śūnyatā*.

The effort to analyse a thing by looking at its parts and trying to call the parts that thing leads us into a philosophic quagmire. The reason being that it is functionality, not the parts, that is important. The order that a carpenter builds the non-essential structures of a house is relatively immaterial. Despite its many parts, once completed it is still a house, because that is its functionality. Though the house contains many appliances and fittings, each with different functions, all interrelate together in *functionality* to be called a 'house'. A calculator is a calculator because of what its does; its component parts, such as resistors and transistors, are not calculators, though they are part of it, their functionality is different. More will be said about this subject in *The Diamond Slivers*. Looking at parts of a thing to try to analyse causes is conventional thought that aims towards the 'absolute valuable reality'. There are *five* ways that one could tackle such a problem philosophically.

- *First,* looking toward the *microcosm,* where much further diversity of detail is seen as we delve into the increasingly microscopic view of parts of things. Scientists have done this with extreme precision. Similar cognition has also helped the Mādhyamika well in their endeavour to conceptualise what does

20 Though the Big Bang theory is the consensus view, there is however considerable debate about this beginning of things.

not pertain to *śūnyatā*. However, they have not understood the nature of the phenomena observed in its true minute detail, and where that would lead them in the atomic and subatomic realm. They could not extricate detailed understanding similar to what physicists nowadays possess. Generalisations and supposition is all that was possible, the complete explanations, such as the paradoxes observed in Quantum Electrodynamics were not imagined by them.

- *Second,* toward the *macrocosm,* leading to universals, and here the philosophy of breaking down or analysing the dependent-origination sustaining a universe in order to try to establish *śūnyatā* is not possible, as nobody has yet been able to ascertain how big the universe is, or where it leads to. This is especially so when we look to both inner and outer universes. Again, science has scored well in analysing the constituency of the macrocosmic universe, but only as far as its physicality is concerned. That associated with the intricacy of the multidimensional interdependence of its component parts is as of yet a closed book, and still lies in the realms of science fiction to them.
- *Third,* to the realm of *consciousness.* This is where most reasoning is based in reality, and within which it stays, as the early philosophers (unless fully enlightened) did not have the tools to go in the other two directions in depth. The enlightened did, but could not explain their revelations properly to their contemporaries, because there was little or no groundwork yet laid for understanding.
- *Fourth,* by residing in *śūnyatā.*
- *Fifth,* looking properly to a combination of any or all of these by means of the awakened all-seeing Eye. The *dharmakāya* visioning then comes into view.

Points one and two show the limitations to the past philosophical methodologies, whilst the third way is really *pratītyasamutpāda.* The fourth method is self-explanatory. (Note the contradiction of terms here, in that the term 'self-explanatory' implies that it requires a 'self' to explain something, whereas in *śūnyatā* nothing is explained at all, because self-less.) The fifth way is only achievable if the facts concerning the other methods are knowable. This is the Dharmakāya Way, producing a true resultant *mahāmudrā* union. This way necessitates using the facts ascertained by modern scientists, that presented by the philosophers and sages of the past, as well as being open to what will be established in the future.

3. *Pratītyasamutpāda ('dependent-existence').* All phenomena is dependent upon the thought that distinguishes them, 'without the thought to designate, the arising of phenomena does not exist'. Here Prāsaṅgikas have rightfully favoured the way of analysing mind-conditioned phenomena. This is conducive to logically produce the perspective of discovering *śūnyatā*. It provides the truism of the ability of the mind to name and to categorise the things that appear as a consequence of Dependent Origination. To the human mind things do not exist, unless it has ascertained that they do by the means available to it. Then using logic in the philosophic investigation of the transient nature of things, one is inevitably led to the conclusion of the reality of *śūnyatā*.

A review of the perspective of the various schools of Buddhist thought might prove helpful here. Lopez states:

> According to the Mādhyamikas, not only is the Yogācārins middle way trifling, it is wrong. Because the Mādhyamikas (with the exception of the Yogācāra-Svātantrikas) assert that objects conventionally exist as separate entities from the perceiving consciousness, they reject the Yogācārin assertion that the duality of subject and object is an extreme of permanence. Because the Mādhyamikas also assert that all phenomenon are empty of true existence, they do not identify the lack of ultimate existence of dependent phenomena as an extreme of annihilation. The Yogācārins come to this view because they assert, in contrast to the Mādhyamikas, that if dependent natures and consummate natures did not ultimately exist, they would not exist at all.
>
> Furthermore, besides contending that the other systems misidentify the extremes, the Mādhyamikas assert that all non-Mādhyamika systems fall to the extremes. The Vaibhāṣikas assert that partless

> particles are ultimate truths and truly exist. The Sautrāntikas assert that impermanent phenomena are ultimately able to perform functions and truly exist. The Yogācārins assert that dependent and consummate natures truly exist. Thus, although the Vaibhāṣikas, Sautrāntikas, and Yogācārins respectively assert that partless particles, functioning things, and dependent natures are impermanent, from the Mādhyamika perspective they have fallen to the extreme of permanence by asserting true existence. Once they assert true existence, they also implicitly fall to the extreme of annihilation, according to Candrakīrti. In his *Clear Words*, he quotes the *Treatise on the Middle Way* and comments on it.[21]

Here we see that the Yogācārin position is the 'assertion that the duality of subject and object is an extreme of permanence' and they 'come to this view because they assert, in contrast to the Mādhyamikas, that if dependent natures and consummate natures did not ultimately exist, they would not exist at all'. Also we have the former statement given by Lopez: 'The Yogācārins, for example, need two separate reasons to abandon the two extremes as they define them. They claim that they abandon the extreme of annihilation because they assert that impermanent phenomena truly exist as the same entity as the consciousness perceiving them. They abandon the extreme of permanence by asserting that impermanent phenomena do not have a nature separate from that of consciousness'.

Their contention, therefore, is that ultimately these things exist in consciousness and it is consciousness (really the I-consciousness) that retains them as memory, or consummate nature, long after their transient forms have disappeared. This subject has already been dealt with, when I stated that if a Buddha can recall such memories at will, then they 'ultimately exist', in accordance with the duration of the omniscience of a Buddha's Mind. No experience, no matter how transient, or forgettable is ever lost; its imprint remains *in perpetuum*. From this perspective the 'duality of subject and object' can be considered 'an extreme of permanence'. The I-consciousness also needs such ability if it is to call forth the *karma* associated in a logical sequence that will produce the desired effect in the long run, over a sequence of many incarnations of personal-I's. The sustainability of 'dependent natures and consummate

---

21 Lopez Jr., *A Study of Svātantrika*, 43-44.

natures' has already been explained in the light of the reasoning of the nature of *māyā* and *ālayavijñāna* (storers of the 'dependent nature') with respect to the reality of *śūnyatā*.

The problem with the Mādhyamika position here (who 'also assert that all phenomenon are empty of true existence'), is that though they observe the process of change of all types of phenomena, they do not perceive the integral Life, which can certainly effectively be called 'true existence', for it is not annihilated with every change, contrary to Candrakīrti's assertion. Such 'integral Life' resides in all stratum of existence from the mineral kingdom to the human and beyond, otherwise evolution to the attainment of Buddhahood could not proceed. Annihilation would then be the only certainty. Nor is the true function of consciousness (which sustains the changes, absorbs the experiences for a purpose, and outlives them) comprehended. It is this Life that undergoes the process known as *pratītyasamutpāda*. The facts that need to be acknowledged are that because of the processes of consciousness (the transformation of *saṃskāras*) we have the Bodhisattva path eventuated, and that the faculties of consciousness are eventually transmuted into the qualities of the wisdoms of a Buddha.

Because there is continuous progressive change in consciousness it necessitates an existing entity that persists through each change, that oversees conscious evolution through successive lives. Such an 'existing entity' is therefore necessary in the equations that concern the making of Buddhahood. It can be stated that this existing entity is the *tathāgatagarbha*, but exactly what this Buddha-germ (I-consciousness) is has not been understood by Buddhists. Highly veiled information was provided in such texts as the *Srī Māla* and *Ratnagotravibhāga*[22] (upon which a commentary shall be presented in Volume 3), however detail has been withheld because the Buddhist mind was not prepared for the revelation of the implications hinted at in these texts. Hopefully this *Treatise on Mind* will provide an appropriate explanation of this highest of yoga Tantras.

The next statement that we should analyse is: 'The Vaibhāṣikas assert that partless particles are ultimate truths and truly exist'. 'Partless particles' may be ultimate truths as far as the field of science

22 Also called the *Uttaratantra of Maitreya*.

is concerned, i.e., that which is relegated to the domain of the intellect and of physical phenomena. (Essentially, this fact holds true on all levels of expression of what may be called substance.) The subject has already been delved into earlier, where a reason for their existence in Nature was established, and also proven by scientific experimentation. The substance of the phenomenal universe has consequently been built up through their properties. But they come under the general law governing all such phenomena, and are thus subject to the changes that befall everything in the material universe. (From this perspective they do not represent an ultimate truth.) The Vaibhāṣika logic was therefore upon the right track when looking to the nature of the physical universe. In the subjective universe, however, we can also say that the Buddha nature can be considered a 'partless particle', from a certain perspective, and this is an ultimate truth. Also, who can say how many such Buddha natures do exist. As myriads of Buddhas have evolved from time-space, and it can be conjectured, taking the rebirthing principle into account, even before this solar system was born, then how this 'nature' is incorporated into the atoms of substance can be queried. Would not such a nature consequently be the basis of all that IS and IS NOT perceived in this universe of wonders?

Finally we have the statement: 'Sautrāntikas assert that impermanent phenomena are ultimately able to perform functions and truly exist'. It is true that impermanent phenomena can and do perform functions, like the eruption of a volcano, and thus do exist, otherwise we would experience nothing, except what our own imaginations concocted up. (Even our imaginations need 'something' to base their concoction of images upon.) They however do not truly exist (except as memory), because once that function has been made manifest they then cease to exist as such. For instance, a dormant volcano becomes a hill. Functionality could be considered an ultimate truth (for consciousness), because that is what we define things in terms of, e.g., *śūnyatā* (by means of the functionality of that which it is not). What, for instance, is the functionality, i.e., the qualities, properties, attributes, of a Buddha or a Bodhisattva? How can we imagine such beings without such considerations? They may simply Be, but this tells us nothing, we might as well be blind, deaf and dumb. If they are to interact with us in any way, and thus have meaning, they must have functionality. Even simply being, existing, can be considered a functionality, because we can learn also from that—to simply Be, like a Buddha. *Pratītyasamutpāda* therefore relies upon the functionality of each entity that interrelates interdependently. Consciousness grasps what is useful to it, experiences it, and then moves on, to experience something else, according to how it functionally relates to it.

We see in all of the above citations the golden thread that runs through them all is the way that *consciousness* deals with all the forms of limited permanency, wherein, the Mādhyamika position of having fallen into the extreme position of 'existence' and consequent 'annihilation' holds true, *except* for what is retained in memory and stored within the constituency of the field of consciousness that I term the I-consciousness. If annihilation does not happen, then this 'golden thread' persists, even through the *śūnyatā* experience, otherwise there could be no Buddha or Bodhisattva who could retain anything after entering such a state, and they do, as they have come back to explain much to us.

10

Chapter one of the *Mūlamadhyamakakārikā*

The Buddha-germ energises Void Element *bījas*[1] with its compassionate thought of what is to be (or rather, 'must be'). The energisation attracts to the *bījas* the appropriate substance (*citta*) from the consciousness-store (*ālayavijñāna*), which then moves according to the inherent constitution of the *bīja* and the quality of the substance attracted. This movement concerns the conveyance of the winds/*prāṇas* of the *naḍīs* incorporating the 'I' that manifests in *saṃsāra*. The *naḍī* system is the real or true corporeal form of a human unit, the physical body is but an automaton of the *prāṇas* that flow within the *naḍīs*. The *naḍī* system is constituted of the Earthy Void Element, and the elementary Winds (*prāṇas* in the form of the Void Elements) it conveys are the breath of compassion of the downward focussed Mind of the *tathāgatagarbha*. The Winds (of which there are five) are then utilised by a personal-I as the base energies for the conscious volitions that interrelate with *saṃsāra* via the five sense-perceptors to produce the *saṃskāras* manifesting as elementary mind, and the *karma*-formations that perpetuate the wheel of Dependent Origination. The unreal is thereby produced that constantly changes according to the vicissitudes of the play of the *māyā* of which it is a part.

This is an outline of the formation process of *saṃsāric* activity in relation to the Void. Nāgārjuna's opening statement in his *Mūlamadhyamakakārikā* can now be analysed, which is concerned with the conditions of existence.

---

1 Here taken as seeds, seed syllables, the focal point of a *yogin's* meditation, and for every act of creative endeavour.

> No existents whatsoever are evident anywhere that are arisen from themselves, from another, from both, or from a non-cause.[2]

'Existents' here refers to 'things' pertaining to *saṃsāra*. They do not arise from themselves, nevertheless, when the subject is analysed appropriately one must conjecture a primal substance (*mūlaprakṛti, svabhāva)* that is the foundational matrix that is utilised by an originating Mind to start the process of *karma*-formations in Nature. This substance has not 'arisen from itself', rather is a pre-existing primordial matrix of elementary inchoate and universally prevalent substance, which is incorporated into the *maṇḍala* of that which must be. Therefore it does not arise 'from another', except in the way that phenomena interrelates in the cause-effect paradigm explained above, all of which is bound in illusionality. In establishing the pre-existing matrix of substance, there can be no 'other'. From the point of view of conventional truth, one thing arises from causes generated by other things, but from the point of view of ultimate truth inevitably all things are 'empty', thus there is no such 'arising'. Things therefore cannot arise 'from both'. The last point of this quaternary relating to arising from a 'non-cause' is obviously true from a conventional point of view, because the cause of something cannot arise from that which is not a cause. However, from the point of view of ultimate truth this both is and is not the case, as 'a non-cause' can be considered the Void, via which the impetus to produce phenomena has emanated. However, by definition, the Void is void of the phenomenal, of things that can produce *saṃsāric* interaction of their own accord. Thus Nāgārjuna's statement is correct from this viewpoint. However, something must account for the phenomena, for its appearance, and thus we must look to the *dharmakāya* for this impetus. Here we have our answer, as explained above. So this realm produces both the cause of the origination of *saṃsāra* and the clause for its annulment. From another viewpoint it is 'a non-cause'. This is because the originating source is a Buddha-Mind, so the effect remains *karmaless,* or rather, it concerns the rectification of the *karma* still inherent in *saṃsāra*. In such a way a Buddha-field is enriched. Such a Mind works effortlessly

2 David J. Kalupahana, *Mūlamadhyamakakārikā of Nāgārjuna, The Philosophy of the Middle Way,* 105.

with the law of cycles in order to activate that which already exists, the *bīja* of what is to be. It is therefore not 'a cause', but rather part of the process of the continuum of driving the all to Buddhahood.

In the second verse Nāgārjuna presents 'four conditions':[3]

> There are only four conditions, namely, primary condition, objectively supporting condition, immediately contiguous condition, and dominant condition. A fifth condition does not exist.[4]

From the perspective of my presented philosophy the 'primary condition' refers to the prima-matrix from which all emanated, or else to the Void Elements utilised by the *tathāgatagarbha*. The 'objectively supporting condition' represents establishing the *bīja* of what is to be. The 'immediately contiguous condition' refers to the substance of the *ālayavijñāna*, the abstract Mind from which the driving impetus to manifest phenomenal activity originates. The 'dominant condition' concerns the conditionings of *māyā* wherein all is enacted.

Verse three states:

> The self-nature of existents is not evident in the conditions, etc. In the absence of self-nature, other-nature too is not evident.[5]

This is evident from the point of view of the entire activity stemming via the Void, which is freed from such a nature, and also an expression of a Buddha-Mind, which is likewise freed. From the point of view of conventional truth however, a form of such a 'self-nature' is seen in the *bīja*, and from another perspective the *ālayavijñāna*, and we have already

---

3 In relation to the philosophy to which Nāgārjuna was referring Kalupahana states (Ibid., 107): 'while the four causal theories mentioned in 1.1 are categorically denied by Nāgārjuna, no such denial is made of the four theories of conditions *(pratyaya)*. Thus, unlike Candrakīrti, Nāgārjuna seems to have accepted the Abhidharmika theory of four conditions, without characterizing it either as self-causation or as external causation. After stating the Abhidharma theory, Nāgārjuna then proceeds to analyse the views of the *interpreters* of Abhidharma, and, as the verse that immediately follows (1.3) seems to indicate, he found that these are the ones who produced theories of self-causation *(svata-utpatti)* and external causation *(parata-utpatti)* out of the Abhidharma theory of conditions *(pratyaya)*'.

4 Ibid., 106.

5 Ibid., 107.

seen that various 'selves' abound in the *māyā*, if one interprets 'self-nature' as the limited duration of the existents that manifest as appearing phenomena. Being transient there is however no true 'self-nature' of this phenomena. Kalupahana however points out that the phrase the 'self-nature of existents' refers to *svabhāva*. We had earlier stated, quoting from Napper, that the word *svabhāva* admits of two meanings: 'one is inherent existence, the object of negation, which does not exist in the least; the other is emptiness, the final nature of each and every phenomenon'. So if the first meaning is intended, then Nāgārjuna is correct, but if the second (which I elaborated in terms of five Void Elements), then these Void Elements are empty of 'self-nature', but replete with the nascent attributes of the wisdoms of the Dhyāni Buddhas.

'Other nature' can be considered to refer to the substance of the phenomenal world, and that which clothes the physical body. Once we have a state (i.e., *śūnyatā)* where 'self' is not evident, then there is nothing to register the existence or otherwise of form, of the substance that constitutes the *mayāvirūpa* of people's lives. This too, ultimately, 'is not evident'.

Verse four states:

> Activity is not constituted of conditions nor is it not non-constituted of conditions. Conditions are neither constituted nor non-constituted of activity.[6]

This statement presents two attributes to activity, that which is not constituted of conditions and that which is constituted of conditions. In utilising Jñānagarbha's methodology presented earlier we can analyse the causes of activity. Five types of activity can be discerned.

a. That of the organs of action—hands, feet, mouth, etc., wherewith sensory data is incurred via the sense perceptors. This category is constituted of conditionings of an Earthy nature.

b. That associated with *siddhis*, clairvoyance, etc., which do not rely upon the physical organs of actions, but rather upon the internal ones, the *chakras*. This category is constituted of conditions of a Watery nature.

---

6 Ibid., 108.

c. That associated with the ordinary empirical mind, the sixth sense. This category is constituted of conditions of a Fiery nature.

d. That associated with the abstract, enlightened Mind, producing the emanation of higher faculties, *bodhicitta,* wisdom. This category is constituted of conditions as well as non-conditions, depending upon whether the Clear Mind acts as a base for the experience of *śūnyatā,* or is directed towards revelation of any aspect of the vicissitudes of *saṃsāra.* Here we find the Airy Element utilised.

e. That associated with the *dharmakāya*, supportive of the activity of a Buddha-field. This category is not constituted of *saṃsāric* conditions. The synthesising Aetheric Element is the principle utilised here.

One can now observe the conditionings to which these five types of activity can manifest. We are told that each such condition either constitutes of activity, or is not constituted of activity, or we can look to a combination of these two. This makes assignment to either of these categories easy. We can see here that the first three categories are constituted of forms of *saṃsāric* activity, as they call forth the *saṃskāras* of the associated Element and their various permutations. The fourth category posits conditionings that are both constituted and 'non-constituted of activity', which can be considered a definition of the serene abiding of its natural state. The fifth category is not constituted of (*saṃsāric*) activity.

Verse five states:

> These are conditions, because depending upon them these [others] arise.
> So long as these [others] do not arise, why are they not non-conditions?[7]

Like many of Nāgārjuna's verses the first line of this statement is somewhat paradoxical to the average reader, because earlier Nāgārjuna appears to have been postulating the existence only of non-things, such as the lack of the 'self-nature of existents'. However he is not just satisfying the rules of debate here, but also informing us that much can be analysed concerning the 'conditions' associated with the

7 Ibid., 109.

demonstration of the Elements, the *skandhas* and *saṃskāras*. Indeed, entire treatises can and have been written concerning the above. Once the pure Elements of any past life consequences appear, then the phrase 'depending upon them these [others] arise' refers to the clothing of the elemental *bīja* of the action to be with the panoply of *saṃskāras* that are karmically bound to the seed.

The second question concerns the nature of the *saṃskāras*. It is posited that if *saṃskāras* do not arise at any given time, 'why are they not non-conditions?' Here we are asked to analyse the fundamental difference between *śūnyatā*, which is a non-condition, and that which conditions *saṃsāra,* which is conditioned by all the abovementioned forces. Essentially, the difference is that *saṃsāra* is conditioned by a karmic potential, a force or residue of past actions, which must bear fruit, whereas *śūnyatā* is not. Even if the *saṃskāras* do not arise, they are still not non-conditions because they exist potentially, like the potential energy stored in a battery. Nothing happens whilst the battery is just sitting there, but once the ends are connected to form a circuit then energy flows from the negative to the positive terminal, wherewith work can be accomplished because of the potential difference between the two ends.

If we stick to the simple doctrine of the Void (wherein 'these [others] do not arise'), then the question in the second sentence becomes valid only in the context of the *śūnyatā-saṃsāra* integration.

We see therefore that in asking such questions Nāgārjuna is manifesting a plea for us to properly utilise our minds to analyse correctly his entire *kārikā*, as there is more to it than appears through cursory examination. In proper discursive and thence non-discursive thought will lie the keys to liberation, the attainment of that state of being wherein non-conditions apply. No more really needs to be said. However, because very few will have the ability to correctly analyse the five key statements above, so he compassionately presents nine more in this chapter.

Verse six states:

> A condition of an effect that is either non-existent or existent is not proper. Of what non-existent [effect] is a condition? Of what use is a condition of the existent [effect]?[8]

---

8 Ibid., 110.

With respect to this Kalupahana states:

> The question is: In terms of what kind of effect should a condition be defined? An existent effect or a non-existent effect? An effect existent in terms of self-nature needs no support for its arising and, as such, a condition would be meaningless. An effect that is non-existent in the sense of being absolutely different from the condition will not be related in any way to a condition.[9]

One can also add that an 'existing effect' can be considered to refer to aspects of *saṃsāra* and a 'non-existing effect' can (at first glance) be considered to refer to *śūnyatā*. *Śūnyatā* is not an effect of anything, therefore, as far as effects go, it is 'non-existing'. *Śūnyatā* however, is 'proper', therefore Nāgārjuna is not referring specifically to it, but rather, to illusions, mirages, which may have effects in consciousness, but nevertheless are non-existing. Such an effect definitely is 'not proper', effectively meaningless.

It should be noted that throughout Nāgārjuna's *kārikā* one of the mechanisms of interpretation to be utilised is the teaching of the two truths. The effect exists conventionally, and he is asking 'of what true value or use is such an effect, steeped as it is in illusion?' The most elementary interpretation is if a non-existing effect is considered to be an expression of the Void, so then how can one describe any conditions associated with it?

If we perceive the questions to relate to the nature of the Void and of the types of conditionings (i.e., 'effects') that may be found in relation to it, then we find that to properly analyse the Void needs meditation. Thus it is to the development of the meditation-Mind or enlightenment that Nāgārjuna is referring. There is a link from *saṃsāra* to *śūnyatā* that must be found, and this is the nature of the true quest of all upon the Bodhisattva path. The esoteric flow of the questions with respect to conditions and existents brings us to the state where both *saṃsāra* and *śūnyatā* are existent in relation to each other. From that stance it is possible to find the answers to life's quest.

However, the question actually posed is, 'out of all the possible categories of non-existent effects, which one can be considered

---

9 Ibid.

to be a condition?' Here we must look to *saṃskāras*. A *saṃskāra* can be considered an effect, in that it is the effect of a past action, however is non-existent in the present moment of action unless it is the specific *saṃskāra* that calls forth that action. The *saṃskāras* are held in potential, as above stated, and therefore for the most part are non-existent in the life of the personal-I. Only that aspect of their multidiversity that accounts for any present action are recalled at any time. Until then they are not part of the consciousness of the individual and consequently are effectively 'non-existent'. However they manifest as conditions governing every aspect of the life of the personal-I.

Nāgārjuna thus asks us to seriously ponder the nature of *saṃskāras* and of how they are engendered and effectively transmuted into the qualities of the wisdoms of the Dhyāni Buddhas. This obviously is a worthy meditation to pursue.

The next question concerning what use 'a condition of the existent [effect]' may be involves an analysis concerning the nature of *pratītyasamutpāda*. Effectively the reader is implored to think deeply concerning it. This is because 'the existent effect' is what turns the wheel of *saṃsāra* and the twelve links of Dependent Origination. We can confidently answer that the use of *pratītyasamutpāda* is to turn ignorance into wisdom and to thereby gain liberation from *saṃsāric* toil.

This is one answer we seek, however another is needed to successfully answer this question with respect to the five types of causes of activity and their conditions, as explained in verse four.

a. With respect to the organs of action the condition of the existent effect allows the ingathering of sensory data wherewith intelligence is developed. We can then gain the first lessons concerning the nature of the illusionality of phenomena and of the role of pain in *saṃsāra*.

b. Next, the development of *siddhis*, clairvoyance, etc., is possible. The role of the existent effect can then clarify the aura through which one visualises. The refinement of the *prāṇas* that one utilises in so visualising allows the images of Buddhas and *mahābodhisattvas*, their auric fields and *maṇḍalic* structures, to appear. The corresponding direct instructions and gift-waves from the guru will allow the higher stages of the path of liberation to be trod.

c. With respect to the ordinary empirical mind the existent conditions have to be cleansed from defilements so that yogic processes in meditation can be pursued to enlightenment.

d. Concerning the abstract, enlightened Mind and the emanation of *bodhicitta,* wisdom, the 'condition of the existent' needs to be stabilised in unwavering *dhyāna.*

e. With respect to the *dharmakāya* the awakened one must manifest the will to sustain the 'condition of the existent' that is his meditation-Mind for the duration of its purpose.

In analysing the overall context of the verses, we find that they move from exemplifying the *dharmakāyic* realm or form of activity as presented in the first two verses, to the *śūnyatā* state in the second and third verses, to the *ālayavijñāna* in the fourth and fifth ones, where Nāgārjuna talks principally about conditions (of the mind, leading to activity of the form). The sixth verse explains the condition relating to the clear separation or distinction ('the conditions') between *śūnyatā* and *saṃsāra.* Finally, verse seven properly grounds us in the realm of 'things', *saṃsāra* proper.

The seventh verse:

> Since a thing that is existent or non-existent or both existent and non-existent is not produced, how pertinent in that context would a producing cause be?[10]

Here 'effects' have concretised into 'things', therefore the focus is specifically upon conventional truth for interpretation. A thing that is 'existent' according to such an interpretation is anything we see around us in the phenomenal world. One that is non-existent refers to the subjective or formless realms, i.e., not perceived by means of the senses. This can therefore refer to a) psychic phenomena, b) imaginings, c) the Void.

That which is 'both existent and non-existent' refers to the domain of the mind, where:

a. Thoughts can be considered 'things', thus existent, but not substantially so, hence non-existent.

---

10 Kalupahana, *Mūlamadhyamakakārikā of Nāgārjuna, The Philosophy of the Middle Way*, 110.

b. To the realm of enlightened being wherein the Mind has been cleansed of 'things', perceptions now being beyond conceptualising thought.

Because each category is stated to be 'not produced', so Nāgārjuna asks 'how pertinent in that context would a producing cause be?' In determining what such a cause may be in the realm of illusion we find sequences of cause-effects manifesting from the hoary mists of time to the present, where nothing can really be pinned down as an originating cause of and in itself. We find therefore, that a 'producing cause' is not pertinent if we cannot find that which lies at the start of all effects. Such a query would bring us to the origination of the universe, and of what existed before it, taking into account also the multidimensionality of that universe and the universal applicability of the process of rebirth. However, we can determine the origination of relativities, such as the birth of a child, when a house was built, etc. Vaster scenarios, such as the origination of a solar system, or of the earth globe, the appearance of the human kingdom in it, are more indeterminate to an unenlightened mind. The causes and conditions associated with the appearance of such 'relativities' is what is important for a human unit and his/her quest for enlightenment. The quest for the absolute origination of 'things' is a side issue, but the origination of phenomenal things within the vaster scenario can be easily ascertained in the all-seeing Eye of an awakened one.

The question also has a reference to the concept of a 'self', which could be considered causative of all things enacted by a personal-I. If the personal-I is transient as well as all forms of actions that it manifests, so it stands to reason that such a causative 'self' would also be considered transient. There is a pertinence with respect to the effects of the nature of the phenomena which is part of a chain of dependent originations, which will inevitably lead to Buddhahood. However, being transient, the self-concept has only a limited duration for all forms of activity, and therefore is pertinent only to the extent of the duration of the illusional phenomena created.

From such analysis we get the syllogisms of the 'Many and the One' and the 'Non-Production from Other' etc., already discussed.

The perspective of being allured by the bewildering world of psychicism and to imaginings can now be analysed, as well as the 'things' found there.

The production of psychic phenomena is not perceptive to the physical senses and therefore can be considered 'not produced' by them. Such phenomena however can portend of things to happen, relegate deeper understandings as to the nature of the world of sensorial experiences, and the inner world of reality, and therefore can be pertinent to enlightenment's quest.

Again, if considered as imaginings, or to take anything else imagined into account, then such phenomena is effectively non-existent because though they are produced by the mind for the purpose of its own reverie, they are not produced in the world of tangible things. Being illusional they are not pertinent in the sense that they are not aspects of anything that can be directly experienced by means of the five sense perceptors. However, if acted out in the mind as if real they can produce experiences of educational value, therefore are often pertinent to the development of wisdom.

A 'producing cause' in the Void would be meaningless, thus is also not produced, and is not perceptible to the world of the senses. However, in the light of the *saṃsāra-śūnyatā* nexus a liberated one having experienced *śūnyatā* can utilise experiences for the gain of all sentient beings, which would be pertinent for such a one.

One can produce similar arguments with respect to the realm of ideas, and to that of the Clear Mind, where one discovers that which is not produced in a tangible sense, but experiences which can be pertinent. However, in each of the above cases what has been discovered to be pertinent is not within the guideline set by Nāgārjuna because they are not within 'that context', i.e., of 'being not produced' upon the physical domain. Here he appears to be arguing against the contentions of outright materialists.

In relation to this verse Kalupahana states:

> This is an examination of the first of the four conditions referred to in 1.2, namely, a primary condition *(hetu-pratyaya)*[11]....In defining the primary condition, the Abhidharma refers to five of the six causes *(hetu) (Abhidharmakośa 2.61).* They are (1) a "co-operative cause" (*sahabhū-hetu*) or factors that work together in producing another; (2) the "complementary cause" *(sabhāga-hetu),* which is

11 Ibid.

> a cause helping other causes of its kind; (3) the "associated cause" *(saṃprayuktaka-hetu);* (4) the "all pervading cause" *(sarvatrage-hetu)* and (5) the "fruitioning cause" *(vipāka-hetu).* However, the interpreters of the Abhidharma defined a primary condition *(hetu-pratyaya)* as a producing *(nirvartaka)* or root cause[12]....Nāgārjuna, in the hope of clarifying the implications of this definition, raises the question as to whether this condition is supposed to give rise to an existent *(sat)* phenomena or a non-existent *(asat)* phenomena or something that is both existent and non-existent (*sad asat).*[13]

Placing the text within historical context, is a valid method of interpretation, as Nāgārjuna may indeed have aimed his text to meet the exegetical needs of the time. However, as an enlightened being he also had an esoteric itinerary to which he acceded, as per my explanation. As before mentioned, there are often many levels of interpretation to any text that is written by the enlightened. Therefore, there are many scholarly interpreters with (differing) valid contributions to the understanding of sacred texts.

The eighth verse:

> A thing that exists is indicated as being without objective support. When a thing is without objective support, for what purpose is an objective support?[14]

We saw that the last verse had to be primarily viewed in terms of conventional reality, verse eight is therefore appropriately primarily to be interpreted in terms of the ultimate truth. The 'thing that exists' here refers to any form of phenomena, and the 'objective support' referring to a 'self' concept that could do so, or to *śūnyatā.* As *śūnyatā* is not an objective (or active) support for any 'thing', so such a 'thing' is without objective support. It does however, subjectively support phenomena by the mere fact of its existence/non-existence. If phenomena exists, then it must be supported by something, there must be some type of base for that which is material to rest upon, such as our feet upon the solid earth, or the eye supported in the body for the function of seeing.

12 Ibid., 110-111.

13 Ibid., 111.

14 Ibid.

We thus have the concept presented above of the base being the Void Elements. The concept of the existence of a permanent 'self' that could act as such a support has been found lacking in conventional Buddhism. However, if the objective support is actually *śūnyatā*, which is void of the phenomenal, then Nāgārjuna is asking us 'for what purpose is an objective support', i.e., for what purpose is the *saṃsāra-śūnyatā* interrelation? This then is the major question to be asked. It postulates the lifestyle for liberation whereby one inevitably must detach oneself from the forms of ephemera so that liberation is eventuated.

The secondary meaning of the question to the Abhidharmists as to the purpose of 'supports' for phenomena, other than the Void (which can be argued from one perspective is no support at all) can now be investigated. This introduces the role that consciousness plays in all of this (as it can also be argued to be the support). We then have the entire Yogācārin doctrine, and the teaching concerning the *saṃsāra*—I-consciousness—*śūnyatā* arrangement as explained in this book. As per usual Nāgārjuna presented this entire problem in a deceptively simple statement. In fact this is the manner that all of the Buddhist philosophers wrote in this period of history. Terse mnemonic verses were used to convey the maximum meaning to those who were astute enough to analyse them correctly. Because they are so terse and esoteric in import, so they have caused virtually endless debate. To rightly interpret, however, we need to approach with the same type of mind as the author, and this is rarely done. We thus have the ways that Nāgārjuna is normally erroneously interpreted.

Verse nine:

> When things are not arisen [from conditions], cessation is not appropriate. When [a thing has] ceased, what is [it that serves as] a condition? Therefore, an immediate condition is not proper.[15]

The 'conditions' have been explained in verse two, where it was stated that they related to the Void Element, the *bīja*, the *ālayavijñāna*, and the activity of the *māyā*.

We can begin by stating that there is no cessation when residing or viewing from the Void because nothing has arisen from there by means

15 Ibid., 112.

of conditions. When something enters into *śūnyatā* and consequently 'has ceased' where then can a condition be found? 'When all possible supports for a condition have been removed, then how can one find an immediate condition?' is the query with respect to *śūnyatā.*

This 'immediate condition' has a reference to time and therefore refers to the activities associated with *saṃsāra/māyā,* or more specifically to consciousness (the 'immediately contiguous condition' referring to the substance of the *ālayavijñāna*), which governs our perception of things therein. Nāgārjuna thus now asks us to properly examine consciousness. So what consciousness is and how it functions, is now our query.

When something has not arisen with respect to consciousness then this means that mental images have not been evoked by the perspective thinker. Actions that evoke a conscious response have not been made. Therefore there are no modifications of the mind to cease. Such a condition exists during deep sleep, an unconscious or unaware state, or in meditation. Of these points only the last is worthy of our investigation here. In the *samādhi* that is posited, the seed thought *(bīja)* of any form of activity has not been activated because 'things' have not arisen from (latent) conditions, therefore 'cessation is not appropriate'.

Next Nāgārjuna depicts the process of entering *samādhi,* namely, the cessation of the activity of that mind (the thing that has ceased). He then asks that when such activity has ceased, 'what is [it that serves as] a condition?' The condition here is the natural state of that portion of the *ālayavijñāna* contained by the mind. Serenity is the state, and Clear Light that is poised to act upon any seed impression is the condition. This condition, however, is not the 'immediate condition', because the process of immediacy implicates time, whereas that which is serene is timeless. What is 'not proper' is the volatility of the substance of the lower empirical mind (the intellect), being in fact an 'immediate condition'. This is because it has an immediate function, of gathering and collating information from *saṃsāric* activity, and to clothe the *bījas* of thought, once activated.

The intellect is also 'immediate' because it is born anew with each new incarnation of a personal-I. It is even born anew with every new discursive thought, or visual imagery derived from the world of the senses, or from its own revelry. Consciousness, on the other hand, wherein the *samādhi* is enacted, outlasts such births and deaths, and consequently cannot be considered an immediate condition. In this verse Nāgārjuna therefore asks us to seriously question the functions and qualities of our personal 'selves', as bound or conditioned by intellects, or rather, by desire-mind, which produces the 'self' concept. He considers such activity as 'not proper' or worthy of manifesting. Instead one should strive to stay in a state of *samādhi* where there is no ceasing or arising. That which enters into it from the *dharmakāya* neither arises or ceases, but impresses the Clear Light with revelation of what eternally IS. This is that which must be for all involved with *saṃsāra* (which represents the immediacy of the past). The relegating of the one (*dharmakāya*) to the other (*saṃsāra*) connotes the manifestation of great wisdom, which is forged in *samādhi* as a consequence of the *saṃsāra-śūnyatā* nexus. This nexus can therefore also be considered the 'condition' that Nāgārjuna refers to here.

From the above we can infer that the remaining five verses are concerned with the question of consciousness. This is appropriate, as the number five relates to the five Elements, *prāṇas,* senses, sense-perceptors (and their transmuted correspondences) that help to gather information for the development of consciousness. If we add this verse then we get the number six, which also allows us to include the intellect as the 'sixth sense'.

Kalupahana adds here:

> Nāgārjuna, realizing the difficulties inherent in such speculations,[16] raises questions regarding the very conception of 'arising' in such a context. Neither the momentary events, nor the substances that were posited to account for the continuity of series of such events, according to Nāgārjuna, can be described as "arisen" *(utpanna).* If they are not arisen *(anutpanna),* their cessation is also inconceivable. If they were to cease momentarily, they could not serve as conditions *(pratyaya).*[17]

Kalupahana's statement consequently refers only to the conditioning of *samādhi* experiencing the Clear Light or the Void.

---

16 Of the Sautrāntikas and the Sarvāstivādins.

17 Ibid., 113.

Verse ten states:

> Since the existence of existents devoid of self-nature is not evident, the statement "When that exists, this comes to be," will not be appropriate.[18]

As we are now to look to the qualities of the five senses, Elements, or *prāṇas* in turn for each successive verse, it is obvious that when speaking of 'existents' we are here focussed upon the Earthy Element, that directly concerning physical plane phenomena. The statement 'When that exists, this comes to be' was said to be spoken by the Buddha,[19] therefore Nāgārjuna was referring to applications when it would 'not be appropriate'. I have earlier posited that everything in Nature can be considered in terms of unities, in terms of singularities, which from one perspective can be considered as 'self-natures', but from another perspective they are part of organic wholes, of complete systems. There is a multiplicity or diversity in the unity. Viewed conventionally therefore, Nāgārjuna's statement that 'existents devoid of self-nature is not evident' is correct. From this perspective he is not arguing against the Buddha's teaching. This is the way that things appear to consciousness.

However, when viewed from the perspective of ultimate truth, then the statement is incorrect, as all existences can be found to be void of self nature, and from such a perspective the Buddha's statement 'will not be appropriate'. He is speaking here of the inevitable turn about in the seat of consciousness that happens once a person strives to ascertain the truth and looks inwards or upwards towards verities stemming from the realms of enlightenment rather than directly empirical observation. 'Existents' however are appropriate for the deluded ones who still have much to gain with identification with the self-nature of existents, no matter how transient. For those upon the path to enlightenment however, the opposite is the case. Their task is to convert the Earthy *saṃskāras* associated with the five sense perceptions into their higher, Aetheric, correspondences of the wisdoms of the five Dhyāni Buddhas.

Regarding this verse Kalupahana states that 'Nāgārjuna's criticism, therefore, leaves the Buddha's general formula of causation untouched,

---

18 Ibid.

19 See Kalupahana, Ibid., 114.

for it was not the Buddha's intention to reify either "this" or "that"'.[20] The Buddha was careful to speak to all in a language people could understand, thus to the average person he spoke in terms of what they understood, and for the *saṅgha* he spoke in different terminology.

Verse eleven states:

> The effect does not exist in the conditions that are separated or combined. Therefore, how can that which is not found in the conditions come to be from the conditions?[21]

Following the general sequence of the Elements from the densest to the subtlest, we find that this verse is directly concerned with the Watery Element of the emotions, or what can be described as the desire-mind. These Watery *saṃskāras* fluidly and instantly combine and separate according to the object of desire. Whatever consciousness thinks about in a desirous way is sought after, and this causes the problems of attachment that later necessitates the painful process of learning nonattachment. Nāgārjuna informs us that there is no true effect in the conditions that produce attachment and nonattachment. The conditions are illusional, ephemeral, with an ever-changing scenario of desire impulses. The effect is not in the field of desire, but rather in consciousness (the Fiery Element), which learns through experience what not to attach to and in which direction to proceed. 'The effect' therefore 'does not exist in the conditions'. Consciousness gains wisdom as a consequence, thereby lessening contact with the field of desire until the Waters are entirely cleansed of murkiness. Inevitably this allows a reflection of a version of the *śūnyatā* experience.

The question Nāgārjuna therefore asks is 'how does consciousness, which is not found in the conditions, actually become derived from the conditions?' This incorporates the entire logic concerning the nature and functions of the organs of sensation, emotions, desire, aspirations, and inevitably the energy of love in relation to consciousness. Being unhappy with the nihilistically orientated Mādhyamika position, the Yogācārins tried to solve this question by means of the introduction of the doctrine of *kliṣṭamanas* (defiled mind), as well as that of the

---

20 Ibid.

21 Ibid.

ālayavijñāna, which shall be elucidated later.

From the more superficial view or analysis of this verse in light of the doctrine of the Void (which here really represents an example of shallow thinking) we can say that 'nothing can be found in the conditions because ultimately all is Void'.

Verse twelve states:

> If that effect, being non-existent [in the conditions] were to proceed from the conditions, why does it not proceed from non-conditions?[22]

Now we are to examine the Fiery Element, the realm of the mind, of intelligence and consciousness. We are directed to look at the effect gained in consciousness through the process of pain and suffering in *saṃsāra* as one learns to detach from the forms of illusion. Nāgārjuna states that if such an effect were to proceed from the conditions (the psycho-physical domain) where it is in fact non-existent, then why does it not (also) proceed from non-conditions? The term 'non-conditions' concerns that which is associated either with a state of *samādhi* or with *śūnyatā*, wherein the field of desire-sensation does not exist. The question therefore really is 'what is the relation of consciousness to *śūnyatā*, as experienced in a state of *samādhi?'* The answer is obvious, as one must eliminate all forms of clinging and desire/emotion, all irritations or disturbances of the mind, if *samādhi* is to ensue. Therefore there is no effect because the substance of the mind is not active.

Also, why is there not a reciprocal approach from *śūnyatā* to consciousness that consciousness can also gain from? The answer is that the Void would actually destroy the (actively manifesting 'conditioned') consciousness that would approach it. (This destructive functioning of the Void is actually what the Herukas[23] symbolise. They are protectors of the *dharma* for those whose consciousnesses are not adequately prepared for what *śūnyatā* will present.) One must actually develop a serene Mind to do so, wherein its natural luminescence can experience the real. Here the sum of the philosophy concerning Vajrayāna and the Mahāmudrā is implied. It can therefore only be adequately answered

---

22 Ibid., 115.

23 Wrathful meditation deities, transformative agents protecting the *dharma*. They will be explained in detail in Volume 5.

by those whose consciousness is clearly approaching *śūnyatā*.

On this path there manifests attributes of disquiet, as cherished beliefs and the other things consciousness once held dear are stripped bare of their dross, so that only the essential, the truth/*dharma,* remains. This is the course of the development of wisdom and of enlightenment. Of this process one can have much to say, and the Bodhisattva path is the outcome.

Verse thirteen states:

> The effect is made of conditions, but the conditions are themselves not self-made. How can that effect made of conditions [arise] from what is not self-made? [24]

The terminology of this verse causes us to review verses one and two, with the Airy Element now being implicated, that which directly pertains to *śūnyatā* (where the Airy principle carries the Void Elements). Note also that verse four states that 'activity is not constituted of conditions nor is it not non-constituted of conditions', whereas here we have the apparently contradictory perspective that the effect of such activity is made of conditions. What Nāgārjuna wishes to elaborate here is the nature of all base conditions, rather than that which modifies them, leaving aside consideration of 'non-conditions'. The effect thus refers to the sum total of phenomena (which Nāgārjuna acknowledges as existing, at least conventionally) and of the mechanism of its appearance. The conditionings are the four indicated in verse two: the Void Elements, the *bījas*, the *ālayavijñāna*, and *māyā*. He then states that they are 'not self made'. An interpretation of this statement is that they are always existent in one form or another, which is an important consideration bespeaking of much esotericism. If the four abovementioned conditions were other than 'not self made' then *saṃsāra* simply could not be. The 'not self-made' nature of the Void Elements are the necessary factors that a great Bodhisattva or Buddha residing in the *dharmakāya* can utilise to activate phenomena of the type that we can and do experience.

The subject of the *bījas* and the *ālayavijñāna* is explained in general Yogācāra philosophy. The *bījas* are the results of former experiences, the effects of actions engendered by most people of a primarily emotional-

24 Kalupahana, 115.

mental character. (As they were not made by the present incarnate 'self' so from this context are 'are not self made'.) The presumption here is that everything reincarnates—as it is for a human personality, so it is for all existents in a universe. There is a store of *bījas* for universes, solar systems, world systems, kingdoms of Nature, as well as for human units. Depending upon what is to take rebirth, so the inherent *bījas* are activated by a process the same as or similar to that given above. The phrase 'or similar to' is used because the process of human rebirths has not yet been properly explained, nor of the rebirthing process in general.

It should be noted that the Sautrāntika and the Sarvāstivādin doctrines contain much that is correct, such as the concept of *svabhāva,* which was later extended to produce the two connotations earlier described. There must be a store of substance, not just the *ālayavijñāna* (which deals with consciousness only). Otherwise, forms such as we experience could not be clothed with anything substantially material, as the process of the manifestation of phenomena could descend no further than the *ālayavijñāna*. There would be thought substance, but nothing that anyone in a physical body could touch. There could be no physical body to touch, nor any physical universe within which to experience such a sense in. This universal store, e.g., of Watery substance, is found as *bījas* within the general *māyā* and is likewise not 'self-made', it simply is. This plenitude of substance *(mūlaprakṛti)* is conditioned by karmic law and is drawn upon according to this law and that of thought in motion. Any entity needing rebirth, to manifest a form through which Watery experiences are possible, can then do so. It is also drawn from whenever any person makes a mental-emotional volition, and which is then incorporated in the robes of Watery and Earthy substance people possess. The meditative process can also proceed to produce the concretion of Fiery substance into forms (e.g., as desired by the enlightened Mind). It can sustain the status quo, or work towards the relinquishing, sublimation, or dematerialising of that substance, which inevitably leads to the *śūnyatā* experience.

The previous verses dealt with *māyā* (the Earthy Element), the *bījas* (relating primarily to the Watery Element), and the *ālayavijñāna* (the Fiery Element). The concern of this verse continues the trend, thus we look now principally to the Void Elements (whose essentiality is characterised by the Airy Element) as the conditions from which the 'effect' is made. From the previous explanation of them we know that they are not 'self made'. The final question therefore really asks 'How can effects arise from the Void Elements, which are in fact the base substance *(svabhāva)* of *śūnyatā?'*

When all of the conditions are included, then Nāgārjuna's question concerns the nature of the entire process of rebirth, which emanates from whatever store exists of the rebirthing principle, be this of a human unit, or any other unity up to and including a universe. The question asked is: 'Having been abstracted into *śūnyatā* (at the end of a cycle of whatever was) how can that relating to phenomena appear again?' The question is answerable if one does not conceive of *śūnyatā* as an absolute finality. The answer incorporates a proper consideration of the nature of the *śūnyatā-saṃsāra* relation. This is a process that is faced by all reappearing Bodhisattvas who had achieved absorption into such a state in a previous life, and must now take form again upon a higher cycle that continues their compassionate purpose. Full understanding however only exists in an enlightened Mind.

Another way of posing Nāgārjuna's question is 'What is it that in fact is activated when a high grade Bodhisattva takes rebirth, what part of such a Bodhisattva remains (in *śūnyatā*) and what part is expressed (in phenomena)?' Such incarnatory activity is only possible because the base conditions that must be utilised when incarnation proceeds are 'not self-made'. They also concern the streams of *karma* from former lives that the Bodhisattva must cleanse for the benefit of the all.

If we understand that the expression of *bodhicitta* is also such a base substance (which can be considered a 'not self-made' condition of the *tathāgatagarbha),* then its power to liberate will be to eliminate the imbalances in *māyā.* This translates as the rectification of world suffering, necessitating cleansing the *karma* of the suffering ones. Such *karma* can also be considered to not be 'self-made' as far as the Bodhisattva is concerned, because it is caused by others, within a greater sphere of cause-effect of which he/she is a part. However, there is *karma* that is also made by the Bodhisattva's former lives (but not 'self-made' as far as his/her present life is concerned). This also must be ridden through to conclusion into the Void.

The Void Elements arise as effects because they are incorporated as the seed point of whatever action commences in the three worlds of human livingness. Their substance is agitated through attracting a matrix of *bījas (bindu)*, condensed, and concreted (utilising the substance-store) by the activity of the mind/Mind and/or by desire-emotions. This 'concretion' is then held in place as the *karma* of the action, to be inevitably resolved back into the stillness of the Void. That which agitates and concretes is a 'self nature' when incorporated in *saṃsāra*, as already explained. Thus an effect is made to arise from conditions that are 'not self-made'.

Verse fourteen states:

> An effect made either of conditions or of non-conditions is, therefore, not evident. Because of the absence of the effect, where could conditions or non-conditions be evident?[25]

This is the last verse of Chapter One *('Examination of Conditions')* of Nāgārjuna's treatise, and thus deals with the most abstruse of the Elements, the Aether, directly relating our vision to the *dharmakāya*. Thus it is to this realm or state of being/non-being that these words refer.

Because of people's lack of understanding of the nature of the conditions governing the state that can be considered the Buddha-Mind and because Nāgārjuna is dealing with ordered sequences of statements which are generally not taken into account as philosophical unities, so we have the major reason for the general misunderstanding of what Nāgārjuna's philosophical intent and content actually is. We also have subsidiary reasons, such as provided by Kalupahana:

> The second statement is, indeed, the final conclusion of Nāgārjuna in this immensely significant chapter. A superficial interpretation of this statement is bound to leave the impression, generally popular among the interpreters of Nāgārjuna, that he rejected any form of causation, including the arising of an effect *depending* upon a cause or condition or a group of such causes or conditions *(pratītyasamutpāda)*. Hence, Nāgārjuna is perceived as a transcendentalist who recognized an "absolute" beyond all linguistic expression[26]....A more careful

25 Ibid., 116.

26 Ibid.

> contextual analysis would reveal that the effect *(phala)* Nāgārjuna was referring to in this verse, as well as in the entire chapter, is one that is identical with the cause or different from it. It is only an effect understood in such a manner, as clearly indicated in the present statement, that he was categorically denying. If no such effect is seen, why speak of a condition *(pratyaya)* that is identical with an effect, or a non-condition *(a-pratyaya)* that is different from the effect?[27]

What could Nāgārjuna reveal about the *dharmakāya* during his time? The probability is that anything that he could reveal would only be perceived as an absolute 'beyond all linguistic expression'. Certainly the *dharmakāya* can be perceived thus, wherewith an 'effect made either of conditions or of non-conditions is, therefore, not evident'. How does one define a Buddha-Mind? Does it contain 'conditions', such as the four mentioned in verse two? Here we can agree with Nāgārjuna in saying no, as a Buddha is beyond the need for rebirth and needs not the *bījas* thereof for any form of his absorbed being. What about the 'non-conditions', which as before mentioned, refers to *śūnyatā?* Nāgārjuna is informing us that a Buddha has also transcended such a state of absorption. This is obvious with regards to the Hinayāna *śūnyatā*, but what about the Mahāyāna version? When the facts are carefully analysed and we see that such a state (*śūnyatā*) is attainable by Bodhisattvas, then clearly a Buddha has transcended this also. This state beyond *śūnyatā* is the *dharmakāya.* Relegation of this verse to the *dharmakāya* is therefore the esoteric mode of interpretation. The lower level of interpretation relates the verse to the ultimate truth, which would ascribe to the Void neither conditions or non-conditions.

One could also apply the *catuṣkoṭikā* of Nāgārjuna here and state that *śūnyatā* contains conditions, non-conditions, both conditions and non-conditions, and neither conditions and non-conditions. The justification here is that it acts as a mirror, mirroring the conditions from the *ālayavijñāna* to the *dharmakāya* and the fruits of the *dharmakāya* to the *ālayavijñāna.* When it is reflected upon or integrated with *saṃsāra* and viewed in terms of the Void Elements, then it can be said to contain 'conditions'. When it rests within itself then it can be stated to contain non-conditions. When it is mirroring the *ālayavijñāna* to

27 Ibid., 116-117.

the *dharmakāya* then it contains both conditions and non-conditions, when it expresses the fruits of the *dharmakāya* to the *ālayavijñāna* then it can be said to contain neither conditions and non-conditions.

The concluding line of Nāgārjuna in this verse is: 'Because of the absence of the effect, where could conditions or non-conditions be evident?' The statement is indeed correct for a 'thus gone one'. There are neither conditions or non-conditions in the *dharmakāya.*

Effectively here, Nāgārjuna also asks for those that have the capacity, to deeply ponder upon the nature of the Thusness, that in reality is expressed as the *tathāgatagarbha*, the Womb of the Buddha-nature within us. We must thus query how the *tathāgatagarbha* evolves with respect to the process of the attainment of Buddhahood by the personal-I.

I have explained the meaning of the first chapter of Nāgārjuna's *Mūlamadhyamakakārikā* here in order to show that his philosophy is not different from what is presented in this treatise.[28] What is explained is indeed the *mūlamadhyamaka*, the true 'middle way' between extremes. Everything is a matter of interpretation, and right interpretation is integral to obtaining an enlightened understanding. The integral teachings differ not, though the mode of presentation may, as well as depth of elaboration. Indeed, how could they differ if the source is from the same well of the enlightenment-experience that is found in the realm of the Lords in the Kingdom of Shambhala.

28 The information presented here should help the astute reader to properly interpret his twenty-sixth chapter, which is concerned with Dependent Origination.

11

The Diamond Slivers

The Four-Cornered Proof

The section titled 'The Diamond Slivers' is found on pages 131-150 of Hopkin's *Meditation on Emptiness.* He states that 'The refutation of production of something from self, or from its own entity, is done through demonstrating the consequent absurdity of senseless production'.[1] The sources are stated to be Nga-wang-bel-den's *Annotations*, Jam-yang-shay-ba's *Great Exposition of The Middle Way,* Dzong-ka-ba's *Essence of the Good Explanations* and *Illumination of the Thought* and Geshe Gedün Lodrö's oral teachings.[2] Hopkins states that these slivers are called thus because each is capable of 'destroying the conception of inherent existence'.[3] This is based on the thesis that things are not *inherently* produced, as an expression of Nāgārjuna's 'four-cornered proof', which Hopkins states as:

> Because of not being produced from themselves, from naturally existent others, from both, or causelessly.[4]

What Nāgārjuna really describes here are the qualities that produce *śūnyatā*, or rather, that are expressive of *śūnyatā*. I shall call them *the four*

1 Hopkins, *Meditation on Emptiness,* 136-137.

2 Ibid., 131.

3 Ibid., 133.

4 Ibid.

gates of śūnyatā, and when these four gates or 'corners' are diagrammed and we put *śūnyatā* at the centre, then we get the following Figure.

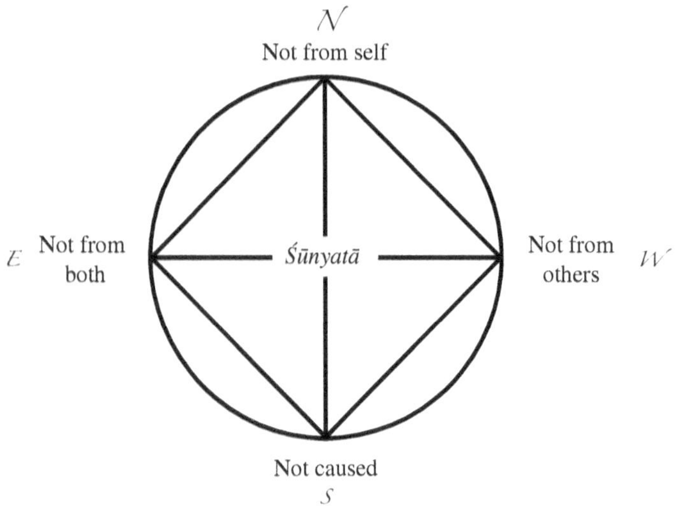

Figure 4. The Four-Cornered Proof

Each of the four negative statements refer to *śūnyatā*, and its non-divisibility or non-accountability with phenomena. These four statements entice us to query 'how does Nāgārjuna depict *śūnyatā*'s relation to *saṃsāra*, as *saṃsāra* is everything that is not represented by this Figure?' The answer is that this relation exists because of actions committed by a 'self', by the actions of others, by the combined action of both, or by causes other than 'self'. This is but an application of conventional truth, which has already been established as a means to enlightenment. Indeed, in order to think about these qualities Nāgārjuna first had to meditate on the qualities of the *saṃsāra* he knew were conventionally existent, and then to apply the opposite in order to deny their existence.

The immediate problem that one should see in the philosophy associated with the above diagram is that one cannot state the co-mutability of *saṃsāra* and *śūnyatā* and then act as if *saṃsāra* does not exist in one's thinking. (The indication therefore is that it came from 'nothing', though such a 'nothing' is philosophically denied.) This diagram is therefore incomplete as it does not explain the relationship of *saṃsāra* to *śūnyatā*. It can imply that *ultimately saṃsāra* can be abstracted into or as *śūnyatā*. If we take this *śūnyatā* to be at the heart of 'everything', and if this 'everything' does not inherently exist, then does this apply to *śūnyatā* as well? In other words, *śūnyatā* may exist, but if there is no consciousness to register the fact of its existence, then does *śūnyatā* factually exist? Here then is a quandary, and it is answerable because consciousness stands between *śūnyatā* and *saṃsāra* in such a way that the 'things' of *saṃsāra* can be particularised, quantified in terms of unities, i.e., in terms of 'I's'. *Śūnyatā* can then be said to be denoted in terms of 'not-I'. *Śūnyatā* may be causeless, but everything in *saṃsāra* has a cause, consciousness will see to that, and it can also define things in relation to what it knows as part of its experiential base.

As already stated, an amorphous consciousness cannot act upon anything thus needs to be particularised if it is to act creatively, or to move things. This moving of things is called the creation of *karma*. Depending upon what is moved, so we get the type of *karma* created. It should be noted that *thoughts are also things*. The substance of thought does have a subtle specific gravity or weight to it, thus we experience such things as the heaviness or lightness of thought.

The particularised consciousness that has moved things must suffer the reverse effect of what has been moved, if equilibrium is to be eventually achieved, allowing *śūnyatā* to ultimately be revealed for what it is, the 'all' that is 'not'. This refers to the end of an evolutionary cycle, but finality may not be what is seen because there is effectively the possibility of rebirth.

As consciousness moves things, so it experiences the process of moving, the gain of where the thing has moved to, and then its resolution into a unity of experience. This process is called the overcoming of ignorance, because as consciousness manifests its directive activity it discovers what was formerly hid, thus was in darkness. As it experiences the process of directing thoughts, consciousness thus sheds light upon the darkness. What was once dark comes to be revealed in the light.

As any particular consciousness approaches *śūnyatā,* the process is one of the release of 'things', of non-attachment to that which has been moved. Being thereby unfettered by things produces a consequent expansion of consciousness. Broad-minded revelations then overcome what once was restricted through attachment to the formed attributes of things. Enlightenment consequently ensues. The release of things is actually achieved by slowing down the rate of activity of the empirical mind, and the process continues until the movement of mundane thoughts is almost imperceptible. All things to which the mind was formerly bonded such as a 'self' concept lose their power to fixate consciousness and are relinquished. The mind disengages from them and they no longer affect the person, except by providing a zone of observation of what once was.

Because the activity of mind has slowed down, where the many often conflicting little racing motions that it formerly contained have been eliminated, there is now but one expanded uniform serene consciousness-form. This allows an exponential speeding up of the animated processes associated with awakened perceptions. Lightning-like do the flashes of perception manifest from the higher Mind. There are now no swirls of thought-moments ('things') blocking or modifying the activity of the rapid thought occurrence. They no longer interfere with the process of thinking. This then depicts the happenings during the process of meditation.

Such swirls can be likened to the congestion of inner city traffic, as compared to a highway unimpeded by traffic and stop lights. Unimpeded natural flow allows the consciousness-unit time to look at the mechanisms of thought, where a number of streams can happen at near simultaneity once the substance of mind has been cleansed of impediments (defilements). The mind has slowed down to virtually imperceptible motion, is serene and therefore can observe and analyse transferences of thought without influencing or modifying them, unless need be. The consciousness can then see the reality of what the thoughts convey, because it does not move (if simply observing) and thus has the capability, i.e., 'unlimited time' to do so. This allows an enlightened being to instantaneously perceive many streams of truth (*dharma*) at once within the rarefied substance that is now Mind.

As the mind slows down, the impression of time becomes indeterminate, as time is reckoned in terms of the speed of the motion of the traffic in consciousness. Once the thought process has slowed down to where its base of substance does not move (has been thoroughly clarified), then 'no time at all' is experienced and *śūnyatā* has been attained. Thought processes within the Clear Light of consciousness then happen with lightning speed, and are instantaneously experienced accordingly. Thus for the meditator it seems that no time at all has passed since first sitting for meditation and upon awakening from it, but to the world of normal conscious interactions much time or many events may have passed. The net result being that the perception of time has actually sped up for the meditator (if one cares to look at it that way), the mental interactions occur much faster than previously, because the former mode of 'moving things' no longer exists. Another way of viewing this point is that one has moved into another, much faster time zone. Consequently the time sequences of the world of enlightened consciousness has sped up considerably. This is part of what allows the perception of multidimensional thought by an enlightened being. Such a one can perceive things on many levels at once, and to be active in all of them. By being detached he/she is not constrained by the time sequences of this world.

Though attachment to things is eliminated nothing is lost, because consciousness bears the imprint of everything experienced, which can therefore be remembered. Consequently much less substance moves in the Mind, but what does move is far reaching and potently effective.

The expansion of the Four-Cornered Proof

Figure 5 expands upon the 'Four-Cornered Proof' and presents five concentric circles that indicate the nature of being/non-being. The dual central zone is that of the *śūnyatā*-Clear Mind interrelationship. The middle zone represents the I-consciousness (effectively also incorporating the Clear Mind). It mediates between the production of *karma*, of what produces deeper *saṃsāric* involvement, and that which eliminates *karma*, leading to *śūnyatā*. The outer two zones represent *saṃsāra*. This zone is inclusive of the empirical mind and concerns the domain of phenomena, of the production and experiencing of the four types of *karma* indicated. The outermost zone represents the place of interaction with the material world, of gathering information by means of the sense-consciousnesses.

The four directions of the *maṇḍala* can be viewed as the four corners or pillars supporting the universe, whereby the phenomena and non-phenomena of everything rests. At each of the 'corners' stands a Mahāraja[5] (the outermost pillars) or Heruka (for the innermost ones,

5 The Mahārajas are the four great Raja (kingly) lords that embody the four directions in space, the four continents or Elements in Buddhist and Hindu philosophy. Their technical names in Hinduism are Virūdhaka (the south), Vessāvana (or Kuvera, north), Dhataraṭṭha

signified by the eight-spoked wheels). They are guardians of the gates leading to the next higher attainment. The Mahāraja of each direction is a Lord of *karma* governing a specific Element; for the east Air, the south Earth, the west Fire, and the north Water, as far as the appearance of phenomena is concerned. The Heruka is a Wrathful Deity that guards the process of transmutation of the nature of the Elements so that only the Void Elements remain within the precincts of the zone of *śūnyatā*. It will not allow any other form of substance to enter.[6] The Mahāraja presides over the domains where there is the formation of *karma*, and the Heruka with its dissolution.

Another way of viewing this Figure is that it is in the form of an Eye, with *śūnyatā* and the Clear Mind in the centre, representing the pupil, which admits light, but to the outer seeming it is dark, veiling what transpires within. The second zone represents the iris of the eye, which is variously coloured (as are the many forms of consciousness states). The iris is essentially a muscle that moves inwards and outwards, thus defining the amount and quality of light that can be safely borne by the pupil. The two-way arrows in the diagram represent its movement, of the ability of the I-consciousness to travel either towards *śūnyatā* or to *saṃsāra*. Finally we have the white of the eye, the general substance, containing the vitreous humour through which the light must travel in order to be processed at the retina. This represents the substance of *saṃsāra*, represented by the third zone.

This entire construct can be called the *Śūnyatā Eye*. The Figure indicates that the functioning of the eyes and the way that *śūnyatā* interrelates with *saṃsāra* is more exact than at first glance. It constitutes an appropriate analysis of what light is and how it is processed.[7]

In analysing from the realm of the I-consciousness we see that in the northern direction actions are produced through self-volition by an individualised consciousness. At first the self-concept is intensified

(east), and Virupāksha (west). In the *Bardo Thödol* they are the four Guardians of the gates of the *maṇḍala* of the Peaceful and Wrathful deities: Vijaya (the east), Yamāntaka (the south), Hayagrīva (the west), and Amṛtakuṇḍalin (the north). These directions are relegated according to the orientation of the Dhyāni Buddhas explained below.

6 The function of the Herukas will be explained in detail in Volume 5.

7 The nature of light would diverge us too much to properly explain here.

N

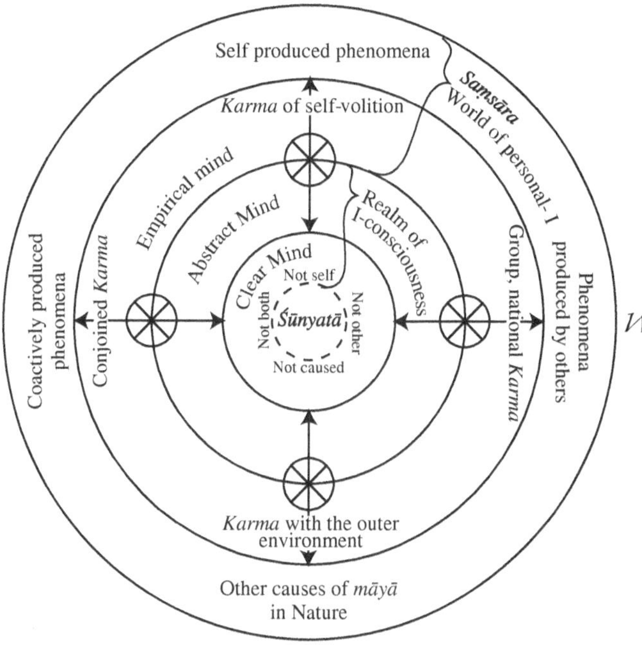

S

Figure 5. The Relationship of *Śūnyatā* to *Saṃsāra*

through the production of much selfish *karma*. The karmic consequences are directly borne by that individual and must eventually be worked off as that 'self' learns the harsh lessons of the transience of *saṃsāra*. When travelling towards *śūnyatā* this self-concept must be eliminated, and forms of action evoked instead that will cleanse all phenomenal *karma*. When focussed upon *saṃsāra* there is a heightening of attachment to phenomena in relation to that which the individualised 'self' desires, increasing selfishness, possessiveness, and material incentive.

The eastern direction demonstrates the *karma* of volitions conjoined to those whom one's consciousness is closely attached to. We thus have family activities, sibling rivalry, the intercourse between lovers. The strongest types of loving interrelations are thus formed. The associated emotions must however be relinquished when travelling inward towards *śūnyatā*. True (sacrificial) love must inevitably stand in place of the emotions. The outward, *saṃsāric* direction, on the other hand strengthens emotional bonds, producing consequent sentimentality, pleasing material comforts, and sexual interactions via coactively produced activity.

The western direction concerns the production of group, national, and international *karma*. Group *karma* generated predominates, as all humans are social beings. This concerns one's interrelation with the society, or nation, and the types of activities people create together. It can include such things as interrelating in a community centre, the part one plays in a national or tribal identity, or even in waging war upon another tribe or nation. We therefore have collectivised *karma* producing myriads of interlocking weavings of karmic strands incorporating group interrelationships. The entire group shares the associated *karma*. Such things as famines, plagues, earthquakes, and other natural and man-made disasters manifest as ways of paying back *karma* for those that had formerly collectively caused suffering to others. Inevitably an entire group can travel inward towards *śūnyatā* by eliminating such tendencies in their societies, by working towards human betterment and not towards group or national greed. This represents an inward motion in the *maṇḍala*. When travelling outward with selfish motives the type of civilisation seen in the world today, with its material incentives, is produced.

The southern direction concerns the *karma* produced by an individualised consciousness interrelating with the outer environment, with the lives incorporated in Nature's kingdoms. This incorporates the *māyā*, the phenomena seen in *saṃsāra*, into which we are all born. To travel inward to *śūnyatā* from this direction involves relinquishing the *karma* one has to phenomena and materiality. Inevitably enlightenment is attained when one enters the causeless zone that is 'the other shore' of the rebirth process.

Information concerning 'the four afflicted emotions' (*kliṣṭamanas*) of the Yogācārin philosophy can be added here. They are the opposing qualities, concerned with *saṃsāric* identifications, to the four 'nots' that represent the gates to *śūnyatā*. These forms of mental-emotions are created by the personal-I manifesting within *saṃsāra*. In relation to this the *Trimśikā-kārikā* states:

> Situated and fully derived from this [*ālaya-vijñāna*], and with that place as its objective support, is [*kliṣṭa-*]*manas*. It is a mind in the

> form of the thought "this is me." It is *nivṛta* ('obscured') which is not the subject of moralizing and it is always assisted by four afflictive emotions: opinion about I *(ātma-dṛṣṭi),* stupidity about I *(ātma-moha),* pride in I *(ātma-māna),* and self-love *(ātma-sneha).* It is of that [level] on which it was born and there are also the other [five mental factors associated with it] such as contact, etc.[8]

'Opinion about I' stands at the northern gate, and is productive of the *karma* of self-volition. It is fundamentally emotional and separative in nature.

'Stupidity about I' is emotional thinking with little true deeply analytical mental import involved. It produces group or mass *karma,* as it involves being swayed by the crowd, by mass public opinion, or of the social or religious mores one is involved with or born into. The position is thus the west.

'Self-love', the production of all types of selfishness, concerns the southern gate of manifesting *karma* with the outer environment as the person manipulates all material resources, money, gold, for his/her own comforts and desires in life.

'Pride in I' involves puffing-up one's ego for other's esteem. This concerns conjoined *karma,* as one tries to bring another into one's own orbit of selfishness and glamour. This can refer to pride in union with one's lover, to the establishment of a worshipping group around one, like a film or rock star does. The eastern gate is the base of its *modus operandi.*

From each of these four afflictive emotions emanate the corresponding emotions derived from the five sense-perceptors, as conditioned by the qualities of these four directions.

The eight-spoked wheels depicted in the *maṇḍala* evoke the Eightfold Path that can be trod in each of the directions, as well as the eight directions whereby people can navigate space.

Each of the eight-spoked wheels can integrate with the central four gates to *śūnyatā,* which can similarly act as a wheel turning, making effectively for each of the four directions the attributes of the twelve petals of the Heart *chakra.* This indicates why the Heart is Life. It is

---

8 Gareth Sparham, *Ocean of Eloquence, Tsong-kha-pa's Commentary on the Yogācāra Doctrine of Mind,* 109.

the centre whereby the highest realisations of universal identity can be obtained, as its various petals are actively and passively concerned with the dynamics of the various transformations that lead to *śūnyatā*, via which comes the higher realisations of the *dharma*.

What is depicted above in reality is the philosophy of the five Dhyāni Buddhas, with Vairocana and the Dharmadhātu Wisdom, embodying the quality of *śūnyatā* in the centre.[9]

Note that I have orientated Figure 5 in relation to the natural manifestation of the Elements, thus the appearance of phenomena. In terms of the demonstration of the wisdoms of the Dhyāni Buddhas (and the assignment of the Jina families) the north and south orientations need to be reversed. Hence the southern direction ('not caused'), and that concerning the *karma* with the outer environment would become north, relegated to Amoghasiddhi. Here his All-accomplishing Wisdom denotes the complete mastery of everything concerning the manifestation of phenomena. The northern direction ('not self') and the *karma* of self-volition would become south and relegated to Ratnasambhava. His Equalising Wisdom concerns the complete mastery of everything involving the 'self' and its translation into selflessness, which is the essence of the path to Buddhahood. Via the reaction of the 'self' to the transitoriness of phenomena, consciousness inevitably turns around from its materialistic and selfish bias to be focussed upwards. It must then master the emotions that are the foundation of *kliṣṭamanas*. This involves the sum of the qualities of *māyā*, which clothes all appearing forms. Ratnasambhava equalises all of this into the vehicle of the enlightenment-stream. The translation of 'self' into selflessness is the essence of the path to Buddhahood.

Akṣobhya, and the Mirror-like Wisdom embodies the eastern direction, of not being produced from a 'self' or of 'others', to overcome the manifestation of conjoined *karma* ('not both'). The reference here is to the functioning of a mirror, which reflects images from one to the other. Amitābha, with his Discriminating Inner Wisdom, refers to the western direction of 'not being produced by others' wherein group and national *karma* are overcome.

9 Buddhist texts often speak of eight petals to the Heart centre. The nature of the different accountings of the petals of the *chakras* will be explained in Volume 4.

From one perspective four petals of the Heart centre deal with the interrelation of consciousness with the phenomena of the material world. Another four petals specifically process the formulations, opinions, and images of consciousness. The final four petals deal with the transmutation of these images in such a way that the grosser *saṃskāras* produced thereby are eliminated. They purify and refine consciousness so that eventually *śūnyatā* at the heart of all can be experienced.

A better way of analysing these twelve is to see that five of the petals are concerned with processing the qualities of the five sense-perceptors and the five Elements pertaining to manifestation. Literally we have four plus one: the four Elements that are the base or support of everything, plus that one which is their synthesis (Aether). This leaves seven petals that deal specifically with processing these experiences and of their abstraction into the heart of Life. These seven can be called *sacred petals* and the other five *non-sacred.*

The non-sacred petals represent the four outermost positions of the *maṇḍala*. They deal directly with *saṃsāric* involvement. The fifth petal can be relegated to the orientation of any of the four inner directions, the quaternary concerning the eight-spoked wheels, depending upon where consciousness is focussed at any time. However, the natural orientation for processing the Aetheric Element is the southern direction of *karma* with the outer environment. The remaining three of the middle tier of Figure 5 (conjoined *karma, karma* of self-volition, group, national *karma)* process purely human-human interrelationships and its *karma*. They convey attributes of three of the seven sacred petals, when integrated with the four innermost qualities pertaining to *śūnyatā*. They are concerned with the cleansing of the gross volitions caused by human interrelationships, as well as for the elimination of the causes for attachment of the *māyā* of the entire outer environment. All of the *chakras* in the body have a similar functions with respect to the particular Element they process, as all are based upon the paradigm of the number twelve.[10] Accordingly the Heart *chakra* processes the *prāṇas* of the Airy Element.

10 This includes the Solar Plexus centre, as shall be later shown, and elaborated on in Volumes 2 and 5A, even though it has ten major petals. Indeed, one of the main purposes of this *Treatise on Mind* is to elaborate the properties and functions of the *chakras* in the body. It is a much misunderstood subject because their qualities are heavily veiled in the Tantric texts that deal with them.

What has been presented with respect to the Dhyāni Buddhas refers to the innermost (*śūnyatā*) level of the *maṇḍala*. The gates associated with the I-consciousness level of the *maṇḍala* would therefore be controlled by the corresponding Dhyāni Bodhisattvas, whilst their Consorts would oversee the general *karma* of the outermost gates.

Five stages to the evolution of the *buddhadharma*

From the above we see that Nāgārjuna presented the foundation for accounting the innermost sphere of this *maṇḍala,* where *saṃsāra* is a non-existent. This inner sphere represents the foundation that allows the framework of the house of incarnate manifestation to be built upon it, and then clad with substance, painted, and furnished. At his time Nāgārjuna could not proceed further. Later Buddhists elaborated the theory of the Dhyāni Buddhas, upon which the *dharmakāya* philosophy sprouted and a whole universe of ideas could be conceptualised. Figure 5 allows a renovation, embellishment, and interior decoration of this house of *dharma*.

Nāgārjuna was well aware of what teachings were possible to promulgate at his time and how they had to be phrased, having also the future development of the *dharma* in mind. The outline of this process is:

- *First* came the Buddha with the core or seed teachings that became the basic Theravāda *sūtras* and the codes of conduct for monks (*vinaya*). He represented the start of the *maṇḍala* of the Buddhist dispensation, thereby expressing the qualities of *Vairocana* and the Dharmadhātu Wisdom.

- *Next,* after much debate, came the necessity of the development of the Mahāyāna, grounded in the philosophy of the Bodhisattva ideal and *śūnyatā*, as taught by Nāgārjuna. This represented the founding of the Mādhyamika school. He thus expressed the stage signified by the Mirror-like wisdom of Akṣobhya for the *buddhadharma*. This wisdom expresses an inherent duality, that of the real (*śūnyatā*) and that which is reflected as an image, the unreal (*saṃsāra*).[11]

11 Here then is the basis for the two truths, where one is mirrored into the other.

- *Third* came the Yogācāra-Vijñānavādin doctrine of the *ālayavijñāna* and Mind Only, as formulated by Asaṅga and his brother Vasubandhu. They expressed the qualities of the Dhyāni Buddha of the western direction of the *maṇḍala*, Amitābha and his Wisdom of the discriminating Inner Vision. *The Lankāvatāra Sūtra* is a well known text representing the doctrines of this school.
- *The fourth* turning of this wheel saw the advent of the various Buddhist Tantric schools, the Vajrayāna proper, epitomised by the teachings of Padmasambhava. Collectively these Tantras, appertaining to the road to liberation, come under the auspices of the Equalising Wisdom of Ratnasambhava, and the Southern gate of the *maṇḍala* because their main expression allows the development of *siddhis*.
- *Fifth* came modern science, with the investigation of the nature of the laws governing the phenomenal appearance of *saṃsāra*, and the nature of the manifestation of the material universe. This investigation materialistically answered some age-long philosophic quandaries, such as the nature of the atom, the motions of the planets with respect to the earth and the sun, the evolutionary process, the organisation of the bio-diversity on this planet, human biology, the laws postulated by modern chemistry, physics and mathematics, etc. Though much still needs to be comprehended by scientists concerning the dimensions of perception and other spiritual verities, this information-explosion can be moulded into the fifth great epoch of Buddhism, that of the Dharmakāya Way. This is epitomised by the All-accomplishing Wisdom of Amoghasiddhi. The northern position of the *maṇḍala* is thereby exemplified. This leads the way of travel into the far reaches of cosmos and all that it signifies in this multidimensional universe. The law of *karma* and the doctrine of the *tathāgatagarbha* can also be properly expounded as the basis to comprehending the higher enlightened domains.

The Diamond Slivers

The Diamond Slivers can now be analysed, starting with the section dealing with the *'non production from self'*. The first statement given is:

> The production again of a sprout is senseless because of having already achieved its own entity. Since the production of a thing means the attainment of its own entity, then if then having achieved its own entity, it is produced again, its re-production is purposeless.[12]

We should first focus upon the statements 'own entity' and 'having achieved its own entity' to try to establish what the statements mean exactly, if this is at all possible. I presume that by its re-production is meant the perfect clone of a 'self', the exact similitude of what a parent was. Actually, little in Nature is that exacting, no two humans are alike, it is doubtful if any two trees are alike, and if we observe closely, generally there is some different observable trait in one member of a species from another, especially so as we progress up the ladder of evolution. (The smaller and less evolved, the more likely there be almost identical natures, but as we get to larger more evolved species, then such similarities disappear.) Sprouts, if grown up under strict laboratory conditions may be raised as clones, but then as they grow into mature plants then differences generally manifest. Variation is the order in Nature. The modern science of genetics relies on this. Without variation there can be no adaptation of the genetic traits of species and the consequent evolution of that species.

The statement that 'its reproduction is purposeless' is only true *if* there is no gain in its sentience, in its reason for existence, or that there is no difference in the growth of any future sprouts, i.e., that all in the foreseeable future are perfect clones of the one observed. But this is not so, thus its evolution slowly progresses. Over time we get genetic mutation and variability, and depending upon environmental conditionings (if left to grow in its natural state), this would mean that in some cases we would get stunted growths, because of famine conditions, and in other cases there would be clear evidences of nutritional deficiencies, diseases, parasite effects, and the effects of competitive struggle for survival.

Also over considerable time we would see the progeny of that sprout evolving into an entirely new species and progress upon the ladder of evolution. This observation is the gain of modern scientific research. When the factor of the sprout manifesting a form of sentience is added (because it is a living entity), we will see that it gradually evolves greater

---

12 Hopkins, *Meditation on Emptiness*, 137.

sentience as part of a collective whole, thereby manifesting greater ability to respond to the impacts of the external environment. (An example is a defence apparatus against its enemies.) It spirals onwards in evolution with respect to all others that it is evolving in relation to. Group *karma* also causes it to evolve towards *bodhicitta* (towards light) inherent in the sunlight towards which the sprout aspires as it grows.

Even a rock 'evolves', changes, as it is slowly weathered away by rain and wind, and by human activity.

From the above perspective the exponent has not understood the purposes of evolution and of *karma* in all things manifest. He has not actually observed from the point of view of the sentience of the sprout as it continues its evolutionary struggle towards light, and greater gains in its sentience stakes, at its own level of evolutionary attainment. There is thus a purpose in seeming 'endless production', and that is evolutionary growth, evolved sentience. It is consequently not an absurd consideration in Nature.

We should note here the fact that the imagery of the growth of a sprout from a seed was used as an example to try to 'refute the production of something from self', but the fact is that no matter what example one could care to utilise as one's example, it falls flat because no 'thing' that reproduces 'its own entity' produces something purely for it to be a clone of itself (except in the mechanised laboratories of human beings, using their self-will to alter the factors in Nature). All lives in Nature are produced for a purpose, and through the related activities, the species as a whole gradually evolves and changes. Even parents never manage to make their children perfect copies of themselves, no matter how hard they try.

So if the exponent did not properly consider what actually exists in Nature when using it as an example, then inevitably it means the theorem will be disproved. Another must be used, as the one called up actually tends to prove the existence of 'self', of individuality, and not the opposite. If the first postulate is groundless, then the remaining argument sinks into it. A foundation for a building built on soft sand inevitably spells the ruination for the entire edifice.

The argument also revolves around as to whether the sprout has destroyed the seed in growing up to become a sprout from its seed form. The opponent thus asserts:

> Having already attained its own entity and needing production are not contradictory.[13]

In relation to this the Mādhyamika states, presenting the 'absurdity of endless production':

> If so, then sprouts, and so forth would be produced again and again because though they have achieved their own entity, they must be produced...[14]It follows that a sprout would not cause its seed to disintegrate because the natures of the seed and the sprout are one. For example, a sprout cannot cause a sprout to disintegrate...[15]It follows that a seed and its sprout would not have different shape, colour, taste, powers, and fruition because the natures of the seed and its sprout are one in all respects.[16]

Note that I will only include what is inferred by the Sāmkhya's arguments if necessary, as they are quickly refuted by the Mādhyamika line of thought.

All that this disparagement between the oneness of the natures of the seed and sprout, and what is actually observed really posits, is the process of *change* as things evolve from an originating principle, just as the fertilised seed in a mother's womb grows into a child. It should be noted however, that the author may be referring to this changeability of everything with respect to the opponent's concept of 'self' as something permanent, thereby pointing out the error in his thinking.

The point also being made is if two things are one, of the same essential substance, then one cannot cause the other to disintegrate. Yet this is what appears to happen in Nature, as the seed disappears when the sprout appears. The next point is that if their nature was one in all respects, then there can be no difference between the form of the seed and the sprout, yet there is. The Mādhyamika is trying to relate this to the opponent's view of 'self' with respect to the personality, indicating an absurd situation if this 'self' is said to be of the same nature as the personality.

---

13 Ibid.

14 Ibid.

15 Ibid., 138.

16 Ibid.

What however is missed is that in reality the seed has not 'disintegrated', it has germinated and the plant formed has evolved from it, in accordance to the type of *saṃskāras* and genetics associated, which is implicit in its form. This means that a new seed can be produced upon maturity of the child, and the entire process started again. If the seed can be reproduced by the sprout after it has matured and the seed can produce a sprout, what indeed has been disintegrated? (From this perspective 'the seed and the sprout are one' in all aspects bar one, for the only real difference is *the point of time* whence we observe the process of the transformation of the one into the other. They are the same, but there is a difference during the process of time unfolding.) There is only evolutionary change, of the appearance of a thing, its reproduction, death, and then repetition of the cycle according to the auspices of the law of *karma* over the fullness of time.

Repetition of past patterns of events is a *modus operandi* of *karma.* The objective is so that eventually new attributes can appear. *Karma* thus manifests in relation to another law affecting *saṃsāra*, the law of cycles. Essentially this means that everything responds to cyclic processes. We have the zodiacal wheel turning because of the procession of the equinoxes; seasonal, and yearly cycles; some plants work according to a diurnal cycle, others according to an annual one, etc. Our hearts beat generally at 72 beats per minute, and we cyclically breathe oxygen in and out in order to stay alive. Every seven years the cells in our bodies are replenished, the sun has an 11 year sunspot cycle, and so forth. Also, as indicated above, there could be no manifestation of karmic law if this cyclic law did not cause happenings of the past to be re-enacted upon a higher cycle, nor can the process of rebirth be a fact. Consciousness also works in this way. Thoughts cyclically appear in consciousness to sustain our lives, such as the thought to eat meals, or to take the next step as one walks. Such thoughts reinforce habit patterns of all types (e.g., those producing social mores) and are generally hard to break.

The sprout is thus obeying this cyclic law (given the right conditions to do so) as it matures from seed to mature plant and back to seed again.

The point being made here is that the entire debate should really be centred around the question of *time,* what is time, how does time effect the transformations from seed to sprout and back to seed again, or the development from a defiled human consciousness to that of

Buddhahood. Seen from this perspective, time means evolutionary change. *Karma* can be considered the process of the progress of time in *saṃsāra*, manifesting according to the related cycles as a means to the resolution of seed causes originated in the mind of a thinker.

As the case for the transformation of a seed into a sprout, so also for an incarnate personal-I. An 'I' can incarnate as a seed and the gain of what it has achieved can later be reborn as a new "I' after its death. The sprout (sentient awareness), can mature into a healthy plant that flowers and the resultant seeds dispersed, carrying that gain. It is not a clone of what has gone before that is dispersed (though can be), rather the possibility of new genetic variance, i.e., new evolutionary traits manifest. The simile holds good for the human kingdom, but it is more than genetic variance that is dispersed here, but new *saṃskāras* and the potential for the development of enlightenment.

The statement 'the natures of the seed and the sprout are one' also has an inherent truism for all things. They are composed of atoms, also all things are subjectively built from any combination of the five Alchemical Elements. Living things are also constituted of integrated cellular units. This produces a coherent organism (or 'own entity') that satisfies the needs of all units composing it. Hence the organism breathes and responds to external stimuli in some way via the utilisation of the organelles of the body. In addition, all living things evolve either sentience, emotions, or consciousness states. Plants share the common faculty of possessing sap, and generally have green foliage. We can continue adding to the list of things shared by any species if we wish, but what is to be pointed out is the inherent oneness of all life, yet nothing causes anything else to *truly* 'disintegrate'.[17] One may prey upon another and cause its death, as happens myriads of times every day in Nature, but the species as a whole (another 'own entity') continues living, evolving, and changes accordingly over the course of time. All however, manifest interdependent actions with all others. They interrelate with each other and assist in the appearance and disappearance of each other. Even then there is oneness (e.g., how

17 Human destructiveness, the application of great heat, or of certain laws of geophysics, such as the effects of a nuclear explosion, may be considered exceptions to this rule. We must however always consider rebirth and forms of renewal of what was destroyed, like the phoenix rising out of the ashes of its own funeral pyre. Even universes can be considered to be reborn after their cyclic death process.

each species acts as a unitary grouping obeying the same instincts), yet there is manifold diversity or individuality within the concept of that oneness, and this point needs emphasising here. Oneness, individuality, and 'self', are virtually synonymous terms.

All factors in Nature posit the existence of unitary selves ('own entity'). Seed and sprout appear from each other, there is thus a oneness in their interrelated action, of the changes caused by genetics, environmental conditions around them, and nutrients, with respect to time. The appearance of one is the death of the other, but such an appearance gives virtual assurance that the other will be produced from it. So no seed in fact is annihilated, for the potential for the appearance of another is always there, as long as the three factors of right environment, nutrients, and necessary time are appropriately met. Natural disasters may even cause the disappearance of species, such as the dinosaurs. Even so, good may come from this. Dinosaur extinction, for instance, has paved the way for the appearance of mammals, allowing them to become the dominant species upon the planet, and from them evolved humans. Also, it has been proved that some dinosaurs evolved into birds. There is always evolutionary gain when the hand of Nature rightfully plays over time.

Change is the most predictable aspect of *saṃsāra*. It would not be *saṃsāra* without it, therefore any concept of a 'self' that does not include the principle of change is immediately questionable. This the Buddhist logician knows well, but the relative permanency of things that change should also be taken into account. This thesis of 'self' is thus based upon *relativity,* and *consciousness*. This concerns the relativity of a consciousness-form existing in the realms of consciousness that changes gradually over a vast evolutionary time in relation to the *saṃskāras* developed by personal-I's incarnate in manifest space. Each 'I' is one of a sequence of many that together help the consciousness-form to evolve. This form manifests in a similar way that the Heart *chakra* does, albeit in the highest realm wherein consciousness is possible.

In analysing the above argument, we can say that 'the seed' is the personal-I planted in the soil of *saṃsāra*, evolving from the mother's womb to become a child (the sprout), then adult (the mature plant). In this analogy the consciousness-form, from whence is emanated the personal-I, is depicted by the flower of the sprout that is capable of producing many seeds. This analogy holds a certain truism in it.

Hopkins states that a Sāṃkhya might respond thus:

> The natures of the seed and its sprout are one, but their states are different; therefore, the state of the seed is abandoned when the state of the sprout is assumed.
>
> Answer:
>
>> It follows that the nature of a seed is not the nature of its sprout because when the phenomenon of the state of the seed is done away with, there is the phenomenon of the state of a sprout. It so follows because the phenomenon of the state of the seed is the phenomenon of the seed and there is no phenomenon of the seed other than the entity of the seed[18]...Just as during the state of the sprout the seed is not apprehendable by a sense consciousness, so it follows that the sprout would be non-apprehendable.
>
> Further:
>
>> Just as during the state of the sprout the sprout is apprehendable by a sense consciousness, so it follows that the seed would also be apprehendable. For, the entity of the seed and the entity of the sprout are one in all respects.
>
> Because these consequences cannot be accepted, one should not assert that the natures of the seed and sprout are one.[19]

In reply we can say that the summary of the argument is not necessarily correct, because we can argue that this is but a corollary, or an adaptation of the fact of the thought that a man grows from being a child in its mother's arms, and from barely being able to respond to its environment, to a highly sophisticated Buddhist philosopher through the course of time. But what has really changed? The inference is that 'the child is the father of the man', it contains within its constitution the *saṃskāras* and *skandhas*, the sum total of the aggregates to come through the course of time. This is conditioned by the type of *karma* that will transform it into a man. It is the seed for all of the transformations to come. So it is also for the seed of the sprout. It has its own type of *saṃskāras* (gathered from past incarnations bound by group *karma*),

18 Ibid.

19 Ibid., 139.

the genetics that will inevitably drive the seed onwards through the process of time and the right environmental conditions, to become a sprout, and for that sprout to grow to become a mature plant, capable of reproducing the seed of its own kind.

The factors are similar in both cases:

1. Seed/child.
2. Time.
3. Genetics/*karma*/*saṃskāras*.
4. Right environmental conditionings/education.
5. Sprout/adolescent.
6. Maturity/reproduction.
7. Death.
8. Rebirth/repeat of cycle with added gain of past accumulation of experiences/sentience/consciousness.

So, is the nature of the child and the man one? The answer is yes and no. No, because the child is not the highly sophisticated philosopher; yes, because the child can become so, given the right fulfilment of the above conditions. For a human, taking the growth of the form from child to man being normally inevitable, there are seven main factors influencing this:

i) Time, ii) Right nutrients to sustain health and growth, iii) Environmental factors, iv) Education, v) Individualised *karma, saṃskāras* and genetics, vi) Intellect/consciousness, vii) Human free will.

For a plant, only four:

i) Time, ii) Nutrients, iii) Environmental factors, such as sun, rain, iv) Group *karma* (which is inclusive of inherent genetics and sentience).

In relation to the statement 'just as during the state of the sprout the seed is not apprehendable by a sense consciousness' we see that the process of the change from seed to sprout *can* be apprehended by a sense-consciousness over the duration of the time of the change, and retained in consciousness. If so, the two can be apprehended to be one, just as the child is in the man, even though the man has evolved beyond the child stage in consciousness and bodily form. The child is in the man because the *saṃskāras* it generated persist, and the actions it manifested can be remembered, and has influenced the progress of the man accordingly. The same goes for the sentience of the plant, on its own accord, on its own level. It does 'remember' its past, in the form of its genetic memory, and related sentience, and this influences its progress through the aeons of evolutionary time.

Even when the seed is a seed, we can easily visualise it as a sprout because we all have seen sprouts come from seedlings, and it is easy to rationalise the future of the seed, given the conditionings above. Everything concerning this process of change is 'apprehendable by a sense consciousness', and modern science has seen to it that we know the minutiae of the process of change from seed to sprout. So, even when a seed is not a sprout, it is prone to change, and in our mind's eye we *can* see it thus, because the mind can perceive things to be in the future, just as it can perceive things as they were in the past. From this we can see that the nature of the seed and sprout *are one,* in that they are part of a process of a continuum of change wherein one is productive of the other, as they have *the same essence/life flux*. It must be the particular life flux of that specific type of species of seed, and not any other, or of a human being, or of animals. It is the continuum of change that is important in life, not a static shot of when a seed is a seed and a sprout a sprout. What is *it* that makes one transform into the other should be the question in the minds of the Mādhyamika philosopher and his opponent. The snapshot view of the difference between a seed and a sprout is irrelevant. What is relevant is the process of evolutionary change as one grows into the other.

Again we have the concept of individuality in uniformity, the seed is an individualised species, though all different types of seeds are capable of producing sprouts. They are individualised, not just because of the different types of seeds, but because the plants that grow from them are all different, to fulfil Nature's marvellous biodiversity. Things are 'apprehendable by a sense consciousness' because they tend to repeat the same (cyclic) patterns of previous activity as members of that species. Thought can therefore predict the processes and outcomes to be. The cyclic changes can be viewed over time and projected, generally unfailingly, to the next generation of entities. The cyclic changes pertainable to human behaviour follow a similar general trend, as a child matures to adulthood.

By such arguments clearly, the production of something from a 'self', or from its own entity is a truism, because of the general predictability of the way all such individualised 'selves' manifest, providing the cycles of genesis, growth, death, and regeneration have been observed over a course of time. So where does this leave this Mādhyamika line of reasoning? Their logic is archaic and technically irrelevant, needing updating to be inclusive of modern thought. Reformation of thinking will produce a higher, more perceptive stance upon the spiry upwards path of constant change to enlightenment.

12

Non-production from Other

Inherently existing otherness and production

Next in Hopkin's book we have the heading *'Non-production from other.'*[1] It utilises the same sources as 'The Diamond Slivers'. The first of three ways to the refutation of the non-production from other is styled, *'Refuting both inherently existent otherness and inherently existent production.'*[2] The presented argument is:

> It follows that thick darkness arises from a tongue of flame and that any effect arises from what are commonly considered to be its causes or non-causes because inherently other effects arise in dependence on inherently other causes.[3]

This 'thick darkness' presumably refers to thick smoke, which obscures light, arising when flammable things are inefficiently burnt. Such smoke actually symbolises the confusion of mind that often ensues when new information (the 'tongue of flame') is presented to those who are set in their old ways and opinions. Resistance to transforming old into new ideas produces the 'smoke' of negative reactionary tendencies in consciousness.

---

1 Hopkins, *Meditation on Emptiness*, 140-148.

2 Ibid., 140.

3 Ibid.

If we eliminate the concept of smoke then it is an error to say that 'darkness arises from a tongue of flame'. Flame exists to dispel darkness and continues doing so even after the flame has gone out, as the waves of light generated continues to move through the darkness and accordingly modifies it, at light speed (186,000 miles per second). This action continues even though not perceptible to our senses. The point to be made here is that no action concerning the engendering of light (which counters ignorance) is wasted or disappears. It remains and continues to modify phenomena, even if the originating perpetuator is not aware of it. The effects of light can be considered waves of *karma* that ripple out as cause-effect deep into the *māyā* that constitutes the substance of things. Mantras effectively work this way. It is the basis of their efficacy.

Despite the imagery of darkness arising from flame, the point made that 'inherently other effects arise in dependence on inherently other causes' is correct. The reasoning is exemplified below, in relation to the objection a proponent of the production of 'other' presents:

> Though cause and effect are inherently other, an effect which is a cause is able to produce is the effect of that cause, and a cause which is able to produce that effect is the cause of that effect. A sprout of rice is not produced from a barley seed and is not produced from its non-producers, such as the future moments of its own continuum. A sprout of rice is produced from that which is included in its same continuum and from producers that are prior to it. Therefore, everything is not produced from everything.

Answer:

> This is not correct; once cause and effect are inherently other, this otherness must be their mode of being. Once otherness is their mode of being, they must be utterly non-related. Thus, it is not possible for a rice seed and a barley seed to be different with respect to whether they can produce a shoot of rice or not because they both are inherently other than a rice shoot.

Further:

> A seed is not inherently other than a sprout because a seed has no inherently existent otherness. It so follows because if a seed were

> inherently other than its sprout, then it could not be a dependent existent or nominal other. It would necessarily have a separate entity of otherness such as is mistakenly propounded by the Vaisheṣhikas.

Further:

> A seed and its sprout are not inherently other because a sprout does not exist simultaneously with its seed. It so follows because if they existed inherently, they would neither depend on nor be affected by anything. They would never disappear, and thus the sprout would have to exist even at the time of the seed. However, they do not exist simultaneously because without a transformation of the seed there is no production of a sprout. Thus, a seed and its sprout are not inherently other, and production of a sprout from a seed does not exist inherently. For this reason, one should forsake the thesis that things are produced from inherently existent others.[4]

It should be noted here that cause and effect are *not* inherently 'other', they are mutually co-dependent and flow from each other, until self will is activated. Then new causes can be created, but on close examination any new cause is the result of any one of a potpourri of former effects. In fact there can be no cause without an effect because if there was no effect it would not be the cause of anything. It goes without saying that an effect presumes a cause. So how can they be 'inherently other', they are mutual extensions of the one thing that has a dual mode of expression (or multiple modes of expression) over time? From another perspective the two sides of a face may appear to be 'inherently other' when viewing them from opposite angles, but when viewed from the point of view of looking at the face as a whole, together they constitute the face, but it would not exist if either of these 'sides' were removed. One half of a face may exist but not the full face. The interpretation of things therefore depends upon the angle of vision one chooses to view those things, or that one may have limited vision through ignorance. The angle of vision, or even the way one chooses to perceive something, is all important. We thus manifest different viewpoints in our analysis of phenomena.

---

4 Ibid., 141-142.

The phrase 'once cause and effect are inherently other, this otherness must be their mode of being. Once otherness is their mode of being, they must be utterly non-related' can now be commented upon.

First, they are not inherently other. (Leaving aside for the moment the definition of the word 'inherently' given above, of neither depending on being affected by anything, causing them to 'never disappear'.)

Second, nothing can be viewed in isolation, everything has its basis in past conditionings, many streams of which can come together to make any one incident of cause and effect. For example, the mere fact that one suddenly closes one's eyes seems to be independent at first glance of any realm of causes, other than the mental desire to act thus, but the underlying cause of closing one's eyes, necessitates having eyes and a physical body to do so. This is a body that must be fed, it must breathe, and possess a consciousness that can think, that has placed that body in an environment which one closes one's eyes to. That environment also has many factors or stimuli affecting the consciousness that shuts the eyes.

If cause and effect were 'utterly non-related' then there would be no such thing as 'cause and effect', nothing could be. It is the very definition of the relation of cause to effect that allows us to define one as a cause and the other as an effect (of that cause), and also to distinguish a time line of past—present—future.

The author has separated cause from effect in his thinking, implying that they are 'other' because one disappears when the other appears, but does not the effect carry the seed of the cause with it? Has not the effect grown from the cause, like the man from the child? Thus there is no real ending of cause, just its continuum in the effect, until eventually all cycles of cause and effect are transmuted and resolved into *śūnyatā*. So how can they be 'utterly non-related', if it is an impossibility? They are constituted of the same *skandhas*, part of the same stream of *saṃskāras* and are related also on the time line, like a seed growing into a sprout, and that sprout into a tree. Therefore the definition of the word *inherently,* that they would neither depend on nor be affected by anything, is not applicable to anything other than *śūnyatā* (except maybe space). But it is not *śūnyatā* that we are analysing here, but aspects of *saṃsāra*, with phenomena, which by definition is affected by things and comes and goes through time. So the argument is correct if it is said that *śūnyatā* is the phenomenon being discussed, with nothing more said or analysed. However, this is not the case. So if the term 'inherently' is interpreted as that which exists as a permanent and inseparable element, quality, or an attribute of something, that 'something' then is *śūnyatā*. If we eliminate the term 'inherently existent', or 'inherently other' from the argument, hence the focus upon absolute truth, then we can continue with a logic demonstrating the veridical nature of conventional truth that is productive of enlightenment.

The past is the cause, the present is the process of cause becoming an effect, and the effect is the future, which is but the seed for a new cause, or sequences of them, because of the multifarious, multidimensional nature of consciousness that must register both cause and effect, if anything, including consciousness, is to exist at all.

In examining the phrase 'A seed and its sprout are not inherently other because a sprout does not exist simultaneously with its seed', we see that the logic here is that some thing can be defined as 'other' (only) if they both exist simultaneously, but have different characteristics. The seed and sprout do not exist simultaneously and therefore cannot be considered 'other'. One can have a seed and a sprout existing simultaneously that are other (by placing a seed next to a sprout), but this is not the point made. The sprout that has grown from a seed is not inherently 'other' from the seed, as already explained. It does not need to be so in order to signify the existence of a 'self', it just needs to be of similar nature and exist on the same consciousness-stream of evolutionary journeying. Within this broad statement there are differences that can be described.

The roots and branches of a tree, for instance, may appear inherently 'other', as one exists under the ground and the other waves in the air. Their natures appear very dissimilar, yet both are part of the same tree; neither could exist without the other. They are mutually co-dependent. The seed first sends down roots and then shoots for the making of leaves. We therefore see a process happening through time, which will inevitably produce a seed again. In this analogy we can even posit the existence of a 'self' that can be considered as the entire tree that produces many cycles of seeds throughout the years, and is capable of observing its seeds grow into trees, and they likewise bear further seeds. (Therefore viewing the cycle repeating itself again and again.)

Is our angle of vision but one still frame of a moving picture, as when looking at a sprout and seed existing non-simultaneously; or are we to view the entire movie, where the transformation of the seed into a sprout, the sprout into a tree, and the tree producing seeds, can be seen in perspective? (In fact the entire process can be viewed in one moment of visual flash in the mind's eye, where the seed and the sprout can be observed simultaneously.)

It should also be noted that a seed is *only* the possibility of a sprout, as it may never mature to sprout, whilst the sprout is the death of the seed, but it has the possibility of producing a new one. They do not have to exist simultaneously to be 'other', they simply have to be seen to exist separately on the time line. For instance, my former incarnation as a woman in a past time zone, is *not* my incarnation now as a man, though the woman incarnation can be viewed as a seed for the later male incarnation. The latter can be said to be produced from the former, with other causes flowing from other sources to make the complete man. A thing that is 'produced from inherently existent others' thus stands correct—*if* mutual co-dependency is acknowledged and placed within a moving time line, and the word 'inherently' is eliminated. There are 'things' and there are 'other things' and they can be interrelated by moving lines of causes and effects to produce new 'things', like a blacksmith forging a sword out of a lump of iron.

The position presented is that all causes and effects are interdependent. A seed cannot grow into a sprout without the right environmental conditions: water, soil, sunlight, all with the right qualifications. Sufficient water is needed for the seed to sprout, but not to flood the leaves, soil with the right nutrients is needed, not too acidic or alkaline, the right amount of sunlight, not too hot if it is a shade loving plant, and so forth.

Because of the interdependent nature of the relation of things, *saṃsāra* can exist and function as it does. Each factor in the chain of interdependence can be considered a cause of the production of any thing. The sum of the biosphere of which we are a part must be taken as a unit if we are to understand the role any entity plays in it. For example, what is known as a human being could not evolve without the factor of air that he breathes, and a fish could not be without the water it swims in. It is all these other things or factors in the environment that defines what we are. We are humans because that over there is defined as a mineral, animal, plant, or 'other'. Because there are animals and plants, so we humans can come to be. From this perspective they produce us, as the food that is digested in our bellies. Thus there really is no 'other', we are basically all One, but within that unity there is the multifarious categories of 'other'. The *karma* of one is integrated with that of the other. There are aggregates (*saṃskāras* and *skandhas*) inherent within the being, and external to the being, and everything is interrelated. Otherwise any human society could not evolve, for all people belonging to that society have *karma* with each other, and that society has karmic interrelations with the sum total of human civilisation on this planet. So the concept of 'non-production from other' is really inconceivable, as all 'others' are helping to produce all 'others' all of the time.

In fact, the path to enlightenment consists in karmically extracting oneself away from the 'others' so that one can rise above the mass conditioning of general human society and master the related qualities. It concerns going inwards to embrace the aggregates constituting the personal-I and riding them forwards in time, via the transmutative process (within the I-consciousness), until they no longer exist in terms of the 'I' and the other.

The statement therefore that 'one should forsake the thesis that things are produced from inherently existent others—if so they would neither depend nor be affected by anything' does not quite hold true, because these 'others' exist all around. They inherently exist whilst *saṃsāra* exists, and such existence is based upon interdependence, which is *all* there really is, making a unity, a oneness. (Even *śūnyatā* and *saṃsāra* are interdependent, according to Nāgārjuna.) As previously stated, that which is 'inherent' is the principle of Life, where 'Life' is defined as that principle that survives the death of the bodily form, and which produces the evolutionary path to Buddhahood.

The truth of the matter is that the way 'things are produced' lies fluidly as a fusion of the existence of others, their non-inherent existence when expressed in terms of *śūnyatā*, and the interdependency between the one and the other, the reality and non-reality, as part of the fabric of space that unifies them all. Thus the 'others' are in reality part of a oneness that is the universe unfolding. But its phenomenological aspects can be transcended through consciousness eliminating its ties to all such conditionings. However, everywhere that consciousness could envision the principle of Life, consciousness persists and is inherent in all.

Inherently existent production

The next subject concerns:

Refuting inherently existent production

> If the entities of the phenomena that are effects, such as sprouts, do not exist in their causes either collectively or individually or as things other than their causes, then the entities of the effects to be produced do not exist prior to their production. If so, how could production from the other exist?[5]

Hopkin's commentary to this (in part) is:

> The activity of approaching production exists at the time of the cause's approaching cessation, and since the effect must exist along with its activity, the seed and the sprout would have to exist simultaneously. This is impossible because simultaneity would rule out that the one produced the other. If the sprout were already existent, what could a seed do to produce it?[6]

The activity of the 'approaching production' may be considered to exist at the time of the causes 'approaching cessation', but such activity is a process of becoming over a time sequence. Until the appropriate moment in time has been reached when production has actually been accomplished, there is *neither* production nor cessation of anything, and indeed this may never be accomplished, as some unforseen factor may come into play preventing such a happening. Therefore to say 'the effect must exist along with its activity, the seed and the sprout would have to exist simultaneously' is incorrect, because if there is *neither* production nor cessation of anything then neither seed or sprout is really existing at that time, maybe something in between, but neither the originating

5 Hopkins, 142.

6 Ibid.

seed nor the finished sprout exists. The seed, for instance, has changed, taken in moisture, and undergone the internal bio-chemical reactions that will transform it into a sprout. Simultaneity, consequently, is not a factor of consideration here, just one of transformation over time. In our philosophical language we can say that the *saṃskāras* of sprout production flow into the etheric-physical aggregates that will constitute the new form, though in a somewhat modified way. The steel that the blacksmith hammers into a sword still remains steel, though now with more tensile strength, and is in the shape of a sword. In a sense the lump of iron and the sword exist simultaneously, in that the iron that made the one is common to the other.

In the case of a seed and sprout, the reality is not the form, as that is illusional, but *its sentience* (like the steel that is both the iron and the sword) exists (simultaneously) in the seed and the sprout. It is that which produces the continuum of transference from seed—sprout—maturation—seed (etc.). The sentience is inclusive of the entire process.

In reality, we have the process of continuous change, the old forms disappear, like snow on the water, to meld into the new form's construction. They do not cease *per se,* because the *saṃskāras* still exist, though modified somewhat. The snow has melted and raised the level of the lake that contains it. If enough melts at once then there is a flood, with dire consequences. So also it is with the *saṃskāras.* Have they been accumulated in the new situation (called 'creation') or modified in such a way as to produce a flowering of pleasant scenery?

The concept of 'approaching production' or 'approaching cessation' is really a misnomer, as there is either production of one (e.g., 'flood') and cessation of the other (e.g., 'snow'), or a transforming flow of one to the other. (There is no real 'approaching' process, though the use of the figure of speech to describe a phenomena that should happen over a period of time, given certain conditions to be in place, is correct.) Both cases prevent the simultaneous appearance of 'seed and sprout', flood and peaceful lake, bar of iron and sword, etc. The phrase 'transforming flow' really means 'inherently existent production' because the process of transformation is inherent in changes of all types, and all changes are a production of something from something else. Change is 'inherently existing', because that is the nature of the *saṃskāras* underlying all forms of manifesting phenomena.

If this 'inherently existing' does not exist, then a Buddha could not predict the future lives of anyone, or of the appearance of the next Buddha to be. The patterns of the future (forms) already exist (i.e., are inherent) in the seeds of the past actions, and are simply to be moulded accordingly as the way that consciousness, or sentience, evolves.

From this perspective, that which is to be, both the seed and the sprout, already exists. (That is, they exist simultaneously.) The sprout/plant is the potential of the seed actualised. The blacksmith already has the idea of the sword in his mind as he hammers the iron. The falling of a sufficient quantity of snow precludes the appearance of a flood. The germination of a seed is productive of the form of the plant to be. The paradigms (i.e., conditionings) for all of these things exist prior to their actualising.

If the philosophy were properly extended, then we would see that it is consciousness of some type that determines the paradigms for each eventuation:

a. The sentience of a plant (yet to evolve self-awareness)—the collective action of group *karma*.
b. The conscious volitions of humanity—the production of individualised *karma;* the personal-I leading to the I-consciousness.
c. The superconsciousness of a Buddha embodying a world sphere, such as ours, as part of his Dharma field, or Body of Manifestation. Individual *karma* has been transcended, and this determines the evolutionary course of Nature as a whole, the laws governing planetary *karma*.

Inherently existing otherness

The third of the ways of refuting production is presented thus:

Refuting inherently existing otherness

> If the effect's own entity does not exist at the time of the cause, then there is no referent in relation to which the causes could become 'other'. Thus, there is no phenomenon of otherness in seeds and so forth, and so no production from other.[7]

7 Ibid., 143.

The problem here is the definition of 'the effect's own entity', as we see that this 'own entity' is both a free flowing mutability of *saṃskāras* as well as the appearance of things, such as sword or sprout. They are then experienced by sentience or consciousness, which delineate the appearance of things into forms. Consciousness then interprets such things in terms of objects of perception. So what then exists; the aggregates, the phenomenal form, or the consciousness/ sentience that contains it all? Or is it a fusion of all of these? All can be considered transient, thus can be said to 'not exist', but at the same time the phenomena appears for a duration of existence. It thus exists conventionally, and for the duration of its existence accordingly manifests as a 'thing'. This appearance can be named by a conscious unit, and when it does so then there is a 'referent', and what is named is 'other' to that which names. (Unless one follows Yogācāra philosophy, in which case all exists within one's mind. Nevertheless within that mind there are things that are delineated from other things.) For such a one the 'other' thus 'exists', because it acts as a *signpost* for consciousness whereby that consciousness can gain its bearings in the material world. It can thus interrelate with it, and accordingly act out its agenda and evolve.

The concept of 'own entity' therefore rests in the field of consciousness, which is not the mind *per se*, but that which inhabits a succession of minds from life to life, which I have termed the I-consciousness, and which will later be exemplified in terms of the *tathāgatagarbha*. If such an entity exists at the time of the cause then it is the referent with respect to that which is caused and consequently must pay the karmic consequences. If 'there is no referent' as this refutation implies then *karma* could not possibly exist because it must manifest in relation to something to which it refers in order to produce its reciprocal action. If one follows the logic of this refutation therefore, the existence of the laws governing the nature of appearance of the phenomena we see around us, both objectively and subjectively considered, would be non-existent, as such laws are also 'referents'. Chaos would be all that exists, and clearly this is not so.

We see therefore that the four possibilities of inherently existent production are *not* proved to be 'non-existent' by the logic presented by the Prāsaṅgika-Mādhyamika, neither are they proved to be existent, except as relatively so because the definition of the term 'inherently' must be substantiated with the philosophy of the integration of the two truths.

When we look to 'ultimate production of an existing effect', then because of the flowing *skandhas* and *saṃskāras* of cause and effect, of transience flowing from transience, we cannot find an *ultimate* existing effect other than *śūnyatā,* or of enlightenment. However, what is known as *śūnyatā* needs to be better defined or clarified in today's Buddhism, because all phenomena, the 'things' of the manifest universe, are inherently derived via it. The seed causes of all phenomena must derive from the real, the permanent; otherwise what is known as the universe and all that is analysed by intellects, known by consciousness and comprehended by the enlightened, could not find any base that would hold it all together long enough for any interrelation to happen in a meaningful way. What is known as the universe is actually far greater than modern science conceives, or perceived by the speculations of Buddhist philosophers. Inner space is vaster and even more meaningful than the outer space observed all around us.

Much like a seed is *śūnyatā,* it can be considered a seed of the sprout of the universe to be. A seed abides in itself, not dependent on anything other than itself for its existence, like *śūnyatā*. We know that the seed can be destroyed by the application of fire (or any strong force), but so also can the condition of *śūnyatā* if the obscuring passions of fiery human emotions arise. Like *śūnyatā*, with the passing of a Buddha to the 'other shore' of existence, the seed has absorbed into itself the fruition of a former cycle of activity. (Indeed, many former cycles of successive generations of incarnations of that species.) It has stored within it the potential for active expression, like the activity of great Bodhisattvas, who though abiding in the *śūnyatā* state, manifest their activities in the realm of forms.

This potential can also become actualised with the appearance of a sprout as a consequence of the application of the five Elements. Thus first it is planted in the Element Earth and we then need moisture (the Element Water), thence warmth (the Element Fire). These two together cause the seed to swell, to germinate and bud. Once the reservoir of nutrients in the seed have been utilised then we need added nutrients (the Element Air), which in the case of the germinating *śūnyatā* seed means the physical appearance of the Bodhisattva-child in the *saṃsāra*-Earth that can grow to the maturity needed to bear its potency (the ability of the plant to make new seeds). The Bodhisattva-child is not content merely to produce one seed (namely his/her own) but to awaken (i.e., produce) many other seeds (sentient beings) to the realisation of *śūnyatā*. This application of *bodhicitta* is the addition of the Element Air that is needed for the consequent growth of the sprout and the plant's proper interaction with the environment of which it is a part. Finally, we have its aspiration, its growth to sunlight, the development of the enlightenment-Mind through the conquering of the darkness of ignorance (represented by the conditions of the soil from which the plant grows)—the added bearing of the fifth Element Aether (the transmuted soil), the awakening to the *dharmakāya*.

The fundamental question is 'what causes the śūnyatā-seed to sprout?' The term 'sprouting' indicates the appearance of all that is known as *saṃsāra*. We see from the above that the first necessitating conditions are the application of water and warmth. We have consciousness implicated here, thus the bearing of 'originating cause' is much concerned with consciousness, its nature, function and purpose, and its relationship to *śūnyatā*. The nature of this relationship still needs to be adequately explored, because the basis to the evolution of what is known as consciousness needs to be investigated.

When analysing the third 'corner' of the 'four-cornered proof', the 'non-production from both self and other', Hopkins states that 'Each part of the dual assertion is refuted by the respective refutations of production from self and production from other already given'.[8] Therefore there is no need to add more here. Also, the fourth 'corner', the 'non-production causelessly', is also a self evident truth, as nothing can come about without causes. But again, the production with causes again posits 'something' to have produced them, i.e., a 'self-concept' utilising the will to do so, as no thing can come into existence, i.e., to move, without some force propelling it thereto. There is no such thing as a spontaneous generation of things coming out of nothing in *saṃsāra*. We do not espouse a nihilistic universe.

8 Ibid., 149.

13

The Four Extremes

Hopkins, in his *Meditation on Emptiness,*[1] presents the sources for this section as: 'Nga-wang-bel-den's *Annotations*, Chandrakīrti's *Commentary on the "Supplement."'*

Hopkins states that:

> The possibilities of inherently existent production are limited to four, and when these four are eliminated, the absence of inherently existent production is established.
>
> The reasoning in brief is:
>
>> An existent effect is not ultimately produced because whatever exists ultimately must always exist, and thus there would be no need for producers, that is, causes.
>>
>> A non-existent effect is not ultimately produced because if a non-existent effect were produced, the horns of a rabbit could also be produced.
>>
>> An effect which is both existent and non-existent is not produced because there is no such thing as an existent and non-existent effect; no one thing possesses contradictory natures.
>>
>> An effect which is neither existent nor non-existent is not produced because there is no such thing.[2]

1 Hopkins, 151.

2 Ibid., 151-2.

The four extremes concern the ultimate, i.e., the consideration from the viewpoint of *śūnyatā*. We thus can see that an existing effect is not ultimately produced as all these effects are transitory. They can not ultimately exist is a true enough statement, because somewhere along the time line they must cease to exist long before the ultimate is reached. Thus, from the point of view of ultimates nothing exists, apart from that which is ultimately attainable—*śūnyatā*, or the *dharmakāya*.

This may be so, but it is not the state or experience of the billions who have not yet achieved such a state. They live in a relativistic universe that exists in between the ultimates of the beginning and the ending of all that is perceivable. We must also look to the expediency of relativistic unities or permanency to find the means of approach to the ultimate. Without the existence of such relativistic unities or 'selves', the ultimate would not be obtainable or experiential.

Alternatively, if only the ultimate existed then there would be no need for the universe of causes and effects, in which case the billions of human lives and trillions of sentient entities upon this earth would immediately disappear. Clearly, this has not happened, and thus a universe filled with relativistic 'selves' is the reality that all philosophers must deal with and account for whilst incarnate in the realm of cause and effects. If they were one of those who actually resided in the ultimate, i.e., were fully enlightened Buddhas or Bodhisattvas, then they still would have to enter the relativistic universe if they wished to communicate with the consciousnesses and sentient entities trapped therein. There is no escaping this condition whilst the phenomenal realms exist with which one needs to be involved.

A non-existing effect is non-existing, thus what more can be said about it? However, we can ask such questions as 'is it a failed effect', i.e., an effect that never matured because the right conditionings for it were not there? 'Is it an effect that is non-existing because our expectations to look for it lie elsewhere?' That is, there was an effect that we did not notice because of:

a. We were looking in a different direction to its outcome.

b. We lacked the developed receptors, e.g., clairvoyance, in order to properly experience it, or to experience it at all.

c. That the entire process is a contrived fiction; there really is no effect.
d. That everything is transitory, therefore a new cause following effect happened so rapidly that it was below or beyond the event horizon of the perceiver.
e. We are thinking in terms of absolutes only; in which case nothing but absolutes exist. Therefore there is no need for consideration of causes and effects. All such are redundant.

We can clearly see from the above that what is non-existing to one can quite clearly be existing to another. Therefore, just because it is deemed to be 'non-existing' does not mean that it is thus. Radio and T.V. waves are non-existing to an ordinary human being until he/she turns on the appliances that can actually receive and translate the waves of energy into experiential phenomena for the human viewer or listener. Even the 'horns of a rabbit' exist in the mind of the one who imagines such a thing, because thoughts are things; otherwise *mantras, mūdras* and *dhāraṇīs* would have no power.

Śūnyatā is likewise imaginary until experienced, then it becomes the real and all things in the phenomenal universe are seen in terms of what is. That is, cause and effect still exist in the flux of mutability, but this is not *śūnyatā*, which exists in a paradigm beyond all that.

From one perspective 'An effect which is both existent and non-existent' exists because that can be considered a definition of *saṃsāra*. It exists conventionally for those that experientially gain from involvement with it, and it does not exist ultimately for those that reside in an ultimate state. We see therefore that everything must be viewed relativitistically, as our angle of vision determines how we define whatever is/is-not. Thus 'An effect which is neither existent nor non-existent' can also be considered to exist as the *saṃsāra-śūnyatā* nexus. We therefore cannot conclude that 'there is no such thing', but rather state that in the enlightened Mind all possibilities for anything are simultaneously existent and non-existent, are produced and non-produced, and therefore are experienced accordingly. All views are one view because no view is excluded, unless irrational.

Oṁ

14

The Four Alternatives and Refuting a Self of Persons

The Four Alternatives

The *Four Alternatives* are one of the main means of refuting 'inherent existence of phenomena' by the Prāsaṅgika. The Sources given by Hopkins are Nga-wang-bel-den's *Annotations,* and Geshe Gedün Lodrö's oral teachings.

> A product such as an eye consciousness is not ultimately produced because ultimately only one effect is not produced from only one cause, ultimately many effects are not produced from only one cause, ultimately only one effect is not produced from many causes, and ultimately many effects are not produced from many causes.

The very meaning of production mitigates against ultimate existence because 'ultimately existing' means 'existing through its own power'. If an entity's existence depends on production, the entity does not exist through its own power. Still, one's mind will not be captivated by this interesting reasoning unless one probes the refutation further[1]... An eye consciousness is chosen as the example because the three causes of the production of an eye consciousness are well known in Buddhist literature. An eye consciousness is caused by three factors: a visible form, an eye sense power, and a former moment of consciousness. A visible object—color and shape—causes an eye consciousness to be produced in the image of that object. An eye sense of power causes an eye consciousness to have the ability to apprehend colors and shapes

1 Hopkins, *Meditation on Emptiness,* 155-156.

> and not sounds, odors, and so forth. A former moment of consciousness causes an eye consciousness to be a conscious entity[2]...The refutation of the first alternative, that ultimately only one effect is produced from only one cause, is based on the fact that an eye sense power not only produces an eye consciousness but also produces its own next moment.[3]

As far as these alternatives go, which again depends upon the way one interprets the word *ultimately,* we are told that something that ultimately exists must be interpreted as meaning 'existing through its own power'. Again what is being referred to as an ultimate is *śūnyatā*, because only it can truly 'exist through its own power'. Consciousness can also 'exist on its own power', but it can also be said to be produced (which prevents it from being an ultimate), and space also 'exists on its own power', but a debate certainly can exist as to whether it is produced or not. Essentially what is being said is that because ultimately there is only *śūnyatā*, so ultimately whatever we look to has no substantiality, no reality, no factuality, and has not even been caused and has no results. In other words, whether it has existed or not is of little concern in the face of this 'ultimate'. Such an approach is like that of a child involved in a game of make-believe, acting out a game 'as if something has happened', i.e., that the ultimate is a reality right now, when in fact it is not immediately perceptible for the great majority of them or for humanity in general. In other words, following this logic is not a road that directly facilitates generating enlightenment, but it does help produce abstract thought, which is a positive step.

If we analyse the reality of the eternal NOW, which includes the past, the present, and the ultimate future, then these times are here viewed in the context of a unity, a plurality in one. From this perspective the concept that 'ultimately only one effect is produced from only one cause' can be refuted on the basis that if one could separate only one cause from the stream of causes and effects affecting anything, then it would be found to manifest a continuum of effects, all of which ultimately will lead to enlightenment. Such a continuum can be considered to 'exist under its own power', the gain of which is enlightenment.

---

2 Ibid., 156.

3 Ibid.

An example of what one could consider as a single cause is if a captain of a ship had suddenly gone blind and as a consequence steered his ship on to rocks and it sank. The cause here can be considered sudden blindness, with one effect, the sinking of the ship. But in reality this is not the case, as the causes for the sudden blindness must be taken into account—former alcohol or drug intake, sudden disease, etc. There are also subsidiary causes for the sinking of the ship, such as the size of the rock hit, the momentum of the ship, for only if there was sufficient momentum could the ship hit the rock with sufficient force to sink the ship, and the strength or weakness of the hull. Many causes to one effect, but that effect produces many subsidiary causes—e.g., the number of people that actually drowned verses those that could swim to safety, or who were rescued. Each then produce subsidiary effects, as those that drown are retrieved, mourned, and buried, and those that survive go on with their lives, totally involved in manifesting a plethora of causes and effects.

An insect lands on a man, and he swats it, killing it. This can be considered a single cause, the swatting of the insect that landed, and a single effect, the death of the insect. The causes, however, again are many, e.g., what caused the insect to land on the man in the first place? Indeed, what caused the insect to be in the area where the man was? What caused the man to be there? What caused the man to automatically swat the insect? Was it because of immediate pain, or because he was bitten before by insects and has an inherent fear of insects? Such considerations of a plethora of causes and effects seed the basis for the concept of the refutation of the 'inherent existence of phenomena'. Continuous changes prevents an inherent existence of the things constituting phenomena, but not the principle of Life that is clothed by that phenomena. Such a principle progressively evolves towards Buddhahood through experiencing these changes.

As previously stated, to find the origination of the causation of things, one would ultimately have to speculate upon the origination of a universe, such as what we all reside in. However in reality one does not have to prove how such a universe was caused, the mere fact that we reside in one and that its effects can be observed by consciousness suffices. From this perspective we find that only one cause for the first alternative is difficult to establish. Of course the key word here is 'inherent', meaning 'permanent', which because of its transience brings us back to the concept of relative permanence.

In theorising only 'one cause' for the second alternative—'that ultimately many effects are produced from only one cause', it cannot conclusively be denied, as there may only be one cause for the beginning of this universe, and we cannot prove what preceded it. As previously stated however, logically the rebirthing principle also governs its appearance. We could similarly also look to a single cause to the appearance of a thing, such as the forging of a sword by a blacksmith. Our analysis would depend upon how we define a single cause.

The third alternative 'that ultimately only one effect is produced from many causes', may be correct if that effect is considered to be enlightenment, liberation *(śūnyatā)*. Of course, a person can make a profound or temporal decision to do something, or change his/her course in life, based on many causes. That decision can be 'singular', e.g., to become a doctor, or to go swimming, but inevitably the effects are many, and the *saṃskāras*, the resultant *karma* flows on.

It should also be noted concerning the 'eye consciousness' that if any of the 'three factors' governing this consciousness are missing, or impaired, then there is no eye consciousness, blindness ensues. To think in terms of phenomena affecting just one of these three factors cannot therefore be considered. All three are necessary for the impact of any perceived phenomena to make impression in the mind's eye, to affect consciousness. It is a truism to say that the person thinks as the eye perceives. The eye consciousness is a central factor to the establishment of an I-concept, as the mind formulates a concept of the 'I' according to what it sees around itself, and which it perceives as different to itself.

The time line and the first argument

The *fourth alternative* preventing a product to be produced is that 'ultimately many effects are not produced from many causes'. There are three main arguments presented. The first is:

> It might be said that a composite of the three causes ultimately produces the three attributes and that the three attributes are not ultimately different but only appear to the mind to be different. Then, because they would actually exist one way but appear another way, they would be false and thus could not be truly existent. Further, if

> the three attributes are not different and do not appear to be different to any mind, the three attributes would be one, and it could not be said that many causes produce many effects.[4]

Here the statement refers to an 'eye consciousness', where 'the three causes of the production of an eye consciousness are well known in Buddhist literature. An eye consciousness is caused by three factors: a visible form, an eye sense power, and a former moment of consciousness'. These three factors can then be applied to all of the sense-consciousnesses. Once the falsity of believing in the 'reality' of a physical form, the mechanism of an eye to perceive phenomena, and the consciousness that registers that perception has been proven, then the illusionality of everything concerning consciousness can be established. So the logic goes, that ultimately there is no true existence of these things. Ultimately the characteristics of all attributes can be stripped bare, to show the 'sameness' or 'oneness' of their being, where *śūnyatā* is all that remains.

What the commentator however misses here is the time line, that this 'ultimate attribute' is far into the future of the manifestation of the presented phenomena. This 'line' involves a consideration of the process that 'strips bare', of how the ultimate is attained.[5] Whichever way this process is analysed it necessitates the (middle) factor of consciousness to manifest an action of continuous refinement of characteristics over time.

What one does when experiencing any phenomena is to experience it in the now. This concerns the way the *saṃskāras* of the thing or cause actually manifest, before the quality called enlightenment is attained, allowing the true nature of the phenomena to be thoroughly ascertained. Such an observation concerns the way phenomena manifests in terms of cause and effect, and of how consciousness interacts with whatever form phenomena presents itself. If ultimates are desired then we would have to negate consciousness, in which case the phrase 'three attributes are not ultimately different but only appear to the mind to be different' would be seen to be redundant, as there would be no mind to perceive anything, either the same or different.

---

4 Ibid., 158.

5 The 'time line' manifests within the context of the law of cycles, which concerns the appearance (rebirthing) of the *karma* of any action upon higher cycles of expression.

So let us not skip the process of getting to the future in our cognition, as if we were already there, but rather, look at the process of getting there. In this process these three attributes actually are different, because that is the way the mind perceives and experiences them, and it is the way the *saṃskāras* manifest and affect consciousness. Maybe consciousness is endeavouring to peel away the *saṃskāras* so that their attributes are thoroughly refined, but the ability for consciousness to evolve such capabilities takes much evolutionary time. During that time we are stuck with a multiplicity of causes and effects affecting consciousness. Ultimately, that consciousness will perceive the non-dual nature of *śūnyatā.*

The line of reasoning presented is like someone picking up a rock and throwing it into yonder lake and then saying that the rock does not exist, because it has sunk into the water and consequently is out of view of the eye consciousness. But this is not so, the rock can be retrieved, and if thrown at the person and it hits him on the head, would he then purport its non-existence? Maybe, after the pain has subsided, or if he had lost consciousness altogether. But the fact is, the rock has had an effect upon his consciousness, has modified his thought process in some way, and thus is an existent irrespective of what he thinks about tomorrow.

It should also be noted that consciousness evolves, and a highly developed consciousness that can transform attributes from things into enlightenment does not simply come from nowhere. It has generated the capacity to do so over time. Very few upon this earth have developed such capacity. Those that have Know, and for them *sūtras* etc., are redundant. The great majority of people however must come to such perception, ultimately, and for them we must write the truth, from all angles of presentation or viewpoints, so that they too can transform *saṃskāras*, so that ultimate truth can be viewed for what it truly is.

The statement 'because they would actually exist one way but appear another way, they would be false and thus could not be truly existent' hints at what generally happens with normal human perception, because something may exist one way but consciousness perceives it in another way. This is especially so when the emotions are involved. Because consciousness perceives something falsely does not necessarily make the consequences wrong. The perceiver's consciousness may be shrouded with ignorance, but the forms of (false) impressions may help paradoxically to eliminate some layer or aspect of that ignorance, as there are differing degrees of ignorance involved with everything concerning *saṃsāra*. That consciousness may perceive something falsely in some way, does not mean that that thing may not be truly existent. Can consciousness cloud over the experience of *śūnyatā* for instance? We can also say that whatever helps consciousness to overcome the shackles or burdens to enlightenment in some way or another is existent enough, and is 'true' for its purposes. In any case absolute truth has already been determined to be truly existent, and conventional truth, which these alternatives are actually endeavouring to deny its factual basis, is simply a method of arriving at the absolute conclusion.

The statement concerning 'a composite of the three causes' that 'ultimately produces the three attributes and that the three attributes are not ultimately different but only appear to the mind to be different' can now be focussed upon. Again the term 'ultimately' is used, referring to the state of *śūnyatā*. Also if the phrase 'truly existent' refers to *śūnyatā*, because only it can be thus, then there is no need for any rhetoric or syllogism, because again we have been led to the ending of things, where nothing whatsoever designated as 'things' can be. If one constantly looks only to the ending then for what purpose do we bother to analyse anything whatsoever? There is then only one word in our philosophic vocabulary—*śūnyatā*, and to talk about anything else is meaningless. The statement 'all things are empty' is a truism from this absolute perspective. If however we are analysing the perception of things, then this statement can be erroneous, because to normal human consciousnesses such emptiness is not perceived at all. If it is perceivable then we must analyse the consciousness that does so.

Also, if somebody is talking about anything at all then *śūnyatā* is not being expressed. Speech comes from consciousness, not *śūnyatā*. Clearly there is more to existence, or to 'true existence' than just *śūnyatā*. There is also the *śūnyatā-saṃsāra* nexus to ponder upon, which should lie at the heart of all our philosophical discussions. The consciousness pertaining to *saṃsāra* may be transcended in an enlightened Mind. Even so, whatever consciousness formerly experienced can be perpetually remembered in the eternal NOW, if need be at the *śūnyatā-saṃsāra* nexus. Ultimately therefore, such experiences are not lost, as *bīja* forms of these consciousness attributes are truly existent in the enlightened

Mind. They may not be experienced in *śūnyatā* (the 'ultimate' referred to above), but one can recollect it all in *dharmakāya*. *Dharmakāya* is what is evoked and lies at the heart of this nexus.

With respect to this, I have already stated earlier, that the 'four conditionings' from verse 1.2 of Nāgārjuna's *Mūlamadhyamakakārikā* can be considered 'truly existent' for the duration of the existence of *saṃsāra*. In relation to this I stated:

> The conditionings are the four indicated in verse two: the Void Elements, the *bījas*, the *ālayavijñāna*, and *māyā*. He then states that they are 'not self made'. An interpretation of this statement is that they are always existent in one form or another, which is an important consideration bespeaking of much esotericism.

It is the factuality of these 'four conditionings' that allows the expression of such things as *mantras* to be effective. Rightly and effectively intoned mantras produce enlightened states of awareness, and do reveal the Void of things. Indeed, they resonate through the Void. For this reason the subject of their invocation and evocation is an esoteric gnosis.

Now, if 'the three attributes are not different and do not appear to be different to any mind, the three attributes would be one' then there could not possibly be any talk of 'three attributes', there could only be mention of one attribute. The entire statement is in the form of a philosophic *en passant*, though to give the author credence, he wrote thus to fulfil the rules of debate of his time.

The second and third arguments

The second argument is presented as:

> If the three attributes are ultimately different, it would follow that an eye consciousness and the three attributes of an eye consciousness would be ultimately different. Then, since the composite of the three causes produces the three attributes, one would have to find a cause for the consciousness which is different from them. Furthermore, an eye consciousness and its three attributes are not ultimately different because if they were, the wisdom realizing suchness would have to perceive them as different since difference would be their mode of being, but it does not.[6]

---

6 Hopkins, *Meditation on Emptiness,* 158.

If the three attributes are ultimately different, would it follow that an eye consciousness and the three attributes of an eye consciousness be ultimately different? (They are of course different, but not ultimately so, because ultimately all rests in the field of consciousness, which persists long after the body, and the eye sense-perceptor, has died and consciousness has moved on from the ephemeral place of sense contact.) This however is irrelevant, because it was earlier stated that if any of the factors concerning eye consciousness are missing or impaired then there is no eye consciousness, blindness ensues. Thus to think in terms of any phenomena affecting just one of these factors is not a consideration. These factors must be viewed as one factor only for the purpose of manifesting consciousness. Also, there would be no possibility of an 'ultimate difference' if the 'ultimate' that is envisioned here is the Void. Ultimately they would all be unified in the being/non-being state associated with the Void.

Two types of 'ultimates' have here been posited, one is a relative ultimate, the I-consciousness, and the other can be considered an absolute ultimate *(śūnyatā)*. How these two ultimates are interrelated is the real question that should be asked here.

Consciousness may acknowledge the existence of 'three factors', but it manifests actions or reactions in the realm of thought as if there is only one. A wisdom realising Suchness in fact will perceive the visible form and instantaneously interpret it from as many different views as is possible. (Such as from the perspective of the two ultimates, and then include the perspective of *dharmakāya.)* The 'eye sense power' and a former moment of consciousness being irrelevant, are below the threshold of awareness for such a wisdom. This does not mean that they do not exist, but that their functioning is automatic and therefore is not part of the consideration of an enlightened being. The truth of the visible form, its past and future, will be viewed concurrently from a multidimensional perspective by one with such wisdom. The wise one could however look at the mechanism of the 'eye sense power' separately and also the nature of the former moments of consciousness that had perceived such phenomena. Because a person with 'wisdom realizing suchness' can do this, it means that these three attributes are separate and distinct, but are viewed as one process of consciousness registering some fact of manifesting or appearing phenomena.

One would not have to 'find a cause for the consciousness which is different from them' because though all perception happens in the field of consciousness, it also differs from that which it is perceiving. This is because what is affected when considering consciousness is the substance of the mind. It has its own laws, relegated to refined subtlety, and moves at the speed of thought, whereas physical plane phenomena obeys different laws relegated to concretion and the speed of light as it travels through space. (Giving us the ability to register colour and form.) Physicists state that this speed (almost 300,000 kilometres per second) is the fastest anything can travel in the phenomenal world. Consciousness is not limited to this finite speed, nor to the laws governing the material universe. A proof of this is that when a body dies, or else is asleep, consciousness persists, though the phenomenal form has ceased to function. Also a person can imagine anything of the far distant past, for instance, or retrieve such information (e.g., images from past lives) far faster than it would take light to travel that time sequence. Indeed, *saṃskāras* are retrieved at speeds concommitent with or faster than that of light, otherwise they would be too late to influence actions involving the eye consciousness and the effects of the physical form as they are happening.

We could also look to the example of an insect biting one at the same time that a rock is thrown towards one's head and broken shards of glass below one's feet that one could tread upon if one is not very careful. All three sets of phenomena must be quickly computed by the indwelling consciousness, to be seen as three different factors, not one, and each responded to in a different way by the consciousness which is definitely different from them, because consciousness has had to simultaneously make the computations of the realistic effects of the rock, glass, and insect upon it, and thence how to respond to each in turn. To do this it has had to consciously identify with the natures of all three and then to ascertain their affect upon the sum total of what makes the person in its response. If it was identical to them, then such computations would not have been made, in fact no response need be made at all because they would not harm him. For example, if he simply imagined such an eventuation of insect, glass, and rock all striking him at once, he will not suffer from it, simply because his consciousness created such images with *its own substance,* but this is not the case when dealing with the external phenomenal world.

The third argument given is:

> Moreover, an eye consciousness would be produced by a visible form because its being generated in the image of the object is produced by the form. Also, an eye consciousness would not be produced by a visible form because its being a conscious entity is not produced from a visible form. An eye consciousness is not a different entity from its attribute of being produced in the image of its object and also it is not a different entity from its attribute of being a conscious entity. Therefore, it would be both produced from a visible form and not produced from a visible form.[7]

The statement 'an eye consciousness would not be produced by a visible form because its being a conscious entity is not produced from a visible form' is incorrect from the point of view of that a conscious entity is largely the result of being produced from an innumerable number of visible forms, many of which it has interacted and responded to in some way. Consciousness is constituted of myriads of such interrelations with visible forms that it contains in its memory banks. When it chooses it can recall any of the individual images that are the basic building blocks of the movies it creates in the mind. It can add to these, distort or remove them, according to the way it chooses to utilise its imaginative faculty, but its basic building blocks to do so are the perceptions gained through interrelation with visible forms. We could also say that without such interactions consciousness as we know it would not exist. (Consciousness is also 'produced' by the data and sensory input from the remaining four sense-consciousnesses, smell, taste, etc.)

The argument implies that the eye consciousness being both 'produced from a visible form and not produced from a visible form' can be considered absurd and allows the inherent existence of phenomena to be refuted. But is it actually absurd? The eye consciousness is produced from a visible form when stimulated by any form of phenomena. But we can also consider a case when the visual stimulus is not there but the imagination steps in and produces images in the mind's eye based upon former sensory input. In such a case one could say that though the revelry may be seeded by the visual form, the resultant imagery is not an expression of that visible form. We therefore see that such a

7 Ibid.

consciousness can be produced and not produced by a visible form. A visual form can certainly stimulate a recollection of a similar image, or inspire a completely fabricated revelry. However we see that there is an inherent time line of a stimulus producing an immediate effect rather than simultaneity. Simultaneity therefore is a non-happening, and if a simultaneous occurrence of the appearance of production and non-production from a visible form is implied, then the author is correct. Consciousness always functions via sensory input with respect to a time line. It can also function meditatively within the eternal Now, where time is not a consideration, but then higher factors are expressed than that of the sense-consciousnesses. Simultaneity is then possible as sensory input may not be a factor of expression.

Hopkins states with respect to the above three statements that:

> The pivot around which these consequences turn is that if an eye consciousness were ultimately the same entity as its attributes, it would be one with its attributes in all respects. Such are the conditions that an object findable under analysis must fulfil; if the sameness of an eye consciousness with its attributes is its inherent nature, how could it also be different from these attributes?[8]

However, the argument given is irrelevant, because we are considering *a conscious entity*; it can function whether that visible form is there or not to stimulate consciousness. To prove that, one needs simply to close one's eyes and see with the inner eye, the visual stimulus of memory and imagination. The imagination is a combination of what has been gained from the visual form, plus that which has been added by the mind. Both are utilised, therefore what is in the mind's eye is a concoction made up of its own creative will and the images derived from physical form. One does not stop thinking simply because the visible form is not there. The eye consciousness is the consciousness gained from what the eye perceives, so if the eye perceives nothing, then the consciousness gains nothing at that time from the eye, that is all; but if the eye perceives an image then consciousness can work with that and build upon it if need be. But the eye consciousness is not those attributes, it is more than those attributes when the mind is

8 Ibid., 158-159.

involved, which can add to what was perceived at will, and to define them according to other attributes in its persona. The impressions received from sense contact produce modifications of the substance of the mind and these modifications can be further altered according to the will of the thinker. Therefore there is no identity between the external phenomena and the internal response mechanism.

Next we have the statement 'An eye consciousness is not a different entity from its attribute of being produced in the image of its object and also it is not a different entity from its attribute of being a conscious entity'. It should be pointed out that the 'conscious entity' utilises the 'image of its object' to further the progress of the development of its consciousness. The images are necessary, otherwise consciousness could not perceive anything and thus not grow and expand towards Buddhahood. Images without consciousness[9] to interpret them are meaningless. Consciousness organises these images into useful input by choosing which of the myriads of images that it perceives (via the eye) that it regards as valuable in its progress in life, and disregarding others as relatively meaningless. For example, are the images it chooses to focus upon the words of a *sūtra* or the ramblings on a T.V.? Both are choosable, and a choice can be made, depending upon *saṃskāras* and the factor of free will. The choices produce different effects upon consciousness. Therefore the image formed in the mind's eye and the consciousness that utilises it are *not* two distinct entities once the consciousness decides to utilise it in some way. All images become incorporated into consciousness *as consciousness.*

What an eye consciousness perceives may in fact be both produced from a visible form and not produced from a visible form. A visible form will produce an eye consciousness, providing the 'three factors' are working as a unity and are not impaired in any way. The mind then automatically chooses which aspect or aspects of the 'visible form' derived from the eye consciousness it wishes to include in its consciousness-building repertoire, and to disregard the rest. What it disregards then does not produce an effect upon consciousness, and what it accepts will. For instance, there are many words to the pages of a book, the eye can see them all at a glance, but only a few may enter

9 Note that consciousness also includes the functions of the intellect.

consciousness in a meaningful way if the mind chooses to read and interpret them. Only what the mind chooses to focus upon out of the myriads of visual inputs is important as far as consciousness-building is concerned, the rest becomes a blur that is quickly forgotten. (What that consciousness chooses not to incorporate as an image in its conscious repertoire is then stored in the 'unconscious' mind.)

Refuting a Self of Persons

In the section entitled *'Refuting a Self of Persons'* it is stated that 'the fivefold reasoning' found in Nāgārjuna's *Treatise on the Middle Way* is[10]:

> The self does not inherently exist because of (1) not being the aggregates, (2) not being other than the aggregates, (3) not being the base of the aggregates, (4) not depending on the aggregates, and (5) not possessing the aggregates. An example is a chariot.

The reason is fivefold, and thus it is called the fivefold reasoning. Candrakīrti added two more "corners" to the reason:

> (6) not being the shape of the aggregates, and (7) not being the composite of the aggregates.

In a slightly longer form the sevenfold reasoning is:

> Except for only being imputed to be the aggregates which are its basis of imputation, there is no self-subsistent self, for:
>
> 1. the aggregates which are the basis of the imputation are not the person
> 2. the person is not an entity other than the aggregates which are the basis of its imputation
> 3. the person is not the support of the aggregates which its basis of imputation
> 4. the person ultimately does not depend on the aggregates which are the basis of imputation
> 5. the person ultimately does not possess the aggregates
> 6. the person is not the shape of the aggregates which are its basis of imputation

10 Ibid., 175-196.

> 7. the person is not the composite of the aggregates which are the basis of its imputation
>
> For example, if a chariot is sought analytically, there is no self-subsistent chariot to be found[11]...Applied to a chariot the reasoning is:
>
> A chariot does not inherently exist because of not being its parts, not being other than its parts, not being in its parts, not being that in which its parts exist, not possessing its parts, not being the composite of its parts, and not being the shape of its parts.
>
> These seven reasons must be established as qualities of the subject, a chariot.
>
> A chariot is not inherently the same entity as its own parts (axles, wheels, etc.) because if it were one with them, just as its parts are many, so the chariot would also be many. Or, just as the chariot is one, its parts also would be one. Furthermore, the agent—the chariot as the whole which conveys its parts when it moves—and the object—the conveyed parts—would absurdly be one.[12]

I shall briefly analyse this sevenfold reasoning here, because many of the points have been elaborated elsewhere. It should be noted that these seven are in conformity with the qualities of the seven Ray lines,[13] which also utilise the five Elements via the lower five Rays.

1. **'The aggregates which are the basis of the imputation are not the person'**. Here one can agree, because obviously consciousness

---

11 Ibid., 178-179.

12 Ibid., 179-180.

13 They are introduced here because the analysis of such lists is incomplete without consideration of them. The Ray qualities are found veiled throughout Buddhist doctrines, and in all sacred scriptures. They thus need to be understood by Buddhists to better interpret their texts. I shall consequently denote their appearance in the texts quoted from throughout this series. Referencing these examples astute students will find many other examples in the texts they are studying. The source material concerning their properties is derived from the works of A.A. Bailey, such as *Esoteric Psychology,* Volumes I and II, and *The Rays and the Initiations* (Lucis Press). I have defined the Rays as: the first Ray of Will or Power, the second Ray of Love-Wisdom, the third Ray of enlightening, Mathematically Exact Activity, the fourth Ray of Harmony overcoming Strife, the fifth Ray of Scientific Reason, the sixth Ray of Devotion, and the seventh Ray of Ceremonial or Cyclic Activity, Materialising Power.

persists after the births and deaths of many containers of such aggregates, and develops Tathāgata qualities as a consequence. Also the person can use the will (the first Ray) to direct such streams of aggregates according to desired outcomes, making him above or beyond the aggregates, in a similar way that the driver of a car is not the car itself.

2. **'The person is not an entity other than the aggregates which are the basis of its imputation'.** Here one must make a distinction between a low grade personality, who is totally conditioned by the nature of the relatively coarse aggregates and related *karma*, and a high grade one on the Bodhisattva path, who has developed *bodhicitta* and Tathāgata qualities. The universality (the expressed love and wisdom of the second Ray) and freedom of thought in such a case is not a condition of base aggregates, and therefore makes such a person an entity that is 'other than the aggregates which are the basis of its imputation'. It is the nature of the mind that does the imputation that determines how conditioned by or freed from control of the aggregates the personal-I is. When thoroughly attached to *saṃsāra* then the aggregates rule, but when *bodhicitta* (Love-Wisdom) governs consciousness then freedom from the aggregates ensues. Our analysis here is limited to a particular incarnation rather than a succession of incarnations, as was the case with point 1.

3. **'The person is not the support of the aggregates which are its basis of imputation'.** That which supports is that which holds something together, sustains its existence, like the foundation of a house or the scaffolding upon which the sum of the structure is built. (Similarly the third Ray of enlightening, Mathematically Exact Activity supports all aspects of consciousness.) Here the Aetheric Element is implied because it supports the viability of all of the qualities mentioned below. The person is not the support of the aggregates, because they flow through as the continuum of the bodily form and mind, but consciousness is. This is because the enlightened consciousness actually directs the flow of what is to be (via mathematically correct activity) with respect to the aggregates of the personal-I. Whatever directs or controls the flow of something can be considered its support or base.

4. **'The person ultimately does not depend on the aggregates which are the basis of imputation'.** Dependency here is a long-term characteristic that can involve many lives of development and continuous transformation of the aggregates. The fourth Ray characteristic that produces harmony in the midst of conflict (the interrelation between the aggregates delineating the normal experience of *saṃsāra*) is now brought into play. The Airy Element is implied because of the subtle nature of the impressions that cause the transformations of what is 'depended' upon. This Element is the carrier of the *prāṇas* that convey the aggregates as *saṃskāras*. Eventually this produces the Bodhisattva path. Here it can be said that a person may not *ultimately* depend upon such aggregates, but practically they are needed for everyday experience and consciousness growth until liberation is attained. The I-consciousness utilises them for its growth towards enlightenment. Without such developed aggregates, from which the Airy essences pertaining to wisdom can be derived or wrought, a Tathāgata could never evolve from out of the *māyā*. Such dependency is based upon the necessity for progressively more refined change, which is eventually synthesised into the changeless state of the *tathatā*. Ultimately therefore there is no dependency, but the process to achieving the 'ultimate' necessitates dependency.
5. **'The person ultimately does not possess the aggregates'.** That which 'possesses' things, or attempts to do so is the mind. (Which is governed by the fifth Ray attribute of intelligent or scientific reason.) Consciousness stores the images and feeling-perceptions of all things that it possesses as the *bījas* of memory. Here the Fiery Element, which governs the mental domain, is implicated. To this assertion we can say therefore that consciousness does and does not 'possess the aggregates'. This is because they continuously change and are transformed by the mind as experiences evolve and the perception of things change. From this perspective, though they are ephemeral, they are manipulated by consciousness, hence are temporarily possessed, but not ultimately. However, memory of them is possessed ultimately, and ultimately their refined essences are kept as the fundamental wisdom of an evolved Tathāgata.

6. **'The person is not the shape of the aggregates which are its basis of imputation'.** Imputation refers to the perception of things by the mind, and is generally the product of the assessment of a defiled (desirous, emotive) mind. (We therefore have the ramifications of the sixth Ray of Devotion.) The Watery Element is implied here, because that which is perceived to be a shape has to act like a container of the *skandhas* and *saṃskāras* in a similar fashion that the fluidity of water has to be contained. Again we can agree that a person is not this shape. However, we will make a proviso that consciousness which persists after its eventual demise, must be contained in some way for it to be effective with respect to its rebirth.
7. **'The person is not the composite of the aggregates which are the basis of its imputation'.** This refers to the composition of the gross form (the Earthy Element), the nature of the attributes that constitute phenomena. This assessment is correct. Such phenomena is governed by the expression of the seventh Ray of Ceremonial or Cyclic Activity that oversees the cycles of life in the realm of form.

With respect to a chariot, it can be said that it may not inherently be the same entity as its own parts, however a chariot can be described to be the sum of the parts, each of which exists to produce the *functionality* of a chariot. Also, it is not absurd to say that the entity consisting of component parts (such as a human unit) exists as a 'one' as it moves. This is the way that each human being functions. In the pedantry provided we are told that 'a chariot does not exist' because :

1. **'Not being its parts'.** This is a moot point. Who, for instance, can truly assert that a human being (symbolised by a chariot) is not identified with his parts? Would it be a human if the form had a cows horns, a chicken's body, but a human's feet? Scientists can microscopically examine the genetics in a minute portion of any life form and say that this specimen is a dog's, that one a cat's, and that of a human. A human being may not be his parts *per se,* but the parts of a human are readily identifiable from whence they came, and how they are distinguished from other entities or things. If deceased, and human parts are separated from a body, an arm over here and a leg over there, we can say that such a memberless corpse was a human, but is it now

a 'human'? The reality is that it is the possession by consciousness, a mind, that distinguishes a human unit from any other form. If such a mind is not there it is not human, and if it has a functioning mind and is minus a part, such as an arm or leg, it is still human.

2. **'Not being other than its parts'**. This phrase is both true and false. It is false in the sense that a human is 'other than his parts', for consciousness is not a part *per se,* because that is what survives after the 'parts' of the observable body have perished. However, from another viewpoint we can say that consciousness is a part of that which it utilises for its expression.
3. Consciousness, the integral factor that makes us human, is **'in the parts'**, otherwise those parts would not function to assist consciousness. There could be no sensory stimulus modifying consciousness in any way, no painful or pleasurable sensations. Wherever sensorial stimulus occurs there also is consciousness.
4. Consciousness incorporates that in which the parts exist. Without the factor of conscious integration the parts would have no function in a human. Such a one would be said to be 'brain dead', insane, or deceased. The form may possess the gross attributes of a human, but the human part is no longer there.
5. **'Not possessing its parts'** is true from one perspective, because of transience, but from another untrue, as those parts are really the expression of the moving winds of the *saṃskāras*, which consciousness 'possesses' and must learn to transmute into the wisdoms of the Dhyāni Buddhas. Such 'possession' allows the experience of *karma* to manifest.
6. **'Not being the composite of its parts'**. Consciousness is certainly not the composite because of being more than that. It can however be an extended expression of the composite if consciousness and even *śūnyatā* are considered parts.
7. **'Not being the shape of its parts'**. There is no argument here.

The explanation provided above is an outline of what will be detailed when *The Seven Cornered Reason* is analysed. One can also observe what a wonderful mechanism language, coupled with a proper mode of interpretation, is for the analysis of any subject.

What gives credence to what something is, is firstly its purpose (functionality) and secondarily its form, and that it is composed of several parts. The functionality of a chariot is what is perceived in the mind's eye as a chariot, not the wheels, nuts or planking that constitutes it. One would not dream of entering a toy car to try to drive it, even if one could get into it, despite the fact that its appearance is identical in every way to that of a car, and has the appearance of similar types of parts. The functions are different, one is a toy to be played with by children, and the other is the real thing that can be driven. People know it to be so because they have educated themselves appropriately. Does a car then inherently 'exist', well yes, as long as its functionality persists and can carry the person to work, etc. It persists as long as a human consciousness experiences it as a factor in its experiential quota. It does not however inherently exist ultimately. Also, it is not a truck, even though a truck can carry a person to work, and possesses wheels, chassis, headlights all similar to that of a car. It has a different function, namely the haulage of goods, rather than people, thus it is 'a truck'. A car is a car because of its functionality, a truck is a truck, similarly because of its functionality, and a zebra is different from the two, even though it could theoretically carry people to work. But that is not its function in a human society, rather it is viewed as an exotic animal, seen on the plains of Africa, or quietly eating grass in some zoo.

'Things' therefore exist in accord with the credence that human consciousness gives to these things, and thus have an existence, seen in functional terms, for the human mind that experiences and utilises them in some way to further the progress of human consciousness. This can be further illustrated by the existence of a distant view, e.g., of mountains. The mountains cannot be touched, smelled, heard, or tasted whilst a person is sitting on a veranda sipping tea. They can only be seen, thus the eye consciousness alone is effected. It could be a mirage, like a photo of the same mountains, but the reality of the mountains *is* the effect it has upon one's consciousness, in other words its functionality. It is pleasing to the consciousness, and brings on lofty images of sages meditating in the snow, etc. Of course, the mind has been educated to understand the functionality of the component parts of the mountains, the hard rocks, the cold soft snow, cold hard slippery ice, etc. Such aggregates make up the mountains, but they are more than that. They are a means for experiential growth for those that perceive them to be a 'thing'. The existence of others depend upon them, like the snow leopard, or because of the water flowing from the melting ice upon it.

The person also knows, because the existence of yonder mountain has been proven to him through logical deduction via his eye consciousness, and the testimony of the stream of the experiences coming from past activities, that he could, if he wishes to go, to the mountain to experience all aspects of its phenomena.

Also, a wheel is a wheel because it is designed for its function, its ability to roll and to be able to bear an axle. If the 'wheel' were square, then it would not be considered a wheel, and certainly would not be attached to a chariot for the function of the chariot to be utilised. The description of the chariot would be changed, 'a chariot with square wheels' maybe, to designate its dysfunction as a chariot. It could not be considered a chariot because it will not roll, and the other essential ingredient of the horse that pulls it by being attached to it in a specific way can not function in the way designated by the term 'chariot'. It has not this functionality, hence it is not a chariot.

Nowhere in the arguments given is the concept of functionality even considered, so when the major factor defining anything is ignored in an argument, the rest of the argument falls flat. Ultimately, all things are transient, thus illusional, this is an undeniable truth. Even the mountain will eventually be ground down by the forces of Nature, or sink into the ocean during a cataclysm, but they have a temporal reality that can be perceived by consciousness, or by sentience, and this also is undeniable. So why manifest arguments that ignore such a conditioned reality? It is indeed real for the duration of the time it is imputed to exist with the functionality for that thing intact.

The word 'ultimately' refers to the time line, to the far distant future. It is not the present reality, but continuously the arguments relate to ultimate truth, not present reality. So what if we are told that 'the person ultimately does not depend on (or possess) the aggregates'? Such a statement does not convey much to one thinking in terms of conventional truth, such as when the person dies. What aggregates exist then? The term 'ultimately' in the context utilised is so far away in the future that for most upon the earth it is a thought hardly worthy of consideration, except as a addendum to the account of the evolutionary process. (We are not considering the death of a personal-I here, but rather, the death of consciousness.) Much like physical plane death is the attainment of *śūnyatā* for the consciousness experiencing it. It refers to the ending of things, but the process of getting there is the important thing to consider.

What about humans? What makes us human is the *functionality of our consciousness,* not whether we have arms and legs etc., for monkeys also have these. Such functionality concerns the human ability to self-identify, rationalise, and philosophise about diverse subjects, to be able to utilise the creative imagination, and the ambidextrous hands. Only then is one possessing two arms, two legs, torso, and head, considered human. If a person cannot do this, then we use such terms as 'a person with split-personality', 'a person that is insane', a 'person who is unconscious', 'a person who is dead'. Some determining label is given to describe what is an anomaly. All other creatures that possess such appendages we call animals, or more specifically, anthropoid apes.

So how do Prāsaṅgika-Mādhyamika philosophers make a distinction between us and the anthropoid apes by their system? They don't. It is all the same to them, 'not inherently existing'. Our consciousness tells us they are different, our experiences tell us that they are different, and our instincts affirm to us that our lives would be in danger if we lived in the natural environment with them. The Prāsaṅgika-Mādhyamika philosophers however do not allow such testimony in the above reasoning, they would deny the existence of an I-consciousness that allows such distinctions to be made. They do say that there is such a thing as 'existence', but how consciousness distinguishes 'this' from 'that' is countered through a system of denials and of ultimates. They may purport a belief in conventional truth to explain such phenomena, but in fact do not give the reality of such a truth much credence. What is not the ultimate is categorically dismissed as illusional, hence denigrated.[14]

The 'self of persons'

Not all Buddhist schools refute a 'self of persons' in the same way as the Prāsaṅgika, and there are many differing assumptions concerning the way to view this subject, and we should look at some of these before

---

14 Leaving aside the Tsongkhapian version of the two truths in this discussion.

delving in depth into the Prāsaṅgika 'seven-cornered reason'. For this purpose I shall quote at length, from *A Study of Svātantrika:*[15]

> According to the Svātantrikas, Yogācārins, Sautrāntikas, and Vaibhāṣikas, the term 'self' *(ātman, bdag)* in isolation, and not in phrases such as "selflessness of phenomena" *(dharmanairātmya, chos kyi bdag med),* refers only to an attribute falsely ascribed to the person *(pudgala, gang zag);* it does not refer to other phenomena. It should be noted that self, in this context, is not a synonym for person as it usually is; when these tenet systems refute the existence of a self, they are not refuting the existence of persons. Rather, they are negating a special type of person, a person which can appear to the mind independent of the appearance of other phenomena.
>
> The Prāsaṅgikas apply the bare term "self" to a wider context than merely the false nature of the person. Buddhapālita says that self is a word for entityness, the inherent existence which is falsely ascribed to all phenomena, including persons. Candrakīrti says in his *Commentary to Ārayadeva's "Four Hundred" (Catuhśatakaṭīkā)*:
>
> > Regarding this, "self" is the entity of things that does not depend on another, [it is] inherent existence. The non-existence of that is selflessness. Through the division into phenomena and persons it is understood as twofold, the selflessness of phenomena and the selflessness of persons.
>
> Thus, for the Prāsaṅgikas, self does not refer merely to a falsely attributed quality of just persons, but refers to an independent entity, an entity which exists under its own power, the existence of an objective mode of subsistence which is not merely imputed by terminology. A person's quality of being an independent, inherently existent entity is a self of persons. Such a quality superimposed on phenomena other than the person is a self of phenomena. The non-existence of those two false qualities of persons and phenomena is the selflessness of persons and the selflessness of phenomena. In the Prāsaṅgika system there is no difference in the subtlety between the two selflessnesses.[16]

We thus have two different types of 'self' to contend with in Mahāyāna philosophy: 1) 'a person which can appear to the mind independent of the appearance of other phenomena'. 2) An independent

15 Lopez, Jr., *A Study of Svātantrika,* 107 ff.

16 Ibid., 107-108.

entity which 'exists under its own power'. Note that a person is limited to the membership of the human kingdom, whereas an 'independent entity' can belong to any other kingdom in Nature or exist upon any other realm of perception. The Prāsaṅgika conception, therefore, is inclusive of a far larger arena of visioning.

When analysing phenomena that can appear to the mind other than that relegated to a person, the conception is difficult, because it presupposes that the person and this 'other phenomenon' can exist in a different time or space-continuum—if the person has to be differentiated from the phenomena of the natural world that sustains him/her. This introduces concepts of the multidimensional realms of perception, especially the realm of the mind, of consciousness, which must make such discernment. The other Buddhist Schools contend that there is no such thing that can be conceived of as a 'self' under these conditions. The conditions being what consciousness (the mind) actually perceives to be true, other than the conditionings of its own substance (the aggregates thereof). Now, if we observe the empirical mind *per se* and its view of the world and the people in it, there can be no independent inherent 'self' that can appear thus, as this mind is limited to considerations of the transience of form only. We consider this empirical mind (the intellect that concretises) to be the mode of thinking of ordinary people (when coupled with the emotions).

However, when observing that which is above or beyond the intellect, the abstracted formless realms of consciousness, then the existence of a 'self' can be posited real or non-real, because it is outside the scope of the empirical mind's domain, which occludes the pathways to ascertainment. The definition of the non-Prāsaṅgika schools fail to account for such a possibility, their consideration lies within the empirical domain, where they can clearly refute the existence of a 'self'.

Not understood by these schools in their query regarding a 'self' is that they are querying the nature of the manifestation of *karma* and how it is directed. What the subjective driving cause is for the *karma* of an appearing 'self' is unanswered. After all, the phenomena of a 'self' is governed by *karma*. Their query really concerns the question 'what is *it* that drives a human consciousness-stream to ultimately gain liberation?' Failing to think abstractly concerning this issue they have extended the logic of the impermanency of phenomena to *'it'* ('self'), without taking into account a concept of relative permanency of a 'self' that could 'exist under its own power', thus direct consciousness through myriad rebirths. They have failed to account for the existence of the *tathāgatagarbha*. Concerning the definition of the 'self' as 'an independent entity which exists under its own power',[17] the existence or non-existence of such an entity must consequently be proven in the abstracted domain of the I-consciousness. This can be considered the *sambhogakāya* type of *karma*. The Prāsaṅgika added consideration of the *dharmakāya* type of *karma* that drives all sentient lives onwards along their evolutionary path. They refute a directing 'self' that does so, but cannot account for this evolutionary progression of all lives constituting Nature to eventual Buddhahood through a system of negations.

Utilising considerations derived purely from the domain of the empirical mind is doomed to failure, unless the right keys are discovered. Hence the properties of the dual aspect of mind; the empirical mind and the enlightened abstract Mind must be thoroughly investigated. Concerning the ramifications of the *dharmakāya* type of *karma,* the consideration lies in a higher domain than the abstract Mind, and necessitates an analytical comprehension of the subject of causation (of phenomena) viewed upon a vast scale of expression, and not just that associated with a human mind. The true nature of the *dharmakāya* must be comprehended[18] if the Prāsaṅgika contention is to be refuted or validated.

Causality, mutability, relativity, co-dependency and evolutionary growth are the keys to the understanding of the nature of all phenomena. All forms of phenomenological interrelation happen via 'selves', and *saṃsāra* is built because of the interrelations of such 'selves'. Co-dependency means that the way that Candrakīrti refutes the existence of 'self' is correct, however, the Prāsaṅgika philosophy does not relegate importance to the existence of co-dependent selves as the key ingredient in the establishment of the *saṃsāra-śūnyatā* nexus. From this point of view there is a reality to the 'self' concept, but from the point of view of mutability it is transient and thus unreal. A 'self' concept is thus both real and unreal. If the concept of 'self' (within a person) is relegated to be the *tathāgatagarbha/I-consciousness* then we will later see that

17 Or as Candrakīrti states above, 'the entity of things that does not depend on another'.

18 The first three volumes *(The I Concept)* of this *Treatise on Mind* introduces the basic premises of the *dharmakāya* view. Volumes 4 and 5 provide a more detailed analysis.

such a concept also both does and does not 'depend upon another'.

The above view of 'self' then, is what the first three volumes of this series is set to explicate, and in doing so will broaden the scope of vision of Buddhist thought and lift its level to new heights. This will awaken Buddhists to epistemic and ontological views that were previously only hinted at by the enlightened amongst them. This means that what was formerly deemed esoteric, 'ear-whispered', can now gain logical acceptance for those fortunate enough to be able to coordinate their eye consciousness with the I-consciousness through the medium of a clarified consciousness. They can thereby gain the faculty of the inner Eye to vision for themselves, and the inner Ear to hear the silent whispered Voice that can thunder in the fray of slothful utterances.

Again quoting from *A Study of Svāntantrika:*

> The Svātantrikas reject the existence of a substantially existent person that is something other than the aggregates and assert that the person is merely designated to the aggregates. They find support in this statement from sūtra:
>
> > Just as, for example, chariot is designated,
> > To a collection parts,
> > So, in dependence on the aggregates,
> > Conventionally, a sentient being is named.
>
> Thus the Svātantrikas reject the existence of a self-sufficient person but do not reject the existence of a person. Bhāvaviveka says in the eighteenth chapter of his *Lamp for (Nāgārjuna's) "Wisdom"*, "Thus, we also actually impute the term self to consciousnesses conventionally because, since consciousness takes rebirth, it is the self."[19]... Bhāvaviveka reasons that consciousness is the conventionally existent self because consciousness is that which takes rebirth; it appropriates the other aggregates which, together with consciousness, serve as the basis of designation of the conventionally existent person in the new lifetime.[20]

One can agree with this, and add the proviso that consciousness must be properly analysed in order to gauge exactly what aspect of consciousness it is that takes rebirth. For, out of all the innumerable

19 Lopez, Jr., *A Study of Svātantrika*, 109-110.

20 Ibid., 110.

experiences of myriads of former incarnations of the personal-I's that have gone to make up consciousness, how can 'it' select (or what part of consciousness thus acts to select) a particular, tiny quantified part of this superabundant amount of former experiences to take rebirth as the next personal-I? What happens to the remainder of consciousness that is not incorporated into the karmic structure of the *selected* bundled aggregates of that personal-I? How is it contained, and in what way does it take part in the evolutionary progress (towards Buddhahood) of each successive personal-I that must come into and out of existence, if the Bodhisattva path to Liberation is to be successfully trod?

These are weighty questions that need to be answered, and are certainly not answered by the Buddhist supposition of 'universal flux', as was explained in *Karma and the Rebirth of Consciousness.* Neither do any of the Buddhist Schools answer these questions in the material so far presented to the West that I am aware of. However, this question of a 'self' in relation to consciousness definitely raises them and they must be answered satisfactorily. The 2,000 odd year silence in Buddhism along this line can now be broken, effecting a thundering roar of Lion-Hearted applause from the Council of Bodhisattvas.[21]

We should note also that the metaphor of *a chariot* is selected above because it aptly symbolises the nature of a human 'self', or sentient being (the personal-I), constituted of bundles of aggregates (the chariot's parts) that can be pulled by the horse of mind. The chariot can bear a load, the (human) 'container' of consciousness that can rightly direct the horse/mind along the enlightenment trail. It alone knows which direction the chariot is to be pulled, and how hard the horse is to be whipped (coaxed) to pull it, when to rest, and when to feed it. It knows the needs of the horse and the capacity of the chariot to pull its load in accord with the type of conditions found upon the trail, rough and muddy, full of ruts and pot holes, or a smoothly laid out paved road. It also can change horses when needed.

Previously the debate has revolved around the more exoteric aspects of the chariot, as to whether or not its component parts symbolises a

21 The purpose of such a statement is to focus the reader upon the domain of the abstract Mind, and access the type of reality that exists there. The Bodhisattva-Mind is non-separative and inclusive of all correctly timed and positive efforts to enlighten humanity—hence the applause. Indeed, such efforts are but expressions of their united meditative activity.

'self' or not, however the true overall significance of the symbolism should not be overlooked.

Continuing with *A Study of Svāntantrika*:

> Those who assert that the five aggregates are the person, citing the quotation above about the chariot are not saying that all five aggregates are the person nor that the five aggregates individually are the person. Rather, they assert that the collection of the five aggregates is the person. Furthermore, when Bhāvaviveka states that the mental consciousness is the person, he is not implicitly denying that the collection of aggregates is the person. Rather, he holds that the main mental consciousness is the traveller continuously migrating through cyclic existence and, therefore, is appropriately designated with the term "person." The positions on the conventional status of the person of the non-Prāsaṅgika Buddhist schools may be summarised in a general way as follows:

School	***Conventionally Existent Person***
Kashmiri Vaibhāṣika	continuum of the aggregates
Sautrāntika Following Scripture	continuum of the aggregates
Sautrāntika Following Reasoning	mental consciousness
Yogācāra Following Reasoning	mental consciousness
Yogācāra Following Scripture	mind-basis-of-all *(ālayavijñāna)*
Sautrāntika-Svātantrika	mental consciousness
Yogācāra-Svātantrika	continuum of consciousness

> Dispensing with the qualification "continuum" *(saṃtāna),* which here refers to the possessor of a series of moments, (for example, the continuation of moments of the mental consciousness over time) the non-Prāsaṅgika schools posit either the collection of the five aggregates or some form of the mental consciousness as the person...[22]
>
> The Prāsaṅgikas deny that the collection of the aggregates is the person and that the mental consciousness is the person. They reject the view that the collection is the person by analyzing the relationship between a chariot and its parts.
>
> The Svātantrikas assert that the collection of the axle, nails, wheels, car, and so forth of the chariot is the chariot and that when one searches for the object designated by the term "chariot" the collection

22 Lopez, Jr., *A Study of Svātantrika*, 110-111.

> of the parts of the chariot is found...[23]
>
> The Prāsaṅgikas do not negate the existence of the chariot; they negate the existence of the chariot as the collection of its parts. They assert that the collection of the parts of the chariot is the basis of the designation of the term "chariot", but the chariot is merely imputed to those parts.[24]

What is presented by the various schools refers to the principle that takes rebirth. Those that posit a 'continuum of the aggregates' (taking also the intellect as an aggregate) are looking only to what constitutes the personal-I, and not as to what incarnates into it, using this 'shell' as a chariot or vehicle for its purpose. The aggregates certainly manifest as a continuum from life to life, but as before stated, something *must* direct the portion of them needed for each incarnation. Without such direction and conscious selection of what is needed the river of aggregates will flow on and on until it has reached some faraway ocean of detritus without having been modified or grown at all, for nothing could have taken rebirth to do so.

Those that state that it is the 'mental consciousness' that takes rebirth are on the right track, because it is the mental consciousness that seeks out the necessary aggregates needed for the next incarnation of the personal-I, but the conception is too generalised.

The Yogācāra following scripture asserts that it is the 'mind-basis-of all *(ālayavijñāna)*', and from one perspective it is so, (as the mental consciousness is incorporated as part of this *ālayavijñāna*), but the *ālayavijñāna* as a consciousness-store alone will not do this, because something within the *ālayavijñāna* must cause the *bījas* of consciousness to muster the *will* to cause the manifestation of a new personal-I. But here is posited a type of container of consciousness, and this is correct, because without such a 'container' (as previously discussed) there could be no store of the *skandhas* and *saṃskāras*, nor for the consciousness *bījas* that are needed to be recalled for each successive incarnation of a personal-I.

The reason for the impossibility of the Yogācāra-Svātantrika position, which posits a 'continuum of consciousness', and the concept

23 Ibid., 111.

24 Ibid., 112.

of *santāna,* or a river of consciousness-moments that takes rebirth manifesting as an actuality, has been presented earlier. Namely, some force must act upon the flow and to appropriately organise it if rebirth is to happen. This presumes that there is an overriding directive of consciousness, a subtle form of 'self' for rebirth to occur.

As the Prāsaṅgikas speak both of a selflessness of persons and of phenomena, and 'deny that the collection of the aggregates is the person and that the mental consciousness is the person', it is difficult to know *exactly what,* according to their system, actually takes rebirth. However, they do assert that rebirth does happen, conventionally. In the quotation given above, the chariot is taken to symbolise what is called the personal-I in this book. Here we see that the existence of such an entity is not denied by the Prāsaṅgika, but its aggregates are, so how does such a 'chariot' come to exist in the Prāsaṅgika system, and what exactly is *it* that sustains its existence? Can Dependent Origination really do it, if there are no aggregates that such origination can work with? If nothing has been originated or caused, how can Dependent Origination actually be an 'origination' and also be 'dependent'—it must be dependent upon something? Such questions have appeared and have been answered previously in this book, however repetition can bring the point home with increasing understanding as to the subtleties of the nature of the query.

The subtle 'self' of persons

To find more answers one needs to closely analyse the Prāsaṅgika and Svātantrika philosophy:

> The fact that consciousness has a distinctive character that separates it from the other aggregates is implicit in Bhāvaviveka's statement that consciousness is the person; when one searches among the aggregates for the conventionally existent person, it is Bhāvaviveka's[25] contention that one will find consciousness. Thus, there must be some special quality of consciousness which sets it apart.
>
> What then is the person? In Candrakīrti's sevenfold reasoning, the person is shown not to exist inherently because when the object

25 Bhāvaviveka is a Svātantrika philosopher, whilst Candrakīrti is Prāsaṅgika.

> designated by the term "person" is sought, it is not found to be inherently the same as the aggregates, different from the aggregates, the basis of the aggregates, based on the aggregates, the possessor of the aggregates, the shape of the aggregates, or the collection of the aggregates. According to the Prāsaṅgikas, the self or person is the mere I which serves as the basis for the generation of the awareness thinking "I" in dependence on the aggregates. The person is merely imputed in terms of the aggregates and is not established by way of its own entity but nonetheless exists, performing the functions of accumulating actions and experiencing the fruition of those actions.
>
> The Prāsaṅgikas assert that the conception of the person as existing by way of its own entity and not merely being posited conventionally is the subtle conception of a self of persons. In reality, the person is merely posited by the power of convention; when the object designated by the verbal convention "person" is searched for, it is not found because the person and the aggregates do not inherently exist in any of the seven ways, which are considered to be exhaustive[26]...Even though the Svātantrikas, at least in terms of their own assertions, realize the person's lack of being substantially existent in the sense of self-sufficiency, they are incapable of abandoning the conception of the person as established by way of its own character because they hold that the person does in fact exist by way of its own character conventionally in the sense that the person is analytically findable among the aggregates. Thus, according to the Prāsaṅgikas, the Svātantrikas retain the subtle conception of a self of persons.[27]

It has already been established that the Prāsaṅgika assertion that 'The person is merely imputed in terms of the aggregates and is not established by way of its own entity but nonetheless exists' is incorrect, in that there is more than just the aggregates working through and affecting the actions of a conventionally existing person. This 'something more' is also responsible for directing the various incarnations of a person along the road to eventual liberation in a progressive evolutionary manner. Furthermore, *The Sevenfold Reasoning* has been found to be flawed, and thus cannot be used as a basis to deny the 'self' of a person, except maybe for the most menial or base type of person, who has not yet evolved the

26 Lopez, Jr., *A Study of Svātantrika*, 113-114.

27 Ibid., 114.

capacity (in that life) to rise above the aggregates in his awareness of things. His form of sensual, emotional thinking is exclusively directed to the 'self-concept', around which his entire universe is centred. For such a being the Prāsaṅgika analysis might be appropriate, but not for a future incarnation of that 'I' wherein it can be argued that higher reasoning faculties, and the intuition, would have been developed as a normal course of evolutionary attainment along the road to Bodhisattvaship. This is inevitable for all human units, otherwise the *tathāgatagarbha* inherent in each human unit would be meaningless.

The statement relating to the Prāsaṅgika assertion that 'the conception of the person as existing by way of its own entity and not merely being posited conventionally is the subtle conception of a 'self of persons'' may indeed be correct as indicative of the existence of such a 'self'.

However, where is the error in admitting the possibility of a subtle version of a 'self', especially when the logic and empirical facts overwhelmingly supports such an assertion? Why are the Prāsaṅgikas specifically, and Buddhists in general, so fearful of, or manifest such inherent hostility to such logic, *contrary* to the position that the Buddha took?[28] Certainly we can point to the historical development of Buddhism as a cause. But such an erroneous line of development in Buddhist history ought to be rectified, to bring the logic closer to the Buddha's own view. The old Brahmanical adversaries, with their concept of an *ātman*, are no longer a contentious issue for them. Buddhists have won their debate regarding *that* form of 'self'. Indeed, Buddhism *must* change its course if it is to truly be a bastion of truth for the world, and to be able to wave the banner of Bodhisattvaship high for all to witness and to utilise as a mechanism for them to gain liberation. If Buddhism persists in the form it presently exists in then very few Bodhisattvas will be able to utilise it as a mechanism for the right education of people. Buddhists may think that they have high grade Bodhisattvas incarnate within their ranks, but this will be an (egotistical) illusion, except for the few that will try to reform the religion, and suffer much ostracism as a consequence. Bodhisattvas will of necessity have to find more fruitful ways of presenting the *dharma* to those aspiring to gain enlightenment.

---

28 As explained in Volume 3, chapter 5.

In fact, if the truth be known, or rather, the teaching of a subtle 'self' be properly understood, then we see that the school of Buddhism known as the Prāsaṅgika, or any other, exists manifesting a 'self of its philosophical content'. Whatever can be defined in some way to be separate or distinct from another entity (such as the various schools of Buddhism, or any other philosophy) can be considered a 'self', i.e., having a defined identity, is 'substantially existing' and can perform functions. In this case the philosophy is being used to educate many students of the system. The philosophy can do nothing of itself, but the student's consciousness can utilise what is inherently there to perform a function. Being a 'self', the Prāsaṅgika system is therefore also transient, and must inevitably change to accommodate new views, for that is the way it is with transient things.

Like the human personality, the Prāsaṅgika system has aggregates consisting of a physical corpus of the monasteries, ritual implements, Buddha images and printed texts that can be examined by the sense of touch and read by the eye consciousness. It contains the bundles of emotional aggregates that many Prāsaṅgika devotees have built up around the system of thought throughout the centuries of its existence, and which they carry through as the force of their convictions to others. It also contains the mental *saṃskāras* that are the result of its accumulated thought structures built by its many philosophers, such as Tsongkhapa, and which have been carried forward by successive generations of adherents to the philosophical system. There have also been different *incarnations* of the system, an example would be the new directions that Candrakīrti gave to Nāgārjuna's original impetus, and then later the reforms of Tsongkhapa. The modern direction can also be seen as a 'fresh' incarnation, as it now has to deal with different circumstances, and the contentions of the modern scientific and technological world, that was not present before. In this manner the 'self' of the Prāsaṅgika school presents itself to the world.

If there were no such 'self' there would be no Prāsaṅgika's and the word itself would disappear into the pages of history, of what once was, i.e., of a 'self' that was. Such a 'self' may be 'conventionally imputed', nevertheless, it obeys all of the characteristics that we attribute to a 'self', including existing 'under its own power', and technically it is not even 'dependent' upon other schools of Buddhism, thus fulfilling Candrakīrti's criteria of a 'self'. Such a dependency is of course debatable, because it exists within the corpus of all Buddhist schools of logic, but the Prāsaṅgika do like to think themselves as a distinct entity.

Just like the human personal-I, the Prāsaṅgika 'self' also responds to higher forces, to higher influences guiding its evolutionary direction emanating from the realm of enlightened being. The heart of the Prāsaṅgika system is *śūnyatā* (as with all other schools of Buddhism), but its guiding principle emanates from the realm of the Council of Bodhisattvas (which effectively 'en-souls' the Prāsaṅgika purpose). Ultimately the guiding principle stems from the *dharmakāya,* which is more than *śūnyatā.* So the analogy is complete from every perspective. Buddhists must begin to extend their thinking concerning the existence of 'self' to much more than just considerations of the human personality, or to the world of external phenomena in general.

It can be said that the denial of a 'subtle conception of a self of persons' is one of the distinguishing characteristics of the Prāsaṅgika. This may be so and from their perspective the logic is valid, and there is a line of reason, viewed in terms of 'ultimates' that allows such a conclusion, but such ultimates should not be the *sine qua non* of their thinking, but rather a proviso of the nature of enlightenment. Their distinction from other schools also lies principally in the commendable methodology of training students via debates and analytical deduction. Thus the term Prāsaṅgika literally means 'consequentialist', referring to the emphasis of their form of reasoning.

Much progress would be gained upon their road to enlightenment if they did not arbitrarily deny 'the subtle conception of a self of persons', but rather analysed the related phenomena properly. Along this line the Svātantrika contention is therefore closer to truth when 'they hold that the person does in fact exist by way of its own character conventionally in the sense that the person is analytically findable among the aggregates'. We should also extend this view of 'person' here to the broader definition of 'self' as indicated above for everything (i.e., every integrated unitary system, organism, or grouping of things) that is 'analytically findable among the aggregates'.

Summary of the Prāsaṅgika and Svātantrika opinions

The summary by Lopez, Jr. can now be presented:

> In summary, what the Svātantrikas assert to be the innate subtle conception of self, the Prāsaṅgikas call artificial and coarse. There is an innate coarse conception of self which the Prāsaṅgikas say is not identified by the Svātantrikas, but even this is coarse. The subtle conception of a self of persons is the conception of the person as inherent existent, and this conception is identified and abandoned only by the Prāsaṅgikas.
>
> The Svātantrika-Prāsaṅgikas schism on the question of self and selflessness relates directly to their assertions concerning the two obstructions. The obstructions to liberation, literally the afflictive obstructions *(kleśāvaraṇa, nyon sgrib),* are those factors preventing liberation from cyclic existence. The obstructions to omniscience, literally the obstructions to objects of knowledge *(jñeyāvaraṇa, shes sgrib),* prevent the achievement of a Buddha's omniscient consciousness which simultaneously cognizes all objects of knowledge *(jñeya, shes bya).*
>
> According to the Vaibhāṣikas, Sautrāntikas, Yogācārins, and Svātantrikas, the conception of the person as substantially existent in the sense of self-sufficiency, having a character different from the aggregates, is the conception of a self of persons and is the chief of the afflictive obstructions, the others being desire, hatred, pride, and so forth[29]...The Prāsaṅgikas assert that Bodhisattvas must first abandon the obstructions to liberation—the afflictive obstructions—before beginning to work on the obstructions to omniscience, but the Svātantrikas assert that Bodhisattvas begin to abandon the two obstructions simultaneously, beginning on the first Bodhisattva ground *(bhūmisa).* The Sautrāntika-Svātantrikas hold that the afflictive obstructions are fully abandoned by the eighth ground, with the last three grounds devoted entirely to removing the remaining obstructions to omniscience.
>
> The Yogācāra-Svātantrikas hold that the abandonment of both obstructions and the achievement of Buddhahood are simultaneous. According to the Svātantrikas, Hīnayānists do not realize the emptiness of true existence. For the Prāsaṅgikas, the conception of true existence together with its seeds are the afflictive obstructions, and mistaken dualistic appearance—the false appearance of phenomena as truly existent—together with its predispositions are the obstructions

29 Lopez, Jr., *A Study of Svātantrika*, 116.

> to omniscience....[30]
>
> Candrakīrti is saying that the Svātantrikas and all others who merely realize a coarse selflessness of persons are incapable of abandoning the afflictive emotions and being liberated from cyclic existence because they have not destroyed the conception of true existence, the chief of the obstructions to liberation[31].....It is the Prāsaṅgika position, then, that everyone who seeks liberation from cyclic existence must realize the subtle selflessness—the emptiness of inherent existence of persons and phenomena—whether that liberation is sought for one's own sake, the Hīnayāna motivation, or for the sake of others, the Mahāyāna motivation.[32]

As far as the statement that 'the chief of the afflictive obstructions' is 'the conception of a self of persons' is concerned, the thesis that I present agrees. There is no other way of obtaining enlightenment than by slaying such a concept at its very root or foundation, when looking to the personal-I. This is because an identification with such an 'I' is really the source of all pain and suffering, as well as to the cycles of existence. Next, the much more difficult presentation of the 'self' related to the I-consciousness must be tackled. This is done upon the Bodhisattva path in the realm of consciousness, and can only be achieved through a succession of lives developing the highest of the Bodhisattva grounds *(bhūmis)* in *dhyāna* (as the Sautrāntika-Svātantrikas posit). The object here being the transmutation of the related qualities into the wisdoms of the five Dhyāni Buddhas. The means to this is the *mahāmudrā,* (or the *vajrayāna),* properly interpreted and practised. Transmutation and transmogrification being the keywords in this process, not 'annihilation' (which is a term often found in Western translations for the concept of the final elimination of 'self'). The nature of this process will be explained as this treatise progresses.

---

30 Ibid., 117.

31 Ibid., 118. The statement is in reference to the quote given from his *Supplement to the Middle Way* (VI.131):

> [According to] you, yogis perceiving selflessness
> Would not realize the reality of forms and so forth.
> [Therefore,] due to seeing forms [as inherently existent] and relating [to them as such]
> Desire and so forth are produced because their nature has not been understood.

32 Ibid., 119.

Concerning the debate between Prāsaṅgikas, who state that 'Bodhisattvas must first abandon the obstructions to liberation—the afflictive obstructions—before beginning to work on the obstructions to omniscience' and the Svātantrikas, who 'assert the Bodhisattvas begin to abandon the two obstructions simultaneously', it should be noted that Bodhisattvas always use the most skilful means available to them to overcome whatever obstacle there is on their path. Thus if first they work upon obstructions to liberation and thence obstructions to omniscience, or simultaneously, or if they spend a little time doing one course and then the other, shuffling as needed, does not matter in the least bit. What matters to them in reality, is not their own welfare, but rather, how they can best help sentient beings gain liberation from suffering, and to properly strike at the root causes, i.e., by revealing to them what such root causes may be. This happens within the context of their own lives lived out as examples for others.

The reality is that they do things according to the way that the relevant *karma* and *saṃskāras* present themselves. They are not freed from such and are tested by the Lords of Liberated Life as to how they handle the emergence of such phenomena out of the available reservoir of realisable aggregates for any life. Whether the *karma* is such that they must work upon the problems at hand simultaneously, or if they must first work upon their own afflictive obstructions to liberation, is a matter of the way that *karma* presents itself. It is obvious however, that in each life some work must be done upon one's afflictive obstructions before some of the qualities relegated to omniscience can be developed. Then more afflictive obstructions can be eliminated, and so forth. This is actually (logically) the normal course of Bodhisattva development.

The Prāsaṅgika position: 'that everyone who seeks liberation from cyclic existence must realize the subtle selflessness—the emptiness of inherent existence of persons and phenomena' is however correct, ultimately, because such emptiness is *śūnyatā*. No person can gain liberation without the *śūnyatā* experience being integral to his/her being. *Śūnyatā* liberates without itself acting in any way. Upon this, I think the Buddhist schools can agree, and therefore is a fundamental supposition. The energies acting via *śūnyatā* (such as *bodhicitta)* are another matter however, and must be evoked by all upon the path to enlightenment. The debate is really upon how one gets 'there', how one actually becomes liberated, and exactly what liberation means, whether spoken in terms of 'omniscience' or 'extinction of characteristics'.

The problem with Candrakīrti's argument as presented[33] is that the way to enlightenment is not specifically the 'abandonment of afflictions' ('desire and so forth'), but rather their transmutation into the principle of Love-Wisdom, namely the development of the Bodhisattva grounds *(bhūmis).* Also, one does not destroy the 'conception of true existence', one develops a refined understanding of the nature of 'existence', of what is and is not a 'self' in relation to the *śūnyatā-saṃsāra* nexus. This involves a fully enlightened comprehension of the nature of the *tathāgatagarbha* and how it develops to become a Tathāgata. I shall continue detailing what it is. Here it can be noted that it is composed of organised substance *(svābhava)* that is a container or store of *Love/ bodhicitta* that organises successive incarnations of personal-I's towards and then along the Bodhisattva path. Therefore such a 'store' can be characterised as 'true existence', a subtle form of 'self'. 'Existence' here refers to the principle of Life.

Quoting from *A Study of Svātantrika* again:

> It is the position of the Prāsaṅgikas that as long as one misconceives the nature of the aggregates, one misconceives the nature of the person because the aggregates are the basis of designation of the person; in order for the person to appear to the mind, the aggregates must appear first. Thus, if the basis of designation is conceived to be truly existent, the object designated, in this case the person, is conceived to be truly existent. The conception of a truly existent person arises from the conception of the aggregates as truly existent. However, in practice it is said that the emptiness of the person is to be realized before the emptiness of the aggregates. Candrakīrti says in his *Clear Words:*
>
>> Because the I is not observed, the mine, the basis of designation as the self, also would not be observed at all. Just as when a chariot is burned, its parts are also burned and thus are not observed, so, when yogis realize the selflessness

33 That all 'who merely realize a coarse selflessness of persons are incapable of abandoning the afflictive emotions and being liberated from cyclic existence because they have not destroyed the conception of true existence'.

> [of the person], they will also realize the selflessness of the mine, the things that are aggregates.
>
> How can this be, if the Prāsaṅgikas also wish to maintain that one continues to misconceive the nature of a person as long as the aggregates are misconceived and that without realizing the emptiness of the aggregates, one cannot realize the emptiness of the person? In answer, it is said that the consciousness realizing the emptiness of the person can, without relying on another consciousness, remove superimpositions, misconceptions about the aggregates, and thus induce ascertainment of the emptiness of inherent existence of the aggregates. However, as long as the consciousness actively misconceiving the nature of the aggregates has not been abandoned, it is impossible to generate a wisdom consciousness understanding the emptiness of a person.
>
> A more satisfying solution to the problem would be to say that Candrakīrti's contention that yogis first realize the selflessness of the person means that they initially realize the selflessness of the internal aggregates *(nang gi phung po),* which are the basis of designation of the person. They thereby come to understand that the person is also selfless, at which point they go to investigate the selflessness of other phenomena.[34]

One can relatively easily ascertain the selflessness of the personal-I, and if the personal-I, constituted of aggregates, is the definition of 'person' we utilise, then the Prāsaṅgikas are correct. ('One misconceives the nature of the person because the aggregates are the basis of designation of the person'.) However, if the I-consciousness is also included in this definition, then much more work and philosophic investigation has to be done than the Prāsaṅgika, or any other Buddhist school has hitherto exoterically done, before the nature of such 'selflessness' can be understood, with the subtle provisos that need to be added for proper comprehension. In fact, before selflessness is to be understood for what it truly is, the nature of the I-consciousness must be first comprehended, for how can something be denied if its properties and functions are not known?

The Buddhist Schools have long manifested a doctrine of categorical denial of all logic relating to a soul concept, which however, is one of the

---

34 Ibid., 120-121.

most basic aspects to phenomenological life. We can say that because all life is en-souled so there is evolutionary progression in Nature, and a human consciousness can utilise a precious human vehicle as a means for striving to liberation. Human consciousness has in fact en-souled the cellular constituency of the form that it has appropriated for any incarnation. The factuality of a 'soul' is an aspect that the Buddha did not explicitly deny. A categorical denial of such a concept, however, has consequently led later Buddhists into a quagmire of muddied thinking, where there should be clear light.

We have already discovered that to analyse the nature of the 'selflessness of the person' leads us to many subtle levels of investigative reasoning, which do not automatically preclude the denial of a soul concept, as the Prāsaṅgika think. Therefore to ascertain the 'selflessness of other phenomena' is even more difficult, because there is much more to the appearance of the external universe than the outer seeming. The sum of what *yogins* perceive esoterically has to be taken into account. Very little thought has been given in Buddhist circles as to *what* has constructed and ordered the marvellous biodiversity in Nature where every species has its rightful ecological niche, and evolutionary characteristics, all working in perfect harmonious interdependence. Much lies hidden to their eyes as how, for instance, *ḍākinīs* evolve and the role that they play in the systemisation of evolutionary space.[35]

In continuing this enquiry as to the nature of what a 'soul' may be or its mode of existence, how it incorporates the concept of the *tathāgatagarbha,* and how such a concept relates to liberation from *saṃsāra*, the last of Prāsaṅgika arguments denying an inherent 'self', the *'seven-cornered reason'* must now be analysed.

35 Their role shall be properly explicated in Volume 5.

15

The Seven-Cornered Reason

The first reason

The Prāsaṅgika *'seven-cornered reason'* for the 'quality of a person' runs as follows:

> 1. The self and the aggregates are not inherently one because the assertion of a self would then be senseless. For, 'self' would only be a synonym of the aggregates, just as 'rabbit-bearer' (that which has the figure of a rabbit in it) is a synonym of 'moon'. Also, just as the aggregates are many, so the selves would be many. Or, just as the self is one, so the aggregates would only be one. Also, because the aggregates are entities which are produced and which disintegrate, the self also would be produced and would disintegrate.
>
> If it is accepted that the self is nominally produced and nominally disintegrates, there is no fault. However, if the production and disintegration of self naturally existed, then there would be three faults: memory of former births would be impossible, deeds done would be wasted, and one would meet with actions not done by oneself. These three faults arise because the selves of former and later births would be naturally individual and thus would be unrelatedly other. Moreover, it is impossible for those which are naturally other to belong to one continuum, just as the being named Maitreya and the being named Upagupta who are other and are contemporaries are not one continuum[1].

1 Hopkins, *Meditation on Emptiness*, 183-184.

'Self and the aggregates are not inherently one', if by 'self' we are referring to the I-consciousness because the aggregates alone do not make the appearance of the new personality awareness. However, if we are looking at the personal-I that is created anew each life, then the aggregates are one with it, but the consciousness that oversees the evolutionary goal of the personal-I is not. The awareness of 'I' is slowly evolved from the aggregates in response to the experiences gained from the new environment in which the child grows up. The personal-I slowly matures as the child grows, with the aggregates continuously being modified by the I-consciousness. Therefore the 'self' here is not the aggregates, but includes them as it builds upon the foundation of whatever aggregates are called forth to express the *karma* of the moment, and all mature together. The personal-I then dies and a new incarnation manifests, based upon past accumulations of aggregates, including those of the life that has just passed. The new personal-I slowly matures, according to the new civilisation and environmental conditions that the child that bears the *saṃskāras* of the past must mould into the moving present.

Here we can see that there is a truism in the statement 'Also, just as the aggregates are many, so the selves would be many. Or, just as the self is one, so the aggregates would only be one'. This is because the aggregates are quantified by each incarnation of a personality. But there are many such incarnations, each dealing with cleansing or mastering one or other of the (many) bundles of aggregates. From another perspective, just as the personal-I is a unity, so the aggregates constituting that personal-I also manifest as a unity, in order to keep the bodily integrity and consciousness intact. Without such a unity of the aggregates there would be but chaotic atoms spread out in space and no such thing as a human being appearing at all.

When building a new personal-I structure, each and every time via the I-consciousness, the continuum of births allows memory of former lives to be possible, as deeds done in a life are not to be wasted, and the *karma* must follow from life to life. Here the collected impressions of all previous births are stored within the containment of the overriding consciousness. In fact, if one takes a proper non-blinkered philosophical view upon the subject, then one will find the logic impeccable, as only something like an I-consciousness can possibly do so, so that memory from past lives can be retrievable. (The basic reasons why have already been given.) Interrelation with this or that 'I' over there (an 'other') would then also be possible. They would not exist within the same continuum of the I-consciousness, as each such continuum is unique to each person. (Except as in so far as everything can be considered to exist in consciousness, and inevitably that consciousness becomes omniscient and timeless.) Such considerations would however exist within the continuum of the I-consciousness that is the result of the integration of all I-consciousnesses that constitute the collectivised *maṇḍala* in the realm of consciousness (the *ālayavijñāna* environment) of which they are a part. A universal consciousness is a necessity for those that are responsible for the *karma* of the sum of a civilisation, of the past, present and future of each individual who is to incarnate therein.

We will also see that though 'the selves of former and later births would be naturally individual' they would not be 'unrelatedly other' because they share a continuum of *saṃskāras* flowing from one to the other. This flow is controlled by an 'over-self' of consciousness that directs their interrelated progressive *karma* with the view in mind of ultimate liberation from that *karma.*

Note that the Prāsaṅgika system of denials has not presented us with any mechanism that would account for these eventuations. Other than saying that these things happen, and indeed are necessary (memory of former lives, non wastage of past deeds, and governing *karma),* zero mechanism is provided to accommodate their existence, as they cannot account for what 'it' is that causes the rebirthing process in such a way that these three factors unfailingly manifest. That which ties one personal-I to its next incarnation, that causes the sequences of personalities to flower from one existence to another, so that the eventuation of *bodhicitta* is promoted, as part of the appearances and disappearances of communities and nations, is *not* explained by this Prāsaṅgika-Mādhyamika logic. The personal-I dies, and then, according to their philosophy, how do the aggregates by themselves determine when and where a new personal-I is to manifest, and *how is the karma arranged* to produce this eventuation? Aggregates alone will not do it, and the death of the personal-I at the death of the form prevents this. Aggregates have no self will to choose how they will manifest, neither can one rely on the reincarnating 'I' to choose. Consider for instance, why one who was a lesbian in one life would wish to be a man in the next (for *karma* to be rectified, balanced); or for a person that one may have hated in one life to now be their wife or husband, so that the lessons of how to love is generated; or that the *karma* of having killed or injured someone necessitates incarnating in such a way that you are to be killed or injured in the life to come. What normal person would choose to become a beggar to pay off *karma*, instead of choosing a life of opulence? Most people are too selfish, indolent, avaricious and fearful to consciously choose such options if they had a choice.

An agent for such absolutely exact deterministic choices for rebirth, that is completely detached from normal human considerations, is obviously necessary. So then, what agency for choosing the necessary *karma* to be cleansed in any life for people, do the Prāsaṅgika, or any of the Buddhist schools, provide to account for the proper explication of this law? Some greater enlightened 'I' must exist to propel the continuation of the pearls of the 'I's' into a string of lives that form part of a continuum of cause and effect towards enlightenment. There is clear logic here for the need of such an agency. It should be obvious that if there was no (enlightened) greater 'I' then the process of rebirth that leads to the actuality of cleansing of *karma* would be an impossibility. Only in this way will one avoid meeting 'with actions not done by oneself'. This is because the entire functioning of the I-consciousness, the greater enlightened-I, is designated or manifests in such a way that will only allow the *karma* engendered by one's previous actions that has been selected for the next life to be experienced in that life. This statement will become obvious as the reader learns more about this functioning in terms of the constitution of the *tathāgatagarbha.*[2]

The second reason

The second of the 'Seven Cornered' reasons given by Hopkins is:

> The self and the mental and physical aggregates are not different entities because if they were, the self would not have the character of the aggregates such as production, disintegration, abiding, form,

2 Later, in Volume 3, I will utilise the term Sambhoghakāya Flower, once that concept has been explained. The foundation for proper comprehension of what such a 'consciousness-form' may be is presently being laid.

> experiencing objects, and so forth. In that case, there would be no basis for the designation 'self', and there would be no object to apprehend as a self because the person would be a non-product.[3]

It has already been stated that the 'self' that is the personal-I is not just simply the emotional-mental and physical aggregates (though it may start this way), but also evolves its own identity, a concept of 'self' during a specific lifetime, allowing it to add to those aggregates or to transmute them. Thus this 'self' and the aggregates are integrated, yet different. Even though 'different', a 'self' does have the character of the aggregates, such as production, experiencing objects, etc. In fact the aggregates cannot do these things by themselves. The mental *saṃskāras* for instance, simply do not flow from the past life *in situ*, otherwise the new personality would simply be exactly the same as it was in the former life. An example would be that a woman in the former life could only manifest as a woman in the next life, manifesting a simple continuum of the same thoughts as what was demonstrated in the past, for there is nothing that could change them, in the above logic. (Being a man, for instance, would be impossible under this scenario.) Such a situation *could not* produce the evolution of a Buddha. For such an eventuation (where a panoply of experiences that must be developed and mastered to make world conquerors out of all humans), new personal-I's must form that are of either sex, and generally of an entirely unrelated national identity from the past one. All is based on the *saṃskāras* of the past that act as seeds for the evolutionary growth of each 'I'. That which changes or acts upon the appearing mental *saṃskāras*, however, is a newly formed 'self' that has evolved from out of the new environment the consciousness-stream finds itself in. Moreover the *karma* that governs such incarnations is mostly group *karma,* because all of us are social beings and have karmic interrelations with a large number of beings. The karmic pull of the entire group causes a necessity to be reborn in a certain locality so that the karmic repercussions of their former existence can be experienced by all.

The *fundamental question* still remains to be answered however, to repeat—out of the myriads of lives that one has led, how exactly, or

---

3 Hopkins, *Meditation on Emptiness,* 185.

what exactly causes the specifically *needed skandhas* and *saṃskāras* to be experienced in the life in order to gain Buddhahood at the end of the succession of lives? What is 'it' that causes the *skandhas* and *saṃskāras* of each life to be processed in such a way that only those aggregates needed (out of the myriads possible) for that particular incarnation are experienced and are sequenced the way that they do? Also, such sequencing has to be planned right from the start, whilst the child is still in the womb, or rather, at a time previous to when the seed is planted in that womb. What for instance, chooses that woman and that man to be one's parents out of the billions of choices, within the context of a specific cultural situation to be born into? The complexity of the entire interrelated *karma* of the family and cultural situation up to the time of death and beyond must also be fully taken into account. There is certainly a difference if one is born into a rich materialistic Western society, a poor Buddhist one, or into the Middle East as a Muslim.

Something, or rather, *some entity must choose when, where, and why for a certain purpose.* It must do so by analysing the billions of possibilities, and so manifesting each incarnation of the personal-I's in such a way that the evolutionary goal is properly eventuated. How can *karma* alone do it, because there will be billions (probably an underestimation when looking at the sum of unresolved karmic actions of all past lives) of karmic bits of information to hamper the selection process? If it is said that *karma* can, and by observing the uncounted billions of human units in and out of incarnation, then the presented philosophy must explain how it does so. In other words how is *karma* organised to allow it to manifest such a mind-boggling function?

Thus the fact that *prevision* is necessary, determining why a person is sometimes incarnated as a woman and then as a man (maybe even for a sequence of lives) in relation to a specific cultural situation is never analysed in extant Buddhism. Sure they can blithely say that it is the law of *karma*, but how does *karma* determine these things for that particular incarnation to be, and then segregate that incarnation from all other personal selves evolving in *saṃsāra*, so that each eventually, ultimately, become Buddhas? Such *karma* must take into account each new manifesting 'I' and of the types of actions that it is to take (i.e., the past, present, and the future) in its scope, taking the emotions and consciousness into account also. It must foresee how a person is going to react emotionally and mentally in the distant future for the eventual proper resolution of a *saṃskāra*. Multiply this by the many billions incarnate and disincarnate, and so we see that the entire process of the way *karma* is organised is staggering. There must be a proper mechanism to account for it all, and for such a mechanism Buddhism really has no answer. An accounting methodology however shall be provided in this series.

If the Prāsaṅgika philosophy is taken and applied to the context of such phrases as I used above: 'each eventually, ultimately, become Buddhas', then problems immediately arise. In other words, how can Buddhas appear if there is no such thing as the segregation of determinatives signified by the term 'each' manifesting in the first place? If nothing organises the phenomena of 'selves' in such a way that the destiny of becoming a Buddha is acceded to, then the entire objective of *saṃsāric* experience (to gain liberation from it) is not possible. The absolute (the Buddha) and conventional ('selves') truths must have a nexus that allows one to evolve into the other.

The commentary to the above quote states:

> Also, if the self were a different entity from the aggregates, then just as the character of consciousness can be apprehended separately from the character of form, so a self without the character of mind and body would have to be apprehendable. However, since the self is not apprehendable separately from the aggregates of mind and body, the self is not a separate entity from the aggregates.[4]

The passage refers to a composite of the aggregates of mind and body, whereby the reference is that which constitutes the dense form, emotions, and the empirical mind. If this is all that is considered a 'self' then the presented deductions may be sound. However it has already been established that a consideration of a directive 'self', viewed in terms of the I-consciousness, and consequently characteristics pertaining to the abstract enlightened Mind, is more than this, but inclusive of it. If the personal-I is considered thus, then the aggregates can at first be considered to be the sum of the mind and body, until the personal-I begins to be receptive to impressions from the I-consciousness. In any case, the

4 Ibid., 186.

life of even a totally ignorant personal-I is directed from the domain of the I-consciousness, to ensure that over time the needed characteristics are developed along the path of gaining wisdom. Also the resultant *karma* of all actions by the personal-I must be appropriately directed.

The remaining reasons

Continuing the presentation of the text of the 'Seven Cornered Reason':

3. The self does not act as the base of the aggregates like a bowl for yoghurt or like snow that exists throughout and surrounds a forest of trees. For, in that case the self and the aggregates would be different, and this position has already been refuted.
4. The self does not inherently exist in or depend on the aggregates like Devadatta living in a tent or a lion living in a forest. For, in that case the self and the aggregates would be different, and this position has already been refuted.
5. The self does not possess the mental and physical aggregates either as a different entity, as in the case of a man possessing a cow, or as the same entity, as in the case of a man possessing his body or a tree possessing its core. For, in the first case the self and the aggregates would be different entities, and in the second case they would be the same entity. Refutations of these positions have already been stated.
6. The self is not just the composite of the aggregates of mind and body because the composite is the basis of the designation 'self' and, therefore, cannot be the self...[5] Furthermore, the composite of the mental and physical aggregates does not inherently exist because the composite is undefinable as either inherently one with or different from the aggregates[6]....The reasoning that the object imputed cannot be the basis of the imputation also refutes the view that the self is the continuum of the aggregates because then object imputed and the basis of imputation would be one. Also, if the self were the composite of the aggregates, then the self as the agent of the appropriation, or assumption, of the aggregates would be one with the aggregates which are its appropriation[7]...

---

5 Ibid., 190.

6 Ibid., 191.

7 Ibid.

If the composite of a person's various consciousnesses—eye, ear, nose, tongue, body, and mental consciousnesses—is asserted to be the person, then the absurdity of the plurality of the composites and the person would follow. Similarly, if it is said that only the mental consciousness is the person, each moment of the mental consciousness would absurdly be a different person because each moment of the mental consciousness is different.

7. The self is not the shape of the aggregates because shape is physical, and if a self were merely shape, then the mind, etc., would not be posited as the self. If it were said that both the physical shape and the mind are the self, then either the self would be two, or shape and consciousness would be one.[8]

Most of these points have been analysed in the logic so far presented, either implicitly or directly in relation to the existence of a 'subtle self', including the meaning of the word 'inherently'. I will consequently not reiterate the information. An understanding, however, of what exactly is the 'subtle self', from the esoteric perspective, shall be fully explicated in Volume 3. I will demonstrate that the 'subtle self' does indeed act as the base for the aggregates, like a bowl for yogurt, or like snow that exists throughout and surrounds a forest of trees. In such a case 'the self and the aggregates would be different', but they will also have similar characteristics. What is known as 'aggregates' become transmuted into refinements of consciousness and the attributes of the Clear Light, by the 'subtle self' *(tathāgatagarbha).* This form of 'self' is viewed as the entity that causes the various incarnations of the personal-I to manifest like pearls upon a string so that Buddhahood is eventually attained. 'Transmutation' means that only that concerning the qualities associated with *bodhicitta* can then exist, otherwise *karma* could not ultimately lead one to enlightenment.

The next statement to be analysed is 'If the composite of a person's various consciousness—eye, ear, nose, tongue, body, and mental consciousness—is asserted to be the person, then the absurdity of the plurality of the composites and the person would follow'. Such a 'plurality of the composites and the person' does not happen because firstly the I-consciousness is not the various sense-consciousnesses.

8 Ibid., 191-192.

They are but mechanisms for the input of sensory data into the mind. Secondly the I-consciousness may govern such a composite, but does not exist as the composite itself. It integrates all into a unity and absorbs the gain or fruit in such a way that the successive personal-I's can be projected into manifestation at the appropriate cycles for their realisation. Such a composite of the sense-consciousnesses would not be a 'person' because a person is more than this. Even the most base person has the capacity to rise above his crass desire-mind state to receive impressions from his/her higher consciousness.

It should also be noted that the mind exists as an organising mechanism for the five sense-consciousnesses. Its function is to integrate the data obtained from them, to store and direct that data in such a way that the ordinary physical life of the person is possible. Because of this organising activity, expressions such as 'the plurality of the composites and the person' are in fact not demonstrated in a normal person. They can however manifest in those whose consciousnesses are impaired in some way, wherewith we have the English term 'insane' to account for this possibility. The fact of the relatively rare occurrence of insanity amongst the human family agrees with the 'absurdity' of the plurality of the presented thesis. This thesis however needs to take into account the role that consciousness plays amongst the six—the five sense-consciousnesses and the intellect.

The term 'sense-consciousnesses' is a convenient term utilised to help define the role the senses play in the acquisition of consciousness. They act as mechanisms to bring to the intellect sensory data obtained through contact with the external universe. The data can then be processed and stored (as memory). These five senses and their mechanisms of receptivity are not 'consciousnesses', rather, they are the mechanism that helps bring consciousness into play in relation to any aspect of the data or impressions received by them. They help modify consciousness at any moment in the continuum of time whereby they manifest. If any of them are impaired at any moment, e.g., as in blindness, then consciousness does not cease, it merely adapts so as to obtain the data needed to function in another way. For example, in the case of blindness the other senses, especially that of touch and hearing, are made more sensitive, to compensate for the lack of visual input. Also the factor of memory retention is increased significantly.

Consciousness may choose to disregard aspects of such data. For example, of all the visual input happening at any moment the mind focuses only upon that which it is interested in, such as when reading the pages of a book. What is happening in the background of the room one is sitting in is then of little interest. Generally the consciousness has defocused the eye mechanism from obtaining too much data from that source in order to focus upon the meaning of the words in print, plus upon the images that they happen to bring into activity in the mind. Generally the images concocted by the words are more important than the sensory data from the surroundings whilst one is reading. Even though the images are merely imputed they are the reality at that time, whilst the data from the factually existent objects become the momentary (*de facto*) illusory world; illusory because irrelevant.

The statement 'the self is the continuum of the aggregates because then object imputed and the basis of imputation would be one' is true, if the 'self' were simply 'the continuum of the aggregates'. Things however, are not as simple as that, and as stated, it is 'more than the aggregates'.

Also, the statement 'that only the mental consciousness would absurdly be a different person because each moment of the mental consciousness is different' may or may not depict the true nature of consciousness. A 'different person' may occur if 'each moment of the mental consciousness is different' because each different moment of mental consciousness changes the person accordingly, there are new thoughts and impressions, which the mind must adapt to and consider, no matter how menial the impressions may be. However, each incremental change is rarely discernable in the overall constitution of the person, any more than the tiny amount of water coming in from a small stream changes the overall constitution of the lake it flows into, or a river into the ocean, though there are measurable effects. Some thoughts, such as the effects of momentous happenings upon the physical plane (e.g., the effects of war) may profoundly change the person's consciousness, because of trauma and the opportunity for revelations to occur. A completely changed person could be the result. There is nothing absurd about incremental or sudden change, as they are integral aspects of the evolutionary process, and such a process is essential to lay the foundations in consciousness wherein Bodhisattvahood can arise.

Bodhisattvahood flowers from the soil of such changing moments of consciousness where a 'different' person is produced.

This does not mean that the person has obviously changed in outward appearance, though that does certainly happen incrementally with the ageing process. Even so, sometimes momentous happenings may drastically change such an appearance, e.g., the loss of a limb after an accident.

The phrase 'each moment of the mental consciousness is different' is philosophically erroneous, because there is really no such thing as 'each moment' of mental consciousness. There is instead a continuum, a flux or flow of consciousness, wherein seconds, minutes, or moments do not exist (though consciousness may choose to register such considerations of time). Consciousness can just as easily register aeons or epochs of evolutionary time in any 'moment' of revelation. The flux may flow into different mental spaces within the continuum, producing different images, conceptualisations and revelations. This may even happen within the context of the 'same' moment. It may envision the future, the past and present at once. If we have a flux or flow of consciousness, rather than moments of consciousness then the statement that there would 'absurdly be a different person because each moment of the mental consciousness is different' does not follow. We may also add that if one shuts out the senses from one's considerations, as in the act of meditation, therefore residing purely in a consciousness-stream, it does not mean that that person is a different person. We simply have the person engaged in an act of meditation now when formerly he was eating or speaking, etc. Of course, if the person is absorbed in *dhyāna* there may be no 'self' that one could observe during that absorption. One could then assert that the meditation is the meditator. The entire process is held in situ in the Mind of the meditating one for the duration of the *dhyāna.* The bodily form has been dispossessed of its normal governing inhabitant during this process. When not in *dhyāna,* consciousness normally identifies with a bodily form it normally regards as a 'self', which though illusional performs a valid function. When one is asleep or dreaming then also the mental consciousness has vacated the form, but still the same person exists. Finally, upon the attainment of death, the mental consciousness remains (as well as the subtle bodies). The deceased may still identify with what he/she was whilst incarnate and consequently is not a 'different person', though will be upon taking rebirth. One should not make quick deductions when analysing the field of consciousness, as many ontological quandaries present themselves, to which the existence of many Buddhist schools testify.

Summary

This concludes the analysis of the Prāsaṅgika-Mādhyamika conception of denial of 'self', where certain flaws in the logic presented have been found. However, the logic is sound from a certain viewpoint (if the part the field of consciousness plays is omitted and only the aggregates and the empirical mind is assessed), otherwise it would not have survived for as long as it has. Some of the problems or errors arose because of the fact that modern scientific information was denied to the philosophers concerned. They could consequently only reason with part-truths. This was not their fault. Other errors arose because of the way that Buddhism deviated from an ideal course set by the Buddha's own wisdom after his *parinirvāṇa*. By taking a view on an arena the Buddha very wisely refused to enter, the extremism of denial of any concept of 'soul' was generated, rather than *truly following* the precepts of his Middle Way teachings. Perhaps this was unavoidable, given the charter of Buddhism to completely explore the nature of *śūnyatā*, where *śūnyatā* is conceived as the extinction of 'self' and 'things'.

Another problem also lay in the fact that Buddhists had only the Hindu concepts of 'soul' (*ātman*) to work with, which was undeniably flawed, from which they evolved their resultant concepts of the necessity for 'selflessness'. In doing so they disallowed any doctrine to appear over the course of time wherein a concept of a 'self' was considered as viable, and ostracised any philosopher as non-Buddhist that would seriously consider such a concept. Therefore the early Vātsīputrīya-Sammitīyas sect (Pudgalavadins) of Buddhism that did so were later fervently suppressed (though very popular during their time), despite the fact that their philosophy was logical and basically sound.

Other bases to errors in logic are founded upon lack of comprehension of the way *karma* works, or of a proper accounting of the functioning of the higher abstract Mind, with such factors as memory, the intuition and previsioning to account for. They had to provide a proper mechanism as to how the mind becomes enlightened, taking a succession of many rebirths into account. The entire mechanism of the rebirth process has consequently been skewered in their accounting or not understood at all.[9] 'The Seven-Cornered Reason' is viewed in mechanistic terms, similar to how a materialistic universe manifests, without taking into account the transformative (alchemical) role that consciousness plays in the scheme of things. Consequently the nature of the *śūnyatā-saṃsāra* nexus is ignored, with the question 'what is "it" that resides at the nexus' not answered. This produced the limitations of the logic relating to mechanistic considerations of *skandhas* (aggregates) when analysing the 'self'. As has been shown, the subject is clearly much more complicated than is presented.

S.K. Hookham states:

> When reality is seen as it is, both nonexistence and existence are seen to be mere concepts. That is why the *Ratnagotravibhaga* says it is Supreme Self because it is free from both self and non-self. However, it is useful to say Nirvana exists, because it remedies the idea that it is the mere extinction of something else.
>
> It is interesting in this connection to consider the position of the Pudgalavadins. According to Fa Hsien, there were, at one time, more monks of this school than of any other. They were a tradition at least as ancient as the Theravadin and they accepted that the mind *(citta)* was not in the *skandhas*, outside them or both in and out, or neither in nor out and so forth. Edward Conze suggested that this is the kind of view that gave rise to the Tathagatagarbha and Cittamatrin doctrines. It is interesting that according to Conze the Pudgalavadins were virtually condemned by all other schools. One wonders to what extent their doctrine was or ever will be understood.[10]

The later volumes of this *Treatise on Mind* shall explore further ramifications of the philosophy so far presented, as well as introducing many new concepts. Before doing so, however, I shall first analyse the

---

9 See Volume 5 on the *Bardo Thödol* for further detail concerning this subject.

10 S.K. Hookham, *The Buddha Within: Tathagatagarbha Doctrine According to the Shentog Interpretation of the Ratnagotravibhaga*, (Sri Satguru Publications, Delhi, 1992), 103.

Pudgala doctrine of the Pudgalavadins to find out what flaws there may be. (From the little that has survived the course of time, and from destructive ostracism by rival canonical sects.) Wherever you get fanaticism or fundamentalism of any type, there you have the process whereby the fanatics endeavour to destroy, distort or misquote the opponent's doctrines, to kill the proponents, or to paint the blackest picture possible concerning that which they disapprove. When such a sect becomes the dominant one then the ability to act thus becomes near absolute. This has happened many times in the course of the world's religious history. Buddhism is not an exception to such activity.

Oṁ

16

The Pudgala Doctrine

The core doctrines

To properly consider the nature and higher ramifications of the 'I' concept, of the way it manifests via the I-consciousness, we should analyse the concept of *pudgala* (personal 'self', individuality). For this aim the arguments of the controversial early Vātsīputrīya-Sammitīyas sect of Buddhism are worthy of consideration. To derive an understanding as to what this doctrine posits I shall quote at length from an article by S. N. Dube.[1]

> The cardinal doctrine of this school is that in addition to the impersonal *dharmas* (i.e., elements composing a being) there is still a *'pudgala'* (person, *jīva* or self) to be reckoned with. This *'pudgala'* can be got at *(upalabbhati)* as reality in the ultimate sense *(paramatthena)* and it can become the object of true experience *(saccikattha).*[2]
>
> Further, the *'pudgala'* is neither identical with nor different from the *skandhas*[3]. The relationship between the two is said to be indefinable (*avaktavya*). The '*pudgala'* is a kind of substance which

1 S.N. Dube, 'Genesis and Development of Pudgalavāda in Buddhism'. Ed. Prof. Kewal Krishan Mittal, *Perspectives on Karma and Rebirth*. (Dept. of Buddhist Studies. Delhi University, Delhi, 1990), 98-105.

2 Author's note: Puggalo uplabbhati saccikatthaparamatthena ti-Kathāvatthu, (Nalanda edition), p. 3; *Abhidharmakośa, IX,* p. 230.

3 Author's note: *Kathāvatthu* (Nal. Edn.) pp. 12ff; *Abhidharmakośa,* IX, p. 231.

provides a common ground for the successive processes occurring in a self-identical individual. According to the Pudgalavādins, the idea of this '*pudgala*' is evidently clear in the events of one life from birth to death. It also extends over many lives, and not only is it the same '*pudgala*' who reappears again in every new rebirth, but also the same '*pudgala*' who is first an ordinary man and then, at the end, totally transformed by Nirvāṇa. They emphasised, therefore, the identity of the man who had won salvation with the man who had sought it.

To support their theory, the Pudgalavādins quote the Buddha who, at times, expressed himself in such terms which would lend support to a personal construction. For example, the Buddha had said: 'This sage Sunetra, who existed in the past, that Sunetra was I'.[4] Similarly the Buddha said: 'In the past I have had such a body'.[5] Here the word 'I' can only refer to the '*pudgala*'. Further, in the opinion of the Pudgalavādins, transmigration is inconceivable without a '*pudgala*'. It is the '*pudgala*' who wanders from one existence to another in the sense that he gives up the old *skandhas*, and takes up or acquires new ones. The Buddha had himself said: 'He rejects one body and takes up another'.[6] The existence of '*pudgala*' as upheld by the Pudgalavādins is formulated as an identity-in-difference, that is to say, a unity in combination with the diversity of states. It is the '*pudgala*' which exists and survives the change in psycho-physical elements. The '*pudgala*' is thought out as a mechanical and organic whole.

The Pudgalavādins argue that in each individual there are a number of factors which appear to survive the fleeting moments, e.g., memory. How is it possible for a thought-moment which has instantly perished to be remembered later? How can it remember and how can it recognize? There must be an 'I' which first experiences and then remembers what it has done. If there were none, how could one possibly remember what one has done[7]? A similar reasoning is also applied to *karman* [*sic*] and its retribution.[8] Moreover, a '*pudgala*' is needed to provide an agent or instrument for the activities on an individual. It is the '*pudgala*' who sees, the eye being merely the instrument.[9]

---

4 Author's note: See *Kathāvatthu-Aṭṭhakathā*, p. 23; *Abhidharmakośa*, IX, p. 271.

5 Author's note: *Abhidharmakośa*, IX, p. 253.

6 Author's note: Ibid., V, pp. 259-60. Cf. *Saṃyutta Nikāya* (Nal. Edn), IX. p. 56.

7 Author's note: *Abhidharmakośa*, IX, p. 271.

8 Author's note: *Kathāvatthu*, p. 33ff; *Abhidharmakośa*, IX, p. 271.

9 Author's note: *Abhidharmakośa*, IX, p. 243ff.

Then, again, if there were no '*pudgalas*' the practice of friendliness would be unthinkable.[10] Is it possible to be friendly to a conglomeration of impersonal and substantial elements? According to the Pudgalavādins, the denial of appearance requires reason. And for them, '*pudgala*' is such an appearance whose denial is difficult to be substantiated by cogent reasons. It is in this strain that they argue that if '*pudgala*' were not there who indeed would fare through the beginningless *saṃsāra?*[11]

The Pudgalavādins also draw attention to such canonical passages which seem to lend support to their theory of '*pudgala.*' They frequently quote: 'One person *(eka-pudgala)* when he is born in the world is born for the weal of many.'[12] Who is that one 'person'? It is the Tathāgata.[13] Similarly, we have: 'After he has been reborn seven times at the most, a '*pudgala*' puts an end to suffering, and becomes one who has severed all bonds.'[14] Then there are some *suttas* classifying the '*pudgalas.*' Even in the *Abhidharma* the eight types of saints are generally known as the 'eight personage' *(pudgalas).* Special attention is also drawn to the *Bhārahārasutta* which provides the Pudgalavādins their strongest argument. On the basis of this *sutta* the Pudgalavādins contend that *bhāra* (burden) refers to the *skandhas* (constituents) while the *hāra* (carrier) is the '*pudgala.*' Unloading the burden is effected by the cessation of desires, attachment and hatred. This '*pudgala*' bears a name, belongs to a family and is enjoyer of happiness and unhappiness. If *bhāra* (= *skandhas)* included *hāra* (= *pudgala)* there was no need of distinguishing the two and so '*pudgala*' exists apart from the *skandhas,* it is neither identical with, not different from *skandhas.*[15]

The Pudgalavādins also adduce some positive arguments of a philosophic character. If there were no '*pudgala*', how can the omniscient Buddha be explained?[16] If all acts of knowledge were instantaneous, none could know all things. A lasting personality, on

---

10 Author's note: *Abhidharmakośa-Vyākhyā,* p. 11; Buston, *History of Buddhism,* Vol. I, pp. 49-50.

11 Author's note: *Abhidharmakośa,* IX, p. 271.

12 Author's note: *Aṅguttar-Nikāya,* I, p. 22.

13 Author's note: *Abhidharmakośa,* IX, p. 259.

14 Author's note: Cf. Kathāvatthu, XII, 5, 9.

15 Author's note: See N. Dutt, *Buddhist Sects in India,* p. 211.

16 Author's note: *Abhidharmakośa,* IX, p. 25ff.

> the other hand, would provide a possible basis for omniscience.[17] It is further pointed out that if *'pudgala'* is only a word to designate the five *skandhas* then why did Buddha not identify *jīva* with *śarīra*?[18] Similarly, why did the Buddha declare *'pudgala'* to be indeterminable or undefinable? If it did not exist, then why did he not say in clear terms that *'pudgala'* does not exist at all?....[19]
>
> The *Vātīsīputīya-Sammīyas* came to uphold the existence of *'pudgala'* in order, perhaps, to meet aforesaid difficulties. Their notion of *'pudgala'* or self is, however, altogether different from the *Sāṃkhya, Vaiśeṣika* and other Brāhmanical systems as also from the worldly *pudgalas* of the *Sarvāstivāda*. They seem to have divided the earlier and contemporary theories of *ātman* or *'pudgala'* into two categories, viz., (1) *Pudgala* as identical with the *skandhas* and (2) *pudgala* as different from the *skandhas*. They rejected the two and established their own category of *'pudgalas'* according to which a *'pudgala'* is neither identical with the *skandhas* nor different from the *skandhas*.[20]

The above passage is quoted in detail because it shows that the Vātīsīputīya-Sammitīyas (Pudgalavādins) were on the right track concerning the understanding of the nature of how *karma* works with respect to the rebirth process. That they 'lost' the arguments with the Sarvāstivādin and Mādhyamika philosophers lies *not* so much in the fact that their philosophy was overly flawed (the logic utilised to refute them were similarly flawed) but that it was *incomplete*. They did not have all of the keys (in the little that has survived of their teachings), to properly explain the doctrine to conclusion. Some of these keys have already been presented, as for instance why a *'pudgala/I-consciousness'* is neither identical with the *skandhas* nor different from the *skandhas*.

The short answer is that they both evolve together, but that the *skandhas* are modified when the successive personalities incarnate and evolve, and finally must become transmuted into enlightenment-attributes if they are to be absorbed into the I-consciousness. (Which is here likened to the *pudgala*.)

---

17 Author's note: *Ibid.*, IX, p. 254ff.

18 Author's note: *Ibid.*, IX, p. 262ff.

19 Dube, 99-101. Author's note: Ibid., IX, p. 264ff.

20 Dube, 103-4.

Correlation of the *pudgala* doctrine to the I-consciousness

The main arguments found in the *pudgala* doctrine, which are similar to what I have presented are:

1. The *'pudgala'* is neither identical with nor different from the *skandhas*.

This relationship has already been ascertained for the I-consciousness. The arguments that the Pudgalavādins give with respect to this concerns 'the expression "fire in relation to fuel" means that the fire has fuel as its basis, or that the fire coexists with fuel.'[21] Notwithstanding the arguments presented in the writings of Vasubandhu, which analyse the characteristics of fire, wood, heat, and fuel, we must look to the 'fire' as referring to the substance of consciousness, and the fuel referring to the experiences derived from the five senses by means of the *skandhas* and directed by the desire-will of the personal-I. This consciousness is dual, with a concreted portion, where the *skandhas* are the same as the intellect, and an abstract-consciousness aspect, wherein the *skandhas* are not identical to it because this consciousness is not an expression of the concept 'I' that is the leitmotiv of the personal-I.

When the process that produces the transformation of the I-consciousness into the wisdoms of the five Dhyāni Buddhas is analysed then it will be seen that consciousness is ultimately not different from the *skandhas* and *saṃskāras* as part of the process that demonstrates the Void Elements. Everything phenomenal becomes relegated transmutatively and is included in the development of a Tathāgata-Mind. The five developed wisdoms find application in the I-consciousness/*tathāgatagarbha*. The zone of the I-consciousness also finds application in the *saṃsāra-śūnyatā* nexus.

---

21 Louis de La Vallée Poussin, *Abhidharmakośabhāṣyam*, Vol. IV. English trans. by Leo M. Pruden, (Asian Humanities Press, Berkeley, California, 1991), 1316-17. Here the 'fire' refers to the *pudgala* and the 'fuel' to the *skandhas* and the argument centers around the relationship of fire to fuel. The opponent answers (Ibid., 1317):

> This means that the *pudgala* coexists with the *skandhas* or that it depends on the *skandhas*: this then admits that it differs from the *skandhas*. And logic demands also that, as fire does not exist when fuel is absent, likewise the *pudgala* does not exist without *skandhas*. You do not admit these conclusions; then your explanation is worthless.

Chapter nine of this book is an essay by Vasubandhu that refutes the *pudgala* doctrines, which is my source for the dialogue analysed.

2. The '*pudgala*' is a kind of substance which provides a common ground for the successive processes occurring in a self-identical individual.

   With respect to this Vasubandhu queries:

   > If the *pudgala* is an entity that one cannot define as being matter (the *rūpa skandha*) nor as being non-matter (the four non-material skandhas, *vedanā skandha*, etc.), why did the Blessed One say that "matter and the other *skandhas* are not self?"[22]

Such 'substance' can be considered the Void Elements of consciousness, as that is the base quality of the *ālayavijñāna*, which when qualified becomes the *bījas* of a thought sequence. When contained within *maṇḍalas* the origination of the *tathāgatagarbha*/I-consciousness can also be discerned. It cannot be defined as matter in the sense of the *rūpa skandha (rūpa* refers to the form, that is visible) that constitutes the substance of the physical body of the personal-I. Neither can it be seen in the 'four non-material *skandhas, vedanā skandha*, etc', which refer to the subjective forms of substance utilised by our emotions (*vedanā*) and intelligence (*manas*). All of these qualifications relate to the *manasic* (intellectual) functioning of the incarnate personal-I, which is definitely not the 'self' that we are here analysing, but do relate to the 'self' that the Buddha referred to.[23] Consciousness, however, incorporates an entire succession of such personal-I's in its embrace, as well as the various Bardo states they transpire through. As it directs them it is above or beyond their lower mind substance, therefore it obeys the laws of its own (higher, abstract Mind) conditioning as applicable to its zone of expression.

3. The idea of this '*pudgala*' is evidently clear in the events of one life from birth to death. It also extends over many lives, and not only is it the same '*pudgala*' who reappears again in every new rebirth, but also the same '*pudgala*' who is first an ordinary man and then, at the end, totally transformed by *Nirvāṇa*.

Thus it is also for the I-consciousness, except it is never an 'ordinary man', but rather that which seeds the ordinary person's existence and

---

22 Ibid., 1320-21. The footnote Poussin gives is to compare also *Saṃyutta, iv. 166.*

23 When he said that 'Matter and the other *skandhas* are not the self'.

gains the accumulated experiences from many such successive seedings. Here, therefore, the Pudgalavādin-Vātīsīputīyas have their doctrine slightly skewered through not properly conceptualising the subtle, transcendental nature of a *pudgala ('soul-form').* However a subtle truism exists because we saw above that the *skandhas* and *saṃskāras* can be transmuted by the I-consciousness utilising the *saṃsāra-śūnyatā* nexus (thus *nirvāṇa)* to produce an enlightened Mind.

4. It is the *'pudgala'* which exists and survives the change in psycho-physical elements. The *'pudgala'* is thought out as a mechanical and organic whole.

Here again we can replace the term I-consciousness for *pudgala*, but the word 'mechanical' is inappropriate as that relates to something that is physical, manifesting automatically as if done by machines, therefore is not influenced by the mind, whereas with the I-consciousness we are concerned with the activity of consciousness. It does not mechanically or automatically function according to a set, rigorous, established pattern, but is inventive and changeable. We can however utilise the concept of 'organic-whole' to include the mechanism whereby consciousness utilises the bodily awareness. The term 'organic' is correct, in the sense of it having a systematic coordination of parts, of it having the characteristics of an highly organised organism.

5. How is it possible for a thought-moment which has instantly perished to be remembered later? How can it remember and how can it recognize? There must be an 'I' which first experiences and then remembers what it has done.

This is one of the most powerful arguments for the existence of an I-consciousness, especially when the sequence of thoughts of any particular life can be recalled many lives later by an enlightened being. There must be a store for such collectivised thoughts (or rather images) existing as *bījas* in an unbroken stream of thought sequences[24] for each individual life stream. If this were not so then the collectivised thoughts of all humans since the foundations of time would be a madly mixed up jumble from which no one could retrieve anything

24 Incarnations of a particular entity.

relating to past lives. Furthermore, the thought-structures must be allocated to a logical hierarchical system (such as pertaining to quality of substance, or nature of content), in a similar fashion that records are kept in a large governmental institution (but here that 'institution' is the I-consciousness), otherwise it would take an impossibly large amount of time to retrieve any specific image from any specific past life. This would be obvious to any thinking person who has had to deal with a mass of records of some kind, but appears to have never entered the mind of Buddhist logicians as to how, precisely, enlightened beings can do such near instantaneous retrievals after entering *samādhi*.

The presented argument basically runs as follows. First a definition of memory is provided,[25] which can be summarised whilst the memory is generated after recognising something, as it is part of the same series of a particular mind-continuum (which distinguishes it from another mind-continuum). The Vātīsīputīyas say 'in the absence of a soul, who remembers?'[26] Also that 'Memory does not die out; it is then not transmitted. One causes it to be produced.'[27] In response to this logic Vasubandhu states:

> Since the cause suffices as master, why require a self to which you could attribute memory? Memory belongs to whatever causes memory. Complexes of *saṃskāras*, or the five *skandhas* forming a homogeneous series, are called "Caitra" and "cow[28]." One says that the Caitra-series possesses the cow-series, because the Caitra-series is the cause of the geographic displacement and the various changes of the cow series. There is not there any one, real entity "Caitra," nor another entity called "cow;" there is not, for the Caitra-series, any quality of owner or master outside of its quality of cause.

25 As is given in the text by Vasubandhu, Ibid., 1339-40.

26 Ibid., 1340.

27 Ibid., 1341.

28 This is stated in relation to the earlier statement (Ibid.):
[Vasubandhu:] Explain by an example how you understand that someone is the master of memory. [The Vātsīputrīyas:] As Caitra is the master of the cow.
[Vasubandhu:] In what is Caitra the master of the cow?
[The Vātsīputrīyas:] In that he directs and employs the cow as he pleases.
[Vasubandhu:] To what then is the memory directed and employed by a master, for whom you search with great pains?
[The Vātsīputrīyas:] It is directed and employed on the object that one wants to remember (that is to say, it is employed on remembering).

[As with memory, so too with recognition.]

> We would answer *mutatis mutandis*, to the questions: "Who knows? To whom do we attribute consciousness?" and to other similar questions, "What feels, what makes ideas?" as we have responded to the questions, "What remembers? To whom do we attribute memory and recognition?"[29]

One can ask here: 'What keeps a homogeneous series maintaining itself as such a series?' Explain precisely as to what prevents this series from commingling with other series, because of similar, if not identical *skandhas* and *saṃskāras*, as all would have a jumbled mess of images. The *saṃskāras* are shared because, for instance, everyone in the vicinity can get an image of the cow over there grazing on grass. The images may be from slightly different perspectives, but all can recall the image of seeing yonder cow when needed. In other words, what is it that defines one 'homogeneous series', making it distinct from another, if there is no agent of distinction, no 'soul-form'? What defines the 'borders' or 'edges' of one stream from another, so that they do not commingle? Indeed, do they have 'borders' or 'edges', if really the best way to describe such series is similar to the flowing eddies in a river, or as streams of consciousness-attributes carried through the air? If they do then how does one explain the commonality of the experience of 'cow', etc? If they do not, then how do you prevent commingling, like the commingling of different streams of water (some of which may be muddy for instance) after having entered a river?[30]

If you naïvely say *karma*, then detail precisely and with exactitude how *karma* does this. Again I ask 'what is the precise mechanism of *karma*?' Here the proponents of 'homogeneous series' will fall silent, for they can only murmur vague platitudes re *karma*. Also, I have already explained in my book *Karma and the Rebirth of Consciousness* why 'homogeneity' in such a series is impossible. A series that flows in a state of uniform motion will continue to do so *ad infinitum* unless acted upon by some external force. This is a basic law of physics. (One of Newton's laws of motion.) So what 'external force' can act upon and thus

29 Ibid., 1341-42.

30 See Volume 2, chapter 6 for further analysis concerning the simile of a river.

modify such a series in order to produce the experiences that become memories? Is it another series flowing over there that somehow acts upon (and thus commingles) with this series? How does one series take elements from another series to produce a memory retention? How can they correlate if there is no regulatory consciousness (i.e., 'soul-form') governing the process? Plainly such is not possible. If the series is acted upon from within (to change the flow or pattern of it) then this admits of an ego, an actor, an 'I' that does so.

A series is much like a river. If there is one type of memory floating in it, say represented by a twig floating in its motion many miles downstream (implying a past action, hence *saṃskāra*) how can something that happens many miles upstream bring that twig to the fore at that precise moment so as to add its specific memory-*saṃskāra,* as it is still floating back there? In other words, what mechanism (other than an overriding or presiding consciousness that can wilfully direct things to bring memory about) can produce such a miracle in the natural ordering of the flow of the series, especially if it is homogeneous?[31]

In his statement that 'memory belongs to whatever causes memory' Vasubandhu has simply avoided answering the question 'How is it possible for a thought-moment which has instantly perished to be remembered later?' In other words, to the question 'what has caused memory in such a case', Vasubandhu answers that memory happens because it has been caused to happen 'by complexes of *saṃskāras* or the five *skandhas* forming a homogeneous series'. The problems with a homogeneous series have already been described. The answer to the question 'What remembers?' with respect to the present life is that it is the consciousness of a personal-I that remembers activities undertaken by that personal-I whilst incarnate. Consequently it is an 'I' that remembers, possessing the wilful volitions to draw images from the memory pool to do so. It has the ability to make conscious volitions to choose what to experience in the form of memory-producing activities. A homogeneous series cannot manifest volitions of its own accord, it can only flow as a series and react in accordance with the flow of another series that may happen to flow into or contact its flow. Then we have

31 See also Volume 2, chapter 4: 'The Vijñānavādins on the existence of "Self"', for further analysis of the implication of this subject of 'homogeneous series' and other aspects of the Vijñānavādin doctrine.

the problem of commingling of the substance of the flows, such as the nature of a muddy stream flowing into a clear one. Certainly a murky mess is then produced in consciousness for Buddhist metaphysicians to somehow sort out.

With respect to past life memories, another form of 'I' is needed to draw forth memories from a vast consciousness-pool, the I-consciousness. It holds all attributes of the past consciousness-stream in the form of *bījas.* The I-consciousness can manifest wilful volitions to choose which past life images are needed to be impressed upon the mind of the personal-I to produce opportune, desired effects. Without the use of the will no memory can be retrieved from out of the consciousness store. This is an important consideration. To the personal-I, memories may flood into consciousness triggered by various stimuli, often without exercising such a wilful input, however, the mind-substance in such cases is of immediate proximity to images caused in that life. When not of such 'immediate proximity' then the *bīja* forms must be wilfully selected. The personal-I cannot do this of its own accord, because such *bījas* lie outside of its memory pool, but not for the overshadowing *tathāgatagarbha,* that has a capacity to project into the consciousness of the personal-I impressions from the distant past elucidating the causes of the *karma* manifesting in the then 'now'. An awakened one has fluid access to the awareness of the *tathāgatagarbha,* thus has access to past-life memory recall. The *bījas* are systemised in an organic hierarchical structure that allows the subtle 'soul-form' to choose the memories to be remembered by its instrument, the personal-I in *saṃsāra.* It can also be deduced that when *karma* is a consideration then memories are generally remembered in accordance with the most propitious time for the appearance of the respective *saṃskāras.*

The fact that the memory of that cow, or some sudden life-changing intuition (or memory) can suddenly pop into the mental space of a person when he/she was not thinking about such a subject at all also belies against a 'homogenous series' as something that instigates memory. Flashes of revelation are directed to a receptive mind from a higher agency responsible for the overall evolutionary growth of that mind. Past life recollections can come *only* from such a source, as there is nothing in the mind-structure of a personal-I developed in a particular life that possesses the mind-continuum of actions or thoughts manifested in an earlier life.

The I-consciousness and the personal-I are therefore the two agents that can 'cause' memory through conscious memory recall.[32] Memory belongs to that which can manifest actions that can draw from the general consciousness-streams images of actions manifested in the past. *Saṃskāras* from former activities can then awaken to modify the desired purpose. The will is evoked to reveal memories from past activities, or is utilised by the overriding I-consciousness to project the images needed to educate the personal-I at the appropriate time. (The images may then come in the form of remembered, or intuited impressions, *déjà vu,* from the activities of past lives.) That which possesses the will to evoke controls the memory process. In *déjà vu* the mind of the personal-I need only be passive in these circumstances. The appearing *saṃskāras* can then stimulate memory recall of events that caused the manifestation of the *saṃskāras* in the past. The personal-I can also wilfully seek out memories for itself.

With respect to the phrase 'Memory belongs to whatever causes memory' one could ask 'to what else can memory belong?' It certainly does not belong to yonder 'cow' (with respect to Caitra's ability to recall the image of seeing a former cow eating grass). In other words, the appearance of a new 'twig' on a river flow will not suddenly cause a similar 'twig' floating some miles back to suddenly come to appear right there, which is what is supposed in Vasubandhu's system of accounting for memory. The memory is contained by the 'twig'/*saṃskāra*, but is possessed by the consciousness that can *wilfully* recall that some miles (or years) back there was a cow grazing. The *bījas* of *saṃskāras* are then activated to release the images that they are constituted of. The *saṃskāra* possesses the aggregates of the memory but not the composite picture of the memory recall. In *déjà vu* the images are directed via a higher Mind because of the appearance of the higher cycle of a karmic action of the past.

6. Moreover, a '*pudgala'* is needed to provide an agent or instrument for the activities of an individual. It is the *'pudgala'* who sees, the eye being merely the instrument.

---

32 A third agent exists in the *chakras*, wherein consciousness (*saṃskāras*) is stored. The subject is vast, as the *chakras* are gateways to subjective and supramundane dimensions of perception. Their function is explored in detail in the later volumes.

It is so for the I-consciousness, but its main instrument is the intellect of the personal-I, whilst the eye functions only via the personal-I. However, both the Head lotus and the Heart *chakra* of the personal-I that the I-consciousness functions through are organised similar to the way that an eye functions. The esoteric all-seeing Eye[33] is of great importance and much more information than was ever hitherto revealed concerning the arrangement of its petals, with respect to the way it functions, will be provided in Volume 5.

The presented argument continues:[34]

> If the *pudgala* is the cause of the eye consciousness, it will be impermanent, because the Sūtra says, "All causes and all conditions that produce consciousnesses are impermanent."
>
> [The Vātīsīputīyas:] We admit then that the *pudgala* is not an object as condition (*ālambana*) of consciousness.
>
> [Very well; but then it is not discernible *(vijñeya)*, an object of *vijñāna*; if it is not discernible, it is not cognizable *(jñeya),* the object of *jñana*; if it is not cognizable, how can one prove that it exists? If one cannot prove that it exists, your system collapses.]
>
> You have said that the *pudgala* is discerned by the six consciousnesses. But, if it is discerned by the eye consciousness, it will be, like physical matter and shape, different from sound; if it is discerned by the ear consciousness, it will be, like sound, different from physical matter and shape. And thus for those (consciousnesses) that follow.

The problem re the arguments presented concerning 'eye consciousness' is that they all refer to the awareness gained by the physical eyes only. This has little bearing upon whether or not an I-consciousness exists, except for the fact that it is responsible for the appearance of the form (the personal-I), of which the eye consciousness is only a part. The person may even be born blind, or lose his/her sight later, according to the vagaries of *karma,* nevertheless the purpose of the I-consciousness persists.

---

33 Technically the Head/Ājñā centre combination.

34 Louis de La Valée Poussin, *Abhidharmakośabhāṣyam*, Vol. IV, 1321-22.

It is not the physical eyes (or of the other sense-consciousnesses) that should be the focus of the enquiry here, but the subjective ones. Yoga philosophy admits of subjective eyes (*chakras*), and specifically of the Ājñā centre (the 'third eye'). The I-consciousness can only be discerned by these subjective eyes, when the *chakras* have been appropriately awakened and rightly directed. They produce modifications in consciousness, once the experiences have been assimilated. Certainly therefore, such experiences cannot be discerned by the eye consciousness or any of the other sense-consciousnesses. Their transmuted correspondences (*siddhis),* obtained through yogic direct perception, however, will produce corresponding revelations and images related to the nature of the appearance of the *tathāgatagarbha.*

7. If there were no '*pudgalas'* the practice of friendliness would be unthinkable. Is it possible to be friendly to a conglomeration of impersonal and substantial elements?

Yes it can be agreed that 'friendliness would be unthinkable', and also to show hatred, etc., but this really concerns recalling *saṃskāras* to the surface of consciousness, to be experienced by the personal-I in accordance with its new emotional environment. However, it is the mind of the personal-I that coordinates what has been recalled with respect to the new stimulus of the present karmic affiliation and then manifests the action of 'friendliness' etc. Without the integrating, coordinating, and directing function of a central 'I' or 'self' no such action could manifest. There would be nothing that would call forth *saṃskāras* and direct them in a new cultural, etc., situation to gain from the interaction and make volitions to produce new *saṃskāras* if desired. *Saṃskāras* will not produce new *saṃskāras* by themselves.

8. If '*pudgala'* were not there who indeed would fare through the beginningless *saṃsāra?*

This is a major reason for advocating the existence of a subtle 'soul-form'. A great deal of the logic as to why this must be so has already been presented. The real subject in question here is 'how does a Buddha evolve from a consciousness-stream if there is no overriding guiding principle that works upon that stream so that liberation and a Buddha-Mind is inevitably achieved?' What is 'it' that evolves thus? As previously stated, the mechanism causing the appearance of each individual personal-I from out of the general consciousness-stream has not been provided, but needs to be if the philosophy is to be accredited as sound.

9. If there were no *'pudgala'*, how can the omniscient Buddha be explained? If all acts of knowledge were instantaneous, none could know all things. A lasting personality, on the other hand, would provide a possible basis for omniscience.

Here we must replace the term 'personality' for a lasting quantified consciousness that outlives the succession of personal-I's and is responsible for engendering them.

Vasubandhu's argument concerning this point is interesting. It starts with a series of quotations from *sūtras*, with the Vātīsīputīyas quoting the phrase: 'But the same Sūtra[35] says, "In the past, I was handsome (literally: I possessed physical matter)."'[36] Vasubandhu's answer to this is:

> This declaration is for the purpose of indicating that the saint capable of recollecting his past lives remembers the varieties of the characteristics of his series of these existences. But the Buddha does not mean that he sees a real *pudgala* possessing, in a past life, such a physical matter, etc.: for to think such is to fall into *satkāyadṛṣṭi*.[37] Or rather, if such is the meaning of this sentence, then its sole purpose is to reject it as non-authentic. We conclude that the Sūtra, insofar as it attributes the possession of physical matter, etc., to a soul, has in view "a self of designation", as one speaks of a pile which, being only an accumulation, has no unity; or of a current of water which being only an accumulation, has no unity; or of a current of water which, being only a succession (of waters), has no permanence.[38]

The fact that the early Buddhists could earnestly liken the highly organised, diversified, and hierarchical, centrally coordinated structures of all sentient beings, to an 'accumulation', like a heap or pile of stones[39]

35 The *sūtra* quoted from is the *Aṅguttara-Nikāya*.

36 Louis de La Valée Poussin, *Abhidharmakośabhāṣyam*, Vol. IV, 1327.

37 Belief in an existent *(sat)* self possessing a form or body *(kāya)*.

38 Ibid.

39 Though this may be the most literal translation of the term *skandha*.

produced many vexatious and problematic syllogisms, such as that of many *dharmas*, homogeneous flux, and naïve teachings of *karma*. The concept mocks the entire processes of living, of the acting out of evolutionary sequences of events, as witnessed by all sentient beings. How can an *uncoordinated* heap (of 'things') move of its own accord to produce positive gain for itself, to produce some factor to sustain its life and to propagate its species, to say nothing of the accumulation of further experiences to benefit the species as a whole? (In the case of humans such actions can also manifest to wreak havoc and destruction upon our civilisation and the environment.) The postulate gets incredulous when the descriptive phrase 'has no unity' is used. Where in Nature can one find one living thing that 'has no unity'?

The phrase 'has no permanence' is true for the nature of the vicissitudes of *saṃsāra*, but *not* for that which is the gain of the living process—which can be recalled by any that have developed the facilities to do so. Rightfully the Vātīsīputīyas would find objection to such a statement:

> The Blessed One would then not be omniscient, since the mind and mental states are not capable of knowing all the *dharmas*,[40] seeing that mind and mental states change, arising and perishing from moment to moment. Omniscience can only belong to a soul, a *pudgala*.
>
> [Vasubandhu:] We would reply that the *pudgala* would be eternal if it does not perish when the mind perishes: a thesis which contradicts your theory of a *pudgala* about which one can only say that it is eternal or non-eternal. We do not say (as do the Mahāsāṁghikas) that the Buddha is omniscient in the sense that he knows all the *dharmas* at one and the same time: "Buddha" designates a certain series: to this series there belongs this unique ability that, by a single act of modulating his mind, he immediately produces an exact consciousness of the object relative to which a desire for knowing has arisen: one then calls this series "Omniscient." One moment of thought is not capable of knowing everything. On this point there is a verse: "As fire, by the capacity of its series, burns all, so too does the Omniscient One—but not by a universal simultaneous knowledge."[41]

40 The factors (elements) of existence in Vaibhāṣika and Sarvāstivādin philosophy.

41 Ibid., 1327-28. Poussin states (Ibid., 1367):
The *Buddhabhūmi*, TD 26, p. 309c9, refutes this stanza.
"Those are vain words. The *paracittajñāna* (knowledge of the mind of another), at the moment when it grasps a thing, does not grasp other things; because it

The first part of Vasubandhu's query is answerable in terms of relative permanence, which has been explained elsewhere in this book. Now, when one talks about the Buddha then one enters into a minefield of opinion, none of which can really be 'proven' because none that possess such opinions are Buddhas. However, we can say that a Buddha can only be presumed 'unique' in that he possesses a greater penetrative wisdom, far-seeing insight and accompanying *siddhis*, than any Bodhisattva; as well as having exhausted his *karma* with our earth system, which they have not. In answer to Vasubandhu's assertion re the Buddha, that he has a 'unique ability' to 'by a single act of modulating his mind, he immediately produces an exact consciousness of the object relative to which a desire for knowing has arisen: one then calls this series "Omniscient"', we can ask the question how did this 'unique ability' come about, and to describe the mechanism that allows the Buddha to do this? It must also be proven conclusively that a Buddha's ability *did not come* from prior having had a subtle 'soul-form'/*tathāgatagarbha* that has organised the consciousness-sequence in such a way that allows him to do this, the gain of which can now be utilised as part of his omniscience. It is obvious that such a mechanism will not be forthcoming by means of the ineffective philosophy presented to us.

Also, how can there be such a 'series' in the Mind of a Tathāgata, a 'thus gone' one, 'an exact consciousness of the object relative to which a desire for knowing has arisen'? This implies that he still retains *karma* with phenomena, and if so he would not be a Buddha. He in fact does not produce 'an exact consciousness of the object' because nothing material in fact is produced in the Mind of such a liberated one. Rather, he can vision that which actually exists, the *skandhas* and *saṃskāras* of the life stream he is observing in the field of consciousness, i.e., what exists as the mind of the I-consciousness concerned (which is inclusive of the three times). Then he can expound his vision with his exemplary gnosis to a receptive audience. This is certainly a much simpler scenario explaining the workings of a Buddha's (or any enlightened one's) Mind than the elaborate schema devised by Vasubandhu, especially in the light of what was previously elaborated concerning the nature of a 'series'.

---

does not know other things, it is not universal knowledge. The series also does not grasp (all), because it knows present being. In your system, it knows solely the general characteristics of a part of the *dharmas*. And if this is the case, it is only by metaphor that the Tathāgata is called omniscient..."

What is 'One moment of thought' in the light of enlightenment-consciousness where 'moments' as such do not exist? Timeless, all-embracive lucidity about all things can exist in such a non-existent 'moment'. The meditation-Mind of such beings is a continuum of intrinsic non-dual revelation within itself, that can relegate instantaneously any truth related to a sequence (of *saṃskāras*) external to it. The all-seeing Eye allows such a One to visualise the all, and the expression *is* omniscience with respect to phenomenon of any type.

The Vātīsīputīyas also find objection in his assertion:

> How do you prove that (the word "Omniscient" should be understood as a series, and not as a particular self of universal knowledge)?
>
> [Vasubandhu:] It is spoken of in the Scriptures, on the subject of the Buddhas of the past, present and future. For example the verse: "Buddhas of the past, Buddhas of the future, and Buddhas of the present destroy the sorrows of many." But, in your system the *skandhas* of existence belong to the three periods of time, but not the *pudgala*.[42]

The point that Vasubandhu makes here is that if the *skandhas* do not belong to the *pudgala* then it cannot 'destroy the sorrows of many' because these sorrows are composed of *skandhas*, which the *pudgala* does not possess, and hence cannot act upon them. His logic may be right from this perspective. However, from the perspective of the I-consciousness, this is not so, because it contains the transmuted *skandhas*, as well as the *bījas* of all past and future possibilities. Therefore, indeed, it can thus work to 'destroy the sorrows of many'. The process of 'destroying' however, is really one of transformation and then transmutation. Even the Prāsaṅgikas do not posit annihilation as an ultimate outcome of the life process. The I-consciousness does this by means of the process of seeding the development of *bodhicitta* in the personal-I, from whence evolves the Bodhisattva after many lifetimes of such seedings of personal-I's. (The I-consciousness-*tathāgatagarbha* is therefore a source of *bodhicitta*, as well as necessarily being an agent of *karma*.)

---

42 Ibid., 1328.

The role of *jīva*

The tenth point of our enquiry is styled thus:

10. It is further pointed out that if *'pudgala'* is only a word to designate the five *skandhas* then why did Buddha not identify *jīva* with *śarīra?*

By *jīva* is generally meant life-force and *śarīra* means the 'skin' or containment of form. *Jīva* vitalises a form so that it retains a particular identity, sustaining its coherent activities by keeping the form in an integral unity that can adapt to the external environment and hence evolve. The question is therefore, why did the Buddha not identify the life force of an individual (which is the energy that establishes a new birth) with the form nature? Note that the life force and the principle of Life earlier explained are different. The principle of Life is that which seeks rebirth via periodical vehicles and must be defined by terminology other than the word *jīva,* hence the terms 'subtle soul', I-consciousness, *tathāgatagarbha* have been used. *Jīva* is that energy utilised by the Life principle to vitalise the aggregates so that a new incarnation is possible. Much confusion and erroneous logic arose in the minds of the early philosophers when they identified the life force with the principle of Life. Vasubandhu is a case at hand.

One can see therefore that *jīva* cannot simply be that representing the 'skin' or containment of form because it is the energising principle of that form. The form nature *(śarīra)* is rebuilt afresh each life, but *jīva* is that force which incarnates into the construct via the Heart centre so that it can be utilised for a purpose. Continuity of consciousness is not retained between lives because this is not the best way to gain new experiences, and because a new mind is constructed and contained within the observable form *(śarīra).* The aggregates of that mind are sustained by *jīva* so that a self conscious identity develops. Once it has been so organised, consciousness can make the links via the pathways established by *jīva* to retrieve past life experiences.

The dialogue presented concerning this subject is that first the Vātīsīputīyas ask that if 'the *pudgala* is only a word serving to designate the five *skandhas*, why did the Buddha not declare that the vital principal (*jīva*) is the body?'[43] Vasubandhu's answer is as follows:

> Because the Buddha takes into consideration the intention (*āśaya*) of whoever asks him questions. The person who asks this question of the Buddha understood by *jīva*, not a being, a simple designation of the *skandhas*, but a person, a real living entity; and he was thinking of this person when he asked if the *jīva* is identical to the body or different from the body. Now this *jīva* does not absolutely exist; and so the Buddha only maintained that this is neither identical to nor different from the body, and then the Blessed One condemned the two answers. In a like manner one cannot say that the hairs of a tortoise are hard or soft.[44]

When one presumes to know what is in the mind of a Buddha when one is answering a question then one is treading upon very dangerous philosophical grounds. Clearly the Vātīsīputīyas had a different interpretation of the Buddha's intent than did Vasubandhu. The Buddha answered truthfully, because the reality lies somewhere in between *jīva* being a real living entity, and part of the designation of *skandhas*. *Jīva*[45] partakes of both. If *jīva* is defined as 'a person, a real living entity' then Vasubandhu's assertion that such a '*jīva* does not absolutely exist' is correct. It is however defined as 'inherent life force, a vitality that integrates the factors of existence of a sentient or conscious being by means of that force'. The concept of *jīva* as 'life force' is what is important here. It is *not* the person *per se*, hence Vasubandhu is incorrect in his assertion. It is the *prāṇa* that has become assimilated by an entity and converted into his own life force (or *prāṇic* fluid) by the action of the Heart centre. It is that which distinguishes one's *prāṇic* emanations from all others. It is a certain type of energy (*prāṇa*) that has been incorporated from the external to the system, through food intake and the breath, (therefore it is a *skandha*), as well as from the I-consciousness, and made integral to that living evolving personal-I by means of a process necessitating the functioning of the I-consciousness via the Heart centre

43 Ibid., 1332.

44 Ibid.

45 Leaving aside here momentarily the interpretation of *jīva* as referring to the entire human individual, namely as the energy that animates one, causing one to be an integral being.

(therefore it is more than just a *skandha*). Here the external *prāṇa* and the internal indigenous life force (from the I-consciousness) are integrated. This makes an integral unity of the two and this unity is termed *jīva*. If the *prāṇa* was not properly integrated in this way it could not be utilised by the person concerned. It would remain alien to his system, in a similar sense that a piece of fruit is alien to a human until eaten. The Buddha's answer to this question was therefore correct.[46]

This subject of exactly what *jīva* is, is quite important, because there is a line of energy from the *tathāgatagarbha* to the central point in the Head centre (the *antaḥkaraṇa* or consciousness-thread), and another similar thread anchored in the Heart centre which is the Life-line *(sūtrātmā)*. The blood stream and its functioning is the exoteric externalisation of this thread. For this reason the Heart is Life. These links between the I-consciousness and the personal-I are necessary, allowing transmittance of *saṃskāras (prāṇas)* from one to the other, otherwise there can be no such thing as rebirth. The links consequently facilitate the expression of *karma* unique to that individual, plus the faculty of prevision, intuition, and the attainment of all attributes of an enlightened Mind. Because of the existence of these links the *guru* is said in yogic texts to be revealed in the Heart and above the Head. It is essential for those who consider the personal-I to simply be a 'heap' of aggregates to ponder *how exactly* consciousness can transcend those aggregates. They must query why meditation techniques purporting to liberate one invariably teach of focussing or entering within the Heart centre, or to journey upwards from the Base of the Spine to the Head lotus (and beyond), to gain liberation.

From this perspective, contrary to Vasubandhu's assertion, *jīva* exists because it thereby segregates one 'heap' of *skandhas* here (representing one personal-I) from another over there (another personal-I), allowing the expression of personal *karma*. If there was no individual life force behind any action, then all *karma* would be impersonal and answerable to any 'heap' of *skandhas* anywhere. In other words what I do in the now can manifest as someone else's *karma,* no matter how evil or depraved it may be. Clearly the notion of karmic justice is dispelled if there is no

---

46 See below for an explanation of Vasubandhu's statement 'then the Blessed One condemned the two answers'.

method for its accounting, if there is no life force distinguishing one individuality from another.

The concept of *jīva* introduces a complexity of aetiological concern as to the nature of what constitutes a 'self' or 'not-self', which the Buddha was not prepared to delve into at that time. Hence, according to Vasubandhu, 'the Buddha only maintained that this is neither identical to nor different from the body, and then the Blessed One condemned the two answers'. This is because *jīva* is the force of Life allowing a body to be sustained, hence it is something other than being identical or different from the body.

Vasubandhu manifested a skewered reasoning in trying to make it comply with his philosophy, where he stated that in 'a like manner one cannot say that the hairs of a tortoise are hard or soft'. This is a way of stating that because in his opinion *jīva* did not exist, it was immaterial or wrong to designate it with imaginary qualities. He then continues with an illustration to prove his point, which concludes with the statement 'In the same way, Oh King, the vital principal does not exist: one cannot then answer your question and say that it is identical to the body or different from the body'.[47] Such vitality however can be seen by anyone who is clairvoyant, and also has been proven to exist by means of Kirlian photography,[48] where not only is it shown in the missing portion of a leaf that has been cut in half (etc.), but also radiating from the finger tips, and clearly showing changes in energy states in accordance with mood states, health and sickness.

The Vātīsīputīyas did not agree with him and so asked: 'But if the *pudgala* does not exist, why didn't the Blessed One answer that the *jīva* absolutely does not exist'. [49] Vasubandhu's answer:

> Because he took into consideration the intention of the questioner, that questioning on the *jīva* may be with the idea that the *jīva* is a series of *skandhas*. If the Blessed One answered that the *jīva* absolutely does not

---

47 Ibid., 1333.

48 See for instance such books as that by L. Gennaro, F. Guzzon and P. Marsigli. *Kirlian Photography, Research and Prospects*, (East West Publications. San Francisco, 1980). Also, Dennis Milner and Edward Smart, *The Loom of Creation* (Neville Spearman, London, 1975).

49 Louis de La Valée Poussin, *Abhidharmakośabhāṣyam*, Vol. IV, 1333.

> exist, the questioner would have fallen into false views. Furthermore, as the questioner was not capable of understanding "dependent origination" (*pratītyasamutpāda*), he was not a fit receptacle for the Good Law: the Blessed One then did not tell him that the *jīva* exists except by way of designation.
>
> The explanation that we have given here is the same that the Blessed One formulated: "Ānanda, the wandering monk Vatsagotra came to me to ask a question thusly: 'Is there, or is there not a soul (*ātman*)?' I did not answer him. In fact, to answer that there is a soul is to contradict the truth of things, because no *dharma* is a soul nor has any relationship with a soul; and if I had answered that there is no soul, I would have increased the folly of Vatsagotra, for he would have thought: 'I had a soul, but this soul does not now exist.' For, in comparison to the folly of the belief in the existence of a soul, this second folly is graver. Whoever believes in a soul falls into the extreme view of eternity; whoever believes that the soul does not exist falls into the extreme view of annihilation.[50]

Vasubandhu goes on a little further in his explanation of the subject of the *jīva*, but the above suffices. As the quote in relation to Vatsagotra is explained in detail in the chapter entitled *The Buddha and the Soul Concept*[51] in Volume 3, it need not be delved into here. The Buddha's intended meaning is always open to interpretation. It is all too easy to relate to an exoteric interpretation in such dialogues, which is almost universally done, rather than an esoteric one, which shall be explained in that chapter.

Fire and its fuel

It should be noted that many of the arguments put forth by Vasubandhu to repudiate the *pudgala* doctrine centre on it being immortal (like the doctrine of the *ātman*), hence he can prove his conjectures, as immortality is not a property of any phenomenal 'thing'.

The argument runs as follows:

> [The Vātīsīputīyas:] The *pudgala* really exists, as it is said, that 'To say that I really, truly do not have an *ātman* is an incorrect opinion."

---

50 Ibid., 1333-34.

51 There the Pali name Bachchhagotta is used instead of the Sanskrit Vatsagotra.

> [Vasubandhu:] This is not a proof, for it is also said that it is an incorrect opinion to affirm the existence of an *ātman*. Scholars of the Abhidharma think that a belief in the existence of an *ātman* and a belief in its non-existence are two extreme opinions, as they identify them with the two branches of "the opinion that consists in believing in extremes." This doctrine is certain, as it is formulated in the *Vatsagotrā-sūtra,* "Ānanda, those who affirm a soul fall into the extreme of the belief in permanence; those who deny a soul fall into the extreme of the belief of annihilation...[52]"

The doctrine concerning the I-consciousness, as presented in this treatise, explains precisely how one can indeed avoid the traps of falling into either of these two extremes, of permanence or annihilation, in accord with the proper interpretation of this *sūtra*. In continuing with the quote, we have:

> [The Vātīsīputīyas]: If the *pudgala* does not exist, what is it that wanders in *saṃsāra?* In fact, one can only allow that *saṃsāra* itself wanders. Further the Blessed One once has said, "Beings misled by ignorance, bound by thirst, wander here and there, either among beings in hell, among animals, among *pretas,* humans, or the gods; thus for a long time they experience all suffering".[53]

The phrase 'one can only allow that *saṃsāra* itself wanders' is a correct assumption when one is analysing the doctrine of 'homogeneous series', because here we only have the various categories of *saṃsāra* moving. If the only categories that change relate to the phenomena and illusion flowing in myriads of streams of homogeneous series (as each 'human unity', I presume, has its own individual 'series'), then indeed, what is it that aspires to gain enlightenment? Also, how can such aspiration arise out from that which is flowing homogeneously in the form of *saṃsāric* activities. The presumption is that *saṃskāras* (carrying the *skandhas*) come to the fore when activated by *karma*, but it already has been proven that *karma* needs 'something', an 'it', or 'self' to act upon that which is responsible or 'owns' the karmic repercussions. Otherwise the concept of *karma* acting is meaningless, as there is nothing

52 Ibid., 1336-67.

53 Ibid., 1337. The author states that this quote is from *Saṃyukta Nīkaya, Taishō Canon* 2, 42b3.

upon which *karma* can act. Plainly, *saṃsāra* will only produce *saṃsāra* out of itself, as that is all that can flow in this uninterrupted series of *saṃskāric* expression. Vasubandhu at first cleverly *avoids answering* this most vexing of questions by asking a related question:

> How does the *pudgala* wander in *saṃsāra?* Would you say that this wandering consists in abandoning old *skandhas* and in taking up new *skandhas*? But we have shown that this explanation is inadmissible. A good explanation is simple: one says that when a flame burns a field it travels, although they be only moments of flame, because it constitutes a series; in the same way the harmony of the *skandhas* which is constantly repeated receives, metaphorically, the name of being; supported by thirst, the series of *skandhas* travels in *saṃsāra*.[54]

Vasubandhu's example is not a correct analogy, because as a flame travels it acts as a wave of fire, utterly consuming everything in its path, leaving only a blackened scene of where it has been. With a series associated with a human personality such is not the case, the *saṃskāras* of the past must be able to come to the fore at any moment of this series (not blackened remains) as resuscitated by *karma*. Memory must thereby be accounted for. In other words, the past cannot be irrevocably eradicated. Also a flame is driven by the availability of its fuel and *can only* travel that way, but with a human series such is not the case; it is partly driven by its 'fuel' (thirst, desire, craving), but is also capable of *wilfully* manifesting actions or movement leading to the ending of one series and the starting of another one that leads to the transmutation of the concept of 'series', the attainment of enlightenment. Thus it can change direction any way it wishes for any whim, to even go over old ground—where it has been, where the fuel that formerly sustained it no longer exists, or to new ground. The physical flame can only consume, leaving behind death and destruction, and itself die. Consciousness-growth on the other hand is the result of the flow of *saṃskāras* directed towards an evolutionary goal—enlightenment. Such enlightenment is inevitable for all because all have the Buddha-germ (*tathāgatagarbha*) within. This is a basic postulate for the Mahāyāna. But how this Buddha-germs acts thus is obviously not clearly understood, thus needs to be clarified.

A *pudgala*, in the form of a personal-I, wanders via the expression

---

54 Ibid.

of resurfacing *saṃskāras*, which can also be altered by taking up new *saṃskāras*. The important thing here is that this process necessitates the use of the will/desire, but such conscious choice is impossible in the process of a 'homogeneous stream'. Something (a *'pudgala') must so choose,* and this but validates the Vātīsīputīyas logic. The debate continues:

> [The Vātīsīputīyas]: If only the *skandhas* exist, we do not see how one can explain these words of the Blessed One, "In the past, I was the teacher Sunetra." In fact, in the hypothesis of the existence of individual *skandhas* metaphorically termed "soul," past *skandhas* are not the same as present *skandhas*, and so the Blessed One cannot express himself in this manner.[55]

The use of the Buddha as an analogy is of importance here, because he has transmuted the qualities of what are described as *skandhas* above. The Vātīsīputīyas argument is that it can't have been the same *skandhas* in the teacher Sunetra as in the Buddha now, but what is it that moved to produce this complete transformation; how can such a transformation come about in a homogeneous series? Vasubandhu's answer is:

> But what is the thing that the Blessed One calls "soul"? The *pudgala*, you would say: then, since the "soul" is permanent, a past "soul" is identical with a present "soul". For us, when the Blessed One said, "I was the teacher Sunetra," he teaches us that the *skandhas* that constitute his present "soul" formed part of the same series as the *skandhas* that constituted Sunetra. In the same way one says, "This fire has been burning here."[56]

Once both sides admit to a 'permanent soul',[57] then Vasubandhu can

55 Ibid. The reference given to the quote is: *Vibhāṣā, Taishō Canon 27,* 424c15.

56 Ibid., 1337-38.

57 Arguments relating to the concept of 'permanent soul' are found throughout the text, as on page 1346: 'you cannot admit that the soul is in partial conjunction with the *manas*, for, according to you, the soul is an entity without parts'. A concept such as 'an entity without parts', or rather, discernable differentiation (no matter how subtle the differences of distinguishing features are) is a philosophic oxymoron, because all forms have parts or divisions. (Except maybe the smallest speck of 'matter', a quark or photon, but then they come under the laws of quantum mechanics, such as also being part of a wave front.)

Even *śūnyatā* can be considered to be constituted of 16 or 18 different forms, as explained earlier. In a similar vein Vasubandhu can state: 'Whence it follows that the soul is not omnipresent: and this contradicts your system'. (Ibid., 1346.) In this series it shall be shown that the I-consciousness is only omnipresent with respect to the personal-I that is its incarnate instrument, as it must be if all aspects of *karma* and associated *saṃskāras* are to be expressed thereto via the three times of the evolving personality.

win the debate, but my Thesis only admits to 'relative permanence', so the debate continues. Also that the series of *skandhas* as Sunetra being the same as that of Gautama Buddha, is highly debatable, because in Gautama the series of *skandhas* has ended, but not that which is the essence of the series, namely the enlightened liberated being we term the Tathāgata, the 'thus gone one'. Clearly there is a difference, and what 'it' is that has caused the change to come about is what the debate is truly about.

Also there is much bandying about of different *sūtras* between the two camps, bringing up the question of what is authoritative.[58] In response to this one should refer to the *Anguttara Nikaya iii. Vii 65,* which was commented upon in Chapter one.[59]

Therefore, let us first look to logic for proof substantiated by *pratyakṣa* (direct non deceptive perception). A *sūtra* may present such logic, but let us first verify that the sequence of the teachings of that *sūtra* is clearly understood and veridical. The eleventh point made is:

11. Similarly, why did the Buddha declare *'pudgala'* to be indeterminable or undefinable? If it did not exist, then why did he not say in clear terms that *'pudgala'* does not exist at all?

This is a good point, well worth answering by Buddhists who deny the existence of such an entity. Why did the Buddha, who is so much more enlightened than they, *not deny* the existence of a *pudgala?* If

---

However it is not everywhere in the external universe, within which the personality structure must evolve. Hence Vasubandhu's arguments are invalidated here because the I-consciousness/*tathāgatagarbha* has a relative permanence with respect to the life of the personal-I. It is also constituted of 'parts'.

58 [The Vātsīputrīyas] These texts are not authoritative, because they are not read in our tradition.

> What then is the authority in your system, your tradition or the words of the Buddha? If it is your tradition, then the Buddha is not your teacher, and you are not a child of the śākyan. If it is the work of the Buddha, why do you not recognise the authority of all the words of the Buddha!

Ibid., 1325-6.

59 Do not simply believe whatever you are told, or whatever has been handed down from past generations, or what is common opinion, or whatever the scriptures say. Do not accept something as true merely by deduction or inference, or by considering outward appearances, or by partiality for a certain view, or because of its plausibility, or because your teacher tells you it is so. But when you yourselves directly know. From the *Anguttara Nikaya* iii. Vii 65, *Kesamutti Sutta (Kālāma Sutta)* iii, ix (Pali Text Society).

he had done so it would have established the conclusive basis for their assertions, but this was not the case.

I shall present further arguments in the next two volumes, extending this doctrine of the nature of the I-consciousness to its conclusion, and accordingly define what exactly a human 'soul'/*tathāgatagarbha* is and the mechanism of its activity.

What Hopkins says about the difference between the Prāsaṅgikas and non-Prāsaṅgikas should be noted, before starting a detailed enquiry into the subject of 'self'.

> The cardinal difference between the Prāsaṅgikas and non-Prāsaṅgikas, as defined by Dzong-ka-ba, Jam-yang-shay-ba, and so forth, is the Prāsaṅgikas' uncommon notion that the *existent* person is not any or all of the mental and physical aggregates. The other Buddhist schools accept either the composite of the aggregates, or the continuum of the aggregates, or the mental consciousness, or the continuum of the mental consciousness as the self. For them, actions could have no cause or effect if the self were merely imputed in the sense of being totally unfindable among the bases of designation of the self. The Prāsaṅgikas answer that if objects were analytically findable as the concrete entities they seem to be, cause and effect would be impossible.
>
> According to the Prāsaṅgikas, even Hearers and Solitary Realizers cognize the same emptiness as Bodhisattvas; all Superiors realize that persons and other phenomena do not inherently exist. It is necessary to be freed from the afflictions achieve nirvana, which is the passage beyond the afflictions, and the chief of afflictions is the conception that persons and other phenomena inherently exist. Thus, without destroying this conception, liberation from cyclic existence is impossible. Chandrakīrti clearly states that the emptiness of both the person and other phenomena must be cognized in order to achieve liberation. The reason is that the conception of a self of phenomena causes the conception of a self of persons. For Chandrakīrti, to be liberated from cyclic existence means to have destroyed the conception that persons and other phenomena inherently exist.[60]

To the Prāsaṅgika assertion that 'if objects were analytically findable as the concrete entities they seem to be, cause and effect would be impossible', it can be answered that they are findable (for limited durations of existence), thus we have 'cause and effect'. If they were not findable then cause and effect would be impossible, because there would be nothing that could

60 Hopkins, 195-196.

manifest a cause and nothing that could experience an effect. *Karma*, in the Prāsaṅgika way of viewing things would thus be a meaningless impossibility, a non-event, rather than being a prime means whereby each human unit can find his/her way home to liberated domains of Mind.

The phrase 'analytically findable' needs to be properly defined, otherwise we can only presume that by 'analytical' the Prāsaṅgikas are referring to the logic presented in their 'Seven Cornered Reason' and 'Diamond Slivers' etc. But this again brings us to concepts of inherent non-existence, which also means the non-existence of *karma*. So how can cause and effect and the evolution of Bodhisattvahood be possible under these conditions of 'non-existence'?

I have already agreed with Candrakīrti's assertion that 'to be liberated from cyclic existence means to have destroyed the conception that persons and other phenomena inherently exist', but this does not mean that such phenomena does not exist. One can say on this score that: they do exist (as phenomena); do not exist (in *śūnyatā*); simultaneously do and do not exist (in the I-consciousness); and neither exist and do not exist (in *dharmakāya*). It all depends upon our point of view and where upon the time scale we are viewing what is/is not.

Enlightenment means much more than just the destruction of concepts such as 'the conception that persons and other phenomena inherently exist'. Enlightenment really means being able to comprehend many viewpoints concerning anything at once and to deduce the related reality. That nothing is destroyed, but everything is retained in one form or other, is another truth to the enlightened Mind that is just as valid. All forms of phenomena transmogrify into other forms of being and so evolution spirals on into subtler and subtler states of existence, until everything disappears into *śūnyatā*. *Śūnyatā* may be the base of the enlightened Mind, but that it not all there is to it. Everything can be relegated to memory, thus the ability to envision the three times is established, but *śūnyatā* represents an emptiness of mind, hence an abeyance of this 'memory'. It however sets the conditions whereby anything of the past can be instantly retrieved, thus manifests the enlightened Mind. How memory is retained, and the vastness of its scope, is the great mystery of being/non being. Welcome to the *dharmakāya*.

Now let us continue with the next volumes, to see what part the I-consciousness plays in this spiral dance to Bliss.

Oṁ

Bibliography

Anacker, S. *Seven Works of Vasubandhu.* Delhi: Motilal Banarsidass, 2005.

Bailey, Alice A. *Discipleship in the New Age II.* New York: Lucis Publishing Company, 1968.

——. *Esoteric Astrology.* New York: Lucis Publishing Company, 1968.

——. *Esoteric Psychology Vol. 1.* New York: Lucis Publishing Company, 1968.

——. *Esoteric Psychology Vol. 2.* New York: Lucis Publishing Company, 1970.

——. *The Rays and the Initiations.* New York: Lucis Publishing Company, 1988.

Balsys, Bodo. *A Treatise on Mind, Volume 4* Sydney: Universal Dharma Publishing, 2014.

——. *A Treatise on Mind, Volume 5a* Sydney: Universal Dharma Publishing, 2015.

——. *A Treatise on Mind, Volume 5b* Sydney: Universal Dharma Publishing, 2015.

——. *Karma and the Rebirth of Consciousness.* Delhi: Munshiram Manoharlal, 2006.

Chang, G.C.C. Trans., *The Hundred Thousand Songs of Milarepa, Vol 1.* London: Shambhala, 1977.

Chokdan, Shakya. Trans. and Komarovsilaroslav. *Three Texts on Madhyamaka.* Dharmamsala: Library of Tibetan Works and Archives, 2000.

Coleman, G. Ed., *A Handbook of Tibetan Culture.* London: Rider, 1993.

——. *The Handbook of Tibetan Buddhism.* Delhi: Rupa & Co., 1995.

Dudjom Rinpoche, *The Nyingma School of Tibetan Buddhism.* Translated by Gyurme Dorje and Matthew Kapstein. Boston: Wisdom, 1991.

Eckel, M. D. *Jñānagarbha on the Two Truths.* Delhi: Motilal Banarsidass, 1992.

Garfield, Jay L. *'Taking Conventional Truth Seriously: Authority Regarding Deceptive Reality'.* Philosophy East and West, University of Hawaii Press.

Gennaro, L, Guzzon, F, and Marsigli, P. *Kirlian Photography, Research and Prospects.* San Francisco: East West Publications, 1980.

Govinda, Lama Anagarika. *Foundations of Tibetan Mysticism.* London: Century Paperbacks, 1987.

Gribbin, John. *In Searchh of the Edge of Time. Black Holes, White Holes, Wormholes.* London: Penguin Bools, 1992.

Griffith, P.J. *On Being Buddha, The Classical Doctrine of Buddhahood.* Delhi: Sri Satguru Publications, 1995.

Gyatso, Geshe Kelsang. *Clear Light of Bliss, A Commentary to the Practice of Mahāmūdra in Vajrayana Buddhism.* Boston: Wisdom Publications, 1982.

Hookham, S. K. *The Buddha Within: Tathagatagarbha Doctrine According to the Shentog Interpretation of the Ratnagotravibhaga.* Delhi: Sri Satguru Publications, 1992.

Hopkins, J. *Meditation on Emptiness.* London: Wisdom Publications, 1983.

Inada, Kenneth. K. *Nāgārjuna. A Translation of his Mūlamadhyamakakārikā with an Introductory Essay.* Delhi: Sri Satguru, 1993.

Kalupahana, D.J. Trans. *Mūlamadhyamakakārikā of Nāgārjuna. The Philosophy of the Middle Way.* Delhi: Motilal Banarsidass, 1999.

La Vellée Poussin, Louis. *Abhidarmakośabhāṣyam, Vol. IV.* California: Asian Humanities Press, Berkley 1991.

Lopez, D.S. Jr. *A Study of Svātantrika.* New York: Snow Lion Publications, 1987.

——. *Buddhist Hermeneutics.* Delhi: Motilal Banarsidass, 1993.

Milner, Dennis and Smart, Edward. *Loom of Creation*. London: Neville Spearman, 1975.

Mittal, Kewal Krishan. *Perspectives on Karma and Rebirth*. Delhi: Dept. of Buddhist Studies, Delhi University, 1990.

Mukhin, K. N. *Experimental Nuclear Physics, Volume II, Elementary Particle Physics*. Moscow: Mir Publishers, 1987.

Napper, Elizabeth. *Dependent Arising and Emptiness*. Boston: Wisdom Publications, 1989.

Nyanatiloka and Nyanaponika Ed. *Buddhist Dictionary, Manual of Buddhist Terms and Doctrines*. Taiwan: The Corporate Body of Buddhist Educational Foundation, Third Edition, 1970.

Pettit, John. W. *Mipham's Beacon of Certainty, Illuminating the View of Dzogchen, the Great Perfection*. Boston: Wisdom, 1999.

Reynolds, J. M. *The Golden Letters*. Ithaca: Snow Lion, 1996.

Rinpoche, Kalu. *The Dharma That Illumines All Beings Impartially Like the Light of the Sun and the Moon*. Albany: State University of New York Press, 1986.

Snellgrove, D. *Indo-Tibetan Buddhism*. Boston: Shambhala, 2002.

Sparham, G. *Ocean of Eloquence, Tsong-kha-pa's Commentary on the Yogācāra Doctrine of Mind*. Delhi: Sri Satguru, 1995.

Tayé, Jamgön Kongtrul Lodrö. *Buddhist Ethics* (Trans. and Ed.) New York: Snow Lion Publications, 2003.

——. *The Treasury of Knowledge; Systems of Buddhist Tantra*. New York: Snow Lion, 2005.

Thakchoe, Sonam. '*Status of Conventional Truth in Tsong Khapa's Mādhyamika Philosophy*'. Contemporary Buddhism, Vol. 8, No. 1, May 2007.

Thurman, R.A.F. *The Speech of Gold; Reason and Enlightenment in Tibetan Buddhism*. Delhi: Motilal Banarsidass, 1989.

Wayman, Alex. *Untying the Knots in Buddhism, Selected Essays*. Delhi: Motilal Banarsidass, 1997.

——. *Yoga of the Guhyasamājatantra, the Arcane Lore of Forty Verses*. Delhi: Motilal Banarsidass, 2005.

Index

A

Abhidharma, 115, 116, 185, 305, 436
  and eight types of saints, 415
  theory, 297
Abhisamaya, 148
Abhisamayālaṃkara, 32
Abhrānta, 40
Absolute beginning, 224
Absolute reality, 62
Absolutes, 64
Absolute valuable reality, 288–289
Abstract Mind, 18, 120, 297, 410, 418
Accumulation
  Buddhist concept of, 427–428
Activity
  five types of, 298–299
Ādi Buddha, 107
  and Dependent Origination, 284
  Consort, 178, 284
  role in evolution, 70
Ādi śūnyatā, 190
Advaita Vedanta, 100
Aggregates, 170–172, 391, 400
  and a person, 383, 385, 388
  and citta, 256
  and consciousness, 171–172, 386
  and Prāsaṅgika view, 388–389, 390
  and the 'I' or 'self', 236–237, 260–267, 371–375, 398, 404, 405, 408
  and the personal-I, 260–261, 386
  defined, 237
  flow of, 257
  need for direction, 386
Ahamkāra, 243
Ākāra, 212, 213
Akāśa, 190
Ālambana, 425
Ālayavijñāna, 59, 69, 117–118, 120, 148, 150, 163, 166, 177, 189, 251, 252, 292, 295, 297, 307, 308, 312, 314, 331, 365, 418
  and aggregates, 386
  and consciousness, 201, 240, 313–314
  and dharmakāya, 127–128, 154, 317–318
  and Fiery Element, 314
  and kliṣṭamanas, 169
  and self-nature, 297
  and Yogācāra, 34, 277
  as universal consciousness, 164
  definition, 68
  enlightenment, 29, 37
  environment, 400

experience of, 144
Alchemical Elements, 24
Alice Bailey
works of, 112, 372
All-accomplishing Wisdom, 29, 82, 141, 190, 328, 331
All-seeing Eye, 107, 289, 304, 425
and enlightened vision, 430
Āloka, 181
Analysts, 115
Analytically findable
meaning of, 441
Ānanda, 435
Aneka, 201
Anima mundi, 251
Anitya, 271
Annihilation
case for, 81
erroneous term, 393
explained, 77, 80
Antaḥkaraṇa, 433
Anu, 229
Anumāna, 38
Anutpanna, 309
Anuyoga, 105
Anvaya-vyatireka, 181, 193
Apekṣhyasamutpāda, 272, 287
definition, 273
Aprattiṣṭhita-nirvāṇa, 14
Arhat, 37
Arhat śūnyatā, 190
Arising
and Dependent Origination, 271
Arthakriya, 115
Arthasāmānya, 85, 92
Arūpa, 106
universe, 179
Āryadeva, 199, 273
Ārya path, 169
Asaṅga, 2, 33, 39, 117, 122, 154, 331
Asat, 306
Āśaya, 432
Aśraddhā, 165
Aṣṭadiśas, 110, 111, 112, 116
utilisation of, 114
Astrology, esoteric, 62
Asūras, 189
As without, so within, 186–187
Atiśaya, 216
Atiśūnya, 177
Ātma-dṛṣṭi, 327
Ātma-māna, 327
Ātma-moha, 327
Ātman, 69, 89, 133, 163, 172, 200, 249, 265, 380, 416, 435
and pudgala doctrine, 435–436
and 'soul', 410
and the two extremes, 436
as 'self', 389
definition, 36, 93
erroneous concept, 135
Ātma-sneha, 327
Atomists, 115, 116
Atom/s
constituents of, 224
theory of, 227–228
Authoritative, 439
Authoritative persons, 38
Avaktavya, 413
Avalokiteśvara
1000 armed, 193
Avidyā, 177, 271
Awakening
levels of, 45–46
Ayatana, 148
definition, 9

B

Bachchhagotta, 435
Bardo Thödol, 191, 324
tantric precepts of, 77
Bhāra, 415
Bhārahārasutta
and pudgalas, 415
Bhāvavādin, 115
Bhāvaviveka, 70, 84, 89, 90, 119, 227, 383, 385, 387
methodology of, 147–150
Bhavya, 121
Bhinna, 185, 194

Bhūmi/s, 161, 270, 393
  definition, 161
  redefined, 271
  Tathātgata, 189
Big Bang
  and śūnyatā, 91, 288
Bīja/s, 68, 71, 92, 124, 166, 204, 285, 297, 307, 317, 364, 365, 423
  and ālayavijñāna, 154
  and rebirth, 314
  and Watery Element, 314
  clothing, 300
  definition, 69
  explained, 313–314
  of activity, 287
  of consciousness, 386, 423
  of memory, 374
  of thought, 241, 308, 418, 419–420
  of Void Elements, 295
Bindu, 316
Black hole, 223–224
Black magic, 231
Bodhi, 76
  bodhi-tree, 12, 17–19, 76, 238
  definition, 12, 34–35
  enlightened Mind, 17
Bodhicitta, 67, 148, 170, 245, 251, 267, 268, 279, 299, 303, 400
  activation of, 139
  and Bodhisattva bhūmis, 161
  and ignorance, 169
  and intelligence, 160–161
  and intuition, 168
  and karma, 283, 285
  and kliṣṭamanas, 169
  and Love-Wisdom, 373
  and transmutation, 406
  application of, 354
  as light, 333
  definition, 34–35, 61
  energy via śūnyatā, 394
  explained, 280
  expression of, 144, 248
  generation of, 117, 141, 430
  momentum of, 270
  not self-made, 315
Bodhisattva-child, 353–354
Bodhisattva-Mind, 384
Bodhisattva path, 63, 98–99, 149, 270, 301
  and inner voice, 255
  ideal, 141
  progression towards, 242, 374
Bodhisattva/s, 99, 204, 287, 315
  and emptiness, 440
  and karma, 315
  and śūnyatā, 353
  capacity to reason, 234
  compassion of, 170
  consciousness of, 225–226
  council of, 37, 112, 384, 391
  development of, 395
  different, 246
  ideal, 330
  skilful means, 112, 394
Bodhisattvaship
  and reformation, 389
  flowering of, 408–409
Brahṃā, 252
Brahmanical philosophy, 187, 266
Buddha, 83, 84, 129, 234, 252, 414, 427, 434
  and cosmic journey, 247
  and his vision, 429
  and ignorance states, 270–271
  and karma, 136, 351
  and meditation, 286
  and Mind-Space, 107, 132
  and omniscience, 428
  and Theravāda sūtras, 330
  and truths, 75, 132
  appearance of, 404
  as unifier, 235
  contradictions of, 142–144
  definition of, 133
  deviation from, 410
  evolution of, 263, 275
  experiences of, 76
  non denial of a pudgala, 439

not speaking, 46–47, 205, 251
primordial, 247
questioned re jīva, 432–434
thus gone, 131
view on 'self', 389
Buddha-field, 99, 107, 179
Buddha-germ, 275, 283, 292, 295, 437
Buddhahood
attainment of, 146, 192, 221, 259
definition, 260
journey to, 266
Buddha-Mind, 81, 100, 153, 162, 171, 174, 222, 241, 316
and bodhicitta, 161
and karma, 284, 285
and law of cycles, 296–297
attributes of, 247
definition, 317
evolution of, 426
omniscience of, 291
Buddha nature, 87
Buddhapālita, 55, 157, 380
Buddhas
different, 198
Buddhavacana, 20, 32
Buddha womb, 98, 161, 162, 276
Buddhism
charter of, 410
esoteric, 89
fifth epoch of, 331
paradoxes, 130
Buddhist philosophy, 153
Buddhist Tantric schools, 331
Byang-chub kyi sems, 280

C

Caitasika, 177
Caitta, 169
Cakṣur-vijñāna, 181, 183
Candrakīrti, 9, 55, 78, 80, 82, 100, 103, 119, 157, 188, 204, 240, 241, 250, 264, 266, 291, 297, 371, 380, 387, 390, 393
arguments, 93–94, 198–199, 292, 395
refutation of 'self', 380, 382
view on liberation, 440
Cārvākas, 227
Catuṣkoṭikā, 90, 158
and śūnyatā, 317
Causative Agents, 202–203
Cause and effect, 180–184, 202, 344–345
Causeless condition, 204
Causeless zone, 203
Cause/s
and continuum, 345
single, 358, 360–361
Centrist/s, 7, 115, 117, 118–119
Candrakīrti, 9
Tsongkhapa, 9
Cetanā, 269
Chakra, 192–193
Ājñā, 29, 30, 36, 37, 107, 123–124, 425, 426
Base of Spine centre, 24, 31, 34, 35, 36, 123, 193
Head centre, 29, 30, 33, 34, 36, 37, 107, 123, 125, 425
and liberation, 27
Heart centre, 31, 33, 34, 61, 123, 140, 169, 193, 327, 337, 425, 431, 433
and Airy Element, 329
and eight petals, 328
and śūnyatā, 33
as 12 spoked wheel, 111
sacred and non-sacred petals, 329
Heart in the Head centre, 33, 61
Sacral centre, 31, 35, 36, 123
Solar Plexus centre, 28, 31, 35, 36, 123, 329
Throat centre, 31, 33, 34, 37, 123
Throat in the Head centre, 33
Chakra furnaces, 184
Chakras, 3, 22, 48, 54, 108, 191, 192–193, 298

and memory, 424
and the schools, 123–125
as fractioning units, 203
as subjective eyes, 426
definition, 22, 30–37, 287
five principal, 189
organisation of, 32
seven major, 30–31, 189, 192
Change
and evolution, 334–335
importance of, 340
inherently existing, 350
Chariot
functionality of, 377, 378
metaphor explained, 384
simile of, 372, 375–379
Child as seed, 338
Christ
as Maitreya, 112
Jesus, 141
Citta, 295, 411
and aggregates, 255–256
definition, 35, 177
Cittamātra, 8–9, 65, 71
doctrine, 273, 411
following reasoning, 113, 118
following scripture, 113, 117
Clear Light, 2, 12, 117, 128, 140, 145, 146–147, 149, 177, 178, 190, 238, 279, 309, 406
and saṃskāras, 177
and speed of thought, 322–323
as condition, 308
definition, 146
Cognitive factor, 209
Cognitive nature, 205–209, 212–213
explanation, 206–207, 213
process, 215
Compassion, 26, 33–34
Conditions
analysis of, 307–308
and activity, 313
and śūnyatā, 317
and their effects, 311–312
explanation of, 299–304
Conscience and intuition, 255
Consciousness, 183, 200–201, 206, 227, 238, 292, 363, 366, 367, 377, 379, 385
action of, 368–371
agent of karma, 283
and aggregates, 171–172, 256, 374
and ālayavijñāna, 240
and being human, 376, 379
and cause/effects, 346
and conditions, 311–312
and Dependent Origination, 279
and emptiness, 90
and intellect, 370
and personal-I's, 418
and rebirth, 238–239, 384–385
and saṃskāras, 437
and 'self', 383–384
and śūnyatā, 233, 321
and the Void Elements, 283
as a continuum, 409
as golden thread, 294
as the person, 387
cleansing of, 243
container of, 386
continuity of, 431
definition, 58–59
examination of, 308–318
expansion of, 232
explained, 208–211
paradigms of eventuation, 351
role played, 239, 307
signposts for, 352
store, 240, 251
Consciousnesses, six, 168, 169
Consciousness-stream
and saṃskāras, 242
Conscious volition, 253, 256
Consequentialists, 119, 391
Container of thought, 286
Continuum
and causes, 345
and 'own power', 359
explained, 87–88

Contradiction, literal, 41, 42, 44
Conventional reality, 75, 76, 287
Conventional thinkers, 64–65
Cosmic Identity, 106
Cosmic Mind, 129
Cross
fixed, 112, 187
mutable, 111
Culmination-of-Light, 190

D

Ḍākinīs, 32, 52, 176, 281
definition, 23
evolution of, 397
Darkness
as ignorance, 51
shades of, 140
Definitive interpretation, 4–7
Déjà vu, 424
Democritus, 227
Dependent-arising, 56–57, 60, 279
and consciousness, 281
as emptiness, 274
as king of reasoning, 272
synonyms of, 272–273, 287–290
Dependent-existence, 273, 290
Dependent Origination, 52, 60, 68, 95–96, 99, 134, 163, 187, 189, 199, 250, 269–275, 290, 295, 302, 318, 387, 435–436
and consciousness, 279
and karma, 284–287
cause of, 253
formula, 269–270
Desire
compassionate, 270
explanation, 168
use of, 438
Devas, 281
Dhāraṇīs, 357
Dharma, 35, 72, 235, 252, 351
as properties, phenomena, 202
definition, 6
eight spoked wheel of, 110–126
esoteric, 109, 125
outpourings of, 126–128
white, 22, 231
Dharmadhatu, 9
Wisdom, 29, 124, 190, 328, 330
Dharmakāya, 13, 14, 29, 52, 56, 62, 83, 84, 107, 109, 120, 146, 151, 154, 189, 191, 192, 234, 243, 247, 252, 253, 259, 282, 289, 296, 299, 303, 309, 313, 316, 354, 391
and ālayavijñāna, 128, 317–318
and Buddha-fields, 100
and consciousness, 201
and cosmos, 17–18
and Elements, 187
and I-consciousness, 237
and karma, 284, 382
and memory, 441
and Oneness, 179
and pratītyasamutpāda, 285
and saṃsāra, 11–13, 74, 87
and śūnyatā-saṃsāra nexus, 365
and Tantric philosophy, 129, 152
and truth, 16, 144
as buddha-body of reality, 121
as Mind, 71, 122
as the All, 48
as ultimate, 77, 86
as universal dharma, 106
beyond śūnyatā, 317
Buddha attributes, 51
definition, 6, 249
matrix of, 190
philosophy, 330
Reasoning, 82, 126, 159
revelation of, 125
way to, 149
Dharmakāya Way, 62, 64, 70, 83, 100, 102, 114, 123, 129, 133, 150, 161, 176
and dharmakāya, 37
and mahāmudrā, 290
definition, 37
explained, 108–109, 125–126
fifth epoch of Buddhism, 331

Dharmakāyic Mind, 12
Dharmakīrti, 117
Dharmanairātmya, 143
Dharmas, 185
    defined, 413, 428
Dharmatā, 63, 191
    definition, 27, 81
Dharmin, 202
Dhataraṭṭha, 323
Dhatu, 9, 143–144
Dhyāna, 106, 303, 409
Dhyāni Bodhisattvas, 330
Dhyāni Buddhas, 26, 34, 63, 83, 124, 154, 177–178, 193, 195, 222, 225, 282, 324, 328, 330
    Akṣobhya, 82, 190, 191, 328, 330
    Amitābha, 190, 191, 328, 331
    Amoghasiddhi, 29, 82, 190, 191, 328, 331
    and chakras, 30–31
    attributes of, 190–192
    colourings of, 141
    gnosis of, 191
    Ratnasambhava, 175, 190, 191, 328, 331
    Vairocana, 29, 190, 191, 328, 330
    Wisdoms, 178, 185, 187, 189, 190, 198, 204, 244, 260, 376, 393, 417
Diamond Fragments, 58
Dignāga, 117
Dimensions of perception, 55
Dīpeṅkara, 175
Directions of space
    cardinal, 112
    east (inward), 112, 117
    eight, 111–112
    northeast (unity), 111, 118
    north (upward), 112, 120
    northwest (goodwill), 111, 120
    south (downward), 112, 114
    southeast (expression), 111, 116
    southwest (understanding), 111, 116
    west (outward), 112, 118
Discriminating Inner Wisdom, 190, 328, 331
Divine, the, 120
Dogmaticists, 119
Dorje, 124, 196, 198, 204
Dragons of Wisdom, 29, 31
Dravya, 113, 114
Dudjom Rinpoche, 104–108

E

Ear, inner, 383
Earthy prāṇas, 29
Ear-whispered truths, 205
Eastern approach errors, 139
East-West integration, 137–144
Effect/s
    conditions for, 215
    continuum of, 359
    dependency of, 342–344
    existing and non-existing, 301–303, 356
Eight consciousnesses, 164
Eight directions of space, 110-120, 150
Eightfold Path, 30, 149, 170, 327
Eka-pudgala, 415
Ekatva, 36
Elements, 204
    18 experiential, 185
    Aether, 29, 31, 185, 187, 191, 299, 316, 329, 354, 373
    Air, 31, 185, 187, 191, 299, 313, 315, 329, 353, 374
    alchemical, 24, 191, 336
    and prāṇas, 196
    and swastikas, 196–197
    definition, 187
    doctrine of, 191, 193
    Earth, 31, 185, 186, 187, 191, 193, 213, 310, 314, 353, 375
    Fire, 31, 185, 187, 191, 197–198, 213, 311, 312, 314, 353, 374
    five, 167, 185–200, 309, 310, 353
        subdivisions, 195–198
        symbolism, 187

Intellect (sixth), 185
pure, 196, 300
seven, 192
transmutation of, 324
Void, 98, 124, 275, 278, 283, 297, 298, 307, 314–315, 316, 317, 324, 365, 417, 418
Water, 31, 167, 185, 187, 191, 213, 311, 314, 353, 375
Emotions
Fiery, 167
four afflictive, 166–167, 326–327
Emptiness, 59, 65, 94, 99, 130, 152, 155
and light, 147
and svabhāva, 188–189
and thoughts, 282
as dependent arising, 272, 274
as experience, 83
as flux, 90
as referent object, 85
as ultimate, 85, 104
definition, 83
extraneous, 11
intrinsic, 11
meaning of, 146
of inherent existence, 103
of person and aggregates, 395–397
two forms of, 122
Emptinesses
five different, 198
Endocrine glands, 30
Energy and the Void, 251
Energy fields, 52, 251
Enlightened, the
teachings of, 45–46
Enlightenment
ālayavijñāna, 29
dharmakāya, 29
differing degrees of, 21, 29, 32
path to, 348
stairway to, 150
śūnyatā, 29
Entityness, 380
Equalising Wisdom, 190, 328, 331
Etheric vehicle, 22
E-VAM, 104
Evolution
and change, 334–335
definition, 275
Existence, 275
dependent, 273, 290
explained, 226
inherent, 274
persistence of, 87
relative, 273
true, 93, 128–136, 392
Existents, 296, 310
Existent things, 303–304
Existent unities, 231
Existing entity
and Buddhahood, 292
Experientalists, 118
Eye
and śūnyatā, 324
inner, 383
white of, 324
Eye consciousness, 362, 365–366, 425
and attributes, 369–370
and I-concept, 361
explanation, 358–359
production of, 368
Eyes, subjective, 426

F

Fa Hsien, 411
Fanaticism, 412
Fire
allegory, 437
symbolism, 417
Fivefold reasoning, 371
Five, relationships, 309
Flame, objective of, 343
Four Alternatives, 358–361
Four conditionings, 365
Four conditions, 297–303, 305–306
Four-Cornered Proof, 319–320
expansion of, 323–326

Four Extremes, 114, 356
Four Noble Truths, 170, 203
Four Reliances, 9
Free will, 163
Fuel symbolism, 417
Functionality
 and pratītyasamutpāda, 294
 as ultimate truth, 293–294
 importance in definitions, 375, 377–379
 importance of, 288
Fundamental question, 402–403

G

Ganges, 172
Gautama, 175, 261
 nirvāṇa, 237–238
Gelugpa school, 112, 130
Gelug Prāsaṅgika, 72, 73
Geshe Gedün Lodrö, 319
Gift-waves, 302
Gluons, 224
God
 belief in, 141
 realm, 189
Go ram pa, 72
Great Madhyamaka, 104, 120–121, 123
Great Perfection, 105
Great Plan, 138
Great seal, 105, 124, 177
Great Symbol, 127
Great Void, 177
Guardians of the four gates, 324
 Amṛtakuṇḍalin, 324
 Hayagrīva, 324
 Vijaya, 324
 Yamāntaka, 324
Guṇa/s, 189–190, 252
Guru, 433
Guruparaṃparā, 39, 153
 definition, 40–41
Gyel-tsap, 130

H

Hāra, 415
Hawking, Stephen, 223
Hearers and emptiness, 440
Heart's Mind, 255
Heart Sūtra, 153
Hell realms, 189
Heruka/s, 312, 323–324
Hetu, 305
Hetu-kāraṇa, 201, 202
Hetu-pratyaya, 305, 306
Hierarchical structure
 and bījas, 423
Hīnayāna, 115, 266, 392
 śūnyatā, 317
Hindu
 concepts, 184
 rhetoric, 100
Homogeneous series, 420–423
 analysis of, 436–438
Humans
 and definitions of things, 348
 definition, 379
Human unit, 376

I

I
 and aggregates, 236–237, 257, 260–267
 and body shape, 267–268
 and consciousness, 171
 and factor of change, 241
 and the mind/body, 244–245
 appearance of, 257
 as base of mind and body, 258–259
 as seed, 336
 awareness of, 399
 concept of, 266
 definition, 163, 261–262
 functioning of, 248
 inherently produced, 239
 many per life, 243
 opinion about, 327
 pride in, 327
 stupidity about, 327
I-concept
 analysis of, 157

and eye consciousness, 361
definition, 54
establishment of, 243
purpose of, 244
I-consciousness, 171, 258, 283, 287, 291, 292, 294, 323, 348, 351, 352, 374, 379, 396, 400, 419–420, 425, 426, 429
and aggregates, 263–264, 399
and Bliss, 441
and composite attributes, 406–407
and deep sleep, 262
and enlightened Mind, 404
and Figure five, 330
and future possibilities, 430
and jīva, 432–433
and karma, 263, 291, 430–431
and kliṣṭamanas, 169
and memory, 261, 263–264, 423
and personal-I, 267
and pudgala, 416–431, 419
and rebirth, 262, 418
and 'self', 382–383, 393
and stored impressions, 239
and substance of mind, 276
and śūnyatā, 246
and tathāgatagarbha, 283
and the Four-Cornered Proof, 324–326
and the lotus, 244
and the two extremes, 436
and transience, 245–246
and wisdoms of Dyhani Buddhas, 417
as enlightened 'I', 401
definition, 163–165
doctrine of, 247
expansion of, 259
not produced, 237
omnipresent, 438
origin of, 418
philosophy of, 253
ralating śūnyatā to saṃsāra, 279
relative ultimate, 366
Idealists, 7–9, 115, 117, 118
hermeneutic, 9, 12
Ignorance
and bodhicitta, 169
and Dependent Origination, 269–272, 278, 285
definition, 134–135, 141, 285
levels of, 10, 51, 60, 76, 138, 364
origin of, 135
overcoming of, 321, 354
Images
and consciousness, 370–372
Imagination, 210
Imaginings, 305
Individuality, 340
explained, 280–281
Individual Way, 115
Inherent
definition, 79
existence, 81
and svabhāva, 188
Inherent life
and evolution, 276
Inherently explained, 237, 239–240, 241–242, 345, 350–351
Initiate, 45
Inner space, 353
Inner voice, 255
Insanity, 259
Integral Life
and true existance, 292
Intellect
as empirical mind, 381
as 'immediate', 308
as mind, 160
moralising, 168
Intended meaning, 41–43, 42
Intention, foundation of, 41, 43–44, 46
Interpretable in meaning, 4, 6–7
Interpretation
of things, 344
question of, 318
seven modes of, 39

Intuition, 389
and bodhicitta, 168
and śūnyatā, 168
functioning of, 255
Iris of the eye, 324
Īśvara, 212

J

Jainas, 227
Jam dbyangs bzhad pa, 72
Jam-yang-shay-ba, 440
Jam yang she pa, 156
Jang-gya, 84–85
Jina/s, 32, 150, 176. *See also* Dhyāni Buddhas
Jīva, 413, 416
and personal karma, 433
explanation, 431–432
interpretations of, 432
role of, 431–435, 433
Jñāna, 38, 177
vs prajñā, 38
Jñānagarbha, 147, 151, 152, 158, 179
methodology, 298–299
on two truths, 180–220
Jñeya, 72, 425
Jñeyāvaraṇa, 392

K

Kadācit, 181
Kalāchakra maṇḍala, 225
Kalpanoparacita, 202
Kalpita, 202, 210
Kamalaśīla, 84
Kāma-manas, 168–169
definition, 26, 54, 55
Karma, 44, 45, 52, 53, 161, 182, 184, 201, 215, 240, 244, 250, 251, 254, 259, 260, 261, 266, 285, 286, 287, 316, 326, 329, 330, 348, 351, 352, 381, 400–401, 405, 410, 423, 433
and a Buddha, 96, 136, 285
and aggregates, 399
and bodhicitta, 285
and coherent unities, 59, 163
and consciousness, 376
and emptiness, 95
and Four-Cornered Proof, 323, 325–327
and I-consciousness, 263, 291
and individuation, 248
and intuition, 255
and jīva, 433–434
and mūlaprakṛti, 314
and Prāsaṅgika view, 441
and pudgala doctrine, 416
and quest for liberation, 394
and saṃskāras, 80, 436
and sentience, 351
and śūnyatā, 136, 243
and svabhāva, 98
and the Bodhisattva, 315
and the ultimate, 211
and the Void Elements, 283
and time, 336
and uninterrupted series, 436–437
and volitions, 154
as binding agent, 276
as conventional truth, 136
as prime directive force, 95–96, 133
conjoined, 328
creation of, 256, 321
directing principle of, 283
erroneous version of, 43
formations, 269, 295, 296
group, national, international, 326, 328, 333, 339, 351, 402
limitations of, 403–404
Lords of, 154, 281, 324
modus operandi, 335, 421
origination of, 284
planetary, 351
streams of, 242–243, 315
waves of, 343
working of, 203, 333
Kashmiri Vaibhāṣika, 385
Kausīdya, 165

Kāya, 100, 427
Kirlian photography, 434
Kleśa/s, 169
  as afflictive emotions, 165, 166
Kleśāvaraṇa, 392
Kliṣṭa, 169
Kliṣṭamanas, 163–170, 177, 311
  and bodhicitta, 169
  and emotional volitions, 167, 169
  and neutral perfumes, 168
  as afflictive emotions, 166, 326–327
  defintion, 165
  explanation, 165–170
  foundation of, 328
  nine mental factors, 167–168
Kliṣṭa-mano-vijñāna, 164
Kṣaṇa, 35, 218
Kuṇḍalinī, 30
  definition, 24
  raising of, 27–28
Kuvera, 323

L

Lakṣaṇa-satya, 13
Lalanā, 25
Laṅkāvatāra Sūtra, 164
Law of cycles, 335, 362
  and Buddha-Mind, 297
Laws as referents, 352
Left eye, activity, 33
Liberation
  drive to, 270
  keys to, 300
  meaning of, 395
Life
  and Dependent Origination, 134–135
  and the Heart centre, 433
  and true existence, 132–133
  definition, 348–349
  principle of, 360, 395, 431
  upholders of, 138
Life flux, 340
Life-line, 433
Light
  and śūnyatā, 51
  effects of, 343
Light śūnyatā, 190
Lion-Hearted applaud, 384
Logoi, 70, 107
Lokas. *See* Planes of perception
Lokavyavahāra, 60
Longcenpa, 105
Lopez, quote, 75
Lords of Liberated Life, 394
Lotus blossom, 244
Love
  and consciousness, 311
  definition, 167–168
Love-Wisdom, 395
  and bodhicittta, 373
  as dual Ray, 26, 34, 280
Lucid dreaming, 262
Lunar wind, 25

M

Madhya, 119
Madhyamaka, 51, 57–58, 65, 71, 100, 144, 147, 200
  argument, 152, 290–291
  as piṇgalā nāḍī, 34
  definition, 12
  doctrine, 122, 154, 172, 174, 198, 311
  outer, 121
  presuppositions, 151
  school as Heart centre, 33
  two kinds of, 105
Mādhyamika, 7, 10–11, 33, 45, 58, 73, 81, 115, 117, 134, 150, 272, 273, 288, 330
  and archaic logic, 341
  and Dependent Origination, 271, 274–275
  and emptiness, 277
  and śūnyatā, 89
  definition, 271
  philosophers, 88, 182, 204, 211, 416

philosophy, 13, 75, 92–93, 118, 119, 130, 178, 182, 200, 271, 294
and ultimates, 215
problem, 292
question of existence, 275
Madhymapratipad, 12, 34
Mahābodhisattvas, 32, 281
eight, 34, 225
Mahāmanvantara, 78
Mahāmudrā, 102, 127, 150, 177, 290, 312, 393
and the two truths, 145–146
definition, 63, 124
Mahāparinirvāṇa
of the Buddha, 238
Mahāraja
as Lord of karma, 324
definition, 323–324
Mahāsāṁghikas, 428
Mahāsiddha, 31
Mahāśūnya, 177
Mahāvibhāṣā, 115
Mahāvirūpa, 92
Mahāyāna, 35, 56, 100, 115
and Bodhisattva ideal, 330
and śūnyatā, 317
doctrine, 191
revelation, 23
schools, 36
syllogisms and predestiny, 261
Mahāyāna śūnyatā, 190
Mahāyānasūtrālaṃkāra, 32
Mahāyoga, 105
Maitreya, 32–33, 39, 127
as Christ, 112
as next Buddha, 33
epoch of, 36
five works of, 32
Manas, 54, 69, 170, 190, 418, 438
as mind, 24
aspects of, 164–165
Manaskāra, 181
Maṇḍala/s, 95, 111, 162, 173
definition, 55
four directions of, 323
of hexagram, 193
of Mind/mind, 191
of pentagram, 193
of square, 193
of Void Elements, 190, 192
Mano-vijñāna, 164, 170
definition, 166–167
Mantra, 27, 105, 133, 357
efficacy, 343, 365
secret, 122, 123, 134, 145, 146, 191
Marpa, 242
Māyā, 251, 292, 295, 297, 298, 307–308, 313, 314, 315, 326, 328, 343, 365, 374
and Earthy Element, 314
definition, 29
Māyāvirūpa, 37, 71
Meditation, 118
and unities, 233–234
process, 314, 322, 409
Meditation-Mind, 108, 153–154
development of, 301
explained, 430
Memory, 237, 240, 258, 291, 294, 374, 422, 437, 441
and permanence, 81
and pudgala, 414
explanation, 420–424
past life, 423
Memory-saṃskāra, 422
Middle way, 34, 119, 126, 129, 150, 155, 200
Milarepa, 23, 31, 131, 242
Mimāṃāsakas, 49, 227
mind
as manas, 24
definition, 262
desire, 166
dual aspect of, 382
emotional, 168–169
empirical, 382
essence of, 282
function of, 407

laws of, 367
possessor of 'things', 374
processes of, 69–71
slowing down of, 322
unconscious, 371
Mind, 70, 141, 164, 190, 240, 264, 296
abstract, 18, 120, 262, 297, 382, 384, 410, 418
and bīja forms, 364
and Herukas, 312
and prevision, 433
and śūnyatā, 43
as dharmakāya, 122
awakening of, 145
Clear, 299, 305, 323, 324
clear light of, 2, 12, 117, 128, 140, 145, 146–147, 149, 177, 178, 190, 238, 279, 309, 406
cosmic, 129, 179
empty, 77, 140
enlightened, 95, 133, 283, 299, 303, 315, 419
and phenomena, 441
evolution of, 77
explanation, 146
higher, 254, 322
and memory, 424
in contrast to mind, 2
of tathāgatagarbha, 295
primal, 91
reality experienced in, 106
supramundane, 78
universal, 106
Mind Only, 33, 122, 331
Mind-Space, 179
Mi-pham, 57, 72–73
Mirror-like Wisdom, 82, 190, 328, 330
Mokṣa, 87
Moments, series of, 385
Monad, 133
Moon, symbolism, 25
Motive, 41, 42, 44
Mountains and functionality, 377–378
Mūdra, 124, 357
Mukhyārthabādha, 42
Mūlamadhyamaka, 318
Mūlaprakṛti, 184, 296, 314
Multiplicity, 182

N

Nāḍīs, 185, 196
cross section of, 196–197
explained, 193
iḍā, 22, 26
and moon, 25
as feminine energy, 24–25
definition, 24–25
of Buddhism, 123
piṇgalā, 22, 26
as son energy, 24–25
as the sun, 25
definition, 24–25
of Buddhism, 124
suśumṇā, 22, 141
as father energy, 27
definition, 27
two major, 24
Nāḍī system, 108, 295
and chakras, 192
definition, 22
Nāgārjuna, 13–15, 22–23, 32, 33, 46, 66, 103, 119, 122, 131, 153, 154, 186, 188, 266, 271, 319, 330, 348, 390
and Abhidharma theory, 297
and Mūlamadhyamakakārikā, 295–318
and pratītyasamutpāda, 278
and serpents, 22–24
arguments, 93–94
catuṣkoṭi, 158
meditation on saṃsāra, 320
rejection of causation, 316–317
statements, 147–148, 156–159
Nāgas, 22, 28, 32
Nāma-rūpa, 269
Nānatva, 36
Newton's laws, 421

Nexus, 184
  śūnyatā-saṃsāra (saṃsāra-śūnyatā), 15–19, 74, 100, 102, 246, 305, 364, 395, 419
Neyārtha, 20, 42
Nga wang bel den, 156, 319
Niels Bohr, 228
Niḥsvabhāva, 143
Niḥsvabhāvavādin, 120
Nirmalā tathatā, 98
Nirmāṇakāya, 71, 146, 249
Nirvāṇa, 92, 100, 191, 237–238, 256, 419
  and saṃsāra, 15, 66–67, 159
  and Sautrāntikas, 116
  and śūnyatā, 15, 67
  as non-product, 253
  definition, 15
  Mahāyāna, 14
  no-fixed abode, 14
  tainted, 191
Nirvartaka, 306
Niṣprapañca, 72
Nītārtha, 20
Nitya, 272, 275, 278
Nivṛta, 165, 327
Non-conditions, 312–313
Non-existence, 200
Non-Prāsaṅgika schools, 381, 385
  view of 'self', 440
Non-product, 402
Non-sacred petals, 329
Not-self and jīva, 434
Now, eternal, 359, 364, 369
Nucleons, 224
Numerology, 111
Nyāya, 151, 158
Nyingma(pa), 64, 104–108, 146, 191

O

Oṁ Maṇi Padme Hūṁ, 192–193
Omniscience
  and pudgala, 416
  and the Buddha, 428
  obstructions to, 392–393
One and functionality, 375
One and the many, 170–179
Oneness, 232, 337
Organs of action, 298
Originating cause
  and consciousness, 354
Other
  categories of, 348
  non-production from, 342–351
Other-nature, 297–298, 298
Other shore, 153
Over-self, 400
Own character, 119
Own entity, 336, 337
  definition, 352
  interpretation of, 332

P

Padmasambhava, 31, 331
Pain, role of, 302
Para-bhāva, 36
Paracittajñāna, 428
Paradoxes in Buddhism, 130
Paramārtha, 151, 152, 158
Paramārthasamudgata, 143
Paramārtha-satya, 13, 50
Pāramārthika, 7
Parata-utpatti, 297
Parinirvāṇa, 55, 99, 136, 153, 205
  of the Buddha, 238
Pariniṣpanna, 191
Particles
  as truly existent, 230
  elementary, 224
  really elementary, 228, 230
Partless entity, 222
Partless particles, 292–293
  definition, 226
  explanation of, 221–225
  impossibility, 226–227
  refutation of, 221–235
Past life memories, 423
Perception
  multidimensional, 381
  of things, 267

Permanence, 80, 361
Personal-I
and aggregates, 256
and memory, 399
as seed, 337
definition, 54, 165
explanation, 167, 256
Persons
selflessness of, 380
subtle concept of, 388–397
Phala, 317
Phenomena
abstraction of, 282
as dependent arisings, 271
genesis of, 284
psychic, 305
selflessness of, 380
Photon, 224–225, 229, 288, 438
Planes of perception, 191
Plurality explained, 173–174
Practitioner needs, 138
Prajñā, 27
as wisdom, 25
definition, 25, 177
vs jñāna, 38
Prajñāpāramita teachings, 37, 155
Prakṛti, 26
Pralaya, 78, 109
Pramāṇa, 38, 165
definition, 97
Prāṇa
and jīva, 432–433
as wind, 146
Prāṇas, 24, 177, 192, 198
Aetheric, 37
and Elements, 187, 196–198
and sickness, 198
and spinal column, 23
apāna, 28, 29
as winds, 196, 295
definition, 177
five types of, 28–29, 54, 189, 309, 310
prāṇa, 28
samāna, 28, 29
udāna, 28
vyāna, 28, 29
Prāṇic streams, 26
Prāpyasamutpāda, 272, 287
Prasajyapratiedha, 278
Prasajyapratiṣedha, 272, 275
Prāsaṅgika, 55, 64, 112–113, 119, 123, 143, 149, 150, 261, 276, 283, 290, 352, 358, 379, 386
and abandonments, 113
and aggregates, 395
and annihilation, 430
and Dependent Origination, 271, 273–274, 279
and I-consciousness, 396
and system of negations, 382
and worldly conventions, 101
concept of 'self', 380–381, 440
denial of 'self', 410
dialectics of, 123
extremism, 72–73
on liberation, 393
philosophy, 72–75, 93–104, 114, 120–122, 128, 156, 175, 198, 268, 382, 387, 400
position on rebirth, 387
rhetoric, 82, 83, 125
view of persons, 388
Prāsaṅgika and Svātantrika opinions, 392–397
Prāsaṅgika system
as a 'self', 390–391
Praṭiccasamuppāda, 270
definition, 56
Pratītyasamutpāda, 270, 272, 285, 289, 290, 302, 316, 435. *See* Dependent Origination
and functionality, 294
and I-consciousness, 287
and Life, 292
as container, 286
begining of, 278
definition, 273
Pratyakṣa, 37, 38, 130, 439
Pratyaya, 215, 297, 309, 317

Pratyekabuddha, 47
Prayajana, 42
Pretas, 189, 436
Prevision
  and rebirth process, 403
Prima matrix, 184, 189, 296, 297
Producing cause, 303–304
Production
  inherently existent, 355–357
  refutation of, 342–354, 351–354
Production/cessation
  and time, 349–350
Psychic phenomena, 305
Pudgala, 380
  and friendliness, 415, 426
  and I-consciousness, 416–431
  and karma, 414
  and memory, 414
  and omniscience, 416
  and rebirth, 414
  and saṃsāric wandering, 436
  and skandhas, 413, 415, 417
  as a substance, 418
  definition, 36, 413
  discernment of, 425
  doctrine, 413–439
  two categories, 416
Pudgala-vāda, 35
Pudgalavādins, 416
  doctrine, 414–416
  suppression of, 410–411
Pudgalavādin-Vātīsīputīyas
  skewered doctrine, 419

Q

Quantum Electrodynamics, 288–289
Quantum mechanics, 438
Quarks, 173, 224–225, 229, 438
Quark theory, 288

R

Rabbit
  horns of, 355, 357
Rāja, 253
Rajas, 190
Rang bzhin, 188
Rangtong, 71
Rasanā, 25
Ray aspects/qualities
  1st ray, 372–373
  2nd ray, 372–373
  3rd ray, 372–373
  4th ray, 372, 374
  5th ray, 372, 374
  6th ray, 372, 375
  7th ray, 372, 375
  explained, 372–375
  seven defined, 372
rDzogs chen, 122, 282
  and bodhicitta, 280
Real, 145
Realists, 115
Rebirth
  and bījas, 314
  and Law of cycles, 335
  not comprehended, 411
  principle of, 386
  process of, 315
Rebirthing principle, 286
Reductionist approach, 288
Referents and laws, 352
Refuge, four points of, 2–6
Relative entityness, 199
Relative permanence, 257–258, 429
  and saṃsāra, 337
Relativity, 9–14, 15–19, 51–52, 68, 84, 131, 271, 337
  factor of, 39–40
  general, 223
  in relation to extremes, 158
  of things, 86
  origination, 304
  philosophy of, 153
  third truth, 16
Revelation
  as lightning, 140
  flashes of, 423
Rūpa, 181, 212, 213, 226, 227, 418
  definition, 54

Rūpa skandha, 418
Rutherford, 228

S

Sabhāga-hetu, 305
Sacred petals, 329
Sad asat, 306
Sahabhū-hetu, 305
Śākyamuni Buddha, 126
Samādhi, 196
  and image retrieval, 420
  and non-conditions, 312
  explanation, 308
Sāmagrī, 193
Samalā tathatā, 98
Samantabhadra, 107
  and Consort, 124
Samantādvaraṇa, 59
Śamatha, 279
Saṃbhāra, 148
Sambhogakāya, 146
  definition, 249
Sambhoghakāya Flower, 401
Samjñā, 54, 55
Sāṃkhya/s, 49, 227, 338, 416
Samkrānti-vāda, 35
Saṃprayuktaka-hetu, 306
Saṃsāra, 73, 93, 120, 132, 158, 182, 236, 239, 266, 278, 337
  and dharmakāya, 87
  and existence, 92
  and force, 92
  and interdependence, 347
  and karma, 300
  and nirvāṇa, 15, 66–67
  and one and the many, 175–176
  and 'selves', 382
  and śūnyatā, 63, 68, 77, 82, 91, 174, 178, 320–321
  and the Four-Cornered Proof, 324
  annihilation of, 159
  appearance of, 133, 285
  as empty, 121
  as existents, 301
  base energies of, 295
  definition, 7
  functionality of, 75, 118
  origination, 174, 275
Saṃsāra-śūnyatā, 53, 172, 175
  as Dependent Originations, 276–277
  experience, 235
  interdependent, 348
  interrelation, 67, 89, 128, 151, 174, 183, 214, 275
  purpose of, 282, 307
Saṃsāra-śūnyatā Nexus, 305, 419
  and effects, 357
  and I-consciousness, 417
  and 'selves', 382
  explained, 15–19
Saṃsāric causes, 211
Saṃskāras, 10, 53, 54–55, 60, 163, 166, 169, 182, 199, 266, 276, 300, 340, 350, 367, 400
  and aggregates, 170–172, 172, 245, 260
  and cause/effects, 345
  and Clear Light, 177
  and consciousness-stream, 242
  and Dependent Origination, 269–270
  and karmic factors, 158, 436
  and meditation, 302
  and memory, 424
  and permanence, 81
  and prāṇas, 22, 196
  and serpents, 22
  and śūnyatā, 50–51, 77
  and the Elements, 310–311
  and the 'I', 160
  as non-existent, 302
  borrowed, 262–263
  definition, 5, 54
  flow of, 198, 402
  growth of, 213
  of elementary mind, 295
  removal of, 16, 117, 203, 216
  transformation of, 243, 256, 259, 376

Samutpāda, 271, 277
Saṃvṛta, 7, 152
Saṃvṛti, 151, 158
 definition, 7, 59–60
Saṃvṛti-paramārtha, 13
Saṃvṛtisatya, 13, 50, 59
 levels of, 60
Samyuksambodhi, 125
Sandhābhāṣa, 125
Sandhyābhāṣa, 125
Saṅgha, 235, 252, 311
Santāna, 163, 218, 387
 definition, 256
 of the Heart, 257–258
Śāntatarakṣita, 172, 173, 221–223
 refutation of permanence, 226
 theory, 225, 227
Śarīra, 416, 431
Sarvajñāna, 37
Sarvāstivādin, 13, 14, 15, 116, 172, 314, 416
Sarvatrage-hetu, 306
Sa skya Paṇḍita, 168
Śāstra/s, 2, 3, 21
Sat, 72, 306, 427
Satkāyadṛṣṭi, 427
Sattva, 190
Satya, 13, 143
 definition, 7, 59
Sautrāntika, 65, 68, 78, 115, 123, 126, 227, 271, 291, 293, 314, 380
 and abandonments, 113
 definition, 116
 following reasoning, 113, 116, 385
 following scripture, 113, 119, 385
 view concerning 'person', 392
 view of Dependent Origination, 272–273
Sautrāntika-Svātantrika-Mādhyamika, 113
Sautrāntika-Svātantrikas, 70, 71, 119, 385, 393
 and abandonments, 113
Seed
 and a 'self', 346
 and sprout as 'other', 346–347
 as child, 338–339
 as personal-I, 337
 as śūnyatā, 353
Self
 and aggregates, 371–375, 398, 405, 408
 and jīva, 434
 and relativity, 337
 and skandhas, 170
 and the four-cornered proof, 320
 as personal-I, 236
 as personality, 334
 as tathāgatagarbha, 406
 concept of, 156, 161, 304, 354, 380
 definition, 163
 independent, 381
 in Mahāyāna, 380–381
 non-existence of, 371–375
 non production from, 331–338
 proof for, 333
 refutation of, 381
 subtle, 390
 truism of, 341
Self-identification
 purpose of, 268
Selflessness
 establishment of, 268
Self-love, 327
Self-nature, 35–36, 297–298, 298
 concreting agent, 316
Self of Persons
 as chief affliction, 393
 explained, 379–397
 refutation of, 371–379, 391
Selves, relativistic, 356
Sentience
 and continuum, 350
 of sprout, 333
Serpent
 and poison, 28

Fiery, 28, 31
Fiery flying, 29, 30, 31
power, 31
prāṇic, 28
small, 29
symbolism, 22–24
Set Theory, 150–151
Seven-cornered reason, 398–412
Sevenfold Reasoning, 58, 114, 157–160, 371–375, 387–388
flawed, 388–389
Seven keys of interpretation, 3
Shambhala, 132
and nāgā Lords, 318
Shantideva, 119
Shentong, 71
Sickness and prāṇas, 198
Siddha, 108, 203
Siddhis, 108, 142, 196, 426
alchemical effects, 77
and chakras, 298
definition, 11
development of, 29
experience of, 302
mundane, 186
of accomplishment, 22
supramundane, 186
Silence
and liberation, 101
teachings in, 48
Singularity, 223, 229
Śiva, 252
Skandha/s, 53, 82, 143–144, 163, 266, 427
and cause/effects, 345
and pudgala, 413, 415–416
and 'self', 411
and the 'I', 160, 417
borrowed, 262–263
definition, 9, 54
esoteric explanation, 54–55
five categories, 170–171
of past lives, 238–239
Skilful means, 394
Sleep and consciousness, 262
Smoke symbolism, 342
Solar wind, 25
Solitary Realizers, 440
Sorcerer, 231
Soul, 251, 396–397, 438
and light, 135
and the Void, 251
as ātman, 93
as unitary existence, 226
Buddhas answer concerning, 435
concept of, 201, 250
definition, 162, 247
form, 240
and consciousness store, 251–252
and pudgala, 419
and the sambhogakāya, 249
as agent of distinction, 421
as intermediary, 249
as tathāgatagarbha, 287
explained, 248–252
permanent, 438–439
Space
three dimensional, 222
two dimensional, 222
zero-dimensional, 222
Space-time, 134
curvature of, 223
womb of, 63
Sphere, 228
Spread-of-Light śūnyatā, 190
Śrāvaka, 41
Staff symbolism, 23–24
Styāna, 165
Suchness, 98
action of, 366
wisdom realising, 365–366
Sunetra, 414
Sun symbolism, 25
Śūnya, 177
Śūnyatā, 6, 7, 17, 18, 52, 53, 75, 76, 80, 83, 87, 88, 89, 90, 92, 149, 152, 154, 159, 176, 183, 199, 229, 246, 257, 266, 271, 276, 277, 290, 298, 301, 312, 317, 321, 324, 326, 359, 362, 394, 410
absolute ultimate, 366

and aggregates, 266
and Airy Element, 313
and alchemical process, 78
and annihilation, 82, 99, 188
and Big Bang, 288
and black holes, 224
and cause/effects, 345
and consciousness, 89–90, 117, 201, 321, 354, 379
and Elements, 187
and empty mind, 77
and enlightened Mind, 441
and evolution, 248
and existence, 348
and formative forces, 68, 91
and four extremes, 356
and I-consciousness, 246
and inherent existence, 81
and karma, 55, 95–96, 243
and light, 51, 147
and memory, 241, 294
and Mind, 43, 52
and perception of things, 364
and primal matrix, 184
and release of 'things', 321
and saṃsāra, 68, 82, 91, 172, 174, 178, 300, 320–321
and saṃskāras, 50–51
and svabhāva, 315
and the eye, 324
and the 'I', 157, 250–251
and the ultimate, 86, 211
and time, 322
and ultimate truth, 56, 144
and Void Elements, 198
as a base, 250, 260
as a unitary, 232–233
as energy state, 78
as experiencable phenomena, 278
as heart of Buddhism, 391
as mirror, 11–12, 82, 284, 311
as 'non-product', 248
as partless, 222, 223
as seed, 63, 353
Clear Mind relationship, 323
defiled aspect, 187
definition, 4, 353
doctrine of, 34, 120
enlightenment, 29, 37
four gates of, 319–320, 327
in svabhāva, 189–190
levels of, 204
non-being, 252
non-dual, 363
not empty, 176
not the All, 48
not, yet is a support, 306–307
paradoxes, 178–179
truth of, 16, 84, 153
without residue, 123
Śūnyatā Eye
explained, 324–326
Śūnyatās
16 or 18 types, 176, 438
different, 237
Śūnyatā-saṃsāra
as Dependent Originations, 276–277
interdependent, 348
interrelation, 67, 74, 174, 191, 192, 204, 235, 275, 278, 315
Śūnyatā-saṃsāra nexus, 15–19, 74, 246, 364, 395, 411
Supreme Self, 411
Sūtrānta, 35
Sūtra/s, 116
definition, 2, 21
interpretation of, 20–21
Sūtrātmā
definition, 433
Svabhāva, 35, 36, 57, 99, 143–144, 184, 190, 204, 296, 314
and self-nature, 298
and śūnyatā, 315
and tathāgatagarbha, 395
as elementary substance, 97–98
definition, 52, 187
explanation of, 188–189
two meanings of, 188–189

Svabhāvātiśaya, 194
Svabhāvena, 148
Svalakṣaṇa, 143–144
Svātantrika, 72, 119, 121, 122, 123, 143, 147, 380
  and abandonments, 113
  assertion, 385–386
  compared to Prāsaṅgika, 391
  critique, 70
  philosophy, 387
  view, 74, 83–93, 383, 388
Svātantrika and Prāsaṅgika opinions, 392–397
Svātantrika Mādhyamika, 64, 158
  attributes, 124
Svata-utpatti, 297
Swastika, 196–198, 204

T

Tamas, 190
Tantrapaṭika, 108, 122
Tantras, 105
Tantrayāna, 36
Tantric philosophy, 129, 152
Tapas, 250
Tathāgata
  and memory, 374
  and skandhas, 439
  as person, 415
Tathāgatagarbha, 18, 87, 98, 151, 155, 161, 162, 188, 242, 250, 287, 292, 315, 352, 389, 401, 411, 417, 426, 429, 433, 439, 440
  and Ādi Buddha, 284
  and bodhicitta, 280, 430–431
  and consciousness growth, 437
  and dharmakāya, 154
  and I-consciousness, 283
  and karma, 284, 331
  and memory, 423
  and phenomena, 275
  and 'self', 382, 382–383
  and 'soul' concept, 397
  and the Void Elements, 283, 297
  as mediator, 276
  as subtle 'self', 406
  definition, 8, 80
  development of, 395
  evolution of, 276, 318
  origin of, 418
  school, 10, 71
Tathāgata-Mind, 417
Tathāgata/s, 53, 131
  and consciousness, 282
  and the lotus, 244
  bhūmis, 189
  families, 124
  properties of, 174–175
Tathatā, 43, 87, 374
Tathātagata-Womb, 64
Tattvā-rthena, 202
The Diamond Slivers, 114, 319, 331–341
Theravāda sūtras, 330
Theravādin schools, 37
  Sarvāstivādin-Vaibhāṣika, 35, 36
  Sautrāntika, 35, 36
Thoughts
  and emptiness, 282
  as things, 173, 321
  container of, 286
  moments of, 422
  swirls of, 322
Three Natures, 7, 8, 65–71, 143, 144, 154
  paratantra (dependent), 7, 8, 9, 11, 14, 65, 66, 68, 73, 143
  parikalpita (imaginary), 7, 8, 10, 12, 14, 60, 65, 66, 143
  pariniṣpanna (consummate), 7, 8, 9, 66, 71, 73, 143
Thus gone one, 89, 131
Thusness, 87, 188, 318
Time
  and cause-effect, 217, 345
  and evolutionary change, 335
  and thoughts, 241
  and transformations, 335–336
  factor of, 218
  fast, slow, atomic, 207–208

production/cessation, 349–350
reckoning of, 322–323
relativity of, 249
Time line, 369
and cause/effects, 345
and sprouting seeds, 347
explained, 362–363
Traditionalists, 115
Transmigration, fellacious, 124–125
Trikāya, 146, 221, 249
Trimūrti, 252
True existent, 172
True existentence, 271, 395
and emptiness, 272
and integral Life, 292
and phenomena, 290–291
Truly
as qualifier, 225
conception of, 230
existent, 365
Truly unitary existence, 225
Truth, 6, 13
conventional, 13, 47, 50–109, 83, 115, 129, 130, 131, 144, 145, 148–149, 159, 200, 214, 235, 296, 303, 320, 364, 378
and enlightenment, 346
and self-nature, 297
definition, 16, 60
ear-whispered, 125
five truths, 84
four truths, 56–57
keys to, 62
paths to, 142
relative, 76, 84
the three, 13
third, 64, 84, 88
ultimate / absolute, 13, 17, 47, 50–109, 68, 106, 115, 118, 119, 120, 129, 131, 144, 145, 148, 149, 159, 200, 214, 287, 292, 296, 306, 317, 346, 363, 364
and Buddha nature, 293
and existents, 310
and karma, 136
and śūnyatā, 56
Tsongkhapa, 9, 16–17, 55, 64, 131, 188, 201, 206, 243, 279, 319, 379, 390, 440
and Prāsaṅgika, 72, 93–104
pragmatism, 102
Twilight language, 125
Two extremes, 272
Two obstructions, 392
Two truths, 50–109, 119, 128–136, 144, 147, 151–152, 154, 159, 301, 352
and śūnyatā, 235
and the Mahāmudrā, 145–146
as dichotomy, 61
in civilisation, 138
simultaneous arising of, 94

U

Ultimate, 75, 85, 86, 87–91, 203, 362
and causation, 203
and four extremes, 356
definition, 72
existence, 89
two types, 366
Ultimately, 182, 183, 184, 210–211, 231, 278
and Madhyamaka philosophy, 207
and śūnyatā, 364
and time line, 378
improper use of, 211
interpretation of, 359
relative, 207
Ultimates, 65–66, 84–85, 175, 176, 391
Unconscious mind, 371
Unitary
existences, 225
explanation, 225
Unities, 321
in meditation, 233–234
Unity
concept of, 173, 174
Universal flux, 384
Universal Life, 106

Universal Void, 178
Universal Way, 115, 118
Universe
expanding, 223
origination of, 304
relativistic, 356
Upādhi, 197
Upalabhdika, 177
Upāya, 25, 65, 177
Utpanna, 309
Uttamaprajñā, 40, 41

V

Vaibhāṣikas, 78, 113, 114, 115, 116, 123, 126, 226, 227, 380
and abandonments, 113
view, 290–291, 292–293
view concerning 'person', 392
view of Dependent Origination, 272–273
Vaiśeṣikas, 227, 344, 416
Vajra, 124, 196, 204
Vajrachhedeka, 153
Vajrārka, 177
Vajrayāna, 266, 312, 331, 393
definition, 124
teachings, 150
Vāsanā, 68, 82, 88, 135
definition, 10
Vastutaḥ, 202, 210
Vasubandhu, 33, 154, 158, 331, 431, 432, 434
and pudgala doctrine, 417–438
question of memory, 422
Vātīsīputīyas, 420
dialogue re jīva, 431–432
Vātīsīputīya-Sammitīyas, 416
Vatsagotra, 435
Vātsīputrīya-Sammitīyas, 410, 413
Vedanā, 55, 418
definition, 54
Vedanā skandha, 418
Vedāntins, 227
Vessāvana, 323
Vidyā, 271
Vijñāna, 201, 202, 205
definition, 54
object of, 425
Vijñānavādin, 118
Vijñānavādins and Self, 422
Vijñeya, 425
Vipāka-hetu, 306
Vipassanā, 279
Viper, 28, 29, 30
Virūdhaka, 323
Virupāksha, 324
Viṣaya, 72
Viśeṣaṇa, 13, 47
Viśnu, 252
Visual cognition, 197
Viśvavajra, 204
Void, 48, 66, 74, 77, 82, 92, 99, 129, 132, 133, 135, 172, 174, 177, 178, 191, 199, 201, 233, 235, 300, 301, 312, 316, 366
and Dependent Origination, 275
and energy, 251
and formation process, 295
and partlessness, 222
and producing cause, 305
and saṃsāra, 159
and 'things', 250–251, 365
as no-thing, 182
attainment of, 204
definition, 296
Elements, 98, 124, 177, 178, 187, 189–190, 199, 275, 278, 283, 297, 298, 307, 316, 317, 324, 365, 417, 418
and Airy principle, 313
and effects, 314–315
and phenomena, 313
and śūnyatā, 198
Earthy, 295
experience of, 75, 186
five levels, 203
of being void, 135
seven types, 178
Vyāvahārika
definition, 7

W

Watery prāṇas, 29
Western approach, 139
Wheel
  eight-spoked, 327
  fourth turning, 331
  functionality of, 378
Will
  and memory, 423, 424
  and the 'I', 256–258
  conscious, 258
  use of, 213, 438
Wind, 177
  as prāṇa, 146
Winds, 376
  five, 295
Wisdom
  and right timimg, 102
  antidote to kliṣṭamanas, 166
  development of, 313
  evolution of, 275–276
  gain of the two truths, 101
  not illusional, 283–284
Wisdom and method, 25–26
Womb
  of Buddha Consort, 83
World-soul, 251
Wrathful Deity, 324

Y

Yathādaśana, 151, 158
Yin-yang, 34
Yogācāra-Cittamatra, 7–9
Yogācāra Following Reasoning, 385
Yogācāra Following Scripture, 385
  and rebirthing principle, 386
Yogācāra Mādhyamika, 64, 146
  attributes of, 124
Yogācāra philosophy, 9, 10, 32, 33, 64, 68–71, 119, 120, 144, 164, 205, 290–291, 313, 326, 352
  and abandonments, 113
  as iḍā nāḍī, 34
  as Throat centre, 34
  syllogisms, 307
  three natures of, 65–71
Yogācāra-Svātantrika-Mādhyamika, 113, 120, 128
  view of Nyingmapa, 104–108
Yogācāra-Svātantrikas, 290, 385
  and two obstructions, 392
  position on rebirth, 386–387
Yogācāra-Vijñānavāda, 152, 154, 331
Yogācārins, 14, 78–79, 115, 123, 143, 200, 227, 271, 272, 311, 380
  and ālayavijñāna, 277
  and Dependent Origination, 277
  middle way, 290
  view concerning 'person', 392
Yogic philosophy, 185
Yogins, 54–55

Z

Zero-dimensional space, 222

About the Author

BODO BALSYS is the founder of The School of Esoteric Sciences. He is an author of many books on subjects centred on Buddhism and the Esoteric Sciences, a meditation teacher, poet, artist, spiritual scientist and healer. He has studied extensively across multiple traditions including Esoteric Science, Buddhism, Christianity, Esoteric Healing, Western Science, Art, Politics and History. His advanced esoteric insights, gained through decades of meditative contemplation, enable him to provide a rich understanding of the spiritual pathway toward enlightenment, healing and service.

Bodo's teachings can be accessed via the School of Esoteric Science's website:
http://universaldharma.com

For any other enquiries, please email
sangha@universaldharma.com

About Universal Dharma Publishing

Universal Dharma Publishing is a not for profit publisher. Our aim is make innovative, original and esoteric spiritual teachings accessible to all who genuinely aspire to awaken and serve humanity. The books published aim in part to provide an esoteric interpretation of the meaning of Buddhist *dharma* with view of reformation of the way people perceive the meaning of the related teachings. Hopefully then Buddhism can more effectively serve its principal function as a vehicle for enlightenment, and further prosper into the future. A further aim is to provide the next level of exposition of the esoteric doctrines to be revealed to humanity following on the wisdom tradition pioneered by H.P. Blavatsky and A.A. Bailey.

Cover Design by
Angie O'Sullivan & Kylie Smith